Miracles

Miracles

An Encyclopedia of People, Places,
and Supernatural Events
from Antiquity to the Present

Patrick J. Hayes, Editor

ABC-CLIO™

An Imprint of ABC-CLIO, LLC
Santa Barbara, California • Denver, Colorado

Library of Congress Cataloging-in-Publication Data

Miracles : an encyclopedia of people, places, and supernatural events from antiquity to the present / Patrick J. Hayes, editor.

    pages cm

  Includes bibliographical references and index.

  ISBN 978-1-61069-598-5 (alk. paper)—ISBN 978-1-61069-599-2 (ebook)

1. Miracles—Encyclopedias. 2. Supernatural—Encyclopedias. 3. Marvelous, The—Encyclopedias. 4. Religion—Encyclopedias. 5. Religions—Encyclopedias. I. Hayes, Patrick J., 1966- editor.

  BL487.M574 2016

  202'.117—dc23   201502574

ISBN: 978-1-61069-598-5
EISBN: 978-1-61069-599-2

20 19 18 17 16 1 2 3 4 5

This book is also available on the World Wide Web as an eBook.
Visit www.abc-clio.com for details.

ABC-CLIO
An Imprint of ABC-CLIO, LLC

ABC-CLIO, LLC
130 Cremona Drive, P.O. Box 1911
Santa Barbara, California 93116-1911

This book is printed on acid-free paper ∞
Manufactured in the United States of America

Contents

Alphabetical List of Entries

Guide to Related Topics

New Thought
Newman, John Henry
Pomponazzi, Pietro
Price, Richard
Sherlock, Thomas
Spinoza, Baruch
Warfield, Benjamin
Whately, Richard
White, Ellen G.
Woolston, Thomas

BY GEOGRAPHIC LOCATION
Asia
Asia, Miracles in
Hinduism and Miracles
Jerusalem
Our Lady of La Vang
Our Lady of Subang Jaya
Sikhism and Miracles

Caribbean
Caribbean, Miracles in the
Voodoo

Europe
Convulsionnaires of St. Médard
Council of Trent
Dancing Sun
England, Miracles in
Eucharistic Miracle of Lanciano
Eucharistic Miracle of Siena
France, Miracles in
Germany, Miracles in
Ireland, Miracles in
Italy, Miracles in
Labouré, Saint Catherine of
Lepanto, Battle of
Lourdes
Lourdes
Lourdes Water

Low Countries, Miracles in the
Medjugorje
Miracule/Miraculee
Miraculous Medal
Northern Europe, Miracles in
Our Lady of Aglona
Our Lady of Czestochowa
Our Lady of Fatima
Our Lady of Knock
Our Lady of LaSalette
Our Lady of Lourdes
Our Lady of Mount Carmel
Our Lady of Pontmain
Our Lady of Walsingham
Poland, Miracles in
Reformation Europe, Miracles in
Shroud of Turin
Spain, Miracles in
Thomas of Cantilupe

Latin and South America
Latin America, Miracles in
Our Lady of Guadalupe
Solemnity of the Lord of Miracles (El
    Señor de los Milagros)

Middle East
Africa, Miracles in
Islam and Miracles
Jerusalem

North America
Bayside Apparitions
Canada, Miracles in
Chimayo Chapel
Georgetown Miracles
Holy Hill
Maria Stein Shrine of the Holy
    Relics
Mission Church

Pomponazzi, Pietro
Price, Richard
Sherlock, Thomas
Spinoza, Baruch
Thomas of Cantilupe
Warfield, Benjamin
Whately, Richard
White, Ellen G.
Woolston, Thomas

Subjects/Objects

Agency
Amulet
Apparitions
Asceticism
Art and Miracles
Beatification
Bilocation
Blindness
Blood
Body Shaped Relquaries
Canonization
Charms
Clairvoyance
Compunction (tears)
Congregation for Saints' Causes
Congregation of Rites
Corpus Christi
Creatio Ex Nihilo
Cult
Deafness
Desert
Dirt
Divinus Perfectionis Magister
Dreams
Exorcism
Ex Voto
Faith
Fasting
Fertility

Fire
Flight
Fragrance
Glossolalia
Grace
Hagiography
Healing
Heroic Virtue
Holiness
Icons
Incorruptibles
Indulgences
Lactation
Levitation
Long Life
Lourdes Water
Magic
Manna from Heaven
Martyrs
Medical Miracles
Mesmerism
Miracle Plays
Miraculé/Miraculée
Miraculous Medal
Movies, MIracles in
Novena
Odor of sanctity
Oil
Orthodoxy and Miracles
Our Lady of Perpetual Help
Physics
Pilgrimage
Postulator
Prophecy
Relics
Reliquary
Resurrection/Resuscitation
Revelation
Retablo
Scala Santa

Introduction

When fiction writer Flannery O'Connor wrote that "the supernatural is an embarrassment today," she struck at a perennial concern. Why, in a culture so vividly pluralistic, does the supernatural come to such disdain? Why does it polarize? Why does it separate the believer into one camp and the unbeliever into another?

The difficulty is all the more pronounced when considering manifestations of the supernatural—miracles—as either proof of some divine being or action in the world, or indeed, of divinity itself. When miracles are considered as phenomena within the natural order, the context or understanding of that order necessarily shapes the strength of the claims. A snowfall in a tropical climate could be explained if weather patterns suggest an anomalous but not impossible confluence of events. It would not be a miracle. But once the phenomenon passes the threshold of explicability and reasonability, it might be viewed as extraordinary or a violation of the natural order, and this people rightly call a miracle.[1]

This encyclopedia tries to approach the concept of a miracle from different perspectives, in part according to ethnic traditions, geographical locations, and time periods as well as through the writings of theologians and philosophers and the lens of modern science. The authors aim to give some insight into how miracles have been treated over the centuries, by whom, and to what ends. Necessarily, each encyclopedia entry is circumscribed by the constraints of space, but together with the bibliographical information supplied in each entry, the reader should have a good starting point for further research. This secondary literature is vast and deep, but as any encyclopedia is meant simply as a tool, this one is a very good survey of what is presently available. In fact, it has been well over a century since the last attempt at assembling a similar volume.[2] We hope that this encyclopedia will fill a gap in the literature and will be useful to students and their teachers but also pastors and historians.

The types of entries that readers will find in this book are reflective of time period or eras, geographic location, and theological and philosophical worldviews. They are explicative of a scientific approach to supernatural data. The authors here do not treat these things as if in opposition to one another but as dialogue partners. We have assembled an international team of scholars whose fields of expertise are divergent and whose interests are eclectic. We eschew a dominant religious perspective on miracles, and while it may seem that Christianity holds pride of place in these pages, mainly by dint of the quantity of material devoted to that religious interpretation, it is essential to see how other faiths take up the problem of miracles in a comparative light, if only to accurately name and draw meaning from classical Christian conceptions of the term. Especially when viewed historically, the concept of miracle becomes radically differentiated by time and place. This is an important insight and helps us to gain greater purchase on the human condition and its relation to the divine.

Defining Miracles: Theology, Philosophy, Science

Miracles have plenty of meanings and are defined variously according to discipline, but they also have a function and so are often defined accordingly. For instance, Peter the Venerable, the twelfth-century abbot of Cluny (1094–1156), made miracles a buffer against the trials of his age: Judaism, paganism, Islam, and other "heresies." They were not a remedy per se but a testament or proof of what is good and honorable about the Christian faith; that is, miracles had an apologetic function. Concomitantly, they also carried with them the politics of proselytization. They were a theological affirmation of the power of Jesus as Son of God. Such claims are not without consequence.

Anyone using the power of reason would likely find the claim that miracles bring us to the threshold of belief in God or Jesus to be a challenge. So, in the thought of Saint Augustine of Hippo, the term *miracle* applies to "anything which appears arduous or unusual, beyond the expectation or ability of the one who marvels at it" (*De utilitate credenda*, XVI, 34; see *Patrologia Latina*, XLII, 90). In this view miracles are a shock, a strangeness, an emptying of reason. With Christ, it is an all or nothing proposition: believe in him and believe in the miracles; don't believe in him and forego any belief in the miracles. Of course, Jesus was fairly clear on which way to go. Jesus says to his apostles in the Gospel of John: "Amen, amen, I say to you, whoever believes in me will do the works that I do, and will do greater ones than these, because I am going to the Father. And whatever you ask in my name, I will do, so that the Father may be glorified in the Son. If you ask anything of me in my name, I will do it" (John 14:12–13). He was plain about what they should do: "Cure the sick, raise the dead, cleanse lepers, drive out demons. Without cost you have received; without cost you are to give" (Matthew 10:8). Their works were spectacular. In the Acts of the Apostles, Peter raised Tabitha from the dead (Acts 9:40), and later Paul raised Eutychus from the dead (Acts

20:12). Converts were numerous, in part owing to the apostles' own miraculous gifts, which they drew upon liberally and authoritatively.

Though the faithful are not required to believe in miracles as necessary for salvation, it is difficult to avoid their impact on both the tradition and the lives of concrete individuals. To what degree, then, does the presentation of a miracle or a miraculous experience impose upon us the need to believe in their truth or facticity?[3] Churches insist that one should not check one's brain at the door of experience. We have to think about what life throws at us and discern its truth or falsehood. Should we, for instance, believe that there was such a thing as a resurrection that happened to a first-century Palestinian Jew? For many Christians, this is a sine qua non. Do we have to believe in a person's ability to change water into wine, to walk on water or calm seas, or to heal hemorrhages, blindness, or lameness?

Should we hold similarly and with the same degree of force the resurrection stories of subsequent generations of saints? Isn't a resurrection miracle performed by Jesus tantamount to the same accomplishment of others? In his book *Saints Who Raised the Dead*, Father Albert J. Hebert documents accounts of some 400 recorded resurrection miracles. Among these are several performed by a well-known missionary, the Jesuit Saint Francis Xavier (1506–1552). His miracles are numerous. His labors took him to Goa in southern India, Sri Lanka (then Ceylon), Bengal, Cape Comorin, the Moluccas, the Spice Islands, Malacca, and through the China Sea to Japan, where he died on the island of Sancian while waiting for a ship to China. The saint's canonization process notes several resurrection miracles. They included those of a catechist bitten by a venomous snake, a child drowned in a pit, and a young man who died of pestilential fever. Each vignette is fascinating, in part because it conveys a singular truth—a reliance on the knowledge that whatever miracle occurs, its source is of divine origin and utterly beyond the kin of the holy person, who is a mere instrument.

On the Fishery Coast as he was about to begin Mass in a small church at Combutur, a crowd entered with the corpse of a boy who drowned in a well. His grief-stricken mother pleaded with Xavier to restore the child. Francis said a short prayer, took the lifeless boy by the hand, and told him to get up. The child rose and immediately ran to his mother. While traveling, Francis had two companions serving as catechists. During the night one of them was bitten in the foot by a cobra. In the morning the youth was found dead. Francis took some saliva from his own mouth, touched the foot of the poisoned catechist, made the sign of the cross over him, took him by the hand, and bade him arise in Jesus's name. The youth responded without hesitation, ready to carry on the journey. The third resurrection miracle occurred in Mutan, where Francis met a funeral procession bearing the enshrouded body of a youth who had died of a malignant fever. The parents were inconsolable, and this moved the saint to kneel down to pray for the boy. He sprinkled the body with holy water and asked that the funeral shroud be removed. When the body was visible, Francis made the sign of the cross over it, took the youth by the hand, and bade him in the name of Jesus to live. The parents were ecstatic, and the child's friends later erected a large cross on the spot.

A final miracle occurred while Francis was preaching at Coulon, near Cape Comorin in Travancore in southern India. He encountered much resistance among the Christians there, and as a way of piercing their hearts, he prayed that they would be shown a sign. He called for the corpse of a man buried only the day before, and when the body was disinterred, its odor was powerful. As before, Francis dropped to his knees before God and begged that the man would be made alive again. Instantly he came back, and the crowd was won over. In this last instance the miraculée himself testified for the canonization cause, and while it was incorporated in the documents, another miracle was used to satisfy the requirements.

In each of these instances, the miracle also points to very definite salvific elements: the hope and joy promised in the resurrection. It may be that theologians today have lost this sense of meaning. The status of miracles in present theology is hardly of the sort that stirs much controversy, and theologians since the 1950s have contented themselves with recounting the tradition in aid of apologetics.[4] The subject, however, has taken on a renewed interest among those in American studies and for whom the saints supply ample insight into the workings of religion in American culture. One thinks of Robert Orsi's *Thank You, St. Jude* (1996), about women's devotion to the cult of Saint Jude Thaddeus; Nancy Lusignan Schultz's *Mrs. Maddingly's Miracle* (2011), about a transatlantic cure in Washington, D.C., in 1824; or Paula Kane's *Sister Thorn* (2014), which relates the story of an alleged stigmatic nun in Peekskill, New York.[5] In the philosophy of religion as well, the concept of miracle has been examined seemingly from every angle.[6] Skeptics have also raised clever arguments that mitigate both the reality and the perception of miracles. In 1920 the famous magician Harry Houdini published an expose on "miracle mongers," and more recently Joe Nickell has provided a body of work that tries to debunk miracles with detectivelike precision.[7]

In the twentieth century, Catholic theology especially sought to give an accurate—even elegant—exposition of what constituted a miracle. Cardinal Alexis-Henri-Marie Lépicier laid out several requirements for a miracle:

- The event must take place comparatively rarely. God did not create the world to interfere constantly with its laws.
- Since it is divine in origin, the event must be of a reasonable and moral nature, with no trace of the fantastic or suspicion of sleight of hand.
- It must always have a recognizable spiritual purpose.
- It must bring about a general or individual good.

- It is often instantaneous, but it can be progressive (i.e., where God uses secondary causes).
- Before giving approval the Church normally insists that a miracle's effects should be lasting, but that is not absolutely indispensable. Miracles are of their nature limited in time. A cure may be granted to demonstrate the existence of God or the efficacy of prayer or to permit some useful action to be performed; its purpose once achieved, the disease, arrested as though by an antibiotic, may resume its natural course.
- Miracles, in general, correspond to prayer.[8]

The theological prerequisites went hand-in-glove with an accompanying set of regulations in canon law. The apparatus of the Roman Catholic Church in deciphering the truth or falsehood of a miracle stretches to the first millennium, but the present structures have been in place for hundreds of years. The bureaucracy surrounding miraculous phenomena is not so much to satisfy an insatiably inquisitive public as much as to determine the sign's value for understanding ourselves in relation to God. The Church has learned to establish this elaborate (some would say baroque) system to hedge against fraud. It is a healthy skepticism that helps to keep one's feet on the ground.

Even though the Catholic system of saint making, with its dual requirements of proof of heroic virtue and of miracles, has changed over time, the process is not immune from politics. The story of America's saints and blesseds is illustrative. How American could they be if their loyalties were less to their citizenship and more toward a pope in Rome or God in heaven? In the eras of Know-Nothingism in the mid-nineteenth century and the American Protective Association in the mid-twentieth century, one finds a shrill and inhospitable cry against the possibility of Catholic saints from America—whether they are native born or from immigrant stock. Talk of their miracles would not be immediately acceptable; they had to prove their credibility as citizens first. Their worth as vehicles for sainthood came second.[9]

Miracle: A Short History

Without exploring the more ancient religious traditions, tracing the history of the notion of a miracle might begin with pre-Christian conceptions in its monotheistic predecessor. The Hebrew Bible speaks of signs and wonders but not in a way that tries to prove God's existence. Instead, miracle references were used to explain God's purposes in relation to Israel.[10] First-century Palestine had its share of philosophical, magical, and medicinal savants. When Jesus of Nazareth began his public ministry, he stepped into a world already charged with miracles and the expectation that such a world would be utterly transformed by a messianic prophet.[11] Subsequent to the apostolic period, when the prospect of martyrdom was all too real, the loyalty generated for the Christian movement was inspired by the sheer disregard for religious convention or legal dictate. The Christian was radically free, liberated from the confines of life and death. The visible and tangible reminders were the relics of the saints.

In Saint Augustine's thought on miracles, they are events that inspire *admiratio* (wonder) at divine majesty, especially the power of God to sustain the created order. "We say that all miracles are against nature," writes Augustine, "but they are not. For how can anything that is caused by God's will be against nature, since the nature of every created thing is nothing else than the will of its Creator?" (*De Civ. Dei*, XXI, viii, 2). Augustine turns a person's *admiratio* back on himself:

> Man sees extraordinary things happen, and he admires them, while he himself, the admirer, is a great wonder, and a much greater miracle than any things which are done by the intervention of man. There is nothing more marvelous done in the world, which is not less wonderful than the world itself. All nature is full of what is miraculous; we seem unconscious of it, because we see those things daily, and because this daily repetition lowers them in our eyes. And this is one reason why God has reserved to Himself other things out of the common course of nature, on which He shows His power from time to time, in order that their novelty may strike us; but when we consider attentively, and with reflection, the miracles we constantly see, we find that they are far greater than others, however surprising and uncommon these may be.[12]

In the Late Antique period, monasticism took up the problem of miracles with deep reflection. Miracles show up in books such as the *History of the Monks in Egypt* and the *Lausiac History*. These texts attempt to give some data on the events they describe, but to illustrate them the texts are loaded with what moderns might call "fairy tales." According to William Harmless, "such tales can be off-putting. . . . While we love the outlandish in our fiction and applaud special effects in our movies, we want sobriety in our spiritual literature. Ancient Christians felt no such inhibitions (nor did their medieval successors)."[13] Harmless continues that there is a need for clarification of our presuppositions about history and about miracles. "People today," he notes, "both scholars and non-scholars, tend to work from the Enlightenment's definition of a miracle: namely, an event that violates or overturns the laws of nature. Since many historians presume that no event can violate or overturn the laws of nature, they presume that miracles reported in ancient texts could not possibly have happened. One may interpret matters that way, but in doing so, one is staking out not a historical position, but a philosophical one."[14] In fact, the ancients used a number of different terms to denote miracles, including *teras* and *miraculum*. Greeks used words such as *dunameis* (deeds of power), *semeia* (signs), or *thaumatos* (the amazing). In Latin the words would be similar—*virtutes, signa*, and *prodigia*. Pointing to the miracles of Abba Apollo, the wonders wrought through the hands of the holy man "defy description" yet maintain a corroborative confidence in their telling, since the stories are told "according to what we heard from the old men who were with him."[15] Miracles were not aspects of some curative power within the holy person. Rather, they were merely vessels or conduits of the divine power working itself out by their hands. Harmless illustrates this by another story from the *History of the Monks in Egypt:*

> Once a great famine swept through the Thebaid, and the people approached Apollo for relief. So he ordered the monastery's last three baskets of bread to be brought forward and then assured everyone that the Lord would multiply these loaves for the famine's duration. For the next four months, these three baskets sufficed. Satan then came to Apollo and chided him for his arrogance: "Are you Elijah, or one of the prophets or apostles . . . ?" Apollo replied: "Were not the holy prophets and apostles, who have handed on to us the power to do such things, men themselves? Or was God present then, but is now away on a journey? God can always do these things, for with him nothing is impossible."[16]

Not all were impressed by such stories. John Cassian, the great Eastern monk, had little patience for miracle tales. "Reading such things produces nothing more than wide-eyed wonder and instills nothing toward instruction in perfect living" (*De institutis*, prol. 7). It didn't matter. Many were convinced of the power of miracles, even after long delays in the execution of a miracle. In fact, some accounts actually note that beneficiaries were not completely healed or that the healing process continued for some time after the provocation of wonder. French scholar André Sigal surveyed 1,102 miracles in the high Middle Ages with chronological indicators: 428 occurred immediately after a petition, 202 occurred on the same day, 191 occurred one to two days after, 81 occurred three to seven days after, and 146 occurred more than seven days after.[17] It would not be difficult to correlate the strength of belief in a saint's miraculous powers, for instance, with the time frame that Sigal lays out.

The early medieval concept of a miracle embraced a wider variety of events than the late medieval or modern concept. In the twelfth century, theologians began whittling away at it by differentiating between wonderful events that occur according to nature or by human artifice and wonderful events that occur against the normal operation of nature, or *contra naturam*. Eventually, late medieval intellectuals regarded only *contra naturam* events as true miracles. By contrast, in the early Middle Ages people believed that miracles took place *praeter* or *supra naturam* (alongside or in addition to the course of natural events). The suspension of natural laws is attributed to God's power exclusively, as Saint Thomas maintained: "Miracles are effects wrought by the power of God alone in things which have a natural tendency to a contrary way of producing it" (*De Potentia*, q. 6; *De Miraculis*, art. 2). Further, "those effects are rightly to be termed miracles which are wrought by divine power apart from the order usually observed in nature" (*Summa Contra Gentiles*, III, 102).[18]

A Time and Space for Hagiography

French historian of religion Ernest Renan once remarked that "miracles happen only in times and places in which people believe in them."[19] Astute readers will note that mention is sometimes made about relics or relic chapels in these pages. Nothing could be more indicative of how miracle stories can grow, transcend temporal boundaries, and yet occupy finite space both in the imagination and in a dedicated physical zone. Examples include those in Maria Stein, Ohio, and Saint Anthony's in Pittsburgh, Pennsylvania. The reliquary chapel in St. John's Abbey Church in Collegeville, Minnesota, was specially designed when the church was built to house the many relics in the abbey collection. In the center is an altar built over the complete remains of the martyr, Saint Peregrine (not the patron saint of cancer patients), a boy martyr who was tortured to death in Rome in the year 192. His body was translated to a Benedictine abbey church in Neustadt-am-Main, Germany, but when fire destroyed the church in 1854, his relics were saved and later passed into the possession of the noble Lowenstein family in Bavaria. In 1895 Benedictine Father Gerard Spielmann, a monk of St. John's Abbey, successfully petitioned Prince Karl-Heinz to care for them. The relics reposed at St. Anselm's Church in the Bronx, New York, until they were solemnly enshrined in the former St. John's Abbey Church on May 6, 1928. They were later placed with other relics in the room-like relic shrine in the crypt of the present abbey church. Bones and tombs move; they have built environments that invite an onlooker's gaze or a client's petitions. They are, in a manner of speaking, alive.

Additionally, the importance of place is crucial. What passes today for an out-of-the-way spot holds the story of something that, for a brief moment, was the stuff of a miracle. In the port city of Palermo, Sicily, a church was built in the Cássaro Morto that today has no record of its foundation. Named Santa Maria della Catena, it was the home of a miracle that took place in 1391:

> Three criminals on their way to the scaffold were overtaken by a violent tempest, and were carried for shelter to this chapel, where, the storm not abating, they were compelled to remain the night. Repenting of their crimes, they made earnest prayer to the Virgin for pardon, when, lo! their chains fell from them, the doors blew open, and, their guards being asleep, they walked forth. They sought not,

however, to escape, but to make known the miracle; and King Martin, who then ruled Sicily, recognizing the will of Heaven, granted them a free pardon. In commemoration of this miracle, Martin erected the present church, for which he and his queen Mary piously contributed the funds.[20]

Few if anyone in Palermo knows of this story, but it is the reason there is a church in that spot today.

The role of hagiography, then, is not merely to understand the narratives behind the cult of a saint or to parse the details of how the miracles were used in a canonization proceeding but instead to see how time and place are coordinated to give a better sense of how we ourselves fit in. What is our own reader response to these seemingly innocuous details, if anything?

Persons and Miracles

When we discuss miracles, we discuss people—either the beneficiaries or witnesses. It is important to name the miraculée in order to present the facticity of miracles. Thus, in one of the parish annals for the Redemptorist Church of the Most Holy Redeemer in lower Manhattan, we find the following entry from July 1895:

> A miraculous cure effected by the use of the water of Lourdes is the following: A man by the name of Joseph Kelly suffered from a terrible skin disease which no doctor seemed able to cure. This man obtained a bottle of this holy water of Lourdes, and after having used only one bottle of this water was entirely cured to the great surprise of all the doctors.[21]

Apart from the rather formulaic rendition, we know that a miraculée from the late nineteenth century relied on a water cure to heal an ailment that medical science could not adequately treat. This man was not anonymous or blotted out from history; his story carries forward. Someone took the time to report on the event, the person, his condition, and how multiple physicians were dumbfounded by the transformation in their patient's condition (or his reliance upon the Lourdes water). The miracle may have been the occasion for recording these lines, but without a real person, there would be less reason to notice.

People are tied to their stories, and their lives are in turn shaped by them. When we are at our most visceral, our most passionate, we sometimes place our bodies at the heart of our emotions, thoughts, and actions. To achieve connection especially in those instances that baffle us—those instances that defy our logic and are not merely or ordinarily confusing—we place the living tissue of our body's experience into a reality that can be overwhelming. When a miracle occurs it is the reverse of a trauma, but just as that is a radical undoing of normalcy, the miracle is a refashioning or reassemblage of reality that carries with it an equally jolting experience. Parents whose prayers are favored with a miracle occurring to their sick child are not subject to a cerebral accounting unless they are some sort of automaton. Rather, they go from being torn by grief and suddenly lifted in ecstatic happiness. There is a shift in physiognomy: a shock to the system—both psychological and physical.

In our time, news of reported miracles are frequent, fast, and filled with variety. We do not know when or where the miracle will take place; no part of the world seems immune. We find multiple episodes of the miraculous even within the United States. All of the miracles used in the canonization cause of Saint Peter Claver took place in the nineteenth-century United States (and all to German Catholic immigrants). Several American causes of saints have had the benefit of support of miracles that have occurred to fellow Americans, but not all reported miracles emerging from the United States are accepted. Closer to our own time, in 1998 Rachel Baumgartner Lozano, a Saint Louis native, was diagnosed with a rare cancer of the spine. A round of chemotherapy put it into remission, but the cancer returned. She underwent a bone marrow transplant, and after a short time in remission the cancer returned between the heart, lung, and spine. Her doctors diagnosed her new crisis as terminal, but a decision was made to perform a dangerous surgery to remove a football-sized tumor. Later, the pathology report stated that this tumor was merely noncancerous scar tissue. Rachel believed that her cure was thanks to Blessed Guillaume Joseph Chaminade, a founder of the Society of Mary or Marianists who, she holds, interceded on her behalf. In 2011 her case was adjudicated negatively. Similarly, while some maintain that a statue of Our Lady of Smiles wept on several occasions at St. Elizabeth Ann Seton Parish in Lake Ridge, Virginia, the local bishop has not issued any statement on the matter since the beginning of this curiosity in the 1990s. Very often the Church is unwilling to respond to these matters for reasons that are not always evident. It is often frustrating to individuals who want to see action or hear confirmations, but there ought to be at least some room for prudential judgment to guard against felonious claims.

The Literature on Miracles

If the literature on miracles is any indication, the historical development of the concept of miracles is a vast, sprawling sea. The ancients had their own views that frankly look primitive to modern eyes. Indeed, we seem to know more about miracles that occurred in biblical times than those who were originally on the ground to witness them. The study of what miracles have done to and for people has become a science: hagiography. The particular province of hagiography—at least through the twentieth century—has belonged almost exclusively to those studying the Middle Ages. Medievalists have by far made the best use of miracle narratives and collections for deciphering the lives of their subjects as well as the institutions operating in that epoch. In part this is owing to their ubiquity. The standout works are notable, from Peter Brown's *The Cult of the Saints* (1981) to Benedicta Ward's *Miracles and the Medieval Mind* (1982) to André Vauchez's *La sainteté en Occident aux derniers siècles du Moyen Age* (1988, 1997).[22]

Modern conceptualizations of the miraculous have been steadily engaged with the challenges of scientific inquiry. Advances in surgical techniques, the application of herbs, the imposition of hands, relief for swellings or inflammations—all began in earnest in the Middle Ages but accelerated in the sixteenth and seventeenth centuries. The accompanying written texts on disassociations from miraculous cures can be considered a branch of the developing literature.[23] The Medical Bureau at Lourdes is notoriously scrupulous in its examination of cases of alleged cures at the shrine.

Without doubt, the dawn of the Enlightenment in Europe changed the way people thought about miracles, their sources, their purpose, and their reality. Philosopher David Hume's work on miracles opened the flood gates for replies attacking his rationalism. Some books on the subject had more legs than others. Bishop Joseph Butler (d. 1752) made arguments still employed today in his book *Analogy of Religion, Natural and Revealed*, initially published in 1736:

> The notion of a miracle, considered as a proof of a Divine mission, has been stated with great exactness by divines; and is, I think, sufficiently understood by everyone. There are also invisible miracles, the incarnation of Christ, for instance, which, being secret, cannot be alleged as a proof of such a mission; but require themselves to be proved by visible miracles. Revelation itself too is miraculous; and miracles are the proof of it. . . . Miracles must not be compared to common natural events; or to events which, though uncommon, are similar to what we daily experience, but to the extraordinary phenomena of nature.[24]

Similarly, John Douglas (d. 1807), the bishop of Salisbury, published in 1757 the first edition of his book *The Criterion or, Rules by which the True Miracles Recorded in the New Testament Are Distinguished from Spurious Miracles of Pagans and Papists*.[25] Over a century later, it was still in print and routinely consulted. Far more authors faded into obscurity. The seventeenth and eighteenth centuries are littered with now forgotten treatises on miracles.[26]

As the nineteenth century arrived, the literature became more defined, critical, and rule bound. Writing on the question of miracles also started to make great strides in the United States. On these shores, the noted Unitarian preacher William Ellery Channing gave the Dudleian Lecture on "evidences" at Harvard University in March 1821. Channing takes the view that "Christianity is not only confirmed by miracles, but is in itself, in its very essence, a miraculous religion."[27] By century's end, the problem of "evidences" for Christian authenticity and truth was renewed by professors in the Princeton Theological Seminary, whose scholarly journals entertained a flurry of dialogue on the subject. They were urged on in part by major church historians such as Philip Schaff of the Union Theological Seminary, who expressed deep reservations over the Catholic conception of miracles. By this time, however, and prodded by critical methods adopted by European biblical scholars, proponents of the miracles of Jesus were on the defensive.[28]

The twentieth century has not had any slowing of the voluminous literature on miracles. Much of it is of the scholarly sort and can be somewhat esoteric, but the study and practice of virtue and the working of miracles has been tied up at least since Jesuit Father R. J. Meyer's book *The Science of the Saints* (1902).[29] In part as an assimilation of the more positivistic methods then gaining ground, Meyer's book draws upon both psychology and the best of traditional spiritual writing to create a program for character formation even while remaining open to holiness of life. In this way he stood in a long line of scholars who made room for valuing religious conceptions of holiness and for systematically studying how the human personality can realize it. By incorporating scientific methodologies into his argument, he was in part deflating the type of challenge offered by people such as Andrew Dixon White, the long-serving president of Cornell University (1866–1885) and former ambassador. White's most famous book, *A History of the Warfare of Science with Theology in Christendom* (1895), went into many editions and was widely digested.[30] It gave room to critics such as Henry Charles Lea, whose target was the inquisition in medieval Spain.[31] Their indictments joined others in castigating medieval thinking and the superstitions they generated. Miracles held no place in any society that would call itself modern.

Into this abbreviated history comes our own humble contribution. It is an exceedingly partial examination of miracles and one meant to be a ready reference tool and not a comprehensive guide. We hope that it generates further thinking on one of the most perennial religious and philosophical problems in the catalog of human experience.

Patrick J. Hayes

Notes

1. Thus, the miracle of the snow in Rome in August 358 or 359 (accounts differ), when Pope Liberius dedicated a site for construction of what would become the Basilica of Santa Maria Maggiore. During Rome's hottest month, the city experienced its only snowfall, apparently predicted by the pontiff from a dream.

2. See E. Cobham Brewer, *A Dictionary of Miracles: Imitative, Realistic, and Dogmatic* (Philadelphia: J. B. Lippincott, 1894).

3. The First Vatican Council made a distinction that contextualizes miracles in and with the more general category of revelation. Miracles are signs that are undeniable and can be recognized as such with certitude. They establish the credibility of revelation. However, the fact of revelation is not established by the miracle, only revelation's credibility is. See Vatican Council I, *Dei Filius*, 3.

4. See John Hardon, "The Concept of Miracle from St. Augustine to Modern Apologetics," *Theological Studies* 15 (1954): 229–257.

5. See Robert Orsi, *Thank You, St. Jude: Women's Devotion to the Patron Saint of Hopeless Causes* (New Haven, CT: Yale University Press, 1996); Nancy Lusignan Schultz, *Mrs. Maddingly's Miracle: The Prince, the Widow, and the Cure That Rocked Washington City* (New Haven, CT: Yale University Press, 2011); and Paula Kane, *Sister Thorn and Catholic Mysticism in Modern America* (Chapel Hill: University of North Carolina Press, 2014).

6. For a sampling, see the bibliography for this encyclopedia as well as the one assembled by James Arlandson, "Bibliography on Miracles," Biblical Studies, http://www.biblicalstudies.org.uk/pdf/jma/miracles_7_arlandson.pdf.

7. See Harry Houdini, *Miracle Mongers and Their Methods: A Complete Expose of the Modus Operandi of Fire Eaters, Heat Resisters, Poison Eaters, Venomous Reptile Defiers, Sword Swallowers, Human Ostriches, Strong Men, Etc.* (New York: E. P. Dutton, 1920); Joe Nickell, *The Science of Miracles: Investigating the Incredible* (Amherst, NY: Prometheus Books, 2013); and Joe Nickell, *Looking for a Miracle: Weeping Icons, Relics, Stigmata, Visions and Healing Cures* (Amherst, NY: Prometheus Books, 1999).

8. See Alexis-Henri-Marie Lépicier, *Le Miracle* (Paris: Desclée de Brouwer, 1936), cited in François Leuret and Henri Bon, *Modern Miraculous Cures: A Documented Account of Miracles and Medicine in the Twentieth Century* (London: Peter Davies, 1957), 22.

9. For the dynamics of this political and religious struggle, see Kathleen Sprows Cummings, "The Making of an American Saint," *Commonweal* 140(10) (June 1, 2013): 7–10.

10. See Kenneth Woodward, *The Book of Miracles: The Meaning of the Miracle Stories in Christianity, Judaism, Buddhism, Hinduism, and Islam* (New York: Simon and Schuster, 2000), 35. See also John C. Cavadini, ed., *Miracles in Jewish and Christian Antiquity: Imagining Truth* (Notre Dame, IN: University of Notre Dame Press, 1999).

11. See, e.g., Howard Clark Kee, *Miracle in the Early Christian World: A Study in Sociohistorical Method* (New Haven, CT: Yale University Press, 1983); Howard Clark Kee, *Medicine, Miracle, and Magic in New Testament Times* (New York: Cambridge University Press, 1986); and Gerd Theissen, *The Miracle Stories of the Early Christian Tradition* (Philadelphia: Fortress Press, 1983).

12. As quoted in Candide Chalippe, *The Life and Legends of St. Francis of Assisi* (New York: P. J. Kenedy and Sons, 1919), viii.

13. William Harmless, *Desert Christians: An Introduction to the Literature of Early Monasticism* (New York: Oxford University Press, 2004), 291.

14. Ibid.

15. Ibid., 291–292, citing *Historia Monarchorum in Aegypto* VIII.2.7, in A.-J. Festugière, ed., *Subsidia Hagiographica* 53 (1971): 49.

16. Harmless, *Desert Christians*, 292, citing *Historia Monarchorum in Aegypto*, VIII: 45–47, in A.-J. Festugière, ed., *Subsidia Hagiographica* 53 (1971): 64–65.

17. André Sigal, *L'homme et le miracle dans la France medieval, XI–XII sièle* (Paris: Editions du Cerf, 1985), 69.

18. On Thomas's conception of the miraculous, see further Alois Van Hove, *La Doctrine du miracle chez Saint Thomas et son accord avec les principes de la recherche scientifique* (Wetteren: J. De Meester et Fils, 1927).

19. Ernest Renan, *The Life of Jesus* (New York: Modern Library, 1927), 59.

20. George Dennis and John Murray, *A Handbook for Travelers in Sicily: Including Palermo, Messina, Canaia, Syracuse, Etna, and the Ruins of the Greek Temples* (London: John Murray, 1864), 54.

21. Redemptorist Archives of the Baltimore Province, Brooklyn, New York, Most Holy Redeemer House Chronicle, 1891–1905.

22. See Peter Brown, *The Cult of the Saints* (Chicago: University of Chicago Press, 1981); Benedicta Ward, *Miracles and the Medieval Mind* (Philadelphia: University of Pennsylvania Press, 1982); and André Vauchez's *La sainteté en Occident aux derniers siècles du Moyen Age d'après les procès de canonization et les documents hagiographiques* (Rome, 1988), English translation by Jean Birrell, *Sainthood in the Later Middle Ages* (New York: Cambridge University Press, 1997).

23. For instance, Henry Stubbe, *Miraculous Conformist: Or, An Account of Severall Marvailous Cures Performed by the Stroaking of the Hands of Mr. Valentine Greatarick; With a Physical Discourse Thereupon; In a Letter to the Honourable Robert Boyle, Esq.,* . . . (Oxford, UK: H. Hall, 1666); John Browne, *Adenochoiradelogia; Or, An Anatomick-Chirurgical Treatise of Glandules and Strumaes, or Kings-Evil-Swellings; Together with the Royal Gift of Healing, or Cure Thereof by Contact or Imposition of Hands, Performed for above 640 Years by Our Kings of England Continued with Their Admirable Effects, and Miraculous Events, and Concluded with Many Wonderful Examples of Cures by Their Sacred Touch* (London: Printed by Thomas Newcomb for Samuel Lowndes, 1684); Anonymous, *The Ceremonies for Healing of Them That Be Diseased with the King's Evil, Used in the Time of King Henry VII* (London: Henry Hills, 1686); William Beckett, *a Free and Impartial Enquiry into the Antiquity and Efficacy of Touching for the Cure of the King's Evil* (London: J. Peele, 1722); and Douglas B. Price and Neil J. Twombly, eds., *Phantom Limb Phenomenon: A Medical, Folkloric, and Historical Study; Texts and Translations of 10th to 20th Century Accounts of the Miraculous Restoration of Lost Body Parts* (Washington, DC: Georgetown University Press, 1978).

24. Joseph Butler, *The Analogy of Religion, Natural and Revealed, to the Constitution and Course of Nature* (London: SPCK, 1848), 155, 159.

25. John Douglas, *The Criterion or, Rules by which the True Miracles Recorded in the New Testament Are Distinguished from the Spurious Miracles of Pagans and Papists*, 4th ed. (Oxford: Oxford University Press, 1832).

26. For example, Zachary Pearce, *The Miracles of Jesus Vindicated*, 4th ed. (London: J. Watts, 1732), and Henry Stebbing, *A Defence of the Scripture-History So Far As It Concerns the Resurrection of Jairus's Daughter; the Widow of Nain's Son; and Lazarus: In Answer to Mr. Woolston's Fifth Discourse on Our Saviour's Miracles* . . . (London: John Pemberton, 1730).

27. William Ellery Channing, *A Discourse on the Evidences of Revealed Religion, Delivered before the University in Cambridge at the Dudleian Lecture, March 14, 1821* (Boston: Cummings and Hilliard, 1821), 4.

28. See, for instance, Richard Chenevix Trench, *Notes on the Miracles of Our Lord*, 2nd ed. (London: John W. Parker, 1847), and 11th ed. (London: Macmillan, 1878); Joseph William Reynolds, *The Mystery of Miracles* (London: C. Kegan Paul, 1879); and Franz Ludwig Steinmeyer, *The Miracles of Our Lord in Relation to Modern Criticism* (Edinburgh, UK: T. and T. Clark, 1875).

29. R. J. Meyer, *Science of the Saints* (St. Louis: B. Herder, 1902).

30. Andrew Dixon White, *A History of the Warfare of Science with Theology in Christendom*, reprint ed. (New York: Free Press, 1965).

31. See, for example, Henry Charles Lea, *History of the Inquisition in Spain*, 4 vols. (New York: Macmillan, 1906–1907).

Timeline

ca. 1500–500 BCE	The Hindu Vedas and later the Upanishads (starting in ca. 1200 BCE) begin to be collected and transcribed.
ca. 1300–516 BCE	Beginnings of the Jewish exodus experience, the codification of laws, the emergence of kings, and prophetic literature to the consecration of the Second Temple in Jerusalem.
ca. 600 BCE	Birth of the Buddha.
ca. 500 BCE	Buddhist canonical texts are assembled.
ca. 33 CE	The death of Jesus outside of Jerusalem. Known for his prodigious miracle working and unique theological outlook, his followers begin to spread the story of his life and message in what comes to be known as the Gospels.
ca. 35–130	Emergence of canonical scriptures of the Christian New Testament and growth of early Christianity across the Mediterranean world; widespread martyrdom, including the protomartyrdom of Stephen. Disposition of Marian legends take rudimentary form but is subdued until the fourth century, when Christianity becomes licit across the Roman Empire.
325–787	The first seven ecumenical councils are recognized by churches of the East and West to establish doctrine and practice for the worldwide Christian movement.
ca. 426	St. Augustine of Hippo completes his masterful *City of God against the Pagans*.
ca. 570	The birth of Muhammad the prophet. Around 610 he receives the first vision on Mount Hira outside of Mecca, the message of which he would later recite to followers. In the coming decade the message would become the birth of Islam.

594	The death of Gregory of Tours, whose miracle collections and narratives begin to influence Gallican political relations in Late Antiquity.
600–700	The rise of pilgrimage sites in the Byzantine Christian world, particularly in relation to those saints' tombs or other holy places connected to healings.
1100	The Muslim philosopher Al-Ghazali takes up the issue of miracles in the Qur'an in his writing.
1199	The first papal bull of canonization is issued, proclaiming sainthood for Homobonus of Cremona.
1126	The death of St. Francis, the stigmatic of Assisi.
1153	The death of St. Bernard of Clairvaux, whose mysticism included encounters with a living corpus of Jesus on the crucifix and the *Maria lactans*.
1223	The Cistercian monk Caesarius of Heisterbach (d. 1240) pens the *Dialogus Miraculorum*, a treatise on miracles and history of the Church in Germany that quickly becomes one of the most widely read books in Europe.
1290s	Appearance of Jacobus of Voragine's *Golden Legend*.
1300–1400	A proliferation of Eucharistic miracles throughout Europe and the subsequent establishment of commemorative shrines occurs.
1492	Christopher Columbus, an explorer from Genoa sailing under a Spanish flag, lands at Hispaniola, bringing with him the introduction of Christianity into the New World.
1530–1550	Reformers such as Luther and Calvin develop their theologies apart from Roman Catholicism, protesting against what many saw as an abuse of church traditions, the subordination of Holy Scripture, and the scandal of indulgences.
1531	Our Lady of Guadalupe appears to Saint Juan Diego at Tepeyac, Mexico, and miraculously imprints her image on his *tilma*, or cloak.
1545–1563	The Council of Trent sets theological policy and church structures in place as a response to Protestantism. The council's effects on the Catholic Church would continue for the next four centuries.
1588	A new branch of the Roman curia, the Congregation of Rites, begins. It is responsible for judging the validity of miracles and how they attach to the causes of canonization of saints.

1665	Jean Bolland, founder of the Bollandists, the Jesuit compilers of the *Acta Sanctorum*, dies.
1727	At the tomb of the Abbe François de Paris (1690–1727) in the poor Parisian parish of St. Médard, numerous healing miracles begin, which accelerate after 1731.
1749	Philosopher David Hume publishes his *Enquiry Concerning Human Understanding*, which contains an important section that argues against belief in miracles.
1758	Pope Benedict XIV, the "scholar pope" known for his masterwork on the process of adjudicating causes for sainthood, dies.
1790s	Appearance of Our Lady of La Vang in Vietnam.
1824	The miraculous cure of Ann Mattingly of Washington, D.C., through the prayerful intercession of Prince Hohenlohe of Bamberg, Germany.
1827	The birth of Ellen G. White, advocate for the curative power and healthful effects of vegetarianism.
1848	The birth of modern spiritualism occurs in Hydesville, New York, when the three Fox sisters claim to be communicating with spirits. Eventually they expose their hoax, but their movement would not be denied.
1871–1885	Over 300 cures are recorded at Boston's Our Lady of Perpetual Help Basilica.
1917	The miracle of the dancing sun occurs in Fatima, Portugal.
1937	Saint André Bessette, known in his lifetime as "The Miracle Man of Montreal," dies.
1947	C. S. Lewis publishes his book *Miracles*.
1969	Establishment at Rome of the Congregation for Saints' Causes.
1986	The Roman Catholic Diocese of Brooklyn issues a definitive statement denouncing the so-called Bayside Apparitions of Veronica Lueken, a housewife and visionary from Queens, New York.
2005	On April 2, Pope John Paul II (born Karol Wojtyla) dies. During his pontificate, he beatified 1,340 people as blesseds and canonized 483 as saints—the most of any pontiff to that point. His own canonization as a saint took place April 27, 2014, after papal recognition of the validity of two miracles—to a French nun and a Costa Rican woman.

A

Africa, Miracles in

Locating particular cases of miracles in Africa presents challenges for researchers, partly for want of extant records and cooperation between subjects and investigators but also because of the vast expanse, tribal diversity, and cultural migration of the people. Some are hard to pin down. For instance, the so-called Black Virgin— Saint Efigenia of Ethiopia—is today venerated in East Africa as someone who was recruited by Saint Matthew the Evangelist, one of the original apostles of Jesus. But she is also well known among Catholics in Brazil and Cuba, where dark-skinned images are widespread owing to the connections of these countries with the African diaspora. But this saint's visage is also present in Peru, on the Pacific coast of South America, which was largely immune from the forced migration of Africans. How did she get there? The mere presence of the Ethiopian saint beyond its national borders is suggestive of the power of the miraculous cult that attached itself to her and eventually transported her to the New World. In tracing the concept of miracle in Africa, then, it is not merely a problem of isolating a tradition at a particular locus; its genesis may go beyond tribe or nation and reify in the admixture of other cultures.

Christianization in Africa—a feature of many tribal regions after 1500— necessarily incorporated worship of Catholic saints into a local idiom and frequently borrowed or played upon a "mythical" panoply of gods and goddesses already found in the indigenous population. Even outside the continent, leaders of a *cofradia*—a kind of catechist group drawn from converted Africans who had been enslaved in Cuba—could instruct their fellow slaves on the particulars of miracles and their wonder-workers. It was easy to associate these with traditional African spirits so that, according to Ócha'ni Lele, "they could, in secret, hide worship of their spirits behind the guise of the saints." Indeed, Catholic statues were hollowed out and stuffed with material found in *orisha*, or Yoruba spirit religion. This style of saint-worship became known as *Santeria*.

Within many African nations, however, the belief in miracles is not something that tests credulity but instead is accepted as a part of the natural order. This extends to all manner of visions. As late as 2001, Rwandan Catholics readily accepted the pronouncements of a local bishop on the authenticity of a Marian apparition at Kibeho, a considerable pilgrimage center that has sprung up around the site where the visions are reported to have occurred. These apparitions appeared on November 28, 1981, at a girls' school to a group of teenagers. In August of the following year all of these young women spoke of the horror of their visions, which foretold many genocidal acts between the Tutsi and Hutu clans. Some of these visions lasted for eight years, and one of the visionaries, Marie Claire Mukangango, was slain during the bloodshed of 1995. Kibeho itself was the site of a massacre of refugees who had assembled to shelter from the violence. Today the sanctuary is named the Shrine of Our Lady of Sorrows.

For many Catholics in Uganda, the annual pilgrimage to another site of martyrs is especially important. Their shrine at Namugongo, where the Ugandan Martyrs were executed by Kabaka Mwanga due to their faith, hosts thousands each year. These martyrs were 22 young men who had been instructed by the white fathers. Their final miracle for their sainthood cause occurred in 1941, when two nuns contracted the bubonic plague after they had buried one of their sisters with the same disease. They both became the subject of a novena to the martyrs, and on the third day of their illness they were completely cured.

Many come to Namugongo to give thanks for favors received, while others place their requests before the shrine. In one report, pilgrims described how they would walk from their village, often at great distance, and pray. "The first time I came here to pray was in 2009. Then, I walked from Mbarara to Namugongo. I came to pray for my daughter to get married and for my family to have a better life. After that, my prayers were answered and I came back in a bus with lots of gifts like matooke (bananas) and other necessities that pilgrims would need while here." Another stated that "It took me 12 days to walk to Namugongo from Ibanda. Last year, my daughter had an internal illness and I prayed for her as I started my journey to Namugongo. While I was still on my way, she called to inform me that she was well."

The heroism of some Christians in Africa is often without parallel around the world. Among the more incandescent heroines is Saint Josephine Bakhita from Sudan, who was canonized in 2000. Born in 1869, when she was around eight years old she was kidnapped and sold as a slave. She was repeatedly trafficked and beaten before being bought by an Italian in 1883. She was brought to Italy and eventually entered the Conosian Daughters of Charity. She died in 1947. Both miracles used in her cause—one for an Italian nun and the other for a Brazilian woman—involved cures of leg ailments.

In some African cultures, the role of the witch or healer in traditional religious belief is not unusual. Their power is such that they move the forces of nature to achieve a particular effect—in the visitation of either evil or good upon a subject. Thus, in certain West African cultures the firing of "witch guns" with "witch bullets" can cause injury or worse to the recipients. Bad luck, often accompanied by some malady or even death, can be traced to their spells. Healers, by contrast, possess special knowledge on how the body responds to herbs, touch, smells, and plasters to restore it to health. Additionally, some hold almost magical power over nature itself. For instance, the rainmaker of Kpan, a member of the Dowayo of Northern Cameroon, uses pots, skulls, and "rain stones." These stones are splashed with water and collected in the pots containing skulls so that at the slightest incantation, a heavy rainfall will commence.

As certain Protestant denominations made inroads in Africa, the so-called gifts of the Spirit have also blended well with local cultures. In Zimbabwe, for example, Pentecostals at the Apostolic Faith Mission are expected to engage in glossalalia. The pastor must speak in tongues in order to affect healings and miracles; lack of such power indicates a charlatan or interloper. Spirit possession is common, and pastors are routinely called upon to exorcise demons. In each of these instances, one can find similarities to the practices endemic to indigenous religion, particularly as they manifest themselves around the sacred bush—typically an anomalous growth well outside the village.

Belief in the mystical and magical elements of miracles remains a prerequisite among many African tribes. Western modalities of science and reason do little to undercut their power, nor do they serve to dismantle the abilities of those who are instrumental in cures and curses.

Patrick J. Hayes

See also: Amulet; Charms; Trees

Further Reading

Bowie, Fiona. "Miracle in Traditional Religions." In *The Cambridge Companion to Miracles*, edited by Graham Twelftree, 122–137. New York: Cambridge University Press, 2011.

Faupel, J. F. *African Holocaust: The Story of the Ugandan Martyrs*. Kampala: St. Paul Publications, 1984.

Gordon, David M. *Invisible Agents: Spirits in a Central African History*. Columbus: Ohio University Press, 2012.

Haar, Gerrie ter. "A Wondrous God: Miracles in Contemporary Africa." *African Affairs* 102 (2003): 409–428.

Heike, Behrend, and Armin Linke. *Resurrecting Cannibals: The Catholic Church, Witch-Hunts, and the Production of Pagans in Western Uganda*. Woodbridge, Suffolk, UK: Boydell and Brewer, 2011.

Lele, Ócha'ni. *The Dillogún: The Orishas, Proverbs, Sacrifices and Prohibitions of Cuban Santería*. Rochester, VT: Inner Traditions/Bear, 2003.

Love, Velma. *Divining the Self: A Study in Yoruba Myth and Human Consciousness*. University Park: Penn State University Press, 2012.

Lukwago, Juliet. "The Journey of the Uganda Martyrs." *New Vision*, October 22, 2010, http://www.newvision.co.ug/D/9/183/735826.

Manchingura, Francis. "The Significance of Glossolalia in the Apostolic Faith Mission, Zimbabwe." *Studies in World Christianity* 17(1) (April 2011): 12–29.

Nambowa, Carol. "Finding Answers at the Uganda Martyrs' Shrine." *Daily Monitor*, June 2, 2013, http://www.monitor.co.ug/Magazines/Life/-/689856/1868284/-/f0i989/-/index.html.

Sanchez, Roberto. "The Black Virgin: Santa Efigenia, Popular Religion, and the African Diaspora in Peru." *Church History* 81(3) (September 2012): 631–655.

Turner, Edith. *Experiencing Ritual: A New Interpretation of African Healing*. Philadelphia: University of Pennsylvania Press, 1992.

Agency

The concept of miracle presupposes the reality of agent causation, inasmuch as miracles are only possible on the assumption of an agent with the capacity to act or refrain from acting. Miracles are understood to be acts of an agent, not mere happenings. They presuppose, therefore, the legitimacy of a concept of causality whereby agents can initiate—that is, be the origin of—causal chains.

Agent causality is often contrasted with event causality. Commitment to event causality is characteristic of the naturalistic perspective wherein all caused events are understood to be caused by a prior event, never by an agent. There are important differences between agent causation and event causation, but it is arguably a mistake to see them as so radically different that they cannot be subsumed under a common understanding of causality.

In a causal disposition theory, substances have causal powers that are a result of their natures. In such a theory, both agent causation and what is termed event causation involve causation by substances, that is, substances producing effects by virtue of their inherent causal powers. The crucial difference between event causality and agent causality is that some substances are essentially passive, in the sense that their causal powers are only, and automatically, exercised in response to a triggering event (event causality), whereas other substances, that is, agents, may choose whether and how to exercise their causal powers (agent causality). Despite this crucial difference, both agent and event causality are instances of the exercise of the inherent powers of substances.

A miracle, of course, may involve both agent and event causality. If God directly causes an event, say the ex nihilo creation of a spermatozoan in the body of a virgin named Mary, this initiates a causal chain—perhaps better, a causal web— that in conjunction with event causation results in the miracle of the Virgin Birth. Mary's pregnancy, apart from the way in which it was initiated, may follow an entirely natural path and be explicable in terms of event causality right up to the point of God's directly creating a spermatozoan. C. S. Lewis makes this point very nicely when he observes that

> If God annihilates or creates or deflects a unit of matter He has created a new situation at that point. Immediately all Nature domiciles this new situation, makes it at home in her realm, adapts all other events to it . . . the divine art of miracle is not an art of suspending the pattern to which events conform but of feeding new events into that pattern.

The fact that miracles presuppose agent causation suggests that the concept of miracle can only find its metaphysical home in theism. Naturalist metaphysics can find no place for the reality of agent causation, and similarly pantheism and panentheism do not allow agency to be an ultimate feature of reality. Given that polytheism is not a viable option, this leaves theism as providing the only metaphysic capable of accommodating the concepts of agency and miracle.

Robert Larmer

Further Reading

Larmer, Robert. *The Legitimacy of Miracle*. New York: Lexington, 2013.
Lewis, C. S. *Miracles: A Preliminary Study*. New York: Macmillan, 1947.

Amulet

The knowledge and usage of an amulet is as old as man's existence on Earth, but the meaning attached to the object by those who first used it is not quite clear. However, various scholars have tried to explain the word in different ways. The word "amulet," first used by Pliny, is derived from the Latin word *amuletum*, which means an object that protects man from trouble. Other scholars who link the word to a similar Latin origin, *amoletum*, describe it as a means of defense. Yet some scholars suggest that it is derived from the Arabic *himala*, which is the word for the cord that suspends an amulet from the neck and for the amulet itself. The two Latin derivations suggest that the inventors of the amulet may have used it for the purpose of self-preservation because of its magical or supernatural powers.

Man invented or discovered the amulet because of fear—fear of the environment, fear of dangerous animals, fear of his fellow man, and fear of unknown dangers. People also wear amulets for magico-religious reasons, such as discerning evil spirits and curing diseases. The invention of the amulet came as a result of man's natural instinct to protect himself, his family, and his belongings and to ensure the continuity of his offspring. Its usage cuts across different geographical locations and religions in the world. Despite its ancient origin, people today still consider it as a means of protection. In the Christian world, for instance, amulets exist in the form of chaplets, crucifixes, rosaries, and scapulars. People who do not belong to any religious group also use amulets for some kind of protection. Among the wearers, the amulet is a symbol of refuge and assurance. Amulets inspire unshakable faith among their possessors, and without faith their supernatural power cannot work.

There are two types of amulets: personal and general. Personal amulets protect the possessors from evil attacks, sicknesses and diseases, and the inability to have children. Amulets exist in different forms and shapes. Some are made of stone, leaf, bark, wood, animal skin, animal tooth, copper, iron, gold, or silver. Amulets also exist in liquid form. For example, the holy water used by some religious groups to ward off evil spirits is a liquid form of amulet. Different groups of people wear amulets for different purposes. In some places in Africa, for instance, pregnant women wear amulets to avoid miscarriage caused by evil spirits. Children wear them to avoid encounters with harmful spirits that may cause sickness or death. Hunters wear them to protect themselves from dangerous spirits and animals in the forest. Business people on the other hand, wear amulets for the success of their business and to avoid loss of their money and goods. Traditional wrestlers and warriors believed in the power of amulets to defeat their opponents. People also wear amulets to be able to foresee the future and prevent dangers.

General amulets are not often worn or carried from place to place. Most times, they are buried at central places in a village or hung at main entrances of people's compounds or villages. Such amulets are used to ward off evil spirits that may harm members of a group. Members of such groups usually perform occasional sacrifices in places where their amulets are buried or hung. Such sacrifices are meant to keep the power of the amulet active. General amulets are also buried in farmlands to ensure a good harvest and protection of the crops from pests.

Arua Oko Omaka

Further Reading

Budge, E. A. Wallis. *Amulets and Magic*. London: Kegan Paul, 2001.
Gonzalaz-Wippler, Migene. *The Complete Book of Amulets and Talismans*. Minneapolis: Llewellyn Publications, 2003.
Maurya, Jyotsna. *Amulets and Pendants in Ancient Maharashtra (3rd C. BC to 3rd C. CE)*. New Delhi: D. K. Printworld, 2000.

Annet, Peter

Peter Annet (1693–1769) was one of the later Deists. His writings on miracles include *The Resurrection of Jesus Considered* (London, 1744) and *Supernaturals Examined* (London, 1747). As R. M. Burns notes, Annet was fundamentally a polemicist, and his writings display little philosophical expertise. He nevertheless anticipated, as did the earlier Deist William Wollaston (1659–1724) in his *The Religion of Nature Delineated* (1722) Hume's argument of Part 1 in *Of Miracles*, asserting that since miracles contravene the laws of nature, any testimony in their favor is undermined by the evidence in favor of the laws of nature. Annet's version of the argument appeared in print too late to have exerted influence upon Hume, but Hume would have read Wollaston's *The Religion of Nature Delineated*. Regarding the question of Wollaston's influence upon Hume in Hume's formulation of the argument of Part 1, Burns suggests that "Wollaston's treatment of the argument had sunk into Hume's unconscious, to be retrieved at La Flèche [the location where Hume tells us he first thought of the argument] by Hume accompanied by the sincere conviction that he was inventing the argument." Annet, as did many other deistic writers, employed Hume's fourth *a posteriori* argument of Part 2 in "Of Miracles." In employing this argument, Hume could make no claim to originality, since the argument was well known to anyone acquainted with the deistic writings.

Robert Larmer

Further Reading

Burns, R. M. *The Great Debate on Miracles*. East Brunswick, NJ: Associated University Presses, 1981.

Apparitions

Apparitions—also known as visions—are experiences of seeing a person or object that is not actually there in three dimensions. Although the apparition appears realistic, there are clues to its nonphysicality: it may be hovering in midair, bathed in light, framed in an oval, or only part of a larger body. Finally, it may disappear into the air or ascend out of sight. The Society for Psychical Research in the United Kingdom carried out research into apparitions and suggested that as many as 10 percent of the population may have experienced one. A frequent case that they cite is a vision of a person who has recently died when the visionary does not yet know of the death. There are also locutions, when someone hears a voice rather than sees a person or object.

The fact that apparitions are not real in the sense of being physical entities leads to the common supposition that they are hallucinations, created by the mind. This idea is supported by the fact that one or more visionaries may see an apparition while everyone else present does not. This would put them into the same category as waking dreams. It does not follow that they are not meaningful: psychoanalysis identifies the importance of dreams as clues to inner psychic states, and apparitions may have the same function.

Most religions take both dreams and apparitions very seriously; they are seen as potential communications from the divine or spiritual sphere. In the Bible, the Josephs of the Old and New Testaments had important dreams, and prophets were recipients of divine visions. Given their potential importance, such phenomena are interpreted by specialists in the religious tradition to decide, first, whether or not they are genuine messages from the divine and, second, what guidance is being given to the community through them.

The most prominent apparitions in religions worldwide are those in the Roman Catholic tradition, particularly those of the Virgin Mary (sometimes visions of Christ, saints, or angels are seen). Apparitions often draw large crowds, which may lead to a new place of pilgrimage, or the visionary or visionaries becoming celebrities or even saints. In the modern period, the most popular Catholic apparition shrines include Lourdes, Fatima, and Medjugorje. These are places where seers claim that the Virgin Mary appeared to them and passed on messages through them.

The Roman Catholic Church rejects or ignores many more cases than it accepts; the numbers of approved apparitions are relatively few. The church is not keen to approve apparitions that might become diversions or embarrassments in its mission. When an apparition is reported and crowds begin to gather, the local bishop has the task of deciding whether to investigate the apparition; if it is regarded as worthwhile, he then appoints a commission of priests, theologians, and psychologists to help him make a decision as to the authenticity of the case. In the modern period, the Church hierarchy has been more sympathetic to children or adolescent girls than to adults, in accordance with a general belief that they are more likely to be innocent of political agendas.

The Catholic curial office responsible for questions of faith and morals, including the legitimacy of Marian apparitions, is the Congregation for the Doctrine of the Faith. It has developed guidelines for assessing alleged appearances. In its document *Normae de Modo Procedendi in Diudicandis Praesumptis Apparitionibus ac Revelationibus* (1978), there are tests that are applied to Catholic apparitions, which include the following:

a. *The trance state itself*. It is a positive sign if the seer or seers remain peacefully at prayer during the vision and do nothing to embarrass or offend onlookers.
b. *The demeanor of the visionaries*. The visionaries' reputation is not important *before* the visions, but increased moral effort and wisdom should result from a genuine vision rather than egocentricity or attempts to gain financially. In other words, a true vision should lead to a transformation.
c. *The orthodoxy of the messages*. They should conform to church teaching and the Bible.
d. *Prophecies by visionaries*. Any prophecies by visionaries should be shown to have been accurate, and if there are any claimed healings central to the case, they should be demonstrated to be genuine.
e. *Church dissent and politics*. The event should not lead to dissent against the Church and should not be clearly political in intent.
f. *Explanation of the case*. There should be no obvious explanation that tells against the divine origin of the case, such as mental illness, hallucination due to hunger, physical illness or the taking of drugs, or illusion caused by atmospheric effects.

Catholic Church responses to apparitions are not uniform across time and place. The period and country most favorable to apparitions in the modern period was France between 1830 and 1876, although even there only five cases led to approved shrines (Rue du Bac, La Salette, Lourdes, Pontmain, and Pellevoisin). The period of the greatest number of apparitions of Mary that were not approved was 1947–1954, when political instability, the Cold War, and the advent of the nuclear age brought communal anxiety to Catholics in Europe and North America. Sometimes when there is an outbreak of visions, particular apparitions of the Virgin Mary are selected as genuine and differentiated, the rest being regarded as inauthentic or copies of the original. This was the case at Lourdes in 1858 and Belgium (Beauraing and Banneux) in 1933.

Recent Catholic writers on apparitions have argued that apparitions can be understood as paranormal phenomena, and while the effects may be dramatic, such as accurate prophecies and telepathic knowledge, this does not necessarily mean a divine origin. The Jesuit Herbert Thurston wrote in 1934 that while visionaries usually described their experiences honestly (he gave examples of bishops who had apparitions), they were subject to what he called "auto-suggestion"—in other words, seeing what their own subconscious had prompted them to see. This was true even in collective cases where several people were witnesses.

Another Jesuit, Karl Rahner, wrote in 1963 that psychic ability is not supernatural but natural. Some people enjoy spiritual faculties more than others, but this does not prove that God is working a miracle. In the tradition of Saint Thomas Aquinas in which Rahner worked, God works through humans' natural abilities, and to believe in miracles is only a last resort. God works through, for example, good teachers, family love, and social justice—these are no less the product of divine action than sensational phenomena such as apparitions. Rahner draws on the mystic tradition of Saint Teresa of Ávila and Saint John of the Cross to argue that the most important aspect of all human experiences is the underlying relationship with God.

In the 21st century, the Vatican itself made a statement that accorded with the cautious view of apparitions. Cardinals Joseph Ratzinger—later to become Pope Benedict XVI—and Tarcisio Bertone wrote a commentary on the famous apparitions at Fatima, Portugal, in 1917 and the subsequent tradition of "secrets" there. While they confirmed the authenticity of Fatima, they also reminded Catholics that apparitions were private and subjective experiences. Even when accepting certain cases as genuine divine revelations, the Church did not guarantee the divine origin of each and every one of their messages, nor did it require Catholics to believe in them. As Ratzinger put it, while apparitions such as Fatima are "the result of a real perception of a higher and interior origin," the visionary "sees insofar as he is able, in the modes of representation available to him." The images are symbolic. Nevertheless, the most prominent apparitions *are* seen as representing a divine initiative to the Church at a particular time and place, often characterized by hardship and crisis. According to devotees, God wishes to console, warn, lead, and guide, often communicated through the Virgin Mary. Therefore, shrines draw millions of pilgrims, including priests, bishops, cardinals, and popes.

The relationship between apparitions and context is explored by several anthropologists. Scholars have shown how apparitions are more likely to occur at times of social unrest and stress on the local community. In many cases, this has included ideological conflict with nonbelievers and sometimes also political repression. Others have focused on the individuals involved: both visionaries and pilgrims understand the experience as a divine response to suffering through the maternal mediation of Mary.

Still other scholars describe the process by which the visionary messages become established. This is not a simple case of Mary passing a message through the medium of a visionary but rather a complex process in which messages are edited and shaped by a local community, including priests and laypeople. The visionary is the focus for this activity but is not the only contributor. Therefore, the whole community's beliefs in the presence of Mary and her consolation during times of suffering and anxiety are expressed and articulated in apparitions. This means that idiosyncratic statements and elements that do not accord with general belief are usually omitted in reports and testimonies.

This community shaping occurs through time, and the understanding of a vision evolves. The original apparition may be thought originally to be a departed spirit (as at Lourdes), the devil (Fatima), or a witch (Banneux). The possibility that it might be Mary, while suspected at first, only emerges through the discarding of other possibilities, including demonic origin (hence the practice of throwing holy water at the place where the vision is occurring). Local people, especially the visionary's own family, may doubt that a person they know could be the object of a divine visitation, and so they need to be convinced by, for example, the durability of the visionary under pressure, the shared testimony of a number of witnesses, or belief displayed by outside visitors.

The Internet has made it easier to locate places where apparitions are occurring; modern jet travel facilitates visiting those places. Therefore, the number of pilgrims at apparition shrines is greater than at any time before, and there is worldwide interest in new visions, even before any approval process. In recent times, the United States, with its large Catholic population, has taken over from Italy as the nation with the most widely reported claims of apparitions of the Virgin Mary. The Church in America has responded by authenticating an apparition by a Belgian immigrant nun, Adele Brise, in Champion, Wisconsin, originally occurring in 1859. The Marian apparition tradition in the twentieth century has been characterized by more apocalyptic messages in which great miracles and severe punishment on humanity are foreseen, prophecies that could prove embarrassing for the Catholic Church if it approved the visions.

Chris Maunder

See also: Bayside Apparitions; Medjugorje; Our Lady of Akita; Our Lady of Beauraing; Our Lady of Fatima; Our Lady of Guadalupe; Our Lady of Knock; Our Lady of LaSalette; Our Lady of La Vang; Our Lady of Lourdes; Our Lady of Pontmain; Our Lady of Subang Jaya

Further Reading

Apolito, Paolo. *Apparitions of the Madonna at Oliveto Citra: Local Visions and Cosmic Drama.* Translated by William Christian Jr. University Park: Pennsylvania State University Press, 1998.

Bertone, Tarcisio, and Joseph Ratzinger. *The Message of Fatima*. Vatican City: Congregation for the Doctrine of the Faith, 2000.

Blackbourn, David. *Marpingen: Apparitions of the Virgin Mary in Bismarckian Germany*. Oxford, UK: Clarendon, 1993.

Christian, William, Jr. "Religious Apparitions and the Cold War in Southern Europe." In *Religion, Power and Protest in Local Communities: The Northern Shore of the Mediterranean*, edited by Eric R. Wolf, 239–266. Berlin: Mouton, 1984.

Christian, William, Jr. *Visionaries: The Spanish Republic and the Reign of Christ*. Berkeley and Los Angeles: University of California Press, 1996.

Congregation for the Doctrine of the Faith. "Normae de Modo Procedendi in Diudicandis Praesumptis Apparitionibus ac Revelationibus," 1978, The Vatican, http://www.vatican .va/roman_curia/congregations/cfaith/documents/rc_con_cfaith_doc_19780225_norme -apparizioni_en.html.

Green, Celia, and Charles McCreery. *Apparitions*. Oxford, UK: Institute of Parapsychological Research, 1989.

"History." The Miracle Hunter, http://www.miraclehunter.com/marian_apparitions.

"Marian Apparitions of the Twentieth and Twenty-First Centuries." University of Dayton, http://campus.udayton.edu/mary/resources/aprtable.html.

Maunder, Chris. "Apparitions of Mary." In *Mary: the Complete Resource*, edited by Sarah Jane Boss, 424–457. New York: Continuum, 2007.

Rahner, Karl. *Visions and Prophecies*. Translated by Charles Henkey and Richard Strachan. New York: Herder and Herder, 1963.

Thurston, Herbert J. *Beauraing and Other Apparitions: An Account of Some Borderland Cases in the Psychology of Mysticism*. London. Burns, Oates and Washbourne, 1934.

Zimdars-Swartz, Sandra. *Encountering Mary: From La Salette to Medjugorje*. Princeton, NJ: Princeton University Press, 1991.

Art and Miracles

The representation of miracles in Christian art stretches back to the earliest examples of fresco painting found in the Roman catacombs. These images, which date from the early third century CE to the fifth century CE, depict the respective liberations of Daniel, Jonah, and the youths in the fiery furnace alongside images of Jesus's miraculous multiplication of loaves and fishes and the transformation of water into wine at Cana. These scenes, understood as prefiguring the sacraments, also feature the sole representation of a Christian saint performing a miracle in early art: Saint Peter drawing water in his prison cell. The overwhelming majority of scenes from Christ's life, however, illustrate miracles of healing. In Dura Europos, the house church (*domus ecclesia*) from 235 CE contains the only surviving example of a house church decoration, Christ healing the paralytic, as he does in innumerable catacomb frescoes where he is also depicted curing a blind man and hemorrhaging women. These same representations of miracles continue into the period of the legalization of Christianity in 313 CE, when the production of carved sarcophagi becomes the richest source of artistic treasures.

The Middle Ages projected Christ high into apses and altarpieces as universal ruler or Pantocrator, and the saints became thaumaturges (wonder-workers) in his name. At this point in time it became necessary to distinguish the artistic representation of miracles from images believed to have miraculous powers. The latter, generally icons of saints or the Savior, grew in number and were soon encased in shrines and framed with medals, gifts, and even vestments. In artistic representations, miracles of healing, resurrection, and exorcism proliferated among the saints of both the East and the West. The cult of relics that exploded in the era of the Crusades gave rise to images of miraculous healings through the many holy objects circulating throughout the Mediterranean basin. The lively discussions around the Fourth Lateran Council, with its reference to the doctrine of transubstantiation, also stirred artists to represent Eucharistic miracles, and Jacobus de Voragine's codification of hagiography in the *Golden Legend* gave the artists of the fourteenth century a treasure trove of miraculous subjects. The life of Saint Francis, however, as recounted by the *Fioretti* (Little Flowers), furnished a seemingly endless supply of artistic inspiration and was mined for frescoes, murals, and manuscripts. The frescoes of the Upper Basilica of Assisi illustrate apparitions, healings, resurrections, and exorcism—a veritable encyclopedia of miracles both during his lifetime and after the saint's death. Of the 28 images of Francis, fifteen represent miraculous apparitions and events. The final four panels focus on his posthumous miracles, forming the hagiographic iconography of saints for the next two centuries.

The Renaissance exalted the empirical and downplayed miracles. The human existence of Christ on Earth and the rendering of the natural world where God entered acted and dignified it with his presence and put narrative in the forefront of art and the supernatural slightly behind. Leonardo da Vinci never painted miracles, although he would delve into the representation of mysteries, nor did Michelangelo, although Raphael painted the *Room of Heliodorus* in the Vatican to recount miracles from the Old Testament through the thirteenth century. In Germany, the excitement of the discovery of the New World brought profane marvels to the forefront of artistic imagination. Albrecht Dürer wrote of the Aztec treasure sent by Hernán Cortés to Holy Roman emperor Charles V that it "was much more beautiful to me than miracles." As the Renaissance gave way to Mannerism, scenes of miracles diminished still further, to be replaced with the wondrous virtuosity of the artist's hand. One notable exception can be found in the *Gallery of Maps* in the Vatican Museums, where Girolamo Muziano's 1583 ceiling celebrated saints and miracles in every region of the Italian peninsula.

Miraculous imagery returned in full force during the seventeenth century. The Baroque era, however, with its emphasis on vision and visibility, favored ecstatic visions above all other divine favors. The gaze of the saint penetrates the curtain of the mortal world through prayer. Bernini mastered this imagery in his *Ecstasy of St. Teresa* (1647–1652), where he combined architecture, sculpture, and painting to re-create for viewers the experience of Teresa's visions. Soaring scenes of rapture proliferated into the Rococo era, becoming standard fare for vaults and ceilings throughout Europe. Not all were swept up in visionary fervor, however. The Netherlands remained fairly impervious to the representation of miracles, and among Italians, Caravaggio always favored narrative over visionary.

The Enlightenment all but called a halt to images of miracles. The few exceptions, found mostly in Italian and Spanish art, regard the miraculous with an almost clinical eye, grounding the disruption of natural law in remarkably ordered space. Miracles are painted and with as much surrounding fact and detail as possible, whether in Giovanni Paolo Panini's *Miracle at Cana* (1725) or *The Ecstasy of Beata St. Catherine de' Ricci*, by Agostino Masucci (1750).

The academic art of the nineteenth century chose to marvel at the wonders of the ancient world or the independent genius of history's great figures rather than illustrate a cooperation with the divine. The more creative artists lauded nature, landscapes, and even machinery in art, and any visual deviation from the real was the product of man's capacities, not God's.

The modern age has challenged religious painting on every level; as figurative grew out of fashion, the ability to narrate the life of Christ and the stories of the saints has impeded the capacity to recount the marvelous in art. Contemporary art's reliance on sensation may kindle the amazement of the miraculous but fails to recount the joy and belief awakened by the vision of God working in the human world. Even in the vast collections of the Vatican Museums, miracles make only the rarest of appearances. At the time of the present writing, it appears that only a miracle will renew the artistic richness of miracles in art.

Elizabeth Lev

Further Reading

Barone, Giulia. "Immagini Miracolosi a Roma alla Fine del Medio Evo." In *The Miraculous Image in the Late Middle Ages and Renaissance: Papers from a Conference Held at the Accademia di Danimarca in Collaboration with the Bibliotheca Hertziana (Max-Planck-Institut für Kunstgeschichte), Rome, 31 May–2 June 2003*, edited by Erik Thunø and Gerhard Wolf, 123–133. Rome: L'Erma di Bretschneider, 2004.

Bartlett, Robert. *Why Can the Dead Do Such Great Things? Saints and Worshippers from the Martyrs to the Reformation*. Princeton, NJ: Princeton University Press, 2013.

Connor, Carolyn. *Art and Miracles in Medieval Byzantium: The Crypt at Hosios Loukas and Its Frescoes*. Princeton, NJ: Princeton University Press, 1991.

Derbes, Anne. *Picturing the Passion in Late Medieval Italy: Narrative Painting, Franciscan Ideologies, and the Levant*. New York: Cambridge University Press, 1996.

Fallani Giovanni, Valerio Mariani, and Giorgio Masherpa. *Collezione Vaticana d'Arte Religiosa Moderna*. Paris: Silvana Editoriale D'Arte, 1974.

Grabar, André. *Christian Iconography: A Study of Its Origins*. Princeton, NJ: Princeton University Press, 1968.

Hall, James. *Dictionary of Saints and Symbols in Art*. New York: Harper and Row, 1974.

Jefferson, Lee M. *Christ the Miracle Worker in Early Christian Art*. Minneapolis: Fortress Press, 2014.

Lunghi, Elvio. *The Basilica of St Francis of Assisi*. Florence: Scala, 1996.

Millburn, Robert. *Early Christian Art and Architecture*. Berkeley: University of California Press, 1991.

Waldema, Deonna. *Du Miracle Grec au Miracle Chrètien: Classiques et Primitiviste dans l'Art*. 3 vols. Basle: Les Éditions Birkhausen, 1945–1948.

Wittkower, Rudolf. *Art and Architecture in Italy, 1600–1750*. New Haven, CT: Yale University Press, 1999.

Asceticism

Asceticism refers to the practice of denying oneself physical comforts or inflicting discomfort or pain on oneself as a form of spiritual discipline. Examples of asceticism include but are not limited to fasting, celibacy, exposure to the elements, sleep deprivation, flagellation, and wearing garments that injure the skin. The purposes of these practices include penance, purification, expressing humility, showing contempt for the physical world, vitalizing the spirit through a rejection of the body, or, in the case of Christianity, imitating the poverty and suffering of Christ.

Ethnographic evidence suggests that ascetic practices date back to the earliest human societies. In many Native American societies, young men go on a vision quest as a rite of passage. Initiates of the vision quest go alone into the wilderness to fast and deprive themselves of sleep until they reach a transcendental state. Other Native American ascetic practices include the Sun Dance, in which participants attach themselves to a vertical pole with straps that are pierced through their skin and dance until they collapse. Other traditional societies in Africa and the Pacific Islands practice ritual scarification and teeth chiseling as a rite of passage or purification ritual.

Asceticism plays an important role in India, where many sects believe that the body and its material needs entrap the soul. The Jainist sect in particular believes that the body must be conquered (the Sanskrit verb *jin* means "to conquer") through fasting, solitude, and meditation. In the past some Jainists even fasted to death in a practice called *sallekhana*. Although the Middle Path of Buddhism avoids such extremes, the Shingon school of Buddhism in Japan once practiced *sokushinbutsu*, a form of fasting until death that if successful resulted in the mummification of the monk's body.

Greek contact with the Indian world may have influenced some of the Hellenistic schools of philosophy. Diogenes the Cynic's teachings included an embrace of poverty, while both Stoicism and Epicureanism advocated self-control and physical discipline as a means of focusing the mind. The Romans likewise valued moderation and self-control as virtues.

Evidence of asceticism in the Judeo-Christian tradition dates at least as far back as the Old Testament prophets, who often lived and fasted in the wilderness and there communed with God. In the Hellenistic era the Essene sect of Judaism formed monastic communities in the desert, where they practiced celibacy and voluntary poverty. John the Baptist's ministry and Jesus's 40 days in the desert are examples of early Christian asceticism, and Christ endorsed voluntary poverty in his teachings.

In the early centuries of Christianity, martyrdom was a common outlet for ascetic impulses. After the end of persecution, many devout Christians turned to hermetic practices as a means of achieving a kind of living martyrdom. Prominent early Christian ascetics include Anthony of the Desert, Jerome, Simon Stylites, and Mary of Egypt. Their practices included solitary living in the wilderness, celibacy, fasting, nudity, or spending long periods of time atop a tree or column. Many of these were influenced by Neoplatonism, which argues that the ephemeral world of the body is an imperfect shadow of the eternal world of the spirit. Some early ascetic movements, such as the Adamites who practiced communal nudity, provoked the condemnation of church officials. The monastic traditions of the Eastern and Western churches, each with rules for communal life, grew out of efforts to maintain orthodoxy among those inclined toward spiritual practices.

In the Middle Ages asceticism was perceived as a sign of sanctity, particularly when practiced by the social elite. Royal saints such as Louis IX of France and Margaret of Hungary wore cilices and spiked girdles. Pious urban merchants such as Peter Waldo of Lyon and Francis of Assisi rejected their wealth to imitate Christ's poverty. Mystics such as Hildegard von Bingen and Teresa of Ávila practiced harsh regimens of fasting to achieve their visions. While Protestant leaders rejected the use of asceticism as a form of penance or a good work, they viewed it as evidence that a person was endowed with divine grace.

Like other Abrahamic religions, Islam also contains ascetic traditions. Muhammad himself was an ascetic and received his visions while fasting and praying in the desert. Muslims are enjoined to fast during the month of Ramadan, and on the Day of Ashura many Shiite Muslims cut their flesh. Sufism also uses ascetic practices to achieve a mystical union with God.

Eric F. Johnson

See also: Fasting

Further Reading

Wimbush, Vincent L., and Richard Valantasis. *Asceticism.* New York: Oxford University Press, 2002.

Asia, Miracles in

From the steppes of Russia to the tip of India and from Tokyo to Istanbul, miracles stretch across a vast Asian landscape, cutting through multiple ethnic and language groups, religious traditions, and economic and social strata.

The preponderant forms of Buddhism take anomalous phenomenon as a matter of course and so do not seek explanation as much as interpretation. Wang Yan, a medieval Chinese scribe, wrote down some of the well-known Buddhist miracle tales in a work called *Mingxiang ji* (Records of Signs from the Unseen Realm). In them are *zhiguai*, or accounts of anomalies. While the stories are light on details, many of them try to convince through the testimony of witnesses, thus laying the foundation for epistemic veracity of the claims and giving credence to the moral force of the stories. The miracles occur when a particular class of individuals not only does their job or fulfills their vocation—as monks do in fulfilling the five precepts—but in the ordinary course of their actions do so in an exemplary and spectacular way, usually overcoming great obstacles in the process. The upshot is not that the miracles are so freakishly out of the ordinary that they raise even a shadow of doubt but that they encourage the faithfulness of the reader to persevere.

In India, religious belief and practice is highly varied. Muslim shrines commemorating that faith's saints and martyrs—such as the one at Madhya Pradesh known as Tekri (Husain Hill), which recalls the memory of the martyrs at Karbala, Iraq—often produces the hallmarks of spirit possession among the devotees. Hindu shrines, similarly, are sites in which commemorative practices are central, particularly for those places connected with miraculous legends. The deities who inhabit these shrines are often associated with healing stories and lend credibility while boosting the fame of their shrine. Devotees identify a particular problem with a god or goddess who will protect or intervene such as Mariyamman, long thought to be the goddess of smallpox (before its eradication from India in the 1970s). Her *sakti*, or supernatural powers, can break into human affairs and help keep children safe from other diseases—and find lost wallets.

For Sikhs, the Golden Temple at Amritsar in the Punjab, with its massive bathing tank, is the ultimate pilgrimage destination, renowned for its beauty and serenity. Pilgrims are able to connect with deceased gurus who composed their holy books and worked wonders at the site. Particularly favored is Guru Nanak, the founder, who is said to have stopped an oncoming boulder with the palm of his hand, though the reason for his veneration has more to do with breaking barriers between Hindus and Muslims through his preaching of a common humanity and unity in the quest for the divine.

Relics and their healing powers are ubiquitous. The hair of the Prophet Muhammad, considered sacred to Muslims, is in the Hazratbal Mosque in Kashmir. In Sri Lanka at the Dalada Maligawa temple, pilgrims come to pay homage to the tooth of the Buddha, which is annually paraded. In Japan, another tooth relic of the Buddha was held in less esteem. Found to be offensive to the local ruler, it was ordered destroyed. But in an attempt to smash it between a hammer and anvil, both implements of destruction broke in the effort.

For Christians, numerous shrines devoted to Mary can be found across the continent. Due to the Chinese government's intolerance for unsanctioned religious activity, believers are often constrained in reporting miraculous phenomena, but at the Marian shrine at Dong Lu in China's Hebei Province, one finds reports of numerous apparitions of Our Lady of China. Like the supernatural occurrences at Fatima, on May 23, 1995, some 30,000 underground Catholic witnesses saw the sun rotate and exude multicolored rays. The local bishop also confirmed that the Blessed Virgin Mary had strengthened the community of underground Catholics through these signs.

In India in Tamil Nadu, one can find the Basilica of Our Lady of Snows, a wedding cake of a church in the Portuguese style that is now over 300 years old. Contained in the basilica is the statue of Our Lady of Snows—a reference to the Roman basilica of Saint Mary Major, site of a miracle of snow in summer. The statue is ornately decorated and is believed to hold protective power. This stems from an incident involving the priest who built the present church, Father Vigilius Mansi, whose home was struck by lightning on April 4, 1707. The priest believed that he was unharmed owing to the presence of the statue in his house. Other miracles were conveyed in 1709 by the Jesuit Francis Vaiz, such as the cure of a Dutch officer who drank the water that washed the feet of the statue of Our Lady of Snows.

Marian shrines are plentiful in the mainly Catholic country of the Philippines. A principal and monumental church dedicated to Our Mother of Perpetual Help in

Baclaran, in the city of Manila, hosts one of the largest pilgrimage destinations in the world. Tens of thousands come each Wednesday to the Perpetual Help novena seeking favors.

The intrusion or insertion of Christianity into the territories controlled by Sino-Japanese rulers often meant harsh treatment for missionaries. The 26 martyrs slain for the faith in Nagasaki were skewered with various implements and crucified. Their bodies hung for nearly three months, with many reported miracles associated with ravaged corpses. Back in India, the body of Saint Francis Xavier lies in a glass casket in Goa, at the Church of the Bam Gesu. This Jesuit missionary is nearly wholly intact except for a forearm (now at the Church of the Gesu in Rome) and a small toe, excised for a relic, allegedly bitten off by a devotee when the deceased saint's corpse passed through the city.

Japan's own Shinto shrines are protected by the *kannushi*, those placed in charge of the shrines and who serve as intermediaries between mortals and the spirit world. Though this functionary is commonplace, Japanese call to mind *kiseki* (miracles) when describing extraordinary or surprising phenomena (*reigen*). Pilgrimage, however, is frequently at the heart of miracle tales, and the stories assembled by pilgrims in their diaries help to build the strength of belief in the power of particular shrines, among which the shrine at Shikoku is perhaps the most famous. Most stories focus on curing illness, but many fit the particular hopes of the spiritual traveler.

Finally, throughout Russia's vast territory and often promoted by monastic communities of Russian Orthodoxy, the miraculous streams into the mortal realm through veneration of icons and relics. Part talisman, part conduit to God, these material objects serve a variety of purposes, from protection to healing. Icons especially convey the grace of a saint to an onlooker as if heart speaking to heart. But at bottom, what the miraculous object does is provide some relief to a body pained by sin and allow a respite from the harshness of the world.

Patrick J. Hayes

Further Reading

Bathgate, Michael. "Stranger in the Distance: Pilgrims, Marvels, and the Mapping of the Medieval (Japanese) World." *Essays in Medieval Studies* 25 (2008): 129–144.

Campany, Robert Ford. *Signs from an Unseen Realm: Buddhist Miracle Tales from Early Medieval China*. Honolulu: University of Hawai'i Press, 2012.

Dempsey, Corrine, and Selva Raj, eds. *Miracle as Modern Conundrum in South Asian Religious Traditions*. Albany: SUNY Press, 2009.

Harris, Richard H. *Images, Miracles, and Authority in Asian Religious Traditions*. Boulder, CO: Westview, 1998.

"History of the Church." Our Lady of Snows Basilica, http://www.snowsbasilica.com/index .php/component/k2/item/160-hoc.

Kivelson, Valerie A., and Robert H. Greene, eds. *Orthodox Russia: Belief and Practice under the Tsars*. University Park: Penn State University Press, 2003.

Reader, Ian. "Pilgrimage as Cult: The Shikoku Pilgrimage as a Window on Japanese Religion." In *Religion in Japan: Arrows to Heaven and Earth*, edited by P. F. Kornicki and I. J. McMullen, 267–287. New York: Cambridge University Press, 1996.

Strong, John S. *Relics of the Buddha*. Princeton, NJ: Princeton University Press, 2004.

Van Voorthuizen, Anne. "Mariyamman's Sakti: The Miraculous Power of a Smallpox Goddess." In *Women and Miracles Stories: A Multidisciplinary Exploration*, edited by Anne-Marie Korte, 248–270. Leiden: Brill, 2004.

Augustine, Saint

Among the most important Christian thinkers, Augustine of Hippo (354–430 CE) profoundly influenced Western philosophy and theology. Raised in Romanized North Africa by a pagan father and a Catholic mother, the young Augustine was attracted to Manichaeism, a syncretic form of Gnosticism deeply suspicious of the material world. An encounter with Neoplatonic philosophy, however, and its emphasis on the intellectual ascent of the mind to God in part led Augustine to return to the church of his childhood in 387. Though intending to dedicate himself to monasticism and the production of treatises on the liberal arts, Augustine was forcibly ordained to succeed the elderly bishop of Hippo Regius. Committed to the care of his people, Augustine still became deeply involved in the doctrinal debates of his time, arguing for the goodness of creation yet also the sinfulness of humanity and the need for God's restoring grace and membership in the Catholic Church.

An older scholarly consensus portrayed Augustine as an aspiring philosopher whose youthful rationalism collapsed into the fideism of a bishop close to his country flock and concerned with the sinful weakness of human nature; by this telling, the young Augustine denied the occurrence of miracles while the aged Augustine used them to coerce conversions from the people of Hippo. The consensus has moved toward new appreciation of the continuity between the early and late Augustine, a general shift that demands a more careful reading of Augustine's statements about miracles. He wrote his longest treatment of miracles, a passage in *The City of God* (22.8), three or four years before he died, but there he describes miracles witnessed around the very time of his conversion. In earlier works, he says that miracles such as those Christ performed have ceased (e.g., *On the Usefulness of Belief*, 34; *On the True Religion*, 47), but later he did not deny the continuation of less numerous, great, and renowned miracles (*Retractions*, 1.13.5).

It is his perception of the frequency and the importance of miracles, not their possibility, that changed over time. Rather than a collapse from reason into superstition, the story of the miraculous in Augustine is the story of a former Manichean's growing appreciation for the value of the bodily experience.

Three themes capture the role which the miraculous played in Augustine's thought.

An apologetic against the unbelief of philosophers. When faced with objections over the rational plausibility of Christian beliefs (e.g., Christ's ascension into heaven), Augustine invoked *mirabilia* (marvels) of both divine and natural origin to demonstrate that the world was not a closed system of causes easily grasped by human reason (*City of God*, 21.5 and 22.5). For Augustine, who viewed the philosophers' continuing rejection of a Christianity that had miraculously grown to embrace the whole world as an act of pride, these marvels constituted a call to intellectual humility (*On the Usefulness of Belief*, 31; *On the True Religion*, 47).

A sign to excite faith. Augustine frequently refers to miracles not as marvels but as *signa* (signs), a word he applied broadly to external things (sacraments, Scripture, martyrdoms) that excite but do not cause faith. He believed faith to be a gift from the Holy Spirit, without which nothing could persuade one to believe (*City of God*, 22.7); yet he also believed relationships developed through the exchange of signs, and in faith the marvel is recognized as a sign of God's power and love (*Confessions* 4.8.13; *City of God*, 22.5). Precisely because Augustine believed that the miraculous could promote faith, he ordered accounts of all miracles that occurred in Hippo to be widely distributed.

A demonstration of eschatological power. Miracles are manifestations not simply of God's power but also of the coming of the end times. Miracles demonstrate that the eschatological power of God is already at work in the world particularly through eschatological bodies, whether the sacramental Body of Christ or the *memoriae* (shrines) and relics of the martyrs (*City of God*, 22.9). If Augustine continued to believe that a spiritual ascent remained the heart of Christianity, physical miracles testified to God's care for the sick: miraculous relief from physical suffering adumbrates the final transformation of the body at the end of time by a God who loves not only soul but body (*Sermons*, 317.1).

Andrew Salzmann

See also: Early Christianity, Miracles in; Jansenism

Further Reading

Augustine. *City of God*. Translated by Henry Bettenson. New York: Penguin Classics, 2003.

Brown, Peter. *Augustine of Hippo: A Biography*. Berkeley: University of California Press, 2000.

Lancel, Serge. *Saint Augustine*. London: SCM Press, 1999.

van der Meer, Frederick. *Augustine the Bishop*. Translated by Brian Battershaw. New York: Sheed and Ward, 1961.

B

Bayle, Pierre

Pierre Bayle (1607–1746) was a French-born Calvinist who was a widely respected philosopher and expatriate of the late seventeenth century. Having fled France in 1670, he was a professor of philosophy in Rotterdam until 1693, when he devoted himself to writing. Bayle's *Réponse aux questions d'un provincial* (1704) observed that tradition viewed miracles as interruptions of the ordinary course of nature, events that do not follow natural laws but directly depend on God's intervention. Bayle's opinions on miracles and the order of nature were influenced by the Catholic philosopher Nicolas Malebranche, whom he esteemed highly. Adopting this view, Bayle thought that the natural order reflects God's immutable and constant control on his creation. Then, "if He sometimes suspends it in favor of man, it is for pure grace, it is pure mercy" (*Oeuvres diverses*, I:532–533).

In the light of Malebranche's defense of nature's intelligibility and Christian purity, Bayle strongly criticized what he considered the Catholic abuse of miracles. According to the Calvinist Bayle, the incredible amount of miracles attributed by Catholics to figures such as Marc of Aviano, Francisco Xavier, and Ignatius of Loyola is a sign of the prevailing pagan idolatry among the papists. Distrustful of Catholic propaganda and sceptical of human credulity, Bayle considered the Scriptures the only real source of miracles.

In his *Dictionnaire historique et critique* (5th ed., 1740), Bayle noted that "credulity is the cause of proliferation" and that Protestants are not immune from the superstition, ignorance, and human weakness that produce idolatry. To credulity, he opposed the philosophical investigation of the natural causes of phenomena. Embracing a mechanistic philosophy, he identified nature with the laws dictated by God and believed that the formation of the world was utterly dependent upon them. For Bayle, natural explanations of miracles do not deny God's place in nature. On the contrary, the image of a clockwork cosmos refers to the great clockmaker, governing his creation by means of rigid mechanical laws.

Some irregularities, such as monstrous births, are part of the usual course of nature and can be explained by the usual laws. In this view there is no place for intermediaries, such as *anima mundi* or plastic natures, because the secondary causes directly depend on the prime cause, God. Bayle extended his skepticism also to biblical miracles. The story of Noah's deluge, for instance, did not need a supernatural intervention. Nor did survival of Jonah in the belly of the whale. Furthermore, Bayle denied any efficacy to miracles in what was maintained their first aim, the conversion of disbelievers. Thus, he entirely questioned the legitimacy of miracles in the Christian religion, which has not been able to liberate humanity from superstition.

Notwithstanding the influence of Malebranche's philosophy and Bayle's Calvinist creed, the observations on miracles contributed to the affirmation of Bayle's later materialist system of philosophy, "stratonism," which largely departed from his sources.

Francesco G. Sacco

Further Reading

Bayle, Pierre. *Oeuvres diverses*, Vol. 3, 2nd ed. La Haye, 1737.
Bouchardy, Jean Jacques. *Pierre Bayle: La nature et la "nature des choses."* Paris: Honoré Champion, 2001.
Mori, Gianluca. *Bayle philosophe*. Paris: Honoré Champion, 1999.
Whelan, Ruth. *Anatomy of Superstition: A Study of the Historical Theory and Practice of Pierre Bayle*. Oxford, UK: Voltaire Foundation, 1989.

Bayside Apparitions

In the years following World War II as the Cold War between the atheistic Soviet Union and the free world of Europe and the United States intensified, a number of apparition sites emerged and gained attention in Catholic Europe and in the United States. Centered on appearances and prophetic messages given by the Virgin Mary, the Mother of Jesus would comment on social, cultural, and religious crises facing the world. One especially fascinating set of late Cold War visions—extreme apocalyptic responses to anxieties generated by fears of godless Soviet-generated world atheism, the reforms of the Catholic Church after the Second Vatican Council, and the cultural changes of the late 1960s in the midst of American troop losses during the war in Vietnam—became known as both "Our Lady of the Roses" and "Our Lady of Bayside."

Dubbed also by followers "the Lourdes of America," the Bayside apparitions have their origin with the activities of Bayside, New York, Roman Catholic housewife and visionary Veronica Lueken (1923–1995). Lueken's mystical experiences began in 1968 with her detection of the "odor of sanctity" in her car during prayerful responses to the news of the assassination of Senator Robert F. Kennedy. She soon began seeing and receiving messages from Saint Theresa of Lisieux. In 1970, Lueken reported visual and auditory communication with the Virgin Mary herself, first in her home. Other saints and even Jesus communicated with her as well. She began to hold public prayer vigils on the grounds of St. Robert Bellarmine Church in Bayside, New York, until the pastor of the parish asked her to move these occasions, which were attracting greater public attention, to a location more accessible to the parking of cars. Communications from Mary and Jesus in 1975 instructed Lueken to move the visionary events to a spot in Flushing Meadows–Corona Park, Flushing, in the borough of Queens, New York City, which had been the site of the Vatican Pavilion during the 1964 World's Fair. Thus began two decades of visionary experiences and communications from the Virgin, Jesus, and other Catholic saints along with associated prayer rituals held on the eves of feast days of Roman Catholicism. Among the mystical messages and prophecies were critiques of the church's reforms of liturgy, practices, and theology; public behavior with a specific emphasis on the immorality of popular culture such as rock-and-roll music; and the demonic nature of late Soviet-era behavior and discourse. All such evils were observed as precursors of the revelation that the Antichrist and a great chastisement would mark the destruction of civilization prior to a new era of peace in this conservative Catholic reading of the Christian apocalyptic tradition.

An exemplar of contemporary vernacular Catholicism, the Bayside believers held that Lueken's visions complemented, expanded on, and updated communications from Mary and Jesus at such famous established postindustrial Marian shrines as Lourdes, Fatima, and LaSalette. The messages that poured from Mary via Lueken condemning such contemporary media activity as television viewing were often paradoxically accompanied by moneymaking ventures incorporating television viewing, such as the sale of Bayside shrine–based videos and DVDs. The financial needs of the developing Bayside devotion also included the production of holy cards, pamphlets, and books containing transcribed messages from the visionary and celebrating the presence of the holy at this special site. The organization of the Bayside devotion also communicated widely its prophetic messages throughout the United States and elsewhere in French, Spanish, and Italian translations and advertised the series of pilgrimage dates when believers would come to pray and watch Lueken in trance. At times, Bayside believers would stand outside institutional Catholic parishes and distribute literature for and about the shrine, to the distinct irritation of local pastors. The search for evidence by believers and visitors to the apparition site regarding the authenticity of the visionary's experiences resulted in a tradition of reading Polaroid photographs taken in situ for messages complementing Lueken's pronouncements.

Upon the death of Lueken, a power struggle between her husband Arthur (d. 2002) and a band of assistants led to a 1997 schism among the followers so that in the 21st century two separate groups, Our Lady of the Roses Shrine and St. Michael's World Apostolate—both claiming an authentic connection to the visionary—hold divergent devotions and vigils of prayer, often concurrently, at the site in Flushing Meadows Park. The Archdiocese of Brooklyn in 1986 investigated the apparitions and announced that they lacked proper authenticity and were contrary to church teachings. The fact that the messages condemned the Second Vatican Council's pronouncements and reforms naturally did not make the institutional church respond positively to the Bayside experience.

Leonard Norman Primiano

See also: Apparitions

Further Reading

Cuneo, Michael. *The Smoke of Satan: Conservative and Traditionalist Dissent in Contemporary American Catholicism.* New York: Oxford University Press, 1997.
Laycock, Joseph. *The Seer of Bayside: Veronica Lueken and the Struggle for Catholicism.* New York: Oxford University Press, 2014.
"Statement on the Alleged Apparition of 'Our Lady of the Roses' and the Bayside Movement." Diocese of Brooklyn, March 25, 2014, http://dioceseofbrooklyn.org/wp-content/uploads/2014/04/Bishop-DiMarzio-Statement-on-Alleged-Apparition-of-Our-Lady.pdf.
St. Michael's World Apostolate, www.smwa.org.
These Last Days Ministries, http://www.tldm.org/default.htm.
Wojcik, Daniel. *The End of the World as We Know It: Faith, Fatalism, and Apocalypse in America.* New York: New York University Press, 1996.

Beatification

Beatification is the formal acknowledgment by the pope of an individual's public ecclesiastical cult, that is, when a blessed may enjoy both the title and the celebration of a feast day officially placed on the liturgical calendar. Since 2005, celebrations of beatifications have typically been confided to the prefect of the Congregation of Saints' Causes, who acts on behalf of the supreme pontiff. Though they may take place in the Vatican, the usual practice is now to hold the beatification ceremony in the local diocese that promoted the cause. This is done in the context of a Eucharistic celebration or Mass, but it may also occur within the celebration of the Word or Liturgy of the Hours.

Beatification raises the Servant of God to the last level before the dignity of sainthood. Papal approval of the venerable's sanctity and life of heroic virtue usually precedes the proof of a miracle wrought by God through the intercession of the beati; one more miracle is required for sainthood, although martyrs are exempt from this two-miracle rule, and some saints may have their miracles waived by papal decree.

For at least the first six centuries after the birth of Christ the beati were, for all intents and purposes, treated as saints. So profuse were their miracles, especially at their tombs, that local popular proclamation was sufficient to establish their holiness, with the spread of their fame to nearby regions enough to establish their universal devotion. This was especially true of martyrs. Local bishops weighed in merely to confirm the vox populi. Spontaneous cults around such people developed well into the medieval period, during which time control of the process was slowly taken from the hands of the local bishop and reserved to the pope. With Pope Urban VII's decree *Celestis Hierusalem Cives* of 1634, the public cult was strictly prohibited until such time as the formal beatification was announced. For those beati who already enjoyed the favor of a public cult, however, *Celestis Hierusalem Cives* grandfathered them into the catalog of the blesseds and allowed their cult's continuance—at least for the next century—despite not having been formally beatified. However, it abolished the practice of local recognition of holy people as saints as well as any new developing public cults. Recognition of any public cult would henceforth be determined by the supreme pontiff.

The rationale for Urban VII's action is important for the credibility of the process. It stems from the Church's interest in protecting the faithful from the snares of the Devil who, Pope Alexander III (1159–1181) believed, would have the simple fooled into placing their prayers before a man venerated as a martyr but who died, nevertheless, while in a drunken stupor. One could not logically invest belief in someone in an objective state of sin.

Urban's decree had the added effect of raising the theological question of the infallibility of papal decisions on the beatification and canonization of saints. Most Catholic theologians and canonists agreed with the possibility of inerrancy in such pronouncements for canonization, and so their solemnity was often placed into the category of beliefs that had to be held by faith, that is, with an absolute assent of mind and will. Saint Thomas Aquinas, for instance, notes that the honor paid to saints is in a certain sense "a profession of faith" and that "we must piously believe that in this matter also the judgment of the Church [i.e., the pope] is not liable to error" (*Quodlibet* IX, art. 8). An instinct of the Holy Spirit, Thomas held, guided the pope in such pronouncements. However, for beatification, there is far less theological certainty in the inerrancy of the pronouncement, at least insofar as the decree is less solemn and does not impose the same liturgical requirements as does a canonization. In other words, it is not necessary to give formal assent of mind and will to the decree of beatification.

Today beatification is necessary before a canonization may take place for a nonmartyr. The theological rationale for beatification, however, is ultimately pastoral in nature. By declaring someone a blessed, the pope asserts publicly that the individual may be considered worthy of emulation by the faithful of a diocese, region, or religious community. It further authorizes the local ordinary to supervise an exhumation of the venerable Servant of God and the extraction of a relic that will assist in the development of a public cult for widespread veneration by the Church.

Patrick J. Hayes

See also: Canonization; *Celestis Hierusalem Cives;* Postulator

Further Reading

Azevedo, Emmanuel de. *Doctrina de servorum Dei beatificatione et beatorum canonizatione in synopsim redacta.* Brussels: Typis Societatis Belgicae, 1854.

Benedict XIV. *De servorum Dei beatificatione et beatorum canonizatione.* Vatican City: LEV, 2010–.

Blaher, Damian Joseph. *The Ordinary Processes in Causes of Beatification and Canonization: A Historical Synopsis and a Commentary.* Washington, DC: Catholic University of America Press, 1949.

Indelicato, Salvator. *Il processo apostolic di beatificazione.* Rome: Scientia Catolica, 1954.

Indelicato, Salvator. *Le basi giuridiche del processo di beatificazione: Dottrina e giurisprudenza intorno all'introduzione delle cause dei servi di Dio.* Rome: Officium Libri Catholici, 1944.

"Sancti Thomae de Aquino: Quodlibet IX." Corpus Thomisticum, http://www.corpusthomisticum.org/q09.html#68749.

Veraja, Fabijan. *La beatificazione: Storia, problem, prospettive.* Vatican City: Libreria Editrice Vaticana, 1983.

Benedictines and Miracles

The Benedictine tradition cannot escape miracles for the simple reason that they inundate the biography of its founder, Benedict of Nursia (ca. 480–547). The only account of Benedict's life is *De vita et miraculis venerabilis Benedicti* (The Life and Miracles of St. Benedict), which comprises the second book of the *Dialogues* attributed to Pope Saint Gregory the Great (540–604). Next to Benedict's *Regula* (Rule), Gregory's vita has influenced the development of Benedictine spirituality, culture, and history since at least the ninth century. Nevertheless, the bizarre miracles of this vita have posed questions about its authenticity, leading some modern scholars to question its Gregorian authorship and, by extension, the very existence of Benedict. This scholarly debate signals the enduring relevance of miracles for the Benedictine tradition. More important, however, Gregory's vita presents a window into how the miraculous has shaped Benedictine history.

Two places are important for Benedictine miracles, both the sites of Benedict's relics: Monte Cassino, the first monastic foundation, and Fleury. While Gregory assembled his vita of Benedict in the sixth century and drew on commonplaces in hagiographic literature (Benedict was able to penetrate dreams, receive visions, and have acute and prophetic insight), the relic miracles associated with Monte Cassino were drawn up by Abbot Desiderius in the mid-eleventh century and concentrated on his posthumous miracles. Those at Fleury were assembled by several writers from the ninth to twelfth centuries and described both pre- and postmortem miracles.

The Benedictine reception of miracles naturally begins with Gregory's vita. The pope's presentation of Benedict's life is no less inseparable from miraculous events than the other biographies of Italian ascetics that fill the four books of the *Dialogues*. The reader finds Benedict miraculously repairing a sieve even before he departs the world for his cave near Subiaco. As Gregory's narrative progresses, the miracles become more numerous. In fact, the chapters of the vita correspond to particular miracles. Benedict shatters a chalice filled with poison upon blessing it, commonly symbolized in Benedictine iconography. He miraculously creates a spring from a mountain and makes one of his disciples (Maurus) walk on water in order to save his drowning brother (Placidus). Benedict further resurrects several children, discerns monks' transgressions before they are reported, and prophesizes both the rise of the Ostrogoth Totila (d. 552) and the destruction of Monte Cassino by the Lombards. Toward the end of his life, Benedict witnesses the ascension of his twin sister, Scholastica (ca. 480–542), into heaven and finds himself raised above the entire world in ecstasy.

Many of these miracles allude to various biblical stories and portray the holy man as possessing many of the same powers as Christ. This biographical archetype of life and miracles repeats itself in the following centuries with a colorful array of medieval Benedictine vitae. The most famous is the *Life and Miracles of St. Maurus*, likely authored by the ninth-century abbot Odo of Glanfeuil. Aside from initiating Maurus's cult among the Benedictines, it further champions Gaul (and thus later France) as the first daughter of Saint Benedict through the mission of his first follower, Saint Maurus. Benedictine hagiography continued this tradition of miraculous monks and nuns in the biographies of Oda, Dustan, and Oswald in England and Boniface and Walburga in Germany.

The centrality of miracles in Benedictine biographies waned with the Enlightenment, only to see a renaissance with the Benedictine revival in the nineteenth century. Thus, the Wolter brothers who founded Beuron, a German center of Benedictine liturgy and art, assumed the names Maurus (1825–1890) and Placidus (1828–1928) in the spirit of Gregory's vita. Their contemporary confrères promoted the sainthood of the French Benedictine Paul of Moll (1824–1896) with a biography arranged according to miraculous anecdotes, similar to Gregory's vita. The late nineteenth century also witnessed the Benedictine popularization of the Medal of St. Benedict and its miraculous protection against the Devil, still prompted among the sons and daughters of Saint Benedict to this day.

Paul G. Monson

Further Reading

Cavadini, John. "A Note on Gregory's Use of Miracles in *The Life and Miracles of St. Benedict*." *American Benedictine Review* 49(1) (1998): 104–120.

Clark, Francis. *The 'Gregorian' Dialogues and the Origins of Benedictine Monasticism*. Leiden: Brill, 2002.

Dal Santo, Matthew. *Debating the Saints' Cult in the Age of Gregory the Great*. New York: Oxford University Press, 2012.

De Vogüé, Adalbert. "Is Gregory the Great the Author of the *Dialogues*?" *American Benedictine Review* 56(3) (2005): 309–314.

Eadmer of Canterbury. *Lives and Miracles of Saints Oda, Dunstan, and Oswald*. Edited and translated by Andrew Turner and Bernard Muir. New York: Oxford University Press, 2006.

McFadden, Brian. "The Elements of Discourse: Orality, Literacy, and Nature in the Elemental Miracles of Bede's 'Ecclesiastical history.'" *American Benedictine Review* 55(4) (2004): 442–463.

Moorhead, John. "Taking Gregory the Great's *Dialogues* Seriously." *Downside Review* 121(424) (2003): 197–206.

Odo of Glanfeuil. *The Life and Miracles of Saint Maurus: Disciple of Benedict, Apostle to France*. Translated by J. Wickstrom. Collegeville, MN: Liturgical Press, 2008.

Rinear, Mona. *Benedictine 'Miracles': Benedictines for Benedictines and Others*. 4 vols. St. Meinrad, IN: Oblates of St. Benedict, 1984–1987.

Speybrouck, Edward. *The Very Rev. Father Paul of Moll: A Flemish Benedictine and Wonderworker of the Nineteenth Century, 1824–1896*. Translated by E. Hetzinger. Clyde, MO: Benedictine Convent, 1910.

Ward, Benedicta. *Miracles and the Medieval Mind.* Philadelphia: University of Pennsylvania Press, 1987.

Biblical Miracles

To speak of miracles in the Bible is a conundrum, since the word "miracle" never occurs in the text. Even in the Vulgate, a fourth-century Latin translation of the Bible, the Latin equivalent of miracle, *miraculum*, never occurs. Notwithstanding, it can be surmised that a miracle in the Bible represents an extraordinary event that would have a dramatic impact on the audience in and/or of the biblical text.

Several terms in the biblical languages can help in identifying and describing the miraculous. These words, when referring to miracles, fit into three semantic categories: wonders (פֶּלֶא, נִפְלָאוֹת, τέρας, παράδοξος), mighty deeds (גְּבוּרָה, גְּדֹלוֹת, δύναμις), and signs (אוֹת, מוֹפֵת, σημεῖον). While their semantic ranges overlap, they emphasize respectively: astonishing deeds, a demonstration of overwhelming power, and a reminder of God's authority.

The words describing miracles can also point to other phenomena. Furthermore, miracles also occur in contexts devoid of particular miracle terminology. Such ambiguity problematizes a proper identification and definition of "miracle" in the Bible. A literary definition may offer a solution. Miracles are divine interventions, either overt or concealed, that leave strong impressions in a literary text. In other words, it is not the wondrous or supernatural quality innate to an event but rather the response in the text or that expected of its audience (nowadays the reader) that defines the miracle. This literary definition can be juxtaposed with a theological one, which emerges as follows. God created creation yet also continuously sustains and directs it, as can be surmised of his involvement in mundane natural processes, such as rain (Job 5:10, Matthew 5:45). A miracle takes place when God, beyond His regular involvement in creation, profoundly interacts with mankind. Such a miracle can take place by direct divine action or indirectly, such as through nature. In other words, a miracle is thus not per se a direct supernatural manifestation. In principle, though, miracles come from God (or sometimes the supernatural more broadly), who is the creator and ruler of creation.

The interplay between the natural and supernatural occurs, for example, in the book of Job. There, the slaughter of Job's servants by Sabbean marauders appeared natural. However, the reader knows that this misfortune was caused by a supernatural adversary—that is, Satan (Job 1:6–14).

The vast corpus of biblical miracles allows for various categorizations, of which a limited number follow. One category pertains to miracles wrought through nature, such as the case where the sun went back (2 Kings 20:9–11; see also Acts 4:31, 16:26). Another group of miracles revolves around timing, including answered prayers, foretold events, or occurrences happening at the right place at the right time, such as the east wind causing the parting of the Red Sea (Exodus 14:21; cf. Genesis 21:19, Luke 5:1–11). A third group of miracles is typified by the use of instruments, such as Moses's staff, Elijah's cloak, Paul's handkerchiefs or aprons, and even Peter's shadow (Exodus 4:3–4; 2 Kings 2:8; Acts 19:11–12, 5:15). Another distinction can be sought in the agent of the miracles. Next to nature, agents are animals, humans, angels, or even directly God. Two more categories follow, which are especially theologically significant in terms of disobedience and obedience, good and evil, and God's sovereignty. The first category relates to miracles of death and resurrection or sickness and healing, and the second relates to false miracles.

Punitive miracles bring about affliction, which typically occurs in three scenarios: following sin (Deuteronomy 28:22, 27–28; 1 Corinthians 11:27–32), mocking God's agent (Numbers 12:10; 2 Kings 2:23–25), and opposing God's word (Acts 13:11). However, God being the ultimate healer can also bring about restorative miracles (Exodus 15:26). An example is seen in Miriam's restoration of leprosy after Moses's intercession (Numbers 12:13–15; cf. James 5:15–16). Not all healing miracles are, however, clearly restorations of subjects having been afflicted by sin (John 9:5). In fact, the purpose of several healing accounts is to aid the preaching of the gospel (Acts 3:6–10, 4:5–10, 30).

Beyond miracles of sickness and healing are those of death and life. Death can follow judgment (Joshua 7:25; Acts 5:1–11, 12:23), whereas the obverse situation brings about salvation (Numbers 21:6–9). This is clearly depicted in the crossing of the Red Sea through which the Israelites were saved yet where Pharaoh and an Egyptian army met death (Exodus 14:26–31). Similarly, in the last of the Egyptian plagues, God smote Egypt's first born, whereas the first born in the Israelite homes that had applied the blood of the Passover lamb were spared (Exodus 12:21–29). Consequently, this event became a type of the New Testament expectation of the salvific miracle of redemption of the wrath of God, in which Jesus was identified as the Passover lamb (John 1:29; 1 Peter 1:29; 1 Corinthians 5:7). Parenthetically, it should be noted that just as not all sickness followed sin, not all premature death followed judgment. Several resurrection accounts show God's sovereignty, even as the giver of life (1 Kings 17:17–24; Acts 20:9–10).

Next to miracles ascribed to God, the Bible also speaks of false miracles. While the Bible strongly condemned these miracles (Exodus 22:18; Deuteronomy 18:10–12; Micah 5:12; Malachi 3:5; Galatians 5:20; Revelation 9:20–21), their efficacy is not denied. A miracle becomes false not per se by whether it affects something or not but rather by whether it honors God and God's word (Deuteronomy 13:1–3, but see also Deuteronomy 18:20–22).

While the Bible does not deny the potential workings of the occult (Acts 16:16; 2 Thessalonians 2:9–10; Revelation 13:13–15), the false supernatural workings do manifest themselves as being inferior to God's power. For example, the occultists at the pharaoh's court could only imitate two of the ten signs Moses performed (Exodus 7:11–12, 20–24). At other times occultists seemed powerless altogether when confronted with a challenge, in contrast to God working through his servants (Genesis 41:8; 25–36; 1 Kings 18:17–40; Daniel 2:1–45).

In the New Testament, two particular instances reveal something about the dynamics of the kingdom of darkness and the kingdom of light. After seeing the apostles perform miracles, a former magician, Simon, who had come to believe the gospel, sought to buy the ability to work miracles. Peter condemned him because God's gifts cannot be bought. Simon's request presumably reflected his former experience as magician, where the supernatural could be manipulated with gifts (Acts 8:9–24). While this story does not explain whether Simon wanted to use God's gifts to acquire wealth, Peter clearly opposed receiving payment for performing a miracle. Also elsewhere, the Bible appears to condemn the acquisition of riches through thaumaturgy (2 Kings 5:20–27; 2 Peter 2:15).

A second example concerns seven sons of a Jewish high priest who wanted to perform an exorcism. Whereas they ventured to use the right formula, they could mount no authority over an evil spirit. The spirit said, "Paul I know, but who are you?" (Acts 19:13–16). The miracle's efficaciousness thus depends not only on the ritual but also on the miracle worker's spiritual position in Christ (Matthew 12:22–30). It should further be noted that the frequent reports of exorcisms in the New Testament do not attest to dualism, in which there is a battle between good and evil. It instead shows the superior power vested in the kingdom of heaven confronting an age beset by dark forces.

The Old Testament also highlights God's sovereignty in the context of false miracles. Balaam, who had been hired to curse Israel, was not able to do so because God prohibited him. Further, in the book of Job, God permitted Satan only to afflict but not to kill Job. Once again, the Bible portrays a monotheistic rather than a dualistic worldview. False miracles and malevolent powers exist. However, their dominion is limited and eventually still subject to the limits set by the sovereign God.

The function of miracles becomes apparent when considering the repetition of miracles. Already within the Old Testament, repetitions created a relationship between events and individuals. Accordingly, God authenticates his agent Moses with the splitting of the Red Sea. Joshua and Elijah as types of Moses are related to similar, though inferior, miracles. This pattern persists in the New Testament, where Jesus as Second Moses has a superior miracle ministry, fulfilling numerous foretold messianic prophecies (Deuteronomy 18:15; John 6:14; Hebrews 3:1–6).

Numerous other Old Testament miracle types reappear in the New Testament, such as the miraculous manna and water provision during the Exodus and the Egyptian plagues that correspond to the Eucharist and to the terrible events in the last days (Exodus 16–17; 1 Corinthians 10; Exodus 7–11; Revelation 16).

Miracles not only can divinely authenticate a leader but also can affirm God's people and/or judge the wicked. Some periods marked by abundant miracles are those of the Exodus, the conquest of Canaan, Elijah and Elisha, Jesus, the early church, and the last days. During these periods, respectively, the Egyptians were judged and the nation of Israel was born, the Canaanites were judged and Israel possessed its land, and wicked Israelites were judged yet the faithful were spared (1 Kings 19:15–18). In the New Testament, Jesus's miracle ministry authenticated the proclamation of the kingdom of heaven as well as Jesus as the expected Messiah and Son of God. Depending on the reception, Jesus's message brings salvation or condemnation (Matthew 10:5–15; John 3:1–21). Numerous miracles affirmed the early church as God's people following in the footsteps of Jesus Christ. Incidentally, miraculous manifestations also confirmed the inclusion of Gentiles in this new Jesus movement. A final battle marks a final rebellion of the wicked against God and his elect. The wicked will perish, yet the righteous will live. In effect, miracles not only authenticate God and show affirmation of God's people and judgment of the wicked but also eventually speak of the sovereignty of God himself.

In the New Testament, the book of Acts records most miracles—not counting Jesus's miracles. The bulk of these miracles took place during the ministries of Peter and Paul. However, miracle working did not limit itself to the apostles only but continued beyond the first generation of Jesus's followers (Galatians 3:5; 1 Corinthians 12:10, 28; James 5:14–15). The overwhelming concentration of miracle accounts happening during the first generation of Jesus's followers, in contrast to the sporadic later accounts, have led some denominations within Christianity to embrace Cessationism, which holds that the gift of miracles ceased after the apostolic period. On the other side, the bulk of Christianity continues to highly regard contemporary occurrences of miracles, including the Catholic Church, the Orthodox Church, and certain streams in Protestant Christianity, such as Pentecostalism and the cross-denominational Charismatic movement.

Not only within Christianity but also in contemporary society at large, the debate about biblical miracles is far from settled. The situation will be illustrated with an analogy. The text under discussion that records miracles, the Bible, can itself be considered miraculous. Just as the miraculous can be differently perceived, the same applies to the Bible. Some consider the Bible a divinely inspired work speaking of a miracle-working God who announces redemption from a darkened world and offers eternal life. Others view the Bible merely as a literary creation, devoid of any divine inspiration. What counts for the Bible also counts the miracles recorded therein. Jesus's words seem to be applicable to this conundrum: "Whoever has ears, let that one hear" (Matthew 11:15).

Stefan Bosman

See also: Jesus, Miracles of; Judaism and Miracles

Further Reading

Ervin, Howard M. *Healing: Sign of the Kingdom.* Peabody, MA: Hendrickson Publishers, 2002.

Hacking, Keith J. *Signs and Wonders, Then and Now: Miracle-Working, Commissioning and Discipleship.* Nottingham: Apollos, 2006.

Keener, Craig S. *Miracles: The Credibility of the New Testament Accounts.* Grand Rapids, MI: Baker Academic, 2011.

Lewis, C. S. *Miracles: A Preliminary Study.* New York: Macmillan, 1947.

Lockyer, Herbert. *All the Miracles of the Bible.* Grand Rapids, MI: Zondervan, 1961.

Williams, Benjamin E. *Miracle Stories in the Biblical Book Acts of the Apostles.* Lewiston, NY: E. Mellen, 2001.

Zakovitch, Yair. *The Concept of the Miracle in the Bible.* Tel-Aviv: MOD Books, 1991.

Bilocation

Bilocation is the ability of an individual to occupy two or more different locations at the same time. Also known as multilocation, out-of-body travel, and astral travel, the concept of bilocation has appeared among a host of ideational and faith-based traditions inclusive of classical Greek philosophy, several Indic religions, mysticism associated with Abrahamic religions, New Ageism, and psychical studies of the paranormal.

Many scholars attribute the popularity of bilocation to the emergence of spiritualism and theosophy. In these belief systems an assumption exists about the dual composition of the human body, divided between material and nonmaterial characteristics. Spiritualists hold that individuals possess an astral double, or spiritual component, that accounts for such phenomena as ghosts, hauntings, and other paranormal activity. Similarly, for theosophists, the spirit takes the form of several bodies throughout its development within the life course, with each body more advanced and substantively definitive than the last before eventually culminating in one's own physical body. Thus, beliefs in bilocation for both spiritualists and theosophists are based upon divisions between the material foundations of the body and nonmaterial notions of a spirit.

The vast majority of cases of bilocation, however, have been associated with Catholicism. Among these cases are the bilocations of Saint Anthony of Padua (1195–1231), the Italian bishop Saint Alphonsus Maria de' Liguori (1696–1797) and his Redemptorist confrère Saint Gerard Majella (1726–1755), and, more recently, Saint Pio of Pietrelcina (1887–1968). All of these men were witnessed in two places at once, with no possibility of their being transported to locations that were at the same time at great distances from one another. Additionally, and in perhaps one of the most well-known cases of bilocation, the seventeenth-century Dominican Saint Martin de Porres (1579–1639) was said to have repeatedly experienced bilocation. Despite having lived the entirety of his life in Latin America, de Porres was reportedly seen in various parts of Africa and Asia, simultaneously. Moreover, he allegedly possessed the ability to describe these locations beyond Latin America in great detail.

Among psychical study circles, investigators of paranormal activity have argued that bilocation provides evidence of astral doubles. In particular, somewhat of a research focus emerged about individuals who claimed to have the ability to project their astral doubles. Indeed, throughout the twentieth century, proponents of psychical studies such as Sylvan J. Muldoon (1903–1971), Hereward Carrington (1880–1958), and Hugh G. Calloway (1885–1949) produced a rather extensive literature on the topic of these astral abilities, most of which was based upon their own personal claims of bilocation.

Salvador Murguia

Further Reading

Fox, Oliver. *Astral Projection: A Record of Out of the Body Experiences*. New York: Citadel Press, 1993.

Monroe, Robert A. *Journeys Out of the Body*. Garden City, NY: Doubleday, 1973.

Muldoon, Sylvan Joseph, and Hereward Carrington. *The Projection of the Astral Body*. New York: Samuel Weiser, 1972.

Webster, Richard. *Astral Travel for Beginners*. St. Paul, MN: Llewellyn Productions, 1998.

Blindness

Miracles involving blindness are very common. Together with motor skills problems, they constitute the majority of miracles that have been reported throughout history. In any society, blindness, understood here as a general term for sight problems, would constitute a dramatic and potentially life-threatening situation for anyone, and this crisis, this rupture in the body's balance, justifies the need for a miracle. Because they are invoked to restore balance and end a state of disorder, miracles can only occur in societies where the line between what is natural and what isn't has been clearly marked. Blindness, as a profoundly debilitating affliction for which traditional medicine has had few answers, provides a fertile ground for such miracles.

Blindness is a complex medical issue and has been represented in ways that often seem to oppose one another. While it is sometimes described as a light deprivation, as a state of perpetual darkness and obscurity in the Bible (Matthew 6.22), it is also a physical state that allows a few chosen people to see better, or rather to have the gift of clairvoyance. This is at the heart of the story of the man born blind in John 9, where the blind person is liable for chastisement owing to his malady. When Jesus heals him, the Pharisees question the miracle and show their disbelief. Jesus turns the tables on them and suggests that it is they who are now blind.

Descriptions of blindness, as suggested, can contribute to the fact that it is a disease that ostracizes its carriers and therefore puts them on the fringe of society. In Egyptian mythology, the eye is a very strong symbol of the Sacred, one that embodies the antagonist nature of sight and illustrates the reconciliation of opposites. It is the symbol of balance and sovereignty. Blindness is charged with this profoundly polarized energy and can be understood by all as a problem of opposition between day and night, light and darkness. The blind person is thus perceived and described as a social outcast, a troubling disturbance.

To be cured by a miracle, blind people would have to invoke a deity or a sacred person, one who is charged with the power to intervene in an unnatural way. In Christianity a large number of saints have been known to cure blindness, and they are usually recognized as such because of an association with their name and words related to light or sight. In Italy, for example, Saint Lucy is prayed to (*lux*), while Saint Claire is popular in France (*clarity*), and Saint Augustine helps the blind in Germany (*die Augen*). Miracles involving saints often occur when the afflicted or his/her family gives an offering, a promise in exchange for healing. Such gifts, known as *ex voto*, are central to the transaction and symbolize the organ that needs to be cured. Some parents would hang silver eyes on the statue of Saint Cataldus for their child to regain sight, while others would promise a pilgrimage or prayers.

The link established between physical blindness and spiritual blindness makes it that much more spectacular when a miracle occurs. Perceived as a sign of positive or negative value, blindness has been associated with mystics in best cases and with the work of the Devil in bad cases. To be cured is therefore a sign of divine illumination from within, a manifestation of a divine presence and will.

Blindness is often associated with fertility in traditional societies and in past Western worlds because of the inability of the blind to participate and to provide for his family and social group. Many sacred places such as lakes and hot springs sanctuaries, such as those devoted to Sara, patron of Gypsies, suggest that they can cure blindness as well as sterility. Greek mythology also provides rich tales of blindness and sterility (Phineas), and water, as a symbol of regeneration and life, is used to cure both afflictions in all cases by direct contact with the body (eyes, stomach).

Geneviève Pigeon

See also: *Ex Voto*

Further Reading

Kim, Stephen S. "The Significance of Jesus' Healing the Blind Man in John 9." *Bibliotheca Sacra* 167 (July–September 2010): 307–318.

Blood

For all of human existence, blood has occupied a significant place in all spheres of life across cultures and eras. Its power, both as a symbol and a biological life force, has been a key component of miraculous phenomena since it has come to be understood by many as a holy substance.

In the Jewish tradition, the Hebrew term for blood, *dām*, refers to life or vitality (Leviticus 17:11, 14), an idea also shared in the ancient Near East. In the Old Testament alone, the word "blood" appears about 360 times. In some of the contexts, blood is associated with rituals. The Passover tradition notes how blood is smeared on the lintels of doors to Jewish homes, and this gives protection from a destroyer (Exodus 12:7, 22–23). Similarly, sacrificial rituals using the blood of an animal as a sin offering are deemed to have an atoning or cleansing effect.

In the New Testament, *aimatos* (αιματος) is the Greek term for blood. The blood of Jesus on the cross created a theology of the cross (*theologia crucis*). A special meaning was attached to the blood of Jesus. It is the blood of no ordinary man but rather one who offered spiritual regeneration as a sacrifice of atonement that reconciled people and God (Romans 3:25; Colossians 1:20) and brought salvation. The ritual recollection of Jesus's death is portrayed in Holy Communion. Similarly, the blood of Christian martyrs also becomes redemptive insofar as the martyr demonstrates a similar love for his/her faith in Christ (Revelations 14:20, 16:3–6, 17:6).

The miraculous power of blood is tied up with this theology. Some blood miracles relate to liquification as a sign of some favor shown by God. Consider Saint Januarius (sometimes called San Gennaro), the fourth-century bishop of

Benevento. He suffered a martyr's death (decapitation), and devotion to the bishop grew accordingly. His remains and two vials of his blood were brought to Naples, and it was around his tomb that the present-day cathedral was built. Each year on his feast day the vials are brought out for veneration, and without fail the coagulated blood continues to liquefy. This has been a regular occurrence—sometimes happening over a dozen times a year—since the translation of this relic in 1389.

Late medieval blood miracles are often found in German contexts. Blood pilgrimages and miracles of bleeding hosts were largely dominant in this part of the world. Corporals—the linens used during celebrations of the Eucharist to wipe the chalice, the receptacle of Christ's blood—would be gathered for veneration by the faithful; so precious was the liquid that ritual precautions were taken against the possibility of one drop being lost. In this regard the search for the chalice that caught Christ's blood on Golgotha—the so-called Holy Grail—has come to symbolize the mythical lengths that believers have gone to in order to collect and treasure the blood of their redeemer.

In England the Holy Blood relics at Westminster, said to belong to Christ and deposited there by King Henry III in 1247, have been stimulants for political and spiritual controversies. A gift of the Patriarch of Jerusalem and borne to London by the Knights Templar and Hospitaller, the Holy Blood relics were processed from St. Paul's Cathedral to Westminster by the king himself, whereupon the abbey's monks took possession. The cult that arose around these relics were minimal, despite the generous indulgences attached to them. While meant to rival the blood relics of King Louis IX of France, they fell into disrepute, in part because the French were expert at distributing theirs to a variety of strategic pilgrimage sites. Insofar as Christ's blood had come into contact with his other Passion relics—a thorn from his crown here, some splinters of the cross there—the ability of the French sovereign to control the flow of relic traffic far outweighed the capacities of the English king. Henry's hopes for Westminster's precious relic of the Holy Blood were circumscribed by the fact that those who sought to make pilgrimage to view it could only migrate to an expensive city to do so.

Fortune Sibanda

See also: Blood and Trees in Old English Miracles; Relics

Further Reading

Atkinson, James. "Theology of the Cross." In *A Dictionary of Christian Theology*, edited by Alan Richardson, 82–83. London: SCM Press, 1969.

Attridge, Harold W. "Blood: New Testament." In *Encyclopedia of the Bible and its Reception*, edited by Hans-Josef Klauck et al., 219–225. Berlin: de Gruyter, 2012.

Bynum, Caroline Walker. *Wonderful Blood: Theology and Practice in Late Medieval Northern Germany and Beyond*. Philadelphia: University of Pennsylvania Press, 2007.

Eberhart, Christian A. "Blood: Ancient Near East and Hebrew Bible/Old Testament." In *Encyclopedia of the Bible and its Reception*, edited by Hans-Josef Klauck, 201–212. Berlin: de Gruyter, 2012.

Vincent, Nicholas. *The Holy Blood: King Henry III and the Westminster Blood Relic*. New York: Cambridge University Press, 2002.

Blood and Trees in Old English Miracles

When Cain slays Abel in Genesis, God says to Cain, the world's first kin killer, "The voice of your brother's blood cries out to me from the earth" (Genesis 4:10). In the anonymous Old English poem known as *Genesis A*, however, Abel's blood does more than cry out; it produces a tree with "wrohtes telgan" (branches of strife). The crimes of fratricide, jealousy, and malice are transferred through blood to the earth, and there grows a tree that gives fruit to sorrow and hostility among humankind. This extraordinary tree is both literally and figuratively the root of murder and hatred in the world.

In *Andreas*, another anonymous Old English poem, Saint Andrew is tortured by the Mermedonians, and his blood falls onto the ground. He prays to God for deliverance, and God tells him he will be made whole. The saint heals, and when he looks at the ground behind him, he sees "geblowene bearwas" (blooming groves) adorned with flowers where his blood had poured forth. Saint Andrew's blood, the tangible embodiment of his holy soul, soaks into the earth, and from it grows God's sacred creation—trees of spring, life, and rebirth. The saint's soul produces beautiful holy trees when planted through the medium of blood into the earth.

The Old English term "sawul-drior" translates to "soul-blood," and soul-blood is closely linked to a person's characteristics, qualities, and actions. Blood's power of transference can damage and harm when evil and sin are involved, but it can also heal and beautify in the presence of true faith. Trees that grow from soul-blood represent murder and sin as well as sanctity and sacrifice.

Hana Videen

See also: Blood; Trees

Further Reading

Brooks, Kenneth R. "Andreas." In *Andreas and the Fates of the Apostles*, 1–55. Oxford, UK: Clarendon, 1961.

Doane, A. N., ed. "Genesis A." In *Genesis A: A New Edition*, 109–221. Madison: University of Wisconsin Press, 1978.

Body-Shaped Reliquaries

One type of reliquary is the body-shaped (also known as body-part or speaking) reliquary. It is commonly assumed that the shape of this reliquary reflects the body part it contains. However, there is no strict correlation between the appearance and contents of the body-shaped reliquary. A body-shaped reliquary could contain the remains of several saints or even contact relics. There are body-shaped reliquaries designed to look like separate body parts (hands being the most common); there are also body-shaped reliquaries known as majesties that look like an entire body. Perhaps the most famous majesty is that of Saint Foy (held at the Abbey of Sainte-Foy, Conques, France), which contains a skull fragment. In the early eleventh century, Bernard of Angers investigated the body-shaped reliquary of Saint Foy in the *Liber miraculorum sancte Fidis*. Bernard recounts a vision experienced by a petty thief in which Saint Foy makes an unusual posthumous appearance, demanding that he return what he stole: "it seemed to him that Sainte Foy appeared to him in a vision, not in the form of a girl but, contrary to her usual custom, in the form of her sacred image. . . . On the next night she seemed to appear again in the same terrifying way." Although miraculous appearances of animate speaking majesties are rare, this vision nevertheless hints at the ambiguous divide between human relic and body-shaped reliquary. There is also uncertainty as to whether the shape of the reliquary determines how a relic's miraculous power is manifested or indeed creates this power. Cynthia Hahn has written on body-shaped reliquaries and describes instances where hand-shaped reliquaries were used and performed as if they were saintly hands, regardless of the relics they contained. Guibert of Nogent's memoirs, for instance, record that his cousin was cured when touched by the arm-shaped reliquary of Saint Arnoul.

Sophia Wilson

Further Reading

Bernard of Angers. "Book I of *Liber miraculorum sancte Fidis*." In *The Book of Sainte Foy*, edited and translated by Pamela Sheingorn, 39–111. Philadelphia: University of Pennsylvania Press, 1995.

Hahn, Cynthia, "The Spectacle of the Charismatic Body: Patrons, Artists, and Body-Part Reliquaries." In *Treasures of Heaven: Saints, Relics, and Devotion in Medieval Europe*, edited by Martina Bagnoli et al., 163–172. London: British Museum, 2011.

Bollandists

The Société des Bollandistes, based sporadically in Belgium for over 350 years, is a collective of church historians who have sought to bring the historical-critical method to the study of hagiography. The group is responsible for the 68 folio volumes of the *Acta Sanctorum*, the most complete rendition of the lives of saints from antiquity to the Middle Ages. Its publication schedule spans three centuries, from the first volumes (saints' feasts for January) in 1643 to the 1940s. The organization's foundations are linked to the Society of Jesus. Father Heribert Rosweyde (d. 1629 in Antwerp), a Jesuit, was the inspiration for bringing together the best learned hagiographical manuscripts in Belgian libraries and who, after assembling several studies such as the *Vitae Patrum* (1615), endeavored to collect in a multivolume work all those vitae of the Servants of God before the year 1500.

Rosweyde's death necessitated the transfer in 1630 of fellow Jesuit Jean van Bolland (d. 1665), for whom the society takes its name. Before he died, Bolland assigned confrères Godefroid Henskens (Henschen) and Daniel van Papebroech to search for and collect copies of manuscripts in Germany, Italy, and France, and the library soon rivaled those of Rome. Work proceeded haltingly on the *Acta*, particularly because of the suppression of the Jesuits in 1773, which also disbanded portions of the library that had been located in Antwerp. The incunabula, medieval manuscripts, and thousands of books were transferred to the Royal Library at Brussels. The Bollandists formally reconstituted in 1837 in Brussels with the intention of reactivating the production of the *Acta Sanctorum*. For this purpose four Jesuits were released to reorganize the society. Thanks mainly to Jesuit Victor De Buck (1817–1876) and collaborators in Russia who did careful studies on Slavonic saints, the rebirth of the Bollandists began. With financial and material assistance from local abbots and scholars from across Europe, they again amassed the most significant library on saints in the world. Today it numbers about a half million volumes, with about 100 incunabula. Gradually, the Bollandists embarked on a massive survey of the most important libraries in Europe to obtain a definitive bibliography of all those works pertaining to saints written before the year 1500.

In the last century, Father Hippolyte Delehaye not only contributed extensively to the workings of the society but also broadened the scope of their work from Latin, Greek, and Oriental texts to the Slavic, Nordic, Asian, and African texts. His work on the critical study of hagiographic texts set the standard for the day. Today Bollandists publish the prestigious journal *Analecta Bollandiana* (begun 1882), which updates the *Acta Sanctorum* (albeit no longer slavishly bound to completing the saints' feasts by day of a given month), and a series of books, *Subsidia Hagiographica* (begun 1886). The Bollandists today are directed from offices located at the College St. Michel in Brussels. The library is slowly being cataloged and linked to the online catalog of the Université Catholique de Louvain, with new accessions since 2003 fully integrated in the catalog, which is presented in both English and French. The Bollandists maintain a separate web site.

Patrick J. Hayes

Further Reading

Analecta Bollandiana: Inventaire hagiographique des tomes 1 à 100. Brussels: Société des Bollandistes, 1983.

Delehaye, Hippolyte. *The Work of the Bollandists through Three Centuries, 1615–1915*. Princeton, NJ: Princeton University Press, 1922.

Godding, Robert, Bernard Joassart, and Xavier Lequeux, eds. *De Rosweyde aux Acta Sanctorum: La recherche hagiographique des Bollandistes à travers quatre siècles; Actes du colloque international (Bruxelles, 5 octobre 2007)*. Brussels: Société des Bollandistes, 2009.

Op de Beeck, Bart, and Ann Rouzet. *La bibliothèque des Bollandistes à la fin de l'Ancien Régime*. Brussels: Société des Bollandistes, 2009.

Peeters, Paul. *L'oeuvre des Bollandistes*. 2nd ed. Subsidia Hagiographica, 24. Brussels: Société des Bollandistes, 1961.

Société des Bollandistes, www.bollandistes.org.

Brownson, Orestes

A convert to Catholicism, Orestes Brownson (1803–1876) was a former Transcendentalist divine who wrote sporadically on miracles and their use in apologetics. His most extensive work, however, came between 1865 and 1866 when he published a short series of articles on Catholic veneration of the saints and the Blessed Virgin Mary for the magazine *Ave Maria*, published from Notre Dame, Indiana. These were later gathered by Brownson's son Henry into volume eight of the *Collected Works of Orestes Brownson*. An earlier separate treatise titled "The Worship of the Virgin Mary," published in 1853, also bears on Brownson's views on miracles and the saints who work them.

As was typical for nineteenth-century America, Catholic apologists were routinely engaged in putting to rest the canard that veneration of the saints or their relics was, as Protestant critics put it, idol worship. Brownson not only addresses this matter but also devotes several pages to miracles, which tend to rely on a kind of scholastic understanding. Miracles are things that should not surprise us, he holds, given the status of saints in the Catholic worldview. These are men and women who have the ability to intercede before God, and this is "no anomaly in the Creator's plan." Divine Providence is such that it honors creatures in their dignity to be able to complete or perfect God's works through the agency or ministry of secondary causes. If God is the first cause of everything in nature—that is, its sole master—and so is not bound by it, then supernatural intervention "is not illogical or capricious."

Brownson understands a miracle, then, as "the direct and immediate action of God in the universe, . . . because it is inexplicable by any natural laws or secondary causes, as the conception of the Lord in the womb of the Virgin Mary." A principle value of miracles, he notes, "is that they vindicate to us the freedom of God, and prove to us that the laws of nature, so called, depend upon him, and not he on them."

Insofar as God's character is such as to permit direct action in nature, which itself can be considered miraculous, their performance also reveals something about God's actions. For Brownson the inseparable qualities of being and action lead him to hold that a miracle "is the act of a power above the laws of nature and not explicable by them; it leaves them to their ordinary operation, and simply proves that they do not exhaust the activity of the Creator, and that he survives them in all his infinity, and in all his inexhaustible freedom of action."

All of this Brownson recognized as being opposed to the worldview of natural scientists. Miracles, for them, cannot be admitted, for the regularity and immutability of the laws of the natural world are sacrosanct. The supernatural effects of religion are totally out of bounds and deviate from what can be known. Should the miraculous somehow intrude, it is of little consequence and easily dismissed. For Brownson, this is a fundamental flaw in logic:

> Their difficulty arises from not knowing or not reflecting upon the truth that the miracles and supernatural facts are in the order of the supernatural, and that this supernatural order does not carry on in the same line and complete the natural; or in other and more precise terms, that grace simply fulfills nature (or completes what is not ultimate, but inchoate or initial, in the world they study), and is not more nor otherwise supernatural than the creative act itself. Nature is supernatural in its origin and end, and the natural is only that which God does mediately, through the ministry or agency of second or created causes. There is in what we here assert the principle of the harmony of faith and reason, of the truths of revelation and the truths of science. The principles of both are the same, and they differ only in the fact that faith reveals their origin and ground in the divine mind, and is the medium of their development and application beyond the power of human reason.

Patrick J. Hayes

Further Reading

Brownson, Orestes A. *Saint-Worship: The Worship of Mary*. Edited by Thomas R. Ryan. Paterson, NJ: St. Anthony Guild Press, 1963.

Buddhism and Miracles

Beginning with the gestation and birth of Siddartha Gautama, the Buddha (b. ca. 483 BCE), the presence of miraculous favors has been endemic to the character of Buddhism. Though the stress is laid on reaching enlightenment, the process by which one attains it is often fraught with supernatural phenomena such as miraculous visions, relics, and omens.

Though the details vary depending upon the text consulted, one can find the birth narrative of Gautama being fashioned in a number of ways. As a young bodhisattva—already perfect in wisdom—he was sent from heaven and impregnated in the womb of his mother, Queen Maya. She had no birth pangs and is said to have conceived without having had sexual relations with anyone, including Suddohodana, head of the Shakya clan, from whom Siddartha was to inherit both wealth and stature. The boy's supernatural persona courses through various traditions: both Mahayana Buddhists and Theravadans raise the status of the Buddha to a being other than a normal human.

While endowed with superhuman abilities, the Buddha is also famed for his birthplace, sites visited, and funerary remains. He is believed to have been born at Kapilavastu in what is today Nepal. While in Sri Lanka, the Buddha is said to have breathed his last, and various relics—a tooth here, a neck bone there—were removed for veneration after his immolation. Not coincidentally, Gautama gave notice before he died that Sri Lanka would be disposed to carry on the Buddha's teachings for another two and a half millennia after his death. Today large temples are built around the sacred teeth (in places such as Kandy and Columbo in Sri Lanka, the Chinatown section of Singapore, and even Lu Mountain Temple in Rosemead, California). In 2007 the sacred hair relics of the Buddha were sent from Bangladesh to Sri Lanka, and when the strands arrived at the stupa where they would be housed, the heavens burst with an unseasonable rainfall, ending a seven-month drought. Today they are enshrined in the Gangaramaya Monastery in Columbo.

In addition to the feats of supernatural power caused by the minds of Buddhist masters, there are physical transformations in nature associated with their saintlike works and given lustrous detail in their hagiography. In Tibetan Buddhism there is the story of the first *dodrupchen* (great adept) Jigme Thrinle Özer (1745–1821) causing a stream to flow from dry land for a community that was without water. His disciple, Do Khyentse Yeshe Dorje (1800–1866), once encountered two attacking dogs—one white and one black. He sliced each down the middle with his sword, killing them instantly. When an angry crowd set upon him for this deed, he placed the carcass of the black dog alongside that of the white dog. The animals were then miraculously knit together as healthy black and white dogs and ran away, to the amazement of all.

Bodies of saints in Buddhism often hold miraculous powers, especially their incorruptibility. Burgyat Lama Itigilov, for instance, a Russian Buddhist lama, died in 1927, though his body remains relatively immune from decay to this day. Before ceasing to breathe, he asked that his body be exhumed upon death after 30 years. It was buried in a cemetery in Khukhe-Zurkhen in Siberia. In 1955 the monks of the Burgyat's monastery at Ivolginsk brought his body out of the ground, and its imperishability was in evidence. It was reinterred after being packed in salt. An exhumation was repeated again in 1973 and 2001, and each time he was found just as he died and was buried, in the lotus position without signs of natural decay. After this last exhumation the Hambo Lama ordered Itiglov's body to be brought to Ivolginsk, where it remains on the second floor of the monastery behind curtains and locked doors. The monks pray on the first floor, faithfully keeping vigil throughout the day. Scientific examination of the body yields a baffling set of data (constant temperature, cellular structure remains intact) such that many believe that the lama continues to live.

A similar scenario played out in January 2015 in Mongolia, where a mummified lama in a *tukdam* state—a very deep meditation—emerged for sale. Forensic scientists examined the body, still supple after decades of being wrapped in cattle skins and crouched in the lotus position. To many devotees, it is believed that such deep meditation allows for a person to reach the final stages before Buddhahood.

Not all scholars agree whether there is any fervor among Buddhists for miracles or whether they associate the classical concept of the miraculous with Buddha. For them it remains on the periphery. But several Buddhist texts on the miraculous have become the object of study for their allegorical or metaphorical meanings. Manifestations of wondrous and superhuman powers dot the Pali canon. The most sustained discussion can be found in a long *sutta* (*Digha Nikaya* 11, Kevatta) in which the Buddha gives a discourse on miracles (psychic power, telepathy, and instruction) and the prospect of conversing with heavenly beings. He does not exclude the possibility of obtaining wisdom from these beings, let alone of having some dialogue with them, but he cautions that they are subject to the same infirmities of the mind as any being, and so they are sometimes untrustworthy. Thus, in the Theravada tradition the teaching on miracles is given with prudence and reserve. By contrast, in the Mahayana canon the sutras are written in highly symbolic language, especially in their descriptions of how Buddhas and bodhisattvas liberate their own minds and those of others using superhuman capabilities. Insofar as the texts employ symbolism as a literary device, the teaching on miracles is hewn less in rationality and more in the imagination.

Imparting the knowledge and deeds of the Buddha—whether subject to Western reason or the Asian imagination—relies on both memory and creativity of expression. The lineal transmission of story remains central to the goal of enlightened consciousness.

Patrick J. Hayes

See also: Asia, Miracles in

Further Reading

Fiordalis, David. "Buddhist Miracles." Oxford Bibliographies, http://www.oxfordbiblio graphies.com/view/document/obo-9780195393521/obo-9780195393521-0116.xml.

Fiordalis, David V. "Miracles in Indian Buddhist Narratives and Doctrine." *Journal of the International Association of Buddhist Studies* 33(1–2) (2010): 381–408.

Fiordalis, David V. "Miracles and Superhuman Powers in South Asian Buddhist Literature." PhD dissertation, University of Michigan, 2008, http://deepblue.lib.umich.edu/bitstream /handle/2027.42/61721/dvf_1.pdf?sequence=1.

Gómez, Luis O. "On Buddhist Wonders and Wonderworking." *Journal of the International Association of Buddhist Studies* 33(1–2) (2010): 513–554.

Myers, Steven Lee. "Ivolginsk Journal: A Russian Lama's Body, and His Faith, Defy Time." *New York Times*, October 1, 2002, http://www2.kenyon.edu/Depts/Religion /Fac/Adler/Reln260/Russian%20lama.htm.

Nakamura, Kyoko Motomochi, trans. *Miraculous Stories from the Japanese Buddhist Tradition: The Nihon Ryōiki of the Monk Kyōkai*. Cambridge, MA: Harvard University Press, 1973.

Thondup, Tulku. *Masters of Meditation and Miracles: Lives of the Great Buddhist Masters of India and Tibet*. Boston: Shambala, 1999.

Bulgakov, Sergei

Sergei Bulgakov (Сергей Николаевич Булгаков in Russian) was an influential Russian Orthodox theologian, philosopher, and economist at the beginning of the twentieth century. He was one of the founders of the religious philosophical system called *sophiology*. It is often stressed that his "religious insights and religious experience seem important for the understanding of the age as a whole."

Sergei Bulgakov was born on June 16, 1871, in the family of an Orthodox priest in the town of Livny, Orlovskaja guberniya, Russia. He started his learning at the seminary of Oryol. However, at that time he was influenced by Marxism and became a student of political economics at the Law School of Moscow University. He returned to religious faith after he read the books of such Russian religious thinkers as Fyodor Dosotyevsky, Vladimir Solovyov, and Lev Tolstoy. Bulgakov described this return to Orthodoxy in his books *From Marxism to Idealism* (*Ot marksizma k idealizmu*) in 1903 and *The Unfading Light: Contemplations and Speculations* (*Svet nevechernii: Sozertsaniia i umozreniia*) in 1917. In *The Unfading Light* he also presented his teaching of sophiology for the first time. Bulgakov's teaching was a synthesis of ideas of Vladimir Solovyov, Pavel Florensky, and his own perceptions concerning Russian religiosity. Bulgakov was ordained to the Orthodox priesthood in 1918.

During the Russian Civil War Bulgakov was in Crimea and worked on books of philosophy: *Philosophy of the Name* (*Filosofiia imeni*) and *Tragedy of Philosophy* (*Tragediia filosofii*), both published in 1920. On December 30, 1922, the Bolshevik government expelled some 160 prominent intellectuals, and Bulgakov was among them. In May 1923 he became professor of church law and theology at the School of Law of the Russian Research Institute in Prague. Then he went to Paris, helped established the St. Sergius Orthodox Theological Institute, and became professor of dogmatic theology and dean of the institute until his death on July 12, 1944.

Bulgakov's views on miracles originally were presented in his manuscript *On Holy Relics* (*O sv. moshchakh: Po povodu ikh poruganiia*), written during 1918–1919. This work, fully published in Russian only in 1992, was Bulgakov's response to Bolshevik mockery of the relics of Russian saints. According to Bulgakov, all that is divine has a flesh, is clothed in a body. Although relics of saints remain connected to the physical body of saints as a cover, they are not corpses: they are bodies of resurrection. As transfigured nature of the body and as a source of divine energy, they could be venerated like an icon. Bulgakov emphasized that all Christian altars include a relic at their core because the culmination of every liturgy is the Eucharist—veneration of the greatest of all relics.

Afterward Bulgakov developed his views on miracles in the work *On the Gospel Miracles* (*O chudesakh Evangel'skikh*), published in 1932. For Bulgakov the foundation of miracles lays in God's providence of the world and in a special causality of His created nature. Besides, Bulgakov's conception of miracles was closely related with his faith in works of Christ and the doctrine of Christian resurrection. Therefore, miracles as the graceful reinforcement of nature are not supernatural but really natural, and Bulgakov brought miracles to an almost mundane level. Bulgakov's vision that everyday life is wonder-filled became an integral part of his conception, termed "religious materialism."

Solveiga Krumina-Konkova

Further Reading

Bulgakov, Sergius. *Relics and Miracles: Two Theological Essays.* Translated by Boris Jakim. Grand Rapids, MI: Wm. B. Eerdmans, 2011.

Evtuhov, Catherine. *The Cross and the Sickle: Sergei Bulgakov and the Fate of Russian Religious Philosophy, 1890–1920.* Ithaca, NY: Cornell University Press, 1997.

S. N. Bulgakov: Religiozno-filosofskii put'. Mezhdunarodnaia nauchnaia konferenciia, posviashchennaia 130-letiiu so dnia rozhdeniia. Nauchnaia redakciia A. P. Kozyreva. Moskva: Russkii put', 2003.

Butler, Bishop Joseph

An Anglican churchman, Bishop Joseph Butler (1692–1752) became one of the principal architects of modern Christian apologetics. He understood the persuasive power of appeal to the testimony of witnesses to miracles, the necessity of not using controversial premises, and the advantages of qualifying one's conclusion so that it both follows in strict logic from the premises and is more than sufficient to warrant Christian practice, especially with regard to acceptance of the Bible as the revealed Word of God.

Butler begins his argument with the observation that in his time, the Christian religion had become an object of ridicule deserving punishment for having interrupted the pleasures of the world. Butler never assumes the existence of God, as is often claimed, but does call on his opponents to grant that the existence of God has been proved. No doubt he had in mind such demonstrations of God's being and attributes as had recently been put forth by his mentor, Samuel Clarke. Once God's existence is acknowledged, the world must be admitted as the work of God, though the world seems filled with defects and irregularities. Those who deny the possibility of moral and rational living in this imperfect world are seen as insane. Looking now at the Bible, the alleged Word of God, Butler acknowledges the irregularities and apparent defects, but he claims, following Origen, that the Bible as a revelation whose author is also the author of the world should naturally resemble the world in its general character, at least when inspected from the perspective of our vast ignorance. According to the analogy of nature and religion, the Bible presents us with moral and intellectual challenges of the same general character as does the natural world, and the parallel is nowhere more striking than with regard to the testimony regarding miracles.

Following biblical usage, Butler sees genuine miracles as signs of divinity. His opponents and even some of his allies sometimes fail to follow on this point. Applying the adage that for us probability is the guide to life since certainty would require a degree of knowledge reserved for God, Butler stresses the consequences of his grand strategy, especially so far as practice is at stake. What we see as our best hope of attaining the best outcome must morally and logically be pursued as if it were a sure thing.

Butler's strategy follows Pascal's wager and James' will to believe, but for Butler all our calculation of the probabilities must be conducted while bearing in mind that what we know is but a point to what we do not know. Butler completes his argument by asserting that since God's existence is not in question and since we have no knowledge of the meaning, nature, and ends of human life beyond what we can infer from natural and revealed theology, we cannot assign a probability to the alleged miracles relative to the whole teleology of nature. Butler concludes that all we can do reasonably is apply the best tests of credibility, the best hermeneutical science, to the whole of the surviving reported data and respond in terms of what seems to be the best explanation of the rapid spread of early Christianity. Reductive naturalistic speculations are available, but as long as the existence of God is admitted as possible, critical inquiry favors an explanation that acknowledges the truth and credibility of the testimony found in scripture.

Those who are critical of Butler see his work as yet another modernizing attempt to reduce the certainty of faith to a mere probable, if that, inference, but those who are sympathetic will recognize in Butler a contribution of continuing value to the immense cumulative endeavor of attempting to interpret all manifestations of divinity into an integrated vision accessible to all.

Butler's exposition of his argument on miracles is in his *Analogy of Religion*, Part 2, initially printed in London in 1736.

David White

Further Reading

Brown, Colin. *Miracles and the Critical Mind*. Grand Rapids, MI: Wm. B. Eerdmans, 1984.

Butler, Joseph. *Bishop Butler's Analogy of Religion: Natural and Revealed, to the Constitution and Course of Nature*. New York: Harper and Brothers, 1868.

Byzantium, Miracles in

Byzantine society (330–1453) was deeply Christian, and saints and holy biblical figures, such as prophets, the Virgin, and the apostles, were extremely important. The largest part of Byzantine artistic and literary production is devoted to saints whose divine powers are mostly demonstrated through the miracles they perform during their lives and posthumously. However, as attested by a number of Byzantine texts, miracle working was not the sine qua non of Byzantine holiness, and the Byzantines did not always believe in miracles even though religion was an essential part of their lives.

Miracle accounts can be found in all Byzantine hagiographical genres: martyr legends, saints' lives, encomia, homilies, collections of miracle stories, *apophthegmata patrum*, beneficial tales, and collective biographies. The miracle genre par excellence, however, is the miracle collection that flourished in the early and late Byzantine periods (ca. 330–650 and 1204–1453), while it declined in the middle period (ca. 650–1204). At this time there was no need for the composition of independent collections, since most hagiographers who wrote saints' lives provided an account of posthumous miracles at the end of their texts. About half of the Byzantine miracle collections are anonymous, while the rest are eponymous. As for the known authors, the large majority are bishops.

The genre of miracle collection might have originated from the records of miracles that were kept in saints' shrines in an attempt to promote their cult and to attract pilgrims by advertising the shrines' miraculous powers. These purposes were further promoted when at some point a hagiographer, who was related to the shrine, would produce a miracle collection by making a selection of the shrine's material, collecting oral testimonies, and committing to writing his own personal experiences of the saint's miraculous powers.

In general, a miracle collection is a text with an external framework within which a number of independent narratives are included. These are selected miracles performed posthumously by the same holy person or the same pair of saints, such as the holy unmercenaries Cosmas and Damian, who were martyred together. The framework of the miracle collection is created by a prologue and an epilogue where the hagiographer's voice is established. In the prologue, the hagiographer introduces himself, addresses his audience, states his intention, makes clear his role as the collector of the saint's miracles, and presents emphatically the utility and authority of his work. In the epilogue, the hagiographer reappears to address his audience for the last time and to offer a doxology to the miraculous saint(s) and, of course, to God, who manifests His power through His saints. Sometimes the hagiographer asks for the saint's miraculous protection as a reward for his undertaking to collect and write down his or her miracles.

The prologue is followed by a number of miracles. This is not fixed but varies from collection to collection. The largest collection consists of about 70 miracles, and the smallest includes about 10 miracles. The miracles in a collection are sometimes arranged according to their type (therapies, punishments, defending of cities, solution to daily problems, promotion of the saint's cult, etc.), their importance (from the personal to the general), the social milieu of the protagonists (churchmen/monks, laymen, aristocracy, lower social classes), their age (children, adults, and elderly people), and their gender (men, women, eunuchs). Each miracle story normally focuses on one incident; it has a single plot, a single setting, and a limited number of heroes or heroines.

The genre of miracle collection might be divided into two sub-genres according to the variety of miracles it includes: the monothematic and the polythematic collection. Monothematic is the collection that includes only one type of miracles, such as the anonymous miracle collection of the aforementioned Cosmas and Damian (sixth century) that consists of healing miracles only. The polythematic collection has more than one miracle category. An example is the anonymous miracle collection of Thecla (fifth century), the oldest Byzantine collection that has come down to us and one of the two miracle collections that are devoted to female saints. The other collection, which was composed in the eleventh century, includes a selection of the miracles of another female martyr, Saint Photeine, who specializes in healing eye diseases.

The most common miracle type in both monothematic and polythematic collections is the thaumaturgical one, that is, the cure of an illness or other bodily infirmity. The miraculous saints' clientele suffers mostly from the following afflictions: paralysis, blindness, eye diseases, dropsy, hernia, leprosy, cancer, dysentery, fever, sterility, hemorrhage, respiratory illnesses, urinary problems, kidney stones, skin diseases, and deafness. As for the most common methods of healing, these are through dreams, visions, and contact with or proximity to the saint's relics or icon. Additionally, anointment with or consumption of water or the miraculously exuded oil from the saint's relics, icon, or coffin can also be used. Miraculous water might be also found in a holy spring that is located in a shrine, while miraculous oil might be taken also from the lamp that hangs above the saint's tomb or icon.

In early miracle collections, sufferers are mostly healed through incubation—that is, the practice of sleeping in a shrine to achieve a cure. In most cases, these people come to healing shrines after realizing the physicians' inability to offer them a cure. They stay in the shrine until they are visited by the healing saint in a dream, who either prescribes a healing treatment or cures them while they sleep. In the miracle collections of later periods, however, incubation as a method of healing is very rare. In these texts, healings are mostly achieved through the patients' immediate contact with the saints' miraculous coffins, tombs, relics, and icons and also by the consumption of holy oil or water, or their application on the patients' afflicted bodily parts.

It seems that from the middle Byzantine period onward, the objects and liquids related to a saint acquire greater importance as healing means than dreams. The reason for this change might be associated with the development of saints' cults in the later periods, when the Late Antiquity practice of incubation might have lost its popularity. Additionally, healing dreams are much fewer in later hagiography because people's attitudes toward them seem to have changed. There are hagiographers who along with their audiences appear to question the divine source of dreams and effectively their function as healing vehicles.

The cured pilgrims of Byzantine sanctuaries expressed their gratitude to the miraculous saints by giving donations to their shrines. The richer ones offered golden jewelry and Eucharistic vessels adorned with pearls and gems. They also commissioned the composition of icons and mosaics. Poorer pilgrims offered nomismata, votive lamps, and woven hangings. All pilgrims could take back home with them little containers of the miraculous oil or water. These *eulogiai* not only functioned as souvenirs of the pilgrims' cures but also, as healing means, could be used again in the future for both themselves and for sick relatives and friends.

Stavroula Constantinou

Further Reading

Constantinou, Stavroula. "Grotesque Bodies in Hagiographical Tales: The Monstrous and the Uncanny in Byzantine Collections of Miracle Stories." *Dumbarton Oaks Papers* 64 (2010): 43–54.

Constantinou, Stavroula. "Healing Dreams in Early Byzantine Miracle Collections." In *Dreams, Healing, and Medicine in Greece: From Antiquity to the Present*, edited by Stephen Oberhelman, 189–197. Aldershot, UK: Ashgate, 2013.

Constantinou, Stavroula. "The Morphology of Healing Dreams: Dream and Therapy in Byzantine Collections of Miracle Stories." In *Dreaming in Byzantium and Beyond*, edited by Christina Angelidi and George Calofonos, 21–34. Aldershot, UK: Ashgate, 2014.

Csepregi, Ildigo. "Who Is Behind Incubation Stories? The Hagiographers of Byzantine Dream-Healing Miracles." In *Dreams, Healing, and Medicine in Greece: From Antiquity to the Present*, edited by Stephen Oberhelman, 161–187. Aldershot, UK: Ashgate, 2013.

Dagron, Gilbert. "L'ombre d'un doute: L'hagiographie en question, VIe-IXe siècle." *Dumbarton Oaks Papers* 46 (1992): 59–68.

Delehaye, Hippolite. "Les premiers *libelli miraculorum*." *Analecta Bollandiana* 29 (1910): 427–434.

Delehaye, Hippolite. "Les recueils antiques de miracles des saints." *Analecta Bollandiana* 43 (1925): 5–85, 305–325.

Déroche, Vincent. "Pourquoi écrivait-on des recueils de miracles? L'example des miracles de Saint Artemios." In *Les saints et leur sanctuaires à Byzance: Textes, images, et monuments*, edited by Catherine Jolivet-Lévy et al., 95–116. Byzantina Sorbonensia 11. Paris: Publications de la Sorbonne, 1993.

Déroche, Vincent. "Tensions et contradictions dans les recueils de miracles de la première époque byzantine." In *Miracle et Karama: Hagiographies médiévales comparées*, edited by Denise Aigle, 145–166. Turnhout: Brepols, 2000.

Efthymiadis, Stephanos. "Collections of Miracles (Fifth–Fifteenth Centuries)." In *The Ashgate Research Companion to Byzantine Hagiography: Genres and Contexts*, Vol. 2, edited by Stephanos Efthymiadis, 103–142. Aldershot, UK: Ashgate, 2014.

Efthymiadis, Stephanos. "Greek Byzantine Collections of Miracles: A Chronological and Bibliographical Survey." *Symbolae Osloensis* 74 (1999): 195–211.

Kaplan, Michel. "Le miracle est-il nécessaire au saint Byzantin?" In *Miracle et Karama: Hagiographies médiévales comparées*, edited by Denise Aigle, 167–196. Turnhout: Brepols, 2000.

Kazhdan, Alexander. "Holy and Unholy Miracle Workers." In *Byzantine Magic*, edited by Henri Maguire, 73–82. Washington, DC: Dumbarton Oaks Research Library and Collection, 1995.

Talbot, Alice-Mary. *Healing Shrines in Late Byzantine Constantinople*. Toronto: Hellenic Canadian Association of Constantinople, 1997.

Talbot, Alice-Mary. *Miracle Tales from Byzantium*. Cambridge, MA: Harvard University Press, 2012.

Talbot, Alice-Mary. "Pilgrimage to Healing Shrines: The Evidence of Miracle Accounts." *Dumbarton Oaks Papers* 56 (2002): 153–173.

C

Calvin, John

Born in the northern French town of Noyon, John Calvin (1509–1564) is most famously known for his role in the sixteenth-century European Reformation. After studying law in Paris, Calvin converted to a form of Protestantism and eventually settled in the Swiss town of Geneva, where he would establish a training school for pastors and write, among a multitude of other works, his *Institutes of the Christian Religion* (*ICR*). Calvin's role as a Protestant Reformer colored much of what he taught concerning miracles.

Calvin held that miracles were divinely ordained "seals" of the gospel and "true" doctrine (*ICR*, "Prefatory Letter," sec. 3). In this role, they facilitated the knowledge of God by the testifying of those who mediated the Word of God. In the ministry of Moses, suggested Calvin, God used miracles to commend his servant as an "undoubted prophet" through whom he established the divine law (*ICR* 1.8.5, 4.12.20). As the incarnate Word of God, Christ bore a self-referential testimony of his divinity through miracles (*ICR* 1.13.13); therefore, in Christ and his resurrection, the purpose of miracles found their fulfillment. To this degree, the miraculous activity of the apostles was a "temporal gift," which confirmed their role in establishing the church and affirmed the teachings of Christ (*ICR* 4.19.19). Calvin believed that the miraculous still occurred in his day but not in the same form as found with the apostles. Present in Calvin's definition is the early Protestant tendency to orient the works of God in the revelation of the Son. In every circumstance, miracles served to direct individuals to the Word of God. The French Reformer's critique that his Catholic counterparts "corrupted the works of God, by separating his word from miracles," should be understood in light of this tendency.

Nevertheless, Calvin's insistence on what he called the "efficacy of [Christ's] word" in the miraculous led him to emphasize the spiritual implications of Jesus's healing ministry. In this, the French Reformer reflected the common tendency of sixteenth-century Protestants to spiritualize the meaning of biblical miracles for the sake of elevating their teachings on *sola Scriptura* and justification by faith. Ordering the spiritual before the corporeal in his interpretation, Calvin allowed for a twofold spiritualization of miracles: "They are intended either to prepare us for faith, or to confirm us in faith." In Calvin's anagogical interpretation, miracles were divine declarations of inner healing from spiritual evils, sin, and decay, available to the individual through faith.

Calvin did not neglect the historical, physical implications of miracles. They served as earthly testimonies to the person of Christ. His miraculous works had the effect of forcing unbelieving Jewish leaders to declare cleansed those whom Christ healed and therefore to indirectly witness to his lordship (*ICR* 3.4.4). Nevertheless, Calvin positioned himself against the Catholic teaching of a miraculous transubstantiation of the corporeal elements of the Eucharist. He dismissed such a belief as a "delusion . . . [drawing] people away from the true worship of their God to vanity" (*ICR* "Prefatory Letter," sec. 3). Though admitting that God acted sacramentally through miracles, Calvin relegated such divine intervention to the Old Testament (*ICR* 4.14.18). Against the Catholic critique that he had rationalized away the miraculous in the sacrament, Calvin argued that his position of the mystical presence of Christ in the Lord's Supper expressed the divine miracles of bridging the insurmountable distance between heaven and Earth and of uniting believers with Christ and his benefits (*ICR* 4.17.24).

Calvin's tendency to primarily read New Testament miracles in a spiritual way, which focused on the inner transformation that Christ's earthly ministry represented, played a determining role in the cessationist position on miracles that would pervade most of later Reformed Protestantism. His spiritualizing of miracles should primarily be understood in light of his role in the Reformation. Like his Protestant counterparts, Calvin interpreted biblical miracles with the underlying intent to recover what he felt to be the true meaning of Christian faith and worship.

Peter James Yoder

Further Reading

Calvin, John. *Commentary on the Gospel according to John.* 2 vols. Translated by William Pringle. Grand Rapids, MI: Baker, 2003.

Calvin, John. *Commentary on the Harmony of the Evangelists.* 3 vols. Translated by William Pringle. Grand Rapids, MI: Baker, 2003.

Calvin, John. *Treatise on Relics.* 2nd ed. Translated by Count Valerian Krasinski. Edinburgh, UK: John Stone, Hunter, and Col., 1870. Reprinted without translator's notes but with an introduction by Joe Nickell. Amherst, NY: Prometheus Books, 2009.

Campbell, George

George Campbell (1719–1796) was a minister, philosopher, and professor of divinity. He is best known for his work on rhetoric and his responses to David Hume's rejection of miracles.

At the age of 15 Campbell entered Marischal College, and by the age of 19 he had earned an MA in philosophy. His areas of study included logic, metaphysics, pneumatology, ethics, and natural philosophy. After hearing lectures at the University of Edinburg, Campbell became interested in theology. He enrolled in the University of Aberdeen, pursuing a doctorate of divinity. He was able to complete it in 1746, delayed by the second Jacobite rising, which began in 1745. He was ordained in 1748 and obtained a parish in Banchary Tenon.

Campbell published two chapters of his well-received *The Philosophy of Rhetoric* in 1750. He then obtained a ministry position in Aberdeen in 1757. Campbell became the principal of Marischal College in 1759. He was among the founders of the Aberdeen Philosophical Society, a group that produced a number of published works. They were fans of Bacon and were concerned with the sciences of the mind.

In 1762 Campbell produced *A Dissertation on Miracles* as a response to Hume's *An Enquiry Concerning Human Understanding*, which was published in 1748. The two publicly admired each other.

In 1770 Campbell became professor of divinity at Marischal. His other published works were *Lectures on Ecclesiastical History, Lectures on Pulpit Eloquence*, and his translation of the gospels. Campbell taught until 1795. He died within a year of retiring.

Campbell was fully engaged in Enlightenment learning as well as fully embracing Christianity. For him, "that we may reflect light upon others, we must ourselves be previously enlightened." Campbell held that faith gave rationality a purpose and contended that faith required rational proof.

Campbell's response to Hume centers upon Hume's assertions concerning testimony. Succinctly, Hume says that all evidence for miracles is based on the testimony of others. Miracles for him are violations of laws of nature. To accept the testimony of a miracle is to accept something that is contradictory to experience, meaning that all the evidence one has accrued through the sense data of experience is to be rejected in favor of testimony to the contrary of what one otherwise knows to be true. One must in light of the testimony of a miracle ascertain which is more likely—that the witness is deceived or is deceiving the audience or that the testimony is true and that one's experiences are violated and irrelevant. The improbability of discarding this knowledge in favor of testimony is so great that it is almost definitional that no miracle testimony is trustworthy.

Campbell rejects the notion that testimony is some sort of lessened evidence. In actuality, he holds that testimony corresponds to an innate recognition of truth. He uses the example of children as they are building their mental worlds. They are prone to accept the testimony of those who have experienced what they have not. Only later do they develop the ability to question. The default response to testimony is acceptance among children. This response is closer to pristine, innate knowledge than is experiential sense data. Thus, testimony is closer to evidence from consciousness than is experience. Hume reverses this order in his assertion, as one is to start from a point of skepticism. Campbell thinks that it is much harder to overturn this order than Hume thinks.

Campbell further illustrates his point with an example from experience. Suppose he has witnessed a ferry crossing a body of water 2,000 times without a mishap. If someone approaches him and tells him the ferry has sunk, he will have no problem accepting the testimony of a person, despite thousands of counterexamples to that testimony. He has never experienced this ferry sinking, though he is immediately willing to accept this testimony without question. This eyewitness testimony is truth and is certain. Thus, Hume's assertion that testimony is subject to credulity of experience is just false. One of Campbell's Aberdeen Philosophical Society friends, Thomas Reid, states that the way we know the world is through senses and testimony, mostly the latter.

Campbell holds that the most important factor in determining the veracity of testimony is witnesses. If one is certain that there is no evidence of collusion, then numbers attesting to the same miracle or type of miracle makes testimony more reliable. Indeed, absolute certainty can be established by the testimony of enough witnesses.

Campbell does see one issue with credulity and miracles that Hume does not address. Rationality has to be the guide to protect against emotion and bias. One can be too ready to receive eyewitness testimony that his or her belief. Likewise, one can also be too ready to reject miracles witnessed by those of other religious traditions. Rationality will reveal the truth of miracles.

Mark Anthony Phelps

Further Reading

Broadie, Alexander. "Scottish Philosophy in the 18th Century." *The Stanford Encyclopedia of Philosophy*, Fall 2013 Edition, http://plato.stanford.edu/archives/fall2013/entries/scottish-18th/.

Suderman, Jeffrey M. *Orthodoxy and Enlightenment: George Campbell in the Eighteenth Century*. Montreal: McGill-Queen's University Press, 2001.

Canada, Miracles in

In all of Canada's vast reaches, there are several places that account for miracles, but three of the nation's most favored and fertile are found in the Province of Quebec. Located just outside Quebec City is the oldest of these places, dedicated to Saint Anne-de-Beaupré; another is in Montreal, in the Shrine of St. Joseph, within which is the tomb of Saint Andre Bissette; the last, the Shrine of Our Lady of the Cape (Notre Dame du Cap) in Trois-Rivières, is nearly equidistant between the two.

Located on the banks of the St. Lawrence River, the Basilica of the Shrine of Ste. Anne-de-Beaupré houses the forearm of the mother of the Blessed Virgin Mary, a sacred relic to Catholics. Every year thousands in search of cures flock to the shrine. Favors received are meticulously cataloged, and many are printed in the shrine's monthly publication, the *Annals of Saint Anne*. From its pages come stories of favors received, such as the woman from St. Vallier who traveled to the shrine as a pilgrim in 2006. She came to give thanks on the tenth anniversary of a cure for breast cancer. Another relates the cure of a young boy from Bellechasse who had meningitis. Without any medical hope, a novena to "good St. Anne" was commenced, and on the ninth day the physician pronounced him cured. Other reports run the gamut—from a desired pregnancy for a couple stymied for ten years after receiving a special benediction at the shrine to a healing of dropsy, blindness, or perpetual hiccups. Today hundreds of crutches and canes, artificial limbs, and prosthetic shoes are stacked in testimony of the efficacy of this sacred place.

Cures have been affected in a number of venues at the shrine. In addition to the reliquaries containing the finger, wrist, and forearm of Saint Anne (a gift of Pope Leo XIII and Pope Saint John XXIII), miracles have also been attributed to the statue of Saint Anne (around which the faithful pray in groups), the waters from an exterior fountain, and a tomb in the basilica where Venerable Father Alfred Pampalon, CSsR, is interred. He is a patron for those with addictions.

The cures began almost immediately after the initial chapel was erected. Louis Guimont (or Guimond in some accounts) placed a few stones in the foundation of the chapel around 1658 and prayed to Saint Anne to remove a steady back pain due to protracted kidney disease. The cure was instantaneous, and today Guimont's case is considered the first of many miracles attributed to Mary's mother. Redemptorists, who have been in charge of the shrine since the 1870s, note that about 30 miracles are recorded each year.

Notre Dame du Cap, Canada's national shrine, grew from a somewhat lackluster parish to an invigorated pilgrimage site thanks to the foresight of Father Luc Desilets, the pastor from 1864 to 1888. His method was to instill a devotion to the rosary in his congregation. So many were attracted to the little church that a larger one was necessitated. Stone to be used in the construction was quarried on the other side of the St. Lawrence River, and the plan was to bring these materials over the river in the winter, when it typically froze. But in 1879 the winter was mild, and building was held up. Parishioners commenced the recitation of the rosary, and the first miracle—an ice bridge—allowed the fieldstones to be carried across the river in a span of about a mile and a half.

A second miracle took place shortly after the consecration of the church in 1888. A parishioner named Pierre Lacroix and Father Desilets and his curate, Father Frederic Janssoone, OFM, noticed that a statue of the Virgin Mary that had been placed on the main altar had "opened its eyes." The witnesses all so testified, and today the statue is crowned by papal decree. As for Father Janssoone, he was beatified on September 25, 1988.

On the peak of Mount Royal in the city of Montreal rests an enormous oratory shrine dedicated to Saint Joseph. The work of Saint André Bessette, CSC, it is also one of Canada's most popular places of pilgrimage, drawing about three million annually. Among its most important attributes is the heart of Saint André, which is encased in glass behind an iron screen, as well as the tomb of the saint. Apart from the oratory is a smaller wooden chapel formerly used by Saint André as a kind of lodging, chapel, and headquarters to receive visitors. First erected in 1904, it is adorned with *ex votos* for some of the numerous favors granted, which some have estimated to be around 125,000.

While Quebec is often considered the province of Canada with the deepest miracle tradition, mainly due to the preponderance of Catholics, the nation's other provinces have also experienced supernatural phenomena. In Alberta, about 75 kilometers from Edmonton, Lac Ste. Anne has been reported to have curative powers. The lake's clear, cold air probably alleviated numerous cases of tuberculosis. Like the Shrine of Ste. Anne-de Beaupré, the lake is visited in large numbers especially on the saint's feast day, July 26. It became a pilgrimage destination through the efforts of an Oblate priest, Father Jean-Baptiste Thibault, who led a group in prayer asking for rain in 1889. Today many come to bathe in the lake, not unlike Hindu pilgrims to the Ganges for the Kumbh Mela festival.

Canadians have been the recipients of miracles, but a select number have had their cases especially scrutinized. For instance, in the cause of the first of Canada's saints, Saint Marguerite d'Youville (d. 1771), it is attested that she interceded on behalf of three Canadians who were healed: two "Grey Nuns" from tuberculosis and blindness and another woman, Lise Dormand, from untreatable myeloblastic leukemia.

Patrick J. Hayes

See also: Saint André Bessette's Heart and the Oratory of St. Joseph Shrine, Montreal

Further Reading

Dunn, Mary Corley. "Sainte-Anne-du-Petit-Cap: The Making of an Early Modern Shrine." PhD dissertation, Harvard University, 2008.

Dunn, Mary Corley. "The Miracles at Sainte-Anne-du-Petit-Cap and the Making of a Seventeenth-Century Colonia Community." *Canadian Historical Review* 91(4) (December 2010): 611–635.

Gillet, H. M. *Famous Shrines of Our Lady*, Vol. 2. London: Samuel Walker, 1952.

Lefebvre, Eugène. *Ste. Anne de Beaupré: Its Shrine, Its Spirit*. Quebec: Shrine of Ste. Anne-de-Beaupré, 1964.

Lefevre, Marie Cecilia. "In Honor of Saint Marguerite We Will Celebrate!" *Grey Nuns Regional Voice* 34(4) (Fall 2005): 1–2, at: http://www.grey-nuns.org/Newsletters /GNRVFall05NL.pdf.

Simon, Steve. *Healing Waters: The Pilgrimage to Lac Ste. Anne*. Edmonton: University of Alberta Press, 1995.

The Miracles of Beaupré: A Collection of the Most Remarkable Cures Wrought at the Far-Famed Shrine of Ste. Anne de Beaupré, Compiled by a Redemptorist. Quebec: Ste. Anne de Beaupré, 1908.

Voisine, Nive. "Luc Désilets et la foundation du centre de pèlerinage de Notre-Dame-du-Cap." In *Les Pèlerinages au Québec*, edited by P. Boglioni and B. Lacroix, 111–122. Quebec: Les Presses de l'Université Laval, 1981.

Canonization

Canonization is the final step in the recognition by the Roman Catholic Church of a person's sanctity and virtue. Only a pope may issue the bull of canonization publicly proclaiming a saint. The ceremony of the canonization of a saint is the formal act that pronounces the candidate as unquestionably in heaven. It is among the most solemn acts of the magisterium, and theologians almost universally hold it to be an infallible act. At that moment, the whole Church acknowledges one of its own as enjoying the beatific vision. They acclaim it by their "Amen."

For nearly a millennium, the prospect of canonizing a saint rested with the local church. The honor of the first canonization belongs to Saint Ulric, bishop of Augsburg (d. 973). He was the first person to be declared a saint, in this case by Pope John XV (d. 996), who intervened in the proceedings outside of Italy. Within a generation the rules for canonizations were collected and codified, beginning a long process of effectively stamping out local and popular control of the canonization proceedings. Pope Alexander III (d. 1181), in a brief to King Kol of Sweden titled *Aeterna et incommutabilis* and written around 1171, assumed the exclusive right to canonize for the papacy. With Saint Ubaldo's canonization brief in May 1191, Pope Celestine III acquiesced to the pleadings of Bishop Theobaldo of Gubbio to raise Ubaldo, his predecessor, to the dignity of the altars—a process that signaled the bonds between the pope and the local bishop in canonization processes. However, it fell to Pope Innocent III (d. 1216) to actually put these measures into effect by codifying them. The norms he developed held sway for the next few centuries, though he took the papal prerogative, still in force, to create a saint without bothering to investigate the candidate's sanctity or demonstrate that he was the object of a public cult. His legate, Peter of Castelnau, was deemed a martyr who could bypass these formalities; his canonization rested on the papal fiat.

History repeats. While he made some attempt to fine-tune the method of investigation by giving detailed requirements for all inquiries into the merits of a case for sanctity, Pope Gregory IX (d. 1241) dispensed with them when Francis of Assisi's nomination to the altars was at stake. Francis was so holy and so universally loved that the pope believed it would be a waste of time to inquire any further.

From 1198 to 1431 these strictures slowed the practice of canonizations down considerably. Only 37 saints were decreed, and 72 processes for canonization were opened. This often had more to do with the political dramas of European royals and their dealings with the pope than with the individual's reputation for holiness. As the papal court grew in power, however, it became politically useful to centralize the function of the canonization procedure. It also served as a vehicle for acknowledging causes to which popes had a personal sympathy, as in the case of the Franciscan pope Sixtus IV (d. 1481). Sixtus IV canonized the Franciscan martyrs in Morocco who died in 1220, a cause that had not had any traction for hundreds of years. In the aftermath of the Council of Trent and the establishment of the Roman Curia, Pope Sixtus V issued *Immensa aeterni Dei* (1588), which placed the function of determining heroic sanctity with the Congregation of Rites.

In 1642, Pope Urban VIII began to refine the function of the Congregation of Rites. He issued a bull reserving the beatification of saints to the Holy See and prohibited the display of a candidate's image with a halo or nimbus before that person was officially canonized. Indeed, any public cult or other mode of publicizing prematurely the beatus miracles could be sufficient for scuttling a case.

Benedict XIV, while still Cardinal Prospero Lambertini, wrote *De servorum Dei beatificatione et beatorum canonizatione*, in which he laid out in scrupulous detail the procedures to be followed in arriving at a truthful and edifying dossier. His work as the Devil's Advocate for the Congregation of Rites earned him the respect of the Curia, both for his learned attention to detail and his zeal for ferreting out fakes. Those who did pass muster were then surely assumed to be saintly. These were listed on extensive rolls of the holy, such as the *Codex canonizationum*,

Porsi, Luigi. "Cause di canonizzazione e procedura nella Cost. Apost: Divinus perfectionis Magister; Considerazioni and valutazioni." *Monitor Ecclesiasticus* 110 (1985): 365–400.

Rodrigo, Romualdo. *Manuale per istruire i processi di canonizzazione.* Rome: Institutum Historicum Augustinianorum Recollectorum, 1991.

Sarno, Robert J. *Diocesan Inquiries Required by the Legislator in the New Legislation for the Causes of Saints.* Rome: PUG, 1987.

Vauchez, André. *Sainthood in the Later Middle Ages.* Translated by Jean Birrell. New York: Cambridge University Press, 1997.

Veraja, Fabijan. *Le Cause di Canonizazione dei Santi: Commento alla Legislatione e Guida Pratica.* Rome: Congregation of the Causes of Saints, 1992.

Woestman, William. *Canonization: Theology, History, and Process.* Ottawa: Saint Paul University Press, 2002.

Caribbean, Miracles in the

The Caribbean region historically is a space were diverse cultures encountered each other and assimilated to both the environment and each other in order to live together with some measure of harmony. The inability of the European colonists to maintain a sufficient source of inexpensive labor through the use of the indigenous aboriginal inhabitants meant that they turned to Africa; India; various countries in Europe, China, and the Middle East; and the United States. There is also a history of migration within the Caribbean. Each of these groups had their own religions and religious practices, but as often happens, the physical space and human interaction lead to a transformation.

Usually the various European colonists insisted that immigrants and the indigenous populations adopt some form of Christianity. For example, the Spanish issued the *Cedula de Population* in 1783 to encourage immigration to Trinidad; one of the requirements mandated that all migrants be Roman Catholic. East Indian immigrants were the one exception of forced conversion because they were initially expected to return to India. Colonial representatives and the official religious authorities carried a lot of power and prestige within the society; hence, for many there was a benefit to adopting the state religion. Others, however, were able to retain their indigenous religious practices, merge Christianity with other religions, create brand new religions, or practice Christianity in public and another religion in private.

One early example of a miracle occurred on the island of Hispaniola (modern-day Haiti and the Dominican Republic), where Christopher Columbus had erected a large wooden cross in December 1492 in order to dedicate the New World to the Christian God. In his absence, some Spaniards who remained on the island came down with fever, but when they touched the cross, their illness dissipated. As months passed and the Spanish administrator Bobadilla proved increasingly belligerent toward the natives of the island, they contrived a plot to burn down the cross. But it withstood a fierce conflagration, only to emerge unscathed the next day. Finally, in 1553 an earthquake rattled the island and particularly the fort at Conception. Only the chapel housing the cross withstood the disaster. If two beams of wood symbolized the importation of miraculous events into the New World, it was Columbus himself who pronounced that the whole of Hispaniola was a miracle.

Such wonders are not contained by any one island. In Puerto Rico, a wooden figurine of Nuestra Señora de La Candelaria from Seville has its own cult. Another, Nuestra Señora de Bethlehem from a Dominican convent on Hispaniola—the first such image to appear in the Indies—is attributed to the resuscitation of Doña Juana Guilarte who, deceased for six hours and placed in her coffin, suddenly sat up singing the Virgin's praises. Nuestra Señora de Monserrat supposedly appeared to the sexton of the chapel in the town of Hormigueros in 1599. Giraldo Gonzáles found himself confronted with an attacking bull. Invoking the aid of the Virgin, the animal's legs suddenly buckled and, brought low as if in prayer, left Gonzáles unharmed. As repayment, he erected the Chapel of Our Lady of Monserrat and installed a statue in her honor. It is a curious admixture of Catholic piety and Yoruba belief whereby the Europeanized figure of the Christ child sits on the lap of the dark-skinned Virgin, clad in a yellow dress, as is typical of the orisha Oshun, a benevolent deity. Throughout the Caribbean, miracles are as diverse as the religious landscape to which they belong. On the island of Trinidad, for example, in the town of Siparia at the Roman Catholic Church of la Divina Pastora, miracles have been tied to the statue of the Madonna beginning with her arrival on the island in 1784. Devotees of many faiths come to the church to request assistance from this representation of the Holy Madonna, who is locally referred to as la Divina Pastora, Suparee Ke Mai (Soparee Mai), and Kwon Yin. Catholics along with a variety of orthodox Christian sects, Spiritual Baptists, and Protestant Evangelicals as well as orisha believers, Chinese Buddhists, Warao Amerindians, Muslims, and Hindus all appeal to her for assistance. Many personal miracles are attributed to la Divina. For many worshippers, favors for personal health and well-being and that of their family members are requested most often.

There are two big celebrations of la Divina. The Hindu celebration begins on Holy Thursday and continues until just before the Good Friday service, while the Catholic celebration occurs on the second Sunday after Easter. These are large-scale events when thousands of pilgrims come to pray before her. At other times, devotees visit her in the church where they have access throughout the day. Typically, followers stand before the statue and pray in their own religious tradition. Some offer gifts of money, jewelry, flour, olive oil, or flowers. There is no prescribed format for worship, but many interviewees insisted that if a promise in the mountain range of Carmel, near Haifa, in present-day Israel. The Carmelites, as they came to be called, followed a rule of life written by Saint Albert, the Latin-rite patriarch of Jerusalem, and approved by Pope Honorius III in 1226. Due to military conquests in the region by Muslims, the Carmelites soon migrated to various parts of Europe and were transformed into a mendicant order, although their rule specified a preference for the contemplative life. Initially they had difficulty justifying their status as a mendicant order, since their origins were shrouded in mystery without a clear founder. Because the prophet Elijah had lived a solitary and contemplative life on Mount Carmel, the Carmelite order claimed him as their founder. In fact, a legend developed that the order could trace its origin in an unbroken line of contemplative hermits living on Mount Carmel since the time of Elijah to the 1200s. Thus, in a sense the many biblical miracles associated with Elijah, including the miracle of the widow's oil, calling down fire from heaven during the confrontation with the prophets of Ba'al, the raising of the widow's son from the dead, and his ascension to heaven in a fiery chariot, could be considered Carmelite miracles.

In 1321, Saint Peter Thomas reportedly had a vision of the Virgin Mary in which she admonished him to "have confidence, Peter, for the Carmelite Order will last until the end of the world. Elijah, its founder, obtained it a long time ago from my Son." To this day, Carmelites have lived and worked in a spirit of confidence and faith.

Female branches of the Carmelite family gradually emerged. The founder of the Discalced Carmelite reform, Saint Teresa of Ávila, had many mystical experiences during prayer, such as visions, locutions, and raptures, and occasionally she even levitated off the ground during prayer, to her great embarrassment (*The Book of Her Life*, ch. 20, no.5, and *The Interior Castle* VI, passim). She received a mystical piercing or "transverberation" of her heart (*The Book of Her Life*, ch. 29, no. 13), which is depicted in Bernini's famous sculpture in Rome. However, Saint Teresa warned that having such mystical experiences was not necessarily a sign of holiness and could even be a source of spiritual pride. Rather, true holiness always finds its expression in charity toward one's neighbor (*The Interior Castle*, VI:9, VII:4).

One of the most famous saints of the Discalced Carmelite Order, Saint Thérèse of Lisieux, experienced a miracle during her childhood through the intercession of Mary. While suffering from an illness that made her appear delirious, she prayed for deliverance before the statue of Our Lady of Victories in her family home. She saw the statue come to life and smile at her, and at that instant she was cured (*Story of a Soul*, Manuscript A, ch. 3). This particular statue of Mary, preserved in the Carmelite convent in Lisieux, has come to be known as Our Lady of the Smile.

The best known miracles associated with the Carmelite order are the granting of the scapular medal by Our Lady of Mount Carmel to Simon Stock in the mid-1200s and the association of Carmel with the apparitions of Our Lady of Fatima in 1917. It should be noted that the only Fatima seer to survive into adulthood, Sister Lucia of Jesus, joined the Discalced Carmelite Order. Furthermore, Saint Pope John Paul II was an honorary member of the Carmelite Order and attributed his survival during the assassination attempt of May 13, 1981, to the miraculous intercession of Our Lady of Fatima. Thus, the miracles associated with the Carmelite order span the time of Elijah to our own day.

Jason Bourgeois

See also: Our Lady of Fatima; Our Lady of Mount Carmel; Scapular; Statues

Further Reading

Baukal, Charles E. "Pyrotechnics on Mount Carmel." *Bibliotheca Sacra* 171 (July–September 2014): 289–306.

Clarke, John, trans. *Story of a Soul: The Autobiography of Saint Thérèse of Lisieux.* Washington, DC: Institute of Carmelite Studies, 1996.

Copsey, Richard, trans. and ed. *The Ten Books on the Way of Life and Great Deeds of the Carmelites (Including the Book of the First Monks).* Faversham, UK: Saint Albert's Press, 2005.

Healy, Kilian. *Prophet of Fire.* Rome: Institutum Carmelitanum, 1990.

Kavanaugh, Kieran, and Otilio Rodriguez, trans. and eds. *The Collected Works of St. Teresa of Avila*, Vol. 1, *The Book of Her Life, Spiritual Testimonies, Soliloquies.* Washington, DC: Institute of Carmelite Studies, 1976.

Rodriguez, Otilio, and Kieran Kavanaugh, trans. and eds. *The Collected Works of St. Teresa of Avila*, Vol. 2, *The Way of Perfection, Meditations on the Song of Songs, the Interior Castle.* Washington, DC: Institute of Carmelite Studies, 1980.

Rohrbach, Peter-Thomas. *Journey to Carith: The Story of the Carmelite Order.* New York: Doubleday, 1966.

Celestis Hierusalem Cives

A papal brief was issued by Pope Urban VIII on July 5, 1634, establishing procedures for the canonization of saints and the confirmation by the pope, *in forma specifica* (that is, by his express wish), of prior decrees of the Holy Office of the Inquisition. These decrees, issued on March 13 and October 2, 1625, forbade the public cult and veneration of those who were not yet beatified or canonized by the Holy See. With the exception of martyrs, candidates had to meet three tests: doctrinal purity, heroic virtue, and miraculous intercession after death. Martyrs, however, required no miracles as proof either of their orthodoxy or heroic virtue. By the seventeenth century, these standards were the minimum tests for sainthood.

The document had a lasting impact among canonists and on those writers who sought to make a contribution to hagiography. In many of these volumes a prefatory page signaled the writers' assent to the teaching contained in Urban's text. Especially inviolate were those writings touching upon the authority of the pope to make decisions on matters of a supernatural nature. Authors would therefore have to make a declaration that their work contained no pretense toward possessing such authority and that "no other credence is to be given to the contents of this volume than that given to human authority, especially in relation to supernatural gifts and graces where the Church has not intervened by her judgment."

Patrick J. Hayes

Further Reading

Blaher, Damian J. *The Ordinary Processes in Causes of Beatification and Canonization: A Historical Synopsis and a Commentary*. Washington, DC: Catholic University of America Press, 1949.

Pope Urban VIII. "Apostolic Letter *Celestis Hierusalem Cives*." In *Bullarium Romanum*, Vol. 14, edited by Taurinensis, 436–440. Rome, 1868.

Pope Urban VIII. *Decreta servanda in beatificatione et canonizatione Sanctorum*, March 12, 1642.

Sacred Congregation of the Holy Office. "Decree of March 13, 1625." In *Codicis iuris canonici fontes*, Vol. 4, edited by Petri Gasparri. Rome: Typis Polyglottis Vaticanis, 1926.

Sacred Congregation of the Holy Office. "Decree of October 2, 1625." In *Codex pro postulatoribus causarum beatificationis et canonizationis*, 4th ed., Appendix I. Rome: Ex Typographia Agostiniana, 1929.

Charms

Charms are one of the significant agents of miracles. By design, charms are objects with the potency of supernatural or magical power to heal or to remedy a situation. Charms could be in solid states (e.g., bracelet, amulet, ring, parchment, necklace, pendant, staff, clothing) and/or liquid form (e.g., water, oil, perfume, lotion). In modern and general terms, charms can also be defined as remedial medicine. However, unlike orthodox medicine, charms are used for both physical and spiritual healing. The result emanating from the use of a charm could be either spontaneous or gradual. Thus, charms have several components that work together for their efficacy. These include conjuration, incantation, adjuration, recitation, repetition, gibberish speaking, muttering, meditation, and bathing. The modus operandi of charms points to their potential intangibility. These modalities may also occur through orality or performance.

Charms have been part of human cultural practices and especially spirituality for ages. Although there is no firm evidence on when exactly mankind introduced charms, records from ancient Egypt show that certain forms of charms were used in the process of mummification. Archaeological evidence has also demonstrated the occurrence of charms among the Vikings, Native Americans, and the early inhabitants of Africa over several centuries. However, knowledge of charms in the medieval period proliferated from the eighteenth through the twentieth centuries. Through the studies of ancient and medieval manuscripts, scholars have researched the use, characteristics, and constituents of charms. For instance, exorcism, herbal charms, and charms that transfer one characteristic for another (typically evil for good) are characteristic of Anglo-Saxon charms. Additionally, the Anglo-Saxons used amulets as remedies for fevers, wounds, and other maladies. Each type of charm was used for specific ailments, and their employment was provided by individuals believed to have the technical knowledge on their application. One finds a diversity of ailments and of charms used in healing them. These include stanching blood loss as well as healing toothaches, ague and fever, scalds and burns, swelling and inflammation, snakebite, strains and sprains, wounds and fractures, and stomach-related diseases, among many others.

For healing, a patient will often go to charmers or invite a charmer to his or her residence, where the procedures for healing are carried out. In medieval Anglo-Saxon cultures, pagan use of charms was widespread. With the emergence of Christianity, a syncretized practice combining elements of pagan and Christian practices can be found. For instance, the incantation or recitation accompanying charms was based on invocation of the names of biblical saints. One could also hear echoes of miraculous events in the Bible. Many theologians of medieval and early modern Europe illustrated this syncretism in healing practices but also for domestic protection—that is, household goods and flocks; protection against evil-doers and spirits, bad luck, and mortality; and fertility, which encompassed procreation or a crop yield.

Conversely, in African literature there is a stark contrast in the way charms are discussed. Whether in the disciplines of history, philosophy, anthropology, sociology, or theology, European writers tend to contextualize the use of charms within the realm of folk religion. This genre of intellectual thought paradoxically labels charms, in the context of African traditional religion, as either a fetish or a cruel hoax. They are often associated with the notion of blackness, as opposed to whiteness. For example, charms in African religions are believed to have mystical and mysterious powers capable of causing evil. They are often condemned as demonic. Although many acknowledge that charms in African religion can be used for good, they tend to present them as elements of perpetual evil doing. Yet in terms of the efficacy of the use of charms, there is no difference between some Christian and African religion practices. For example the Catholic Christians use *medas*, rosaries, and crucifixes, among others, for protection. The Pentecostal Christians use a white handkerchief and anointing oil for miraculous purposes. Similarly, charms in the Yoruba religion—practiced among the Yoruba people of southwestern Nigeria—can take the shape of the *onde* (amulet) or *oruka* (ring).

Charms in any form (as object, orality, performance) exist in all human societies, religions, and cultures. For instance, in Yoruba religion, sometimes a procession of groups of healers is required to improve the potency of a charm. It is believed that dancing in a place where multitudes gather to watch or be part of a feast will facilitate the expediency of the charm.

Charms can also be used for an individual, a group of people, or an entire community. A good example of this is the use of charms to cure a community of a plague. Frequent deaths due to unknown causes in a community could be a plague, especially when an agricultural region produces a low harvest due to infertile soil or drought. Likewise, in urban centers, high unemployment and poverty due to bad governance can be seen as a plague. These situations can be remedied with the use of charms.

Abidemi Babatunde Babalola

Further Reading

Awolalu, Omosade. J. *Yoruba Beliefs and Sacrificial Rites*. Essex, UK: Longman Group, 1979.

Davies, Owen. "Healing Charms in Use in England and Wales: 1700–1950." *Folklore* 107 (1996): 19–32.

Grendon, Felix. "The Anglo-Saxon Charms." *Journal of American Folklore* 22(84) (1909): 105–237.

Obinna Elijah. "Life Is Superior to Wealth? Indigenous Healers in an African Community, Amasiri, Nigeria." In *African Traditions in the Study of Religion in Africa: Emerging Trends, Indigenous Spirituality, and the Interface with Other World Religions*, edited by Adogame Afe, Chitando Ezra, and Bateye Bolaji, 135–148. Burlington, VT: Ashgate Publishing, 2012.

Olsan, Lea. "Latin Charms of Medieval England: Verbal Healing in a Christian Oral Tradition." *Oral Tradition* 7(1) (1992): 116–142.

Roper, Jonathan, ed. *Charms, Charmers, and Charming: International Research in Verbal Magic*. New York: Palgrave Macmillan, 2009.

Chaucer, Geoffrey

Among the most inventive and engaging poets of late medieval England, Geoffrey Chaucer (ca. 1340–1400) is best known for his *Canterbury Tales*, left incomplete at the time of his death but still embracing a wide range of medieval genres, topics, and concerns, including that of miracles. His treatment of miracles falls under two headings, one explicit and the other implied, both attached to the Christian faith that Chaucer practiced and endorsed.

Chaucer's most explicit treatment of miracles appears in the "Prioress' Tale," spoken by an ambiguously described prioress, one of three women narrators in the *Canterbury Tales*. The tale itself is described as a "miracle," being an example of a subgenre referred to as "Miracles of the Virgin," popular devout narratives showing the Virgin Mary's divine power and also her merciful intervention on behalf of those who pray to her; Chaucer's tale is the most accomplished of the genre.

The miracles in the "Prioress' Tale" center on a seven-year-old boy living in an unnamed Asian city who, because of his sung devotion to Mary, has had his throat cut by certain unnamed Jews through whose ghetto he walks, innocently if provocatively singing the *Alma redemptoris mater*, a hymn in praise of the Virgin, as he does so. His distraught mother is finally able to locate his hidden body when inspired by Christ where to look. Thanks to a miraculous seed that the Virgin placed on his tongue as he was attacked, the boy has been able to continue his song, and, once discovered, is able to describe the circumstances of his martyrdom to an assembled audience. The treatment throughout, though starkly anti-Semitic, is also orthodox and sadly traditional, probably attached to the fraternity of Young Hugh of Lincoln, to which both Chaucer's wife, Philippa, and his patron, John of Gaunt, had been admitted.

But Chaucer's representation of miracles extends to other circumstances too, including unnoticed divine intervention in human affairs. Thus, in the "Man of Law's Tale," the long voyage of the saintly female protagonist, Constance, is undertaken in a rudderless boat and involves many acts of divine protection, all thanks to Mary's intervention. Less obvious divine intervention appears as well in the apparently coincidental meeting at sea of Constance and the victorious Roman senator sent to avenge her treatment in Syria and the coincidental meetings and revelations with which the tale ends. The dramatic "Second Nun's Tale," a life of Saint Cecilia, also contains representations of unremarked divine power that both protects the Christians and directs their activities and also leads the protagonist to a triumphant martyrdom.

The divine manifesting itself through apparent coincidence is a continuing theme in Chaucer and appears in both religious and semireligious narratives. Other less evident instances include the young "rioters" meeting of the old man in the

"Pardoner's Tale" and their subsequent discovery of eight bushels of gold coins, and the meeting of the summoner and the yeoman in the "Friar's Tale." Although not averse to the use of coincidence in certain finally secular tales, as when Palamon and Arcite meet outside the city walls, and then are discovered in combat, in the "Knight's Tale"—though even these occurrences appear to be brought about by the gods of antiquity—apparently chance meetings and other coincidences often hold out the possibility of miraculous intervention.

The tales in which miracles figure unmistakably, however—the "Man of Law's Tale," the "Prioress' Tale," and the "Second Nun's Tale"—constitute three of the four tales universally agreed to be religious in tone, meaning, and implication. There is throughout an edge to their miracles, which are neither static nor simply revelatory, though they often reveal meaning and advance the plot. But they also accomplish or complete important matters and testify to a divine presence that, observed or not, is everywhere present, everywhere attentive to those who love and honor God and his saints. Taken together, the tales constitute a serious and complex meditation on the role of divine agency in human affairs—whether explicitly revealed or implied—and attest to a degree of not uncritical Christian faith that runs through the *Canterbury Tales* as a whole.

John C. Hirsh

Further Reading

Brown, Carleton. *A Study of the Miracle of Our Lady Told by Chaucer's Prioress.* London: K. Paul, Trench, Trubner, 1910.

Chaucer, Geoffrey. *The Canterbury Tales: Fifteen Tales and the General Prologue.* New York: Norton, 2005.

Malo, Robyn. *Relics and Writing in Late Medieval England.* Toronto: University of Toronto Press, 2013.

Chimayó Chapel

The Santuario de Chimayó, an adobe chapel in northern New Mexico, is a popular site of pilgrimage. Legend holds that a layman named Bernardo Abeyta discovered a crucifix emerging from a hole in the ground in the village of Chimayó. He repeatedly took the cross to the local parish church, only to have it return during the night to its original location in the ground. In 1810 Abeyta built a chapel around the site and named the crucifix the Cristo de Esquipulas after a well-known crucifix of the same name located in Guatemala. Dirt from the original hole soon came to have miraculous powers to heal. Today thousands of pilgrims and tourists come to Chimayó every year, nearly 40,000 of them during Holy Week alone. Visitors extract great quantities of dirt from the hole, located in a tiny side chapel, and many still use this holy earth to cure pains and illness, rubbing it on the parts of their bodies that are in need of healing.

Brett Hendrickson

Further Reading

De Borhegyi, Stephen F., and E. Boyd. *El Santuario de Chimayo*. Santa Fe, NM: Ancient City Press, 1982.

Christian Science

Christian Science rejects medicine but also rejects miracles, traditionally conceived, preferring instead the remedies of a certain brand of "science" based on supernatural intervention. The instantaneous physical healings it induces are not, in its view, divine contraventions of natural laws. Rather, they are the perfectly reasonable workings out of divine laws, as properly understood by the healer and the healed. Even to use the word "heal" when talking about Christian Science is misleading, because it suggests that something was wrong with the material, physical body. But Christian Science denies that this is so: matter and the body do not actually exist, so how could anything be wrong with them? All of Christian Science rests on three basic premises—(1) God is, (2) God is all, and (3) God is Spirit—from which follow two basic conclusions—(4) Therefore, all is spiritual, and (5) Nothing is material. Christian Science means for these five propositions to be taken literally.

Christian Science was founded in the last third of the nineteenth century by Mary Baker Eddy. Mary Baker was born and lived all her life in New England. She grew up in the Congregational Church, whose Calvinism she detested but never fully escaped. In 1843 she married George Glover, who died just before she bore their first and only child. Her second husband deserted her after 13 years of marriage. Chronically ill ever since she was a child, she abandoned conventional medicine as an adult for various alternatives. In 1862 she sought the help of mind curer Phineas Quimby of Maine. Through hypnosis, mental suggestion, and healing touch, Quimby alleviated many of Mary's symptoms, yet they kept recurring. Over the next four years Mary studied Quimby's healing techniques as he treated her. She eventually concluded that Quimby's practice had no biblical or spiritual grounding; he relied on personal charisma and mind-manipulation, not God.

Soon after Quimby died in 1866, Mary fell and hit her head on the ice in Lynn, Massachusetts. After regaining consciousness, she found herself crippled and dying. She asked for a Bible, read Matthew 9:2—Jesus healing "a man sick of the palsy"—and found herself instantaneously healed. She came to understand this healing as God's revelation to her of the divine science that Jesus demonstrated in his healing ministry. As Isaac Newton discovered the immutable natural laws of the universe by an apple falling on his head, so Mary Baker Eddy discovered the immutable divine laws of being by her head falling on the ice. "In the year 1866," Eddy writes in the Christian Science "textbook" *Science and Health*, "I discovered the Christ Science or divine laws of Life, Truth, and Love, and named my discovery Christian Science."

Eddy makes clear in *Science and Health* that Christian Scientific religious experience consists in instantaneous healing—of sin and death as well as sickness and injury. Gradual healing results from the individual's corrupt understanding of the divine laws governing existence. The better one understands spiritual mechanics, the quicker one is able to "demonstrate" their truth by "healing" oneself or others. Jesus healed not because he was God or God's Son or because God infused him with unique power, but because he grasped divine law as clearly as, say, Newton grasped natural law. Jesus did not create but instead *revealed* eternal and immutable divine law. Jesus showed human beings how to avail themselves of this law so that they too could do what he did. Jesus did not mark the beginning or end of some sort of special dispensation. He exemplified what humanity is and always has been capable of. As Eddy writes, "the so-called miracles of Jesus did not specially belong to a dispensation now ended, but . . . they illustrated an ever-operative divine Principle."

Authentic religious experience consists of metaphysical principles working through the mind to effect instantaneous healing by correcting mistaken thought. To have such an experience, one must fully *understand*, not merely believe, *Science and Health*'s metaphysics. One may enlist the help of a practitioner—a metaphysical "doctor" licensed by the Christian Science Church—to aid one in understanding. Several notorious court cases have found Christian Science parents prosecuted for manslaughter because they refused to take their children to doctors and then subsequently failed to heal their children through Christian Science. For each of these tragedies, however, hundreds of dramatic healings weigh in the balance. Still today, Christian Scientists gather at church every Wednesday night for a testimony meeting in which anyone, member or not, may share a healing accomplished through Christian Science.

Guy Aiken

Further Reading

Christian Science Publishing Society, ed. *A Century of Christian Science Healing*. Boston: Christian Science Publishing Society, 1966.

Eddy, Mary Baker. *Science and Health with Key to the Scriptures*. Boston: Writings of Mary Baker Eddy, 2000.

Schoepflin, Rennie B. *Christian Science on Trial: Religious Healing in America*. Baltimore: Johns Hopkins University Press, 2003.

Cistercians and Miracles

The Order of Cistercians of the Strict Observance—communities of monks and nuns seeking a more rigorous practice of the Benedictine Rule—originated in France, Germany, and Spain and experienced astonishing acceleration in the twelfth century. Many of their early leaders became saints, and their accompanying miracles remain vital to their legend and important for their contemplative charism.

According to the *Golden Legend*, Saint Bernard of Clairvaux's miraculous abilities were legion, and many focused on the ability to speak. Known as the Doctor Mellifluous for his own preaching prowess, in 1121 Bernard performed his first miracle. While celebrating Mass he restored to Josbert de la Ferte, a relative who was dumbstruck, the power of speech. Josbert's death was imminent, but with Bernard's healing, he was able to confess shortly before.

The *Golden Legend* reported two other miracles related to Bernard's control of nature. The first involved the dictation of a letter in the open air. It suddenly began to rain and the scribe began to pack away the parchment. Bernard ordered that he continue to write, and so he did, with the rain falling all around him, except at "that spot the power of charity warded off the annoyance of the rain." Finally, one of Bernard's monasteries was once infested by flies. "I excommunicate the flies!" he declared, and the next morning the pests were all dead. These supplement a string of wonders recorded while Saint Bernard was on his way to the Diet of Étampes in 1146. As he rode through France, Belgium, and Germany he cured dozens of various afflictions—palsy, blindness, deafness, and the inability to speak—irrespective of age or gender.

When a certain Herbert composed the most extensive collection of Saint Bernard's miracles, he included Bernard's most famous legends. The first relates Bernard's prayer before an image of the Virgin. "Monstra te esse matrem" (show that you are a mother), he demanded, and the image, coming to life, squirted breast milk into Bernard's mouth. Other versions have him in the same posture with the milk of life shot into his eyes to cure a vision ailment. The second conveys the saint's intensity in prayer. While kneeling before the image of Christ on the cross, the corpus bent over from the wood and embraced him. A similar narrative accompanies the legend of Saint Francis of Assisi, too.

Other Cistercian saints have miracles to their credit. Abbot Robert of Newminster (d. 1159) had miracles reported at his tomb, and subsequently his relics were translated to the church at Newminster, which became a place of pilgrimage. Blessed Waltheof of Melrose (d. 1160), an abbot known for his unbounded generosity, was found incorrupt after 47 years as further proof of his sanctity. Waltheof's miracles also include the ability to multiply food. Saint Peter of Tarantaise (d. 1191)—not to be confused with Pope Innocent V of the same name—was a Cistercian archbishop known for aiding the poor and serving as an adviser to popes and kings. His chronicler, Geoffrey of Auxerre, noted that Saint Peter could cure the sick and, in time of famine, could multiply foodstuffs. The real testament to his observance of the Cistercian life, however, was a deep-seated renunciation of fame, demonstrated by his unwillingness to remain in the public eye as an archbishop. Saint Maurice of Cornoet, a twelfth-century abbot, resuscitated a young boy presumed drowned when he was brought near to the abbot's tomb. According to the monk Guy of Molesmes, Abbot Robert of Molesmes was spiritually espoused to the Blessed Virgin Mary. Shortly before his birth, Mary appeared to his mother, Ermengarde, with a ring for the betrothal. According to the *Acta Sanctorum* (IX, 677), henceforth Robert was dubbed the "spouse of Mary." His affinity to the divine was hardly static. Paralytics who made pilgrimages to his tomb were made to walk erect.

Cistercian nuns were also wonder-workers. Sister Margaret of England (d. 1192), a nun at Seauve-Bénite, had many miracles at her tomb. Saint Lutgard of Aywières, a Flemish-speaking sister, prayed to the Blessed Virgin Mary to impede her from learning French. To most who knew her, she was always clumsy in that language, though when circumstances warranted, such as the provision of consolation to a grief-stricken woman, she spoke it fluently. Her ecstatic visions produced spontaneous bleeding. Finally, Saint Juliana of Cornillon (d. 1258), while not formally connected to the Cistercians, was a visionary throughout her life and, like so many of her contemporaries, held the Eucharist in high esteem. It was mainly through her efforts and prompted by her visions that the Church is graced with the Feast of Corpus Christi. She is buried in the Cistercian cemetery at Villers.

Patrick J. Hayes

Further Reading

Berlioz, Jacques. "La lactation de saint Bernard dans un *exemplum* et un eminiature du *Ci nous dit* (début du XIVe siècle)." *Cîteaux, Commentarii cistercienses* 39 (1988): 270–284.

Bredero, Adrian H. *Bernard of Clairvaux*. New York: Continuum, 2004.

Chen, Sheryl Francis. "Bernard's Prayer before the Crucifix That Embraced Him." *Cistercian Studies Quarterly* 29(1) (1994): 23–54.

Gineste, Bernard, ed. "Geoffroy de Clarivaux: Miracles of St. Bernard on the Road to the Diet of Étampes (1146)." Corpus Étampois, http://www.corpusetampois.com/cls-12 -geoffroy1146bernard.html.

Holdsworth, Christopher. "Reading the Signs: Bernard of Clairvaux and His Miracles." In *Writing Medieval Biography, 750–1250*, edited by David Bates, Julia Crick, and Sarah Hamilton. 161–172. Woodbridge, Suffolk, UK: Boydell and Brewer, 2006.

Picard, André. *La thaumaturgie de Bernard de Clairvaux d'après les Vitae*. Montreal: Université de Montréal, 1991.

Thomas of Cantimpré. *The Collected Saints' Lives: Abbot John of Cantimpré, Christina the Astonishing, Margaret of Ypres, and Lutgard of Aywières*. Edited by Barbara Newman and Margot King. Turnhout: Brepols, 2008.

Clairvoyance

Clairvoyance is a form of extrasensory perception with which individuals are said to exercise certain supernatural abilities in the acquisition of information about other people, places, and events. The term itself refers to the combination of two French words: *clair*, meaning "clear," and *voyance*, meaning "vision." Occult and paranormal experts have noted three categories of clairvoyance: (1) retrocognition, in which clairvoyants can view the past; (2) premonition, wherein they can see the future; and (3) extant states, where current conditions beyond one's natural range of sensory perception can be viewed. As this perception challenges conventional understandings of basic natural sensory abilities, clairvoyance is often deemed to be pseudoscience by much of the larger scientific community.

Early notions of clairvoyance emerged in Europe during the late eighteenth century along with other protoscientific movements such as hypnotism, magnetism, and mesmerism. The French hypnotist Marquis de Puysegur (1751–1825), a student of Franz Mesmer (1734–1815), first popularized clairvoyance after claiming to have observed the phenomenon among trancelike behavior in one of his subjects. After Puysegur's documentation several other European researchers pursued the topic, including chemist William Gregory (1803–1858), ophthalmologist Rudolf Tischner (1879–1961), and physiologist Charles Robert Richet (1850–1935)—the works of which made major contributions to what is known today as the field of parapsychology.

Perhaps the most well-known follower of this parapsychology movement that studied clairvoyance in depth was Joseph Banks Rhine (1895–1980). Rhine's laboratory, once affiliated with Duke University, created a methodology for testing the validity of extrasensory perception and even ran experiments in which he concluded that clairvoyance was possible. Yet no other major study at any other research institution was able to reproduce Rhine's findings.

Despite the conclusions of the broader scientific community, researchers of parapsychological phenomena as well as practitioners of clairvoyance have refuted such conclusions. In what may be viewed as an attempt to broaden the scope of clairvoyance as a real and perhaps legitimate phenomenon, some researchers of parapsychology have identified a typology of "clair" that includes (1) clairsentience, in reference to touch; (2) clairaudience, in reference to hearing; (3) clairalience, in reference to smell; (4) clairgustance, in reference to taste; and (5) claircognizance, in reference to mental cognition. Nonetheless, given the similarities between such a typology and natural sensory perceptions, arguments that find little scientific credibility in such reasoning have reduced these notions to a whole host of faulty analyses, such as confirmation bias, expectancy bias, and subjective validation.

Salvador Murguia

See also: Understanding, Miracles of

Further Reading

Hines, Terence. *Pseudoscience and the Paranormal*. Amherst, NY: Prometheus Books, 2003.

Melton, J. Gordon. *Encyclopedia of Occultism and Parapsychology*. Detroit, MI: Gale Group, 2001.

Taves, Ann. *Fits, Trances, and Visions: Experiencing Religion and Explaining Experience from Wesley to James*. Princeton, NJ: Princeton University Press, 1999.

Compunction (Tears)

Compunction, from the Latin term *compunctio*, or a puncturing sensation of conscience, refers to one's ceaseless effort to produce tears, which in turn inspires awe in others. These tears of compunction are said to accompany moments of regret, remorse, repentance, or spiritual renewal. Although tearing is commonly thought of as the fundamental feature of compunction, to produce tears may be only one indication of such moments of penitence. In at least one example, John of Cassian (360–435 CE) in his spiritual treatise *Collationes patrum in sectica eremo*, or

Confessions, described other forms of compunction including fits of joy, prolonged commitments to silence, and even inarticulate sounds associated with grief and sorrow.

As a religious phenomenon, compunction is largely associated with Christianity through the concept of *penthos*, or a type of purifying compunction. References to this form of compunction can be found within both the Old Testament and the New Testament. In the former, penthos refers to a form of mourning or lamentation, while in the latter it has a more rehabilitative or corrective function whereby such compunction engenders repentance through change.

Some scholarship suggests that compunction was popularized by the fourth-century asceticism of Desert Fathers. Perhaps one of the most well-known ascetics that wrote of compunction was Evagrius of Pontus (345–399 CE). Although asserting that tears in this form were an indication of sincere repentance, he also cautioned that they were merely a means to an end and should not be confused with the goal of establishing a genuine discourse with God. Although the writings of Evagrius of Pontus appear to be some of the first that attempt to characterize the function of producing tears, later interpretations established a breadth of compunction's significance. John Climacus (525–606 CE) in his *Scala Paradisi*, or *Ladder of Divine Ascent*, wrote of the parallels between the sacrament of baptism and tearing during prayer. According to this work, compunction during prayer could be viewed as a form of cleansing oneself of postbaptismal sin, adding that the tears that are produced are signs that God has accepted one's prayers.

Beyond the traditions of Catholic and Orthodox Christianity, forms of compunction loosely associated with penitence can be found in several other traditions. In Judaism, for example, the practice of visiting the Wailing Wall in Jerusalem is accompanied by weeping that conveys a wide array of religious and perhaps political commitments. A number of Pentecostal traditions incorporate the production of tears as part of their worship and prayer ceremonies. For instance, the followers of La Luz del Mundo, or Light of the World Church, partake in collective expressions of sorrow and crying as one of the more important stages of each mass. Additionally, in Islam there is at least one group of Muslims known as the Weeping Sufis who make the hajj pilgrimage to Mecca annually and demonstrate their mystical experience through compunction.

Salvador Murguia

Further Reading

Corrigan, Kevin, and Gregory Yuri Glazov. "Compunction and Compassion: Two Overlooked Virtues in Evagrius of Pontus." *Journal of Early Christian Studies* 22(1) (Spring 2014): 61–77.

Hausherr, Irénée. *Penthos: The Doctrine of Compunction in the Christian East*. Translated by A. Hufstader. Kalamazoo, MI: Cistercian Publications, 1989.

Lutz, Tom. *Crying: The Natural and Cultural History of Tears*. New York: Norton, 2001.

Patton, Kimberley Christine, and John S. Hawley. *Holy Tears: Weeping in the Religious Imagination*. Princeton, NJ: Princeton University Press, 2005.

Ramsey, Boniface. *John Cassian: The Conferences*. Mahwah, NJ: Paulist Press, 1997.

Sinkewicz, Robert E., trans. *Evagrius of Pontus: The Greek Ascetic Corpus*. New York: Oxford University Press, 2003.

Congregation for Saints' Causes

With the suppression by Pope Paul VI of the old Congregation of Rites in 1969 by the apostolic constitution *Sacrae Rituum Congregatio*, the Congregation for Saints' Causes came into being. The pope mandated that the Congregation of Rites be split into two new entities—the Sacred Congregation for Divine Worship (now Divine Worship and Discipline of the Sacraments) and the Congregation for Saints' Causes.

The new Congregation for Saints' Causes would assist local dioceses in the preparation of its causes, especially in their observances of the universal laws of the church. It was itself divided into three distinct offices: a judicial branch, a promoter general of the faith, and the historical-hagiographical office, which continued the historical section created by Pope Pius XI in 1930 to do all the necessary spade work for causes that do not rely on testimony of living witnesses or "ancient" causes.

Shortly after he promulgated the 1983 Code of Canon Law, Pope John Paul II issued an apostolic constitution, *Divinus Perfectionis Magister*, on January 25, 1983, that simplified the rights and obligations of bishops in the instruction of saints' causes. It was followed on February 7, 1983, by *Normae Servandae*—particular norms developed by the Congregation for Saints' Causes for the guidance of bishops. This was a step-by-step manual of sorts to enable the bishops to follow carefully crafted rules in determining the validity of a cause—with respect to the proofs of a candidate's life of virtue, martyrdom, or miracles—or whether the diocesan inquiry has followed the necessary procedure for advancing it toward a final disposition by the pope. Assistance by the congregation in this process is given in numerous ways, but among the most crucial is the development of the positio on the Servant of God, a detailed exposition of the person's life and virtues.

The Congregation for Saints' Causes runs semester-long workshops for postulators—those who are responsible for seeing the case through the process. In 2014 the 30th such studium was presented, covering the theological, historical, and juridical phases required by the congregation. The branch of the congregation that schools postulators is also responsible for updating an important database called the *Index ac Status Causarum*—a collection of numbered active cases of Servants of God that are presently before the congregation.

On May 17, 2007, José Cardinal Saraiva Martins, the then-prefect of the Congregation for Saints' Causes, issued with Pope Benedict XVI's approval a comprehensive instruction for conducting diocesan or eparchial inquiries in the causes of saints. These new norms supplanted those published in 1983 with the hope of establishing closer collaboration between diocesan officials and the Holy See in the conduct of a saint's cause. Among its new features are refined norms for verifying alleged miracles, which experience of the previous two decades indicated was not always clear or could be easily misunderstood by local bishops. Decisive questions need to be asked with respect to the Servant of God's reputation for holiness and proof of intercessory power, that is, the reputation enjoyed by the candidate for interceding for a supplicant in the dispensation of God's grace and favors. Postulators are responsible for collecting the data that will satisfy such questions, but it is left to the competent bishop to investigate any alleged miracle. Competence does not necessarily rest with the petitioning bishop but rather with the one in whose diocese the miracle is purported to have occurred.

Medical experts are to be appointed and allowed to freely render an opinion in a written report on a particular case of a cure attributed to a miraculous healing. The medical expert may also participate in the sessions that solicit testimonies from witnesses to these cures by asking probative questions and helping the tribunal interpret technical data supplied by such witnesses, including other physicians.

According to the norms, relics are to be given special consideration. Not only are the remains of the Servant of God to be authenticated and translated to a designated place for public veneration, but the relics themselves should receive the utmost care in preservation. As it is an ancient practice of the church, tombs of saints are often places of pilgrimage. While the Congregation for Saints' Causes has ultimate responsibility for authentication and preservation of relics, the Congregation for Divine Worship and Discipline of the Sacraments has authority in matters related to saints' public cults.

Patrick J. Hayes

See also: Congregation of Rites; Postulator

Further Reading

Congregation for Saints' Causes. *Miscellanea: In occasione del IV centenario della Congregazione per le Cause dei Santi (1588–1988).* Vatican City: Congregation for Saints' Causes, 1988.

"Sanctorum Mater." The Vatican, http://www.vatican.va/roman_curia/congregations/csaints
/documents/rc_con_csaints_doc_20070517_sanctorum-mater_en.html.

Congregation of Rites

The Sacred Congregation of Rites was established as an office in the Roman curia by Pope Sixtus V's constitution *Immensa Aeterni Dei* on January 22, 1588. It served as the culmination, to that point, of the Roman centralization of the canonization process. It was suppressed by Pope Paul VI in 1969 with the apostolic constitution *Sacrae Rituum Congregatio*. The function of the congregation was left to an interim body established after the Second Vatican Council, known as the Congregation for Saints' Causes, whose function was circumscribed until the revision in 1983 of the Code of Canon Law. When those changes took effect the congregation retained its name, but its powers were more strictly defined, especially in relation to local bishops.

As an important agency for the promotion of saints, the Congregation of Rites had within its competence all those instances where questions of a liturgical nature arose, together with the ability to counsel local bishops on the proper method of instruction on determining the reputation for holiness of a proposed Servant of God. Its ultimate function was to provide a definitive judgment on the Servant of God's reputation for holiness and miracles and report that to the pope. It was also the dicastery responsible for the collection and preservation of sacred relics and the placement of the Church's saints on the liturgical calendar.

Only with the promulgation of the 1917 Pio-Benedictine Code of Canon Law did Latin Rite Catholics have a two-pronged policy for canonizations set in place, that is, the episcopal (or local) inquiry and the apostolic (or papal) inquiry, though the former was always subordinate to the latter. In order to meet the standards of contemporary historical criticism, Pope Pius XI, in his Apostolic Letter *Già da qualche tempo* of February 6, 1930, established the "Historical Section" within the Sacred Congregation of Rites and entrusted it with the study of historical causes, that is, those cases where there were no living witnesses. On January 4, 1939, the same pope published the *Normae servandae in construendis processibus ordinariis super causis historicis*, which made the apostolic process no longer necessary. Instead, a single process would then be conducted in order to streamline the process connected to historical causes.

Historically, the existence of the congregation can be broken into four phases: from the foundation in 1588 to 1634, when new legislation by Pope Urban imposed universal norms for the methods of instruction of cases; from 1634 to 1740, when all known processes were codified by Prospero Lambertini, the future Pope Benedict XIV; from 1740 to 1917, with the incorporation of saint making in the universal Code of Canon Law; and 1917–1983, when the apostolic letter *Divinus Perfectionis Magister* introduced new legislation for saints' causes in accord with the methods of modern historical criticism. Cutting across each phase, however, are the personnel who examine the cases—the prefect, the secretary, the promoter of the faith, and a battery of consultors expert in theology and canon law. The medical experts were usually consulted beginning in the late nineteenth century, though a formal office, the Consulta Medica, was not formally instituted at the congregation until October 22, 1948.

Patrick J. Hayes

See also: Congregation for Saints' Causes

Further Reading

Congregation for Saints' Causes. *Miscellanea: In occasione del IV centenario della Congregazione per le Cause dei Santi (1588–1988).* Vatican City: Congregation for Saints' Causes, 1988.

Frutaz, A. P. *La sezione storica della Sacra Congregazione dei Riti: Origini e metodo di lavoro.* Vatican City: Tipografia Poliglotta Vaticana, 1963.

McManus, Frederick R. *The Congregation of Sacred Rites.* Washington, DC: Catholic University of America Press, 1954.

Papa, Giovanni. *Le cause di canonizzazione nel primo period della Congregazione die Riti (1588–1634).* Vatican City: Urbaniana University Press, 2001.

Pope Sixtus V. "Apostolic Constitution *Immensa Aeterni Dei.*" In *Bullarium romanum*, Vol. VIII, Section cxvii, 985–999. Rome: Augustae Taurinorum, 1863, http://www.icar .beniculturali.it/biblio/pdf/bolTau/tomo_08/02g_T08_966_1025.pdf.

Convulsionnaires of St. Médard

The tomb of Abbe François de Paris (1690–1727) in the cemetery of the poor and obscure parish of St. Médard in the city of Paris became the site of a series of healing miracles beginning in 1727, although the number of claimed miracles quickly accelerated after 1731. The same year also saw the first cases of people going into convulsions at the tomb, a phenomenon that would come to eclipse the healing miracles in notoriety and cultural significance. The St. Médard miracles took place in the context of the split dividing the French Catholic Church between the Jansenists, a theologically rigorous faction, and the mainstream church authorities, particularly the Jesuit order, whose fully reciprocated hatred of the Jansenists was legendary. The proclamation of the papal bull *Unigenitus* (1713) had condemned many Jansenist propositions and led to a government crackdown on surviving Jansenists. The Abbe Paris himself had been a Jansenist. Jansenists had frequently referred to miraculous evidence to demonstrate their innocence when persecuted by authorities in church and state. However, not all Jansenists would be supporters of the St. Médard miracles.

The miraculous healing of an elderly single woman, Anne Lefranc, from paralysis and blindness in late November 1730 was held by Lefranc herself as well as other Parisian Jansenists to be a rebuke for the dismissal of the Jansenist curé, Father Guillaume Lair, pastor of Saint-Barthélemy, a parish filled with upstart constitutionalists. Ecclesiastical authorities refused to investigate the miracle, but an anonymous pamphlet, *Dissertation on Miracles, and Particularly on Those at The tomb of M. de Paris, at the Church of St. Médard in Paris*, published in March of the following year along with a *Relation* of Lefranc's cure, widely publicized it. The *Dissertation* argued that the miracles at Paris's tomb were testimonies to his faith, and particularly to his Jansenism. Publication was followed by an official diocesan investigation casting doubt on Lefranc's miraculous healing. The archbishop of Paris, Charles-Gaspard-Guillaume de Vintimille, issued a decree against visits to the tomb of Paris. The controversy spread with a revolt of much of the Paris clergy against Vintimille, pamphlet debates, and increased crowds from all social classes and different regions of France visiting the tomb in spite of the prohibition. The number of miracles recorded at the tomb exploded, with around 70 recorded in 1731.

Beginning in July 1731, the miracles were increasingly accompanied by convulsions, which in some cases seemed to lift the convulsionaries off the ground and came to eclipse the miracles themselves. Most convulsionaries were women and girls. Opposition continued from both the French state and the papacy. On August 22 the Roman Inquisition, which had no direct jurisdiction in France, declared that the miracles at the tomb were fraudulent. This brought the dispute into the long-standing Gallican controversy, in which many French lawyers and ecclesiastics asserted the independence of the French church, the so-called Gallican liberties. The Parlement of Paris, the supreme legal authority, suppressed the inquisitorial decree, although the pope continued to press the French government to shut down the St. Médard cemetery. Efforts to suppress the miraculous gatherings were also conducted through secular channels, including the Paris police. On January 27, 1732, when visits to the cemetery were fewer due to winter weather, a royal decree closed the cemetery indefinitely. The decree was carried out with little opposition by the police on January 29.

The closing, which was accompanied by a pamphlet campaign to impugn the miracle cult, did not end the controversy. Parlement continued to press the matter of an investigation of the miracles, resulting in a royal decree forbidding them to discuss the subject. The convulsionary movement continued in Paris and other parts of France, with an increased open hostility to authority in church and state coupled with apocalyptic expectations. Although without central direction, the convulsionaries remained united by common belief and a shared reverence for M. de Paris, whose relics were cherished by many. The movement's increasing radicalism, however, led some Jansenist theologians and other early supporters to distance themselves. The government banned all convulsionary activities in a decree in February 1733. The convulsionaries persisted, in increasing obscurity, for decades.

The convulsions were frequently used as an example of superstition and irrationality by the champions of the French Enlightenment, including Voltaire and Diderot. The miracles became known beyond France and were cited by antimiraculous writers, including Scottish philosopher David Hume and Anglican clergyman Conyers Middleton.

William E. Burns

See also: France, Miracles in

Further Reading

Kreiser, B. Robert. *Miracles, Convulsions and Ecclesiastical Politics in Early Eighteenth-Century Paris*. Princeton, NJ: Princeton University Press, 1978.

Maire, Catherine. *Les convulsionnaires de Saint-Médard: Miracles, convulsions et prophéties à Paris au XVIIIe siècle*. Paris: Gallimard, 1985.

Radner, Ephraim. *Spirit and Nature: The Saint-Médard Miracles in 18th-Century Jansenism*. New York: Crossroad, 2002.

Corpus Christi

Literally "Christ's body," the term "Corpus Christi" is also used to refer to a feast of the liturgical calendar for the Latin Rite churches celebrating the institutional banquet enacted by Jesus and his apostles at the Last Supper. For many, it also commemorates numerous Eucharistic miracles that have brought people to a deeper faith or converted the hard of heart. In either event, it draws attention to the miracle of the Eucharistic host, transformed sacramentally from ordinary unleavened bread into the real presence of Christ.

Long before the development of the medieval doctrine of transubstantiation, with its use of supporting Aristotelian language, Eucharistic miracles had their place in firming up the significance of the Christian sacramental system. Tales of miraculous phenomena were already well rehearsed by Gregory the Great in his *Dialogues* and in Venerable Bede's *History of the English Speaking People*. Paschasius Radbertus, among the more important sacramental theologians of the first millennium, incorporated four miraculous stories in his *De corpore et sanguine domine*, including one where a child appeared in the Eucharist held aloft by Saint Basil, with the effect of converting a Jew. Such tropes found their way into several later miracle collections.

As a devotional movement for a recognized feast honoring the gift of the Body of Christ, the origins of the cult go back to Juliana of Mont Cornillon (d. 1258), a prophetess from the city of Liège. Her preternatural visions of the Eucharist were linked to spiritual perfection. In one, she interpreted a full moon with a portion missing as a revelation from Christ symbolizing the lack of a proper feast in the Church accorded to the Eucharist. Slowly she began circulating the content of these visions to powerful friends, who widened the circle of confidants up to and including the bishop of Verdun, who eventually became Pope Urban IV. The Dominican Hugh of St. Cher and others consulted one another and found no impediment to such a feast. On August 11, 1264, Pope Urban promulgated *Transiturus de hoc mundo*, which set the feast in the liturgical calendar, and in 1317 Pope John XXII established it as a feast of the universal Church. Juliana's cult began shortly after her death, though it was not until 1869 that the Holy See recognized her as a saint.

Saint Thomas Aquinas was tasked with developing a suitable set of office texts for the feast's liturgy. These works became essential to later debates on transubstantiation of the Eucharistic species of bread and wine, a central element of Catholic doctrine on the sacrament that holds that Christ's body and blood are made truly present.

Some have been confounded by this doctrine. In 1263, a German priest on pilgrimage stopped in the town of Bolsena. While consecrating the bread and wine in the Church of Santa Cristina, he was consumed by doubt about the real presence. Immediately the host became bloodied, and a few drops fell onto the corporal, a small cloth used to wipe the chalice. This caused such a stir in the village that the congregation carried it in procession to nearby Orvieto, where Pope Urban was in residence. The corporal today rests in the Cathedral at Orvieto, where the pontiff had it installed.

While there are no contemporary attestations of this miracle, including from Pope Urban himself or any of his biographers, later popes have made reference to it in connection with the proliferation of the feast. As recently as 2010, Pope Benedict drew attention to the special role the miracle has in the feast's narrative, which continues to prompt practices such as Eucharistic adoration.

Where a "miraculous mood" prevailed in medieval culture, there was also a ubiquity of exempla literature—those stories, often Eucharistic, that promoted right living. The Body of Christ could defy senses, take on new forms, enthrall believers, and make new converts. Though each Mass was an everyday miracle, the occasional spectacle and their legends helped the faithful remain convinced of the power of God.

Patrick J. Hayes

Further Reading

Levy, Ian Christopher, Gary Macy, and Kristen Van Ausdall, eds. *A Companion to the Eucharist in the Middle Ages*. Leiden: Brill, 2011.

Rubin, Miri. *Corpus Christi: The Eucharist in Late Medieval Culture*. New York: Cambridge University Press, 1993.

Walters, Barbara, Vincent Corrigan, and Peter T. Ricketts. *The Feast of Corpus Christi*. University Park: Pennsylvania State University Press, 2006.

Council of Trent

The Council of Trent was an ecumenical council convened by the Roman Catholic Church in the sixteenth century from 1545 to 1547, then from 1551 to 1552, and finally from 1562 to 1563. In these years, the council fathers discussed an array of subjects, including scripture, original sin, the sacraments, the communion of saints, and the contentious issue of indulgences. The motivation for a council emerged within an environment of intense religious debate that defined most of sixteenth-century European religious culture.

The German reformer Martin Luther (1483–1546) not only rejected traditional Catholic practices but also defied papal authority resulting in the promulgation of Pope Leo X's (r. 1513–1521) castigatory papal bull *Exsurge Domine* of 1520. The French theologian John Calvin (1509–1564) also challenged Rome by demanding a return to the more authentic church of the first century. The nature of these controversial teachings required clarification from the Church, prompting demands for the organization of a council.

In his papal bull *Laetare Jerusalem*, the convener of the council, Pope Paul III (r. 1534–1549), explains that the purpose of the council is both to address the recent religious challenges and the possibility of implementing changes to the Church. The first major topic discussed at the council were the issues surrounding scripture. The council rejected the proposition that the layperson could understand scripture without commentary and moved to place the teachings and authority of the Church on the same level as scripture.

While the council eliminated the more contentious practices that had elicited significant condemnation from the church's critics, such as the practice of benefices where high-ranking clerics ruled multiple sees and the position of the arms collector for indulgences, it retained others. Most notably, it promulgated decrees on the subjects of relics, icons, and miracles.

The council fathers confirmed the importance of showcasing the relics and images of the saints in respected places of honor. In the case of miracles, the council fathers affirmed the duty of the bishop to confirm or deny a possible miracle that has allegedly occurred in his diocese. In uncertain instances, the council requires the bishop to consult with his superiors and fellow bishops. The decrees of the final session of the council declared that

> no new miracles are to be acknowledged, or new relics recognized, unless the said bishop has taken cognizance and approved thereof; who, as soon as he has obtained some certain information in regard to these matters, shall, after having taken the advice of theologians, and of other pious men, act therein as he shall judge to be consonant with truth and piety. But if any doubtful, or difficult abuse has to be extirpated; or, in fine, if any more grave question shall arise touching these matters, the bishop, before deciding the controversy, shall await the sentence of the metropolitan and of the bishops of the province, in a provincial council; yet so, that nothing new, or that previously has not been usual in the Church, shall be resolved on, without having first consulted the most holy Roman Pontiff.

The council was officially closed in 1563. In early 1564, Pope Pius IV (r. 1559–1565) formally recognized and officially promulgated the decrees of the council. In addition to papal approval, several texts were later released. Among these are *The Catechism of the Council of Trent* (1566) and a liturgical book, the *Roman Missal* (1570), both of which retain reference to the Church's teaching on the miraculous, particularly in regard to the role of sacraments and invocation of the saints and the veneration of their relics.

The Council of Trent had many supporters but none more ardent than Saint Charles Borromeo, the archbishop of Milan. His reputation for holiness has been amply documented, but the resulting miracles from one so zealous in pursuit of conciliar implementation is noteworthy. Among the thousands of miracles to his credit is the gift of sight to an infant born without eye balls.

The legacy of the Council of Trent, along with its declarations and documents, proved to be lasting. They remained firmly in place until the mid-twentieth century, when many new reforms were instituted at the Second Vatican Council (1962–1965).

John Cappucci

See also: Reformation Europe, Miracles in

Further Reading

Hughes, Philip. *The Church in Crisis: A History of the General Councils, 325–1870.* Garden City, NY: Hanover House, 1961.

Jedin, Hubert. *A History of the Council of Trent*, Vol. 2, *The First Sessions at Trent, 1545–47.* Translated by Ernest Graf. London: Thomas Nelson and Sons, 1961.

O'Malley, John W. *Trent: What Happened at the Council?* Cambridge, MA: Harvard University Press, 2013.

Schroeder, H. J., trans. *Canons and Decrees of the Council of Trent.* London: B. Herder, 1941.

Creatio Ex Nihilo

Creatio ex nihilo is the doctrine that God made all of created order including space, time, and matter "out of nothing." This belief is typically derived from Genesis 1:1, which states that "In the beginning, God created the heavens and the earth." This belief concerning creation sets Judaism apart from other ancient Near Eastern religions, which taught that a deity formed creation out of a preexisting state of chaos. Some scholars, however, have recently suggested that the Hebrew of Genesis 1:1 should be understood as a temporal clause, thus reading "When God began to create the heavens and the earth, the earth was void and formless." This alternative translation would suggest that the divine act of creation began with a preexistent formless and empty Earth. If this is true, then the earliest explicit reference to *creatio ex nihilo* does not appear until 2 Maccabees 7:28 in the second century BCE. Although scholars note that the doctrine is found in the ancient foundational texts of the Tanakh (Hebrew Bible), the New Testament (see Hebrews 11:3), and the Qur'an (see suras 19:19, 66–67), *creatio ex nihilo* remains a ubiquitously taught doctrine of Judaism, Christianity, and Islam.

Nicholas R. Werse

Further Reading

Niehoff, Maren R. "*Creatio ex nihilo* Theology in *Genesis Rabbah* in Light of Christian Exegesis." *Harvard Theological Review* 99(1) (January 2006): 37–64.

O'Neill, John Cochrane. "How Early Is the Doctrine of *creatio ex nihilo?*" *Journal of Theological Studies* 53(2) (October 2002): 449–465.

Torchia, Natale Joseph. Creatio ex nihilo *and the Theology of St. Augustine.* New York: Peter Lang, 1999.

Cult

A cult is a type of popular devotion in which worship or veneration is directed toward a particular location, object, or individual associated with a miraculous event. Cults are distinct from other types of worship in three ways. First, a cult is not directed toward a supreme deity but is directed toward a person, object, or place that has either been involved in a miracle or is perceived to be closer to a supreme deity. Second, cults usually include the construction of a shrine, statue, ceremony, or some other marker of veneration. Third, cults develop and operate outside of an established religious hierarchy.

Cults are as old as religion itself. Some of the first recorded cults venerated ancient Greek heroes and gods. The Greek hero Achilles, for example, was venerated throughout the ancient Mediterranean world. Venerators constructed shrines and temples to Achilles and directed prayers toward his statues. In the Roman Empire, it was common for cults to develop around emperors. Romans venerated their emperors by worshipping in specially built temples, constructing altars, and building statues. Imperial cults operated alongside the existing religious hierarchy. Romans were still expected to worship their traditional gods, but they were also expected to venerate the emperor.

One of the most popular modern cults is the cult of Saint Pio of Pietrelcina, an Italian priest who lived from 1887 to 1968. In 1910 "Padre Pio" began to experience the stigmata, a miraculous phenomenon in which a person displays the wounds suffered by Christ during his crucifixion. Until his death, Padre Pio was regularly afflicted with the stigmata. Believers in his supernatural abilities held that he could also bilocate (appear in two different places at the same time), read people's souls, and communicate personally with Jesus, the Virgin Mary, and angels. As word of Padre Pio's supernatural abilities spread throughout Italy and the world, devotees began traveling to his monastery in Puglia, Italy, to seek his blessing. Over time, this veneration turned into a cult.

Cults often develop outside of clerical authority. In the case of the cult of Padre Pio, the Catholic Church alternated between trying to suppress the cult and encouraging it. In 1960, the Catholic Church investigated the cult of Padre Pio. The subsequent report remains unpublished, but is believed to be suspicious of Padre Pio's miraculous abilities and critical of the cult that venerated him. In 1982, the Catholic Church launched a new series of investigations into Padre Pio's abilities. This time, it was concluded that he indeed had performed miracles, and in 2002 he was canonized as a saint.

Cults similar to that of Padre Pio have a long history in the Catholic Church. Kateri Tekakwitha was an Iroquois woman who was converted to Catholicism in the seventeenth century by French Jesuit missionaries. Tekakwitha led a life of extreme religious disciple. She took a vow to remain a virgin and frequently practiced self-flagellation. Tekakwitha served as an important cultural ambassador between French Canada and her Iroquois people and earned respect from both communities for her highly disciplined ascetic lifestyle. In 1680, while still in her early 20s, Tekakwitha fell ill and died. Witnesses claim that her body began to shine brightly upon her death. Others believed that they were visited by the spirit of Tekakwitha in the weeks following her death. Because of these purported miracles, a cult developed around Tekakwitha that was especially popular among the French Canadians of Montreal. Relics from Tekakwitha's grave have been used in miraculous healings. Dirt collected from her grave has been sold to devotees and tourists for decades and has also been linked to miracles. Shrines to Tekakwitha still operate in upstate New York and Canada. Like Padre Pio, Tekakwitha's cult has contributed to her canonization. She was made a saint in 2012.

Images, relics, and statues are an important component of cults. The cult of Our Lady of Guadalupe developed around an image of Mary that miraculously appeared in 1531. Over the nearly five centuries since the image appeared, Our Lady of Guadalupe has become a symbol for Catholicism in the Western Hemisphere and is one of the most recognizable images in the world. Every year, millions of devotees make the pilgrimage to the Basilica of Our Lady of Guadalupe in Mexico City to see the original image. The image comes in many shapes and sizes and can be purchased as figurines, jewelry, or paintings. Often, Guadalupaños (adherents to the cult of Our Lady of Guadalupe) have a representation of the image in a home shrine.

Cults can also develop around a specific location. Since 1885, Italian Catholics have gathered every year in Harlem, New York, to celebrate the annual feast of Our Lady of Mount Carmel. The Festa, as it is known, is a lively celebration of religion, culture, and community that involves fireworks, food, singing, storytelling, and a parade. The Festa is both a celebration of the Italian Catholic community in Harlem and a manifestation of the cult of la Madonna del Carmine, a statue of the Virgin Mary that, over the course of a century, became a symbol of the Italian American community in New York City. The statue, which is housed in the Our Lady of Mount Carmel Shrine Church on 115th Street, has been linked to dozens of miracles. Believers have reported that praying to the statue led to miraculous healings. The cult of the statue of la Madonna del Carmine and the annual Festa are popular religious devotions that serve community purposes as well. The annual Festa is a reunion for parts of the Italian American community. In the late nineteenth century, most Italian Americans were recent immigrants and lived along the East Coast, primarily in New York City. Today, the Italian American community is much more widespread. The cult of Our Lady of Mount Carmel in the United States is a way of reestablishing Old World Italian religious traditions. For these reasons, scholars view cults and other types of popular religious devotion as a way of building religious community outside of a formal church hierarchy.

Richard Kent Evans

Further Reading

Carroll, Michael P. *Madonnas That Maim: Popular Catholicism in Italy since the Fifteenth Century*. Baltimore: Johns Hopkins University Press, 1992.

Greer, Allan. *Mohawk Saint: Catherine Tekakwitha and the Jesuits*. New York: Oxford University Press, 2005.

Orsi, Robert A. 2010. *The Madonna of 115th Street: Faith and Community in Italian Harlem, 1880–1950*. 3rd ed. New Haven, CT: Yale University Press, 2010.

Smoller, Laura Ackerman. "From Authentic Miracles to a Rhetoric of Authenticity: Examples from the Canonization and Cult of St. Vincent Ferrer." *Church History* 80(4) (2011): 773–797.

D

Dancing Sun

On October 13, 1917, before some 70,000 people gathered at Fatima, Portugal, several witnesses repeated that they saw the sun "dance" in the sky. The testimonies, some by witnesses observing many miles from the fields outside Fatima, fed already curious devotees of the Blessed Virgin Mary who had heard of her apparition to three young shepherds near the little Iberian town. Today, thanks to the World Apostolate of Fatima, millions recall that day when the sun danced and celebrate it as a divine affirmation of the stories the children relayed about their visions.

If the dancing sun was a validation of the children's words, who were these young people, and what was the message? Two siblings, Francisco (age 8) and Jacinto Marto (age 7) joined the elder child, their cousin Lucia Santos, age 10, in the experience of six apparitions that took place over the course of several months beginning in May 1917, culminating with the sun miracle. It has been Lucia, a future Carmelite nun, who has been the most prolific and descriptive. Though she remained cloistered for nearly 60 years, she has had a worldwide cult following and was visited by Pope John Paul II.

Timing mattered for the narrative. The precision of the apparitions (usually on the 13th day of each month at noon) lent an air of routine normalcy to the visions. They would become predictable were it not for other elements. The hovering lady, dazzling white, told the children that their penances would save sinners. The rosary, she said, was the key to their penitential practice. At the beginnings of World War I in Europe, the reparations of children over against the sins of their elders took on a political character and was invested with symbolic power. The lowly were meant to fight a spiritual war and took on the Goliaths of their age, including communist Russia, whose conversion became an object of special concern for Fatima devotees.

According to the traditional narrative, on the day of the sixth and final vision a miracle had been assured. While the children beheld some delightful images of

97

the Holy Family, the sun became contorted and moved. Rather like a pinwheel of fire, it changed colors and sparkled in a rotating motion, dipping and bobbing as it did so. Thousands noted these phenomena; thousands more remained unconvinced and saw nothing. Written testimonies were not solicited, and so few survive. Skeptics searched for a rational explanation—from unusual weather to mass hallucination to temporary blindness resulting from looking at the sun. Regardless, it set off a sweeping fascination and regular pilgrimages. An official investigation was launched by the local bishop, Dom José Alves Correia da Silva, who in 1930 decreed that the visions of the children were worthy of belief and that a cult of the Lady of Fatima had ecclesiastical approval. However, no comment was made about the dancing sun.

It is worth noting that the popularity of the cult of Our Lady of Fatima around the world emerged from a locale with high illiteracy rates, at a time when the government cracked down on what it believed was superstition among the people. Accordingly, it curbed publicity of the Fatima events through conventional media. Asserting the truth of the apparitions—and especially of the dancing sun—became a form of resistance to a culture that was proving hostile to the religion of simple people. That the story took on such strength in the years since is perhaps the true miracle.

Patrick J. Hayes

Further Reading

Bennett, Jeffrey S. *When the Sun Danced: Myth, Miracles, and Modernity in Early Twentieth-Century Portugal*. Charlottesville and London: University of Virginia Press, 2012.

Santos, Lucia. *Fatima in Lucia's Own Words*. 2 vols. Fatima: Secretariado does Pastorinhos, 1998–1999.

Deafness

When Jesus called out to the deaf man "Ephphatha!" he commanded that his ears should literally "be opened" (Mark 7:31–37). Where sound was once forbidden, a new sensation would take hold in consciousness. The terms "deaf and dumb" or "deaf mute" are often conjoined insofar as the inability to hear inhibits the proper annunciation of vocal sounds into intelligible words. People who have labored under both conditions are sometimes referred to as deaf-mutes, even though their impairments are not necessarily connected. In the Gospel of Mark cited above, for instance, the healing occurs to someone referred to as a deaf-mute even though he could communicate imperfectly. Whether as a result of hearing loss or deafness from birth, speech patterns and mispronunciation associated with deafness was thought to be some sort of divine punishment. As a result, their inability to communicate has been the source of much social stigma and in many places a gross injustice. To win the freedom of hearing was tantamount to a miracle.

Saints have been known to restore both hearing and speech to the afflicted. Saint Foy, the French virgin whose miracles are as spectacular as they are manifold, was known to cure a boy who was blind, lame, deaf, and mute from birth (*Liber miraculorum* I, 28). At another time, Saint Foy cured a deaf-mute from birth named Stephen, who clutched the arms of the bearers of the image of Saint Foy on its golden throne as it was processed through Auvergne. Stephen pushed his fingers into his ears, with the result that blood came out and rose up from his throat. The flow discharged the blockage to his hearing and speech so that his first words were "Saint Mary, help me!" The witnesses noted that he had never heard any word before and took his exclamation as proof of Saint Foy's aid (*Liber miraculorum* II, 4).

A saint's tomb could also be associated with curing deafness. The relics of the eleventh-century hermit William Fermat, by order of a local count, were translated to a tomb at Mortain in Normandy. There the deaf had their hearing restored and other maladies rectified. John of Salisbury, one time secretary to Saint Thomas Becket (d. 1170), testified that his tomb was a source of cures of a variety of maladies and that "the deaf hear." However, some were dubious of the power of a saint's tomb to aid supplicants. One skeptic of the curative power associated with the medieval canonist Raymond of Peñaforte declared that "whoever is blind stays blind, whoever is deaf stays deaf, and he who comes to his tomb lame goes away lame."

Generally, Saint Francis de Sales (d. 1622), the former bishop of Geneva, is considered by many to be the patron saint of the deaf. He learned to communicate with them through sign language and often gave instruction to deaf children. Some holy people were themselves hearing impaired, such as Saint René Goupil, a lay brother who was the first of the North American martyrs, all of whom were canonized in 1930.

Other saints whose intercession has been invoked or relied upon to affect cures for hearing loss include Saint Gerard Majella, a Redemptorist saint better known for his miracles assisting women in difficult pregnancies. On April 17, 1906, an Ursuline nun named Sister Patrick wrote from her convent in York, Nebraska, to the pastor of Most Holy Redeemer Church on East Third Street in New York City, extolling the assistance of Saint Gerard for miracles taking place in and around York. On this occasion Sister Patrick noted that "another client was threatened with deafness, and on applying the medal of St. Gerard and invoking the Saint, the hearing returned. She is perfectly well. This happened in one night, when the medal was applied in the evening. All traces of pain and deafness had gone by the next morning."

Two miracles used in the canonization cause of Mother Katharine Drexel, a Philadelphia heiress and foundress of the Sisters of the Blessed Sacrament, were cures of deaf people. As a child in Bucks County, Pennsylvania, Amanda Wall had no startle reflexes even with the assistance of powerful hearing aids. Two years after her birth in 1992 her family began to pray to Drexel, and the young girl received her hearing. A second case involved Robert Gutherman, whose hearing was restored when he was a teenager. The miracle was decreed in 1988.

Patrick J. Hayes

Further Reading

Bartlett, Robert. *Why Can the Dead Do Such Great Things? Saints and Worshippers from the Martyrs to the Reformation.* Princeton, NJ: Princeton University Press, 2013.

Goldwyn, Ron. "Miracle Girl Because Amy Wall Can Hear, Katherine Drexel Will Become a Saint; Sainthood Is Next 2nd Miracle, Is Linked to Katharine Drexel." *Philadelphia Daily News*, January 28, 2000, http://articles.philly.com/2000-01-28/news/25598198_1 _drexel-university-amanda-amy-wall-nerve-deafness.

Wagner, David. *The "Miracle Worker" and the Transcendentalist: Annie Sullivan, Franklin Sanborn, and the Education of Helen Keller.* Boulder, CO: Paradigm Publishers, 2012.

Della Porta, Giambattista

Della Porta (1535–1615) was a prolific writer on topics such as natural magic, physiognomy, and various experiments as well as an author for the stage. He did not write explicitly about divine miracles but was interested in the production of seemingly miraculous events that worked without demonic, angelic, or immediate divine intercession. Accordingly, he developed a strictly natural theory of magic, in the sense that the formal principles constituting the moving agents of the cosmos were actually to be seen as occult. In short, many causes of marvelous things have properties that are per se unknowable to us. By eliding discussion of the metaphysical and religious implications of his experiments, he directed attention to the physical preconditions that would allow for spectacular manifestations of portentous qualities in physical bodies, whether human, animal, or vegetable. In this universal hierarchy of being, all things are moved by the (irrational) forces of attraction and repulsion they feel for one another. Knowledge of such procedures allows the magician to exercise considerable power in ordering and disposing bodies so that they appear in new and amazing features.

Della Porta maintained that in the strict hierarchical order of Creation the transcendent forms are directly affiliated to God and are then projected into the world in various manifestations––first to the angels (or demons), subsequently into the souls of human beings, and ultimately into qualities that, via the elements of celestial origin, shape matter (*Magia* 1558, I:4). Central to these interrelated ideas is the doctrine of universal animation and the belief that the superior celestial influx is mirrored in material objects. Hence, these forces may be channeled at will into the inferior creatures on Earth (*Magia* 1558, I:5). Della Porta thus bypasses questions of "proper" miracles produced by divine intercession. The marvelous becomes a source for amusement, a means of deceiving other people, and a way of demonstrating the dexterity of the magician.

The wonders that Della Porta produced onstage or in his laboratory had a decidedly histrionic character. This topic of the marvelous (*meraviglia*), and emotions elicited by attendant stupefaction, is essential. He necessarily projects it onto the whole of creation, thus endowing it as a universal law. In a crucial passage from the *Magia* of 1558, he writes that Nature herself—the great female magician—creates all her wonders because of her delight in her own showings (*Magia* 1558, I:9).

Della Porta's account thus has the marked and unorthodox tendency to eclipse human agency. The figure of the natural magician, by dint of his natural talent, erudition, and wealth, is in a position to manipulate and to command the natural properties of many substances and objects. This approach to human agency was geared to the naturalization of the human being, both in body and mind, and sought to lay aside notions that magic was inexplicable.

There is good reason to believe that Della Porta's naturalist stance and his concomitant resistance to theological speculation was actually a consequence of ecclesiastical persecution. The censors disapproved of his works on divinatory arts such as physiognomonics (the art of predicting character traits from the faces of humans). This was compounded by the distrust of more orthodox intellectuals such as Jean Bodin, who would have loved to see Della Porta burn at the stake for naturalizing the Witches' Sabbath. Della Porta had divulged a recipe for the witch's unguent (*Magia* 1558, II:26) in which nocturnal flights and orgiastic encounters with demons and the devil were consequences. While this was supposed to be witchcraft's stock in trade, for Della Porta they were in fact mere hallucinations caused by *belladonna*, a material substance with occult but nondemonic properties.

When seen in their proper historical context, Della Porta's literary and scientific activities can appear as a novelty meant to fascinate an emerging class of courtiers who sought to curry favor with absolutist rulers. By using his philosophy and techniques, they could impress at court. The practice of deception and dissimulation—qualities valued by these rulers—is tied to the crafty staging of all things marvelous.

Sergius Kodera

Further Reading

Balbiani, Laura. *Giambattista della Porta*. Frankfurt am Main: Peter Lang, 2001.

Biagioli, Mario. *Galileo, Courtier: The Practice of Science in the Culture of Absolutism*. Chicago: University of Chicago Press, 1991.

Borrelli, Arianna. "Giovan Battista Della Porta's Neapolitan Magic and His Humanistic Meteorology." In *Variantology 5: On Deep Relations of Arts, Sciences, and Technologies*, edited by Siegfried Zielinski and Eckhard Fürlüs, 103–130. Cologne: Walther König, 2011.

Clubb, Louise George. *Giambattista della Porta, Dramatist*. Princeton, NJ: Princeton University Press, 1964.

Daston, Lorraine, and Katharine Park. *Wonders and the Order of Nature, 1150–1750*. New York: Zone Books, 1998.

Della Porta, Giovan Battista. *Magiae naturalis, sive, De miraculis rerum naturalivm libri IIII*. Naples: Matthias Cancer, 1558; Anverse: Plantin, 1560.

Della Porta, Giovan Battista. *Natural magick* [London, 1658; anastatic reprint of the English translation of the 1589 edition of the *De magia*]. New York: Basic Books, 1957.

Eamon, William. *Science and the Secrets of Nature: Books of Secrets in Medieval and Early Modern Culture*. Princeton, NJ: Princeton University Press, 1994.

Kodera, Sergius. "Giambattista Della Porta's Histrionic Science." *California Italian Studies* 3 (2012): 1–27.

Picccari, Paolo. *Giovan Battista Della Porta: Il filosofo, il retore, lo scienziato*. Milan: Franco Angeli, 2007.

Snyder, John. *Dissimulation and the Culture of Secrecy in Early Modern Europe*. Berkeley: University of California Press, 2009.

Torrini, Maurizio, ed. *Giambattista della Porta nell'Europa del suo tempo*. Naples: Guida, 1990.

Valente, Michaela. "Della Porta e l'inquisizione: Nuovi documenti dell'Archivio del Sant'Uffizio." *Bruniana et Campanelliana* 3 (1997): 415–445.

Desert

The association of the desert or wilderness with miraculous events is prominent in the Judeo-Christian religious tradition. The Hebrew Tanak (Christian Old

Testament), prominently roots the symbolic function of the desert in religious imagery to the period of Israel's 40 years of wandering in the wilderness after the Exodus event (Exodus 12:31; Joshua 2:24). The Hebrew word *midbar* is often translated as "desert" but is more broadly representative of a general uninhabited and uncultivated wilderness area (Hebrew *yeshimon* and *iyyah* are also used). The desert was characterized by numerous threats to life, including thirst, hunger, and wild animals (e.g., Deuteronomy 8:15; Jeremiah 2:6). The period of Israelite wandering is remembered for being both a time when the Lord miraculously intervened in Israelite history (e.g., providing food and water for the Israelites in the desert in Exodus 16 and 17) and a period in which Israel, burdened with the hardships of desert survival, complained against God and the prophet Moses (e.g., Exodus 16:1–4, 17:1–4, 32–33; Numbers 11, 12, 14, 16). For this reason, the biblical tradition often presents the wilderness in one of two ways. First, the wilderness is identified as the origins of the people of Israel, since it was in the wilderness that the Lord established his covenant with them, transforming the group of slaves into a nation. Thus, several prophets refer to the wilderness as a place of purification to which Israel may be drawn for the Lord to refashion and purify the people (Jeremiah 2:2–4:6; Hosea 2:16–17, 9:10, 13:5). Second, the wilderness is remembered as the place of Israelite sin against God (Psalm 78:14–41, 106:14–33; Ezekiel 20:4–26).

The Christian New Testament places the temptation of Jesus in a desert setting. Jesus withdrew to the desert for a 40-day period of fasting and prayer at the beginning of his earthly ministry, during which time Satan appeared to him offering three temptations (Mark 1:12, 13; Matthew 4:1–11; Luke 4:1–13). After Jesus resisted each temptation by quoting from the Hebrew Scriptures, the tradition reports angels appearing to tend to him. The site of the temptation is located above the Jordan Valley on the way to Galilee, traditionally associated with modern-day Mount Quarantana.

The desert tradition is further observed in the Egyptian Christian traditions of the Desert Fathers that gave rise to monasticism. The Desert Fathers were a group of hermits (ca. 250–500 CE) who withdrew to the Egyptian desert to live a life of solitude devoted to prayer. As reports of their devotion spread, so did rumors of miracles, which drew both religious followers and curious spectators. Paul of Thebes (ca. 227–340) was the first attested hermit who is credited by Jerome in *Patrologia Latina* (23:17–28) with initiating the tradition of the Desert Fathers. Anthony of Egypt (ca. 250–356) was perhaps the most popular of the Desert Fathers because of his hagiography written by Athanasius of Alexandria titled *The Life of Anthony*. Athanasius presented Anthony as the archetype of orthodoxy and devotion, focusing considerably on the miraculous stories of Anthony battling demons in the wilderness, healing the sick, and performing miracles of nature, all by means of prayer in Christ's name. *The Life of Anthony* became so popular that its themes and miraculous narratives served as inspiration for the retelling of medieval hagiography for the next 1,000 years. Pachomius of Thebaid (ca. 320) is commonly considered the founder of Cenobitism (official monastic communal living). Coptic stories of his life feature numerous miracles, mostly involving the ability to read the hearts of men. From the third century on, thousands migrated to the desert following the teachings of the Desert Fathers in the pursuit of God. These followers formed small communities governed by rules that eventually gave birth to Christian monasticism.

Islam preserves an additional religious tradition in which the desert provides a conduit for communication with the divine. The Prophet Muhammad customarily retreated to a cave (Hira) in the wilderness for periods of prayer. During one of these wilderness retreats in the month of Ramadan, the Angel Jibreel (Gabriel) appeared to Muhammad, commanding him to recite the text of the Qur'an and commit it to memory. Thus, this desert location is held precious in Islam as the place where the Qur'an was delivered to Muhammad.

Nicholas R. Werse

Further Reading

Harmless, William. *Desert Christians: An Introduction to the Literature of Early Monasticism.* Oxford: Oxford University Press, 2004.

Dirt

Dirt often plays a role in miracles, especially miracles of bodily healing. Paradoxically, dirt often indicates a lack of purity in religious contexts even while soil can represent the building blocks for life and serve as a receptacle for the holy. Indeed, religions around the world recognize sacred precincts in which oftentimes even the dirt is imbued with holiness. The ritual consumption of soil or clay, also called geophagy, is a practice common to many cultures and has occurred throughout human history. Research on ritual geophagy suggests that it may have origins in the nutritional needs of impoverished people, an assertion that is supported by the fact that pregnant woman have consumed clay as part of ritual practice in many parts of the world. Geographer John M. Hunter has found that clay sold in markets in West Africa is often used for both nutritional and ritual purposes. In the latter case, the clay is ingested to accomplish miraculous healing. Likewise, holy earth is consumed in Guatemala in association with a sacred crucifix there named

Nuestro Señor de Esquipulas for the miraculous healing of several maladies including blindness, leprosy, malaria, and paralysis. Similar use of holy dirt, including ingestion but also as a substance applied externally to the body, is well documented in relation to a miraculous shrine in Chimayó, New Mexico.

Brett Hendrickson

See also: Chimayó Chapel

Further Reading

Hunter, John M. "Geophagy in Africa and in the United States: A Culture-Nutrition Hypothesis." *Geographical Review* 63(2) (1973): 170–195.

Divinus Perfectionis Magister

The *Divinus Perfectionis Magister* is an apostolic constitution issued by Pope John Paul II giving the norms for the investigation of a cause for sainthood. On the day it was promulgated, January 25, 1983, it became universal law for Catholics of the Latin Rite. These new rules abrogated all previously applicable norms.

Prior to the enactment of this legislation, canonizations had been governed by rules laid down by Pope Urban VIII in 1634. These remained in effect to a great extent until 1917, when the Code of Canon Law was first promulgated. The Second Vatican Council, a gathering of the world's bishops between 1962 and 1965, had hoped for a change in the Church's canon law. As one step toward reform of the canons, Pope Paul VI issued a *motu proprio, Sanctitas clarior*, on March 19, 1969. In it, he brought the role of the diocesan bishop into greater prominence—effectively restoring a pre-Tridentine procedure for the investigation of saints' causes at the local level.

Divinus Perfectionis Magister applies to the inquiries made by local bishops into "the life, virtues, or martyrdom and reputation of sanctity or martyrdom, alleged miracles, as well as, if it be the case, ancient cult of the Servant of God, whose canonization is sought." Inquiries related to alleged miracles are to take place separately from the inquiry into virtues or martyrdom. The bishop is to receive a report on the entirety of the investigation, be convinced of the reasons for the petition, and send all documentation to the Congregation for Saints' Causes for further scrutiny. Attached to these submissions is a declaration by the bishop that there is no public cult associated with the candidate's cause. The cause is assigned a case number, and the candidate is designated a "Servant of God."

If a candidate has any published writings, a theological censor must be appointed to examine them for doctrinal error. If they are found to be free of heterodoxy, the bishop is to appoint suitable persons to collect other data, such as correspondence or news accounts, related to the Servant of God. If possible, witnesses are to be deposed and their testimonies included in the files.

The entire dossier is further vetted by several committees trained in history, canon law, and theology at the Congregation for Saints' Causes. The constitution lays out the duties of members of the congregation, such as the prefect, secretary, and relators. For historical causes, where Servants of God or any witnesses have been deceased for decades, the relators are charged with the spade work for assembling a *positio*, or digest of the candidate's reputation for holiness and virtue. This can take several years, owing in part to any objections that might be raised by theological consultors.

One of the relators is to be assigned the special duty of preparing a *positio* on miracles and will take part in the meetings with the physicians and theologians who are consulted to weigh the evidence of healings and whether they may be classed as supernatural events. A vote is taken by the prelate members of the congregation on whether to move the cause forward for recommendation to the pope, whose approval is definitive, for raising the stature of the Servant of God to that of venerable. Only then may a public cult be opened. The candidate then awaits confirmation of a further miracle, unless this is dispensed by the pope, as in the case of martyrs. If that occurs, the venerable is eligible for beatification. A final miracle is required, again subject to papal dispensation, for canonization.

The role of this legislation in the papacy of Pope Saint John Paul II cannot be understated. By the time of his death in 2005, he beatified more than 1,300 venerables and canonized more than 500 blesseds—more than any other pope in the history of the Catholic Church.

Patrick J. Hayes

Further Reading

"Apostolic Constitution: *Divinus Perfectionis Magister.*" The Vatican, http://www.vatican
.va/holy_father/john_paul_ii/apost_constitutions/documents/hf_jp-ii_apc_25011983
_divinus-perfectionis-magister_en.html.

Marino, Jeannine. "The Required Canonical Documentation in the Diocesan Phase of Causes of Canonization." JCL thesis, Catholic University of America, 2008.

Paul VI. "*Motu proprio Sanctitas clarior*, March 19, 1969." *Acta Apostolica Sedis* 61 (1969): 149–153.

Zubek, Theodoric J. "New Legislation about the Canonization of the Servants of God." *The Jurist* 43 (1983): 361–375.

Dominicans and Miracles

The Order of Preachers was founded in 1216 by Saint Dominic Guzman (ca. 1170–1221), a Spanish priest from Old Castile in France. More commonly known as Dominicans, their charism centered on orthodox preaching of Christ's gospel as well as formal and rigorous study. Saint Dominic's zealousness on behalf of the Inquisition to combat the Catharist heresy inspired his fellow friars to live lives marked by holiness, virtue, and intelligence.

Typical narratives of the life of Saint Dominic lift up his powers of persuasion, but occasionally the legends are filled with interesting vignettes about his miracles. Even prior to his birth, his mother dreamt of a black and white dog holding a torch that illumined the whole world—presaging his founding of the Order of Friars Preachers. At a colloquy held at Montreal, he challenged the Cathar Guilhabert de Castres by consigning printed matter into a bonfire. All of Guilhabert's books and papers burned to a crisp, but Dominic's would not combust. At Fanjeaux, a similar disputation before a panel of judges found Dominic's treatises in competition with the local heretics. In a test to determine whose faith was superior, the undecided judges threw all of the tracts into a fire. According to the *Libellus* of Jordan of Saxony, Dominic's first biographer, it was recorded that not only did Dominic's book survive the flames, it leaped out of the fire of its own volition. Unsatisfied, the judges repeated the process twice more; each time the friar's book hopped to safety. Such were the first Dominican miracles in the Langueduc, but they produced few believers.

Dominic's abilities to convert the inhabitants of southern France were aided considerably by the Albigensian Crusade, which forcibly and horrifically turned the people away from their heretical views, some of which included the denial of the Holy Trinity and the promotion of vice. Saint Dominic had the ability to ferret out and control the demonic tendencies of anything or anyone he encountered. Prior to the launch of the crusade, he was able to convince nine pious ladies, who eventually became the first Dominican nuns. It was not easy, for they were guarded by the demonic black cat. It was no match for the Hound of the Lord (Domini = Lord; canes = hounds).

Dominic's other miracles included one in Rome at the Dominican headquarters in the Convent of St. Sixtus. Humbert of Romans, sometime after 1235, records the miracle of the bread at St. Sixtus. One day the brothers found themselves without anything to eat when their spiritual father Dominic ordered them all—about 40—to the refectory. All chanted the grace before meals as usual, but nothing was to be found. Dominic entered into prayer, and suddenly there appeared two men, arms laden with bread, which was dispersed to the youngest friars first for their edification. Dominic was served last, but all had their fill.

Humbert of Romans was attentive to the need to keep accurate records of what was happening in the second and third generations of the Order of Preachers. He sent word to every prior to have miraculous phenomena diligently written down and sent to the master-general of the order. Canonization records for the Dominicans' founder note other miracles. At his invocation, he could raise the dead. Other accounts suggest that the very bulls announcing the canonization of the saint were saved by a miracle after the ship in which they traveled became completely wrecked. While living he could multiply food and wine, predict the weather in time of drought, and restore hearing to the deaf, and postmortem he could cast out demons from those visiting his tomb.

Other Dominicans followed suit. Peter of Verona (ca. 1203–1252) took an interest in the complaint of a woman over the absence of her husband. He quelled her worries by predicting that within a year she would be reunited and give birth to a son who would eventually rise to power. Indeed, the birth of Alberto dei Scotti led to his becoming *podestà* (town manager) in Piacenza, where Peter was prior of the Dominican convent. Peter's clairvoyance is recounted in his vita, supplied by Peter Caro in 1340, and helped to form Peter of Verona's cult and his patronage for those women seeking children or those engaged in childbirth.

Due to their zeal in preaching, especially in mission territories, Dominicans were routinely badgered or killed for their faith. A long string of Dominican martyr saints arose, with all the concomitant miraculous wonders. For instance, Peter of Verona, also known as Saint Peter Martyr, is frequently depicted with the instruments of his martyrdom: a sword protruding from his breast and a cudgel lodged in his skull.

Saint Vincent Ferrer (d. 1419) was a Dominican thaumaturge with considerable success in the number of conversions to the Catholic faith (in Granada alone he converted several thousand Muslims). His miracles—at least those given in the depositions for his canonization in 1455—were no less spectacular. His intercessions included healing a man whose intestines hung down to his knees, a boy who passed around 60 stones, or another child cured of the plague. All perhaps pale in comparison to his restoration to health of a child murdered by his mother. The matricide was particularly hideous, for in her dementia she slayed the infant by cutting him up and cooking him.

Dominicans were also careful chroniclers of miracles. Raymond of Peñaforte, a friar in the thirteenth century, was a canonist who compiled the Decretals of Pope Gregory IX, among other works. Raymond supplied the vitae of saints such as Catherine of Siena and also contributed to the canonical rules governing sainthood causes. In addition to Jordan of Saxony, mentioned above, Reginaldo de Lizárraga, OP, in his treatise on Peru, *Descripción breve de toda la tierra del Perú*, mentions the miracles attached to the statue of the Virgin of Copacabana, which includes the first: saving Don Marañón from harm after a processional cross fell on his head.

Finally, two of the most important Dominican saints in the Americas are two contemporaries, Saints Rose of Lima and Martin de Porres. For Rose, her abiding connection to the faith of the native Peruvians was intimated when Dutch pirates took the port of Lima, intending to desecrate all the Catholic churches of the city. When Rose gathered up the Indians inside the church to pray for their safety, the Dutch barged in ready to wreak havoc. Instead they were blinded by the Dominican, who appeared in a bright light carrying a monstrance. Vanquished, they returned to their ships and sailed away. Later, she entered into an ecstasy to find herself on the end of a proposal from Jesus to be his spiritual bride.

Martin, by contrast, had powers over nature. He could communicate with animals and bilocate. While Rose's canonization occurred in 1671, Martin's came much later. The cause was only introduced in 1926 and was not brought to a successful conclusion until 1962. The two miracles used in his cause occurred in Paraguay in 1948 and Tenerife in 1956. For the former, an elderly woman had suffered a heart attack. Meanwhile, her daughter sought the saint's intercession and attended church services. At the same time 1,000 miles distant, the old woman began to show improvement so that in a few days she was completely recovered. In 1956, a young child of four had an accident whereby a cement block crushed his left foot. With gangrene setting in, the doctors believed that the best option would be to amputate. Again Blessed Martin was called upon to work his healing wonder. A small card with a second-class relic was touched to the damaged limb, and the boy kissed the card. Others in the hospital joined a prayer vigil, and within the next two days the leg regained its natural color. In three weeks' time the child walked out of the hospital.

Patrick J. Hayes

Further Reading

D'Apolda, Thierry. *Libellus de vita et obitu et miraculis S. Dominici et de ordine quem instituit.* In *Acta Sanctorum*, Vol. 1, August, 558–628. Brussels: Société des Bollandistes, 1867.

Graziano, Frank. *Wounds of Love: The Mystical Marriage of Saint Rose of Lima*. New York: Oxford University Press, 2004.

Humbert de Romanis. *Legenda sancti Dominici: Monumenta Ordo Fratres Praedicatorum historica*. Edited by A. Walz, Rome: Institutum Historicum Fratrum Praedicatorum, 1935.

"Lives of the Brethren of the Order of Preachers, 1206–1259." Our Lady of the Rosary Province, http://www.holyrosaryprovince.org/2011/media/essencial/lives_of_the%20 brethren.pdf.

"The Miracles of St. Dominic." OP Central, http://opcentral.org/blog/the-miracles-of-st -dominic/.

Purdio, Donald S. "Mothers and the Martyr: The Unlikely Patronage of a Medieval Dominican Preacher." *Journal of the History of Sexuality* 21(2) (2012): 313–324.

Smoller, Laura Ackerman. *The Saint and the Chopped-Up Baby: The Cult of Vincent Ferrer in Medieval and Early Modern Europe*. Ithaca, NY: Cornell University Press, 2014.

Dreams

Etymologically, the word "dream" can be traced to its Anglo-Saxon origin, *dréam*, that in turn developed from the Middle English *dreem*, implying joy and merriment. The word also harkens back to its Proto-Germanic root in which *draugmas* denotes deception and illusion. Dreaming retains a miraculous and mysterious quality that continues to inspire artists and writers, despite being scientifically mapped as a progression of images and sensations through the brain that occur primarily during a sleep stage called rapid eye movement. Notably, in ancient Greece, dreams were considered to be prophetic pronouncements by Morpheus, the god of dreams, and were believed to be a medium by which the gods visited humans to convey their messages.

Likewise, in many aboriginal cultures, dreams are believed to be divine interventions or revelations from supernatural sources and hence understood as innately mysterious or miraculous. In the Old Testament, most dream sequences appear in the book of Genesis. For example, the anecdote of Jacob's famous dream at Bethel of a stairway between Earth and heaven and the tale of Joseph's ability to interpret dreams are some of the most famous biblical references to this phenomenon.

In the Bible, dreams are the means by which God communicates with his believers to warn and guide them through life. Similarly, in the Eastern context, Hinduism considers dreams as prophecies from the Supreme Soul that remind humans of their karma and help them achieve enlightenment through self-knowledge. Notably, *Srimad Bhagvatham* (6.16.53–54, 7.7.25) defines three material stages of consciousness—*jagrata*, or the awakened state; *svapna*, or the dreaming state; and *susupti*, or the deep sleep state—wherein *swapna* (dreams) serve as a platform for reminders about divine retribution for sinful earthly karmas. In Buddhism, dreams refer to *sunyata* (emptiness) that is possibly meant to bring messages from ancestors or instructions from the Creator.

Understandably, dreams have found a powerful presence in imaginative literature across cultures. Examples from English literature include names such as Caedmon, the Anglo-Saxon poet who, according to Bede's *Historica ecclesiastica* (IV:24), had no knowledge of composition but began creating hymns after receiving divine inspiration in a dream that helped him craft hymns in praise of the Supreme Creator. Through the Middle English period the phenomenon of dreams found expression in anonymously composed allegorical poems such as *Pearl* and in Chaucer's works such as *Legend of Good Women, House of Fame, Book of Duchess*, and *The Parliament of Fowls*. Shakespeare too used dreams as the central motif in many of his comedies and tragedies, such as *Midsummer Night's Dream, Romeo and Juliet, Macbeth*, and *The Tempest*. Though the depiction of dreams and miracles in literature took a backseat with the advent of rationalism in the seventeenth century, these literary tropes made a powerful comeback in the nineteenth century with the Romantics, who celebrated dreams as manifestations of human subjectivity. Notable examples include Coleridge's *Kubla Khan*, which is touted to have sprung from an opium induced dream, and Keats's epic poem *The Fall of Hyperion: A Dream*, which follows an elaborate dream sequence.

Arguably, dreams and human psychology are deeply intertwined, and this concept perhaps found its first compelling examination in Sigmund Freud's *The Interpretation of Dreams* (1900). In his pathbreaking analysis of this phenomenon, Freud argued that dreams are "far from being the expression of a fragmentary activity of the brain, as the authorities have claimed," but when interpreted "a dream is the fulfillment of a wish." By conflating dreams with one's deepest fears, anxieties, desires, and repressed childhood memories, Freud dissociates them from the realm of miracle and integrates them into a scientific discourse. Freud's theories have inspired many twentieth-century literary works, such as Franz Kafka's *The Metamorphosis* and *The Castle* and James Joyce's *Finnegan's Wake*, that use the dream theory from a literary and critical perspective. Not surprisingly, the phenomenon of dreams continues to intrigue artists and the wider populace alike, and the huge success of films from Hitchcock's *Spell Bound* (1945) to Nolan's *Inception* (2010) attest to its overwhelming presence in the human imagination.

Swathi Krishna S.

Further Reading

Bar, Shaul. *A Letter That Has Not Been Read: Dreams in the Hebrew Bible*. Cincinnati: Hebrew Union College Press, 2001.

Bede. *Historia ecclesiastica genis Anglorum*. Translated by A. M. Sellar as *Bede's Ecclesiastical History of England*. London: George Bell and Sons, 1907.

Freud, Sigmund. *The Interpretation of Dreams*. Translated by James Strachey. New York: Basic Books, 2010.

Wheatland, Thomas. "Sleep and Dreams in Literature." *Encyclopeda of Dreams and Dreaming*, edited by M. N. Carskado. New York Macmillan. International Institute for Dream Research, http://www.dreamresearch.ca/encyclopedia.php.

E

Early Christianity, Miracles in

For Christians in the early church, that is, the second to the fourth centuries, miracles were most commonly described as wonders, marvels, portents, or signs; events or experiences occurring outside the normal course of nature or society. Predominantly, a miracle was considered to be something that causes amazement or wonder. It was not essentially something supernatural, if by that is meant something that breaks or contradicts nature, but rather something outside the usual course of nature. Interest in wonders was widespread in the ancient world and developed into its own genre of paradoxography. For the early Christians, God, the author of miracles, is the source and cause of nature, so wonders and portents confirm nature as the work and effect of providence while, more important, attesting to or signifying God's actions in the world. Christian interest in the marvelous focused on events and experiences suggested by Scripture—nature miracles such as the flood of Noah and the plagues against the Egyptians as well as works of divine power, such as prophecy, healing, and exorcism. For the early Christians, the scope of the miraculous included events described by the mythologies and literature of the Hellenistic world, such as divine epiphanies, omens and oracles, dreams and visions, and the variety of wonders worked by thaumaturgists. In the Christian mind, miracles are primarily a demonstration of divine power, as can be seen in the accounts of the martyrs, the arguments of the apologists, and the rise of asceticism.

Miracles play a significant role in the emerging martyrology of the early church. For both author and audience, they demonstrate the invisible power of God in providing victory against the apparent power of the persecutor. The early Christian editor of the passion stories of Perpetua and Felicitas says that these "wonders" (*virtutes*) demonstrate that the "one and the same Holy Spirit works ever until now" (*Perp.* 1). An early and formative example is *the Martyrdom of Polycarp*, in which Polycarp, the elderly and holy bishop, is arrested when persecution breaks out in Smyrna. However, when he is to be burned, a "great wonder" (*thauma*) occurred: the fire, rather than consuming his body, folded around it like a sail and baked it golden like bread. He was then stabbed with a dagger, and a dove flew out from the wound. For both author and audience, this demonstrates that though Polycarp was arrested and executed when Quadratus was proconsul, his martyrdom occurred while "Jesus Christ is king forever" (*Mart. Pol.* 21). Miracles as a demonstration of the divine power of the martyr are extended to moral power as well. The *Acts of Paul and Thecla*, a popular second-century account of Thecla, a female disciple of the apostle Paul, records miracles that enable Thecla to preserve her virginity against a series of suitors. Like Polycarp, she is arrested and sent to the arena to be burned but is miraculously rescued by a cloud and an earthquake. A female lion likewise will not attack her but defends her against a male lion and other beasts. Thecla dives into a pool in the arena, and the sea lions are killed while she enjoys the equivalent of baptism. Ultimately she is released and takes up a life of virginity. Later additions to the story have her living in a monastery and protected from a rape attempt by "an incredible wonder" (*to paradoxon thauma*) (Thecla 11). These wonders or powers, for the early church, serve as evidence of God's providence and power in the face of their experience of the oppressing powers of state and society.

Miracles play an important role in early Christian apologetic, which shares in and engages the intellectual world of the Hellenistic period. Origen of Alexandria, whose *Against Celsus* provides extended excerpts from a second-century critique of Christianity, says that the Christian gospel has a "more divine" proof, a demonstration of "the Spirit and of power" (*Cels.* 1.2). The proof from the Spirit consists of fulfilled prophecy, while the demonstration of power is "because of the awesome works of power [*terastious dunameis*]" and "traces of them still remain" (*Cels.* 1.2). For Origen, wonders and marvels are key evidences of the divine character of Christianity. The teaching of Moses was surrounded by miracles, the appearance of Jesus was attested by miracles, and the apostles continued to do miracles after his death. "For without powers and prodigies (*dunameis kai paradoxwn*)," he says, "they would not have been able to convince those who heard new doctrines" (*Cels.* 1.46).

This Christian argument from miracles was contested by Celsus. He cites the widespread stories of wonder-workers and thaumaturgists and argues that such miracle workers are generally frauds who delude the uneducated. The intelligent person, Celsus says, will put wonder-working claims in the context of the common literary and cultural tradition. This tradition includes accounts of wonders, but these should either be allegorized for their moral significance or embraced as part of the time-honored pieties that make up the diverse religious traditions of the Roman world. For Celsus, Christian miracles, especially the incarnation of God into a physical body, are either shameful or novel, arising as bizarre notions with no long-standing pious tradition. Origen, however, defends miracle as an extension of the principle of providence, which he sees as a part of the common second-century assumptions about the world. God, he argues, acts in a variety of ways for the benefit of humanity, and while some of these actions are usual and customary, such as the provision of seasons and the fruitfulness of the earth, some are surprising and extraordinary, properly classified as prodigies or wonders. To deny such wonders is to deny providence as a whole, which, Origen argues, would be irrational. Against Celsus's claim that Jesus and other Christian miracle workers were frauds, like magicians in the marketplace, Origen grants that there are fraudulent and even wicked miracles but argues that the moral benefit of Jesus's teaching and Christian practice demonstrate that Christian miracles are the work of providence. In Origen's view, wonders are real but are either produced by wicked demons who are trying to draw people away from truth and morality or are the product of the power of God, which provides enlightenment and moral progress. He argues that miracles should be judged for their moral benefit, which for him proves the validity of Christian wonders.

Augustine continues this line of argument in the Latin Christian tradition. He affirms the Christian reliance on miracles—they are wonders or marvels that provide evidence leading to faith. They are not contrary to nature. Rather, nature itself is a miracle, and human nature is the most miraculous of all. He cites the paradoxographical tradition of antiquity—the collections of stories of natural wonders and prodigies—to demonstrate the regular occurrence of wonders. He affirms that such wonders are natural—the wondrous substances of the paradoxographies are usually explained by asserting that they are acting in accordance with their nature. For Augustine, however, since God is the author and governor of nature, even though wonders exceed usual and customary observation, they lie within the power of God. While they attended the events of Scripture and the life of Christ, according to Augustine, they continue to occur in his time, centered around baptism and the Eucharist, and around the tombs and relics of the martyrs. However, he laments that present-day miracles are less well known and devotes an entire chapter of the *City of God* to listing miracles that he has either seen or heard reported (*Civ.* 4.22.8).

Miracle as wonder and evidence of divine power is also associated with the rise of asceticism and the holy man in the fourth and following centuries. The model here is Saint Antony, made famous by Athanasius's *Life of Antony*. Marvels and works of power attend the development of Antony as an ascetic and holy man, but the biography attributes his wonders to nature—that is, to the power of his soul purified from the body by asceticism and to providence, the power of the savior made present in the world by Antony's discipline. Citing the casting out of demons and healings, Antony says to his disciples, "To work signs [*semeia*] does not belong to us—it is the work of the Savior" (*Vit. Ant.* 38). Athanasius ends his biography with the affirmation that "Evidence of his virtue and that his soul was loved by God is that he . . . is marveled at by all" (*Vit. Ant.* 93). Participating in a widespread interest in the marvelous in the ancient world, the early Christians saw the miraculous as an affirmation of providence and of God, in harmony with nature, but particularly demonstrative of the truth of Christianity, the divinity of its way of life, and the sovereignty of God.

Robert Hauck

See also: Jesus, Miracles of; Late Antiquity, Miracles in

Further Reading

Dodds, E. R. *Pagan and Christian in an Age of Anxiety: Some Aspects of Religious Experience from Marcus Aurelius to Constantine.* Cambridge: Cambridge University Press, 1965.

Fiorenza, Elisabeth Schussler, ed. *Aspects of Religious Propaganda in Judaism and Early Christianity.* Notre Dame: University of Notre Dame Press, 1976.

Grant, Robert M. *Miracle and Natural Law in Graeco-Roman and Early Christian Thought.* Amsterdam: North Holland Publishing, 1952.

Kee, Howard Clark. *Miracle in the Early Christian World: A Study in Sociohistorical Method.* New Haven, CT: Yale University Press, 1983.

Remus, Harold. *Pagan-Christian Conflict over Miracle in the Second Century.* Cambridge, MA: Philadelphia Patristic Foundation, 1983.

England, Miracles in

While it is difficult to trace the first Christians in the British Isles, around the end of the third century evidence of a Christian presence begins to emerge. This was probably not sustainable or was lackluster for several decades. The polytheism of pre-Christian Anglo-Saxon England was too widespread to immediately dislodge, though the Druid culture at the time of the Roman invasion by Julius Caesar had its share of mystical elements, including miraculous happenings in nature. England was a Roman outpost for centuries and was largely forgotten. Roman legions withdrew in 410, and the island was wide open to attack. Saxon invasions ensued, though not before the inhabitants had grown accustomed to Christians.

When Saint Augustine of Canterbury was commissioned to undertake a formal mission to England in 595, the Church lacked organization, but it was surviving. With the introduction of the first bishop, the English grew quickly into the Christian fold, thanks mainly to the baptism by Augustine of King Aethelbert of Kent in 601. By the Synod of Whitby in 664, practically the entire nation converted to Christianity. In the meantime, Augustine had established monastic houses, including one that grew up around his cathedral at Canterbury—a church he stuffed with relics that were gifts of Pope Gregory the Great.

It is in the sixth and seventh centuries that there is a proliferation of English saints, and we know about the earliest of these through their chief chronicler, Bede the Venerable (d. 735). Some were supplied with new powers, or the ones they already possessed were somehow awakened. Saint Caedmon, for instance, was an unlettered cow herder who, discouraged at his lack of talent, remonstrated with his charges. Falling asleep, he was met in a dream by a man who implored that he sing him some verse about Creation. Caedmon began to sing gloriously of God's wonderful world, and when he awoke he continued the poetry begun in his dream. Knowing this must be from God, his friends took him to see a holy abbess, Hilda, of the abbey at Whitby. She asked that he render some scriptural verses into poetry, which he did. She believed that this talent could only be the work of the divine and so urged Caedmon to seek a life in religion. He became a monk of Whitby and spent the rest of his days composing some of the finest poetry of his era.

Other visions befell Saint Cuthbert (d. 687), who saw the soul of a bishop borne heavenward. He saw "with the eyes of the spirit" angels ascending and descending bearing the soul of a saint in their hands "as though in a ball of fire." He suggested to his acquaintances that it was perhaps the soul of a bishop or some other dignitary. In a few days he was proved correct, because they learned of the death of Bishop Aidan at the very hour of Cuthbert's vision.

As these saints became better known, principally through the miracle collections that began to appear after the invasion of the Normans in 1066 and the installation of French abbots in English abbeys, proof was sought that the relics in their possession were genuine. But once provenance was established, they were often taken on tours—partly to honor their patrons but also as a way of soliciting donors. That miracles would occur on these relic tours was important for the saints' legends, of course, but they also incited people to lavish funds on the abbeys from whence they came. By the twelfth century sufficient income and interest made shrine-based miracles a possibility. Translation of relics to new shrines influenced the liturgical and paraliturgical rites of the church—a process that began in earnest in 1091 when the bones of six abbots of the monastery at Canterbury were ceremoniously translated to specially built shrines at the new abbey.

No other period in English Christianity is so fecund with miracle stories as the High Middle Ages. Some scholars count at least 75 different collections of saints' posthumous miracles between 1080 and 1220. These focused on holy people from the Anglo-Saxon period. Thus, Saints Cuthbert, Edmund, and Swithun joined their later confrères in the communion of saints—Thomas Becket (murdered in 1170) chief among them—as objects for increased veneration.

Benedict of Peterborough brought together the most important and widely used collection of Becket's shrine miracles. Most of the collections were based on oral tradition and so were highly personal and subjective. The difficulty in assimilating these kinds of stories to the cult of a saint was that very often the testimonies were collected for the purpose of a saint's cause. The stories not only had to be valid but also had to be trustworthy, and so the inquiries of ecclesiastics into the merits of a narrative were routinely massaged to elicit just the right replies. As these were gathered and transcribed, the oral tradition—which could be imbued with embellishments—was smoothed over on the printed page. Oral stories could spread and experience accretions. Textualizing these fixed the story for all time.

Around 1135, Benedictine monk William of Malmesbury wrote the *Miracles of the Virgin Mary*, one of many such treatises written by English Benedictines in the 1120s and 1130s. In it he collected numerous accounts of miracles attributed to the Madonna. Later the miracles would be connected to a shrine such as at Walsingham, where the cult was strong and continues to this day.

Scotland was not immune from miraculous phenomena. Saint Margaret, Queen of Scotland (d. 1093), has a number of miracles to her credit. Among the most famous includes a book of the gospels she entrusted to the care of a court priest. While journeying with it, he lost it. Margaret sent a soldier in search of the book, and he found it floating in a stream, unsullied by the water. Today it rests in the Bodleian Library (MS Lat. Liturg. f.5) at the University of Oxford. Other miracles relate to her tomb. The canonization records note that flashes of light could be seen emanating from her grave site at Dunfermline Abbey in Fife. While disinterring her remains for translation to another part of the abbey, a sweet odor could be detected. As she was moved past the tomb of her husband King Malcolm, the bier carrying her suddenly became immovable. Someone suggested that the couple ought to be reunited, and thus the two graves were combined. Nearly a third of the miracles attributed to her involve visions of Saint Margaret by nearly a score of individuals. Saint Margaret's head later was obtained by Mary, Queen of Scots, and then traveled with the Jesuits who were in exile at Douai. Unfortunately, the relic was lost during the French Revolution.

The period of the Reformation was not kind to relics such as these, but perhaps worse still, the treatment of the living was equally reprehensible. Saint Thomas More (d. 1535), the chancellor to King Henry VIII, was beheaded in hatred of the faith and is considered a martyr by Catholics. His head is in Canterbury in the Church of St. Dunstan, while the remainder of his body lies in the chapel of the Tower of London. He was canonized in 1935, without benefit of miracles. More's contemporaries who formed part of the recusant culture were hunted down as viciously. In 1559, the Acts of Supremacy and Uniformity attacked "images, relics, and miracles" and ordered that recusants be handed over to government officials. Tract wars ensued when Catholics exiled to France and Belgium learned that English Protestants were suggesting that the age of miracles ended after the death of the last apostle. Enlightenment figures stretched this even further to say that it was perfectly reasonable to deny miracles altogether, even to those attributed to Jesus.

Before the nineteenth-century restoration of the Catholic Church in the British Isles, it was not uncommon to hear of miracles, though these were anomalous. In 1748, for instance, just as David Hume was making his mark on the philosophy of miracles, a Cheshire woman named Bridget Bostock was reported to be healing hundreds of people of all types of diseases. Her methods were simple (and biblical): fasting, spittle, and prayer. Scottish and English Protestants contended that on occasion the voice of God could be heard or that prophetic utterances could be proclaimed. English soil was hardly without its holy people either. Among them was a Victorian cleric and convert. Through the intercession of Blessed John Henry Newman (d. 1890), a former Anglican clergyman, a Roman Catholic deacon was cured of a spinal cord malady in 2001. Should he be canonized, Newman would be the first English person raised to the altars since the seventeenth century.

Patrick J. Hayes

See also: Annet, Peter; Hay, Bishop George; Middleton, Conyers; Newman, John Henry; Our Lady of Walsingham; Price, Richard; Reformation Europe, Miracles in; Sherlock, Thomas; United States, Miracles in; Woolston, Thomas

Further Reading

Donovan, Leslie A. *Women's Saint's Lives in Old English Prose*. Suffolk, UK: Boydell and Brewer, 1999.

Duggan, Anne. *Thomas Becket*. London: Bloomsbury Academic, 2004.

Keene, Catherine. *Saint Margaret, Queen of the Scots: A Life in Perspective*. New York: Palgrave Macmillan, 2013.

Koopmans, Rachael. *Wonderful to Relate: Miracle Stories and Miracle Collecting in High Medieval England*. Philadelphia: University of Pennsylvania Press, 2011.

Lapidge, Michael. "The Saintly Life in Anglo-Saxon England." In *The Cambridge Companion to Old English Literature*, edited by Malcolm Godden and Michael Lapidge, 243–63. New York: Cambridge University Press, 1991.

Lapidge, Michael, ed. *The Cult of St Swithun*. Winchester Studies 4.ii. Oxford: Oxford University Press, 2003.

Lapidge, Michael, and R. Love. "The Latin Hagiography of England and Wales." In *Hagiographies: Histoire internationale de la littérature hagiographique latine et vernaculaire en Occident des origines à 1550*, Vol. 3, edited by Guy Philippart, 203–325. Turnhout: Brepols, 2001.

Love, R. C., ed. *Three Eleventh-Century Anglo-Latin Saints' Lives*. Oxford: Oxford University Press, 1996.

Malo, Robyn. "Intimate Devotion: Recusant Martyrs and the Making of Relics in Post-Reformation England." *Journal of Medieval and Early Modern Studies* 44(3) (2014): 531–548.

McCready, William David. *Miracles and the Venerable Bede*. Toronto: PIMS, 1994.

Ridyard, Susan J. *The Royal Saints of Anglo-Saxon England: A Study of West Saxon and East Anglian Cults*. New York: Cambridge University Press, 2008.

Ryrie, Alec. "Hearing God's Voice in the English and Scottish Reformations." *Reformation* 17 (2012): 49–74.

Salih, Sara, ed. *A Companion to Middle English Hagiography*. Suffolk, UK: D. S. Brewer, 2010.

Sanok, Catherine. *Her Life Historical: Exemplarity and Female Saints' Lives in Late Medieval England*. Philadelphia: University of Pennsylvania Press, 2013.

Sharpe, R. *Medieval Irish Saints' Lives: An Introduction to Vitae Sanctorum Hiberniae*. New York: Oxford University Press, 1991.

Shaw, Jane. *Miracles in Enlightenment England*. New Haven, CT: Yale University Press, 2006.

Staunton, Michael. *The Lives of Thomas Becket*. Manchester, UK: Manchester University Press, 2001.

Stephanus, Eddius, and Bertram Colgrave. *The Life of Bishop Wilfrid*. New York: Cambridge University Press, 1985.

Thomas, Charles. *Christianity in Roman Britain to AD 500*. Berkeley: University of California Press, 1981.

Van Houts, Elizabeth M. C. "Historiography and Hagiography at St. Wandrille: The *Inventio et Miracula Sancti Vulframni*." *Anglo-Norman Studies 12 (Proceedings of the Battle Conference, 1989)*, edited by Marjorie Chibnall, 233–251. Woodbridge, UK: Boydell and Brewer, 1990.

Ward, Benedicta. *Miracles and the Medieval Mind*. Philadelphia: University of Pennsylvania Press, 1987.

Whatley, E. Gordon. "An Introduction to the Study of English Prose Hagiography: Sources and Resources." In *Holy Men and Holy Women: Old English Prose Saints' Lives and Their Contexts*, edited by Paul Szarmach, 3–32. Albany: SUNY Press, 1996.

Whatley, E. Gordon, ed. and trans. *The Saint of London: The Life and Miracles of St. Erkenwald, Text and Translation*, Medieval and Renaissance Texts and Studies 58. Binghamton, NY: Center for Medieval and Renaissance Studies, SUNY–Binghamton, 1989.

Wilson, S. E. *The Life and After-Life of St John of Beverley: The Evolution of the Cult of an Anglo-Saxon Saint, Church, Faith and Culture in the Medieval West*. Aldershot, UK: Ashgate, 2006.

Winstead, Karen A. *Virgin Martyrs: Legends of Sainthood in Late Medieval England*. Ithaca, NY: Cornell University Press, 1997.

Winterbottom, Michael, and Michael Lapidge. *The Early Lives of St. Dunstan*. New York: Oxford University Press, 2012.

Winterbottom, Michael, and Rod M. Thomson. *Miracles of the Virgin by William of Malmesbury*. Suffolk, UK: Boydell and Brewer, 2015.

Winterbottom, Michael, and Rod M. Thomson. *William of Malmesbury: Saints' Lives*. New York: Oxford University Press, 2002.

Wood, Ian. "St. Wandrille and Its Hagiography." In *Church and Chronicle in the Middle Ages: Essays Presented to John Taylor*, edited by Ian Wood, Eleanor Wood, and Graham A. Loud, 1–14. London: Continuum, 1991.

Wulfstan of Winchester and Michael Lapidge. *Life of St. Æthelwold*. Oxford Medieval Texts. Oxford: Oxford University Press, 1991.

Yarrow, Simon. *Saints and Their Communities: Miracle Stories in Twelfth-Century England*. New York: Oxford University Press, 2006.

Eucharistic Miracle of Siena

The medieval city of Siena, Italy, is replete with religious overtones—from the skull reliquary of Saint Catherine in the Church of St. Dominic to the tomb of Blessed Joachim Piccolomini, the patron of epileptics, in the Servite Church of St. Martin. But in the airy barnlike Church of St. Francis there is housed in a side chapel the ciborium containing 133 consecrated hosts dating from 1730—altar breads as fresh today as the day they were baked.

While the Conventual Franciscan friars stationed at the Church of St. Francis were attending traditional festivities in honor of the Assumption of the Blessed Virgin Mary, August 14, 1730, burglars entered the church, cracked open the tabernacle containing a gold ciborium, and made off with it and its contents. For Catholics, the consecrated hosts underwent a desecration—a literal affront to the real presence of Jesus Christ in the Eucharist. The Sienese were disconsolate, and the local constabulary set to work finding the thieves. On August 17, a priest in the nearby Church of St. Mary of Provenzano noticed that a host was protruding from a collection box. The archbishop and the Franciscans were informed. The box was opened in their presence, and they discovered scores of hosts approximating the number the friars estimated were stolen. The hosts were hurriedly cleaned and processed the following day back to the Church of St. Francis. The presumption was that the Eucharistic species would naturally deteriorate.

Weeks and then years passed with no apparent change. A half century after the return of the hosts, the minister-general of the Conventual Franciscans, Father Juan Carlo Vipera, came to Siena to investigate what many were convinced was a miracle of preservation. He tasted one of the hosts and was convinced. He ordered that the remainder, some 230 hosts, be placed in a new ciborium. They continued to repose in this vessel until 1789, when the archbishop of Siena, Tiberio Borghese, had some of the hosts inspected under a microscope. Again, there were no signs of corruption. He had some of the hosts removed and placed under lock and key in a separate box. A decade later these were found to be mottled, and by 1850 their appearance was nothing like the consecrated hosts in the Church of St. Francis, which continued to be preserved from any deformity.

Periodically church authorities would consume one of the hosts to determine its taste and texture. Each time the Eucharistic species appeared unblemished to the eye and did not taste unpleasant. One would expect deterioration and mold, but the purity of the hosts remained, as if baked that morning.

Another test in 1914 by scientists from the universities at Siena and Pisa confirmed that on one of the fragments the starch content was normal. If unleavened hosts were prepared under ordinary conditions in 1730 and kept as they had been for over a century, the scientists believed that they would decay in less than five years. But they found that no extraordinary measures had been taken to preserve these particles. They were forced to conclude that science could not explain the prolonged preservation of this organic material.

In 1950 the hosts were transferred to a new ciborium. Again in 1951 a thief managed to remove it from the church, though that person left the remaining 133 hosts in the tabernacle. Now with new security measures in place, the hosts are only displayed on occasion but especially August 17, the anniversary of their return after the first theft. They are also processed through the streets of Siena on the Feast of Corpus Christi.

Patrick J. Hayes

Further Reading

Cruz, Joan Carroll. *Eucharistic Miracles and Eucharistic Phenomena in the Lives of the Saints*. Rockford, IL: TAN Books, 1987.

Eucharistic Miracles of Lanciano

Among the many reported Eucharistic miracles, two occurred at Lanciano, Italy. At Mass, Catholics believe that bread and wine are transformed into the Body and Blood of Jesus, yet the appearance of bread and wine remain. In rare miraculous cases, the consecrated bread and wine shed their appearance and take on the properties of flesh and blood.

In the eighth century during the celebration of Mass at Lanciano's Saints Legontian and Domitian Church (now St. Francis Church), a priest of the Basilian order doubted Jesus's presence in the consecrated bread and wine. He was, according to a 1631 document, "not very firm in the faith, versed in the sciences of the world, but ignorant in that of God." When the priest pronounced the words of consecration—*hoc est enim corpus meum* ("This is my body")—over the bread, its appearance is said to have changed to physical flesh and blood. The contents of the chalice also transformed at the words of the consecration prayer. The story of the miracle was handed down through the generations, known locally and eventually throughout Europe.

A second lesser-known Eucharistic miracle—called the miracle of Offida— was said to have occurred in Lanciano in 1280 when a distressed wife, Ricciarella Stasio, took a consecrated host from church, believing on the advice of a witch that it could be used to concoct a "love potion" to win over her emotionally distant husband. Before the sacrilege could be committed, the host transformed into flesh, and the frightened Ricciarella buried it. She was tormented by her decision for seven years before her conscience compelled her to unearth the host, which remained miraculously intact. The miraculous host was eventually transported to the town of Offida, 60 miles north of Lanciano, where it has remained.

At St. Francis Church in Lanciano, the relics of the eighth-century miracle are contained in a reliquary above the altar. The miraculous host retains a circular shape; the dried blood took the form of five distinct globules. The earliest surviving testaments to the miracle date from the sixteenth century. By the seventeenth century, documents from Rome reveal that Lanciano was a place of pilgrimage and devotion.

The relics have long been the subject of inquiry. A marble epigraph from 1636 references the local bishop's "careful examination" of the miracle in 1574. Subsequent inspections of the relics occurred in 1637, 1770, and 1886. Dr. Odoardo Linoli, a doctor and professor of anatomy and pathological histology, conducted a scientific examination of the relics during November 1970–March 1971. He published his findings in an Italian scientific journal, concluding that the flesh and blood are of human origin; the flesh is striated muscle tissue from the myocardium—the heart, and the blood is type AB (the same blood type found in other purported relics of Christ, including the Shroud of Turin and the Sudarium of Oviedo). His analysis determined that neither the flesh nor the blood had signs of artificial preservation.

Though disputed, the relics of Lanciano's first Eucharistic miracle have been submitted to modern scientific inquiry. The relics are reported to be genuine, and their existence is unexplainable—an ironic conclusion to a miracle story that began with a skeptical priest who trusted science more than faith.

David J. Endres

See also: Eucharistic Miracle of Siena; Italy, Miracles in; Shroud of Turin

Further Reading

Cruz, Joan Carroll. *Eucharistic Miracles and Eucharistic Phenomena in the Lives of the Saints*. Rockford, IL: Tan Books, 1987.

Linoli, Odoardo. "Ricerche istologiche, immunologiche e biochimiche sulla carne e sul sangue del miracolo eucaristico di lanciano (VIII secolo)." *Quaderni Sclavo di diagnostica clinica e di laboratorio* 7(3) (September 1971): 661–674.

Nasuti, Nicola. *The Eucharistic Miracle of Lanciano: Historical, Theological, Scientific and Photographic Documentation*. Translated by M. Nicoletta Lanci. Lanciano, Italy: Litografia Botolini, 1995.

"Physician Tells of Eucharistic Miracle of Lanciano: Edoardo Linoli Verified Authenticity of the Phenomenon." Zenit: The World Seen from Rome, May 5, 2005, http://www.zenit.org/en/articles/physician-tells-of-eucharistic-miracle-of-lanciano.

Sammaciccia, Bruno. *The Eucharistic Miracle of Lanciano, Italy*. Translated by Anthony E. Burakowski. Trumbull, CT: Passionist Fathers, 1976.

Exorcism

Exorcism is the act by which a priest expels or casts out a demon or evil spirit that has taken possession of a human being or a form of prayer used to undercut the power of the devil. It is a religious countermeasure against satanic influence, where a man or woman could be possessed as a consequence of the fight between God and the devil. God has equipped his servants with the power to expel the demons, the disciples of Satan, by using the rite of exorcism. There is some scriptural warrant for this, grounded as it is in the life of Jesus Christ (cf. Mark 1:34, 39; Luke 4:35; Matthew 17:18), but it is generally agreed that the ritual that has developed particularly in the Catholic Church has no formal basis in the sacred texts. In 2014, the United States Conference of Catholic Bishops approved an English translation of *De exorcismis et supplicationibus quibusdam*, and the final text of *Exorcisms and Related Supplications* is presently awaiting the confirmation of the Holy See.

Strict protocols govern the administration of the rite. A prior prerequisite is an assessment of the allegedly possessed person. This includes medical, psychological, and psychiatric testing. An actual determination of whether a member of the faithful is genuinely possessed by the Devil is made by the Church, even if individuals claim to be possessed through their own self-diagnosis or psychosis. Non-Catholics may also request an exorcism. The minister of a minor exorcism—by which simple prayers are recited on certain occasions (such as at the baptism of children)—may be a cleric or a lay person; only major exorcisms are performed by a designated priest or bishop.

Nowadays when people think of exorcism, they usually associate the term with *The Exorcist*, the 1973 movie directed by William Friedkin. While the film was one of the most successful horror movies, the rite of exorcism became more commonly known. But the rite itself has its own history and tradition. With regard to the Bible, Satan, who hated God, tried to seduce humans, who were created in the image of God. Despite that fact, humans' belief in God was thought to save them from the devil's tactics. One of his mightiest options had been the possession of a human being whereby a human's body and thoughts are controlled by a demon. The bodily organs and the lower spiritual faculties are controlled by an evil force, and the possessed person is not able to control himself or to remember what has been done.

Around 200 CE the rite of exorcism became part of the baptismal repertoire that could be used against the devil, especially in a case of possession. The rite itself had changed over time to become what it is today, when it was codified against during the Vatican Council II. Today if an exorcism needs to be performed, the priest, in cooperation with a physician, must ascertain if a person is actually possessed by a demon, because a mental illness could be mistaken for a possession. To prevent a mistake, it is imperative to find out the actual reason for the person's strange behavior. The priest must ascertain if the eight symptoms of possession are present:

1. An unclean spirit,
2. Unusual powers,
3. Display of paroxysms,
4. A personality that is split or disintegrated,
5. Resistance or opposition to the faith of the Christian church,
6. Signs of hyperesthesia,
7. Talks with a varying or altered voice, and
8. Displaying an occult transference.

If the person has these symptoms, the priest can be sure that the examined person is actually possessed by a demon.

Once the question of possession has been positively answered, the priest will begin the strict rite; only authorized exorcists are allowed to do this. He has to be a living example of the highest piety as well as prudence and must live a life of integrity in order to be immune to human weaknesses and be able to face the powerful demon. Whenever possible, the rite of exorcism should be undertaken in a church. Using the traditional verse of exorcism, the priest will also need a cross, as a sign of God, and holy water, used to treat possible bodily disturbances. Finally, the demons need to be named by the exorcist, who is then able to expel the evil. The process of exorcism lasts several days, during which the possessed might try to resist the exorcism, vomit out evil signs or amulets, or refuse to name the demon that possesses him or her.

Today the rite of exorcism is not conducted that often, but it is still part of the ritual repertoire of the Catholic Church, which faces regular debates about this practice with regard to former cases. For instance, the case of Anneliese Michel (1952–1976), a young German epileptic who underwent an exorcism because her parents were convinced that she was possessed, was a scandalous reflection on the rite. She was first exorcised in September 1975. Two priests continued to perform the rite during 67 sessions over the next 10 months. In the meantime, her parents refused further medical attention, though Anneliese had been prescribed multiple antipsychotic drugs. She herself renounced any nourishment as a means toward atoning for perceived sinfulness of other young people and apostate priests. She died on July 1, 1976, of malnourishment and dehydration, and the two exorcists were found guilty of negligence.

Frank Jacob

Further Reading

Amorth, Gabriele. *An Exorcist Tells His Story*. San Francisco: Ignatius Press, 1999.

"Frequently Asked Questions about Exorcism." United States Conference of Catholic Bishops, http://www.usccb.org/prayer-and-worship/sacraments-and-sacramentals/sacramentals -blessings/exorcism.cfm.

Goodman, Felicitas. *How about Demons? Possession and Exorcism in the Modern World*. Indianapolis: Indianapolis University Press, 1988.

Ney-Hellmuth, Petra. *Der Fall Anneliese Michel: Kirche, Justiz, Presse*. Würzburg: Königshausen and Neumann, 2014.

Ex Voto

The term "ex-voto" derives from the Latin *ex voto*, short for *ex voto suscepto*, meaning "from the vow made" or "according to the promise that was made." The practice of making and offering *ex voto* objects is ancient and goes back at least as far as the Etruscans, the precursors of the Romans. While there were small offerings made in response to requests concerning health and fertility, votive offerings were also offered for other purposes as well. As far back as the Greek Geometric Period (ca. 900–700 BCE), small bronze figures of gods, animals, and people were made to be left as offerings in temples. It was also common practice among the Romans for military generals make a vow to build or rebuild an entire temple in return for victory on the battlefield.

In the material culture of Christianity, *ex votos* can take various forms including carved or molded objects or painted panels. The destination of an *ex voto* offering is a church, chapel, shrine, or oratory where the worshipper seeks grace or wishes to extend public gratitude. *Ex votos* have had wide appeal for many centuries among many Christians, specifically Roman Catholics and the Eastern Orthodox, throughout the world, especially Europe, parts of Asia, Central America, and South America in such locales as Spain, Italy, Greece, Poland, Germany, Mexico, Guatemala, Puerto Rico, Brazil, Peru, and Bolivia, among others. Sites of Roman Catholic pilgrimage frequently contain any number of forms of *ex voto*, including text-centered plaques, miracle paintings, floral arrangements, crafted wax or wooden correspondences of body parts cured or protected by a saint, and silver hearts honoring the Sacred Heart of Jesus. *Ex votos* can take the form of wooden houses, paintings of ships saved, and even models of ships themselves. Jewelry or precious gems can be offered as *ex votos*—as in the case of the chapel of the icon at the Marian shrine of the Black Madonna at Jasna Góra Monastery in Częstochowa, Poland, where resplendently abundant mounds of amber necklaces adorning the walls of the chapel of the revered image resemble folds of orange fabric. In the last 50 years, the Catholic *ex voto* tradition has changed to include more cost-effective means of vow fulfillment: mass-produced paper ephemera images of Jesus, Mary, and the saints; photographic portraits; and handwritten notes of those who need or were granted heavenly intercession.

Within Christianity, there is a rich historical connection between the practice of *ex voto* offerings and the rise of the cult of the martyrs and saints, the tradition of saintly relic and tomb devotion, the concept of the patron saint, and the human client–saintly protector relationships that developed in Late Antiquity. One of the most vivid expressions of the Christian saint cult was the honor paid to the miracle-producing physical remains: the sanctified bones of these holy men and women. What made this belief in saints even more viable was that complementing the miraculous nature of relics—their bodily remains—was the sense of communion and communication that the saints retained as redeemed personalities in heaven with their Christian brethren on Earth. The apostle Paul had noted in his Epistle to the Romans (12:4–8) "so we, though many, are one body in Christ, and individually members one of another." It only seemed reasonable that if living Christians prayed for each other, the heavenly redeemed would do the same. It was the duty of patron saints to act as a heavenly intercessor at the time of an individual's judgment before God the Father or Jesus as well as manifest earthly protection from the vicissitudes of a potentially violent and disease-filled world. The saint, however, expected the loyalty of his or her charges, which by the Middle Ages was promised in a vow consummated by some formal act that served to express the bond between patron and loyal follower.

By the late Middle Ages, votive images took on a visual pattern of familiarity and communication including the dangerous circumstance below on Earth—whether serious accident/situation or deadly illness—and the miraculous intervention marked by the presence of the saint or the Virgin Mary above in the heavenly clouds. Such a visual framing of saintly intercessor and human votary continued in painted *ex voto* imagery into the late-twentieth century.

Leonard Norman Primiano

Further Reading

Briscese, Roseangela, and Joseph Sciorra. *Graces Received: Painted and Metal Ex-Votos from Italy*. New York: John D. Calandra Italian American Institute, 2012.

Durand, Jorge, and Douglas S. Massey. *Miracles on the Border: Retablos of Mexican Migrants to the United States*. Tucson: University of Arizona Press, 1995.

Jacobs, Fredrika H. *Votive Panels and Popular Piety in Early Modern Italy*. New York: Cambridge University Press, 2013.

F

Faith

"Faith is the assurance of things hoped for, the conviction of things not seen" (Hebrews 11:1). Those who live by faith are deemed to be "righteous" (Habakkuk 2:4) and place themselves in a confident relationship built on trust in God (Psalm 26:1–3; Sirach 32:24). In the New Testament, miracles performed by Jesus are often accompanied by his admonition to those he healed to go their way because it is their faith that has made them well (Mark 5:34; Luke 17:19). The miracles are a ratification of a person's deep and abiding trust, or, as Goethe put it in his *Faust*, "The dearest child of Faith is Miracle." Faith therefore has power to activate the performance of a miracle by Jesus or is in some way the motivating force behind his action. Similarly, when faith is impeded, his miracles are withheld (Matthew 13:58).

The so-called faith cure is an American phenomenon, though it has echoes wherever American missionaries have been a presence. It suggests that the ability to heal oneself of an ailment, no matter how extreme, rests with the strength of one's faith. The community can help the sick to come to faith by praying over them, following the letter to James (5:14–15) in the New Testament: "The prayer offered in faith will make the sick person well." Especially since the nineteenth century, faith healing has had a particularly feminine character, with the vast majority of cases of cures belonging to women. Modern medicine looks askance at faith healing or cures. In the context of the United States, where rights to religious freedom sometimes clash with the medical establishment, periodically there are court cases brought to compel patients to accept treatment over and above their hope in a faith cure.

Some would hold that faith is a test of reason, insofar as there is at least some question of credulity of belief. However, at least until the Enlightenment, miracles provided evidence for the tenets of faith. Today they supply credibility for the claims of "apologetical rationalism" or the "science of faith"—what Pascal called "the reasons of the heart."

Patrick J. Hayes

See also: Christian Science; Televangelists

Further Reading

Barnes, Linda L., and Susan S. Sered, eds. *Religion and Healing in America.* New York: Oxford University Press, 2004.

Curtis, Heather D. "Houses of Healing: Sacred Space, Spiritual Practice and the Transformation of Female Suffering in the Faith Cure Movement, 1870–90." *Church History* 75(3) (September 2006): 598–611.

Dulles, Avery. *The Assurance of Things Hoped For: A Theology of Christian Faith.* New York: Oxford University Press, 1994.

Scott, Robert A. *Miracle Cures: Saints, Pilgrimage, and the Healing Powers of Belief.* Berkeley: University of California Press, 2010.

Farmer, Hugh

Hugh Farmer (1714–1787) was a Rationalist Dissenter pastor. Rationalist Dissenters sought to wed rational thought with theology. The goal was to create a faith that would be buoyed by reason, supported by the emerging sciences. They were independent of the Anglican Church, rejecting its hierarchy and appeal to traditions. For these dissenters, reason and the Bible were the only basis of faith.

Farmer received a classical education during his upbringing. In 1730 he began to study with the Dissenter Philip Doddridge at Northampton. Farmer became the chaplain of William Coward, with a small chapel at Walthamstow, in 1737. He soon took up residency with William Snell, a chancery solicitor and friend of Doddridge, staying there for more than 30 years. He never married but instead spent money on books and little else. The tiny congregation became one of the wealthiest in the Dissenter world. Farmer had a reputation for delivering rational yet spiritual and spirited sermons. He could please a wide range of tastes with his messages. By 1740 Snell had a larger meetinghouse built for him.

In 1762, Farmer began to preach at Salter's Hall in the afternoons once he was released from preaching afternoon sermons at Walthamstow. He also became one of the speakers who would lecture on Tuesday mornings at Salter's Hall. It became the second-largest Presbyterian afternoon congregation in London. Farmer was always an independent.

Farmer's publishing career began in 1746 when a sermon he delivered in the wake of the Battle of Culloden during the Jacobite rebellion (1745–1746), "The Duty of Thanksgiving," was published. In 1761 he published *An Inquiry into the Nature and Design of Christ's Temptation in the Wilderness*. His conclusions were attacked in print the next year. He further fleshed out his conclusions and responded to the criticisms in a reprinted edition. Farmer published additional notes and answered more questions in 1764. A third edition appeared in 1766. In 1775 he published *Essay on the Demoniacs of the New Testament*. He then engaged in a print battle with Richard Worthington, MD. Worthington rejected Farmer's reliance on natural reason and found the whole impetus of Dissenters to be theologically dangerous. In 1783 Farmer published *The General Prevalence of the Worship of Human Spirits in the Ancient Heathen Nations Asserted and Proved*. This began another exchange in print, with John Fell.

His most influential work was *A Dissertation on Miracles*, published in 1771. The catalyst for this work was rooted in a rejection of miracles based upon what Farmer considered to be the faux attribution that miraculous events could be caused by evil forces. He addresses the topic in a lengthy work. For Farmer, the only possible source of miracles was God. Miracles were not only produced by God but were necessary in validating prophetic revelation. It is by this divine demonstration that the revelation can clearly be seen as having the imprimatur of God. Miracles are not impossible for God to do and are ultimately consistent with his nature. He is the only being in the Bible who has this characteristic. Given that God has control over nature and possesses perfection, clearly nothing that goes on in the human realm is beyond his control.

Other sentient beings, good or evil, are never granted this power in the Bible, apart from God's bestowing it upon them. Neither Satan, nor demons, nor other gods have this kind of power. Not a single act of this sort is attributed to an evil being. Thus, there is ultimately no miraculous activities that occur apart from God's control.

Real miracles belong solely to God. Magic is ultimately not the same thing. The confrontation in pharaoh's court is not a battle of miracles. Moses looks with disdain upon what the magicians do. Upon the last miracle, even they have to proclaim that "this is the finger of God." Miracles are the fabric of what makes Christianity appealing. Couple this with the logic of the ordered universe in which God performs miracles, and the system appeals to common sense as well. Common sense is a form of intuitive understanding. Thus, it is completely rational.

He was accused of plagiarizing the work of Abraham Le Moine, which he denied at length in print. His *Dissertation on Miracles* and *Essay on Demoniacs* both were translated into German during his life, and both had English editions published more than a decade after his death. Farmer retired from all of his positions by 1780, though he was forced to continue working during periods until 1785. He was blind by then and had successful surgery to restore his sight. Farmer died in 1787 and was buried in the same grave as his benefactor Snell and Snell's wife.

Farmer had three virtually completed works when he died: new editions of *Miracles* and *Demoniacs* as well as a work on Balaam. Farmer had instructed the executors of his will to destroy them, which they did. Bits of the Balaam work survived, as did a reply to John Fell and a few letters. These latter works were published.

Mark Anthony Phelps

Further Reading

Farmer, Hugh. *A Dissertation on Miracles*. 3rd ed. London, 1810.
Ruston, Alan. "Farmer, Hugh (1714/15–1787)." Oxford Dictionary of National Biography, http://dx.doi.org/10.1093/ref:odnb/9167.

Fasting

Fasting has long been an integral practice in religious and spiritual life in a variety of world religions, and ardent practitioners often are tied to miracles. As a form of austerity, religious adherents undergo fasting for myriad reasons, such as penance or spiritual reflection (as in Catholic Lenten practice), worship and ritual action, protestation (as in hunger strikes by individuals such as Mahatma Gandhi), and as a means toward spiritual liberation or revelation. Typically defined as the conscious elimination of some or all food and drink, religious fasting can be practiced to varying degrees by laity and clergy alike as a means for drawing oneself nearer to the divine. When fasting, the religious practitioner attempts to transcend the desires and cravings of the physical body in order to gain spiritual merit or purification, to be enjoyed in the here or the hereafter.

There are many instances connecting the practice of fasting to ostensible miraculous outcomes from antiquity to the present day. In the Hebrew scripture, fasting was a way for the Israelites, a covenanted people, to renew and repair their extraordinary connection with God when the moral behavior of their community faltered, as in Leviticus 16:29, in which God calls for an annual ritual fast as a means of atonement. In both the Jewish and Christian scriptures, fasting also became a way in which spiritual illumination could be achieved. For instance, in Daniel 10:2–14, the man who famously escaped unscathed from the lion's den refrained from "all choice food" for three weeks, culminating in an angelic vision that only he could see that foretold the future succession of the monarchy and thus the future of the Israelites.

Fasting as a way to connect to divinity is not exclusive to Judeo-Christian traditions. Abstaining from food and sexual relations during periods of religious reflection is one of the Five Pillars, or central practices, of Islam. Following the example of the Prophet Muhammad, Muslim followers engage in strict fasting practices during the holy month of Ramadan in order to bring themselves closer to Allah, or God. Fasting has also historically been used as a gateway to divine experience in the religions of the East. In the Hindu tradition, some practitioners engage in ritual fasts in order to gain favor and earthly assistance from deities such as Vishnu and Shiva. Buddhist monks and nuns who strictly follow the *vinaya*, or monastic code, will sometimes engage in daily or periodic fasts after their midday meal as a way to purify the body and gain merit through self-sacrifice.

Although extreme fasting is deemed detrimental to one's physical and spiritual well-being by most faith traditions, in some contexts (for instance, among some practitioners of Jainism and in the story of the Tibetan monk Milarepa) fasting to the death is considered to be the ultimate form of nonviolence and the surest path toward liberation. While both laity and clergy engage in religious abstinence from food and drink, the fasting exercises of the latter (those who have committed themselves to rigorous religious training and lives) tend to be more austere than that of their lay counterparts.

Stories about the potential for fasting as a means to divine encounters or miraculous experiences are common the world over, regardless of one's faith tradition or status as a lay person or cleric. Saint Mary of Egypt, a Christian penitent of the fifth century, is described in her vitae as having the power of lifting off the ground through fasting. Thus, when describing mystical experiences through fasting, the Dominican Saint Thomas Aquinas could write that when the stomach is empty, "the mind rises more freely to the heights of contemplation of heavenly things" (*Summa Theologica* II-II, q. 147, a. 1).

Emily Bailey

Further Reading

Bynum, Caroline Walker. *Holy Feast, Holy Fast: The Religious Significance of Food to Medieval Women*. Berkeley: University of California Press, 1987.

Maslanka, Christopher. "From Wench to Wonder Woman: Lenten Discipline and Miraculous Powers in the South English Legendary's Life of Saint Mary of Egypt." *Essays in Medieval Studies* 29 (2014): 27–41.

Weddle, David. *Miracles: Wonder and Meaning in World Religions*. New York: NYU Press, 2010.

Fertility

Miracles addressing fertility, or rather a lack of it, are considered the solution to a crisis threatening a collectivity, a nation, or an individual. In a situation where sterility of women, lands, or animals disrupts the balance of life, restoring fertility is necessary. By acknowledging that the harmony between life and death can be broken by human activities such as crimes, wars, or dishonesty, participants in fertility rituals are involved in a transaction in which they must give in order to boost life. Mircea Eliade refers to this intimate relation between man and life as a cosmo-biological solidarity.

Fertility problems and solutions have generally been a female area of expertise. While some societies consider the king to be responsible for his people's ability to produce life, as seen in Hesiod's *Works and Days*, and therefore require him to be fair and wise, most fertility deities and specialists are women. Irish mythology, however, offers a good example of both, as the king united with the Earth goddess in a symbolic sexual relation to ensure the country's wealth.

Earth and fertility deities can be recognized by the objects they carry or are associated with. They display fertility symbols such as eggs, bread, wheat, fruits, babies, and animals. In cases of sterility, these are the deities to whom people will turn with gifts and sacrifices, knowing that in a transaction such as this, one's offering must be as valuable as its request. The implied reciprocity and respect of sacred rules are fundamental to the success of the ritual and the occurrence of a miracle.

The burden of producing descendants has been universally imposed on women, and therefore most individual rituals practiced to resolve fertility issues concern them. Often associated with shame and disgrace, sterility is a tragedy for women in many societies, and the richness of rituals available is a witness to their desire to overcome this intimate crisis. Rituals will often include water or rocks, both closely associated with the life-giving power of Earth. For instance, women will be told to scrape some rock powder from a saint's statue and mix it with wine (Saint Greluchon, France); to lay naked at night on a rock before going back home to unite with their husbands (Lavours, France); and to touch a standing stone, a phallic symbol. Some rituals re-create the reproductive act, with women sitting naked on a mare-shaped rock (*ar gazeg ven*). Sometimes a gift, such as an amulet representing the reproductive organs, is left on the ground as a gift to Earth.

Some rituals take place in consecrated places such as hot springs, caves, or underground churches. They symbolize the womb, as women connect with the bowel of Earth to obtain some of its reproductive powers.

Sterility of land and cattle can be catastrophic and is addressed in powerful ways. To escape famine and death, groups will sacrifice children, virgins, kings, or animals, hoping to receive as much as they give to the concerned deity. Some rituals are repeated yearly to prevent such crises, while others are occasional and only practiced in cases of emergency. The annual Celtic celebration of Beltain, for example, has been interpreted as a fertility ritual by scholars. In Beltain as in other fertility festivals, symbolic and carnal sexual relations may occur to summon fertility powers and to connect with Earth's reproductive soul.

Within a Judeo-Christian framework, (in)fertility and the miracle of birth are exemplified in reference to God's power. The case of Sara, Abraham's wife, is illustrative. Being a woman of advanced age, with her child-bearing years long behind her, when told of her impending pregnancy through God's mercy, she cannot quell her laughter at this cosmic joke. Indeed, she gives birth to her son Isaac, whose name translates as "he makes me laugh."

Geneviève Pigeon

Further Reading

Eliade, Mircea. *Traité d'histoire des religions*. Paris: Payot, 1986.
Green, Miranda J., ed. *The Celtic World*. London: Routledge, 1995.
Mauss, Marcel. *The Gift*. London: Routledge and Kegan Paul, 1965.

Fire

The anthropocentric manipulation of fire is ancient. The control of fire and its power to provide light and warmth and its purifying and transformative capacities have had an incalculable influence on the successive permutations of human civilization and culture. The metallurgical arts and the evolution of the exoteric and esoteric functions of alchemy reflect humanity's earliest conceptual grasp of the influence of fire on life processes. The image of the refiner's fire serves as a metaphor for spiritual transformation to the present day.

Many cultural and religious traditions have sought to conceptualize the importance of fire as more than a physical phenomenon. India's Vedic tradition recognizes five elements; to the classical quartet of earth, wind, fire, and water, Indian spiritualists add the experience of space as a primordial element. Five sacrificial fires are recognized in Vedic India's cosmogony. They are the fires of faith, which in turn feed the fires that produce rain in the heavens, the fires that create food on Earth, and the fires of men and women that create new life. The final fire is the funeral fire, returning the being to the fires of the universe from which he or she came.

The Catholic tradition is replete with expressions of fire and flame as symbols of spiritual awakening. One of the most acclaimed artistic representations of this experience is Gian Lorenzo Bernini's (1598–1680) sculptural depiction of the *Ecstasy of Saint Teresa*, housed above the altar in the Cornaro Chapel in Santa Maria della Vittoria church in Rome. The sculpture illustrates an autobiographical description of the saint's spiritual encounter with an angel who pierced her heart with a flame-tipped arrow. The experience of God's love as a living flame that wounds and purifies the soul echoes in the meditations of Saint John of the Cross (1542–1591), Teresa's spiritual director and confessor.

All spiritual traditions are built on the command to practice compassion, to willingly experience sympathy and a loving awareness of the sufferings and trials of other sentient beings. This realization is beautifully stated by the mystic Saint Catherine of Siena, who in her *Dialogues* characterized God as a fire that burns all selfishness from the soul, freeing it to set the world ablaze with the love of God. Fire is a miraculous spiritual purifier, no more so than in the context of Purgatory, which cleanses the soul of its sins before enabling it to be in the company of God forever.

To have power over fire is likely the most spectacular of miracles. Being able to control its burning effects by walking into and out of it unscathed was an important test of faith and proof to unbelievers both of the sincerity of the witness and the truth of one's religion. Saint Francis of Assisi's encounter with Sultan al-Malik al-Kamil of Egypt in 1219 is rendered by Saint Bonaventure in the following passage:

> Inspired from heaven, Francis continued: "If you wish to be converted to Christ along with your people, I will most gladly stay with you for love of him. But if you hesitate, then command that an enormous fire be lit and I will walk into the fire along with your priests so that you will recognize which faith deserves to be held as holier and more certain." (*Legenda maior*, 9).

Let it be said that Saint Francis was not able to convert the Sultan, nor did he walk through fire. In Islam, the Qur'an (suras 29:24, 37:97) states that Abraham survived being thrown into fire by God's mercy.

Orthodox Christianity boasts an annual fire miracle when, from the inner sanctum of the Church of the Holy Sepulchre (or Church of the Resurrection), the patriarch enters without any combustibles but emerges with large bunches of tapers lit up for dissemination among the faithful gathered outside. Attempts have been made to film the miracle, but the theatrics of the spectacle have always obscured a clear view. Witnesses claim that the spread of the Holy Fire is like a rush of wind whereby fire miraculously races around the sanctuary of the church, gently alighting each of their candles.

Finally, the rite of the barefoot fire walk is also practiced widely, from Polynesia to Greece to the American New Age movement. While it is an intense experience for the performer and spectators alike, demonstrating personal faith, strength, and courage, physicists explain that burning embers are poor conductors of heat, and the duration of contact with the quick walker is not long enough to burn the skin.

Victoria M. Breting-Garcia

Further Reading

Bromley, David G. "On Spiritual Edgework: The Logic of Extreme Ritual Performances." *Journal for the Scientific Study of Religion* 46(3) (2007): 287–303.

Corrigan, Ian. *Sacred Fire, Holy Well: A Druid's Grimoire of Lore, Worship & Magic.* 2nd ed. Lughnassadh: ADF Publishing, 2009.

Dubay, Thomas. *Fire Within: St. Theresa of Avila, St. John of the Cross, and the Gospel, on Prayer.* San Francisco: Ignatius Press, 1989.

Frazer, James George. "The Fire-Festivals of Europe." In *The New Golden Bough*, chap. 62. New York: Criterion Books, 1959, http://www.gutenberg.org/files/3623/3623 -h/3623-h.htm.

Holy Fire, http://www.holyfire.org/eng/.

Knipe, David M. *In the Image of Fire: The Vedic Experiences of Heat.* Delhi, India: Motilal Banarsidass, 1975.

Rosner, Victor. "Fire-Walking the Tribal Way." *Anthropos* 61(1–2) (1966): 177–190.

Tolan, John. *Saint Francis and the Sultan: An Encounter Seen Through Eight Centuries of Texts and Images.* New York: Oxford University Press, 2008.

Flight

Flight, over against levitation, conveys the notion of taking wing instead of merely hovering in place. Those persons or objects capable of alighting from Earth into the sky without aid of mechanical devices defy the natural law of gravity. Magnetic pull has no effect, and mortals who hope to act as birds rank flight as among the more marvelous in any catalog of miracles. Many cultures have flying miracles, with Greek mythology holding out Pegasus, the winged horse, as an early example.

Within Hinduism, the term *vimana* is used to denote a mythological flying palace, replete with mechanical wings and wheels. In the Vedas, the *vimanas* are not so much places to inhabit as aerial vehicles that convey bodies in mystical fashion. To skeptics these contraptions test credulity, but they come as little surprise to Hindus, who have a predisposition to accept as real phenomena outside the natural order, at least as much as that which is inside it.

Christians have known miracles of flight from the time of the birth of Christ. A tradition involving the Holy House of Loreto, a pilgrimage site in an Italian town that continues to be venerated to this day, notes that in 1291 (or 1294) the edifice of this house was transported by a band of angels from Nazareth in Galilee to Loreto. It is the site where the birth of the Virgin Mary and the annunciation to Mary of her impending birth of Jesus occurred and the place where Jesus spent his boyhood. Because of its significance for the biblical narratives, the house is replicated in churches and chapels around the world. In North America, Jesuits erected them in Canada and in the Baha California missions in the late seventeenth century. A statue to Our Lady of Loreto is ensconced in the Holy House, a structure that today is enveloped by the city's cathedral. In 1920, Pope Benedict directed that Our Lady of Loreto be made patron of air travelers. The miraculous flight of the Holy House has been immortalized in a painting by Giovanni Battista Tiepolo (ca. 1744) that hangs in the J. Paul Getty Museum in Los Angeles.

Christ's own ascension into heaven, followed by his mother's assumption, is described both in scripture and tradition. In Acts 1:9–11, Jesus ascends bodily from Mount Olivet, under his own power, in front of several of his disciples. In the Gospel of Luke 24:50–52, Jesus's flight into heaven takes place on the Mount, in Bethany, near Jerusalem. Unlike the ascension, Mary's assumption into heaven takes place not by her own effort but instead through God's grace. A dogma promulgated in 1954 by Pope Pius XII prescribes this as a central tenet of the faith, binding on all of the faithful.

Christians have often depicted angels as winged creatures. Imitation of angelic ability is not unknown among hominoids. Among the most notable are Saint Joseph of Cupertino (1603–1663), a Conventual Franciscan who gave ample proof of his ability to fly. His vita is filled with stories of his disruption of church services during which his confrères were forced to lasso him down. It did not prevent his beatification in 1753 or his canonization in 1763. Another story—not without controversy—comes from the life of Saint Pio of Pietracela, who allegedly flew toward an oncoming fighter plane during World War II. Its mission was to drop bombs on the Gargano peninsula, but Padre Pio foiled their plan. Years later the aviators met Saint Pio and recognized him as the flying friar who forced them to abandon their objective.

Finally, in Islam the cartoonlike notion of a magic carpet in the popular mindset is tempered by the Night Journey (*al-Isrā'*) of the Prophet Mohammad from Mecca to the porch of the Temple Mount—"the most distant place of worship"—in Jerusalem (Qur'an, sura 17:1). It was made possible through *baraka*, a kind of grace dispensed by Allah into creation and through which miracles, such as flying, may occur. Further, Mohammad was conveyed by *al-burāq*, a winged steed in the form of Pegasus but with a woman's head. Upon arrival at the Temple Mount, Mohammad soared into the seven heavens, passing previous prophets such as Moses and Jesus, and ultimately coming into the presence of Allah. Mohammad's ascension is known as the *miraj*, and the Qur'an itself acknowledges that it is a test of belief (sura 17:91). Mohammad returned to his bed in Mecca the next morning.

Patrick J. Hayes

See also: Levitation

Further Reading

Citterio, Ferdinando, and Luciano Vaccaro, eds. *Loreto: Crocevia religioso tra l'Italia, Europa e Oriente*. Brescia: Morcelliana, 1997.

Kugle, Scott A. "Heaven's Witness: The Uses and Abuses of Muhammad Ghawth's Mystical Ascension." *Journal of Islamic Studies* 14(1) (2003): 1–36.

Lewisohn, Leonard, and Christopher Schackle, eds. *Attar and the Persian Sufi Tradition: The Art of Spiritual Flight*. London: I. B. Tauris, 2006.

Luzzatto, Sergio. *Padre Pio: Miracles and Politics in a Secular Age*. Translated by Frederika Randall. New York: Henry Holt, 2010.

Pastrovicchi, Angelo. *Saint Joseph of Copertino*. Rockford, IL: TAN Books, 2009.

Velez, Karin. "Resolved to Fly: The Virgin of Loreto, the Jesuits and the Miracle of Portable Catholicism in the Seventeenth-Century Atlantic World." PhD dissertation, Princeton University, 2008.

Weddle, David. *Miracles: Wonder and Meaning in World Religions*. New York: NYU Press, 2010.

Folk Religion

Folk religion, also referred to as vernacular religion, is classically defined as the difference between what is preached from the pulpit and what is believed in the pew. Church doctrine, for example, holds that animals lack immortal souls, but few pet owners would agree; inscriptions in pet cemeteries staunchly maintain that pets go to heaven. The pew can challenge church doctrine by citing voices such as Matthew 19:26: "with God all things are possible," yet possible only by God's miraculous intervention. The miraculous itself is an area of agreement between pulpit and pew; both see miracles as phenomena that stand above the laws of nature, therefore emanating from the supernatural, or sacred, realm. But each pulpit holds that coming from the God of its own temple, mosque, or church, a genuine miracle will be one that upholds its own doctrine, something each pulpit retains an exclusive right to verify. Therefore, purported miracles that do not convince the pulpit but do convince the pew are those that enter folk religion.

With their festivals, feast days, hosts, and libations, houses of worship are no strangers to physical as well as spiritual nurture, sometimes miraculous nurture given by and received from the pulpit. But the American pew relocates miraculous foodstuff from the pulpit to the hearth, that is, to the nurturing heart of the home, usually the kitchen (or at least the TV snack table). Sacred apparitions are often manifested in mainstream American food ways. Among the most well known include a Virgin Mary grilled cheese sandwich from Florida, a Mother Theresa cinnamon bun from Tennessee, and from Minnesota a Madonna pretzel cradling the baby Jesus. In a nation of ethno-Americans, the sacred also manifests in ethno-American foodways. The southwestern Spanish American tortilla broke ground for this phenomenon in 1978, producing an image recognized as Jesus. On Lake Erie's shore, an image of Jesus similarly emerged on a pierogi, a traditional Central European dumpling, on Easter Sunday in 2005.

Twentieth-century scholars of religion have sought to explain the significance of such images and how they are invested or imprinted with a sacred character. For instance, Mircea Eliade's definition of "hierophany" as "an act of manifestation by the sacred, in ordinary worldly objects," implies that any sacred image that does not occur by human design is, by default, a manifestation of divine providence. The pulpit may resist authenticating such revelations, but the pew requires no convincing.

It is noteworthy that culinary apparitions also differ greatly from church-approved Marian (Virgin Mary) apparitions in the specific type of comfort they provide. Miraculous apparitions authenticated by the church tend to appear in outdoor spaces or public arenas, while family food apparitions appear in private, domestic settings and are free of the prophetic, apocalyptic, and political proselytizing by which church-approved apparitions typically promote church objectives. Instead, apparitions that manifest in aptly termed comfort foods confirm only that sacred beings maintain an ongoing interest and involvement in the everyday lives of true believers. Thus, miracles in folk religion that are autonomous from temple, mosque, and church require no mediation by religious authority and are accessible to any believer; in the case of American culinary apparitions, they are accessible to any believer in possession of a grill, a griddle, a skillet, or even a bag of snacks.

Historically, church-authenticated miracles have stood for and served the varied purposes of the pulpit. Conversely, folk religion is generated, modified, and maintained in the pew and has no broader interest. Rather, miracles in folk religion serve only to fulfill the spiritual needs of the pew, independent of the pulpit. Folk religion functions as a parallel belief system, not always in conflict with temple, mosque, or church but ready to step in and take over if and when the pulpit conflicts with or fails to meet the spiritual needs of the pew.

Judith S. Neulander

Further Reading

Brandes, Stanley. "The Meaning of American Pet Cemetery Gravestones." *Ethnology* 48(2) (Spring 2009): 99–118.

Choron, Harry, and Sandra Choron. *Look! It's Jesus: Amazing Holy Visions in Everyday Life*. San Francisco: Chronicle Books, 2009.

Eliade, Mircea. *The Sacred and the Profane: The Nature of Religion*. New York: Harcourt, Brace, Jovanovitch, 1957.

Primiano, Leonard. "Vernacular Religion and the Search for Method in Religious Folklife." *Western Folklore* 54(1) (1995): 37–56.

Yoder, Don. "Toward a Definition of Folk Religion." *Western Folklore* 33(1) (January 1974): 2–15.

Fragrance

The term "odor of sanctity" applies to the blessed who are somehow conduits for the sweet scent of the divine. Whether on their person, by their presence, or through objects they've handled—and in varying degree of pungency—pleasing fragrances are often observed to be the by-product of holiness. More than a simple adornment, it was a mark of God's special favor, especially for saints, those in their company, or devotees. Often, a wonderful fragrance could be detected postmortem, when ordinarily a decaying body might exude a foul odor. However, the appealing air of those graced by God defies natural processes.

Many Christian saints have been said to have died in the odor of sanctity. Constance Classen has noted that Saint Hubert of Brittany's death flooded his region with such a sweet odor that "it seemed as if God had brought together all the flowers of spring." Some of the living smelled of exotic spices, such as cinnamon and pepper. Lydwine of Schiedam (d. 1433)—a wretched creature to behold but inescapably aromatic to all who touched her—used a hair belt as a discipline while still living. Kept as a relic for decades, the future bishop of Tournai remarked in the early 1600s that he had held it in his own hands and found it to have a "wondrous odor of sweetness," so that "the demons dread it exceedingly."

Canonization records indicate that Saint Rose of Lima's body emitted a miraculous fragrance postmortem and that in the days prior to her burial, her body gave off a scent "like the rose water of angels." Others reported an intermingling of lilies, balsam, and roses. When her tomb was opened in March 1619 and again in May 1632, her remains continued to emit a holy perfume, even though she had died in 1617.

Perhaps the most notable of the saints whose presence gave off a delightful smell are two Discalced Carmelite nuns: Saint Teresa of Àvila (d. 1582) and Saint Thérèse of Lisieux. When Saint Teresa died in October 1582, the Spanish nun was attended by many of her sisters in the convent she founded at Alba de Tormes. Testimonies gathered indicate that the odor of sanctity spread throughout the convent. Prior to her burial, one sister who kissed her feet was cured of headaches, while another was relieved of eye pain. Long after she had been interred, the chapel where she was placed continued to emit a sweet odor, particularly on her birthday. When her body was translated back to Àvila years later, its removal again evoked a powerful fragrance, which the nuns took to be an affirmation of the goodness of virginity.

Saint Thérèse (d. 1897), known as the Little Flower, herself says "du blanc muguet j'ai la fraîcheur l'odeur" (from the lilies of the valley I have the fresh fragrance)! But it is the rose that is associated with this French doctor of the Church, for in her *Autobiography* she promised upon her death to send a shower of roses from heaven. Subsequent to her death a massive worldwide cult arose, and her sainthood cause was introduced. Favors, often accompanied by physical roses or their scent, were seen as confirmation of the nun's assistance. Novenas were developed in her honor and were extraordinarily popular in North America and Europe. In 1923 two cures were acknowledged as coming from her miraculous intercession: to Sister Louise of St. Germain (stomach ulcers) and Charles Anne, a seminarian suffering from advanced pulmonary tuberculosis. Two additional cures were judged miraculous in 1925, prompting Pope Pius XI to declare the Little Flower a saint and according her the title "prodigy of miracles."

Patrick J. Hayes

Further Reading

Classen, Constance. *The Color of Angels: Cosmology, Gender, and the Aesthetic Imagination*. New York: Routledge, 1998.

Ficocelli, Elizabeth. *Shower of Heavenly Roses: Stories of the Intercession of St. Thérèse of Lisieux*. New York: Crossroad, 2004.

Freeman, Charles. *Holy Bones, Holy Dust: How Relics Shaped the History of Medieval Europe*. New Haven, CT: Yale University Press, 2011.

Görres, Ida Friederike. *The Hidden Face: A Study of St. Thérèse of Lisieux*. San Francisco: Ignatius, 2003.

Graziano, Frank. *Wounds of Love: The Mystical Marriage of Saint Rose of Lima.* New York: Oxford University Press, 2003.

Harvey, Susan Ashbrook. *Scenting Salvation: Ancient Christianity and the Olfactory Imagination.* Berkeley: University of California Press, 2006.

France, Miracles in

The presence of Christianity in France extends to the first generation of Jesus's followers. Legend has it that his friends Lazarus, Mary of Magdala, Martha, and two other Marys—Mary the mother of James the Less (Marie Jacobé) and Mary Salomé, mother of James the Elder—landed on the coast near Arles in a boat without sail or oars. They had set off from Palestine to seek refuge from growing persecution of the young Christian community. It was in the region of Marseilles that Lazarus became the first Christian bishop. Across the Mediterranean in southern France they found their haven and in turn made antique Gaul "the eldest sister of the Church."

Technically a part of the Roman Empire, France was thus subject to the same prohibitions as their homeland. The early Christians in France underwent similar trials as those who came from Palestine. Indeed, legend speaks of Lazarus meeting a martyr's end. Yet their leaders produced some of the most profound and cogent arguments for the Christian life. In his panegyric against Gnosticism, for instance, the Greek transplant, Saint Irenaeus of Lyon, called attention to the vacuous currents passing for true religion in his day. The magical elements of Gnostic belief were assailed mightily in his *Adversus Haereses* (e.g., I, xiii, 1). Many early Church Fathers attest to Irenaeus's demise by martyrdom. His tomb thus became a site for pilgrimage and veneration up to the age of the late sixteenth-century Huguenots, who vanquished both the church named for him and his relics contained in it.

Following in the footsteps of saint bishops, Caesarius of Arles (d. 543), a man of inordinate holiness, helped spread the faith. Caesarius's biographers tell of sixteen miracles performed by him during his life (and one more instigated by another at his urging) and sixteen more after his death through the application of his relics. Though formulaic in their execution and publication, the bishop's miracles eschew any pretense toward self-adulation but point instead to the power of Christ. If Caesarius's reputation for curing people had anything to do with his own intervention with the Almighty, it was on account of his humility before God. Perhaps this is what made Caesarius such an effective exorcist. But his therapeutic touch was also an evangelistic tool. In one of his sermons (13, 3) he notes specifically that people should "run to the Church" for healing from sin and any infirmity and not waste their time on "diabolical amulets, or through soothsayers, *haruspices*, diviners, and fortune tellers."

Part of the hagiography that developed in regard to saints' miracles was the writers' ability to amass numerous types of miracles and draw out from them the spectacular from the ordinary. Consider the *Life of St. Martin of Tours* by Sulpicius Severus. In hastening his baptism into the Christian fold, Martin had a vision of a destitute man whom he aided by splitting his own cloak in two and providing the beggar with half. The poor man, who others passed by, became Christ and echoed the words of the Gospel: "Whatever you do for the least of these, you do for me." A simple encounter became an iconic image found in European streetscapes to this day—a depiction urging both religious and civic virtue.

In accounts of Saint Radegundis, a Frankish queen of the sixth century, her powers to cure are equivalent to those of her holy male contemporaries, but that is precisely the point: the saint had broken the gender barriers associated with miraculous cures.

In the post-Merovingian period, miracles abound but are not tied to particular individuals as much as they are to places. Chartres is exemplary. Saint Martin of Tours is purported to have resurrected one child and restored speech to another there. But it is the massive cathedral that has been the region's focal point for nearly a millennium. Both in its architecture—which drew and taught pilgrims the divine mysteries—and in the treasury of its relics, Chartres Cathedral of Notre Dame took pride of place among French houses of worship dedicated to Mary. Among the most prized objects is the reliquary containing the Veil of the Virgin Mary, a silken cloth thought to belong to the Mother of Jesus as she gave birth to him. It had been brought from the Holy Land by the Byzantine imperial couple Nicephorus and Irene of Constantinople and passed to Charlemagne. He, in turn, gave it to his heir, the Carolingian king Charles II (Charles the Bald), who donated it to the cathedral in 876. It is said to have protected the church from destruction by the army of Rollo, the Viking conqueror, and became an object of protection from similar disaster. Rollo later converted and became the duke of Normandy. A catastrophic fire in 1194 compelled some of the cathedral clergy to rescue the chemise by fleeing with it to the crypt of the church. As the fire raged for three days they remained in constant prayer before the sacred cloth and emerged unscathed. In thanksgiving, a magnificent Gothic structure was ordered to honor the Virgin. It draws hundreds of thousands of visitors each year.

Similarly, the cathedral at Autun was also a pilgrimage destination. It too claimed to have the Veil of the Virgin in the twelfth century, but its principal function was to serve as the final resting place of Lazarus of Bethany, the man who was resuscitated by Jesus in the Gospel of John (11:1–44). Thus, the Cathedral of

St. Lazarus at Autun shares in the story of evangelization like its neighbor in Vézelay, where Mary Magdalene's bones were believed to be entombed in the Benedictine abbey church that bears her name. Their respective relics, and the purported miracles that gave prominence to these places, seemed to take on a facticity that wasn't always supported by those in authority. In spite of nearly four centuries of pilgrimage to the penitent's shrine at the abbey, Boniface VIII agreed with a local cult in Aix that it had Magdalene's bones. In 1295 he issued a decree to that effect, and the visitations to Vézelay declined sharply. Autun, by contrast, has had a continuously strong cult, though most who journey there today do so to marvel at the Last Judgment tympanum above the church's main portal on the western facade, a work signed by Gislebertus.

Two further instances of the miraculous in the French Middle Ages belong to the cults of Saint Foy and Saint Louis. Both of these saints' miracles were legion and legendary. Saint Foy was a virgin martyr in the third century whose relics were cherished until the ninth century, when they were stolen. Only in the eleventh century were they presented to the Benedictine monastery at Conques. The saint was given instant fame through the miracle of replacing the eyeballs of a man who had them ripped out a year prior. The restorative power of this saint extended to animals as well as people, in an age when these were considered the life blood of families. Her predilections for assisting the blind, however, were numerous. Today a sumptuously decorated reliquary personifying a seated Saint Foy is enshrined in the treasury of the abbey church.

King Louis IX (d. 1270) became a saintly model for future kings; his virtue was without question. His cult was aided by liturgical innovations that glorified his saintliness, such as *Gloriosissimi regis* and *Beatus Ludovicus*—both of which drew from the canonization records approved by the pope in 1297. Here one can find some of the facts rehearsed from the various vitae submitted for Louis's cause for sainthood, but more important, one can detect how, given the occasion and audience, his virtues were heralded in time and place. As Louis's cult spread, so did the virtues he inspired, but it is the miracles at his tomb in Paris that kept the fame of sanctity alive.

Fifteenth-century Dijon was dazzled by a Eucharistic miracle. A monstrance containing the Eucharistic species was purchased by an unwitting customer, and when she attempted to remove the host lodged inside, her knife cut into it. The story of how droplets of blood oozed forth reached the ears of the pope. Local clergy commandeered the Eucharist, and eventually it was made a papal gift in 1433 to Philip the Handsome, the duke of Burgundy. He supplied it to the city of Dijon, where it remained in the Basilica of St. Michael the Archangel until 1794. It was in February of that year that the church was secularized into a temple celebrating reason, and its sacred contents were all destroyed. The Host of Dijon had already been the object of a huge cult and was strengthened in 1505 when King Louis XII of France received a cure after making a pilgrimage to venerate the host. Multiple images of the host, complete with blood spatters, were replicated in books of hours, stained glass windows, and other objects for decades following its donation to Dijon. Today these comprise a large vein of Eucharistic devotional material for the period.

While it is difficult to say exactly what brings about these kinds of devotional practices among the French, it is at least partly attributable to a spirituality of relationality. That is, the object is both desirable and desired. It attends to a basic want: to be loving and to be loved. A paragon of this type of spirituality is the Carmelite Sister Thérèse of Lisieux. During her short life she repeatedly predicted that she would spend her happiness in heaven by doing good on Earth. Almost immediately after her death in 1897, people began to experience favors through her intercession. First within her monastery and in the Carmelite family but soon among those outside the cloister, records of miracles began to accumulate. These flowed into the Carmel at Lisieux with considerable regularity: a healed relationship, a sudden windfall during financial hardship, a conversion from alcoholism, a quieting of the mind over some distress. By 1925, the year of her canonization, postulators had sifted through thousands of cases.

Since the medieval period, France has enjoyed spiritual favors abundantly, though these have manifested themselves mainly at large pilgrimage centers. The vicissitudes of religious and social upheaval, such as the rise of Jansenism or the dawn of extreme secularism, have marked French culture and its acceptance or rejection of miraculous phenomenon. When in 2006 a French nun, Sister Marie Simon Pierre, was cured of Parkinson's disease through the intercession of Saint John Paul II the world rejoiced, though few in the French press took notice.

Patrick J. Hayes

Further Reading

Blum, Christopher O. "Vézelay: The Mountain of the Lord." *Logos: A Journal of Catholic Thought and Culture* 8(3) (2005): 141–164.

Colomb, Amable. *Notre Dame de Beauregard: Notice sur son sanctuaire, son image, son culte et ses miracles*. Avignon: Typ. F. Seguin, 1877.

Cousin, Bernard. *Le miracle et le quotidian. Les ex-voto provençaux, images d'une société*. Aix-en-Provence: Sociétés, mentalités, cultures, 1983.

"Eucharistic Miracles and Final Ends at the Morgan Library." Ad Imaginem Dei, http://imaginemdei.blogspot.com/2013/06/eucharistic-miracles-and-final-ends-at.html.

Fassler, Margot. *The Virgin of Chartres: Making History through Liturgy and the Arts*. New Haven, CT: Yale University Press, 2010.

Goposchkin, M. Cecilia. *Blessed Louis: The Most Glorious of Kings; Texts Relating to the Cult of Saint Louis of France*. Notre Dame: University of Notre Dame Press, 2012.

Goposchkin, M. Cecilia. *The Making of Saint Louis: Kingship, Sanctity, and Crusade in the Later Middle Ages*. Ithaca, NY: Cornell University Press, 2008.

Goposchkin, M. Cecilia. "Place, Status, and Experience in the Miracles of Saint Louis." *Cahiers de recherches médiévales et humanistes* 19 (2010): 249–266.

"Illuminating Faith: The Sacred Bleeding Host of Dijon." YouTube, http://www.youtube .com/watch?feature=player_embedded&v=HbNhK6fYzbE.

Kahan, Michéle Bokobza. "Ethos in Testimony: The Case of Carré de Montgeron, a Jansenist and Convulsionary in the Century of the Enlightenment." *Eighteenth-Century Studies* 43(4) (Summer 2010): 419–433.

Klingshirn, William E. *Caesarius of Arles: The Making of a Christian Community in Late Antique Gaul*. New York: Cambridge University Press, 2004.

Korte, Anne-Marie. *Women and Miracles Stories: A Multidisciplinary Exploration*. Leiden: Brill, 2004.

Nie, Giselle de. *Word, Image, and Experience: Dynamics of Miracle and Self-Perception in Sixth-Century Gaul*. Aldershot, Hampshire, UK: Ashgate, 2003.

Saxer, Victor. *Le Dossier Vézelien de Marie Madeleine: Invention et translation des reliques en 1265–1267*. Brussels: Société des Bollandistes, 1975.

Seidel, Linda. *Legends in Limestone: Lazarus, Gislebertus, and the Cathedral of Autun*. Chicago: University of Chicago Press, 1999.

Shower of Roses, 1914–1919: Conversions and Spiritual Favors, Cures, Miscellaneous Interventions of Sr. Thérèse of the Child Jesus during the War. New York: P. J. Kenedy and Sons, 1921.

Stancliffe, C. *St. Martin and His Hagiographer: History and Miracle in Sulpicius Severus*. New York: Oxford University Press, 1990.

Thomas, Antoine. "Les miracles de Notre-Dame de Chartres." *Bibliothèque de l'École de Chartes* 42 (1881): 509–550.

Van Dam, Raymond. *Saints and Their Miracles in Late Antique Gaul*. Princeton, NJ: Princeton University Press, 1993.

Franciscans and Miracles

Giotto's *Life of St. Francis* cycle in the Basilica of San Francesco in Assisi under-scores the power of miracle in the Franciscan hagiographical tradition. The basil-ica's walls are frescoed with one miracle after another. Francis (1181/1182–1226) could speak to birds, cast out demons, walk unscathed in fire, command a spring to burst from an unknown source, and bilocate. He was a super saint. Franciscans recognized as bearing the mantle of sanctity often trailed their heroic founder's miracles either numerically or in degree, but they all sought to imitate his virtue.

Saint Francis had his hagiography set in place by Thomas of Celano, a friar who wrote up his life at the direction of Pope Gregory IX shortly after his canonization in 1228. Already by that date a number of chronicles of miracles had been assembled but, by order of the pope, were all destroyed in favor of Celano's more official record. His description of Saint Francis's exorcism of a woman from Narni relates the power of the saint over a demon, which is often depicted as flying out of her mouth. A more modern interpretation would be that she suffered from psychological mania. In a later account by Saint Bonaventure (in his *Legenda maior* of 1263), a more vivid description of demoniacal possession of a Franciscan brother looks to modern eyes to be like a grand mal seizure typical of epilepsy. Whether the devil inhabited these unfortunates or they suffered from some physical or mental ailment is immaterial. In the end, Francis cured them.

Francis's stigmata—the physical imprinting on his body of the five wounds that Jesus bore as a result of his crucifixion—is the saint's hallmark. Francis conformed his life so closely to that of Christ that he became an *alter Christus* (another Christ). Within a generation after his death, the wounds became contentious, both for their reality and their meaning. And yet its mention is nowhere to be found in the saint's canonization process. Thomas of Celano's *Legenda* gives ample testimony, as does the *Legend of the Three Companions*, a text compiled principally through the reminiscences of Francis's closest confrères. Recent scholarship has called into question the legitimacy of these texts on the miraculous stigmata, though the ocular witnesses who testified—especially to the side wound—have never been positively refuted. The proliferation of their stories, largely thanks to Saint Bonaventure, a friar who never knew Francis, either clouds or illuminates the earlier hagiography, depending upon the view one takes on this seminal event. The story goes that while the saint was in ecstasy on Mount Alverna, a six-winged seraph came from heaven and pierced Francis's flesh with the five wounds. Thereafter he tried to keep the visible holes a secret until his death, when the body was prepared for burial and several of his companions and admirers saw them.

Francis's other miracles are too numerous to list, though Thomas of Celano's later work, *The Treatise on the Miracles*, attempts to catalog them. They include healing of a cancer of the mouth and cheeks of a man from Spoleto. Francis kissed his face, and the cure was instant. Francis tamed a wolf in Gubbio, instructing it to cease its harassment of the local populace. Crucifixes came to life such as at the Church of San Damiano, where the corpus communicated to him to rebuild the Church.

Among Francis's contemporaries was the Lady Clare of Assisi, foundress of the second order of Franciscans. Assessing the person of Saint Clare (1194–1253) through her miracles is not always easy. Those who meant to canonize her used their hagiographies to portray someone on par with Saint Francis, and like the poor man, her reality often became obscured. Like Francis, there was a movement that was both widespread and instantaneous that moved quickly to get her on the register of saints. The strength of this movement is typified by the fact that it was initiated by Pope Innocent IV. The investigation of Clare's sanctity and miraculous works took only six days. Within two months of her death, all of the evidence of her sanctity was assembled by the bishop of Spoleto based on the instructions of the pope, whose bias in the case was well known to be in favor of canonization. Clare's sisters and several townspeople who knew her recalled that she turned water into oil, fed all the convent's sisters from half a loaf of bread, and cured her sisters of fistulae, abscesses, and other ailments. But the most spectacular of her miracles are those related to the Eucharist. At one point, a sister overheard the host speak to Clare as she prayed to have the city of Assisi spared by the advancing Saracen army. Today, a statue of Clare holding a ciborium aloft sits outside the Chapel of San Damiano in commemoration of her prayerful heroism.

Other members of the Franciscan family are noted for their miracles. Saint Anthony of Padua (1195–1232), a noted preacher and scholar, has many miracles accredited to him and is often invoked to assist in finding lost objects. Among the most rehearsed miracle is the healing of a severed leg and the obedience accorded him by a donkey that bowed low in the presence of the Eucharist carried by Anthony.

Saint John Capistran (1385–1486), a jurist and preacher with extraordinary talent, was a witness in the canonization cause of Saint Bernardine of Siena (1380–1444), an observant Franciscan whose own preaching drew tens of thousands. Capistran's miracles included the restoration of speech to a mute boy, the healing of a paralytic's hands and feet, and the cure of a possessed Venetian woman whose screams had filled the church where the saint was saying Mass. In Vienna, where he traveled to give missions, he ordered that the sick who went away cured have their names and maladies recorded by his companion, Nicholas of Fara, and later Conrad of Freyenstadt, whose compilation, the *Liber Miraculorum*, eventually contained over 2,500 miracles—among the most extensive accounts of the genre during this period. Capistran, in his humility, ascribed all the cures to the intercession of Saint Bernardine, though it was Saint John who did the blessing.

In the whole panoply of saints, perhaps the most unruly is the Italian Conventual Franciscan Joseph of Cupertino (1603–1663). When he entered one of his ecstasies, the friar would often take flight, at times levitating for several hours, much to the consternation of his brothers in the monastery. His superiors forbade him from certain activities for fear of disturbing the proceedings with one of these levitations. In the *Acta Sanctorum*, which contains the official *acta* of his beatification, some 70 "flights" are recorded. On visiting Joseph in his cell in 1645, the Spanish ambassador to the papal court remarked that "I have seen and spoken with another St. Francis."

Echoes of Saint Francis emerge again and again, as with the stigmatic Capuchin friar Padre Pio of Pietrelcina (1887–1968), renowned for his ability to read minds (especially in the confessional) and bilocate. Saint Pio's cult was spread by Italians around the world and especially in the United States. Another Capuchin, the American friar Venerable Solanus Casey (1870–1957), was a great consoler to lay people in the Detroit area and, while living, relieved the anxieties of a large number of the faithful. Today, people leave prayer requests on his tomb at St. Bonaventure Monastery in Detroit in the hope of a miracle from one whose sufferings were offered "so that all might be one."

Patrick J. Hayes

See also: Stigmata

Further Reading

Andrić, Stanko. *The Miracles of St. John Capistran*. Budapest and New York: Central European University Press, 2000.

Crosby, Michael, ed. *Solanus Casey: The Official Account of a Virtuous American Life*. New York: Crossroad, 2000.

Derum, James Patrick. *The Porter of St. Bonaventure's: The Life of Father Solanus Casey, Capuchin*. Detroit: Fidelity Press, 1985.

Hofer, John. *St. John Capistran: Reformer*. Translated by Patrick Cummins. St. Louis: Herder, 1943.

Huber, Raphael Mary. *St. Anthony of Padua: Doctor of the Church Universal; A Critical Study of the Historical Sources of the Life, Sanctity, Learning, and Miracles of the Saint of Padua and Lisbon*. Milwaukee: Bruce, 1948.

Paciocco, Roberto. "Coscienza agiografica e organizzazione territoriale: I *Catalogi sanctorum fratrum minorum* del 1300." *Laurentianum* 31 (1990): 504–533.

Pastrovicchi, Angelo. *Saint Joseph of Copertino*. Rockford, IL: TAN Books, 2009.

Pattenden, Miles. "The Canonisation of Clare of Assisi and Early Franciscan History." *Journal of Ecclesiastical History* 59(2) (2008): 208–226.

Preziuso, Gennaro. *The Life of Padre Pio: Between the Altar and the Confessional*. Translated by Jordan Aumann. Staten Island, NY: Alba House, 2000.

Schmucki, Octavian. *The Stigmata of St. Francis of Assisi: A Critical Investigation in the Light of Thirteenth Century Sources*. St. Bonaventure, NY: Franciscan Institute, 1991.

Trembinski, Donna C. "*Non alter Christus*: Early Dominican Lives of Saint Francis." *Franciscan Studies* 63 (2005): 69–105.

G

Georgetown Miracles

In Washington City and neighboring Georgetown, a spate of miraculous events took place between 1824 and 1838. The most famous was the dramatic healing of the widowed sister of Washington City's mayor, Thomas Carbery. Thirty-nine-year-old Ann Carbery Mattingly was suffering from end-stage breast cancer and was completely healed on March 10, 1824, through the intersession of a charismatic German priest with alleged supernatural powers, Prince Alexander Hohenlohe. Mattingly's sudden restoration at the moment of the Eucharist was both dramatic and controversial and set the stage for several other cures in Georgetown, many involving Father Stephen Dubuisson and other Jesuits. The attention given to Mattingly's miraculous cure created immense interest in the healing powers of Hohenlohe for the next fourteen years, and numerous additional cures were attributed to him. Of seventeen documented healings of fourteen people in the United States, all but one were women, and ten out of fourteen were members of religious orders. Six of the cures were reported in the Georgetown Visitation Convent.

Nancy Lusignan-Schultz

See also: Hohenlohe-Waldenburg-Schillingsfürst, Prince Alexander Leopold Franz; Miraculé/Miraculée

Further Reading

Curran, R. Emmett. "The Finger of God Is Here: The Advent of the Miraculous in the Nineteenth-Century American Catholic Community." *Catholic Historical Review* 73(1) (1987): 41–61.

Pagliarini, Marie. "'And the Word Was Made Flesh': Divining the Female Body in Nineteenth-Century American and Catholic Culture." *Religion and American Culture: A Journal of Interpretation* 17(2) (2007): 213–245.

Schultz, Nancy Lusignan. *Mrs. Mattingly's Miracle: The Prince, the Widow, and the Cure That Shocked Washington City*. New Haven, CT: Yale University Press, 2011.

Germany, Miracles in

Though miraculous occurrences in Germany predate the conversion by Saint Boniface of the people, it is through his efforts that a deeply Christian understanding and sensibility of these wonders took hold. The famous story of his dispensing with a large oak tree, dedicated to the pagan god Thor, is exemplary. According to Willibald's *Life of Boniface*, the saint showed those who persisted in nature worship that the authority of the Church could not be outdone. At Geismar, a mighty Oak of Thor had stood for generations, but Boniface cut it down and used the wood to build a chapel to Saint Peter. No calamity befell the town—which locals thought was a miracle in itself—and they eventually converted.

Prior to the period of the Reformation in the sixteenth century, approximately 3,800 saints' lives were written and dispersed throughout Europe. Contributing to this literature was one of the few women hagiographers of the Middle Ages. Hrotsvit of Gandersheim (ca. 935–ca. 1002) was a poet, dramatist, historian, and nun from a noble Saxon family. Writing the history of her abbey at Gandersheim, Hrotsvit connected it with the development of the Ottonian kings, whose spouses and offspring excelled in nobility and holiness and whose relics, she recounted, were destined for the abbey's chapels for veneration.

However, no other German writer has done more for the medieval understanding of the miraculous than Caesarius of Heisterbach (ca. 1180–1240). His *Dialogus miraculorum*, written between 1219 and 1223, was the most popular of miracle books—second only to the *Golden Legend* of Jacobus of Voragine. The *Dialogus* was among the first to narrate miracle tales in connection to *exempla*—the literature of the practice of virtue. His narratives circulated and were parsed in monastic communities throughout Europe. As a Cistercian, Caesarius was well aware of his spiritual inheritance, but as novice master for younger monks, he was the primary agent in convincing them to abandon the world for holier pursuits. Thus, the *Dialogus* emulates a typical conversation between an elder monk and a novice, whom he allows to underline the moral by agreeing with the master. In twelve books, the text relates over 700 individual miracle tales of punishment, the restoration of health, or safe passage, among others. In a miracle involving obedient storks, the birds approach the prior of the abbey before departing in order to render thanks for hosting them on the abbey grounds. The prior gives them a blessing, and they depart as models of obedience and refined manners (*Dialogus miraculorum*, X.58).

Medieval piety was rife with stories, some of which coincided with the growth of the royal saint in England and France. Among these are the *legendae* surrounding Saint Wenceslaus (d. 929 or 935), which became ensconced in both Bavaria in the tenth century and Bohemia in the eleventh century. The historical Wenceslaus was a Bohemian duke whose fortunes were thrown in with the German Empire and the Roman church. For his allegiance he was martyred by his own brother, Boleslav, though not before implanting Christianity among the people. On the spot where his murder took place, by a miracle the blood could not be scrubbed away. The writer of *Cresenta fide*, a tribute to the saint written sometime in the 970s, idealized his rule as being both benevolent and just.

Many of the legends surrounding German saints convey both a miracle and a virtue. One story of Saint John Nepomucene, for instance, notes that he was confessor to the queen. When the king asked that he divulge the contents of her confession, he refused in order to protect the seal between priest and penitent. This outraged the king, who had the priest thrown over a bridge, but the saint merely alighted upon the water and could be seen walking to shore. Today he is the patron of many Bavarian bridges.

Some German saints are what might be termed cross-border in that their legends translate easily between cultures. Among these is Saint Wilgefortis, known for the gift of a holy face (*heilige vartez*) and the beard that covered it. Though her legend crops up in Portugal, Spain, and France, her story has common tropes—a virgin who chooses to forego an arranged marriage, asking God to make her unappealing to suitors by the presence of facial hair, and her father's anger and the ordering of her execution by crucifixion. Courageous, strong, pious—these are the values that her image evokes. Artistic works on Wilgefortis, who is often depicted in princely robes pinned to a cross, may have influenced the Devotio Moderna, a Germanic and Dutch movement that ended with the Protestant Reformation.

If the border-crossing life of a medieval saint traverses geographic location, German saints also possess historical durability over time. Consider Saint Hedwig of Andechs (or Hedwig of Silesia, d. 1243), a thirteenth-century duchess canonized in 1267. Hedwig was another border saint insofar as her place of birth was in Bavaria, but her influence later in life was in territory comprising what is today part of the Czech Republic and Poland. Both she and her husband were religious and frequently endowed monastic communities. Their daughter rose to become the abbess of the Cistercian monastery at Trzebnica, and when Hedwig became a widow, she gave all her inheritance to the Church and took the habit in this same monastic house. Her relics went both to the Andechs Abbey and eventually to St. Hedwig's Cathedral in Berlin. Her story's longevity, however, spans seven centuries. Most of what is known about her comes from her canonization process and a later work, the *Legenda maior de beata Hedwigi*, where a biography is supplied.

The remaining two-thirds of the book consist of her miracles, which run from cures of lesser ailments to resurrections. Her notorious allegiance to Silesia was used periodically when that population was under threat, most notoriously in the aftermath of World War II, when 12 million ethnic Germans were expelled by Russian forces from this territory.

German culture has also had particular devotion to its shrines, such as that of Our Lady of Altötting in Bavaria, among the most well-known chapels in Europe. The chapel's existence predates the work of Saint Boniface among the Germans, but the embellishments that adorn the little statue of Mary are from the post-Reformation period. The site became a pilgrimage destination after the miraculous healing of a drowned child who in 1489 was laid before the image of Mary and resuscitated. The Jesuit, Saint Peter Canisius (d. 1597), performed a spectacular exorcism at the site in 1570, spurring a renewal in the number of pilgrimages. Another German Jesuit, Jacob Irsing, composed a Latin collection of nearly 300 pages giving the accounts of miracles at the shrine from 1487 to 1643, many of which dealt with cures for some form of mental disorder. It was in such demand that it went into the vernacular the following year. Those associated with the shrine, such as Brother (now Saint) Conrad of Parzham, OFM Cap (1818–1894), were renowned for working miracles.

Other locations hold deep connection to miraculous phenomena, though this can often become secondary to the physical space. The Cologne Cathedral is an imposing edifice, but housed in a small gothic reliquary are the relics of the Magi—often called the Kings of Cologne. Moritzburg's castle chapel once held 353 reliquaries with over 21,000 relics, among which were the entire bodies of 42 saints—the largest collection in Germany after the Monastery of Reichenau, near Wittenburg, that possessed nearly 19,000. The grandiose nature of these worship spaces had the effect of integrating the miraculous into the culture. During the period of the Reformation, Protestant Christians felt inclined to incorporate much of this into their developing theology. Consequently, Lutherans produced numerous wonder books detailing the inexplicable powers found in nature and how they are brought about by God to discipline a sinful humanity.

Oddities in nature appear in the twentieth century as well. Therese Neumann (1898–1962) lived all of her life in a little Bavarian village called Konnersreuth. As a youth she was plump and hearty, but late adulthood saw her fasting for days. When she was a teenager she helped to put out a fire in a relative's barn but injured her spine. Though she attempted to recover, she repeatedly lost her balance and fell, sometimes causing days-long concussions and diminished eyesight. In March 1919 she went totally blind, and paralysis set in. A local pastor, Father Joseph Naber, served as her spiritual director and took note of her devotion to Thérèse of Lisieux, the Carmelite nun known as "the Little Flower." On the day of the beatification of this sister and after having made a novena in celebration of the event, Neumann's sight was miraculously restored. Upon the nun's canonization in 1925, Neumann was able to walk again.

While these occurrences rely on the testimony of Neumann and her spiritual adviser, the public at large witnessed what followed. During the liturgical season of Lent the following year, 1926, Neumann was favored with the stigmata. Wounds appeared above her heart, at her side, on her feet, and on the backs of her hands. She also suffered bleeding from her head, in accord with the wearing of a crown of thorns, and on her back, where Christ was scourged by the lash. For the rest of her life, the wounds would reappear each week from Thursday to Friday. In 1927 another vision of Saint Thérèse of Lisieux confided that Neumann should no longer take nourishment but instead rely solely on the heavenly bread of the Eucharist, which she consumed each day. Neumann was placed under observation by Church authorities to see if she would break the fast. Over the course of two weeks, Neumann not only managed to survive only on the Eucharistic species but also gained between five to six pounds. Fascination with Neumann during the years of World War II brought a new crop of devotees: U.S. Army chaplains. Largely through the popular press and their own encounters, Neumann developed a small but continuous following in North America. Her canonization cause began in 2005 in the Diocese of Regensburg, Germany.

Patrick J. Hayes

See also: Relics; Reliquary; Stigmata

Further Reading

Alvis, Robert E. "The Modern Lives of a Medieval Saint: The Cult of St. Hedwig in Twentieth-Century Germany." *German Studies Review* 36(1) (February 2013): 1–20.

Blackbourn, David. *Marpingen: Apparitions of the Virgin Mary in Nineteenth-Century Germany*. New York: Knopf, 1994.

Bynum, Caroline Walker. *Wonderful Blood: Theology and Practice in Late Medieval Northern Germany and Beyond*. Philadelphia: University of Pennsylvania Press, 2007.

Friesen, Ilse E. *The Female Crucifix: Images of St. Wilgefortis since the Middle Ages*. Waterloo, Ontario: Wilfred Laurier University Press, 2001.

Irsing, Jacob. *Historia von der weitberühmbten lieben Frawen Capell zu Alten-Oeting in Nidern Bayern*. Translated by Johann Scheitenberger. Munich, 1644.

Kalhous, David. *Anatomy of a Duchy: The Political and Ecclesiastical Structures of Early Premyslid Bohemia; East Central and Eastern Europe in the Middle Ages, 450–1450*. Leiden: Brill, 2012.

Lama, Friedrich von. *Thérèse Neumann: La stigmatisée de Konnersreuth, continue sa vie d'immolation; Suivi d'une letter de M. le curé Naber de Konnersreuth*. Paris: Éditions Alsatia, 1939.

McGuire, Patrick. "Friends and Tales in the Cloister: Oral Sources in Caesarius of Heisterbach Dialogus Miraculorum." *Analecta Cisterciensia* 36 (1980): 167–245.

Merback, Mitchell B. *Pilgrimage and Pogrom: Violence, Memory and Visual Culture at the Host-Miracle Shrines of Germany and Austria.* Chicago: University of Chicago Press, 2012.

Metzger, Konrad, and Franz Metzger, trans. *Das Leben der Heiligen Hedwig.* Düsseldorf: Patmos-Verlag, 1967.

Middlefort, C. Erik. *A History of Madness in Sixteenth-Century Germany.* Redwood City, CA: Stanford University Press, 1999.

Olsen, Karin E., Antonia Harbus, and Tette Hofstra, eds. *Miracles and the Miraculous in Medieval Germanic and Latin Literature.* Leuven: Peeters, 2004.

Soergel, Philip. *Miracles and the Protestant Imagination: The Evangelical Wonder Book in Reformation Germany.* New York: Oxford University Press, 2012.

Vogl, Adalbert A. *Therese Neumann: Mystic and Stigmatist, 1898–1962.* Rockford, IL: Tan Books, 1987.

Glossolalia

The term "glossolalia" (speaking in tongues) has been interpreted both as the vocalization of unintelligible sounds possessing no semantic significance and as xenoglossia, or the purportedly miraculous acquisition of a real language previously unknown to a speaker. The etymology of the word "glossolalia" can be traced back to its Greek roots to the words *glossa* and *laleō*, mean "tongue speech." The Greek reference to this term also appears in the New Testament, and in Christianity glossolalia has been largely associated with the Pentecostal movement wherein the Holy Spirit bestows the "gift of tongues" upon believers. The Christian origins of this phenomenon can be traced back to Saint Paul's Letter to the Corinthians, where in the twelfth chapter the apostle narrates how the Holy Spirit grants gifts such as wisdom, knowledge, faith, healing, power, and prophesying along with the gift of tongues. Notably, this gift has been viewed as a highly sought-after one among many Pentecostal believers.

In most recorded history, glossolalic performances have been specifically linked to women. Research studies on this phenomenon demonstrate that within most glossolalic communities, women are more susceptible to undergoing this experience and greatly outnumber men in displaying such speech patterns. Significantly, research on modern glossolalic communities, including those belonging to the late-twentieth century Appalachian churches, proves that women with this fantastical speech ability enjoy an elevated status within their religious coterie. However, the so-called improved status of glossolalic women is restricted only to the religious sphere of their lives and to moments of inspired speech. More important, seeking the gift of tongues is not always welcome, since some evangelical groups, such as the Missionary Alliance, also believe that this exercise can possibly cause its believers to deviate from the actual aim of attaining proximity with God.

Notably, the phenomenon of glossolalia has been observed not only in Christian communities but also among other religious groups, such as Muslims in India. Despite their lack of prior knowledge of Arabic, they demonstrated an innate power to recite verses from the Qur'an in Arabic, with perfect diction. While glossolalia has largely been associated with religious experiences, some linguists have contested this belief, claiming that similar speech acts may also be observed in other spoken performances, such as vocalization of bebop, jazz, and scat singing. Secularizing the concept, William Samarin defines glossolalia as "a meaningless but phonologically structured human utterance believed by a speaker to be a real language but bearing no systematic resemblance to any natural language, living or dead."

Glossolalia, however, is not simply gibberish, because unlike the latter, which is purely onomatopoeic, the words in glossolalic utterances can be broken down into phonological units, just as in real languages. Understandably, there are numerous debates and controversies surrounding the interpretations of glossolalia. Accordingly, while linguists and anthropologists view this as a phenomenon arising under a trance or a state of mental dissociation after a Christian conversion or baptism by the Holy Spirit, others have contested this by citing numerous recorded instances of glossolalic utterances that have taken place in the absence of trance possession. For them, this is proof that mysticism is merely incidental and not essential to such utterances.

V. Neethi Alexander

See also: Understanding, Miracles of

Further Reading

Cartledge, Mark J. *Charismatic Glossolalia: An Empirical-Theological Study.* Aldershot, UK: Ashgate, 2002.

Cooper-Rompato, Christine F. *The Gift of Tongues: Women's Xenoglossia in the Later Middle Ages.* University Park: Pennsylvania State University Press, 2010.

Goodman, Felicitas D. *Speaking in Tongues: A Cross-Cultural Study of Glossolalia.* Chicago: University of Chicago Press, 1972.

Hine, Virginia. "Pentecostal Glossolalia—Toward a Functional Interpretation." *Journal for the Scientific Study of Religion* 8(2) (1969): 211–226.

Johnson, Lee A. "Women and Glossolalia in Pauline Communities: The Relation between Pneumatic Gifts and Authority." *Biblical Interpretation* 21(2) (2013): 196–214.

King, Paul. "The Early Christian and Missionary Alliance Position on Glossolalia." *Wesleyan Theological Journal* 40 (2005): 184–219.

Samarin, William. "The Linguisticality of Glossolalia." *Hartford Quarterly* 8(4) (1968): 49–75.

Samarin, William. *Tongues of Men and Angels: The Religious Language of Pentecostalism; A Controversial and Sympathetic Analysis of Speaking in Tongues.* New York: Macmillan, 1972.

Sweet, J. P. M. "A Sign for Unbelievers: Paul's Attitude to Glossolalia." *New Testament Studies* 13 (1967): 240–257.

Golden Legend

The *Golden Legend* is a compilation of hagiographies completed circa 1266 by Jacobus de Voragine, the Dominican archbishop of Genoa. Most likely intended as a reference work for Dominican preachers, it drew from numerous written and oral sources including the New Testament, the Church Fathers, and earlier medieval hagiographers. It was one of the most widely disseminated texts of the Late Middle Ages and was translated into several languages for lay audiences.

The original version is divided into 177 chapters of varying length, each devoted to a particular saint. Later versions had additions or were condensed. The chapters are arranged in the order of the saint's feast day on the liturgical calendar. The saints featured are primarily figures from the New Testament, the late Roman Empire, and the early medieval Church, although Voragine also included important contemporary saints such as Francis of Assisi and Dominic Guzmán.

Miracles are very prominent in these accounts and are often given more attention than the saint's proselytizing and other deeds. They range in nature from the truly extraordinary, such as raising the dead or having the earth swallow the wicked, to the more mundane, such as taming wild beasts or stopping inclement weather. In some cases saints miraculously defeat dragons or other fantastical creatures.

Taken together, several common themes emerge from the stories contained within the *Golden Legend*. One important theme is the adversarial confrontation between Christianity and paganism, Judaism, or heresy. These confrontations typically end with the humiliating defeat of the saint's antagonist and either conversion to Christianity or downfall for the antagonist. An example of this theme is the story of Longinus, who was ordered to sacrifice before idols but instead smashed them to release the demons they contained. The demons then possessed the pagan magistrates who were persecuting him. Another significant theme is the heroic endurance of saints in the face of torture and death such as Vincent, who taunted the

Roman governor as his bones were broken and his flesh was torn with iron combs. In many cases saints are miraculously spared from torment or a painful death such as Agatha, who was cast into a fire that split down the center and killed the pagan onlookers instead. While these saints are typically martyred anyway, the failed attempts to torture them and make them abjure Christianity under torture served to humiliate their tormenters, demonstrate the saint's resolve, or win new converts.

Many of these stories also contain gendered themes. Several female saints were persecuted for taking a vow of celibacy and rejecting male suitors. Their virginity was miraculously preserved when male authorities tried to take it by force. When a Roman consul ordered Lucy to be taken to a brothel and raped to death, he was unable to drag her from where she stood with 1,000 oxen. While many male saints were also celibate, this was not a factor in their persecution.

The stories in the *Golden Legend* provided lessons in Christian virtue and the triumph of Christianity. They reaffirmed a theological view of history that was prominent in the Middle Ages and offered encouragement to those who perceived Christendom as being under siege by heretics, Turks, and other infidels in the late medieval era.

Eric F. Johnson

Further Reading

Brown, Peter. *The Cult of the Saints: Its Rise and Function in Latin Christianity.* Chicago: University of Chicago Press, 1981.

Jacobus de Voragine. *The Golden Legend: Readings on the Saints.* Edited by William Granger Ryan and Eamon Duffy. Princeton, NJ: Princeton University Press, 2012.

Grace

Grace is a mark of God's benevolence toward creation, an in-breaking of the supernatural into the natural order. Where reason is stymied, grace permits belief or at least neutralizes doubt. As such, it is an aid to reason and will. Insofar as these may be faulty or otherwise inhibited, grace supplies what is lacking in us. The divine favor of elevating our natural thoughts and acts is not supplementary to faith or to our reason but instead is integral to them.

Miracles do not present a challenge to the notion of grace. Indeed, they are by definition infused with the gracious power necessary to make them manifest to our awareness. These arresting moments invariably draw our attention toward God— our ultimate longing—and away from sin. To be graced is therefore to enjoy a quality of personhood that has a wide-open vista toward the divine. Through an admission of weakness, it permits healing of our broken humanity and fosters the supernatural virtues of faith, hope, and love. Crucially, grace should not be seen as throwing up a road block to freedom, even within our conscience. Instead, it is the catalyst for a rightly formed choice. Applied to belief in miracles, grace is the vehicle by which people may choose to give assent of mind and will to some apparently reason-defying event. A way is shown to skeptics that reason and miracle can be compatible.

Finally, grace is held by many to be sanctifying—that is, by the power of habit, one develops a consistent propensity toward holiness. That God chooses to work miracles through those in a state of sanctified grace has been a staple of the Christian tradition.

Patrick J. Hayes

Further Reading

Duffy, Stephen J. *The Graced Horizon: Nature and Grace in Modern Catholic Thought.* Collegeville, MN: Michael Glazier, 1992.

H

Hagiography

Hagiography is the scientific study of sanctity. The term "hagiography" has two Greek roots: "holy" (*hagios*) and "writing" (*graphe*). Among its various methodologies, it relies in the main on the historical and social sciences, including archaeology and anthropology as well as theology and canon law. As a science, hagiography is interested in distilling the facts from the myths or legends that have arisen from data about saints. This has not always been a critical endeavor undertaken by qualified researchers, nor has it been a body of literature that could be treated in any sort of positivist way, as if every morsel was laden with truth or authenticity. Indeed, early hagiography was interested in doing just the reverse: crafting a cult around the ideal type, a figure whose very being could not be believed as truly saintly unless he or she entered the realm of the fantastic. For this, one did not need to be credentialed in some academic discipline. All one needed was the flare of masterly writing. It would have been highly typical for some person in authority, such as a king or an abbot, to employ these specialists to create so invincible a legend as to persuade even the hardest hearts. That this was often a contest of political importance was hardly inconsequential. Prestige and money were often in the balance. As a narrative art form, the hagiographer was therefore nearly as important as the hagiography.

As a general rule, early Christian hagiography was deeply imbedded in the notion that ours are betters than yours; that is, the miracles of our saints are not just distinct from those of other religious bodies, but they also are more powerful, more spectacular, and more revealing of divine intentions than contemporary pretenders. These are miracles that instill confidence that a person could convert to the truth of Christianity without the least hesitation. Hagiographies therefore have as their purpose the formation of cult. They do not merely occupy space on a page. They are meant to bring about strong emotion and action and unity around a particular narrative.

Apart from a text-critical reading of early miracle narratives, many Greek hagiographers of the fourth to the seventh centuries referred to their writing as *diegesis*, a technique that allows for the narrator to tell how each character in a narrative feels, thinks, or speaks as a plot unfolds. This contrasts with *mimesis* whereby the narrator *shows* how a plot unfolds through action. In either case the reader benefits from a communication that is at once privileged and inviting, including the reader in a kind of club that helps to preserve the saint's memory. If the hagiographer has done his or her job, the reader might become a disciple or client of the saint. Typically, the hagiographer places the whole project before a saint in order that the readership will become as devoted as the writer.

Hagiography does not seem especially bound by the constraints of time or place but shifts with cultural needs. One finds hagiographic texts emerging from the desert regions of the Arabian Peninsula, the mountains of Peru, and the lakes of Ireland. Those who compose the vita remain key to any future interpretation of or participation in a saint's cult. They use memory as a tool and sift the orality of a story for the choice nuggets needed in any given age. As a technique of writing, the superiority of learned monks who had the time and means to create books of *legenda* was given a kind of approbation by a market that sought out their books as aids to piety. In the high Middle Ages, Franciscan and Dominican friars took over where Benedictine monks left off. Among the Dominicans, for instance, Jacobus of Voragine's 1258 hagiographic composition, the *Golden Legend*, was among the most widely circulated books in Europe.

In Irish hagiography, the hagiographic tradition is fueled by story but blends a decidedly Celtic mysticism with historical data. Thus, attention is given not merely to persons and their actions but also to the location where the actions took place. No detail of nature is overlooked. Thus, when Adomnán lays out the life of Saint Columbkille, he makes mention of the sacred space of Iona (and other Irish monastic settlements) and how it is rooted in familiar biblical tropes as well as the flora and fauna of his surroundings.

In examining hagiographic narratives, one might get the impression that there is so much myth making going on that one barely finds any mention of a real person. For this reason, the sixteenth-century English controversialist and playwright John Bale routinely poked fun at the very notion of hagiography and cast considerable doubt on the communion of saints in the process. English evangelical reformers did not particularly warm to such notions, but neither did they condemn them, which paved the way for rabble-rousers to smash the noses off of church statuary with near abandon. If hagiography of pre- and post-Reformation Europe was either too sugary or suffered under the weight of religious change, it also risked being ignored by Christians who sought a more intelligent way of viewing their church. As it was, the eighteenth and nineteenth centuries produced a goodly amount of pious dreck. No one was interested in dismantling the saintly legends; no one called into question the miracle accounts.

Yet recent scholarship has learned to take the narratives with a grain of salt as it were and, by engaging them with a critical framework, mine them for a broader picture of what life must have been like in various contexts. They are not valueless but provide critical clues to a person's life and times. The credit for this shift in understanding belongs to Hippolyte Delehaye, a Bollandist, who originally published his *Legends of the Saints* in 1905. This pathbreaking study began the critical period in scholarly hagiography. Delehaye noted that in hagiography "a new form of literature is born, part biography, part panegyric, part moral lesson."

Admittedly, Delehaye moved the Bollandists in a vastly different direction than their previous iteration. Based in Louvain, Belgium, this Jesuit project, begun in Antwerp in 1607 by Father Heribert Rosweyde, attempted to systematize the collection and publication of the lives of the saints, though without the historical-critical method. Rosweyde's *Fasti sanctorum* (1607) was a broad organizational scheme to gather the extant hagiographic manuscripts in Belgian and other European archives and libraries. Upon Rosweyde's death in 1629 John Bollandus picked up where Rosweyde left off, giving the institute its definite shape. Bollandus saw the first two volumes of saints' lives appear in the 1640s. These biographies corresponded with the festal calendar of the Church, where each day a different saint or saints was celebrated.

Roughly around the same time, in 1645 and 1647 John Colgan, an Irish Franciscan friar also working in Louvain, published two volumes of Irish saints' lives: the *Acta Sanctorum Hiberniae*, on Irish saints whose feast days occurred in January, February, and March, and *Triadis Thaumaturgae*, which brought together the various lives of Saints Patrick, Brigid, and Colmcille. Like the work of Bollandus, Colgan's texts tried to support an ecclesial effort at rendering truth about a saint and thus give legitimacy to the liturgical rites accompanying their feast days. The methodologies of reading a saint's life were not as advanced as in the days of Delehaye, whose own training occurred in the midst of a historiography that looked at miracles as either deficient literary devices, distractions, or outright falsehoods. And yet for Delehaye as well as his predecessors, the purposes are largely the same: to write about the nature of holiness, what accounts for it and what counts as worthy examples.

Scholars have not experienced any lack of new things to say about hagiographies. In fact, the work of medievalists in this field outpaces other branches of history. More sophisticated research tools are now being used to map and locate information on saints across time periods and locations, thanks mainly to the creators of new research databases. A small sampling of the work in this subject area can be found in the bibliography below.

Patrick J. Hayes

See also: Bollandists

Further Reading

Aigrain, René. *L'hagiographie: ses sources, ses methodes, son histoire.* 2nd ed., with supplement by R. Godding. Brussels: Société des Bollandistes, 2000.

Barnes, Timothy David. *Early Christian Hagiography and Roman History.* Tübingen: Mohr Siebeck, 2010.

Brook, Eric. "Hagiography, Modern Historiography, and Historical Representation." *Fides et Historia* 42(2) (2010): 1–26.

Brown, Peter. *The Cult of the Saints: Its Rise and Function in Latin Christianity.* Chicago: University of Chicago Press, 1981.

Carey, John, Máire Herbert, and Pádraig Ó Riain, eds. *Studies in Irish Hagiography: Saints and Scholars.* Edited by John Carey, Máire Herbert, and Pádraig Ó Riain. Dublin: Four Courts Press, 2001.

Delehaye, Hippolyte. *The Legends of the Saints.* Translated by Donald Attwater. New York: Fordham University Press, 1962.

Delehaye, Hippolyte. *Sanctus: Essai sur le culte des saints dans l'Antiquité.* Subsidia hagiographica 17. Brussels: Société des Bollandistes, 1927.

Delehaye, Hippolyte. *The Work of the Bollandists through Three Centuries, 1615–1915.* Princeton, NJ: Princeton University Press, 1922.

Dubois, Jacques, and Jean-Loup Lemaitre. *Sources et méthodes de l'hagiographie médiévale.* Paris: Editions du Cerf, 1993.

Efthymiadis, Stephanos, ed. *The Ashgate Research Companion to Byzantine Hagiography.* 2 vols. Aldershot, UK, and Burlington, VT: Ashgate, 2011, 2014.

Fouracre, Paul. "Merovingian History and Merovingian Hagiography." *Past and Present* 127 (1990): 3–38.

Grégoire, Réginald. *Manuale di Agiologia: Introduzione alla letteratura agiografica.* Bibliotheca Montisfani 12. Fabriano: S. Silvestro, 1996.

Head, Thomas. *Hagiography and the Cult of Saints: The Diocese of Orléans (800–1200).* New York: Cambridge University Press, 1990.

Head, Thomas. "An Introductory Guide to Research in Medieval Hagiography." The Orb, http://www.the-orb.net/encyclop/religion/hagiography/guide1.htm.

Head, Thomas. *Medieval Hagiography: An Anthology.* New York: Routledge, 2000.

"Hagiography." Medieval Studies, http://www.medieval.illinois.edu/resources/library/hagiog _000.html.

Hagiography Circle, http://hagiographycircle.com/index.htm.

Hagiography Society, http://www.hagiographysociety.org/.

Howard-Johnston, James, and Paul Anthony Hayward, eds. *The Cult of the Saints in Late Antiquity and the Early Middle Ages.* New York: Oxford University Press, 1999.

Joassart, Bernard. "Hippolyte Delehaye (1859–1941): Un bollandiste au temps de la crise modernista." In *Sanctity and Secularity during the Modernist Period: Six Perspectives on Hagiography around 1900,* edited by Lawrence F. Barmann and C. J. T. Talar, 1–45. Brussels: Société des Bollandistes, 1999.

Kitchen, John. *Saints' Lives and the Rhetoric of Gender: Male and Female in Merovingian Hagiography.* New York: Oxford University Press, 1998.

Lifshitz, Felice. "Beyond Positivism and Genre: 'Hagiographical' Texts as Historical Narrative." *Viator* 25 (1994): 95–113.

Lifshitz, Felice. *The Norman Conquest of Pious Neustria: Historiographic Discourse and Saintly Relics, 684–1090*. Toronto: PIMS, 1995.

McCready, W. D. *Signs of Sanctity: Miracles in the Thought of Gregory the Great*. Pontifical Institute of Medieval Studies, Studies and Texts 91. Toronto: PIMS, 1989.

Mulder-Bakker, Anneke B., ed. *The Invention of Saintliness*. New York: Routledge, 2002.

Noble, Thomas F. X., and Thomas Head. *Soldiers of Christ: Saints and Saints' Lives from Late Antiquity and the Early Middle Ages*. University Park: Penn State University Press, 2011.

Philippart, Guy. "Hagiographes et hagiographie, hagiologes et hagiologie; Des mots et des concepts." *Hagiographica* 1 (1994): 1–16.

Philippart, Guy. *Hagiographies: Histoire internationale de la littérature hagiographique latine et vernaculaire en Occident des origines à 1550*, Vols. 1–6. Turnhout: Brepols, 1994–2014.

Philippart, Guy. *Les légendiers latins et autres manuscrits hagiographiques*. Typologie des sources du moyen âge occidental 24–25. Turnhout: Brepols, 1977.

Rapp, Claudia. "Storytelling as Spiritual Communication in Early Greek Hagiography: The Use of Diegesis." *Journal of Early Christian Studies* 6(3) (1998): 421–448.

Rennard, Étienne, Michel Trigalet, Xavier Hermand, and Paul Bertrand, eds. *Scribere sanctorum gesta: Recueil d'études d'hagiographie médiévale offert à Guy Philippart*, Hagiologia: Études sur la Sainteté en Occident, Studies on Western Sainthood 3. Turnhout: Brepols, 2005.

Rewa, Michael P. "Early Christian Life-Writing: Panegyric and Hagiography." *Biography* 2(1) (1979): 60–82.

Ryan, Salvador. "Seventeenth-Century Irish Hagiography Revisited." *Catholic Historical Review* 91(2) (2005): 251–277.

Sharpe, Richard. *Medieval Irish Saints' Lives: An Introduction to Vitae Sanctorum Hiberniae*. New York: Oxford University Press, 1991.

Société des Bollandistes, http://www.bollandistes.org/.

Stancliffe, C. *St Martin and His Hagiographer: History and Miracle in Sulpicius Severus*. New York: Oxford University Press, 1983.

Vizzini, Iosepho, et al., eds. *Bibliotheca Sanctorum*. 13 vols. Rome: Pontificia Universitá Lateranense, 1961–1969.

Hay, Bishop George

In 1775, faced with criticism from intellectuals who attacked the biblical accounts of miracles as superstition and self-delusion, Bishop George Hay of Scotland wrote the two-volume *The Scripture Doctrine of Miracles Displayed*. Hay's detailed account used reason and argument to describe and defend a cornerstone of Roman Catholic doctrine—the existence and reality of miracles.

Hay defined miracles as extraordinary events that produced feelings of wonder, awe, and inspiration; if these emotions were not present, the event could not be termed a miracle. Miracles worked for the good of humanity and served as proof that God had wanted the miracle to be created so that false miracles would not be confused with genuine ones. Additionally, miracles were created specifically so that human beings would experience them and perceive them by their five senses. However, human beings could never perform miracles of their own volition.

According to Hay, only supernatural beings such as angels and God could work miracles. He subdivided angels into good angels and demons, describing the works of angels as miracles commissioned by God, whereas the activities of demons were illusions or tricks unsanctioned by God. Endowed with special powers and operating outside the laws of nature, angels might act as agents of a miracle, such as enabling a person to walk on water, or they might be facilitators of a miracle, such as when they communicate something otherwise unknowable to a human being. Angels, however, could neither suspend nor contradict the natural laws of the universe; therefore, Hay assigned the term "relative" to the kinds of miracles that angels performed.

Hay argued that since God had invented the universe and the laws that governed it, only God could act against those laws; therefore, miracles requiring the contravention of natural laws could be only the work of God. Hay called this category of miracles "absolute," such as giving life to someone who had died, changing one substance into another, causing something to exist in two places at once, restoring or giving to someone a physical ability that the person had either lost or never had, and defeating the Devil. God could also employ humans, inanimate objects, animals, and holy relics to work miracles. Examples of these were Joshua's ability to stop the sun's progress, Moses's rod, Balaam's talking donkey, and Elisha's bones that revived a dead man.

Hay presented seven reasons for the existence of miracles. They were meant to convince human beings that the scriptures were the true Word of God and to encourage people to accept them and stay faithful to them. Another purpose of miracles was to serve as a shield and a defense for the scriptures, to protect Catholicism from attack by allowing believers to refute criticism. Additional reasons were that miracles enabled God to show his superiority over other deities, lead people to trust in God and therefore become more perfect, and garner respect for priests, relics, and holy places. Miracles certified that human beings who performed them were credible and should be followed. Finally, miracles encouraged nonbelievers to accept God.

Addressing whether miracles continued down to contemporary times and if they would continue in the future, Hay pointed out that the miracles described in the Bible were necessary because Christianity's existence was threatened under the Roman Empire. After Christianity gained acceptance, miracles did not stop but only became more subtle following the era of the apostles. Referring to his own time, Hay maintained that miracles happened frequently; however, all purported miracles were subject to the strictest judicial procedures by the Catholic Church in order to verify their validity. Thus, Hay concluded, miracles had occurred from biblical times until the eighteenth century, and they would to do so forever.

Hay's explanation of miracles is significant because it provided Roman Catholics with a comprehensive defense of their faith based on an argument from reason. His work is also important historically because it reflected the influence of the Enlightenment on Catholic thought.

Molly Pulver Ungar

Further Reading

Hay, George. *The Scripture Doctrine of Miracles Displayed*, Vols. 1 and 2. Edinburgh, UK: William Blackwood and Sons, 1873.

Healing

As healing may occur physically, emotionally, and spiritually, a miracle may be defined and explained according to the epistemologies and methodologies within any of these spheres. Therefore, medicine, psychology, or religion may independently determine the definition and standard for a miracle. However, in recent years, integrative breakthroughs and collaborations have developed among disciplines for mutual understanding concerning healing miracles.

When terminal cancers disappear, physicians generally may recognize these as statistical improbabilities, referring to them as spontaneous remission and, while calling them "medical miracles," they intend no supernatural explanation. For this group, no further explanation is necessary. Other physicians may reference a miracle—meaning an unexplainable and supernatural event—while still others will seek to identify a causal physical agent or interpret the processes of the mind and consciousness itself as the precipitant for a so-called miraculous healing event.

According to some psychiatrists and researchers, there are twelve reasons why scientists and skeptics reject spiritual healing, prayer, and, by extension, miracles: (1) Western materialistic beliefs reject prayer-based healing based on the established scientific paradigm, (2) human nature resists change, (3) cognitive dissonance,

(4) fear of mysticism, (5) healing occurs outside of conscious control, (6) fear of "power of the mind" control by others, (7) fear of one's own healing powers, (8) healers are strange or different, (9) the lack of repeatability of healing phenomena, (10) healing involves laws different from other sciences, (11) healing is often associated with religions requiring faith and belief, and (12) individual reputations, careers, and financial security are at stake.

In modern times, however, interdisciplinary endeavors through fields such as psycho-neuroimmunology as well as new perspectives about faith and spirituality give rise to the realization that the constructs of these varying disciplines, while significant, are also artificial constructs of the mind that cannot fully comprehend and explain the phenomena of healing and miracles. Reality and the miraculous, as well as healing itself is often elusive, complex, and holistic, eluding the rigors of particular academic disciplines. Healing, much less a miracle, is thus often a mystery.

There is voluminous documentation on healings that occur within spiritual communities, not unlike traditional faith healings, under experimental conditions, concluding that research in body and mind will increase and accumulate, leading traditional scientists to feel more comfortable to embrace holistic approaches that both include and necessitate spirituality and prayer. From this documentation one may conclude the importance of an expanding consciousness, that is, it points health care to two formidable realizations: death of the body will not be their main preoccupation, and awareness of the psyche will no longer be a mere assertion of religions. Both must be taken seriously. A legitimate implication of rational, empirical science will recognize that immortality subsumes preoccupation of bodily death, which does not minimize the task for advances to extend and enhance physical life. Studies that integrate medicine and spirituality expand understanding of healing through a more profound transformation of consciousness, one that recognizes life as inherently miraculous and mystical.

Over the past two decades, several authors have documented how the immune system and mind affect healing and health, related to belief and perception. For example, some have described unconditional love as the most powerful stimulant of the immune system, detailing research in documenting medical and psychological healing with faith-based practices. Such research has been corroborated in body and mind studies through psycho-neuroimmunology—understanding the impact of thoughts, faith, and belief on physical reality—whereby emotions and attitudes, both positive and negative, directly impact healing.

Recent advances in neuroscience reveal how healing changes occur and affect enhanced functioning in the brain through meditation, mindfulness, and prayer. Since earliest recorded history, all cultures and religions, including the great world religions, have aided people in centering themselves through prayer and meditation.

Research in meditation and mindfulness explains how attunement, consciousness, and awareness stimulate and change the brain's circuitry to enhance physical, mental, social, and spiritual well-being. Through meditation, mindfulness, and prayer, transformation of consciousness occurs, integrating the very structures of the brain and resulting in emotional balance and enhanced immunity, in addition to multiple health benefits.

John T. Chirban

Further Reading

Dossey, Larry. *Healing Words*. San Francisco: Harper San Francisco, 1993.

Harrington, Anne. *The Cure Within: A History of Mind-Body Medicine*. New York: Norton, 2008.

Locke, Steven, and Douglas Colligan. *The Healer Within: The New Medicine of Mind and Body*. New York: Mentor, 1986.

Scott, Robert A. *Miracle Cures: Saints, Pilgrimage, and the Healing Power of Belief*. Berkeley: University of California Press, 2010.

Segal, Daniel J. *The Mindful Brain: Reflection and Attunement in the Cultivation of Well-Being*. New York: Norton, 2007.

Siegel, Bernie. *Love, Medicine, and Miracles: Lessons Learned about Self-Healing from a Surgeon's Experience with Exceptional Patients*. New York: Harper and Row, 1986.

Heroic Virtue

The etymological roots of the term "virtue" are the Latin *virtus*, translated as "strength," and the Greek *arête*, meaning the excellence of things. As a strength, virtue is the positive capacity of the human person to craft a morally balanced life through repeated good action. An honest person does not hedge from practicing truthfulness when tempted to lie. A just individual stands firm on one's convictions of right and wrong even when swayed to suspend beliefs of justice. In understanding virtue as the excellence of things, virtue seeks the proper end or, from Greek, its *telos* of something. For example, the excellence of a plane would be that it would fly well and for a racehorse that it would compete well. The telos of the human person is the fullest realization of the nature and potential of all that is human through the integration of human will and reason. For the Christian, telos would extend its range further to include one's ultimate fulfillment in God.

Virtue arises from the human person's capacity in freedom to seek and do the good in order achieve human flourishing, what Aristotle has termed "eudaimonia."

Examples of commonly sought-after virtues include patience, kindness, integrity, honesty, and loyalty. As Saint Thomas Aquinas observed, "virtue is understood as the perfection of a power" (*Summa Theologia*, I–II, q. 55, a. 1). Vice is the opposite of virtue, achieved through the regular practice of bad behavior. Vice obfuscates the classification of goods and corrupts actualized potential. A human life of discovering proper goods and capitalizing on them through virtue can be a long and sometimes arduous journey. Christians have long identified this movement as a pilgrimage to know God, their greatest good, whose Holy Spirit guides them in the exercise and extension of virtue. In the pursuit of moral excellence through the exercise of virtue, the human person seeks to cultivate a proper ordering of all goods that lead to human flourishing. The virtuous person strives to discriminate properly ultimate goods of human nature from subordinate ones.

Virtue seeks the mean between two extremes. According to the Latin phrase *in medio stat virtus*, virtue lies in the middle. It always seeks the balance between excess and deficiency. Chastity as a virtue is the mean between promiscuity and prudishness. Courage is the balance between indiscretion and cowardice. Aristotle emphasized that this mean, what he termed "the golden mean," is not simply an absolute arithmetic mean universally applicable to everyone but instead is proportionate to each person. In other words, this mean is not an objective standard, but contextual and discoverable. For example, the arithmetic mean between a choice of meals of 2,000 kilocalories of energy and that of 800 calories is 1,400 calories. However, for the person who is intent on weight loss, the relative mean will be different than for the person merely eating another meal and not on any diet. Consider also that the arithmetic mean of $50,000 and $30,000 is $40,000 dollars. Yet, the relative mean for a person with a family to support is different from that of a single person. Virtue searches to know and exercise the middle ground. Practice makes perfect, and the ongoing effort to find the virtuous balance takes time, good judgment, and practical wisdom.

An individual is trained in the school of virtue through education and practice. A person could learn patience by being introduced to stories of heroic virtue in the face of challenges and, in turn, seek to incorporate similar virtuous behavior into one's life. Another way to grow in the virtue of patience would be for an individual to position oneself in circumstances where one's virtue—such as persistence, generosity, or tolerance—might be tested or even taxed. Choosing to exercise virtue and militating against temptations toward vice "by similar and repeated activity" (*ST* I–II, q. 51, a. 3) transform a person through "modification of a subject" (*ST* I–II, q. 49, a. 2). Seeking and doing the good through regular practice of virtue can eventually cease to be a burden but can inhabit a person and become a part of one's character. Virtue is its own reward.

Historically, virtues have been grouped in two ways. The first category is the theological virtues of faith, hope, and love or charity, a list having its origin in Saint Paul's first letter to the Corinthians (13:13). These supernaturally infused virtues from God assist people in deepening their relationship with God, their ultimate happiness. The second grouping is the naturally acquired cardinal virtues of justice, temperance, fortitude, and prudence. Prudence or practical moral reasoning has been identified as the "mother of all virtues," for it organizes rightly all the other virtues. The cardinal virtues, directed by human reason, pertain to the achievement of natural happiness with others. This latter collection also has been termed the "hinge virtues," because all other virtues are said to "hinge" upon them.

Supererogation is derived from the Latin *supererogation*, meaning above or beyond (*super*) what is expected (*erogare*) or asked (*rogare*) in action. The supererogatory person exercises more virtue than what is required. Such a person goes beyond the moral minimum to which a person was called, particularly in an effort to build a richer spiritual life and avoid the temptation of sin. Examples of acts of supererogation include the practice of the counsels of perfection or three evangelical counsels (the vows of poverty, chastity, and obedience of religious institutes), the choice of a celibate lifestyle, and performance of certain other charitable activities. Works of supererogation of the saints and the blessed are the warehouse of indulgences from which sinners can draw to be reconciled to God rather than having to endure temporal punishment.

Every human being seeks to achieve a maximum degree of happiness in life. For some, this journey can be an awkward one rich with fits and starts, particularly if there is no clear idea about what happiness consists of. It does not have to be; a clear trajectory toward fulfillment is possible. An unambiguous appreciation of the horizon of happiness prompts the person to discover what the ultimate good consists of and how to act accordingly so that his or her life will be directed toward human flourishing. For the Christian, this ultimate fulfillment is in a dynamic everlasting relationship with God, whose Holy Spirit guides and directs the virtuous person in a profound way. In freedom, this telos has the capacity to propel a person to cultivate dispositions or virtues and lead a virtuous life. A life of virtue is an ongoing quest to learn and ultimately love the good.

Patrick Flanagan

Further Reading

Flescher, Andrew M. *Heroes, Saints and Ordinary Morality*. Washington, DC: Georgetown University Press, 2003.

Heyd, David. *Supererogation*. New York: Cambridge University Press, 2009.

Hinduism and Miracles

Julius R. Oppenheimer, "the father of the atomic bomb," recapitulated the hymn from the Hindu scripture *Bhagvat Gita* (XI, 12) during atomic bomb testing of the Manhattan Project at Los Alamos, New Mexico, on July 16, 1945. While witnessing the mushroom cloud resulting from the detonation, the thoughts of scientists went back to the Mahabharata War. Lord Krishna was persuading Arjun to do his karma, or duty, and took the multiarmed form of Viswarupa—a divine form with vision of the whole universe.

The supernatural elements and miracles of Hinduism give an added fascination to studying and following it. With millions of adherents around the world, Hinduism has caught the attention and fancy of scholars, common people, pop singers, cinema stars, musicians, and others. The philosophical speculation of Hinduism sets the agenda for *moksha* (liberation or enlightenment) from this *samsara* (mundane world/phenomenal existence), which is superior to the other three: *dharma* (duty/moral harmony), *artha* (wealth/fame), and *kama* (sensual/emotional pleasure). For the Hindus, reincarnation of *atman* (soul) under the law of karma is embedded deeply in their religious beliefs. Whether in esoteric tradition of religion or supernatural powers of the divine beings or action of Yogis, unusual happenings constitute an important component of Hinduism.

There are innumerable references in the *Rig Veda* to the myths and exploits of the pantheon of gods and goddesses that comprise Hindu cosmology. The epics such as the *Mahabharata* and *Ramayana* as well as the eighteen Puranas depict the astonishing power of divine beings. Indra, for instance, traversed the skies in a *vimana*, or flying machine, fitted with devastating weapons having destructive powers like modern-day nuclear warheads. In the description of wars in classical texts, the after effects of weapons, called *Brahmastra*, were similar to a nuclear holocaust. Whether it was Arjun or Karna of the *Mahabharata* or Ram or Indrajit of the *Ramayana*, their accomplishments were miraculous. The latter Brahmanic gods and goddesses also performed unbelievable feats. Lord Vishnu took ten incarnations, or avatars, in human, semihuman, and animal forms in order to cleanse evil from this mundane world.

In literature, art, architecture, and popular tradition, the central deity Krishna of bhakti tradition or devotional Hinduism finds a major place. Splitting the Yamuna River, killing the demon Putana, lifting the mountain Govardana, showing the divine form or *viswarupa*, and giving up his mortal body are legends associated with Krishna's superhuman deeds. His miracle saved Draupadi from being humiliated by the Kurus as Krishna kept on extending her garment, or *sari*, infinitely. Yama, the God of death, has many legends in the Puranas woven around him. The most celebrated one is about *sati* and involves the chaste woman

Savitri and her husband Satyavan. She could bring back the life of her dead husband due to the blessings of Yama and became the mother of 100 children. The monkey deity Hanuman, famous for valor and devotion to Rama, possessed many miraculous powers. The goddesses in the Hindu pantheon are represented as *shakti*, or power, with various names such as Durga, Kali, Chandi, and Parvati, among others. Some Hindu deities are not so benevolent, though their narratives are no less imaginative. The story is told of a demon, Raktabija, who was seriously wounded, but a clone of the demon was produced from each drop of blood. The goddess Kali was summoned, and she sucked his blood, devouring the clones. The son of Siva and Parvati, Lord Ganesha, is also credited with many miraculous feats.

The saints of medieval times nurtured in bhakti tradition have influenced the common people as well as the elite with their teachings and supernatural powers. The bhakti saints, with their personal devotion to God, emerged in medieval India out of prevailing social conditions. The saints also influenced the people with their supernatural powers. Adiguru Shankaracharya, the promoter of *advaitavada* (the doctrine of nondualism), traveled throughout India propagating his doctrine. One of the celebrated debates was with Pandit Mandana Mishra, author of the *Brahmasiddhi*. The debates continued for days, with Mishra's wife Ubhaya Bharati acting as a judge. As her husband was losing the verbal duel, she played the last trump card by asking about the *Kama Shastras*, texts on sex and sexuality. The legends mentioned that the ascetic Shankara entered the body of a king to know about this science of love. The dead body of Kabir was turned into a heap of flowers when both Hindus and Muslims claimed the body to burn or bury.

The story goes that the God was accepting offerings from Saint Namdev and visiting his home, taking human form. Nambi Ambar, a swami from southern India, was famous for miracles and once requested Lord Ganesha to partake of his offerings in person. After the death of the seventeenth-century Saint Tukaram, a divine chariot is said to have come to take him to heaven.

Chaitanya was born in 1486 in Navadwip and his parents were inhabitants of Jajpur in Orissa, but had migrated to Bengal in search of a livelihood. A remarkable change had taken place in the life of Chaitanya after experiencing religious ecstasy: he began to chant the name of Hare Krishna. Numerous persons believed that he was an incarnation of Krishna as well as Radha. Chaitanya possessed startling miraculous powers. Chaitnya had appeared in his mother's womb after her prayers. He moved the gigantic chariot of Lord Jagannath by touching his head upon it. The musical chanting of Chaitanya and his believers, known as *samkirtan*, became a form of devotion.

The meaning of miraculous symbols in Hinduism is derived from ancient texts, mythologies, and cultural traditions. Lord Vishnu's chakra, or disk, was a destroyer of evils. The Hindu gods and goddesses were identified with such weapons as the javelin, spear, arrow, trident, club, rope noose, mace, thunderbolt, and sword—all of which had the motive of destroying evil doers. In modern times, some of the symbols are painted in Hindu homes as good signs. The swastika (from Sanskrit, meaning "well-being") image is a powerful symbol in Hinduism of good fortune. On festive days, designs of swastikas are prepared with a mixture of powdered rice, limestone, and colored powders. The lotus flower is another motif in visual arts signifying impending good things of life.

The chanting of *mantras*, or hymns, that are prescribed in Hindu texts performs various functions. The day will be auspicious and free from the hazards of life by the chanting of om, Gayatri, and Mahamrityunjaya mantras. *Japa*, or ritualistic chanting, is a spiritual practice done in prayers. The *asta siddhis* (eight practices for liberation, emancipation, and accomplishment) are magical or supernatural powers gained through spiritual practices. These are *anima* (the power to reduce the body to an atom), *mahima* (expanding the body to a very large size), *garima* (the power of becoming too heavy), *larghima* (becoming too light), *prapti* (access to everywhere), *prakamaya* (accomplishing any wish), *isitva* (unlimited command) and *vasitva* (bringing anybody under one's grip). Krishna in the *Bhagavat Purana* describes various *siddhis* such as *trikala-jnatvam* (knowledge of past, present and future), *paracitta adi abhijnata* (mind reading of others), *aparajayah* (invincibiity), *kamarupam* (changing of body form), *parakaya pravesam* (entering the body of another person), and others. The art of yoga and tantra are also associated with mystical powers and miracles.

Modern-day gurus captivate gullible people by their supernatural powers. The news media is full of deceptive babas hoodwinking people by their deceptive practices. Some amass large fortunes and become infamous by their deviant sexual behavior. Of course, there are a few genuine swamis leading pious lives, imparting religious discourses, assisting people, and performing noble deeds. Swami Vivekananda, Ramakrishna Paramahansa, Swami Chinmayananda, and Swami Sivananda are exemplary. Vivekananda once commented that miracles were the greatest obstacles in the path of truth. The immortality of Hariakhan Baba Maharaj is believed by some. He lives in the icy caves of the Himalayas and frequently comes to northern India to give an appearance. The followers of Mata Amritanandamayi from southern India testify to her healing power. One baba sits in a tree all the time and cures people by simply touching them. Another is a child-god whose disciples perform wonders and astonishing feats.

Sai Baba performed many miracles and claimed that he was God. Amid allegations of pedophilic behavior, millions of dollars worth of property was discovered from personal chambers after his death. The self-appointed "national" saint catapulted to fame owing to his extraordinary power of Yoga, curing people by prescribing herbal medicine, and rousing crowds with sometimes nationalistic discourse. Allegations of land grabbing and amassing huge assets were leveled against him.

Objects are also considered by Hindus to possess miraculous powers. On September 21, 1995, the whole of India was flabbergasted by the phenomenon of a statuette of Lord Ganesha drinking milk. A mass hysteria gripped the nation over the "milk miracle." A repeat of the incident occurred on August 21, 2006. A simple capillary action was the scientific explanation.

In miracles of Hinduism, the demarcation between rationality and irrationality is blurred. Like Hegelian dialectics, rational becomes irrational and vice versa. However, miracles in some aspects of Hinduism pertaining to yogic asana and meditation bring wonders for the human mind and body. All the saints, swamis, and babas are not charlatans. Even the philosophical systems of earlier days such as Carvaka and the Mimamsa have challenged the legitimacy of supernatural happenings.

Patit Paban Mishra

Further Reading

Dadlani, Sanjay. "Sai Baba: A Whiff of Fraud." Nirmukta, October 6, 2008, http://nirmukta.com/2008/10/06/sai-baba-a-whiff-of-fraud/.

Dempsey, Cornnie G., and Selva Raj, eds. *Miracle as Modern Conundrum in South Asian Religious Traditions*. Albany: State University of New York Press, 2008.

Hawley, John S., and Vasudha Narayanan. *The Life of Hinduism*. Berkeley: University of California Press, 2006.

"Hindu Gods & Goddesses." Sanatan Soceity, http://www.sanatansociety.org/hindu_gods _and_goddesses.htm.

Michaels, Axel, and Barbara Harshav. *Hinduism: Past and Present*. Princeton, NJ: Princeton University Press, 2004.

"Miracles." Hinduism Today, http://www.hinduismtoday.com/modules/smartsection/item .php?itemid=3461.

Praphupada, A. C., and Bhaktivedanta Swami. *Krsna: The Supreme Personality of Godhead*. Mumbai: Bhaktivdanta Book Trust, 2004.

Radhakrishnan, Sarvepalli. *The Hindu View of Life*. New York: Macmillan, 1973.

Sharma, Krishna. *Bhakti and the Bhakti Movement: A New Perspective*. New Delhi: Munshiram Manoharlal Publishers, 1987.

Sivananda, Sri Swami. *All about Hinduism*. Shivanandannagar: Divine Life Trust Society, 1997.

Weddle, David L. *Miracles: Wonder and Meaning in World Religions*. New York: New York University Press, 2010.

Hohenlohe-Waldenburg-Schillingsfürst, Prince Alexander Leopold Franz

Alexander Leopold Franz Emmerich, prince of Hohenlohe-Waldenburg-Schillingsfürst (1794–1849), priest, and reputed miracle worker, was born at Kupferzell, Würtemberg, on August 17, 1794. Alexander's father, Karl Albrecht, was the reigning prince of Schillingsfürst, and his mother Judith Freiin Reviczky von Recisnye, was a Hungarian noblewoman. Prince Alexander was the last child of second marriages for both parents. His mother destined him from birth for the church, and his father died when he was two years old. Educated in prominent European schools, Hohenlohe was ordained a priest in 1815. His early assignments were at Stuttgart and Munich in Germany, where he began to develop a reputation as a charismatic preacher. In 1821, he was assigned to a parish at Bamberg. Through the prayers of a devout peasant, Martin Michel, Hohenlohe was healed of an illness, which strengthened his belief in the efficacy of prayer.

In June 1821, Hohenlohe was credited with curing 17-year-old Princess Mathilda von Schwarzenberg, who had been paralyzed for eight years. This sensational cure brought him international fame, and petitioners from various countries flocked to request the grace of his supposed supernatural gifts. Hohenlohe is credited with hundreds of cures of peasants and royalty. Under intense pressure from both civil and church authorities over the miracles, he left Bamberg for Vienna. Pope Pius VII ordered the prince not to attempt any more public cures, but he continued them in private.

Forbidden by both church and civil authorities to hold public healings, the prince engaged an assistant, Father Joseph Forster, to help him send letters to Roman Catholics throughout Europe, the United Kingdom, and the United States. The letters specified a time during which Hohenlohe would pray for those who applied to him, and in this manner he is credited with numerous additional cures. The most famous U.S. healing was of Mrs. Ann Mattingly of Washington, D.C., who reportedly was cured of breast cancer on March 10, 1824. The Vatican investigated but did not pass judgment on these supposed miracles, and Catholics were sharply divided in their opinion of Hohenlohe. The healings caused extraordinary excitement and created polarization among his contemporaries. For critics, the cures signaled a relapse into irrationality and religious fanaticism; for believers, the cures were signs of God's mercy and demonstrative love. Detractors assailed Hohenlohe's character, alleging that he was a charlatan, a gambler, and a womanizer.

In 1824, Hohenlohe was assigned to the Cathedral in Grosswardein, Hungary. He was later promoted to vicar-general. In 1844 he was named *chorepiscopus*, a type of archdeacon, and titular bishop of Sardica, now Sofia, Bulgaria. He died in

Austria in 1849. Hohenlohe is the author of four volumes of sermons and ascetical treatises, most of which were collected and published by Sebastian Brunner in 1851. Hohenlohe's method of curing the sick was continued after his death by his friend and disciple Joseph Forster, who died in 1875.

Nancy Lusignan-Schultz

Further Reading

Schultz, Nancy Lusignan. *Mrs. Mattingly's Miracle: The Prince, the Widow, and the Cure That Shocked Washington City.* New Haven, CT: Yale University Press, 2011.

Holiness

Holiness is a state of being whereby someone or something is set aside or put aside specifically for religious purposes. The etymological root of the term "holiness" is found in the Old English word "hālignes," translated as "without blemish or whole." In Greek, *hagios* is the word for "holy," and in Hebrew, it is *qds*. Both connote a quality of purity and an undefiled state of being whereby something is distinguished for the purposes of consecration.

Rudolf Otto in *The Idea of the Holy* identified the holy as *mysterium tremendum et fascinans*. This classical appreciation of the holy recognizes that in the presence of that which is holy, one can be overwhelmed with a profound sense of fascination and awe. The holy is a tremendous mystery unlike any ordinary experience and one to which the human being is invited to participate. God, who is the refulgence of sanctity (Isaiah 6:3, 1; Psalm 24:3, 99:5; 1 Samuel 2:2; Luke 1:49; 1 Peter 1:15; John 17:11; Revelation 4:8, 6:10), is the ultimate holy one. Aspiring freely toward a life of holiness—in pursuit of sanctity or being a saint—is the human being's response to God's gracious invitation to the mystery of Trinitarian love. Specific locales (Exodus 3:5, 28:29; 2 Chronicles 35:5; Matthew 4:5; 2 Peter 1:18), particular texts (Romans 1:2), liturgical ceremonies (Exodus 20:8–11, 29:33, 30:25; Numbers 5:17; 1 Kings 8:4), and covenantal agreements (Luke 1:72) and laws (see especially "Law of Holiness" in Leviticus 17:1–26:46) are also designated as holy, sanctified, consecrated, or sacred in that they too are set apart in relationship to God.

Throughout the Judeo-Christian sacred scriptures, the call to holiness is clear and resounding. In the Old Testament book of Leviticus alone, compiled by Moses and positioned as the third book of the Pentateuch, there are three directives to be holy:

"For I, the Lord, am your God. You shall make and keep yourselves holy, because I am holy. You shall not make yourselves unclean, then, by any swarming creature that crawls on the ground. Since I, the Lord, am the one who brought you up from the land of Egypt that I might be your God, you shall be holy, because I am holy." (11:44–45)

"Speak to the whole Israelite community and tell them: Be holy, for I, the Lord your God, am holy." (19:2)

"Sanctify yourselves, then, and be holy; for I, the Lord, your God, am holy. Be careful, therefore, to observe my statutes. I, the Lord, make you holy." (20:7–8)

Throughout the Old Testament, obedience to the law was primary in understanding holiness. Externals of relationship formed the primary evaluative means by which holiness was validated. In the New Testament, Jesus, as the incarnate Son of God, moves beyond the exterior to an interior disposition of the heart (Matthew 15:17–20) to describe holiness. In fact, Jesus reprimands the Pharisees and other leaders of the people who cling to cleaning the "outside of the cup" but fail to wash the inside equally clean (Matthew 23:25–26; Luke 11:39). Holiness, for Jesus, originates within the person and expresses itself in charitable action (Mark 7:15). In his very life, death, and resurrection, Jesus models a holy life, always seeking wholeness in God, forsaking sin, and being virtuous in action.

Jesus amplifies this understanding of holiness found in relationship when he declares "Do not think that I have come to abolish the law or the prophets. I have come not to abolish but to fulfill" (Matthew 5:17–18). Holiness is not simply following the letter of the law; it goes *beyond* it. Since Jesus is the "word made flesh" and the law is founded upon the "Word," Jesus, as God incarnate, is the source and summit of all holiness. The law/word cannot be separated from Christ, since "the word was God" (John 1:1). This is evident in John's Bread of Life discourse, when Jesus states "Amen, amen, I say to you, it was not Moses who gave the bread from heaven; my Father gives you the true bread from heaven" (John 6:32) and "Amen, amen, I say to you, unless you eat the flesh of the Son of Man and drink his blood, you do not have life within you" (John 6:53). As John (1:14) teaches, "And the Word became flesh and made his dwelling among us." The Pharisees sought holiness in the law apart of Christ, which is impossible since Christ himself is the law. One cannot know holiness without truly knowing Christ.

All through the apostolic writings of the post-Resurrection church, Jesus's call to holiness is sustained. Paul reminds the Corinthian community that in Christ, humanity has been made holy (1 Corinthians 6:11) and, similarly he reminds the Colossians that Christ completes humanity (2:10). The anonymous author of the letter to the Hebrews testifies to this holiness that has been accomplished by Jesus (Hebrews 10:10, 14). Peter reminds the community of the invitation to holiness. Followers of Jesus are a sanctified people, a "chosen race, a royal priesthood, a holy nation, a people for God's own possession, so that (they) may proclaim the excellencies of Him who has called (them) out of darkness into His marvelous light" (1 Peter 2:9). As a sanctified people, "saints," there is an ethical command to "put on the new self, which in the likeness of God has been created in righteousness and holiness of the truth" (Ephesians 4:24).

In the course of postbiblical history, men and women have chosen a life of holiness by setting themselves apart for consecration through religious life and the observance of the evangelical counsels of poverty, chastity, and obedience. For some the walls of a monastery provided the crucible for growing in holiness, and for others the monastery provided priesthood or membership in active religious congregation. Up until the Second Vatican Council, monks, religious sisters and brothers, and priests were understood to have a higher calling to holiness.

With the promulgation of the council's document *Lumen Gentium*, the dogmatic constitution on the church, the church has taught that all people are called to be holy. It is both a gift and a call. The goal of holiness is union with God and charity toward others. By God's grace, a life of holiness within the life of the Trinity is offered to all. Under this grace, the human being is called to discern and develop his or her innate gifts to build the kingdom of God. As an individual moves beyond sinful preoccupations, one participates more fully in the life of God, who alone is holy, and truly becomes "without blemish and whole."

Patrick Flanagan

Further Reading

Barton, Stephen C. *Holiness: Past and Present*. New York and London: T. and T. Clark, 2003.

Latourelle, René. "Miracle et sainteté dans les causes de beatification et de canonization." *Science et Ésprit* 50(3) (1998): 265–277.

Holy Hill

Rumors swept through southeastern Wisconsin in the 1860s that a hermit was performing penances on the top of a local hill. A few Catholic priests investigated. Finding the hill to be an ideal place for worship, they planted a cross. With that, the Holy Hill pilgrimage was born. An enigmatic hermit and some enterprising Catholics—helped by an international Catholic discourse on the miraculous that stretched from Germany to Wisconsin—made Holy Hill a sacred space.

In the 1860s, the Holy Hill pilgrimage was a local phenomenon. Catholics from nearby parishes, most of them first generation German American farmers, made the initial treks. Gradually, as interest grew, local caretakers made improvements to the shrine. In 1875, local priests had the Stations of the Cross hewn into the side of the hill so penitents could imitate Christ's climb up Calvary.

Holy Hill quickly gained a reputation for miracles. Pilgrims from Milwaukee and Chicago, arriving crippled and chronically ill, walked away cured. They left behind their glasses, bandages, canes, and crutches no longer needed.

By the 1880s, the local press began to take an interest in Holy Hill. Journalists often left the hill convinced that the miracles were real. On August 3, 1883, a writer for the *Milwaukee Daily Journal* claimed to have seen several such miracles: Joseph Hook "came there ruptured and left a sound man," an eight-year-old boy was cured of lameness and walked down the hill, and Mary Burns overcame a "deformity" and promptly entered the convent. Reports of miracles were common in the 1880s. By the mid-1890s, Catholics from all over the United States were making pilgrimages to Holy Hill.

Holy Hill was a product of the tensions of Wisconsin's industrial capitalist modernity. In the late nineteenth century, Wisconsin was undergoing a shift from agriculture to industry. When industrialization changed patterns of work and daily life, it contributed to the outbreaks of nervous and bodily disorders. Pilgrims suffered from epilepsy, paralysis, melancholy, cancer, and stiffness of the limbs. But modernity—particularly the railroad and the press—also aided the hill's mission. Starting in the 1890s, railroads brought pilgrims to the hill by the thousands. Once on the hill, Catholics mixed and mingled markets, good food, devotions, consumerism, sacraments, Mass, and miracles. Priests and laypeople advertised pilgrimages in local papers.

Between 1897 and 1903, reporters continued to describe Holy Hill's power in local newspapers: the cures of Anna Davlen (cured of nervous prostrations in 1897) and Mrs. Robert Small (cured of neuralgia and rheumatism in 1898)—both delivered upon completing a novena—were widely reported.

The shrine's mingling of miracles and commerce proved too profane for one local priest. Father J. J. Keenan thought that local priests told tales of miracles to take pilgrims' money. Local Catholic elites pushed back. Father John Bertram and state senator Herman Kroeger wrote articles claiming that the miracles were real. When the debate appeared on the front page of the *Catholic Citizen* in August 1903, it scandalized Catholic officials.

In 1906 as a solution, church officials handed the shrine over to Carmelite monks. The Carmelites built the shrine into its current form. The contribution of the Carmelites is distinguished by two interrelated trends, one devotional and the other institutional.

Devotionally, the Carmelites achieved a change in continuity: they replaced the communal and dramatic miracles with powerful but surreptitious prayers for Mary's intervention. After the arrival of the Carmelites, the miracles never again entered the public sphere. Mary does her miraculous work quietly, but she still delivers the cures.

Institutionally, the Carmelites have modernized Holy Hill, providing new liturgical space for pilgrims and entwining the shrine more deeply with modernity. Electricity was added to the shrine in 1919, thousands of Wisconsin Catholics made automobile pilgrimages in the 1920s, a $250,000 church was built in 1931, and by the 1960s, according to one brochure, nearly 500,000 people visited Holy Hill annually. A gift shop became the major revenue producer by the 1980s. But Holy Hill's modernization should not obscure its profound connection to the holy: pilgrims have abandoned thousands of canes and crutches. They have no more need for them.

Peter Cajka

Further Reading

Armstrong, William Ayres. *Miracle Hill: A Legendary Tale of Wisconsin*. Milwaukee: Cramer, Aikens, and Cramer, 1889.

Basilica of the National Shrine of Mary, Help of Christians at Holy Hill, https://www .holyhill.com/.

Rohrbach, Peter-Thomas. *Journey to Carith: The Sources and Story of the Discalced Carmelites*. Washington, DC: Institute of Carmelite Studies, 2007.

Homobonus of Cremona

A married lay cloth merchant of twelfth-century Italy (d. 1197), Omobono Tucenghi was canonized by Pope Innocent III on January 12, 1199, as Saint Homobonus. He has the distinction of being the subject of the first recorded canonization bull issued by a pope. In it, the pontiff argued that it was necessary to provide proof of sanctity—something that postulators to that point felt was self-evident—and not just a catalog of virtues. The pope believed that it was apposite to a saint's cause to have both demonstrated satisfactorily, or the Church might fall victim to scoundrels seeking its highest honors without deserving them. Indeed, the pontiff held that signs and miracles observed by heretics would end up confounding them. He further speculated that because Satan's chief attribute was to deceive an otherwise simple faithful, the Devil or his agents might contrive to perform miracles on their own and thus induce a false sense of holiness. Thus, it was essential to any canonization cause that a true saint be denoted by miracles *and* the exemplary engagement of a virtuous life.

Homobonus was illustrious on both counts. One biographer said of him: "While still alive, he demonstrated many other signs of his sanctity. No fewer occurred after his death, when, many heretics, befuddled by evil and disbelief, were converted due to the signs and words of the man of God." Among his miracles is the cure of a demoniac.

Today Saint Homobonus (literally "good man") is considered the patron of business people owing to his reputation for fairness and high ethical standards in the practice of business affairs as well as his desire to earn a living in order to assist the poor.

Patrick J. Hayes

Further Reading

Foglia, Andrea, ed. *Beatus vir et re et nomine Homobonus: La figura di sant'Omobono ad ottocento anni dalla morte (1197–1997); Rassegna di fonti biografiche e testimonianze del culto e della tradizione iconografica, Cremona, 19 dicembre 1997–28 febbraio 1998.* Cremona: Linograf, 1998.

Goodich, Michael. *Miracles and Wonders: The Development of the Concept of Miracle, 1150–1350.* Aldershot, Hampshire, UK: Ashgate, 2007.

Piazzi, Daniele. *Omobone di Cremona—Biografie dal xiii al xvi secolo.* Cremona: Diocesi di Cremona, 1991.

Vauchez, André. *Omobono di Cremona (1197): laico e santo, profilo storico.* Cremona: NEC, 2001.

Vauchez, André. "Un nouveau texte hagiographique du XIIIe siècle sur saint Homebon: Le recueil de miracles *Omnipotens Deus*." In *Amicorum Societas: Mélanges offert à François Dolbeau pour son 65e anniversaire*, edited by J. Elfassi et al., 853–964. Florence: SISMEL edizioni del Galluzzo, 2013.

Hume, David

The Scottish Enlightenment skeptical philosopher David Hume (1711–1776) is known for his argument against the belief in miracles. Hume opposed both Christianity and natural theology, the idea that truths about God could be deduced from nature, although his opposition to Christianity had to be concealed. His contribution came toward the end of a long series of controversial writings in Britain on miracles and particularly the miracles of Jesus and the early church as evidences for the truth of Christianity. Hume's approach to religion in general was naturalistic. In *The Natural History of Religion* and other works, he sought to understand not the truth or falsity of religion but rather why people believed in it. Unlike some of the Deist writers against belief in miracles, Hume was not a crusader against popular credulity and superstition, which he did not believe could be overcome by philosophical arguments.

Hume's discussion of miracles is found in his 1749 *Philosophical Essays Concerning Human Understanding* (better known by its later title *Enquiry Concerning Human Understanding*), although there is evidence that his interest in the subject went back to the mid-1730s if not earlier. Much of "Of Miracles," Section 10 of the *Philosophical Essays*, is not original with Hume but can be found in earlier Deist antimiraculous writers.

Hume's main targets were not fanatical Christian believers but rather practitioners of "reasonable religion" who developed the argument for Christianity from miracles beginning in the late seventeenth century. The discussion opens with praise of the archetypal "reasonable" Christian, Archbishop of Canterbury John Tillotson (1630–1694), for his argument against transubstantiation, but Hume implies that the argument goes much farther than Tillotson would have taken it. Hume defined a miracle as an outright violation of the "laws of nature." By "laws of nature," Hume was not referring to scientific laws but to generalizations such as "all men must die." Divine causation, central to many definitions of miracle, was not important to Hume's overall argument. Although most Hume scholars believe that Hume was claiming that there could never be sufficient testimony to believe in a miracle, a minority believes that Hume made the stronger claim that a miracle could never occur. The question was what testimony was valid to compel belief in a violation of these laws. Testimony for a miracle could only be accepted if the testimony's being false would be even more miraculous. Given the human propensity to deceive and be deceived, this was practically impossible. Reasons for believing in nonexistent miracles or circulating false miracle stories include the human love of wonder and the desire of religious believers to further their cause with miraculous evidence. One argument made by Hume's critics is that he destroys the possibility of believing not only in miracles but also in any extraordinary event, including commonly accepted historical events, on the basis of testimony.

Another problem with using miracles to support religion was that miracles supported diverse religions, not all of which could be true. Hume used the examples of Roman emperor Vespasian healing a blind person by means of his spittle, attested by the revered Roman historian Tacitus; of a Cathedral doorkeeper in Saragossa whose lost arm had been regenerated by the rubbing of holy oil, recounted in the memoirs of Cardinal de Retz; and the Catholic miracles of healing associated with the Convulsionnaires of St. Médard—none of which an Anglican controversialist could accept as legitimate. Historical evidence for the weakness of accounts of miracles and prodigies was also that they were more common in the ancient and medieval worlds and less common, although not extinct, in the more learned and rational world of the eighteenth century, another argument that Hume did not originate.

Although Hume did not directly attack Christianity, he made indirect attacks, using the case of Queen Elizabeth's dying and being resurrected as an example of a miracle very difficult to believe on the basis of testimony. He also discussed the ancient fraudulent prophet Alexander of Abonoteichus, the subject of a biography by the satirist Lucian of Samosata. The progress of the belief in Alexander's supernatural powers, from the ignorant folk of Paphlagonia to Greek philosophers and Roman statesmen, mirrored that of Christianity. In his conclusion Hume ironically portrayed himself as the true defender of Christianity, which can only be supported by faith, not reason.

Hume's argument on miracles has been the most influential contribution to the eighteenth-century British debate on miracles for subsequent philosophers. So controversial was it that the discussion of miracles was left out of some nineteenth-century republications of the *Enquiry*. Although there was little immediate response on publication, it was the subject of several commentaries and polemics in the following decades and remains the subject of lively philosophical debate to the present. The continuing relevance of Hume's argument and the extent to which it divides the modern philosophical community can be seen in the titles of two recent books, John Earman's *Hume's Abject Failure: The Argument against Miracles* (2000) and Robert Fogelin's *A Defense of Hume on Miracles* (2003).

William E. Burns

See also: Locke, John; Middleton, Conyers

Further Reading

Ahern, Dennis M. "Hume on the Evidential Impossibility of Miracles." *American Philosophical Quarterly* (1975): 1–31.

Bayne, Stephen M. "Hume on Miracles: Would It Take a Miracle to Believe in a Miracle?" *Southern Journal of Philosophy* 45(1) (2007): 1–29.

Burns, R. M. *The Great Debate on Miracles: From Joseph Glanville to David Hume.* Lewisburg, PA: Bucknell University Press, 1981.

Earman, John. *Hume's Abject Failure: The Argument against Miracles.* Oxford and New York: Oxford University Press, 2000.

Fogelin, Robert J. *A Defense of Hume on Miracles.* Princeton, NJ: Princeton University Press, 2003.

Garrett, Don. "Hume on Testimony Concerning Miracles." In *Reading Hume on Human Understanding: Essays on the First Enquiry*, edited by Peter Millican, 301–334. New York: Oxford University Press, 2002.

Gaskin, J. C. A. "David Hume and the Eighteenth-Century Interest in Miracles." *Hermathena* 99 (1964): 80–91.

Houston, J. *Reported Miracles: A Critique of Hume*. New York: Cambridge University Press, 1994.

Hume, David. "Of Miracles." In *An Enquiry Concerning Human Understanding*, Section 8, 79–95. New York: Oxford University Press, 2008.

I

Icons

An icon most commonly is a painted likeness of a divine being. For devotees, an icon may possess spiritual power and facilitate a sense of the depicted individual's real presence. Icons are usually created by a trained iconographer, though some icons are reputed to be of miraculous origin. Though many religions claim long traditions of sacred figural images, as a category, "icon"—from the Greek *eikōn*, meaning "image"—derives from Eastern Christianity, both Orthodoxy and Catholicism.

The visual conventions of icons vary according to their contexts. Most feature a vivid single figure, especially Jesus, Mary, or the saints, though narrative biblical scenes can also be depicted. They range in scale from the miniature, if designed for private use in a domestic space, to the life-sized or larger if displayed in a church, such as on the iconostasis, the icon-covered screen dividing the sanctuary from the nave in Eastern churches. While icons remain closely associated with the use of egg-based tempera paint on wood panel, an iconographer may employ various media, such as fresco, mosaic, ceramic, enamel, and textile. Icons also may be stylistically diverse, though the Byzantine tradition had a formative aesthetic influence beyond Byzantium in areas including Russia and the Balkans. One of the most famous and widely copied types of Byzantine icons is the Virgin Hodegetria, in which Mary holds the child Jesus on her arm, drawing the viewer's attention to the right path of salvation by gently gesturing to the child with her other hand.

Controversy over icons played a major role in Eastern Christian history. Trouble began in 726 when Byzantine emperor Leo III declared his opposition to the veneration of religious images and ordered acts of iconoclasm, the destruction of images, throughout the empire. Iconodules, or venerators of icons, were persecuted and exiled and sometimes even brutalized and killed. This policy continued under Leo's successor Constantine V until 787, when Empress Irene called the Second Council of Nicaea, which reestablished the cult of images. Subsequent emperors, however, renewed the persecutions, which occurred from 814 until 843, when Empress Theodora fully restored image veneration. Thereafter, the veneration of icons became an identifying practice of Orthodoxy, which Eastern Orthodox and Eastern Catholic Christians memorialize annually as the "Triumph of Orthodoxy."

The Second Council of Nicaea distinguished between two different kinds of devotion to images. The first kind was *proskynesis*, or veneration, which was deemed acceptable. Veneration given to the image was understood to remit directly to the image's depicted person. The second kind was *latreia*, or worship, seen by the council as a form of idolatry and therefore unacceptable. Worship was to be reserved for God alone and not for God's material representations. The council's theological declarations were drawn from the work of Saint John of Damascus, a Syrian monk and theologian and one of the most famous defenders of icons during the iconoclastic controversy. He and other iconodule theologians also emphasized the idea that icon veneration was a proper consequence of the Incarnation, which enabled matter to serve as a medium for divinity.

Popular religious practice, however, often disregards the fine distinctions of learned theologians. This is true for today's faithful no less than for ninth-century Byzantines, who sometimes respond to icons as if divinity miraculously inheres in the image itself. Indeed, many icons seem to invite these kinds of responses by their composition: a single figure, frontally posed, often appears to meet the gaze of the viewer, which may engender a sense of spiritual intimacy and colloquy. Beholders are known to touch, kiss, carry, and kneel before icons as well as adore them by lighting candles, offering incense, or even washing and clothing them. Sometimes these responses can have incredible emotional depth, if not an erotic charge. This sense of the charged power of icons is further reinforced by stories of miracles they perform. According to various religious communities, icons can save themselves from destruction, heal an ailing pilgrim, and protect cities from invaders.

In recent years, scholars have employed an enlarged understanding of icons and iconicity to describe the visual practices of religions commonly assumed to be aniconic, such as Protestant Christianity. The widely reproduced early twentieth-century painting *Head of Christ* by Warner Sallman, for example, arguably operates as an icon for American Protestants.

Sonia Hazard

See also: Orthodoxy and Miracles

Further Reading

Barasch, Moshe. *Icon: Studies in the History of an Idea*. New York: New York University Press, 1993.

Belting, Hans. *Likeness and Presence: A History of the Image before the Era of Art.* Translated by Edmund Jephcott. Chicago: University Of Chicago Press, 1997.

Cormack, Robin. *Painting the Soul: Icons, Death Masks, and Shrouds.* London: Reaktion Books, 1997.

Freedberg, David. *The Power of Images: Studies in the History and Theory of Response.* Chicago: University Of Chicago Press, 1991.

Maniura, Robert. "Icon/Image." *Material Religion: The Journal of Objects, Art and Belief* 7(1) (2011): 50–56.

Morgan, David, ed. *Icons of American Protestantism: The Art of Warner Sallman.* New Haven, CT: Yale University Press, 1996.

Pentcheva, Bissera. *Sensual Icon: Space, Ritual, and the Senses in Byzantium.* University Park: Pennsylvania State University Press, 2013.

Incorruptibles

The term "incorruptible" is applied to Christian saints whose bodies after death do not appear to suffer decay or for whom decay is significantly delayed. Incorruption is a form of preservation that is neither artificial nor natural; it cannot be explained through embalming, evisceration, or environmental factors. Incorrupt bodies can exhibit other unexplainable phenomena such as producing blood, perspiration, oil, and even a flowerlike scent. Believers attribute these rare occurrences to the divine and view it as proof of the individual's sanctity.

Among the more than 100 saints said to have become incorrupt, the best known include Saints Francis Xavier (d. 1552), Jean-Marie Vianney (d. 1859), Catherine Labouré (d. 1876), and Bernadette Sobiróus (d. 1879). The incorrupts' bodies are often encased in glass and fully clothed in priestly or religious garb, displayed for public viewing and veneration.

The earliest known case of incorruption was Saint Cecilia (d. ca. 177), a martyr of the early church. When her body was exhumed in 1599, it was found whole and intact in the same position in which she had died, inspiring the artist Stefano Maderno to carve her likeness in white marble.

Among the most recent incorruptibles is Saint Pio of Pietrelcina (d. 1968), Capuchin friar and stigmatist. When his body was exhumed in 2008, it was found to be preserved, though some decomposition had occurred. Thousands prayed before the body each day during a period of public viewing in 2008–2009.

Though preserved, the incorrupt are not spared from all decay. The incorrupt whose bodies are displayed for veneration often require a wax, silicone, porcelain, or metallic mask over the face, obscuring facial disfigurement. Bodies once reported incorrupt have later decomposed, as in the case of Saint Pierre Julien

Eymard (d. 1868), whose body was found intact nine years after his death, and Saint Vincent de Paul (d. 1660), who was preserved for at least half a century. Later exhumation revealed only bones.

While viewed by many as proof of sanctity, incorruption is not necessary for sainthood, nor is it considered one of the miracles necessary for canonization by the Catholic Church. When the body of John Henry Newman—on the path to sainthood—was exhumed in 2008, only the brass handles of the coffin and threads from his hat were found. The body had completely decomposed. Among the most revered saints in the church, many have decomposed without any degree of incorruption.

Incorruption is not viewed by all as miraculous. A number of potential causes have been posited. Frequently environmental factors, including air quality, temperature, and the presence of fungi in the soil surrounding the body, are presumed to be the cause, yet incorrupts have been preserved in a variety of environmental conditions even when bodies buried nearby have decayed.

Skeptics accuse the Catholic Church of fraud, believing that bodies were embalmed or eviscerated at the time of death. The bodies of Saints Margaret of Cortona (d. 1297), Catherine of Siena (d. 1380), and Rita of Cascia (d. 1457), long thought to be miraculously incorrupt, show signs of artificial preservation.

It is often reported, however, that incorrupt bodies do not show signs of mummification and can exhibit lifelike qualities, including soft, pliable skin and limbs. Saint Zita of Lucca (d. 1272) remains incorrupt with no signs of artificial preservation. When pathologists examined her body, they found no traces of preservatives on the skin or the existence of incisions. Over 700 years since her death, her body is intact and preserved.

The incorrupt continue to confound and fascinate, prompting prayer and veneration from countless faithful who view them. The phenomenon of the incorrupt remains a disputed question at the convergence of scientific inquiry and popular religious devotion.

David J. Endres

See also: Relics; Reliquary

Further Reading

Cruz, Joan Carroll. *The Incorruptibles: A Study of the Incorruption of the Bodies of Various Catholic Saints and Beati*. Rockford, IL: Tan Books, 1977.

Jeremiah, Ken. *Christian Mummification: An Interpretative History of the Preservation of Saints, Martyrs and Others*. Jefferson, NC: McFarland, 2012.

Pringle, Heather. "The Incorruptibles." In *The Mummy Congress: Science, Obsession, and the Everlasting Dead*, 242–268. New York: Hyperion, 2001.

Indulgences

According to the current Code of Canon Law (1983), for Catholics, an indulgence is "the remission in the sight of God of the temporal punishment due for sins, the guilt of which has already been forgiven" (Canon 992). Any member of the faithful can receive an indulgence, which may be classed as direct or indirect, partial or plenary.

Provided one is well disposed, the indulgence is direct in the sense that it attaches to the living. The mode through which it attaches varies, but recent popes have given particular approbation to certain prayers, pilgrimages (especially to shrines), works of charity, or a combination of these. It is not that these particular acts merit the indulgence. Rather, the indulgence simply serves as an acknowledgment of the reality that the graces acquired through the sufferings of Christ and the saints are such that they render temporal sins, which would otherwise incur a penalty, already forgiven in heaven, thus making moot the need for satisfaction. In effect, the debt to God incurred by one's sins is commuted.

The indirect indulgence may be applied to the dead, by way of suffrage. This means that Christ's satisfaction for one's sins is presented before God together with a plea that any penalty be condoned. In this way, intercessory prayers for the dead, drawing especially from the treasury of satisfactions brought about by the lives of Christ and the saints, has positive effect. The need for the purgation of a soul's sin is therefore minimized or eliminated.

A partial indulgence condones the punishment for temporal sin in part, not in total. A plenary indulgence remits all temporal punishment for sin. In each instance, the distinction is made over the disposition of the one obtaining the indulgence. Naturally, the latter is to be given only to those who have sworn off committing even the most venial of sins, while the former applies to those less scrupulous.

An example of a plenary indulgence is the Portiuncula Indulgence, so-named for the chapel inside the Basilica of St. Mary of the Angels, where Saint Francis of Assisi lived and died. It is the place where Franciscanism began and where in 1216 Saint Francis beheld Jesus, who himself imparted an indulgence to the holy man of Assisi that was later confirmed and promulgated by Pope Honorius III. Today, any pilgrim visiting the Portiuncula may gain this indulgence.

Indulgences have been the subject of much contention—from Abelard, who denied that such power to remit sin existed on theological grounds, to Luther, who saw in their trafficking an egregious abuse. For this he laid blame squarely at the feet of the pope, who, according to Luther's 95 Theses, did not have the power to remit sins. Luther saw in this practice a direct challenge to God's power to forgive as articulated in the Gospels.

Today a periodic *Enchiridion Indulgentiarum* is published by the Apostolic Penitentiary, listing all the available indulgences and their conditions.

Patrick J. Hayes

Further Reading

Apostolic Penitentiary. *Enchiridion Indulgentiarum: Normae et concessiones.* 4th ed. Vatican City: Libreria Editrice Vaticana, 2004.

Lépicier, Alexis. *Indulgences: Their Origin, Nature and Development.* 3rd ed. New York: Benzinger Brothers, 1928.

Swanson, R. N. *Indulgences in Late Medieval England: Passports to Paradise?* New York: Cambridge University Press, 2008.

Ireland, Miracles in

The miracle literature in the British Isles is abundant from ancient times forward, and Ireland has both pagan and Christian examples of heroes, shamans, and saints. During the early medieval period, Irish monks were the major archivists and chroniclers of ancient texts, along with Greek and Roman philosophers and the early Church Fathers. Irish prehistory is full of tales of wonder and miracles, and it is no accident that the miracle-working power of the early Irish saints would be recorded and preserved for posterity.

For many of the early Christian Fathers, differentiating between magic and miracle was a challenge, given that many oral traditions within pagan societies documented the powers of heroes and gods performing feats similar to those of the Christian saints. There are also many parallels between early Irish religious literature, Celtic oral traditions, classical mythology, and miracles in both the Old and New Testaments. These parallels were quite apparent to Irish and European monks writing hagiographic materials related to the early Irish saints. Mary Steinberg does an excellent job of categorizing and documenting the miracles associated with the early Irish Christian saints and their parallels in the literatures indicated above. These categories include malediction (pronouncing a curse on one's enemies), prophecy, power over nature, exorcism, and healing.

The primary recorded sources of miracles by Saint Patrick and many other Irish saints is *The Book of Armagh* (an ancient text copied in the early ninth century), which contains the *Confessio* of Saint Patrick; *Notes of Muirchu Maccu-Mactheni* (late seventh century); *Tirechan's Collections* (late seventh century, referencing a nonextant work of Saint Patrick titled *Commemoratio Laborum*); and *Additions to*

Tirechan's Collections (early eighth century). Other primary sources include *Lebar Brecc* (which only survives in a fifteenth-century copy taken from an eighth-century copy), *The Tripartite Life* (eleventh century, referring back to seventh- and eighth-century saints), the *Vitae Sanctorum Hiberniae* (twelfth-century copies from sixth- through eighth-century hagiographies), and the *Life of St. Columba* (late seventh century from nonextant sixth-century sources).

In addition to the many hagiographic instances of miracles related to the early Irish saints (both insular and the wandering Irish saints, known as the *perigrinatio*, on the continent), there is a rich historical literature related to the Irish navigation legends, or *immram*. These stories involve a hero's series of adventures on a boat. The most famous of these stories is "Voyage of Saint Brendan" about an Irish saint who lived in the fifth and sixth centuries. This story was recorded early in the tenth century and survives in over 100 manuscripts. It is based on other *immram* tales, specifically "Voyage of Bran" and "Voyage of Mael Duin." There are many intertextual parallels and references shared among these tales, and many of these are documented. The mixture of Christian and pagan influences on these tales, fantastic creatures from Irish mythology, and heavenly encounters with beings from the Old Testament, is similar to that of the medieval epic poem *Beowulf*. The *immram* has inspired numerous writers throughout history, most recently C. S. Lewis in his *Narnia Chronicles*.

Finally, Ireland has a long and distinguished history of holy wells and sacred trees, from pagan times through early Christianity and up to the present. These wells and trees are often in close proximity to each other and prompted many early Irish saints to build monasteries beside them in order to provide a smooth and easy transition to the new religion. Veneration of these wells and trees were and still are an active part of pilgrimage in Ireland. Eighteenth- and nineteenth-century accounts record devotees who, on the last fortnight in July or the first fortnight in August, would crawl on their knees around these wells and trees until bloodied and bruised in celebration of the god Lug, Saint Patrick, or other pagan deities and early Irish saints.

Many of these places and objects figure in wider Irish cultural narratives, not least of which are the problems associated with relations between Catholics and Protestants. Throughout the eighth century especially, miracles were employed as polemical devices, generating either incredulity or piety. Whether they were alleged to have occurred on the island or not was immaterial. For instance, on September 1, 1823, the promised miracles of Prince Hohenlohe, erstwhile priest and wonder-worker in Germany, saw believers throughout Ireland staying home from work and flocking to country chapels at the very hour the prince prayed for the sick of Ireland.

In the twentieth century the Marian shrines were politicized into action as well, especially as a spiritual antidote to communism and perceived vulgarisms of a modern secular world. Vigils at Knock by the Blue Army involved incessant repetitions of the rosary to hasten the fall of the Soviet threat and return Ireland to greater faithfulness.

Bradford Lee Eden

See also: Hohenlohe-Waldenburg-Schillingsfürst, Prince Alexander Leopold Franz; Our Lady of Knock; Pilgrimage

Further Reading

Burgess, Glyn. *The Voyage of St. Brendan.* Exeter, UK: University of Exeter Press, 2002.

Burgess, Glyn S., and Clara Strijbosch. *The Legend of St. Brendan: A Critical Bibliography.* Dublin: Four Courts, 2000.

Connelly, Claire. "Prince Hohenloe's Miracles: Supernaturalism in the Irish Public Sphere." In *Scotland, Ireland, and the Romantic Aesthetic*, edited by David Duff and Catherine Jones, 236–257. Lewisburg, PA: Bucknell University Press, 2007.

Donnelly, James S. "Opposing the 'Modern World': The Cult of the Virgin Mary in Ireland, 1965–1985." *Éire-Ireland* 40(1–2) (Spring–Summer 2005): 183–245.

Ghezzi, Bert. *Mystics & Miracles: True Stories of Lives Touched by God.* Chicago: Loyola Press, 2002.

Hamlin, Ann, and Kathleen Hughes. *The Modern Traveler to the Early Irish Church.* Dublin: Four Courts, 1997.

Harbison, Peter. *Pilgrimage in Ireland: The Monuments and the People.* Syracuse, NY: Syracuse University Press, 1992.

Logan, Patrick. *The Holy Wells of Ireland.* Buckinghamshire: Smythe, 1980.

Steinberg, Mary Alice. "The Origins and Role of the Miracle-Story in Irish and English History and Hagiography, 400–800 A.D." PhD dissertation, New York University, 1978.

Wooding, Jonathan. *The Otherworld Voyage in Early Irish Literature: An Anthology of Criticism.* Dublin: Four Courts, 2000.

Islam and Miracles

In Islam, miracles are manifestations of the divine presence to weak humanity. Cognizance of these miracles is grace. According to some scholars, there are two Arabic terms for miracle in the Islamic tradition. The word *karama* means a personal favor granted by God to a saint, living or deceased. Depending upon the region, identifying a saint may be done through his personal conduct. In the Moroccan context, for instance, a person with the quality of *salih* (virtue) has the hallmark of sainthood. Distinct from this mode of being is an act of grace described as *mujiza*, that which overpowers or overwhelms. The root is *'ajaza*, meaning to be overwhelmed. While this act or manifestation is granted by God, it requires no mediation through a saint. It does, however, convey a miraculous message through a prophet that unequivocally demonstrates the truth of his mission and words. In Islam, although several miracles (pl. *mujizat*) are attributed to the Prophet Muhammad, the revelations contained in the Qur'an, and its word-for-word transmission are considered the greatest possible miracles.

Barakah is a general term drawn from Sufi mystic traditions designating the breaking into human reality of the divinity of God. It is variously described as a blessing or a grace. Muslims hold that the miraculous, or *barakah*, may be found in the holy scripture, the *Hadith*, in the actions of the saints, at shrines, or in the ability of individuals to emulate the righteous. These are not believed to be manifestations of anything other than the divine power. Therefore, they are *ayat*, signs, that point to God's overarching control of all human experience.

The Qur'an supplies many examples of miracles. Abraham is thrown into fire, yet at God's command, it becomes cool and safe for him (sura 21:69). Jesus the Prophet is portrayed as an animator of clay birds and a frequent and versatile healer (sura 5:110). Solomon could understand the language of fowl (sura 27:16). With Muhammed, the miracles are numerous: a gazelle speaks to him, and a handkerchief he used to clean his mouth and hands resisted immolation in a furnace. Yet in each instance, God is the cause for the orchestration and the ultimate source of the marvels. Even in the presentation of the Qur'an to Muhammad, the miracle is the gift of eloquence in its recitation. More than one commentator has called the Qur'an itself a literary miracle.

Like the Christian who makes a pilgrimage to Lourdes, for Muslims, the quest for miracles at shrines is known as *zivara*. Typically, the expectation of miracles is accompanied by ritual action, as with pilgrims within Shia Islam who travel to the tombs in Iraq. They come to places such as the tomb of Imam Ali, the cousin of the Prophet Muhammad, in Najaf, where an enormous and copiously decorated shrine is dedicated to his memory. For Shias, it remains the third-holiest place on Earth after Mecca and Medina in Saudi Arabia. Slain for the faith in 661, Imam Ali ibn Abi Talib was the fourth caliph or political head of a Muslim community after the Prophet Muhammad. Various constructions of the sacred site began in the tenth century. It is thought also to contain the remains of Adam and Noah. The present structure dates to the sixteenth century, though extensive repairs were necessitated following damage incurred by the Persian Gulf War in 1991. The site has also suffered from occasional violence within its precincts, including murderous car bombings in 2003 and 2006. Nevertheless, Muslims of the city bring their dead to the mosque and circumambulate Ali's tomb with the coffin in the hope that Ali will guide their loved ones to heaven. The adjacent Wadi Al-Salaam, a massive cemetery, is filled with the remains of Muslims desirous of being raised with Imam Ali at the consummation of the world.

Pilgrims also travel to the grave of Imam Ali's son, Imam Hussain (sometimes Hussayn or Husayn), in Karbala. It is considered by Shias to be the fourth most sacred place and recalls the sacrifice of the martyr and grandson of the Prophet Muhammad. The mosque associated with this tomb dates to the eleventh century, though the dome dates to the fourteenth century. A tree-lined boulevard separates the shrine of Hussain with that of his half brother Abbas, a warrior who died alongside Hussain in the Battle of Karbala in 680. Pilgrims often reenact, with bloody crowns and flesh-tearing cat o'nine tails, the heroic exploits of these men. Veneration of these revered associates of the Prophet reaches well into the millions each year but especially on the Muslim holiday of Ashura.

The goal of pilgrims on the hajj, of course, is to circumambulate the Ka'aba, a large block-like structure said to contain the footprints of Abraham set in stone. Among other holy sites, the Al-Aqsa mosque in Jerusalem contains the porch upon which Muhammad is said to have been transported from Mecca. The winged creature that conveyed him, the Buraq, is often depicted as having the head of a man and body of a winged-steed. The story of the Night Journey (sura 17) in which Muhammad alights from the mosque in Mecca to Al-Aqsa culminates with the Prophet's ascendency to heaven to converse with Allah.

Muslim philosophy and literature have routinely weighed in on the concept of the miraculous. Whether Suni or Shia, Muslims are routinely instructed that miracles are not essential as proof for faith or in testing the veracity of a prophet's words. Muslim philosophers, following Al-Ghazali, do not wish to detract from the edifying effects of miracle narratives either. Many prop them up as counterarguments against the naturalist perspective that holds that natural causes are the only explanation for unusual phenomena. Most, however, do not stress their importance at all and simply relegate them to the realm that lies beyond human understanding. By no means is this an admission of defeat. Rather, it elevates the value of scientific discovery of the natural world and suggests that technological advances will one day clarify that which remains obscure today.

Patrick J. Hayes

Further Reading

Hoffman, Valerie. *Sufism, Mysticism, and Saints in Modern Egypt*. Columbia: University of South Carolina Press, 1995.

Meri, J. W. "Aspects of Baraka (Blessings) and Ritual Devotion among Medieval Muslims and Jews." *Medieval Encounters* 5 (1999): 46–69.

Najarzadegan, Fathullah. "An Examination of the Literary Miracle of the Qur'an as Evidence That a Science of Qur'anic Exegesis Is Possible." *Journal of Shi'a Islamic Studies* 4(2) (Spring 2011): 199–217.

Østebø, Terje. "Claims for Authority at the Shrine of Shaykh Husayn, Ethiopia." *Journal of Islamic Studies* (March 2014).

Schimmel, Annemarie. *Mystical Dimensions of Islam*. Chapel Hill: University of North Carolina Press, 2013.

Takim, Liyakat N. *The Heirs of the Prophet: Charisma and Religious Authority in Shi'ite Islam*. Albany: SUNY Press, 2012.

Waines, David. *The Odyssey of Ibn Battuta: Uncommon Tales of a Medieval Adventurer*. London: I. B. Tauris, 2010.

Yazicioglu, Isra. "Re-Defining the Miraculous: Al-Ghazālī, Ibn Rushd, and Said Nursi on Qur'anic Miracle Stories." *Journal of Qur'anic Studies* 13(2) (2011): 86–108.

Yazicioglu, Isra. *Understanding Quranic Miracle Stories in the Modern Age*. University Park: Penn State University Press, 2013.

Italy, Miracles in

Rare is the town or city in Italy that cannot boast of some miracle or is the host for some saint's tomb or shrine. Whether in urban centers or on rural roadsides, there can be found shrines to the Madonna faithfully tended by the devout. Though not always the case, Italian miracles are frequently hallmarked by their economy of exchange. Prayer is promised to a local saint before the tomb or in the relic chapel in return for favors. When a saint does not make good on the fulfillment of the request, the clients can withdraw their esteem, and the saint's popularity can decrease. The more a saint delivers miraculous favors, the greater the belief in the saint's power to intervene with God and the wider the saint's renown. This type of popular piety has been supported financially by Church authorities. Their rationale is simple: why spend good money on extravagant honorifics to local saints if their miracles are not real? Italian miracles have been routinely subjected to the scrutiny of local bishops from Lombardy in the north to Sicily in the south. Popularity of the cult, however, is often outside their control.

Given the long association with Christianity, Italians have witnessed a highly creative array of spectacles over the centuries. It is also a country of important firsts in the history of miracles. Not only was Italy the first country to have a saint officially canonized by the pope (Saint Homobonus of Cremona in 1199), but the rules for canonization—including the acknowledgment and function of miracles—were established in its territories. Italy, and Rome especially, were the sources for the translation of relics across the Alps, which were ensconced in new altars of churches across Europe. An air of importance arose in Italy. It was a bastion of sanctity, and the merits of its saints had accrued a privileged status throughout Christendom.

Pagan Italy often came to terms with Christian influences through its witnessing and recording of miracles, and these helped to spread the faith. In the second century Milan was evangelized by Saint Juventius, a missionary bishop from Pavia. He performed a miracle among the Milanese and then baptized the crowd of onlookers, who fell into immediate belief. Shortly thereafter he established a church community, ordaining priests before returning to the mother church at Pavia. The *Roman Martyrology* is filled with similar stories of missionary Christians who were able to convert large groups or families and whose fame of sanctity was tested by the sword.

Martyrs' cults, especially in fourth-century Rome, were a means toward legitimating episcopal authority. Those in office were able to use their powers of governance and teaching to discern whose cult was legitimate and whose were not. Sometimes popes were also recipients of supernatural communications, as when Pope Damasus (d. 384) received a vision of a martyr telling of the place of his burial. But it was also the job of bishops to determine if miracles at the tombs could be verified. Catacombs fell under episcopal oversight for their preservation and access. The miracles reported in these places were given approbation by church authorities. Few were declined this privilege.

The importance of bones and other relics cannot be understated for the growth of Christianity in Italy and for the development of Italian culture itself. Saint Gaudentius was a Brescian bishop from 387 to 410. Recalled from a pilgrimage to Jerusalem to be consecrated to this see, he returned laden with relics acquired on this trip and established a basilica to house them called the Concilium Sanctorum, which now forms part of the Basilica of St. John the Baptist in Brescia. Of prime importance for this church was the supposed relic of the Baptist—his head— which the Synoptic Gospels maintain was removed at the request of Herodias's daughter by King Herod (Mark 6:14–29; Matthew 14:1–12; Luke 9:7–9). Oversight of these relics was not an exact science. There have been several places that now claim to possess the head of the Baptist. Provenance over these relics, however, testify to their originality and authenticity. The bodies of Jesus's apostles buried in Italy—nearly the entire group—are spread throughout Rome, Amalfi, and Venice, the most prominent being the tomb of Saint Peter, over which is the main altar of the massive basilica in the Vatican that bears his name.

Eucharistic miracles have been plentiful. In the *Life of Pope St. Gregory the Great*, written about 787 by Paul the Deacon, the story is recounted of the pope's celebration of the Mass at which a communicant was refused the Eucharist for her disbelief in the real presence of Christ. Gregory petitioned God for some sign to convince this person, and the host became like flesh and blood in front of them both. The communicant showed deep remorse at her disbelief, and the scene was ingrained in numerous portrayals over the centuries. The host, which remained enfleshed, is in a reliquary chapel dedicated to the miracle in the Benedictine monastery at Anechs, Germany. Another famed story reproduced in innumerable images is that of Saint Anthony of Padua, who is said to have made a donkey bend its knee at the presence of the Eucharistic species.

Of all the Neapolitan miracles, there are perhaps none more well known than the liquification of the otherwise coagulated blood of San Gennaro (Saint Januarius) of Naples (d. 305). The blood of this martyr is encased in an ampule and enshrined in the cathedral. The regularity with which this miracle occurs—at least three times per year—captivated the English visitor of the eighteenth and nineteenth centuries or became the stuff of their derision of alleged Catholic superstitions. Neapolitans place great significance on this miracle, as they believe that the prosperity of the city depends upon it. When Napolean's army stormed Naples, the cathedral priests declared that the liquification would not take place on the first Saturday of May, as per usual. The Neapolitans did not take the news well, and disorder ensued, resulting in the death of some French soldiers. On the first Saturday at eight o'clock in the evening as the crowds began moving through the streets, a French officer instructed the cathedral rector to produce the miracle or be shot. The blood liquified on cue, but Neapolitans were so disillusioned by the collaboration of their patron saint that his image was thrown into the sea. Some in the Campania region believe that liquification of coagulated blood is, while hardly common, not unusual. The liquification of the blood of Saint John the Baptist and Pantaleo also takes place in this part of Italy.

The festal celebrations of local saints have become part of the Italian norm. On January 17, for instance, several Italian towns, especially in the Abruzzo, celebrate the Festa di Sant'Antonio Abate (Feast of Saint Anthony the Abbot), also known as Saint Anthony the Great. This Egyptian saint is particularly important throughout southern Italy and is the patron saint of butchers, domestic animals, basket makers, and gravediggers. Typically, the feast includes the blessing of farm animals either in the church or on the farm. His intercession is supposed to protect supplicants from skin diseases, especially shingles, known in Italian as "Fuoco di Sant'Antonio" (Fire of Saint Anthony). Saint Anthony the Abbot was a hermit of the third century and is considered the father of eremitical monasticism. His temptations in the desert form the bulk of the legends surrounding him, but despite repeated visits from demons, his prayer life remained firm. The Feast of Saint Anthony the Abbott is celebrated with processions, music, and especially bonfires, as one legend claims that he went to hell to steal the devil's fire—a feat he accomplished with some artistry. Participants in the feast, especially in rural areas, can be seen dancing around with devil masks. The eve of the feast finds peasants going house to house singing for food that will be consumed the following day.

Bodily fluids are often the subject or source of miracles but particularly among Italian saints. Additionally, there is a peculiar oral fixation among some saints and the working of their miracles. Raymond of Capua's *Life of St. Catherine of Siena* notes how Saint Catherine would drink the pus of the sick she nursed. The Franciscan tertiary and mystic Angela of Foligno (d. 1309) would ingest the bath water of the lepers she tended and once commented on a scab stuck in her throat, calling it "sweet as communion." Saint Catherine of Bologna (d. 1463) would lick the sores of her fellow sisters to reach the heights of spiritual perfection, healing them in the process. Her incorrupt body is encased in a glass box and remains on display in the Convent of the Poor Clares in Bologna. In the case of Saint Maria Maddalena de' Pazzi (1566–1607), a Carmelite nun in Florence, she licked the putrefying sores of two of her fellow sisters and sucked the wounds of others. Though she heals them by her actions, the otherwise repugnant tasks show this nun's saintly heroism in overcoming worldly fears and unquestionably raises the bar for what counts for sanctity.

Holiness is not reserved for adults, and Italian children often bear the mark of the miraculous. Saint Catherine of Siena, at the age of seven, went out of the city gates into an imagined desert to pray one day. She sought the permission of the Blessed Virgin Mary to enter a spiritual betrothal to her son Jesus. Soon Catherine found herself levitating in ecstasy while conversing with a vision of Mary holding the Christ child. The Madonna placed a ring on Catherine's finger, sealing the marriage. So close was her relation to Jesus that Catherine later experienced a spiritual stigmata, that is, the actual pain of the wounds of Christ in her hands, feet, and side, though without the visible wounds. In early modern Italy, many young women who sought a holy life were dubbed a "second Catherine" and strove to be living saints. For instance, a Venetian girl, Angela Maria Pasqualigo, began to live a holy life as soon as she reached the age of reason. She soon began to fast three days each week, and one day she swooned and fell head-first into a fireplace. When she was retrieved from the fire, not a hair on her head was singed, replicating an episode that was reported to have happened also to Catherine. The story repeats with the twentieth-century mystic of Lucca in Tuscany, Saint Gemma Galgani (d. 1903), who, like Catherine, experienced stigmata and visions during her brief life. She died at age 25.

Italy is practically a showcase for miraculous objects—the more unusual the better. The so-called Girdle of St. Thomas the Apostle is currently in the Tuscan cathedral in Prato in the Capella del Sacro Cingolo. Legend holds that the Virgin Mary, on the occasion of her assumption into heaven, dropped a cincture into the hands of Saint Thomas as she departed Earth. The relic of this knotted belt has special significance for pregnant women. It eventually became the subject of numerous works of the masters of late medieval and Renaissance art, such as the

Oddi Altarpiece by Raphael and Pinturicchio's *Madonna della Cintola*. Periodically the reliquary of the cincture is exposed by the archbishop for veneration by the faithful.

For all the miraculous objects strewn around Italy—from the Shroud of Turin in the north to the smallest Sicilian chapels—the most important element of their power is the kind of behaviors they elicit from the faithful. People from around the globe are drawn to Rome, for instance, on pilgrimage to the holy sites, among which is the Carceri of Sts. Peter and Paul, near the Forum. This dank cistern was the place in which the apostles were held before their execution for being Christians. It is literally a hole in the ground. There is no grandeur about it, nothing to marvel at except the tablet on the wall indicating the cell's purpose. The stark reality that awaits visitors to this cell places the whole panoply of miracles in perspective. There is a deep connection between the living and the dead.

Patrick J. Hayes

See also: Art and Miracles; Eucharistic Miracle of Siena; Eucharistic Miracles of Lanciano; Homobonus of Cremona; Lepanto, Battle of; Shroud of Turin

Further Reading

Apolito, Paolo. *Apparitions of the Madonna at Oliveto Citra*. Translated by William A. Christian. University Park: Penn State University Press, 1998.

Bell, Rudolph M., and Cristina Mazzoni. *The Voices of Gemma Galgani*. Chicago: University of Chicago Press, 2003.

Benvenuti, Anna, and Marcello Garzaniti. *Il tempo dei santi tra Oriente e Occidente: Liturgia e agiografia dal tardo antico al concilio di Trent, Atti del IV Convegno di studio dell'Associazione italiana per lo studio della santità, dei culti e dell'agiografia. Firenze, 26–28 ottobre 2000*. Rome: Viella, 2005.

Benvenuti, Anna, et al. *Storia della santità nel cristianesimo occidentale*. Sacro/Santo 9. Rome: Viella, 2005.

Cadogan, Jean K. "The Chapel of the Holy Belt in Prato: Piety and Politics in Fourteenth-Century Tuscany." *Artibus et Historiae* 30:60 (2009): 107–137.

Carroll, Michael P. *Veiled Threats: The Logic of Popular Catholicism in Italy*. Baltimore: Johns Hopkins University Press, 1996.

Del Santo, Matthew. "Gregory the Great and Eustratius of Constantinople: The Dialogues on the Miracles of the Italian Fathers as an Apology for the Cult of Saints." *Journal of Early Christian Studies* 17(3) (2009): 421–457.

Garnett, Jane. "Miraculous Images and the Sanctification of Urban Neighborhood in Post-Medieval Italy." *Journal of Urban History* 32 (2006): 729–740.

Garnett, Jane, and Gervase Rosser. *Spectacular Miracles: Transforming Images in Italy from the Renaissance to the Present*. London: Reaktion Books, 2013.

Holmes, Megan. "Miraculous Images in Renaissance Florence." *Art History* 34 (2011): 433–465.

Kaftal, George. *Iconography of the Saints in North East Italy*. Florence: Sansoni, 1978.

Kaftal, George. *Iconography of the Saints in North West Italy*. Florence: Sansoni, 1985.

Luongo, F. Thomas. *The Saintly Politics of Catherine of Siena*. Ithaca, NY: Cornell University Press, 2006.

Morrison, Molly. "Strange Miracles: A Study of the Peculiar Healings of St. Maria Maddelena de' Pazzi." *Logos: A Journal of Catholic Thought and Culture* 8(1) (2005): 129–144.

Peterson, Janine Larmon. "Contested Sanctity: Disputed Saints, Inquisitors, and Communal Identity in Northern Italy, 1250–1400." PhD dissertation, Indiana University, 2006.

Peterson, Janine Larmon. "The Politics of Sanctity in Thirteenth-Century Ferrara." *Traditio* 63 (2008): 307–326.

Saghy, Marianne. "Martyr Cult and Collective Identity in Fourth-Century Rome." In *Identity and Alterity in Hagiography and the Cult of Saints*, edited by Ana Marinković and Trpimir Vedriš, 17–36. Bibliotheca Hagiotheca Series I. Zagreb: Leykam International, 2010.

Sansterre, Jean-Marie. "Praesentia sacrée et virtus entre reliques et images: À propos des miracles des saints au-delà de l'Italie, du XIIIe au XVe siècle." *Hagiographica* 20 (2013): 25–78.

Sansterre, Jean-Marie. "Virtus des saints, images, et reliques dans les miracles de guérison ou d'autres bienfaits en Italie du VIIIe au XVe siècle." *Hagiographica* 20 (2013): 25–78.

Schutte, Anne Jacobson. *Aspiring Saints: Pretense of Holiness, Inquisition, and Gender in the Republic of Venice, 1618–1750*. Baltimore: Johns Hopkins University Press, 2001.

Vocino, Giorgia. "Under the Aegis of the Saints: Hagiography and Power in Early Carolingian Northern Italy." *Early Medieval Europe* 22(1) (2014): 26–52.

J

Jansenism

Jansenism was a theological movement that was based on the principles of Cornelius Jansen (1585–1683), the bishop of Ypres. His digest of the older teachings of Saint Augustine (354–430) aided in driving a wedge among members of the Catholic Church in France during the seventeenth century. Jansen's approach to the miraculous, while not insignificant, grew to be a cause célèbre in the aftermath of his death.

Jansen's doctrine was formulated in his manuscript *Augustinus*. It was posthumously published in 1640 and resembled in some ways parts of Calvinism and Puritanism. His main arguments were that (1) the official theology of his age was too scholastic and not particularly evangelical, (2) theology itself remained too dialectical, and (3) it could no longer have an influence on popular religion. The three main points Jansen set his focus on were used to explain that spiritual and religious experience, and not reason, were the decisive principles of faith. In contrast to the ceremonialists of his time, Jansen stated that it was not the visit to the church and the Mass itself that could save a human from hell; only the love of God himself could lead to salvation. Due to this, Jansen defined the relationship between divine grace and human freedom during the process of the final salvation in a new way.

Miracles, of course, were part of this new understanding. Sitting on the fulcrum between the immanent and the transcendent, they could not but show that God's love was more than abundant for salvation. What was not needed was more Paternosters, Jansenists argued, but deeper faith in supernatural realities. According to these theological reformers, God's plan for the world was already determined; miracles served to prick our awareness of this fact. They underlined that not all human beings were scheduled to be saved. Indulgences—both in practice and theory—were futile.

These ideas were popularly received in France, where Antoine Arnauld (1612–1694) published his book *Communion* in 1643, which provided the first public discussion of Jansenist ideas. These led to a conflict with the Jesuits, who were accused of granting absolution too easily. Additionally, in the following decades there was a criticism of the absolutist ambitions of French king Louis XIV (1638–1715), which would lead to a conflict between the pope and the king of France. In 1653 Pope Innocent X declared Jansenism to be heretical, and his action sparked theological turmoil in France until 1669, when Clement IX reestablished peace.

The papal bull *Unigenitus* (1713) marked the beginning of the end of the new theology in France. It condemned over 100 tenets held by Jansen and his followers. Unable to maintain their community in France, the Jansenists fled to Holland, where some survived further harassment. By 1724 Jansenism and its supporters had broken with Rome, but the influence of the new heretical theology would reach Italy as well, and its influence, although remote, was traceable during the Synod of Pistoia in 1786.

Therefore, it is not possible to say that Jansenism died a quiet death. Rather, it had resurgent moments. About 1728 the miracles at St. Médard presented a new wrinkle in the Jansenist narrative. It was in the cemetery at St. Médard that a deacon, Francois de Paris, was interred. Known for his piety, he was also a fervent opponent of *Unigenitus*, and when claims of miracles began to emanate from those who visited his tomb, Jansenists took it as a sign from God that their position was correct. The government response was decisive. It closed the cemetery in 1732.

Frank Jacob

See also: Augustine, Saint; Convulsionnaires of St. Médard; France, Miracles in; Indulgences

Further Reading

Doyle, William. *Jansenism: Catholic Resistance to Authority from the Reformation to the French Revolution*. New York: Palgrave Macmillan, 2000.

Maire, Catherine-Laurence. *De la cause de Dieu à la cause de la Nation: Le jansénisme au XVIIe siècle*. Paris: Gallimard, 1998.

Strayer, Brian E. *Suffering Saints: Jansenists and Convulsionnaires in France, 1640–1799*. Brighton, UK: Sussex Academic Press, 2008.

Van Kley, Dale. *The Religious Origins of the French Revolution: From Calvin to the Civil Constitution, 1560–1791*. New Haven, CT: Yale University Press, 1996.

Vidal, Daniel. *Miracles et convulsions jansénistes au XVIIIe siècle: Le mal et sa connaissance*. Paris: PUF, 1987.

Jerusalem

While the Hebrew Bible never articulates a precise rationale for the special status of Eretz Yisraeil (Land of Israel) in God's cosmic scheme, rabbinic literature, which coins the term "Eretz Kedoshah" (Holy Land), is replete with claims and narratives about the unique and miraculous nature of the land. The supernatural feats and features associated with Israel only continue to multiple in subsequent religious writings up to the present day.

Jerusalem (Yerushalyim, 'Ir David, 'Ir ha-Kodesh) in particular is regarded as the site of regular miraculous occurrences. Some traditions assume that the numinous nature of the city is grounded in the fact that it was the location of the divinely mandated Temple (Heichel, Beit ha-Mikdash), while other Jewish miracle traditions are premised on the Neoplatonic idea that God initiated the creation of the world at the point that is now Jerusalem and that the formation of Earth radiated out from there, with farther lands possessing decreasing gradients of holiness (*Midrash Tanhuma*, Kedoshim 10; *Gen. Rabbah* 3:9, 8:20; *Leviticus Rabbah* 24:4). Regardless of the premise, Jerusalem is perceived to be the nexus point between heaven and Earth, the earthly counterpart to Yerushalyim shel Malah, the "celestial Jerusalem" (Babylonian Talmud [BT], *Ta'anit* 5a; *Midrash Tanhuma*, Pikudei 1).

The miraculous aspects of Jerusalem were most common when the Temple stood. The city smelled of cinnamon (BT, *Shabbat* 63a), no houses would catch fire, and no woman miscarried (*Avot de Rabbi Natan* 35).

The Temple itself was the product of a miraculous method of construction, the *shamir* worm (*Gen. Rabbah* 2:5; *Pasikta Rabbatai* 6), and continued to be the site of almost daily wonders (M. Avot 5; BT, *Yoma* 21a–b, 37b, 39a; *Lev. Rabbah* 20:4). Divine theophanies on the Temple precinct continued (BT, *Berachot* 7b).

Earthly Jerusalem in the interregnum between the destruction of the Temple and the coming of the eschatological messiah is still a place where more modest wonders (miraculous healings, cures for barrenness, revelatory encounters) occur, most often in association with the Temple Mount and the Western Wall but also with select synagogues (i.e., the Elijah Synagogue in the Old City) and the purported graves of dead luminaries, such as King David's tomb on Mount Zion.

In the Messianic era, clear and manifest miracles will return to Jerusalem: the celestial Jerusalem will descend and merge with the physical Jerusalem (Pirkei de Rabbi Eliezer 21:4), and a purifying river will flow from the Holy of Holies, fructifying the whole world.

The Land of Israel at large is also a place of wonders. Aside from the many supernatural events documented in the Hebrew Scriptures, the land is dotted with the graves of celebrated Jewish figures that, starting in the late Middle Ages, perhaps in imitation of Christian and Islamic custom, became pilgrimage destinations where individuals may petition for intercessory assistance. There are many stories and folkloric accounts of divine responses to these petitions. There are also springs (the Banyah, Tiberius, and Beit Shean), small topographic locations (the Cavern of Elijah), and man-made features (the city of Safed) that are imbued with numinous power and are treated as shrines.

Among the most intriguing miracles of the Christian variety is the annual gift of the Holy Light at Christ's tomb in the Church of the Resurrection. The Orthodox patriarch of Jerusalem enters a small enclosure and, bereft of flint or match, emerges with two bunches of lit candles that are then passed to all the congregants' torches, illuminating the darkened church. The inexplicable ignition of these candles drives the masses into a spiritual frenzy.

Muslims too have enjoyed miracles in Jerusalem, perhaps the most famous being the landing of the Prophet Muhammad on the front portico of the Al-Aqsa mosque during the Night Flight, or Isra. While reposing one evening in Mecca, Allah took Muhammad to Jerusalem and back in the space of a night, a feat quite impossible under ordinary circumstances of the day. Given the sacred character of the mosque and its proximity to other holy sites for Christians and Jews, Jerusalem is counted among the most precious of all the world's cities.

Geoffrey Dennis

See also: Biblical Miracles; Islam and Miracles; Judaism and Miracles

Further Reading

Dennis, Geoffrey. *The Encyclopedia of Jewish Myth, Magic, and Mysticism.* Wooddale, MN: Llewellyn, 2007.

Gratz, Michael. "Miracles." In *Encyclopedia Judaica*, Vol. 12, cols. 74–81. New York: Macmillan, 1974.

Peters, F. E. *Jerusalem: The Holy City in the Eyes of Chroniclers, Visitors, Pilgrims, and Prophets from the Days of Abraham to the Beginnings of Modern Times.* Princeton, NJ: Princeton University Press, 1985.

Vilney, Zev. *The Sacred Land*, Vols. 1–3. Philadelphia: Jewish Publication Society, 1973–1978.

Jesuits and Miracles

The Jesuits may be known more commonly as teachers and preachers than miracle workers, but there are over fifty saints who were members of the Society of Jesus.

Each performed numerous miracles, in life and posthumously, through relics and images. Additional miracles can be attributed to Jesuit Blesseds or are associated with the Jesuits in other ways (including Jesuits as the recipients rather than creators of the miracle). The Jesuits' focus on forming images in the mind may account for the large number of visions experienced by Jesuits. Among the most well known are the vision of Christ in the chapel at La Storta by Ignatius of Loyola, foretelling the establishment of the order a few years later; the premonition of his own death by Luigi Gonzaga; and Francis Xavier's vision of himself in India years before his missionary work began. In addition, there are substantial numbers of miracles, notably healings, chronicled in the canonization records of the Jesuit saints.

An examination of Jesuits and miracles must begin with the Society of Jesus's founder, Ignatius of Loyola. Although the canonization process of Ignatius was stalled briefly in the late sixteenth century because his biography did not adequately emphasize his miracles, he did perform them. Later editions of his life story focused on his miracles to a greater extent, leading to his beatification and canonization. Like most saints, the majority of miracles associated with Ignatius are those of healing. His own life as a religious man may be attributed to the intercession of a saint, Peter, who appeared to Ignatius while the former soldier was recovering from a leg injury suffered at the Battle of Pamplona (1521). Peter cured him, and the life of Ignatius was irrevocably changed. Even before they were canonized, Peter Paul Rubens produced paintings of both Ignatius and his companion, Francis Xavier, performing healing miracles.

The first two Jesuits beatified—in 1605, before either Ignatius or Xavier—were the novices Stanislaus Kostka and Luigi Gonzaga, although they were not canonized until 1726. Due to their youth (they died at ages 17 and 23, respectively), they are the patrons of children and students, and many of their miracles involve healing young people.

The missionary Francis Xavier was a saint much invoked during plague outbreaks in seventeenth-century Naples. This was likely the consequence of the wide distribution of prints with his image that had circulated as the result of an earlier healing he had performed in that city. In 1634 a Jesuit priest, Marcello Mastrilli, was close to death as the result of a head injury when Francis Xavier spoke to him from an image close to the priest's bed. He offered Mastrilli the choice of death or undertaking a planned mission to Japan. Mastrilli returned to life and eagerly embarked on the missionary life. In Goa en route to Japan three years later, he visited the tomb of the saint there. Mastrilli was disappointed in its form, and the commissioning of the silver casket now encasing Xavier's body stems from this visit. Mastrilli proceeded on to Japan and was martyred there in October 1637, still carrying an image of Xavier. Mastrilli's fellow Neapolitans also continued to venerate images of the saint, especially in times of plague (such as the 1656 outbreak).

Francis Xavier is also known for his incorrupt body, and miracles of healing have occurred at the tomb in Goa as well as at the sites of other relics, for example, his arm now in Il Gesu in Rome.

A number of miracles involve Jesuit missionaries beyond Father Mastrilli. Records from the North American missions suggest many healings connected to the Jesuits, although they were also accused of witchcraft when they could not control outbreaks of disease. People still venerate the image of Francis Xavier and leave votive offerings at the Mission Church of San Xavier del Bac in Arizona, established by Father Eusebio Francisco Kino. One very interesting miracle involves Father Ignatius de Azevedo and his 39 Jesuit companions, martyred while sailing to Brazil in 1570. It does not involve them being saved—they did in fact perish after their ship was attacked by Protestants. Without witnesses their case for canonization was stalled, however. Their arrival in heaven was seen by Teresa of Ávila in a vision, and her description led to their eventual beatification. Finally, eight German Jesuits stationed in Japan during World War II survived the atomic blast at Hiroshima, attributing this miracle to their faith.

Alison C. Fleming

Further Reading

Duffin, Jacalyn. *Medical Miracles: Doctors, Saints, and Healing in the Modern World.* New York: Oxford University Press, 2009.

San Juan, Rose Marie. *Vertiginous Mirrors: The Animation of the Visual Image and Early Modern Travel.* Manchester, UK: Manchester University Press, 2011.

Tylenda, Joseph. *Jesuit Saints & Martyrs.* 2nd ed. Chicago: Loyola University Press, 1998.

Jesus, Miracles of

The miracle narratives of Jesus reveal Jesus's salvific power as he intervenes in situations of human misery, bringing peace to those desperate petitioners. In this statement are the two kinds of revelation provided by the miracle stories: the revelation of Jesus's powers over nature and over evil forces and the revelation of Jesus's person in his response of mercy and compassion.

Given that Mark's gospel, the earliest of the four gospels, postdates Jesus's life by over 30 years, the miracle stories that survived until then and are now embedded and contextualized by that gospel had already proved themselves powerfully significant to the Christian communities that went before. The significance of Jesus's miracle stories for early Christians is manifold. Unlike the sayings of Jesus or the parables where he teaches, miracle stories show Jesus in action responding to a variety of petitioners, some of them, it must be said, who are bold and even rude in their behavior. A good example is found in the Markan account of Jesus healing the leper (Mark 1:40–45, cf. Matthew 8:1–4 and Luke 5:12–14). The leper is far too close to Jesus on both social and religious grounds, and we can tell this because Jesus has only to reach out to touch him. The leper is rather rough in his speech as well: "If you wanted to, you could make me clean" (Mark 1:40). Listeners might expect Jesus to reprove this man, but instead he closes the distance between them, touching him and responding to his rough petition with reassurance: "Of course I want to be made clean!" The leprosy instantly leaves the man, but the story has shown us that the narrator desires more of the listener than simply to notice Jesus's power. Jesus's compassion and his recognition of the man's misery took supremacy over expectations of social and religious rules of propriety. The miracle story reveals Jesus, both his power and his person. It also calls for would-be followers to demonstrate the same understanding.

What type of miracle is operative in the narratives? Most deal in some way with mercy. The miracle stories of Jesus can be seen to bear some resemblance to those of the prophets Elijah and Elisha, and these allusions are deliberate, since Jesus is the fulfillment of God's salvific plan in Christian teaching. But the differences are notable in that Jesus does not need to pray for God to intervene but himself wills nature to restore the person, a command instantly affected.

The Greco-Roman world hosted abundant miracle workers: holy prophetic seers, magicians, and the usual marketplace wonder-workers. A listener to a Jesus miracle might at first see little difference between his miracles and those of others, and in fact today's scholarly attempts to distinguish them result in awkward and artificial arguments. Rather, Jesus miracles require the context of the Christian attestation of Jesus as God's only Son. This is made explicit in the beginnings of the four gospels so that all the miracle stories are plainly understood as nature's recognition of Jesus as God's Son on Earth.

It was Rudolf Bultmann who first categorized the various miracles of the Synoptic Gospels (Matthew, Mark, and Luke) into four main classes: healings, exorcisms, raisings from the dead, and nature miracles.

In the healing miracles, Jesus restores wholeness to the person instantly. Since nature was seen as a rational force, the Greco-Roman person would understand that it was completely submissive to Jesus. The overall enormity of any healing miracle for persons in the first century is difficult for us to appreciate today. The only hospitals were located in the Roman army camps, so folk medicine was the refuge of most people. Some could afford to have a doctor come to the house, and the medical field was rather good for that time. Certain cures, however, were outside a doctor's capability. Jesus's cure of a man with dropsy (Luke 14:1–6) saves him from the horrors of the medical treatments so horrific that they caused Emperor Hadrian to commit a kind of suicide to avoid them. Jesus instantly cures a man with total paralysis that was considered fatal (Mark 2:1–12; cf., Matthew 9:1; Luke 5:17–20), and heals a crippled woman (Luke 13:12–17). He stops the twelve-year hemorrhage of a woman impoverished by seeking medical help (Mark 5:25–34; cf., Matthew 9:20–22; Luke 8:42–48) but, even more astonishingly, restores sight to the blind, something considered completely impossible (e.g., Mark 8:22–26, 10:45–52; Matthew 20:29–34, 18:35–43; John 9:1–12). Other miracles show Jesus quietly curing Peter's mother-in-law's fever (Mark 1:29–31; Matthew 8:14–15, 4:38–39) and compassionately restoring a man's withered hand (Mark 3:1–6; 12:9–14; Luke 6:6–11). Moreover, Jesus need not even be present for his will to be obeyed, as made clear in the story of Jesus's cure of the Centurion's houseboy (Matthew 8:5–13; Luke 7:1–10).

An exorcism is the expulsion of an evil spirit, a demon. In the Greco-Roman world there was a widespread belief that evil demons existed and could take advantage of any opening a person gave to possess the person, ridiculing and torturing the person with the intent to kill. Jesus's exorcisms are so instant and so complete that they emphasize the total authority that the demons recognize, instantly capitulating and relinquishing their prize possession at his command or just his very presence. The source of Jesus's authority is made plain when the demons call out his identity as "the Holy One of God" (Mark 1:21–27; Luke 4:31–36) or "Son of the Most High God" (Mark 5:1–20; Matthew 8:28–33; Luke 8:3–9). The circumstances surrounding these exorcisms are terrifying and profoundly poignant. A father has his long-demonized son restored to him (Mark 9:14–29; Matthew 17:14–20; Luke 9:37–43). Jesus does not need to be present for the exorcisms either, as shown in the story of the foreign woman's daughter exorcized at a distance through the will of Jesus (Mark 7:24–30; Matthew 15:21–28). These stories underline the safety to be found when one is united with Jesus.

Modern interpreters who recast these stories as Jesus healing mental illness remove this particular and distinct attestation of his cosmic authority: his supremacy over the personified evil entities. Mental illness was known in the first century, with treatments prescribed. Certainly there must have been confusion between the two situations, but the narrator means that the victim was possessed by a demon. Indeed, Jesus's actions in the story are for the expulsion of a demon, not a healing. Modern difficulties over the veracity of the existence of demons are better to avoid the accounts altogether rather than misinterpreting the attestation as a natural healing.

Jesus's restoration of life to Jairus's dead daughter (Mark 5:35–43; Matthew 9:23–26; Luke 8:49–56) and to the widow of Nain's dead son (Luke 7:11–17) illustrate the ultimate power of Jesus to reverse the greatest of terrors, which is death. These miracle stories also affirm Jesus's recognition of the importance of life itself here on Earth. In the context of the gospel, Jesus's promising of the coming kingdom of God then shows that this kingdom is one that treasures ongoing life to the full with God forever.

In the stilling of the storm (Mark 4:35–41; Matthew 8:23–27; Luke 8:22–25) and the walking on water (Mark 6: 45–52; Matthew 14:22–33; John 6:1–15), it would be plain to the Greco-Roman listener that nature's forces recognize Jesus as having full and complete cosmic power. Thus, Jesus cannot be drowned by a storm or swallowed by waves if he wishes to traverse the waters. The cosmic character of Jesus's power over nature needs to be contextualized by the circumstances whereby human vulnerability is served by these enormous miracles. The fear of the disciples explains both Jesus stopping the storm by ordering the elements to silence and his ending his own walk on the water, at the screams of the terrified disciples who happened to see him. The multiplication of the loaves and fishes (Mark 6:30–44; Matthew 14:13–21; Luke 9:10–17; John 6:1–15) is a response to the adamant crowd who insist on staying to hear Jesus teach and risk fainting from hunger as a result. When modern commentators reinterpret this miracle as an actual sharing of food that everyone had brought due to Jesus's teaching on love, they contradict the narrator, who wishes to say that Jesus's compassion and his great cosmic power come together to serve the people who are so needy for God's word that they risk their own strength to return home unfed. Discomfort over nature miracles is not sufficient method-wise to change the miracle to a story of generous sharing.

In the interpretation of all the miracle story types, the kind of power and authority that Jesus exerts is always in a context of mercy and compassion and respect for each person no matter what their class or status. Thus, the teaching of Jesus that power must always be used in service of the neediest finds its exemplification in these ancient and revealing accounts of his miracles.

Wendy Cotter

Further Reading

Achtemeier, Paul, J. *Jesus and the Miracle Tradition*. Eugene, OR: Cascade Books, 2008.

Cotter, Wendy. *The Christ of the Miracle Stories: Portrait through Encounter*. Grand Rapids, MI: Baker Academic, 2010.

Ferguson, Everett. *Demonology of the Early Christian World*. Symposium Series 12. Lewiston and Queenston: Edwin Mellen, 1984.

Kee, Howard. *Medicine, Miracle and Magic in New Testament Times*. SNTSMS 55. Cambridge: Cambridge University Press, 1986.

Kee, Howard. *Miracle in the Early Christian World: A Study in Socio-Historical Method*. New Haven, CT: Yale University, 1983.

Kertelge, Karl. *Die Wunder Jesu im Markusevangelium: Eine redaktionsgeschichtliche Untersuchung.* SANT 33. Munich: Kösel, 1970.

Pilch, John. *Healing in the New Testament: Insights from Medical and Mediterranean Anthroplogy.* Minneapolis, MN: Fortress, 2000.

Twelftree, Graham. *Jesus the Exorcist: A Contribution to the Study of the Historical Jesus.* WUNT 54. Tübingen: J. C. B. Mohr. Paul Siebeck, 1993.

Judaism and Miracles

The Hebrew Bible is replete with reports of wondrous feats, variously called a "sign" (*nes, ot, mofet*) or "wonder" (*pele', nifla'*), performed on cosmic (Genesis 1–11), national (Exodus 7–15), and personal (Genesis 17–21) scales. Though some books forefront the miraculous (Exodus, Numbers, I Kings), others are virtually bereft of supernatural events (Esther, Ruth, most of the literary prophets).

The postbiblical reception of these miracles, and of numerous reports of contemporaneous wondrous events, varies dramatically throughout Jewish sources. In the absence of any doctrinal or ecclesiastic oversight, Jewish literature simultaneously preserves three fundamental positions: endorsing, skeptical, and apologetic. The endorsing position not only believes in the veracity of reports of marvels in the past but also affirms that signs and deeds of power continue to occur to them and around them. Skeptics question the fundamental truth of all miracle reports, while apologists argue that, properly understood, miracles are on some level not unnatural at all. All three positions are already evident in early rabbinic literature.

Many Jews endorse the reality of the miraculous, an attitude that remains a constant feature of Jewish life right up to modern times (Babylonian Talmud [BT], *Shabbat* 19a; *Midrash Rabbah Ruth*, 3; *Zohar* I: *Shivhei ha-Besht; Or-ha-Emet* 55b). Some Talmudic rabbis, such as Rabbi Akiba, have gone so far as to claim that God's miraculous interventions during the Exodus actually far exceeded the ones explicitly enumerated in the Torah ("Maggid" section, *Pesach Haggadah*). Others make a point of emphasizing the miraculous aspects of the Maccabean Revolt, which pitted the followers of Judah Maccabee against their Seleucid Greco-Syrian overlords (*Seder Rav Amram*). The Maccabees eventually recaptured Jerusalem when, in the course of rededicating the Temple, it is reported that a shortage of dedicatory oil was miraculously overcome (BT *Shabbat* 21a–23b). Even so, several Talmudic sages, with awe of God mixed with some tinge of skepticism, pointedly emphasize that the faithful should not rely on miracles to solve their problems (BT *Pesachim* 64b; *Taanit* 20b; *Kiddushin* 39b).

Other sages, both apologetic and skeptical, have felt bound to offer justification for the continuing value of biblical accounts of wondrous feats, even if such miracles had ceased in their own times. Hence, some put forward the argument that miracles are merely a subjective and perceptual rather than factual reward for the faithful (BT *Rosh ha-Shanah* 29a; *Exodus Rabbah* 23:5).

Other apologetics regarding miracles include interpretations predicated on the claim that marvels are not interruptions of natural mechanics but rather "preordained" natural events, programmed into the natural order by a prescient deity (*Genesis Rabbah* 4:5, 5:45; *Exodus Rabbah* 21:5; Mishna *Avot* 5–6; *Pirkei de Rabbi Eliezer* 19). Alternatively, some resolve the dearth of divine intervention in the recent history of Israel by arguing for a "parenthetical" structure to history; we live in a middle period, deliberately bereft of the wondrous. This is usually explained as the result of inferior devotion among the current faithful, and thus miracles will not return to the world until the messianic era (BT *Berachot* 20a; *Sanhedrin* 94b; *Taanit* 18b). In any case, the rabbis caution against appealing to God for miraculous intervention. Mishna 9:3, for example, pleading for God to reverse a current misfortune or to undo the past, constitutes a "vain prayer."

Even the rabbis who affirm the reality of the miraculous nonetheless continue to struggle with the biblical ambivalence (Deuteronomy 13:2–4) over the question of to what degree a miraculous event serves as proof of divine authorization of a person, theological position, or religious practice (BT *Baba Metzia* 59b). Even those who have embraced the miraculous wholeheartedly lean toward de-emphasizing the value of miracles as proof of a given doctrinal position or even as a tool for affirming belief (Mishneh *Torah, Hilkhot Melakhim*, 11:3). Signs and wonders play, for example, a far less conspicuous role in the Mishna and *Gemara* than they do in the contemporaneous Christian literature of the Gospels and testimonies of the saints.

The recognition that miracles are not to be expected, even for the most devout believer, takes hold postbiblically and is evident, for example, in the stories surrounding the Maccabean revolt against the Seleucid Empire, where stories of martyrdom are virtually bereft of miraculous aspects (I *Maccabees*, chap. 7).

Some effort is made to systematize the nature of the miraculous, though this is at best a sporadic endeavor. One form of miracle typology, articulated by the Bible commentator Nachmanides, is that of the "revealed" and "hidden" feat, with hidden miracles defined as the events that, in their consistency, constitute a wonder of predictability. The Talmud anticipates this taxonomy, labeling such mundane events as recovery from serious illness, or even swallowing, to be innately miraculous (BT *Nedarim* 41a; *Exodus Rabbah* 24:1).

The question of miracles deeply concerned the rationalist philosophers, because these defied the uniformitarianism undergirding medieval science and were predicated on the idea of a created world, a problematic stance in scholastic thought. Again, however, the main ideas staked out in rabbinic literature all find their rationalist champions. Saadia Gaon (d. 942) has no problem conceptually with the reality of marvels, which serve to affirm divine sanction (*Emunah v'Deot* 3:4–5). Maimonides (d. 1204), building on the "preordained natural event" argument found in Talmudic literature, adopts the model of miracles as "preordained" natural causation (*Moreh Nevukhim* II:29, III:25) but also finds some miracle reports to be allegorical rather than factual accounts (II:46–47). Nachamanides (d. 1270), championing ideas rooted in Jewish mysticism, argues that the very condition of the people of Israel is supernatural and that the "ends of Torah" supersede nature. Baruch Spinoza (d. 1677), by contrast, takes up the rabbinic argument for the subjectivity of signs and wonders, though with a more cynical slant.

Since the start of modernity, the diverse literature of Hasidism, composed on the cusp of the revolution of modernity, can either baldly assert the reality of miracles (*Midrash Pinchas* 16:5) or opt to render miracles as figurative reports of psychological and sociological states (*Itturei ha-Torah* 8:129). Martin Buber (d. 1965) and Abraham Heschel (d. 1972) follow Spinoza in acknowledging the subjective experience of their ancestors but with more enthusiasm, hoping that the modern Jew can cultivate a similar receptivity toward a sense of wonder at God's creation.

The skeptical thread of Jewish thought, further reinforced through the crucible of modernity, tends to dominate among modern Jews. Religious thinkers who frankly reject the reality of miracles are best represented by Mordecai Kaplan (d. 1983). While modernists such as Kaplan reject the objective reality of the miraculous, they nevertheless often seek to extract useful teachings from wondrous accounts by interpreting them in nonliteralist ways.

Contemporary faith in the miraculous is largely found among the antimodernity (ultraorthodox) movements of Judaism, the Haredi and the Hasidim. Building on the sixteenth- and seventeenth-century phenomenon of shaman-like *baalei shem* (masters of the [divine] name) and *wunder rebbes* (faith healers), Hasidic groups, in particular, still adhere to a belief, bordering on a doctrine, that the *tzaddik*, the charismatic leader of a given Hasidic community, is a wonder-worker, able to channel divine beneficence to his followers, nullifying or reversing on a small scale the order of nature (*Ohr ha-Emet* 55b). In Hasidic communities in particular, the numerous and oft-repeated miracle testimonies about spiritual leaders such as Baal Shem Tov (Ukraine, d. 1760), Shlomo of Karlin (Belarus, d. 1792), and the Seer of Lublin (Poland, d. 1815) serve an important faith-reinforcing function as Jews have found themselves plunging into the disorienting maelstrom of the Enlightenment and modernity. Several Hasidic thinkers, notably Menachem

Mendel of Kotzk (Poland, d. 1859), nonetheless criticized the Hasidic preoccupation with wonders (*Commentary on Psalm* 106:7).

Geoffrey Dennis

See also: Biblical Miracles

Further Reading

Arkush, Allan. "Miracle." In *Contemporary Jewish Religious Thought*, 621–625. New York: Free Press, 1985.

Buber, Martin. *Moses*. Oxford, UK: East and West Press, 1958.

Dennis, Geoffrey. "Healing," "Miracle," and "Righteous, the." In *Encyclopedia of Jewish Myth, Magic, and Mysticism*. Wooddale: Llewellyn, 2007.

Gratz, Michael. "Miracles." In *Encyclopedia Judaica*, 12:74–81. New York: Macmillan, 1974.

Heschel, Abraham J. *Man in Search of God: A Philosophy of Religion*. New York: Farrar, Straus and Giroux, 1964.

Kaplan, Mordecai. *Judaism without Supernaturalism*. New York: Macmillan, 1958.

Kaplan, Mordecai. *Questions Jews Ask*. Philadelphia: Reconstructionist Press, 1956.

Kohler, Kauffman. "Miracle." Jewish Encyclopedia, http://www.jewishencyclopedia.com/articles/10869-miracle.

Mackler, Aaron. "Eye on Religion: A Jewish View of Miracles of Healing." *Southern Medical Association* (2007): 1252–1254, https://pmr.uchicago.edu/sites/pmr.uchicago.edu/files/uploads/Mackler,%20Eye%20on%20Religion-%20a%20Jewish%20View%20on%20Miracles%20of%20Healing.pdf.

Rabinowicz, Tzvi. *The Encyclopedia of Hasidism*. Northvale, NJ: Jason Aronson, 1996.

Spinoza, Baruch. *Theological-Political Treatise*. Translated by R. H. Elwes. New York: Dover, 1955.

L

Labouré, Saint Catherine

Often a single experience in one's youth becomes an imperative or mission directing one's entire life. Such was the experience of Zoe Labouré (1806–1876), who at age nine was devastated by her mother's death. Resourceful, she climbed on a chair, embraced a statue of the Blessed Mother, and confidently declared "You shall be my mother now." Labouré followed Mary's "little way" of seeking God in humble, simple ways, staying aware of His presence in the events and encounters of the day. Labouré too would be glorified.

The Labourés were productive landowners and respected citizens within the village of Fain-les-Moutiers in Burgundy, France. While Zoe's parents were well educated, she remained illiterate until she entered the Daughters of Charity. After their mother's death, Zoe's sister Marie Louise assumed her mother's responsibilities, while Zoe and her sister Tonine lived with relatives. In 1818 Marie Louise entered the Daughters of Charity, and Zoe at age 12 took her place as mistress of the farm. In 1828, Zoe shared with her father her desire to become a Daughter of Charity. Her father rejected the request, and the next year when she repeated her request, he sent her to Paris to work in her brother's restaurant, where he hoped the excitement of the city would weaken her resolve. In January 1830, Zoe entered the community, with her brother providing her dowry because her father had refused.

Now known as Sister Catherine, she experienced spiritual favors and visions before the two Marian apparitions in 1830. While still at home, she had a dream in which a priest seemed to be calling her. She ran away frightened. The priest, whom she later identified as Saint Vincent, cautioned her that God had designs on her. In April 1830, Catherine participated in the transfer of Saint Vincent's relics to the motherhouse of the Congregation of the Mission on Rue du Sevres. Subsequently in the Chapel of Rue du Bac, Catherine saw a heart changing color, moving from white symbolizing peace to red symbolizing charity to a black that signaled future conflict and destruction. In addition, Catherine reported to her confessor Father Aladel that she often saw the person of Jesus in the Eucharistic host. He attributed these phenomena to her imagination and advised caution and humility.

On the night of July 18–19, 1830, the novice Catherine was summoned to the Chapel by a young child, presumably her angel, where she had the singular privilege of a two-hour conversation as she knelt with her folded hands on Mary's lap. The whole experience was one of brilliance and beauty. Mary told Catherine that God wanted to entrust her with a mission that would cause her great suffering, but she should not fear. Mary also spoke of the future political situation. The king would be toppled, but the communities would survive. When some of these predictions eventuated, Father Aladel listened more carefully to Catherine but still was not sympathetic.

On November 27 while at evening meditation in the chapel, Catherine heard the rustle of silk, and the first apparition of the medal occurred. Again in December, Catherine was summoned in the same way for the second medal apparition. Mary spoke of the delay and told Catherine that she would not see her again but that Catherine would continue to hear her voice. Catherine did not share this vision with Father Aladel.

On February 5, 1831, Catherine was missioned to the Enghien Hospice, where she served the old men in a variety of humble duties. In the fall of 1831, urged by Blessed Mother, Catherine went to Father Aladel and reported that the Virgin was not pleased. Father Aladel became troubled and consulted with his confrère Father Étienne, who then consulted with the archbishop of Paris. The first 1,500 medals were distributed in May 1832.

Her mission completed and her anonymity intact, Catherine continued over four decades to use the hands that rested on Mary's knees for service to the old men in Enghien. On December 31, 1876, Catherine died and was buried in a vault under the chapel at Enghien. Shortly thereafter a young boy regained his ability to walk after being led down to her tomb, and physical and spiritual miracles abounded. Catherine was declared a saint by Pius XII on July 27, 1947, and her incorrupt body lies now in the chapel at Rue du Bac, where hundreds visit each day.

Margaret John Kelly

See also: France, Miracles in; Miraculous Medal

Further Reading

Englebert, Omer. *Catherine Labouré and the Modern Apparitions of Our Lady*. New York: Kenedy, 1959.

Laurentin, René. *Catherine Labouré et la médaille miraculeuse: Documents authentiques, 1830–1876*. Paris: Lazaristes, 1976.

Laurentin, René. *The Life of Catherine Labouré*. London: Collins Publication, London 2001.

Lactation

Breast milk has taken on symbolic features based upon the physical activity of providing nutrition to newborns. It may also be seen as holding curative power or sustaining health. In the Middle Ages, the Christian West invested lactation with numerous curative properties, none of which could compare to the milk of the Blessed Virgin Mary. She is frequently depicted dispensing her milk, either with or without the Christ child suckling at her breast. The Madonna del Latte (Madonna of the Milk) was a common trope among European artists, such as Lorenzetti, Van Eyck, and Da Vinci. Invariably she shows tenderness to supplicants by delivering a stream of milk, usually into their mouths. The topoi of *Maria lactans* became commonplace by the fourteenth century.

According to William of Malmesbury, a twelfth-century theologian, Fulbert of Chartes (d. 1028) was cured when Mary offered him three drops of breast milk. The miracle, though, has less to do with Marian generosity and more to do with a mnemonic toward contemplation of the three persons of the Trinity. The Cistercian abbot Henry of Clairvaux (d. 1179), by most accounts an unlettered man, was filled with knowledge after imbibing from the breast of the Virgin. However, Henry's confrère, Saint Bernard of Clairvaux, is without rival for his association with *Maria lactans*. Around 1290 the first known representation of the Lactation appeared in Palma in Majorca, in an altarpiece showing Saint Bernard of Clairvaux receiving the holy liquid.

Lactation is often facilitated in a miraculous way through the use of amulets as well. Suckling is not always an easy process, and absent a wet nurse or proper instruction, a new mother sometimes employed this device to produce milk, believing that the secretion would flow readily if the talisman was applied. The same effect could also be sought through the ingestion of a small particle invested with sacral quality.

Some scholars have argued that the importance of lactation goes beyond gender. Jesus himself is sometimes portrayed as lactating. In the thirteenth century Thomas of Cantimpré, for instance, noted how the medieval mystic Lutgard of Aywières (d. 1246)—emerging from some delirium in order to do penance—saw Jesus in the doorway of a church, at which point she nursed from his side. By another account, when she suckled from Christ's breast, her saliva became sweet.

Patrick J. Hayes

See also: Cistercians and Miracles

Further Reading

Berlioz, Jacques. "La lactation de saint Bernard dans un *exemplum* et une miniature du *Ci nous dit* (début du XIVe siècle)." *Cîteaux: Commentarii cistercienses* 39 (1988): 270–284.

Bynum, Caroline Walker. *Holy Feast, Holy Fast: The Religious Significance of Food to Medieval Women*. Berkeley: University of California Press, 1987.

France, James. "The Heritage of Saint Bernard in Medieval Art." In *A Companion to Bernard of Clairvaux*, edited by Brian Patrick McGuire, 305–342. Leiden: E. J. Brill, 2011.

Hildburgh, W. L. "Some Spanish Amulets Connected with Lactation." *Folklore* 62(4) (December 1951): 430–448.

Newman, Barbara, ed., Margot H. King and Barbara Newman, trans. *The Collected Saints' Lives: Abbot John of Cantimpré, Christina the Astonishing, Margaret of Ypres, and Lutgard of Aywières*. Turnhout: Brepols, 2008.

Lambertini, Prospero (Pope Benedict XIV)

To those interested in miracles as attributes of sainthood as well as in connection with the natural sciences, Pope Benedict XIV is best known for his seminal treatise *De servorum Dei beatificatione et beatorum canonizatione*. It deals with the prerequisites for a Servant of God to be beatified and thereby recognized as blessed (*beatus*) and for the blessed person to be canonized and thereby recognized as a saint of the Catholic Church. Often referred to in early modern sources as *De can.*, the treatise deals in part with miracles and the testimonies and other proofs required to validate them. It was important for miracles to withstand legal and scientific scrutiny, because they were among the criteria, alongside heroic virtue and others, that allowed a Servant of God to be recognized posthumously as blessed. The same criteria, in addition to at least two proven miracles, then generally were required for a *beatus* to accede to the rank of saint.

Benedict XIV had begun composing the treatise under his birth name, Prospero Lambertini (b. 1675; pope, 1740–1758), when he was *promotor fidei* (promotor of the faith) within the Congregation of Rites. Lambertini was a *doctor utriusque iuris*, a specialist of both canon and civil law, and his work translates his concern for applying the pronouncements of the Council of Trent, especially the reforms of Pope Urban VIII, to ecclesiastical practices of his day. As *promotor fidei*, Lambertini was in charge of testing events that appeared miraculous, mainly unexpected cures but also apparitions, uncorrupted remains, lengthy fasting, heavenly portents, and ejection of demons. In application of the procedures of canonization, one of his duties was to raise any possible objection (*animadversio*) to an event being deemed a miracle. In doing so, he was arguing in effect against the candidate's entitlement to the rank of blessed or saint and therefore was known as the devil's advocate.

The assessment of miracles, as set forth in *De can.*, steers a course between devotional trends that, since the Counter-Reformation, had diverged markedly into mystical and antimystical currents. Lambertini's rationalistic examination of extraordinary phenomena involved appraising them against natural processes, but he also allowed for understanding them in the context of intimate communication with God. Realizing that human knowledge of the natural sciences is imperfect, he nevertheless argued that it was possible to distinguish between an unexplained natural occurrence and a miracle. His classification of types of miracle into those "above nature," "against nature," and "beyond/outside nature" (*supra, contra*, and *praeter naturam*, respectively) follows Thomas Aquinas. In keeping with other scholars of his day, Lambertini additionally devoted attention to the influence of the mind (variously called *phantasia* or *imaginatio*) on the body and things.

The definitive augmented and revised edition of *De can.* was published in Rome (Palearini, 1747–1751) within Benedict XIV's 12-volume complete works (volumes 1–4 contain *De can.*, volume 7 contains its appendices, and volume 8 contains the subject/name index). It was reedited in various forms during Lambertini's lifetime and thereafter, and the reviews and summaries of it that appeared in well-known eighteenth-century journals across Europe indicate that it was known to scholars even outside the Church. Lambertini's work thus offers one comprehensive view into perspectives on miracles among certain ecclesiastical, scientific, legal, and literary elites of the eighteenth century. A recent undertaking by the Congregation for Saints' Causes to translate *De can.* into modern Italian further demonstrates the vitality of Lambertini's work to the present day and is a tribute to its wealth of theological sources on miracles, examinations of miraculous events, and legal reasoning about miracles in the context of canonization.

Raeleen Chai-Elsholz

Further Reading

Fattori, Maria Teresa, ed. *Le Fatiche di Benedetto XIV: Origine ed evoluzione dei trattati di Prospero Lambertini (1675–1758)*. Rome: Edizioni di Storia e Letteratura, 2011.

Haynes, Renée. *Philosopher King: The Humanist Pope Benedict XIV*. London: Weidenfeld and Nicolson, 1970.

Saccenti, Riccardo. "Il *De Servorum Dei beatificatione et Beatorum canonizatione* di Prospero Lambertini, papa Benedetto XIV: Materiali per una ricerca." In *Le Fatiche di Benedetto XIV: Origine ed evoluzione dei trattati di Prospero Lambertini (1675–1758)*, edited by Maria Teresa Fattori, 121–152. Rome: Edizioni di Storia e Letteratura, 2011.

Vidal, Fernando. "Miracles, Science, and Testimony in Post-Tridentine Saint-Making." *Science in Context* 20 (2007): 481–508.

Late Antiquity, Miracles in

The miracles of ascetics, saints, bishops, and their relics and tombs played an important role in the development of Late Antique society and its institutions in both the East and the West. Miracles were most commonly described as wonders, marvels, portents, or signs—that is, events or experiences occurring outside the normal course of nature or society. The literary genre of paradoxography, collections of natural wonders and marvels, developed in the classical period. Hellenistic society displayed an increased interest in access to divine and saving power in the rising focus on theurgy and thaumaturgy as well as in the biographies of wonder-workers such as Apollonius of Tyana. Early Christianity embraced salvific miracles, such as healing and exorcism, and saw particular access to divine power in the heroic suffering and miracles that attended the lives and deaths of the martyrs. Augustine reflects this interest at the end of the fourth century, devoting an entire chapter of the *City of God* to listing the miracles of his own day that he has either heard reported or seen himself (*Civ.* 4.22.8). In the Late Antique societies of Byzantium and Christian Europe, miracles were seen increasingly as evidence of divine power, providing access for ordinary people in need in this period of transition and instability or affirmation for the developing institutions in church and society.

Constantine provides the most signal example of the latter. His Christian biographer Eusebius attributes his conversion and subsequent success in establishing Christian empire to divine power attested by miracles. Eusebius connects this with divine providence leading to the establishment of God's kingdom, quoting the Psalms: "Sing to the Lord a new song, for He has done marvels" (Psalm 98:1; *Hist. eccl.* 10.1). Miracles in this period are particularly associated with the rise of the ascetic as holy man and the role of the holy man in the building of Christian society. If Constantine is the model emperor, the model ascetic is Antony, made famous by the biography of Athanasius. His miracles are likewise signs of the power of God now present in Late Antique society. He says to his disciples, "To work signs does not belong to us—it is the work of the Savior" (*Vit. Ant.* 38). The demons resent Antony's appearance and incursion into the desert. Satan complains to him that "I no longer have a place—no weapon, no city. There are Christians everywhere, and even the desert has filled with monks" (*Vit. Ant.* 41). Peter Brown has argued that the holy man, with his demonstrations of heavenly power, adopted the role of patron to the villagers of Late Antique society. The holy man and his wonders also played a role in validating the institutions of society. Evagrius says of Simeon Stylites, in the Byzantine East, that he "realized in the flesh the existence of the heavenly hosts," and "he was adored by all the countryside, wrought many miracles, and the Emperor Theodosius II listened to his advice and sought his benediction" (*Eccl. hist.* 1.13).

Divine power manifest in the wonders worked by the holy man, and his relics or tomb were equally important in the Latin West. The iconic holy man here was Saint Martin, who unlike the ascetics of the East was also a bishop. In the biography of Sulpicius Severus his miracles are works of divine power, confirming the bishop's role of defending the poor, confounding heretics, converting pagans, and resisting the encroaching interests of the emperor. The power of Saint Martin continued after his death, and Gregory of Tours, in *The History of the Franks*, records the role of the miracles of Saint Martin in the complex relationship between the sixth-century Merovingian chieftains and the Christian bishops. Gregory describes miracles by holy bishops and the relics of figures such as Martin as a sign of divine justice in this unstable military society. Gregory records that Clovis, his model king and builder of the Merovingian royal dynasty, takes Martin as his patron. Martin then serves as the champion of Christianity against pagans and of orthodoxy against Arians. Divine approval is provided by a miraculous sign given at Saint Martin's church at Tours as well as by the appearance of a pillar of fire in the Church of St. Hillary. "It seemed," says Gregory, "to move towards Clovis as a sign that with the support of the blessed Saint he might the more easily overcome the heretic host." Building on classical and Hellenistic interest in wonders and divine power, miracles played a key role in the new societies of Late Antiquity.

Robert Hauck

See also: Early Christianity, Miracles in

Further Reading

Bowersock, G. W., Peter Brown, and Oleg Grabar, eds. *Interpreting Late Antiquity: Essays on the Postclassical World.* Cambridge, MA: Harvard University Press, 2001.

Brown, Peter. *The Cult of the Saints: Its Rise and Function in Latin Christianity.* Chicago: University of Chicago Press, 1981.

Brown, Peter. *Society and the Holy in Late Antiquity.* Berkeley: University of California Press, 1982.

Van Dam, Raymond. *Saints and Their Miracles in Late Antique Gaul*. Princeton, NJ: Princeton University Press, 1993.

Latin America, Miracles in

Central and South America—from the Baha to Patagonia—have borne some of the most freighted histories in the world. Ancient civilizations were altered by the encounter with Europeans and especially Iberian influences, and a mix of cultural religions has emerged in the intervening centuries. Belief in the supernatural was not unknown among the indigenous, but the Christianization of these vast territories placed a decidedly colonialist stamp on them. This had the effect of largely erasing an already tenuous oral tradition among many native populations, making them conform to a faith that was itself beset with diverse oral and printed traditions.

The ancient inhabitants of Latin America often used miraculous phenomena to convey cultural traditions. The Mayans employed dreams or prophecies as part of their mystical relations with the gods. Aztecs and Incas also feared supernatural events and sought to appease their gods through sacrifice or used totems of various kinds to keep peace with the spirit world. This human-divine commerce was not easily dispatched with the introduction of Catholic Christianity, since many of its own practices echoed the natives, but it was assimilated and gradually ingrained. To take one example of the blending of language, religion, and culture, the genesis of the cult of Our Lady of Guadalupe is instructive. The short tract *Nican mopohua* (*Huei tlamahuiçoltica*), first published in 1649 by Laso de la Vega, is a Nahuatl rendition of the events surrounding the Virgin's appearance to Saint Juan Diego in 1531 as Our Lady of Guadalupe. It places the story of the apparition at Tepeyac in a native tongue and specifically states that it is in that language that the Madonna chose to communicate. She also promised to grant the requests of those who ask. Some scholars have suggested that by placing the narrative in Nahuatl the text should be seen as a tool for conversion, but this does not detract from the initial miracle itself or the fourteen others attributed to the image that were described in a later section of the book.

Other incidences of cultural accommodation could be made, such as the sculpture by the Incan Francisco Tito Yupanqui of the Virgin of Copacabana in 1582. The national Bolivian image is delicate and refined, but Yupanqui was continually scoffed at for thinking that a native could make a likeness of the Virgin. So, he took an image from his own people, the sun goddess of the Incas, and made her into the Madonna. The loyalty cultivated by Christian missionaries to the adoration of Marian or feminine images is among the most complex and abiding elements of religious expression in Latin America. Their cultic aspects were enhanced by alleged apparitions, many of which were used as a means of achieving cultural or political unity.

Among the apparitions of the Virgin in Latin America there are several that stand out. The earliest is traced to Quito, Ecuador, in 1594. Coming under the banner of Our Lady of Good Success, four visits by the Virgin Mary to Venerable Mother Mariana de Jesus Torres, a Spanish-born Conceptionist sister, brought the healing of a blind girl and eventual incorruption of Mother Mariana's body. Others are more recent. In Betania, Venezuela, 31 apparitions occurred to the stigmatic, Maria Esperanza, over the course of 14 years, from 1976 to 1990. Mary called herself the "Reconciler of People and Nations." In 1984 over 100 individuals supposedly witnessed one of the apparitions. In 1987 the local ordinary, Bishop Pio Bello Ricardo, approved the authenticity of the miracles. In Cuapa, Nicaragua, the Virgin appeared from April to October to Bernardo Martinez, a church sacristan. Bringing warnings of national suffering if people did not reform themselves religiously, Mary asked that daily recitation of the rosary and increased devotion to the shoulder wounds of Christ be observed. Similarly, from 1983 to 1990 in San Nicolas, Argentina, nearly 80 communications from Christ came to Gladys Quiroga de Motta, an illiterate homemaker and grandmother. She claimed numerous daily visits by the Blessed Virgin as well. An investigation of her encounters began in 1985 and was positively concluded by Bishop Domingo Castagna in November 1990 some months after the last of the apparitions, which totaled over 1,800.

National images of the Blessed Virgin Mary have become normative for Latin American countries since the mid-sixteenth century. *Nuestra Señora de la Evangelización*, a gift to the newly created Diocese of Lima, Peru, was presented by Emperor Charles V from Spain around the year 1540. It is therefore one of the oldest images that is venerated in the region. The *Virgen De Los Treinta Y Tres*, located in Paraguay, is a small image of the Virgin of the Thirty-Three; the image a wood carving originating in the missions that the Jesuits had in Paraguay during the eighteenth century. Around 1779 the image was placed in the chapel in the village of Pintado, and later it moved with the entire village to what is now the city of Florida. In 1962 it was named Patroness of Uruguay. *Nuestra Senora de Comoroto* is a tiny relic that measures 27 millimeters high and 22 millimeters wide. The image is kept inside a richly adorned monstrance, where it is presented for the veneration of the faithful. In 1944, Pope Pius XII declared her patroness of Venezuela.

Argentina's Madonna has a history that goes back to May 1630, when a statue destined for Sumampa was diverted. The delivery men had two figurines in their cart, and they stopped on their journey to spend the night on the shores of the Luján River. The following day they realized that the mules could not move the wagon, even when they got rid of some of the weight. Only by strenuously taking out the box that contained the statue of the Immaculate Conception were they able to move the wagon. They took this as a sign that the Virgin wished to be installed on that spot. The two drivers left it in the care of Don Rosendo Oramas, and for more than 40 years it remained with him. He built a brick chapel, pilgrims came, and it became a center for prayer. One day a sick missionary came to Lujan and was miraculously healed. In 1763 he built a larger church that was eventually expanded; it was named a basilica in 1930. At the time, the little statue was given a solid silver covering and clothed in a white robe and a sky blue cloak—the colors of the Argentine flag. Lujan remains one of the most frequented places of pilgrimage in the world. In 1978 during a period known for national strife, the Argentine national team won soccer's World Cup. The players had invoked the Virgin of La Luján and dutifully sung her praises after their win. In 1982 when the Argentines battled the British for the Falkland Islands, Argentine seaman stowed away images of Our Lady of La Luján.

Mary appears in the strangest places but usually for good reason. For instance, records of the ecclesiastical court of the Archdiocese of Mexico give multiple versions of a miraculous image of Mary appearing in a kernel of corn in 1774 in Tlamacazapa, an Indian village in the parish of Acamixtla in Central Mexico. Bernardino de Mesa, the parish priest, supplied a testimony, and depositions were taken from the principal witness who discovered the image, Anna María, as well as her husband and one of their sons. Their story fits with a burgeoning cult of Our Lady of Sorrows (*Nuestra Señora de los Dolores*) during the seventeenth and eighteenth centuries, especially by pregnant women. According to one version, the apparition was made in a kernel of corn to an Indian woman about to give birth. Before departing for field work, her husband instructed her to separate all the good kernels for planting and to set the bad ones aside. While holding about five kernels in her hand, she suddenly became drowsy and fell asleep. Because her pregnancy was advanced, she felt some discomfort and awoke, imploring the Virgin Mary to help her. At this moment the woman opened her hand to discover that one of the kernels looked like an image of Mary. Her son was called, and he confirmed it. With this came gentle birth pangs and a quiet delivery. When the husband returned from his labors, he was astonished to learn that the Madonna had not only appeared in a kernel of corn but that she had given aid to his wife as she gave birth. Eventually the kernel was brought to the attention of the local priest. He became convinced of the corn's power and displayed it in his residence for two weeks. Every woman in labor who invoked it underwent an easy child birth.

Stories of mystical relationships often migrated from Spain to Latin America through missionaries. The Franciscan friar Juniper Serra (d. 1784) was a devotee of the writings of Sister María de Jesús de Ágreda (1602–1665), whose *The Mystical City of God* was widely read. It is a lengthy book of visions of the Immaculate Conception, but these visions are tinged with exhortations to missionaries to be zealous in their efforts. Although she never left her convent in Spain, sor María had bilocated to America by flying on the wings of Saint Michael and Saint Francis, sometimes making multiple trips in a single day. Protected by angels and dressed as a friar, María de Ágreda spoke to the Indians in their own language, urging them to seek out a Franciscan to perform their baptisms. Serra believed that she was talking about him.

Serra's Franciscanism, hallmarked by self-sacrifice, is replicated among others, including Maria Anna de Jesus de Paredes y Flores (1618–1645), also known as the Lily of Quito. Sor Mariana was the first canonized saint from Ecuador (1950), and though her body rests in the Jesuit church in Quito, her life was devoted to Franciscan simplicity. This stands in stark contrast to her family's prestige and wealth. She sustained herself on the Eucharist alone, and her visions often predicted future events or allowed her to peer into the minds of those she met. When the great earthquake of 1645 rocked the city of Quito, she made of herself a public sacrifice and died soon after. On the spot where she expired a lily shot up through the ground in full bloom.

Dominicans and later Jesuits joined this cavalcade. The Order of Preachers made their mark with Saint Rose of Lima (1586–1617), the first person to be canonized from the New World (1671). Her life experience and willful asceticism mirrored the late medieval mystic and Dominican tertiary Saint Catherine of Siena down to the mystical marriage between herself and Christ. With her contemporary, the Dominican brother Martin de Porres, the resulting miracles were prodigious. One of Rose's included the cure of the Dominican provincial in Peru, Father Augustine de Vega, who though near death recovered to become the bishop of Paraguay.

Among Jesuits who stand out is Saint Peter Claver (d. 1654), the so-called Apostle to the Negro. When they arrived on the docks in Cartagena, newly arrived African slaves faced an uncertain and a largely unwelcome future. But before they were taken into the country or prepared for export, these people had Claver's ministrations made available to them. It is said that he baptized nearly 300,000 people. All of the miracles accredited to Claver's canonization cause took place in the United States, though these do not compare with the more spectacular ones given in his hagiographical accounts, not the least of which is the raising from the dead of a little girl, Agustina de Villalabos, daughter of one of the slave ship captains.

For many in Latin America, Holy Week (Semana Santa) is the preeminent season for processions. Nicaraguans, as others, commemorate the miraculous death and resurrection of Jesus at this time through elaborate theatrical productions of the biblical passages related to the last week of Jesus's life. A statue of Jesus, or a real person dressed as him, is set on a donkey. Believers proceed behind Jesus's representation and the donkey while holding palm fronds and accompanied by philharmonic music (with a band called *chicheros*). This procession is commonly known as the Procesión de las Palmas (Palm Procession), but in Nicaragua it is popularly known as the Procesión de la Burrita (Donkey Procession). It is the statue that crowds invest with miraculous powers. Such was the case with Sacromonte at Amecameca, Mexico, where a cave associated with the Franciscan mystic Martín de Valencia became the home of a miracle-working image of the Santo Entierro (the entombed Christ) and the focus of Holy Week processions.

Latin America has known its share of saints and martyrs. The Spanish-born Franciscan Francisco Solano was one of five canonized saints who lived in Lima around 1600. According to the *Relacion de la vida y milagros de San Francisco Solano*, the friar was revered in life and after death, with some 195 miracles to his credit. According to one miracle story, he healed a dove that had been attacked by a fox. In another, Solano's holiness is shown in the power of his relics when a group of fishermen calmed a raging sea by casting a bit of cloth from Solano's habit upon the waters. He was beatified in 1675 and canonized in 1726.

Latin America's martyrs are found both in the region and abroad. By the late seventeenth century, the cult of San Felipe de Jesús (ca. 1572–97), native of Mexico City and martyr in Japan, had arisen. On February 5, 1597, Father Felipe and 26 others died by crucifixion in Nagasaki. In 1627, Pope Urban VIII beatified the martyrs as a group. Among the more famous twentieth-century martyrs is Archbishop Oscar Arnulfo Romero, Sister Dorothy Stang, Miguel Pro, and all the sons and daughters of the Mothers of the Plaza de Mayo. Many are in line for sainthood, including three missionaries murdered in 1991 in Peru by the Shining Path, a Maoist group. In February 2015 the Polish Order of Friars Minor announced their beatification. These men will also join Archbishop Romero, whose beatification was announced in February 2015.

In Brazil, healers abound. Anthropologists have tracked some of them, who play on their reputation for engaging in surgical therapies without benefit of anesthesia. By placing their patients in trances, these healers are able to repair bones or remove cancers by means of psychical treatments. The popularity of healers such as Zé Arigó (José Pedro de Freitas) and John of God (João Teixeira de Faria) reached international fame. Some healers employ the methods of Umbanda or Candomblé mixed with the Pentecostal laying on of hands, within the proximity of a shrine, to bring about an ecstatic trance. Similarly, a festival of healing takes place in Espinoza, Mexico, that links the words and actions of the traditional faith healer (*curandero*) with Catholic paraliturgy and sacramental vestments. Twice each year, thousands of Mexican pilgrims travel to Espinoza seeking cures from *El Nino Fidencio*, a figure who is chief among the healers. Born in 1898 as José de Jesús Fidencio Constantino Síntora (d. 1938) in Guanajuato, he is like a folk saint. His followers are known as *fidencistas*. They attest to his power to remove ailments such as headaches or insomnia, among other maladies. While living,

Fidencio removed teeth and gall stones without anesthesia but also took away cancer and paralysis. Prayers to his spirit, *fidencistas* insist, are equally as effective. While they get no official sanction from the Catholic Church, most *fidencistas* would self-identify as Catholic, just as Fidencio did. The syncretism of these healers and practices cannot be denied.

Recent wonders in Latin America included the cure of Floribeth Mora Diaz of Costa Rica. This cure of a life-threatening brain aneurysm was used in the canonization cause of Pope Saint John Paul II as the final miracle needed for a declaration of sainthood. She had prayed for John Paul II's intercession for a cure while watching a broadcast of the former pope's beatification on May 1, 2011. In July of that year she later visited a church that hosted some of his relics, and her cure was complete. Even in the present age Latin America continues to enjoy these favors, despite political and ethnic turmoil.

Patrick J. Hayes

See also: Dominicans and Miracles; Franciscans and Miracles; Jesuits and Miracles; Martyrs; Our Lady of Guadalupe; *Retablo*

Further Reading

Brading, D. A. *Mexican Phoenix: Our Lady of Guadalupe, Image and Tradition across Five Centuries*. New York: Cambridge University Press, 2002.

Conover, Cornelius. "Saintly Biography and the Cult of San Felipe de Jesús in Mexico City, 1597–1697." *The Americas* 67(4) (April 2011): 441–466.

Curcio-Nagy, Linda. "Native Icon to City Protectress to Royal Patroness: Ritual, Political Symbolism and the Virgin of Remedies." *The Americas* 52(3) (January 1996): 367–391.

de Oré, Luís Jerónimo. *Relación de la vida y milagros de San Francisco Solano*. Lima: Pontificia Universidad Católica del Perú, 1998.

Freedberg, David. *The Power of Images: Studies in the History and Theory of Response*. Chicago and London: University of Chicago Press, 1989.

Graziano, Frank. *Wounds of Love: The Mystical Marriage of Saint Rose of Lima*. New York: Oxford University Press, 2004.

Graziano, Frank. *Cultures of Devotion: Folk Saints of Spanish America*. New York: Oxford University Press, 2007.

Greenfield, Sidney M. *Spirits with Scalpels: The Cultural Biology of Religious Healing in Brazil*. Walnut Creek: Left Coast, 2008.

Haas, Lisbeth. *Saints and Citizens: Indigenous Histories of Colonial Missions and Mexican California*. Berkeley and Los Angeles: University of California Press, 2014.

Hall, Linda. *Mary, Mother and Warrior*. Austin: University of Texas Press, 2009.

John of God, www.johnofgod.com.

"Latin American Titles of Our Lady." University of Dayton, http://campus.udayton.edu/mary/resources/english.html.

Osowski, Edward W. *Indigenous Miracles: Nahua Authority in Colonial Mexico*. Tucson: University of Arizona Press, 2010.

Poole, Stafford. *Our Lady of Guadalupe: The Origins and Sources of a Mexican National Symbol, 1531–1797*. Tucson: University of Arizona Press, 1995.

Ramsey, Claire L., and Jose Antonio Noriega. "Ninos Milagrizados: Language Attitudes, Deaf Education, and Miracle Cures in Mexico." *Sign Language Studies* 1(3) (Spring 2001): 254–280.

Rodríguez, Jeanette. *Our Lady of Guadalupe: Faith and Empowerment among Mexican-American Women*. Austin: University of Texas Press, 1994.

Sandell, David P. "Mexican Retablos." *Journal of Folklore Research* 51(1) (January–April 2014): 13–47.

Sandos, James A. "Junípero Serra's Canonization and the Historical Record." *American Historical Review* 93(5) (December 1988): 1253–1269.

Stanfield-Mazzi, Maya. *Object and Apparition: Envisioning the Christian Divine in the Colonial Andes*. Tucson: University of Arizona Press, 2013.

Taylor, William B. *Marvels & Miracles in Late Colonial Mexico: Three Texts in Context*. Albuquerque: University of New Mexico Press, 2011.

Taylor, William B. "Our Lady in the Kernel of Corn, 1774." *The Americas* 59(4) (2003): 559–570.

Taylor, William B. *Shrines and Miraculous Images: Religious Life in Mexico before the Reforma*. Albuquerque: University of New Mexico Press, 2010.

Thomas, David Hurst. "The Life and Times of Fr. Junípero Serra: A Pan-Borderlands Perspective." *The Americas* 71(2) (October 2014): 185–225.

Wright-Rios, Edward. "Envisioning Mexico's Catholic Resurgence: The Virgin of Solitude and the Talking Christ of Tlacoxcalco 1908–1924." *Past and Present* 195 (May 2007): 197–239.

Le Moine, Abraham

Abraham Le Moine (d. 1757) was an eighteenth-century controversialist and scripture scholar. A rector of the Anglican community at Everly in Wilts and chaplain to the duke of Portland, his signal treatise on miracles, first published in London in 1747, was a scriptural and theological defense of the veracity of miracles. Le Moine's principal interlocutor was Thomas Chubb, whose own *Discourse on Miracles* in 1741 had caused a stir among philosophers. There Chubb attempted to make a case for the probability of miracles but not their certainty. Le Moine, by contrast, raised the stakes and skewered the argument as being lackluster and illogical. Chubb had fallen into skepticism with all its pitfalls, noted Le Moine. Not only could the probability of miracles be ascertained through the natural reason of human beings, they exhibited a high degree of probability such that an impartial person could attain their certainty. According to Le Moine, the miracles of scripture are of such circumstances as to be divinely revealed and, because of this, "afford a just foundation, not only for presuming, but for being certain, that true miracles exceed the bounds of human power, are always annexed to the truth, and wrought by God himself."

Patrick J. Hayes

Further Reading

LeMoine, Abraham. *A Treatise on Miracles, Wherein Their Nature, Conditions, Characteristics, and True Immediate Cause Are Clearly Stated; and All the Objections and Difficulties Which Have Been Hitherto Raised against Their Credibility, or the Evidence Arising from Them, Especially in Mr. Chubb's Discourse upon That Subject, Are Fully Considered, and Answered: With a Postscript, Containing Some Remarks on Dr. Middleton's Introductory Discourse to a Larger Work, &c.* London: Printed for J. Nourse, 1747.

Lepanto, Battle of

Military battles have often been occasions for the perceived workings of the divine, and success in battle has been seen as a sign of God's favor. A remarkable, perhaps miraculous, naval battle was fought on Sunday, October 7, 1571, in the Gulf of Lepanto just south of present-day Naupaktos, Greece, a key turning point in the battle between Christian and Islamic forces.

Intent upon further expanding the Ottoman Empire, Sultan Selim II already controlled much of the Mediterranean Sea and had likely plans to attack Venice and Rome. To defend Christendom, Pope Pius V (1504–1572) formed the Holy League in March 1571, a weak alliance of forces from Spain, Venice, Genoa, and the Papal States. The Holy League assembled a fleet of ships to meet the advancing Islamic forces, the largest Christian naval force ever assembled: 200 war galleys (large seagoing vessels propelled primarily by oars) and 75 smaller ships. Pope Pius V had asked the Christian faithful to pray and fast for the success of the Holy League's efforts, entreating them in particular to pray the rosary, a time-honored devotion, asking for the intercession of Mary, the mother of Jesus.

The Christian forces numbering nearly 80,000 had an unlikely leader in 24-year-old Don Juan (also rendered as Don John) of Austria (1547–1578), illegitimate son of Emperor Charles V. Before setting sail, each of the Christian soldiers was provided a rosary. Before battle, chaplains celebrated Mass on each of the ships and granted the sailors and soldiers absolution from sin.

The Ottoman fleet of over 200 galley ships and another 100 smaller vessels with more than 80,000 soldiers (including thousands of Christian slaves serving as oarsmen) marginally surpassed the Holy League's forces. As the battle began, the wind switched direction, blowing against the Ottomans, providing an advantage for the Holy League by allowing the use of their sails and thus conversation of the oarsmens' strength. Don Juan's battle plan was to strike at the center of the Ottoman line, concentrating his forces there. After fierce fighting, the Ottoman forces eventually became trapped against Scropha Point as the Christians pressed upon them. Within a few hours, the Christians achieved a decisive victory. The defeat of the Ottoman fleet was total, with tens of thousands killed and perhaps 175 ships lost. The Holy League's losses included 12 ships and 7,500 men. The battle halted the advance of the Islamic forces against Christendom. It is widely viewed as one of history's most significant naval battles.

Pope Pius V was convinced that prayer, in particular the praying of the rosary, had enabled the Christian victory. The battle has lived on in the memory of Christians. It inspired twentieth-century English Catholic writer G. K. Chesterton's poem "Lepanto," which celebrates the role of Don Juan in the battle. The naval victory continues to be remembered in the Catholic Church annually on October 7, celebrating the intercession of the Virgin Mary under the title Our Lady of Victory or Our Lady of the Rosary. The Christian victory at the Battle of Lepanto remains a witness to the power of prayer in providing protection and aiding in victory over one's adversaries.

David J. Endres

Further Reading

Capponi, Niccolò. *Victory of the West: The Story of the Battle of Lepanto*. London: Macmillan, 2006.
Chesterton, G. K. *Lepanto*. Edited by Dale Ahlquist. San Francisco: Ignatius Press, 2004.
Konstam, Angus. *Lepanto 1571: The Greatest Naval Battle of the Renaissance*. Westport, CT: Praeger, 2005.

Levitation

Levitation is the suspension above ground or floor level of a body or object. Levitation is distinguished from flight insofar as the gravitational pull is such that it somehow tethers a person or object to a particular location, whereas miracles of flight allow for maximal freedom in moving across greater distances and for longer periods of time.

Westerners in the nineteenth century enjoyed a fascination with the Orient. Fakirs of the Middle East drew wondrous accolades for the abilities to climb ropes hanging in midair or to command objects to rise. The Flying Lamas of India and Tibet were drawn from the Buddhist sutras, but their fame was their downfall. When he heard about the displays of power to rise off the ground, the Buddha found it distasteful and showy. He punished them by decreeing that each would spend more time in the world to seek greater merit and repent of their misdeeds. The famous spiritualist Alexandra David-Néel noted how Tibetan lamas could sit crossed-legged on a cushion and hold their breath. They would then train themselves to jump up from the cushion at higher and higher distances so that over time they appeared weightless. "These men are able to sit on an ear of barley without bending its stalk or to stand on the top of a heap of grain without displacing any of it."

Levitation in Hinduism relates the feeling of liberation from the constraints that keep us bound. For the ascetic especially, the ability to control one's body by picking it up off the ground is tantamount to gaining control over the whole universe. In the Yoga Sutras of Patanjali, extraordinary powers called *siddhis*—which include levitation—can be developed through yogic discipline. A levitating saint such as Nagendranath Bhaduri found that engaging in Astanga Yoga and employing multiple breathing techniques brought such calm that his weight became anti-gravitational. The realization of power over one's being is often done while in ecstasy or is in fact the cause of that ecstasy. The result is to rise like a helium balloon, what the sutras call *laghami*. Today, yogini in the streets of many European cities may be found "levitating" accompanied by attendants reciting prayers below their feet, but these individuals are merely sitting atop steel platforms connected by rods.

Ecstatic levitation—where a body becomes light as a feather—is also present in many Christian saints. The difference is that the objective is not so much interior control of the self as relation to God, which all bodies are meant to contemplate and crave. Self-control is not particularly worrisome, though in an ecstatic fit the saint might prove embarrassing. Saint Teresa of Ávila, for instance, when engaged in a contemplative rapture could often be found rising from her seat in chapel. When she felt this coming on, she would ask the sisters in her convent to sit on her so she would not float away. While preaching at Foggia in 1777, Saint Alphonsus Liguori is said to have been lifted off in ecstasy toward the tabernacle.

Often the site or location helps to set the stage for a levitation. This is true of séances, which seek to harness psychical energy to produce certain effects. In the United States, a floater of wide renown was Daniel Douglas Home, a nineteenth-century medium and magician. He wowed crowds in his séances that included people such as Mark Twain, William Cullen Bryant, and Czar Alexander II, who could levitate multiple times in each session. Additionally, shamans, writes Mircea Eliade, possess an ability to ascend from the ground. In a Tungus séance, "the shaman becomes 'light' and can spring into the air with a costume that may weigh as much as sixty-five pounds."

Patrick J. Hayes

See also: Flight

Further Reading

David-Neel, Alexandra. *Magic and Mystery in Tibet*. New York: Dover, 1971.

Eliade, Mircea. *Shamanism: Archaic Techniques of Ecstasy*. Princeton, NJ: Princeton University Press, 2004.

Goldberg, Philip. *American Veda: From Emerson and the Beatles to Yoga and Meditation: How Indian Spirituality Changed the West*. New York: Random House, 2010.

Harevy-Wilson, Simon Brian. "Human Levitation." PhD dissertation, Edith Cowan University, 2005.

Oppenheim, Janet. *The Other World: Spiritualism and Psychical Research in England, 1850–1914*. New York: Cambridge University Press, 1988.

Lewis, C. S.

Clive Staples (C. S.) Lewis (1898–1963) was a scholar at both Oxford and Cambridge Universities and one of the most famous and widely revered Christian apologists of the twentieth century. Many people also know him as the author of numerous best-selling children's fiction books such as *The Chronicles of Narnia* series. As an apologist, however, he wrote many books in defense of the Christian faith. One such book, *Miracles: A Preliminary Study*, is of particular importance because it provides an intellectual underpinning for the existence of miracles. As with any intellectual discussion, Lewis's work has many supporters and many detractors, but the work is almost universally seen as a valuable contribution to the debate on faith and miracles.

As a practical matter, Lewis investigated the existence of miracles so as to defend the existence of the supernatural through the existence of the miraculous. In fact, Lewis notes, "Christianity is precisely the story of a great miracle." The linchpin of the entire Christian faith is predicated on the existence of miracles, and so, Lewis argues, it must have intellectual validity. He espouses the point that "the central miracle asserted by Christians is the incarnation," promoting that a divine God the Son would become man. Without incarnation, there is no Christianity. Every miracle is then possible if the incarnation is possible. Lewis argues that "it is unphilosophical, if you have once accepted the Grand Miracle (the incarnation), to reject the stilling of the storm (in Mark 4 and Matthew 8)" or any other miracle, for that matter.

Originally published in 1947 (and then updated in 1960), *Miracles* provides a scholarly defense, utilizing logic and reason, of miraculous events. The major reason for his update was the result of a debate with a contemporary scholar, Gertrude Anscombe, at the Socratic Club at Oxford University in which the two scholars disagreed on sections of Lewis's work on miracles. The debate led Lewis to rewrite chapter three on difficulties within the field of naturalism. The debate, and Lewis's work in general, covers a range of questions such as whether naturalism and supernaturalism can coexist, whether miracles are possible, whether God can perform miracles, and whether the incarnation of God as man is possible, among other questions.

Lewis ultimately argues that there is a central decision that must be made on the issue of miracles. "Miracles in first-century Palestine are either lies, legends, or history," he states, alluding to the point that either miracles happened at the time of Christ or are a fabrication or a myth. This discussion parallels Lewis's trilemma—a means of choosing an option from three often challenging choices—in another work, *Mere Christianity*, first published in 1952, that Jesus is either a lunatic, a liar, or the Lord.

Lewis cautiously presents the idea that "a miracle is . . . the most improbable of all events" but notes that while a miracle is improbable, it is not impossible. In fact, Lewis spends time examining the criteria for accepting miracles that pertain to both the believer and the skeptic—the threshold at which one accepts a given event as a miracle. He concludes that miracles do exist but are rare.

The existence of miracles is an important part of the debate over whether a creator exists. Miracles point to the interjection of a loving God into the world. Lewis notes that what we should really do is decide for ourselves whether or not miracles are possible but not expect ocular proof that one will occur. He reasons that miracles are not to be expected in the everyday lives of people. "God does not shake miracles into Nature at random as if from a pepper-caster." Miracles are reserved, Lewis argues, for great occasions—one would not expect to "be present when a peace treaty is signed, when a great scientific discovery is made, or when a dictator commits suicide," among other extremely rare events—so why should we expect to see a miracle?

Lewis further notes that the miraculous does not have to supersede the natural world; in fact, miracles can follow the order of the natural world. In essence, miracles very seldom occur, but when they do they change the trajectory of human history—the world, Lewis argues, is altered by a Creator who is intimately involved in the lives of everyday people.

Glen Duerr

Further Reading

Lewis, C. S. "Study Guide to Miracles." C. S. Lewis Foundation, http://www.cslewis.org/resources/studyguides/Study%20Guide%20-%20Miracles.pdf.

Lewis, Clive Staples. *Miracles: A Preliminary Study.* New York: Simon and Schuster, 1996.

Locke, John

The English philosopher and physician John Locke (1632–1704) was a champion of "reasonable Christianity," whose argument sometimes seemed close to those of Deists without ever crossing the sometimes thin line that separated Deists from "reasonable" or "Latitudinarian" Anglicans. His principal contribution on miracles, *Discourse on Miracles*, was written in 1702 but published posthumously in 1706. (Locke also discussed miracles in his *Third Letter on Toleration* [1692], *Essay Concerning Human Understanding* [1690], and *The Reasonableness of Christianity* [1695].) *Discourse on Miracles* was an intervention in the controversy over Deists and their sometimes hostile attitude to biblical miracles that had begun with the publication of John Toland's *Christianity Not Mysterious* (1695). It drew from previous Anglican writers on miracles and wonders such as Robert Boyle, Joseph Glanvill, and William Fleetwood. (Locke described Fleetwood's *Essay on Miracles* [1701] as the inspiration for *Discourse on Miracles*, although he thought Fleetwood's definition of a miracle incomplete.)

Locke defined a miracle as an event above the order of nature taken to be divine. Not all events out of the order of nature were miracles, but miracles, as emanating from God, had a power that other "unnatural" events lacked. Locke uses the example of the Egyptian wizards who turned their staffs to snakes, only to be overcome by Moses's truly miraculous power to make this distinction. Locke argued that the wonders ascribed to their gods by ancient Greek and Roman polytheists could not be viewed as miracles, since they did not encourage the worship of one god to the exclusion of all others, nor did they promote any article of faith, a concept alien to ancient and polytheistic religion. Islam, the only religion besides Judaism and Christianity that Locke believed to make truth-claims based on monotheism, did not adduce miracles as evidence—itself evidence of its falsity. He dismissed Asian religions, such as Zoroastrianism and Hinduism, out of hand as "obscure" and "fabulous." This meant that the only religions attested to by miracle were Judaism and Christianity, and since biblical Judaism and Christianity, in Locke's view, reinforced each other's truth, it really reduced to Christianity alone. The many miracles of Jesus recounted in the Gospels were overwhelming evidence of the truth of Christianity—an idea by no means original to Locke, as Christian apologists in the late seventeenth century were putting more weight on the evidence of miracles. (Unlike many of the skeptical writers on Jesus's miracles, Locke does not consider the credibility of the Gospel writers themselves.) Not just the existence but the number and variety of miracles attributed to Christ were further evidence, as a person skeptical of one type of miracle—walking on water, for example—might be convinced by another type of miracle, such as a miraculous healing.

Unlike the Deists, who believed that "natural" or "reasonable" religion was the only kind of true religion, Locke accepted the distinction between natural and revealed religion, both valid but revealed religion offering truths, such as the Divinity of Christ, unattainable by reason alone. Miracles were particularly relevant for revealed religion. However, the identification of an event as miraculous and its acceptance as evidence require the exercise of reason. As overwhelming evidence for the truth of Christianity, miracles were not opposed to a reasonable faith but were its very foundation.

Unlike the skeptics, Locke considered the context of a supernatural miracle, in that one of the criteria for evaluating a miracle is the end to which God might be directing it. Miracles must not only testify to the power of the Christian God but must also address matters of significance, such as Christ's divinity. Miracles testify to the glory of God or to things particularly important for humans to know; therefore, those apparent miracles that do not relate to these issues can be dismissed out of hand, no matter how wonderful they seem. For Locke, this end-oriented view of a miracle was superior to the definition of a miracle as something out of the order of nature only God could do (Fleetwood's definition), as what events precisely lay outside the power of nature or of angels, good or bad, was unknown.

William E. Burns

Further Reading

Burns, R. M. *The Great Debate on Miracles: From Joseph Glanville to David Hume.* Lewisburg, PA: Bucknell University Press, 1981.

Mooney, T. Brian, and Anthony Imbrosciano. "The Curious Case of Mr. Locke's Miracles." *International Journal for Philosophy of Religion* 57 (2005): 147–168.

Shaw, Jane. *Miracles in Enlightenment England.* New Haven, CT: Yale University Press, 2006.

Long Life

The patriarchs from Adam to Noah are attributed supernaturally long lives in the genealogy of Genesis 6. The length of life ranged from 365 years (Enoch) to 969 years (Methuselah). The antediluvian patriarchs are presented not only as living extraordinarily long lives but also as aging slower, as is evidenced by them begetting children between the 65th and 187th years of their lives. This genealogy is attributed to the priestly source, serving the function of linking the account of Adam and the story of creation to Noah and the flood. Genesis 6 bears similarities to an ancient Babylonian king's list of antediluvian rulers (which includes the hero of the Babylonian flood epic), with reigns ranging from 18,600 to 65,000 years. Genesis 6 differs from ancient Near Eastern parallels both in the names, which bear no resemblance to ancient cuneiform lists, and the life length being considerably reduced. Scholars therefore link the long life tradition of Genesis 6 to a broader ancient Near Eastern tradition of exalting antediluvian heroes but recognize a considerable process of adjustment and adaptation before inclusion into the biblical material. Moreover, the length of life differs in different Old Testament textual traditions. The Samaritan Pentateuch only agrees with the Masoretic Text (Leningrad Codex) on the first half of the names, listing shorter lives for the names in the second half of the list. The Greek Septuagint differs considerably, offering longer lives for every figure except Adam, whose 930 years agrees with the Masoretic Text.

Nicholas R. Werse

Further Reading

Rüdiger Heinzerling. "'Einweihung' durch Henoch? Die Bedeutung der Altersangaben in Genesis 5." *Zeitschrift für die alttestamentliche Wissenschaft* 110(4) (1998): 581–589.

Lourdes

The town of Lourdes is a modern pilgrimage site in the foothills of the French Pyrenees. Each year millions of tourists travel to Lourdes to visit the shrine dedicated to the Virgin Mary and to seek cures from the town's water. Since 1858, Lourdes has developed from a village with a local shrine into an international site of Catholic devotion. The debates surrounding the cures and their relation to local religious traditions, science, technology, commerce, and gender stimulated Lourdes's transformation.

In February 1858, Bernadette Soubrious experienced 18 visions of the Virgin in the Masabielle Grotto. Two weeks after the initial vision, the apparition instructed Bernadette to drink from and wash herself in a patch of apparently dried earth before the grotto. Bernadette obeyed, dug into the soil, and, finding it wet, drank from the soil and smeared her face with mud. Villagers dug deeper into the earth and uncovered a flowing spring.

Debates over the water's healing powers engulfed the town's inhabitants. Some local residents promptly accepted Lourdes as a site of healing. Pyrenean religious traditions recognized the connections between saints, healing sites, and local topography. For some, the appearance of the spring at the grotto affirmed Bernadette's visions, the Virgin's presence, and the spring's powers. By July 1858, dozens of villagers claimed that the water healed their ailments. Debates ensued. The local government outlawed worship at the grotto and barricaded the site. Catholic priests warned villagers that recognizing the water's power undermined the Virgin's power. Nevertheless, villagers continued to attribute cures to the water.

Popular attention to the cures prompted an official Church investigation. In July 1858, Bishop Laurence of Tarbes established an episcopal commission to investigate the miracles' divine origins. Government officials reopened the grotto, and informal pilgrimages recommenced. In 1862, Laurence recognized Lourdes as an official shrine devoted to the Virgin and proclaimed seven cures to be miraculous. Laurence initiated building projects—a chapel, bathhouses, a fountain, and a basilica on the hill above the grotto—to promote official Church devotions. Droves of local pilgrims visited Lourdes, washed in the water, and bought religious objects from peddlers now stationed in the town.

From 1866 to 1874, Lourdes developed into a national pilgrimage site. Laurence invited the missionaries of Notre-Dame de Garaison to manage the shrine. The Garaison fathers brought a railway line through Lourdes in 1866 and transported almost 50,000 pilgrims to the shrine. Henri Lasserre, a Catholic journalist, published *Notre-Dame de Lourdes* (1869), which chronicled Bernadette's story and the alleged cures. Railway access and Lasserre's book ignited the nation's interest in Lourdes. The Augustinian Fathers of the Assumption selected Lourdes as the site for their 1872 pilgrimage. They also inaugurated Lourdes's first national pilgrimage of the sick in 1874. Women's associations were enlisted to raise money for these pilgrimages and care for infirm pilgrims. Thereafter, women and the sick became central to Lourdes pilgrimages and devotional life.

By 1900, Lourdes was a site of mass pilgrimage and spectacle. Religious leaders worked with railway companies to secure reduced fares and special compartments for pilgrims. Leaders initiated building projects, including a hospital for sick pilgrims, a new basilica, an electrical plant, a religious boutique, and a printing press. Local priests and entrepreneurs harnessed the power of media to market Lourdes via newspapers, pilgrimage guidebooks, images, and bottled water. Lourdes resembled a resort town with hotels, restaurants, and souvenir shops.

Lourdes's popularity engendered disputes over religion's relationship to commerce and science. Émile Zola's *Lourdes* (1894), a novel that disparaged the town's commercialization, ignited the debates. Anticlerical republicans argued that Lourdes's promotion of miracles stimulated Catholic superstition. The work of the Bureau des Constatations Médicales, established in 1883 by medical professionals to verify cures, did little to allay these concerns. Anticlerical republicans also suggested that Lourdes lured the secularizing masses back to the Church via the marketplace. Catholic priests criticized Lourdes for endorsing popular beliefs and devotions as well as profane commerce. Both Catholic and anticlerical critics attributed this debasement of religion to women. Female pilgrims, they argued, were susceptible to the lures of consumer culture and hysteria that promoted belief in miracles. These controversies culminated in republican authorities' attempts to close Lourdes from 1903 to 1910.

The campaign to close Lourdes betrayed the town's entwinement with private and state interests. Commercial enterprises, banks, and railway companies heavily invested in Lourdes. Closing the site would devastate these businesses. Moreover, a 1908 report revealed that the state-run postal service profited enormously from Lourdes. Instead of closing Lourdes, the government transferred jurisdiction of the site from the church to the city in 1910.

Lourdes thrived in the twentieth century and became an international pilgrimage site. The town reached new heights of notoriety in the 1940s with the publication and film adaptation of *The Song of Bernadette* in the United States. Today, millions of devotees make pilgrimage to Lourdes and donate funds for building projects. Pilgrims continue to attribute cures to Lourdes water. In June 2013, the Roman Catholic Church officially recognized Lourdes's 69th miraculous cure.

Jamie L. Brummitt

See also: Lourdes Water; Our Lady of Lourdes

Further Reading

"Cures and Miracles." The Sanctuary of Our Lady of Lourdes, http://en.lourdes-france
.org/deepen/cures-and-miracles.

Duffin, Jacalyn. "Religion and Medicine, Again: JHMAS Commentary on 'The Lourdes Medical Cures Revisited.'" *Journal of the History of Medicine and Allied Sciences* 69(1) (January 2014): 162–165.

Harris, Ruth. *Lourdes: Body and Spirit in the Secular Age.* New York: Penguin, 1999.

Kaufman, Suzanne K. *Consuming Visions: Mass Culture and the Lourdes Shrine*. Ithaca, NY: Cornell University Press, 2005.

Lourdes Water

Among Catholics in nineteenth-century America, the fascination with Lourdes and its miracle waters was widespread. As far back as 1891, Redemptorists serving the parish of Most Holy Redeemer on Third Street on Manhattan's Lower East Side kept Lourdes water for the faithful. This water, drawn from the spring at Lourdes, France, was supplied liberally to all who asked for it. According to the parish history, on August 25, 1897, a lady came to the rectory and told Brother William that her child had suffered from scurvy of the gums, which several doctors failed to cure. After giving the child Lourdes water three times, it was cured. Elizabeth Lyons of Springfield, Massachusetts, sent a statement to the rectory about her use of this water dated October 11, 1899. "About the middle of September, I was troubled with great pain in my ear. I could hardly stand it. I took a little Lourdes Water, sent to me from 3rd Street, and put it into my ear. Almost immediately the pain left me and I felt cured." In August 1901, a lady from Virginia stopped by the rectory and procured some Lourdes water along with a blessing for the sick. No name was given, nor did she give a reason for making the long journey. What mattered was getting her presence on record and registering the exchange between the priests and the pious supplicant who, like so many others across the country, found relief in a bottle without having to cross the ocean for it.

Patrick J. Hayes

Further Reading

McDannell, Colleen. *Material Christianity: Religion and Popular Culture in America*. New Haven, CT: Yale University Press, 1998.

Low Countries, Miracles in the

The Low Countries have traditionally been considered Belgium, the Netherlands, and Luxembourg. Though no process for canonization was held in the Low Countries during the later Middle Ages, its territories were not without popular saints or stories of miracles. The nation of Belgium has been predominantly Christian—and mainly Catholic—since the first millennium. The faith took hold beginning with early missionaries such as Saint Willibrord (d. 739), whose travels into the Low Countries planted the seeds. His tomb was the site of many miracles in the late eighth century and became a site of pilgrimage associated with an unusual dance that has processed annually through the town of Echternach in Luxembourg.

Proliferation of miraculous phenomena in Belgium occurred in the Middle Ages. Eucharistic miracles, such as those at Bruges (1256) and Herkenrode (1317), became well known throughout Europe. A vial of clotted blood thought to belong to Jesus and shed at the crucifixion has been preserved in the Cathedral in Bruges in an ornate reliquary there. It is processed annually throughout the city and made available for daily veneration by the faithful. At Herkenrode, blood could be seen oozing from a consecrated host, and later witnesses noted that they had seen the face of Christ on it. Until 1796 the host was kept in the Cistercian Abbey of Herkenrode, where it was the object of annual pilgrimages. After the French Revolution, it was transferred to the Cathedral of Saint Quintinus in Hasselt, where it reposes in a reliquary there.

To these instances of Eucharistic piety one might add the power of large clusters of healing saints, particularly those who formed communities in the Low Countries in the early fourteenth century. Their appeal—which included stories of miracles performed at the tombs of their forebears or by visiting shrines—followed an almost formulaic client-patron approach and so could hold the attention of listeners and lodge themselves in memory for generations. In the Ardennes, for instance, Saint Hubert the Hunter is the object of a national pilgrimage on November 3. His stole was said to have miraculously descended from heaven.

Saint Bavo (or Bavon) of Ghent's miracles were written up in the eleventh century, but he became an example of the exchange that takes place between supplicants and saints. One legend states that with invaders causing havoc in the village of Houtem, with the marauders even cursing Saint Bavo, the peasantry beseeched the saint to quell the upstarts. After many prayers to the saint their pleas were heard, and the invaders were brought low. It is practically formulaic, and as some scholars suggest, if a group of aggrieved supplicants (*clamantes*) cries loudly enough, they will "wake up" a saint to cause a miracle.

Reviving a saint in this manner had everything to do with monasteries that promoted this sort of practice among lay people. Not only did people go to their local saint, as on pilgrimages, but Low Country monks began to make reliquaries that were portable so that elaborate processions could be made with powerful saints in tow, a tour known as a *delatio*. An example of this mobile miracle driver was Saint Ursmer (d. 713), among the first to convert the Flemish to Christianity.

The monks who cared for his remains in their chapel were wronged in a property dispute, and hoping to impose penalties on their usurpers and suppress the warring factions that caused the dispute in the first place, they circumambulated the region with their patron saint who, of course, rendered justice and peace.

In the Flemish regions, the female saint who stands out for both her miracles and following is Lutgard (Lutgardis) of Aywières (d. 1246). As a Cistercian abbess she was made blind by the side wound of Jesus, who appeared to her in a vision. She was the recipient of further heavenly privileges whereby in addition to other visions of the Blessed Virgin Mary and Saint John the Evangelizer, she also witnessed the corpus of Christ extend his hand to her from the cross and the Son of God showing his divine heart to God the Father. She could levitate, heal, and exude oil from her fingertips, a balm that cured anyone with problems of the hand or foot.

In the late seventeenth century in the town of Halle, a debate sprang up over human abilities to identify and authenticate miracles reported at the shrine of the Virgin. The controversialist Justus Lipsius (1547–1606) published a short tract, *Diva virgo Hallensis*, that would soon be translated into French, Dutch, and English. *Diva virgo Hallensis* was a devotional work but not in the usual sense of espousing positive pious sentiments. Instead, it was antideterministic in approach to the question of miracles; that is, it did not allow for a natural order brought about by causal determination. Rather, Lipsius sought to make a space for God's utter freedom in bringing about miraculous phenomena, gave wholesale assent to the apparitions of the Virgin reported at Halle and Montaigu, and legitimated the veneration of her shrines. Protestant Europe scoffed at such claims.

That Belgium should be a battleground over the possibility of miracles or of their interpretation should come as no surprise. Since the fifteenth century, it was home to one of the finest theological faculties in Christendom at the University of Louvain. It was in this theological center that the Bollandists rose to prominence as being the most sophisticated collection of researchers into the lives and miracles of saints in the whole of the Christian world. While the academy should be a place for serious scholarship on the lives of saints and their miracles, there is also the lived reality of the people. In the Netherlands alone, between 1380 and 1726 about 1,700 miracle stories were recorded of cures related to blindness as the result of smallpox or measles. Miracles were, in a sense, ordinary.

The depth of piety of the people of Belgium and Holland helped to give rise to a large cadre of missionaries who began to flood Africa and Asia in the eighteenth and nineteenth centuries. They brought with them their favorite local saints and stories associated with them. Neither Belgians nor the Dutch were immune to a kind of religious colonization, but they were also prepared to face spiritism or animism and other occult practices in the cultures they encountered. Many were already well acquainted with extraordinary supernatural forces and how these might brush up against modern scientific truths.

For example, the Belgian stigmatic Louise Lateau (1850–1883), from the village of Bois d'Haine, began to relive the Passion of Christ in her body at age 18. When she began to bleed from the chest, her parish priest asked her to keep it to herself. But over the next several weeks, the blood flowed from her head, hands, and feet in such copious amounts that she could no longer hide it. Her bleedings replicated the wounds of Jesus at the crucifixion with awful regularity, and she endured these painful episodes until her death. Her ecstasies produced an ability to converse in English and Latin, despite having no formal training in these languages. She took no food other than the daily Eucharist from 1871 to 1883. After her death her cult grew, prompting the antiecclesiastical psychiatrist and would-be politician Désiré-Magliore Bourneville to attack Lateau as a fraud and an embarrassment to modern Belgium. His book *Science et miracle: Louise Lateau ou la stigmatiseé belge* (1875) pulled no punches. Her stigmatization was due to hysteria, he claimed. But without proof in the concrete, Bourneville and others remained as much on the periphery as did the supporters of Lateau. Meanwhile, her fame spread throughout Europe and the United States.

Nearly contemporaneous with the emergence of Lateau's critics, at the shrine of Our Lady of Lourdes in Oostakker, Belgium, a miracle is said to have cured Pierre De Rudder, a wood cutter who suffered a severe bone break in his left leg in 1867. He was hobbled for nearly eight years until he visited the Lourdes Oostakker shrine. De Rudder enjoyed the cure until his death in 1898, but it was only in 1908 that the Diocese of Bruges formally announced his cure to be miraculous. In the meantime, the canonical inquiry relied on somewhat dubious testimony of physicians, and several accounts were drawn from distant memory. Nevertheless, the diocesan inquiry still stands.

The Low Countries are rife with such pilgrimage sites. Among these is Scherpenheuvel (Dutch for "sharp hill") in the northern Flemish region. Convincing miracle stories had grown up around a little statue of Mary ensconced in an oak tree, and a large and impressive shrine had grown up around it. Drawing up to 20,000 pilgrims on major feast days, Scherpenheuvel quickly became a profitable locale, and the tiny village emerged as an economic center. The reported miracles continued along with this growth so that in 1602 when Calvinism was surging, the statue is said to have wept bloody tears.

Belgium's importance for Marian piety cannot be understated. Many of its Marian shrines claim miracles to their credit. Reference to two will suffice: Our Lady of Beauraing and Our Lady of Banneux, both of which enjoy the Church's official recognition as apparition sites. The former between November 1932 and

January 1933 enjoyed the presence of the Virgin some 33 times. She visited with five young children, ages 9 to 15. The declaration of the bishop of Namur, Andre-Marie Charue, on the veracity of the sightings came only in July 1949. In Banneaux, the Madonna made eight appearances to Mariette Becco (d. 2011) from January 15 to March 2, 1933. The vision called herself "The Virgin of the Poor," and eventually a little chapel was erected to commemorate the visitation. A miraculous spring is also associated with the site. It was also accorded official sanction by Bishop Louis-Joseph Kerkhofs of Liège a month after the decree for Beauraing in August 1949. Shrines have been erected at both sites.

Patrick J. Hayes

Further Reading

Albertson, Clinton. *Anglo-Saxon Saints and Heroes*. New York: Fordham University Press, 1963.

Coens, Maurice. "Translations et miracles de Saint Bavon au XIe siècle." *Analecta Bollandiana* 86 (1968): 39–66.

De Landtsheer, Jeanine. "Justus Lipsius' Treatises on the Holy Virgin." In *The Low Countries as a Crossroads of Religious Beliefs*, edited by Arie Jan Gelderblom, Jan L. Deong, and Marc Van Vaeck, 65–68. Leiden: Brill, 2004.

Harline, Craig. *Miracles at the Jesus Oak: Histories of the Supernatural in Reformation Europe*. New York: Doubleday, 2003.

Howe, Frances R. *A Visit to Bois d'Haine: The Home of Louise Lateau*. Baltimore: Kelly, Piet, 1878.

Kozol, Geoffrey, trans. "The Miracles of St. Ursmer on His Journey through Flanders." In *Medieval Hagiography: An Anthology*, edited by Thomas Head, 341–358. New York: Routledge.

Krack, Paul. "Relicts of Dancing Mania: The Dancing Procession of Echternach." *Historical Neurology* 53(9) (1999): 21–69.

Lachapelle, Sofie. "Between Miracle and Sickness: Louise Lateau and the Experience of Stigmata and Ecstasy." *Configurations* 12(1) (2004): 77–105.

Lipsius, Justus. *Diva virgo Hallensis* (English title: *Miracles of the B. Virgin, Or, An Historical Account of the Original, and Stupendious Performances of the Image Entitled, Our Blessed Lady of Halle, Viz., Restoring the Dead to Life, Healing the Sick, Delivering of Captives, &c*). London, 1688.

Merton, Thomas. *What Are These Wounds? The Life of a Cistercian Mystic: Saint Lutgarde of Aywières*. Milwaukee: Bruce Publishing, 1950.

Murphy, Edward L. "The Saints of Epilepsy." *Medical History* 3(4) (October 1959): 303–311.

Ritchey, Sara. "Affective Medicine: Later Medieval Healing Communities and Feminization of Health Care Practices in the Thirteenth-Century Low Countries." *Journal of Medieval Religious Cultures* 40(2) (2014): 113–143.

Van den Broek, Hans. "Genezing van blindheid na pokken of mazelen: Nederlandse mi-rakelverhalen, 14e-18e eeuw." *Nederlands tijdschrift voor geneeskunde* 154(43) (2010): 2018–2021.

Wade, Susan W. "Miraculous Seeing and Monastic Identity: Miracles of the Visual from the Monasteries of Lobbes and Nivelles." PhD dissertation, New York University, 2007.

M

Magic

Magic is ritualized behavior and/or language purporting to engage with a nonphysical or extramundane order of reality enacted with a specific purpose. Previous views of magic focused on its supposed inefficacy. This has been challenged by more recent research and remains a contentious subject.

In 1871, Sir Edward Tylor set the initial tone for anthropology by describing magic as properly belonging to rudimentary human culture and working through an erroneous thought process that confuses an association of ideas with a connection in reality. Sir James George Frazer theorized this as "sympathetic magic," operating according to either (or both) of two rules: the law of similarity and the law of contagion. According to the law of similarity, the magician believes that he can produce an effect by imitating it; by the law of contagion, he believes that what has once been in contact remains so and can thus be magically manipulated.

Bronislaw Malinowski challenged this interpretation after intensive ethnography of the Trobriand Islanders led him to the functionalist view that human culture was reducible to the satisfaction of human needs. Accordingly, magic served a psychological function in alleviating anxiety in response to the unknowable and/or uncontrollable.

Early sociologists considered the social role of magic rather than its mechanisms. Marcel Mauss defined magic as taking place outside of organized religion in privacy and secrecy, even approaching social unacceptability. Émile Durkheim took this further to propose a categorical difference between public religion (church) and private magic (clientele). Although both deal with sacred as opposed to profane things, he argued that magic could not create the lasting social bonds essential to the religious moral community.

Max Weber used magic to characterize different societies, especially the development of Western society. Thus, he began with an epoch of enchantment gradually being superseded by disenchantment under the influence of rationalization.

Disenchantment signified a complex of societal dynamics, with the loss of magic as a means to salvation being a central theme. For Weber, enchantment (magic as a social condition) provided existential satisfaction through meaningfulness.

The philosopher Lucien Lévy-Bruhl described magic as belonging to the "mystical mentality" of premodern peoples, not as an error in logic but as a different way of thinking that emphasizes participation over causality. In his later writings, Lévy-Bruhl allowed that mystical and logical modes were simultaneously present, although differently valued in the modern age. This turn from the positivism of Tylor and Frazer marked the beginnings of a new cultural relativism that has facilitated a deeper engagement with magic on its own terms, for example, as a form of consciousness or as having positive existential outcomes in the context of reenchantment.

Leo Ruickbie

Further Reading

Durkheim, Émile. *Les formes élémentaires de la vie religieuse*. Paris: Alcan, 1912.

Greenwood, Susan. *The Nature of Magic*. Oxford, UK: Berg, 2005.

Lévy-Bruhl, Lucien. *La mentalité primitive*. Paris: Alcan, 1922.

Lévy-Bruhl, Lucien. *Les carnets de Lucien Lévy-Bruhl*. Paris: PUF, 1949.

Malinowski, Bronislaw. "Magic, Science and Religion." In *Science, Religion and Reality*, edited by Joseph Needham, 19–84. London: Sheldon Press, 1925.

Mauss, Marcel, and Henri Hubert. "Esquisse d'une théorie générale de la magie." *L'Année sociologique* 7 (1902–1903): 1–146.

Ruickbie, Leo. "Weber and the Witches: Sociological Theory and Modern Witchcraft." *Journal of Alternative Spiritualities and New Age Studies* 2 (2006): 116–130.

Styers, Randall. *Making Magic*. Oxford: Oxford University Press, 2003.

Turner, Edith. *Experiencing Ritual*. Philadelphia: University of Pennsylvania Press, 1992.

Tylor, Edward. *Primitive Culture*. 2 vols. London: John Murray, 1871.

Weber, Max. *Wissenschaft als Beruf*. Munich and Leipzig: Dunckler and Humblot, 1919.

Manna from Heaven

The Bible reports God miraculously providing manna to sustain the Israelites during their wandering in the wilderness in response to their complaints about the lack of food (Exodus 16:1–4, 6–8, 11–12, 35). Unfamiliar with the miraculous food (Exodus 16:15; Deuteronomy 8:3, 16), the Israelites called it "manna," literally meaning "what is it?" (Exodus 16:31). Other biblical traditions alternatively refer to manna as the "bread of heaven" (Psalm 105:40), "bread from heaven" (Exodus 16:4; John 6:31), "grain of heaven" (Psalm 78:24), and "bread of the strong" (Psalm 78:25), and the reference to "spiritual food" in 1 Corinthians 10:3 is often considered to be manna. Comparable to a coriander seed with the appearance of bdellium (Exodus 16:31; Numbers 11:7), manna was like a frost left behind after the morning dew (Exodus 16:14; Numbers 11:9) that melted in the heat of the sun (Exodus 16:21). The Israelites gathered manna in the morning, ground it with mill-stones and cooked it into cakes that tasted like flat cakes with oil (Numbers 11:8). Each person gathered enough to eat for one day according to the size of his or her family (Exodus 16:16–18, 21). On the sixth day they gathered a double portion (Exodus 16:5, 22–26) because no manna fell on the Sabbath (Exodus 16:26–27). Later in the wanderings the people grumble again for their dislike of the manna, thereby incurring divine punishment (Numbers 11:4–6, 21:5).

Nicholas R. Werse

Further Reading

Peder Borgen. *Bread from Heaven: An Exegetical Study of the Concept of Manna in the Gospel of John and the Writings of Philo*. Leiden: Brill, 1965.

Maria Stein Shrine of the Holy Relics

The second-largest collection of Catholic relics in the United States can be found at the Maria Stein Shrine of the Holy Relics in southwestern Ohio. The relics in-clude the skeleton of Saint Victoria and a chunk of the crib that Jesus lay in as an infant. Maria Stein houses the bone fragments of hundreds of saints and martyrs, including Saint Ursula and Saint Thomas Aquinas.

That so many relics came to rest at Maria Stein is the result of a unique histori-cal convergence. Catholic immigration played a crucial role. In the 1850s German Catholics poured into southwestern Ohio, bringing parish structures, devotional regimens, and religious orders. Father Francis de Sales Brunner, leader of the Missionaries of the Precious Blood, founded a convent at Maria Stein in 1845. Sisters of the Precious Blood took up residence in it a year later. The sisters are distinguished by a commitment to perpetual adoration.

The second piece of the puzzle is the rise of the modern nation-state in Germany and Italy. The Kulturkampf and the Risorgimento threatened the monas-teries that stored Catholic relics. Priests such as Brunner, imagining the United States as a repository for such relics, purchased saints' bones and other sacred things in Europe and gave them to the sisters at Maria Stein for safekeeping. They donated relics to Maria Stein in the 1870s and 1880s, and the sisters built a chapel for the relics in 1892.

Maria Stein is still the site of many devotions. Catholics come to the shrine not just to pray in the presence of corporeal abundance but also to see the saints and be in relationship with them. Relics give saints a temporal presence. Some Catholics believe that if they pray in the presence of the relics, the saints are more likely to intervene on their behalf.

Peter Cajka

See also: Relics; Reliquary

Further Reading

Maria Stein Center. *A Guide to the Shrine of the Holy Relics and Retreat House of Maria Stein Center*. Revised ed. Maria Stein, OH: Maria Stein Center, 1989.
Maria Stein Shrine of the Holy Relics, http://www.mariasteinshrine.org.

Marmion, Abbot Columba

Blessed Columba Marmion, OSB, was beatified on September 3, 2000. The miracle that led to his beatification was the cure in 1966 of Patricia Bitzen, a wife and mother from St. Cloud, Minnesota, of inoperable breast cancer that had metastasized to her lungs. Her youngest child at the time was nine months old. The young mother's chance of survival was not good. At the encouragement of a priest, she and her husband visited the tomb of Abbot Columba Marmion at Maredsous Abbey, Belgium. For each of four days they attended Mass at his tomb offered by the vice postulator of Abbot Marmion's cause. When Bitzen first touched the tomb of the abbot she felt an immediate and irremovable bond. When she and her husband returned from the trip, her doctors said that the tumor had receded. After a few months more it had disappeared altogether.

In 1979 the diocese in which the Bitzens live began an inquiry into the cure. An oncologist, four priests, the bishop, and a former Benedictine abbot heard the testimonies of the cured mother, her husband, and a priest friend. Two physicians examined her and determined that she was cancer free. In January 2000, Pope Saint John Paul II declared her healing a miracle. He said that Marmion "offered the Church a treasure of spiritual teaching, following a simple, but demanding path of everyday holiness."

Vincent Bataille

Further Reading

Murray, Placid. "Columba Marmion: A Blessed Dubliner." *Studies: An Irish Quarterly Review* 89(356) (Winter 2000): 380–388.

Tierney, Mark. *Blessed Columba Marmion: A Short Biography*. Collegeville, MN: Liturgical Press, 2000.

Martyrs

A martyr is someone whose life is subordinated by means of a personal sacrifice to some higher principle that is objectively good, whose death is not sought for its own sake, and who dies at the hands of another who is intent on destroying the belief system of the victim. The Greek derivation of the term "martyr," *martus*, means "witness," especially in a juridical sense. Often the martyr experiences torture before death, and this is often described in hagiographic terms as the examplar of holiness.

For Christians, Stephen serves as the protomartyr. The account of his death, recorded in Acts 6–7, stands in direct parallel to the sacrifice of Jesus at his crucifixion and echoes the murder of Abel the Just (Genesis 4:1–16; 1 John 3:12). Centuries later the miracle stories recorded near Stephen's tomb are vivid depictions of the power of righteousness and purity of heart. In Uzalis, near what is today Tunis, Stephen's relics rested. A young woman, Magetia, routinely went to pray before his shrine there. Once she laid her head upon the reliquary, wetting it with her tears. A short time later, her jaw was healed of an ailment that had persistently troubled her.

Early Christians became subject to martyrdom with great frequency under several of the Roman emperors, from Nero (d. 68) to Diocletian (d. 311). Only with Emperor Gelarius was the practice rescinded throughout the empire, owing mainly to its inefficacy. In the meantime, some of the greatest Christian literature and evangelistic writings were produced, which inspired the conversions of thousands. These writings were known variously as the acts of the martyrs and the *passio*, where often the rationale for belief is laid out in copious detail. In short, death as a final consequence of life is a lie. For the Christian, their murder is avenged by a sweeter justice: life with God.

Roman pagan culture looked askance at the willingness of Christians to forego their lives, particularly when given the opportunity to recant. Many did, and it was an early point of dissension within the Christian fold whether to readmit the *lapsi* to full communion. Tacitus notes about the year 57 that the noblewoman Pomponia Graecina was persecuted for the "foreign superstition" and in so doing records the first such account of a Christian woman suffering for the faith (*Annales* 9.3.32). The miracles resulting from the exorcism of demons in preparation for baptism would have assaulted non-Christian sensibilities even while ritualizing the inclusion of neophytes into their adopted religion. Miracles thus destroyed one belief system and built up another.

For the Christian West, the city of Rome quickly became elevated in importance because it was the site of the deaths of Saints Peter and Paul. Walking along Capitoline Hill steps from the Forum, one can enter the *carceri* of Saint Joseph where Peter and Paul were imprisoned—the chains of each now enshrined in two Roman churches. Veneration of their tombs was carried out in secret, but an unbroken tradition kept Christian pilgrims in the city hopeful that they could also walk the paths of these great martyrs.

In the beginning of the second century, Irenaeus of Lyon succeeded the martyr Bishop Pothinus and is purported to have been a martyr himself. In his widely disseminated treatise *Against Heresies*, Irenaeus notes that the performance of miracles by the Apostles are done through the agency of Christ—an important claim that would refute all those engaged in the magical arts who hoped to draw attention to themselves (*Adv. Her.*, XII:1). Ireneaus was predeceased by a number of fellow Christians in Lyon, notably Saint Blandina, who after having been tortured on a grill was thrown into the path of wild bulls to be trampled. In this martyr's death, the miracle of zealous perseverance was a model to all who witnessed these assaults. Saint Ignatius of Antioch, though Syrian, by tradition died while being devoured by beasts in the Colosseum in Rome sometime at the beginning of the second century. His extant letters to nascent churches are among the weightiest Christian testimonies of the period, not least for warning against false prophets "whose bites are hard to heal." His relics, transposed to the Basilica of San Clemente in Rome in the eighth century, have been venerated there ever since.

In the East, Saint Polycarp of Smyrna, martyred circa 154/155, encouraged innumerable followers by his edifying death. His was a martyrdom of vindication, a death that became a cause for those who followed the Christian way. The response was astoundingly effective. Witness the Forty Martyrs of Sebaste, when a group of Roman soldiers became Christian and were condemned in 320. Their extraordinary deaths came by freezing the group during a night of bitter cold. Today two containers of relics repose in the Chapel of the Forty Martyrs in the Church of the Holy Sepulchre in Jerusalem and are visited by pilgrims from around the world. For Orthodox Christians, the Holy 20,000 Martyrs of Nicomedia also hold great importance in the history of the faith. During the reign of Emperor Maximian (284–305), persecution of Christians was widespread. While celebrating the Feast of the Nativity in 302, some 20,000 Christians had gathered in the cathedral at Nicomedia when soldiers were sent to demand that all present were to make sacrifice to the pagan gods or face death by fire. Not one of the 20,000 recanted, and the church was set ablaze.

Many of these early martyrs became fodder for artists interested in their heroism. Saint Sebastian (d. 288), for instance, is a classic example of a Christian martyr whose death by numerous arrows has been made the subject of artistic expression from Late Antiquity to the present day. A member of the Praetorian Guard, Sebastian had become Christian in secret but had great success in converting many Roman officials and their families as well as prisoners over whom he had oversight. Many of these were eventually martyred. Sebastian is often depicted tied to a tree, with multiple arrows jutting out from or through his flesh. The legend states that none of these was enough to cause his death, and a compassionate woman managed to nurse him back to health. When a blind member of her household doubted his Christianity, Sebastian asked whether she wished to be with God. With her affirmative reply came her sight. In the tenth century Sebastian's cranium was removed to Ebersberg in Germany, where it is encased in a silver head reliquary. His cult throughout Europe was especially pronounced during periods of plague, when he was invoked as a healer and an interceder to protect families from this scourge. More contemporary renditions of Sebastian have idealized his ability to suffer the slings and arrows of prejudice of all kinds, making him a favorite, for instance, of homosexuals who have had to fend off stigma attached to their sexuality. His relics have also traveled the world. In 2014 a fragment of his arm was translated to Sri Lanka, where its reliquary now holds a place of honor in a shrine dedicated to him in Kandana.

Similarly, there are many stories attributed to the martyrdom of Saint Lucy, the virgin from Syracuse in modern Sicily. Lucy's mother Eutychia promised her in marriage to a pagan noble. Eutychia suffered a painful illness, but Lucy persuaded her to make a pilgrimage to Saint Agatha's tomb, where she was cured. Her mother abjured the marriage for the sake of her child's wish, sending the nobleman into a rage. He denounced the pair as Christians to the Roman governor, who ordered Lucy to be dragged away. Neither man nor beast could budge her. She was ordered to be burned alive, but the flames would not obey. Finally, she was stabbed through the throat. Other versions of her legend have her eyeballs carved out of their sockets, and she is often depicted holding the two orbs on a dish. With such stories for legends, her cult spread widely. One could multiply these narratives virtually ad infinitum. Perpetua and Felicitas gave ample witness in their *Passio*, written in prison while they awaited their fate (devoured by lions); Saint Lawrence the Deacon was roasted on a spit; and Catherine of Alexandria was crushed by a wheel. They all join other martyrs who were clubbed, stoned, beheaded, or flayed alive.

The theology of martyrdom has also evolved. The Second Vatican Council noted that "martyrdom makes the disciple like the master, who so generously accepted death for the world's salvation; in the shedding of his [or her] blood the disciple is fashioned after the pattern of Jesus. This is why the Church holds martyrdom in such esteem as the most precious gift and the highest mark of his love" (*Lumen Gentium*, 42). As recently as 2015, Pope Francis has expanded the notion of martyrdom to advance the cause of Archbishop Oscar Arnulfo Romero, former archbishop of San Salvador in El Salvador, for his advocacy of the poor and his denunciation of violence. The pope noted that henceforth the definition of a martyr could be understood as one who died as a result of persecution for the principles of the Gospel.

Bloodless martyrdom—so-called white martyrs—testify by their writings or popular conviction to have withstood tyrannical suppression. More commonly, these individuals are called confessors and designated as such by the liturgical calendar. Today the Congregation for Sainthood Causes no longer requires martyrs to have a miracle to their credit. The power of their witness is enough of a litmus test.

Patrick J. Hayes

See also: Tomb

Further Reading

Bale, Anthony, ed. *St Edmund, King and Martyr: Changing Images of a Medieval Saint*. Suffolk, UK: York Medieval Press, 2009.

Buckle, D. P. "The Four Martyrs of Sebaste: A Study of Hagiographic Development." *Bulletin of the John Rylands Library* 6 (1921): 352–360.

"De miraculis sancti Stephani libri duo, II.2." In *Les miracles de saint Étienne: Recherches sur le recueil pseudo-augustinien (BHL 7860–7861) avec édition critique, traduction et commentaire*, edited by Jean Meyers, Hagiologia 5. Turnhout: Brepols, 2006.

Dubois, Jacques. *Les Martyrologes du Moyen Âge Latin*. Turnhout: Brepols, 1978.

Karlin-Hayter, Patricia. "Passio of the XL Martyrs of Sebaste: The Greek Tradition, the Earliest Accounts." *Analecta Bollandiana* 109 (1991): 249–305.

Limberis, Visiliki M. *Architects of Piety: The Cappadocian Fathers and the Cult of the Martyrs*. New York: Oxford University Press, 2011.

Middleton, Paul. *Martyrdom: A Guide for the Perplexed*. London: T. & T. Clark, 2011.

Moss, Candida. *The Other Christs: Imitating Jesus in Ancient Christian Ideologies of Martyrdom*. New York: Oxford University Press, 2010.

Nowak, Edward. "La Chiesa è nuovamente la Chiesa dei Martiri." Pamphlet issued under the auspices of the Studium Congregationis de Causis Sanctorum XXI Corso, 2004–2005. Rome: Congregation for Causes of Saints, 2004.

Workman, Herbert B. *Persecution in the Early Church*. New York: Oxford University Press, 1980.

Medical Miracles

Medical miracles refer to events that are unanticipated and inexplicable, outside the range of medical precedents and the laws of nature as assessed by science. Such miracles often represent remarkable results that are either outside of known medical or scientific expectations or breakthroughs in medical sciences that occur against all odds.

Scientists subscribing to traditional assumptions of the scientific method emphasize that metaphysical topics involving the supernatural or God are, by definition, outside of the scope of science. However, in recent decades, a changing climate of the understanding of science related to limitations in classical physics through quantum mechanics as well as recognition of the healing significance of spiritual practices has expanded the assumptions of scientists. They are now more open to recognizing that the scientific method may consider the impact of metaphysical or supernatural phenomena and how these affect outcomes.

While most of the causes of healing medicine are not fully understood yet are practiced on the basis of outcome results, the rigorous application of the scientific method has propelled the field to significant medical advances and discovery. Some medical educators, however, are appalled that medical research considers prayer, much less medical miracles, as anything more than information that can be explained in physical terms. Atheists will often argue that considering God or prayer in medicine degrades medical or scientific research. While most medical professionals conservatively reference medical miracles as unexplained or unpredictable phenomena, others embrace a holistic integration that includes faith in medical practice, recognizing spirituality as a substantive resource for healing. The case of Dr. Eben Alexander, a Harvard academic neurosurgeon and former agnostic, is notorious. He awoke following a life-threatening and debilitating coma from E. coli meningitis and described a life-changing event. Not only did he meet the traditional criteria of a medical miracle with an unexpected recovery, but he now owes his conversion from faithlessness to faith in heaven, God, and the soul to his bodily restoration. Alexander explained that while he was comatose there arose events confirming for him that God and the soul are real and that death is only a transition: "I was communicating directly with God. I was doing what every soul is able to do when they leave their bodies, and what we can all do right now through prayer and deep meditation."

The role of spirituality in medicine is a growing topic of research and scientific examination because of impressive outcome studies that include issues formerly banned from the criteria of scientific investigation. Widening the exploration of the scientific method to include metaphysical concerns has produced significant research and widening openness to the role of spiritual topics such as prayer, meditation, mindfulness, and intercessory-prayer.

A meta-analysis of over 3,600 quantitative research articles published in scientific journals revealed the overwhelmingly significant and positive role of spirituality and religion for those suffering from serious medical and psychological illnesses. Scientific studies have revealed substantial medical and psychological enhancements, improvements, and healing from prayer, meditation, and mindfulness. Identifying the physiological effects of prayer and spirituality as well as psychological benefits are limited by explanations beyond current measures. Such outcome studies have resulted in the World Health Organization defining health not only as the absence of illness or maladies but also as a state that consists of a person's mental, social, and spiritual well-being. Outcome studies have led 90 percent of U.S. medical schools to require or offer elective classes addressing spirituality and health content. Additionally, health care workers are mandated to recognize the relevance of religion and spirituality for their patients' well-being, to accept their patient's spiritual and religious needs, and to attend to the spiritual needs and concerns of patients, even though these are beyond the typical realm of doctor-patient relations.

The current climate in medicine reflects openness to areas that may be resourceful for healing outside of the medical model, to include openness to a medical miracle beyond the traditional definition "as something occurring against the odds or clear by scientific explanation."

John T. Chirban

Further Reading

Alexander, Eban. *Proof of Heaven: A Neurosurgeon's Journey into the Afterlife.* New York: Simon and Schuster, 2012.

Duffin, Jacalyn. *Medical Miracles: Doctors, Saints, and Healing in the Modern World.* New York: Oxford University Press, 2008.

Gaudia, Gil. "About Intercessory Prayer: The Scientific Study of Miracles." *Med Gen Med* 9(1) (March 2007): 56, http://www.ncbi.nlm.nih.gov/pmc/articles/PMC1924985/.

Koenig, Harold, Dana King, and Verna B. Carson. *Handbook of Religion and Health.* New York: Oxford University Press, 2012.

Schroder, Donn M. "Midwest Surgical Association Presidential Address: Can Prayer Help Surgery?" *American Journal of Surgery* 201 (2011): 275–278.

Medjugorje

Medjugorje, a collection of Croat villages in Bosnia-Herzegovina, is now home to the most popular of the late-twentieth century Marian apparition shrines. The visions began on June 24, 1981, when Bosnia was a region of Yugoslavia; the next day a group of six main visionaries was formed, all aged between nine and sixteen. Thus began a series of daily apparitions that is still continuing, with the visionaries now in their 40s. The messages all begin with a greeting translated into English as "dear children" and end with "thank you for responding to my call."

Why did Medjugorje become so popular when it began in the 1980s? First, by 1981 the processes of global communication had been developed through jet, TV, and video, and the case quickly gained interest through media reports and opportunities for travel. Second, the apparitions occurred in a country on the front line between Catholicism and communism just three years after the ascension of the Polish pope, John Paul II. The villagers of Medjugorje, just like John Paul II, spoke a Slavonic language and were Catholics in a communist country. Third, Yugoslavia was in the news as a country in some turmoil after the death of its strong leader Tito in 1980. There were three different ethnic groups with a history of conflict: Catholic Croats, Bosnian Muslims, and Orthodox Serbians. The 1980s were therefore a time of uncertainty that culminated in the genocidal civil war of 1991–1995 (resulting in the independence of the Yugoslav regions, including Bosnia-Herzegovina, first recognized by the United Nations in 1992).

Into this tense situation came a Croat Madonna (Gospa) who called herself Kraljice Mira, the "Queen of Peace." This was not a new title, having been added to the Loreto Litany by Benedict XV during World War I, but it was very apt in a region where the fault lines of the twentieth century still threatened catastrophe. Indeed, the visionaries were keen to claim that the Virgin called for interfaith and interdenominational understanding in a situation where alienation and enmity had been and were again becoming the norm.

As late as the summer of 2015, the Vatican was deliberating on a decision as to whether the case merits approval. Probably the shrine will be authenticated because of its great number of pilgrims but not the apparitions, as they are too apocalyptic in tone and have been highly controversial: there has been a great deal of Catholic opposition to Medjugorje. This was first stated by the diocesan bishop and his successor, who felt that the Gospa had proclaimed her partiality in a local disagreement between the diocese and the Franciscan order. Bishops of Mostar-Duvno Pavao Žanić (1980–1993) and Ratko Perić (1993–) have been implacably opposed to the Medjugorje apparitions.

Then there is the complicity of the Medjugorje cult in Croat extremism during the civil war, despite the messages of peace. This has led to several investigations that have exposed unsavory elements of the Medjugorje story. There is no doubt that Croat nationalism was present in Medjugorje. The shrine's own periodical, *Mir*, has several examples of this during the early 1990s. During the civil war, Medjugorje was the place where, as reported on many news channels, a United

Nations convoy loaded with food for starving Muslims in East Mostar was prevented from getting through. Additionally, some of the investigators themselves have had their reliability questioned; in particular, Dutch anthropologist Mart Bax, the author of *Medjugorje: Religion, Politics, and Violence in Rural Bosnia*, was found to have fabricated evidence. So, the truth behind Medjugorje is difficult to uncover. In all probability, like much religion, sincere devotion and misrepresentation of facts, beneficial community spirit, and exploitative politics have been mixed together there.

Medjugorje comprises elements both old and new. It stands in a long history of visionary shrines where traditional Catholic practice is encouraged: Mass, confession, and daily prayer. On the other hand, it is also a phenomenon of modern post–Second Vatican Council Catholicism. The Medjugorje Gospa displeased archconservative Catholics, as she echoed the Catholic ecumenism that had emerged after the council, and in the same vein, she asked for Bible study groups. She also deferred to her Son, which reflected the council's reemphasis on the centrality of Christ in all Marian doctrine.

Medjugorje, like Lourdes and Fatima, established a new template for apparitions that came afterward, such as those in Ireland in the mid-1980s. It also echoes visions from the past, most notably the apocalyptic tradition of Ezkioga and Garabandal in Spain (1931–1934 and 1961–1965, respectively). This consists in the visionaries' claim that there will be a great miracle, warning, and chastisement in the future and that they would give a few days' notice of the onset of these events. This tradition departs from Fatima, as there the miracles and chastisements were wrought by God through world events (peace and war, respectively), whereas the Medjugorje miracle and chastisement will come, it is claimed, in a miraculous form. The problem for the Church is that the Ezkioga visionaries said something along the same lines in the 1930s, but now most have passed away, and the prophesied miracles of Conchita Gonzalez of Garabandal, who is now in her 60s, have not yet occurred. For the Church to approve apparitions in which such prophecies are central to the message would run the risk of ridicule when the visionaries died.

Finally, for pilgrims, Medjugorje is a place of many miracles. Visitors have their own visions and see the sun spinning, and many healings are reported. The site has become popular with the Catholic Charismatic Revival, which views it as an irruption of the Holy Spirit into the world through Mary. There are many Catholic organizations worldwide that promote Medjugorje. It is likely to remain a popular shrine well into the future.

Chris Maunder

See also: Apparitions

Further Reading

Laurentin, René. *Medjugorje Testament: Hostility Abounds, Grace Superabounds.* Toronto: Ave Maria Press, 1998.

Zimdars-Swartz, Sandra. *Encountering Mary: From La Salette to Medjugorje.* Princeton, NJ: Princeton University Press, 1991.

Mesmerism

Mesmerism was a popular scientific theory developed by German physician Franz Mesmer (1734–1815). Mesmer believed that the universe was permeated by an invisible fluidlike medium through which natural laws such as gravity, electricity, light, and magnetism operated. Developed initially as a theory of medicine, mesmerism was offered by scientists, physicians, and skeptics as an explanation for supernatural, metaphysical, and miraculous phenomena, including spiritualism, mind reading, ghost apparitions, glossolalia, spirit photography, and automatic writing.

Mesmer was born in Germany in 1734. After completing his medical training at the University of Vienna, he began developing his theory of animal magnetism. Mesmer gave the name "animal magnetism" to an invisible energy force that exists in every person. This energy force was influenced by the environment, can transfer from one person or another, and causes medical problems if out of balance. Mesmer believed that correcting these imbalances in animal magnetism could heal his patients. He began to experiment with healing techniques that included waving powerful magnets or iron rods over his patients. He also developed a technique in which he or a trained assistant would stare into the eyes of the patient while making physical contact. This technique, which was popularly called mesmerizing, proved to be effective for many of his patients. Mesmer believed that mesmerizing was the process of sharing his healthy animal magnetism with his patients and that this exchange led to healing.

In 1777, a controversy between Mesmer and the faculty of medicine at the University of Vienna over the efficacy of his medical treatments forced him to move to Paris. The move proved to be a boon for Mesmer's career. His medical practice was wildly successful, and he began training other physicians in his techniques. While in Paris, Mesmer expanded his theories on animal magnetism to include his thoughts on the structure of the universe. In 1814 he published a book in which he argued that the universe was filled with an invisible fluid called the Odyllic Force. All forces of nature, including animal magnetism, light, gravity, and electricity, traveled through this medium.

As the theory of mesmerism began to spread throughout Europe and the United States, it developed into a popular scientific theory. Mesmerism proved to be a convenient way of understanding supernatural, metaphysical, and miraculous phenomena. Spiritualists (a group that believed in spirit communication through séances, automatic writing, and other means) believed that mesmerism and the Odyllic Force were scientific proof that communication with the spirit world was possible. Mind readers and other paranormal entertainers told their audiences that they were employing the principles of animal magnetism. Many antebellum Americans believed that mesmerism provided a way to permeate the barriers between the natural and the supernatural.

Mesmerism proved most successful as a medical technique. In the nineteenth century, European and American surgeons began mesmerizing patients before surgery. Before the advent of anesthesia, surgery was a very painful procedure that was used only in life-or-death situations. In the 1840s, surgeons began placing patients in a trancelike state that allowed them to undergo surgery without much pain. As mesmerism began to fall out of favor in the late nineteenth century and many mesmerizers were exposed as frauds, physicians using these techniques began referring to the trancelike state as hypnosis. Hypnosis is still practiced by physicians and psychiatrists today.

Richard Kent Evans

Further Reading

Albanese, Catherine L. *A Republic of Mind and Spirit: A Cultural History of American Metaphysical Religion*. New Haven, CT: Yale University Press, 2007.

Darnton, Robert. *Mesmerism and the End of the Enlightenment in France*. Cambridge, MA: Harvard University Press, 1986.

Fuller, Robert C. *Mesmerism and the American Cure of Souls*. Philadelphia: University of Pennsylvania Press, 1982.

Monroe, John Warne. *Laboratories of Faith: Mesmerism, Spiritism, and Occultism in Modern France*. 2nd ed. Ithaca, NY: Cornell University Press, 2008.

Methodism, Miracles in

From its inception in early eighteenth-century Britain, Methodism has always had an uneasy relationship with miracles and the supernatural, one that often troubled its leaders at the same time that it astounded its followers. Methodists held in tension their belief in the power of God and the Devil to act in the world with concerns that such beliefs and behaviors rendered the new faith less than respectable.

While Methodism's founding fathers, John and Charles Wesley, created a faith in which others would find the miraculous, they left room for God's providence but saw his intervention in the world in a more ordinary light. As accomplished open-air preachers, they came to believe that such preaching blessed their ministry more than any other way of delivering the gospel message, but they feared that perhaps the novelty of the delivery triumphed over the message in the end.

Methodists experienced miracles in three main realms. During camp meetings—open-air revivals that lasted for days and even weeks—the saved and unsaved alike experienced various inexplicable phenomena, such as jerks (spasmatic movements of the body) or barking (unintelligible sounds, not to be confused with speaking in tongues). Others danced or sang to unheard songs or fainted. Preachers debated among themselves the origins of these events. Were they the work of the Holy Spirit, the product of overwrought emotions, or simply pleas for attention? Worse yet, some preachers feared that they might be the work of the devil, sent to discredit the young but growing church. With no apparent consensus, ministers struggled to judge individual cases, attempting to determine what force worked within each person. While preachers questioned the origin of these events, ordinary Methodists found in them proof of the transformative work of the Holy Spirit. As Americans increasingly shifted from a belief in predestination to a belief that each individual chose to accept God's offer of salvation, they needed new means of determining who was sincerely saved, and these physical manifestations of the indwelling Holy Spirit provided public proof of the condition of a person's soul.

Lorenzo Dow, the most famous Methodist preacher in early nineteenth-century America, Britain, and Ireland, wrote repeatedly of miraculous occurrences, which he attributed to God's approval and blessing of his ministry. Possessed by the Holy Spirit, Dow solved murders, healed the sick, predicted the future, and commanded the weather, in direct defiance of the regulations of the Methodist Episcopal Church in America. True or not, tales of these events spread wildly, and while the official Methodist preachers renounced him, the ordinary people flocked to hear him preach and perhaps glimpse the wondrous workings of God. Despite the protests of American and British Methodist leaders, Dow introduced camp meetings in Britain and carved out space for the miraculous in British Methodism.

Other official Methodist itinerants had their own supernatural encounters. In their many journals, they recorded nighttime struggles with the devil—physical displays of their own doubts and spiritual failings—overcome through the power of the Holy Spirit. The church leaders rejected such claims, either reinterpreting them as signs of mental illness or eliminating such episodes in the published journals of otherwise respectable itinerants. In his 1791 memoir, prominent itinerant

Freeborne Garrettson vividly described his bodily struggles with the devil, overcome by his reliance on Christ; at the insistence of Bishop Francis Asbury, when the Methodist Episcopal Church published his memoirs in 1794, Garrettson removed all references to the devil and demonic activities. For the next half century in Britain and America, Methodist leaders rejected the miraculous as they tried to make the church more respectable, while most Methodists found in it comfort and evidence of salvation.

Elizabeth Georgian

Further Reading

Andrews, Dee E. *The Methodists and Revolutionary America, 1760–1880: The Shaping of an Evangelical Culture*. Princeton, NJ: Princeton Paperbacks, 2001.

The Doctrines and Discipline of the Methodist Episcopal Church in America . . . Philadelphia, Pennsylvania, 1792.

Dow, Lorenzo. *The Life and Travels of Lorenzo Dow Written by Himself in Which Are Contained Some Singular Providences of God*. Hartford: Lincoln and Gleason, 1804.

Garrettson, Freeborne. Journal, Garrettson Family Papers, United Methodist Church Archives, GCAH, Madison, New Jersey.

Garrettson, Freeborne. *The Life of Freeborn Garrettson: Compiled from His Printed and Manuscript Journals, and Other Authentic Documents*. New York: Carleton and Porter, 1832.

Middleton, Conyers

Conyers Middleton (1683–1750) was a Church of England clergyman and classical scholar who became known for his robustly skeptical attitude toward many aspects of traditional Christianity, including the authority of the Bible, miracles (although he avoided direct attacks on the miracles ascribed to Jesus Christ himself), and prophecy.

Middleton's critique of miracles drew from the long Protestant tradition of attacking "fraudulent" Catholic miracles. Several of his earlier writings were directed at the Catholic Church, and skepticism over Catholics' miraculous claims seems to have turned him in a more broadly skeptical direction. However, he also viewed his work as striking a blow at "enthusiasts," extreme Protestants such as the "French Prophets" and the Methodists. His *A Free Enquiry into Those Miraculous Powers, Which Are Supposed to Have Subsisted in the Christian Church, from the Earliest Ages through Several Successive Centuries* (1749) was very popular. *An Introductory Discourse to a Larger Work*, which set forth much of the program of *A Free Enquiry*, was published in 1747. David Hume blamed the poor success of his own *Enquiry Concerning Human Understanding* (1748), which contained his argument against the belief in miracles, on the competition it received from Middleton's work.

Although *A Free Enquiry* focused on denying the authenticity of the miracles of the postapostolic church beginning in the mid-second century, it was widely understood as attacking the miracles of Christ and the apostles by implication. Historians continue to dispute the nature of Middleton's exact religious position, but many have called him a Deist. Middleton tried to avoid this by emphasizing what he claimed was a roughly 50-year gap after 100 CE in which there were few or no claims of Christian miracles, thus drawing a sharp line between the possibly genuine miracles of Christ and the apostles and the later fraudulent ones. In attacking the later Christian writers, Middleton was striking a blow at the reverence for the Church Fathers present in much Anglican scholarship, treating them as witnesses of their time to be read as historical documents, not as inspired authorities.

Middleton's arguments against specific miracle accounts sometimes ascribed conscious fraud and other times ignorance of natural causes, as the "real" explanation of purported demonic possessions was epilepsy. An admirer of the philosophers and statesmen of pre-Christian antiquity, particularly Cicero, of whom he had published a biography, Middleton also associated Christian miraculous claims with the fraudulent pagan miracles that Cicero and others had exposed. (Middleton had previously argued that many of the ceremonies of the Catholic Church had roots in classical paganism.) He referred to recent Catholic miracles that all Anglican Protestants would agree to have been fraudulent, such as those of the Convulsionnaires of St. Médard, to further discredit early Christian miracles.

A Free Enquiry provoked many responses, including a heated one from founder of Methodism John Wesley. Wesley's "Letter to Conyers Middleton" appeared in 1749 and defended the miracles of the second and third centuries from Middleton's assaults. Wesley had a genuine contempt for Middleton, whom he regarded as a poor scholar as well as a threat to Christianity, and later referred to him as an "ignoramus." With the exception of Wesley, Middleton's opponents represented mainstream Anglicanism. Middleton also had defenders, who claimed that he was a loyal Protestant whose principal target was Catholicism, not Christianity in general, and a fine scholar. Middleton's skepticism on early Christian miracles was an influence on Edward Gibbon's *Decline and Fall of the Roman Empire*, which followed a similar strategy of largely ignoring the miracles of Christ and the apostles to concentrate on the postapostolic era.

William E. Burns

Further Reading

Campbell, Ted A. "John Wesley and Conyers Middleton on Divine Intervention in History." *Church History* 55 (1986): 39–49.

Young, Brian. "Conyers Middleton: The Historical Consequences of Heterodoxy." In *The Intellectual Consequences of Religious Heterodoxy*, edited by Sarah Mortimer and John Robertson, 235–265. Leiden, UK: Brill, 2012.

Miracle Plays

Miracle plays were a type of religious-themed drama that was prevalent in Europe, particularly England, from the tenth century to the thirteenth century. The plays were inspired by the lives of saints, sometimes presenting life histories of individual saints but often focusing on particular events from the life of the saint upon whom the play was based. It was common for a play to depict a miracle or series of miracles performed by a saint or to dramatize the events that led up to a saint's martyrdom. Traditionally, the miracle plays were performed using the Latin language at least in part.

The miracle plays emerged as the Catholic Church lessened its opposition to theatrical performances, which had been considered secular and perhaps not moral. By the tenth century, brief liturgical dramas began to be incorporated into services for such important occasions as Christmas and Easter. These dramas were usually drawn entirely from the Gospels. By the twelfth century, entire parables were being dramatized.

Full-length plays dealing with the first Christmas were being performed in Germany in the eleventh century. These plays were performed by traveling troupes of religious scholars. By 1170, miracle plays were commonplace in England; records of performances exist, although no English miracle plays of this period remain extant. The oldest surviving English miracle play is one titled *Harrowing of Hell*, which was first performed in the 1200s and depicts the descent of Christ into hell. In the 1100s the French Church produced its first miracle play, *Adam*. This play is broader in scope than preceding miracle plays, beginning with the fall of Adam and Eve and continuing through the earliest prophecies that the Savior would arrive on Earth.

By the thirteenth century, miracle plays were less frequently performed in Latin and more commonly performed in contemporary language. They were slightly more secular in nature. Miracle plays were no longer performed just at churches and certainly not just at church services. They had become a type of entertainment, performed at festivals and other gatherings throughout Europe. The festivals themselves were open to the public and were extremely important elements of cultural development; with continental Europe being largely agricultural, these festivals represented the few occasions when individuals saw or interacted with their neighbors, and the miracle plays provided an essential common ground for all. Plays were performed in cycles that could consist of as many as 48 plays. The play cycles were named after the towns in which they were performed. Guilds were formed to oversee the production of the plays.

During this period plays about the Virgin Mary were particularly popular, as Mary herself had a fervent following in Europe. These plays were not always based directly on the events of Mary's life but were often fictitious stories in which Mary intervened on the behalf of someone who had invoked her name and needed her assistance.

Another common subject of miracle plays during the 1200s was Saint Nicholas, the Greek bishop of Myra who is said to have inspired Santa Claus. The plays about Saint Nicholas also usually centered on Nicholas being asked to aid needy people who had called upon him.

During the reign of Henry VIII of England, 1509–1547, miracle plays were banned, and their manuscripts were destroyed, leaving very few remaining today. Modern miracle plays are still performed.

Because so many of the miracle plays depicted the lives of saints, they were often referred to as saint's plays. They are one of the three types of dramas known as vernacular dramas, the other types being the very similar mystery plays and the morality plays.

Randy Clark

Further Reading

Cawley, A. C., ed. *Everyman and Medieval Miracle Plays*. New York: Penguin, 1993.

Hamblin, Vicki L. *Saints at Play: The Performance Features of French Hagiographic Mystery Plays*. Kalamazoo: Medieval Institute Publications, Western Michigan University, 2012.

Patterson, Lee. "'The Living Witnesses of Our Redemption': Martyrdom and Imitation in Chaucer's Prioress's Tale." *Journal of Medieval and Early Modern Studies* 31(3) (2001): 507–560.

Miraculé/Miraculée

A miraculé (male) or miraculée (female) is one upon whom a miracle has been performed. If miracles may be defined as extraordinary events taken to manifest the supernatural power of God fulfilling his purpose or, as C. S. Lewis called them, "an interference with Nature by supernatural power," then the miraculé/miraculée is the iconic manifestation of that power. Those who receive miracles, then, include those who reaped the benefits of Old Testament miracles, such as manna from heaven for the Hebrews or Moses's parting of the Red Sea. They also include recipients of New Testament miracles such as Christ's multiplication of the loaves and fishes on the shores of the Sea of Galilee, turning water into wine at the wedding at Cana, and the multiple cures and resurrections attributed to Jesus. All believing Christians are in this sense miraculés or miraculées graced by the miracle of Jesus's own resurrection from the dead, bestowing the gift of eternal life.

Miraculés and miraculées can be the beneficiaries of healings and other physical phenomena, including nontraditional manifestations such as stigmata, the spontaneously duplicated wounds of Christ's crucifixion on the body of a Christian. Paula Kane notes that "Since the thirteenth century, stigmata have often been accompanied by other spiritual gifts, including the ability to live without food (inedia or 'holy anorexia') or without sleep, as well as bilocation, clairvoyance, exudations, hierognosis (discernment of the authenticity of holy relics), levitation, prophecy, and telekinesis." Miraculés and miraculées include those who have witnessed wondrous appearances of Christ, the Virgin Mary, or sacred relics. They can manifest Pentecostal powers, such as speaking in tongues, prophesying, or taking up serpents. While miraculés and miraculées are symbols of God's power, they themselves are not always gifted with supernatural powers, and some rely on miracle workers to be intermediaries for God's mysterious work.

Two miraculés/miraculées need to be identified for a miracle worker to be canonized, and these miracles need to be directly attributable to God. As part of the investigation of miracles, the Roman Catholic Church makes inquiries into the miraculé/miraculées's character and psychological state and about whether or not there might be a profit motive behind the miracle claim. The miracle itself is closely studied to determine if it contains any elements contrary to scripture or faith, and explorations center on the spiritual fruits of the miracle, such as whether or not it attracts people to prayer. The miraculée/miraculé, then, plays an important role in beatification and canonization.

In the nineteenth-century United States, Mrs. Ann Mattingly was a recipient of a dramatic healing attributed to Prince Alexander Hohenlohe of Bavaria in Washington City in 1824. Cures were also associated with holy water from shrines such as Lourdes and its accompanying devotions to the Immaculate Heart of Mary and the Sacred Heart of Jesus. Recent saints who have had at least two confirmed miraculés/miraculées are Brother André Bessette of Canada and Nathaniel

Hawthorne's daughter, Rose Hawthorne Lathrop, known in religious life as Mother Mary Alphonsa. The testimony of miraculés/miraculées is central to the canonization process of Roman Catholic saints.

Nancy Lusignan-Schultz

Further Reading

Burkardt, Albrecht. *Les clients des saints: Maladie et quête du miracle a tràvers les procès de canonization de la première moitié du XVII siècle en France*. Rome: École Française de Rome, 2004.

Kaufmann, Suzanne. *Consuming Visions: Mass Culture and the Lourdes Shrine*. Ithaca, NY: Cornell University Press, 2005.

Lewis, C. S. *Miracles: A Preliminary Study*. 1947; reprint, New York: HarperCollins, 2009.

Schultz, Nancy Lusignan. *Mrs. Mattingly's Miracle: The Prince, the Widow, and the Cure That Shocked Washington City*. New Haven, CT: Yale University Press, 2011.

Miraculous Medal

Sister Catherine Labouré (1806–1876), a novice in the Daughters of Charity in Paris, enjoyed an intimate conversation with Mary, Mother of Jesus, during the night of July 18–19, 1830. Having been guided by a little child, her presumed angel, Catherine knelt for two hours with her hands on Mary's knees in the motherhouse chapel on the Rue du Bac. This was the fulfillment of a childhood wish. In 1815 when Catherine's mother died, the nine-year-old girl named Mary her mother and developed not only a strong Marian devotion but also a driving desire to see Mary in person.

In that July visit, Mary expressed to Catherine her sadness about conditions in France as well as some irregularities in the religious communities. She told Catherine that the Church and France would suffer greatly and that God had a special mission for her. She was to be Mary's messenger, and she too would suffer. Catherine must maintain anonymity and confide only in her confessor, Father J. M. Aladel. Catherine maintained that pledge of secrecy until, near death in 1876, she identified herself to her superior Jeanne Dufes as the sister who received the medal, claiming "I was chosen because I was nothing."

In a subsequent apparition of November 27, 1830, during evening meditation, Mary revealed to Catherine her mission to have a medal of the Immaculate

Conception struck and propagated. Catherine then saw the medal from a distance, first the front of the medal with Mary's beautiful image as she had appeared in July and the prayer. Then the medal turned to reveal a series of symbols, a veritable catechism. Mary directed Catherine to tell Father Aladel that a medal should be struck. Aladel remained skeptical if not cynical and cautioned Catherine about her "illusions."

Again in December at evening meditation, Mary appeared and expressed concern that the medal had not been struck. Catherine chose not to share this encounter with Father Aladel. This was Mary's last visit to Catherine, although Mary promised that "You will hear my voice." Finally, Catherine shared Mary's concern with Father Aladel, a devotee of Mary himself. He became uncomfortable in his resistance to Catherine's message and sought counsel from his confrère Father Étienne. They took the issue to Archbishop DeQuelen of Paris, who approved the striking of the medal but for prudence sake did not allow discussions of the medal's origin. The medal was crafted and struck, with the first distribution occurring in May 1832. The number of people experiencing "miracles" (conversions, cures, and consolations) caused the Medal of the Immaculate Conception to become known as the "Miraculous Medal," a title it retains today despite the theological inaccuracy.

The front of the oval medal shows Mary standing on the world sphere connecting heaven and Earth and with arms outstretched offering graces to all who seek help. The prayer "O Mary conceived without sin, pray for us who have recourse to you" is engraved around the edge of the medal. The reverse of the medal, a richly concentrated catechesis, presents Mary's role in salvation history. The twelve stars suggest the woman of Revelation and the foundations of the Church. The integration of the "M" with the cross speaks of the related sufferings of Mary and Jesus, her presence at the crucifixion, and their hearts, one pierced by a sword and the other crowned with thorns.

The Miraculous Medal has encouraged Marian devotion globally. In 1854 it helped to spread awareness and scholarship on the dogma of the Immaculate Conception, as did the apparitions of Bernadette at Lourdes in 1858. From the first distribution of 1,500 medals in June 1832 to the circulation of 15 million by 1836 and to our own day, persons worldwide have followed Mary's invitation to wear the medal and seek her help.

Catherine was beatified in 1933 and was canonized by Pope Pius XII in 1947. Her incorrupt body now lies in the Chapel at Rue Du Bac and remains a site of Marian pilgrimage today.

Margaret John Kelly

See also: Apparitions

Further Reading

Laurentin, René. *The Life of Catherine Labouré*. London: Collins Publication, 2001.

Quitano, Fernando. "A Re-Reading of the Message of the Rue du Bac." Presentation during the First International Meeting of the Association of the Miraculous Medal, Rome, October 2001.

Mission Church

The city of Boston's Basilica of Our Lady of Perpetual Help, dubbed "Lourdes in the Land of the Puritans" and the "Mission Church," houses an icon for which the church is named that believers hold to be miraculous. Set on land once known as the Mission Hill section of Roxbury, the church's icon was installed on May 28, 1871, and was placed above the main altar. Between its installation and 1885, 331 cures were documented by the Redemptorists who administer this parish. Many though not all took place within its precincts. When the present basilica of Our Lady of Perpetual Help was dedicated in 1878, the icon was removed to a side chapel, and a shrine was created in her honor. Today it is adorned with the crutches left by those who enjoyed cures wrought by the miraculous picture.

Of the scores of miracle accounts on record, the most famous of these is number 43—the case of Grace Hanley, daughter of Civil War colonel P. T. Hanley of Roxbury, on August 18, 1883. As a five-year-old at play one day, she stumbled and fell upon a rock, causing her back considerable pain. The intensity of the pain grew, and despite medical assistance, her condition did not improve. She was often confined to bed and immobilized by the wearing of a heavy corset to set right her "shattered spine." Her family stormed heaven with novena after novena, often at the behest of Sisters of Charity and Sisters of the Good Shepherd. By the time she was twelve, she had been homeschooled and made her first Holy Communion. While on her way home from church one day she lost the ability to walk and could barely stand at all. Severe headaches followed, and while she was periodically able to endure transport, it was always with the assistance of others or some instrument.

By August 1883, Redemptorist Father Charles Rathke suggested that a novena be made before the Our Lady of Perpetual Help icon, and the next day Colonel Hanley carried his daughter to the Mission Church. "From the moment I began this novena I felt sure I would be cured," she later wrote. She was guided to the altar rail and received communion at the hand of Father Francis Delargy. She states that as she prayed the postcommunion thanksgiving, "I thought perhaps I was going to faint; this had not passed off when another feeling—I never can describe it—passed through me from head to foot, like a thrill (and something like electricity)." She conversed a moment with her aunt, who encouraged her to walk unassisted to the altar. There Grace Hanley knelt down and moments later got up and walked down the center aisle out into the street and did not stop until she reached her mother's room, up one flight of stairs. "I did not even feel tired," she said, "thanks to our Blessed Lord and our Dear Lady of Perpetual Help."

Some versions of this narrative have Hanley dancing down the aisle, but however it is construed, the attention lavished on the story was enough to secure the Mission Church's fame. As for Grace Hanley, she became a member of the Order of the Sisters of Jesus and Mary and died on June 14, 1902.

Patrick J. Hayes

Further Reading

Byrne, John F. *The Glories of Mary in Boston*. Boston: Mission Church Press, 1921.

Currier, Charles Warren. "History of the Church of Our Lady of Perpetual Succor in Boston." *Records of the American Catholic Historical Society of Philadelphia* 2 (1886–1868): 206–224.

Eskildson, J. F. *Our Lady's Shrine: An Account of Some of the Miraculous Cures (with a History of the Miraculous Picture) Performed at the Mission Church, Boston Highlands, 1870–1883*. Boston: Cashman, Keating, 1883.

Movies, Miracles in

Miracles in the movies have encompassed multiple thematic categories, sometimes thrilling special effects, and passionate arguments about fraud, misperception, delusion, natural phenomena, sorcery, divinity, and the inexplicable.

Biblical miracles powerfully occurred within the Old Testament classic *The Ten Commandments* (1923 and 1956, directed by Cecil B. DeMille) when God supplied intense burning bushes that remained unconsumed, parted the Red Sea, and cosmically dictated his divine commandments. Similarly, within the New Testament biopic *The Greatest Story Ever Told* (1965, directed by George Stevens), Jesus healed the blind, sick, and crippled; raised Lazarus from the dead; and dramatically resurrected and ascended. Other miraculous incidents in numerous Old and New Testament films include exorcising demons, turning rods into snakes, turning water into wine, stopping the sun, and walking on water.

Religious miracles have encompassed the (nonscriptural) divine curing of Judah's leprous mother and sister following Jesus's crucifixion within the Roman-Christian epic *Ben-Hur* (1959, directed by William Wyler) and God's commissioning of modern-day congressman Evan Baxter to build a wooden ark that saved residents from a ruptured dam in the comedy *Evan Almighty* (2007, directed by Tom Shadyac). Also, there are movies featuring Virgin Mary apparitions-cum-miraculous events, such as the screen hagiographies *The Song of Bernadette* (1943, directed by Henry King), *Miracle of Our Lady of Fatima* (1952, directed by John Brahm), and *Guadalupe* (2006, directed by Santiago Parra).

The Danish drama *Ordet* (1955, directed by Carl Theodor Dreyer) directly challenged viewers to accept miracles when "crazy" former theology student Johannes (who believed himself Jesus of Nazareth) successfully resurrected his dead sister-in-law from her coffin, while the contemporary Danish-Scottish drama *Breaking the Waves* (1996, directed by Lars von Trier) was profoundly religious *and* inexplicable when huge energetically ringing church bells floating high in the sky, unaided, ended the film.

Miracle versus mundane themes in movies showcased battles between faith and skepticism, truth and treachery, and perplexity and probability. The cynical viewpoint was succinctly stated in the biblical epic *King of Kings* (1961, directed by Nicholas Ray) when Pontius Pilate, upon hearing about Jesus's miracles, scornfully said that "There are no such things as miracles, only fools who believe in them." *The Miracle Woman* (1931, directed by Frank Capra), a romance drama, concerned embittered preacher's daughter-cum-sham evangelist Sister Florence Fallon and her very profitable miracle business. She was trapped by her phenomenal success; however, her Christian faith, good conscience, and pauper's purse were eventually restored by a blind ex-aviator's love and trust.

The "Il Miracolo" vignette from *L'amore* (1948, directed by Roberto Rossellini) depicted disturbed goatherd Nanni drinking to unconsciousness before a stranger whom she believed was Saint Joseph. She was "miraculously" pregnant and claiming God's grace to birth a divine son, and the community contemptuously crowned her the Virgin Mary before ostracizing her. The mystery thriller *Agnes of God* (1985, directed by Norman Jewison) investigated whether naive novice nun-cum-stigmatic Sister Agnes, alongside her dead newborn, was a murderess, was seduced, was raped, was a seducer, or was divinely impregnated.

The drama comedy *Leap of Faith* (1992, directed by Richard Pearce) featured the phony healings of traveling "Miracles and Wonders" showman-preacher Jonas Nightingale until a career-altering "genuine article" unexpectedly occurred. Similarly, *The Third Miracle* (1999, directed by Agnieszka Holland) showcased Roman Catholic priest-postulator Father Frank Shore, "the miracle killer" whose own deepening crisis of faith was cured by uncovering a genuine miracle.

The romance drama *Henry Poole Is Here* (2008, directed by Mark Pellington) starred the terminally ill Henry, who sought home-based solitude but was repeatedly disturbed by his deeply religious neighbor, Esperanza, who saw Christ's face in a brown water stain upon Henry's recently renovated blue stucco wall. Father Salazar and numerous neighbors-cum-pilgrims trespassed, prayed, deposited shrine gifts, and touched the wall, and some experienced cures. The disbelieving Henry angrily washed and destroyed the (repeatedly bleeding) stain but collapsed the wall and ended up in the hospital injured but disease-free with love and a hope-filled future yet still denying miracles.

Science fiction miracles replaced biblical transcendence with alien technology-cum-physiology in *The Day the Earth Stood Still* (1951, directed by Robert Wise) wherein alien ambassador Klaatu is killed by the military but resurrected via his robot, Gort, and hi-tech spaceship. Similarly, in *E.T.: The Extra-Terrestrial* (1982, directed by Steven Spielberg), cute alien visitor E.T. possessed life-restoring powers, died, and was mysteriously resurrected. *War of the Worlds* (1953, directed by Byron Haskin) featured Martian invaders who forced humanity into "praying for a miracle," which worked when the Martians were killed "by the littlest things which God in his wisdom had put upon this Earth"—bacteria and germs—against which they had no resistance.

Anton Karl Kozlovic

Further Reading

Austin, Ron. "Blue Screen: Miracles and Movies." In *Things in Heaven and Earth: Exploring the Supernatural*, edited by Harold Fickett, 45–53. Brewster, MA: Paraclete Press, 1998.

Pardes, Iiana. "Moses Goes Down to Hollywood: Miracles and Special Effects." *Semeia: An Experimental Journal for Biblical Criticism* 74 (1996): 15–31.

Shaw, Tony. "Martyrs, Miracles, and Martians: Religion and Cold War Cinematic Propaganda in the 1950s." *Journal of Cold War Studies* 4(2) (Spring 2002): 3–22.

Staley, Jeffrey L. "How to Read a Gospel by Viewing a Miracle Story in Film: An Exercise in Redaction/Narrative/Feminist Criticism." In *Teaching the Bible: Practical Strategies for Classroom Instruction*, edited by Mark Roncace and Patrick Gray, 273–274. Atlanta: Society of Biblical Literature, 2005.

Tibbetts, John. "The Wisdom of the Serpent: Frauds and Miracles in Frank Cap[r]a's *The Miracle Woman*." *Journal of Popular Film and Television* 7(3) (September 1979): 293–309.

N

Necedah Apparitions

Mary Ann Van Hoof's first claimed encounter with the Virgin Mary came in November 12, 1949, in the form of a vague figure appearing in the bedroom of her farmhouse in Necedah, a small rural village in central Wisconsin of less than 1,000 residents. On Good Friday of the next year, she saw a crucifix glow on her wall and heard a voice speak to her. In late May she began to see proper apparitions of the Virgin Mary as a "beautiful Lady," who returned repeatedly through the summer with messages to deliver to the public.

As Van Hoof's visions continued and word of them began to spread, crowds grew from dozens to hundreds to thousands (with no small help from the local Chamber of Commerce). In mid-August 1950 during the Feast of the Assumption, a massive crowd of people that some estimated as being larger than 100,000 descended upon Necedah to hear the messages. While a few individuals claimed to see the sun dance or rosaries change color, most saw nothing supernatural, and the fervor around Necedah cooled into a routinized core following.

Van Hoof was claimed to not only be visited by the Virgin Mary but to be a seer and mystic who relayed messages from her. A victim soul chosen by God, for three decades she suffered the Passion of Jesus on Fridays during Advent and Lent and displayed the stigmata for a shorter period.

Some aspects of the messages that Van Hoof claimed to receive from Mary were standard religious ones urging Catholics to renew their faith, attend Mass, and pray the rosary. Mentioning Russia, the Cold War, and other Marian apparitions such as Fatima locates them as a product of their political and cultural time. Van Hoof's messages were also awash in apocalyptic paranoia and conspiracy theories that often pointed to priests, the Novus Ordo Mass, and the Roman Catholic Church as part of a diabolical hidden plot. Eventually George Washington, Czar Alexander III, and a litany of saints were included in her visionary universe.

The activities at Necedah were condemned by the Roman Catholic Church in 1955, and interdicts against the shrine were issued in 1970 and then again in 1975. The group around Van Hoof became aligned with the North American Old Catholic Church, Ultrajectine Tradition, and Necedah became a way station for a stream of disaffected and schismatic Catholics on the far margins of the faith. In the early 1980s three men consecrated as bishops by the Spanish antipope Paul VI and a British seeress dwarf named Patricia McElliot regularly traveled to Necedah and illicitly consecrated a priest there.

Van Hoof died in March 1984 at the age of 74. The community was rocked by several scandals during the 1980s and beyond, including shrine priests and affiliates accused of fraud and child abuse.

There is a small but active community at Necedah today that includes a primary school and an orphanage. The shrine is officially known as Queen of the Holy Rosary Mediatrix between God and Man Shrine, and its grounds host a large Christmas pageant, monthly prayer vigils, and several annual prayer vigils on the days that Mary allegedly appeared to Van Hoof. The "House of Prayer" edifice requested by the Blessed Mother in 1950 has been perpetually under construction on the site of the visitations for decades and is still little more than a concrete foundation.

Many have noted the similarities and alleged contact between the legacy of Van Hoof and the Necedah apparitions and Veronica Lueken and the Marian visions at Bayside, New York.

Philip Deslippe

See also: Bayside Apparitions

Further Reading

Kselman, Thomas A., and Steven Avella. "Marian Piety and the Cold War in the United States." *Catholic Historical Review* 72(3) (July 1986): 403–424.

Swan, Henry H. *My Work with Necedah*, Vols. 1–2. Necedah: For My God and My Country, 1959.

Zimdars-Swartz, Sandra L. "Religious Experience and Public Cult: The Case of Mary Ann Van Hoof." *Journal of Religion and Health* 28(1) (Spring 1989): 36–57.

Newman, John Henry

Born in 1801, John Henry Newman demonstrated early academic aptitude while at the Great Ealing School from 1808 to 1816 before entering Trinity College at

Oxford and subsequently attaining a fellowship at Oriel College. After redirecting his education from law to theology, Newman was ordained to the Church of England in 1825. In 1828 he became the vicar of St. Mary's at Oxford, where he gained popularity as a preacher and writer. Newman resigned from his post at St. Mary's in 1843 after falling into disapproval with his superiors at Oxford and several bishops over one of his publications in the reform effort known as the Oxford Movement. In 1845 Newman transitioned into the Roman Catholic Church, and in 1847 he was ordained to the priesthood, receiving a doctorate of divinity. In his writings Newman argued for several reforms of the Catholic Church, many of which did not come to full fruition until Vatican II. In 1879, Newman was made a cardinal by Pope Leo XIII. Newman continued to live and write in England until his death on August 11, 1890. On July 3, 2009, Pope Benedict XVI recognized the first miracle attributed to the intercession of Newman when Deacon Jack Sullivan was healed of a spinal disorder in 2001. Newman has thus been beatified, but a second miracle is necessary before his canonization.

Newman's chief writings on miracles stem from an 1825–1826 essay on biblical miracles. He subsequently wrote an essay on the miracles in early Christianity from 1842 to 1843. In the first essay, Newman presents biblical miracles as instruments of conversion addressed to inquirers. Following numerous Anglican thinkers of his day, Newman's early essay diminished the value of postbiblical miracles in the Catholic tradition. After its publication Newman developed an understanding of the supernatural at work in the ecclesial community, which becomes evident in his second essay. He thus had to rethink his position on postbiblical miracles that were claimed by the Catholic Church during his transition from Anglicanism to Roman Catholicism. Newman eventually concluded against the Reform cessationist tradition that miracles ceased with the apostolic age.

In the second essay, ecclesial miracles are addressed to Christians as rewards of the faith that are different in nature and scope. The two essays were later combined and published as *Two Essays on Biblical and on Ecclesiastical Miracles*, which went into several editions. Newman ultimately claimed a degree of analogous continuity between biblical and ecclesial miracles. In a later more apologetic work, *An Essay in Aid of a Grammar of Assent*, Newman intentionally responded to the critique of miracles from Hume and Gibbon. According to Newman, the argument that miracles are improbable due to the lack of observable parallels in personal experience is invalid, because miracles must be assessed in light of both the physical and moral order. According to Newman, the value of miracles was not their physical effects but rather the influence they had on one's moral consciousness. Formal inference is not the best way to consider miracles, which only serve to defy the application of human logic. God's working of miracles, Newman insisted, "cannot by any ingenuity be imprisoned in a formula, and packed into a nut-shell."

Nicholas R. Werse

Further Reading

Jaki, Stanley Ladislas. "Newman and Miracles." *Downside Review* 115:400 (1997): 193–214.

Ker, Ian. *John Henry Newman: A Biography*. New York: Oxford University Press, 2009.

Newman, John Henry. *An Essay in Aid of a Grammar of Assent*. Notre Dame: University of Notre Dame Press, 1979.

Newman, John Henry. *Two Essays on Biblical and Ecclesiastical Miracles*. Notre Dame: University of Notre Dame Press, 2010.

Rickaby, Joseph. *Index to the Works of John Henry Cardinal Newman*. London: Longmans, Green, 1914.

New Thought

New Thought, a school that believed that one's thoughts and could influence their physical health, material success, and environment, is often thought of as emerging from Christian Science in the late nineteenth century. New Thought reached the height of its popularity in the early-twentieth century, but its lasting mainstream influence can be found within the Positive Thinking movement and the Prosperity Gospel. The similarities between New Thought's central tenets and those of magic were often noted by its critics, and there was significant overlap between New Thought students and teachers and theosophy, esoteric Christianity, the occult, and hypnotism.

The history of New Thought and its immediate predecessors is filled with testimonies of inexplicable healings from illness and dramatic reversals of fortune. William Walker Atkinson claimed that New Thought rescued him from the depths of a nervous breakdown, and Helen Wilmans chronicled her own rags-to-riches story in *The Conquest of Poverty*. Several leading New Thought figures such as Annie Rix Militz, founder of the Home of Truth, and Charles Fillmore, founder of Unity, believed during their lifetimes that they had achieved physical immortality.

With a strong emphasis on universal laws and science, these events were seen as evidence of New Thought teachings and not divine intervention. Many New Thought authors used the examples of miraculous events—from biblical miracles to the astounding success of contemporary industrialists to psychic phenomena—as logical demonstrations of the infinite power of the will and the mind.

Philip Deslippe

Further Reading

Albanese, Catherine. *A Republic of Mind and Spirit: A Cultural History of American Metaphysical Religion*. New Haven, CT: Yale University Press, 2007.

Braden, Charles S. *Spirits in Rebellion: The Rise and Development of New Thought*. Dallas, TX: Southern Methodist University Press, 1963.

Northern Europe, Miracles in

In Northern Europe the stable belief in miracles mostly exists in countries with strong Roman Catholic, Orthodox, and Old Orthodox traditions. That is, such a belief predominates in the Baltic countries, especially in Latvia and Lithuania, and in the United Kingdom with its Catholic background.

Marian apparitions are difficult to catalog, as there have been so many. Appearances of Our Lady that have been reported in the territory of the Baltic countries still are less known among them. According to the chronicle of Syrenez (Vaskarva) in Estonia, Mary appeared in the sixteenth century in the territory of the current Orthodox Pühtitsa Dormition Convent (Kuremäe Convent). In eastern Latvia the appearance of Mary dates back to the seventeenth century, and from that time in the Latvian Roman Catholic Church, Our Lady of Aglona is celebrated. In the beginning of the seventeenth century a similar celebration of Our Lady was established also in Lithuania, where several times many people saw the apparition of a sorrowful Mary on the rock near the village of Siluva. All three above-mentioned places have something else in common. In Pühtitsa and Aglona the churches in honor of Our Lady have been built near springs whose waters had curative power and to this day are associated with healing miracles. In Siluva, healing powers are attributed to the rock on which Mary appeared. All places are connected also with so-called wandering icons. For example, in Pühtitsa the ancient icon of Dormition of the Mother of God was found by locals under a huge oak tree. In Siluva, the icon of Madonna with Child was found by a blind man, more than 100 years old, and after that his sight was miraculously restored. It is believed that all three icons have healing powers, and today Pühtitsa, Aglona, and Siluva are important pilgrimage sites. In the same context should be mentioned well-known Marian apparitions in England and Mary's sanctuaries in Abingdon,

Canterbury, Glastonbury, and Walsingham as well as the pilgrimage sites of Our Lady of Musselburgh in Scotland and Our Lady of Trim in Ireland.

It should be noted also that a number of other places connected with Catholic pilgrimage are often described as sites with wonder-working power. In Lithuania, such a place is the Hill of Crosses located 12 kilometers north of the small industrial city of Siauliai. In 1993 Pope John Paul II visited the Hill of Crosses and proclaimed it a place for hope, peace, love, and sacrifice. Since that time millions of people from all over the world have journeyed to this hill, and the number of crosses reaches 200,000 today. In the United Kingdom, pilgrimage places are shrines of the saints, such as the tomb of Saint Wulstan in Worchester Cathedral and St. Winefride's Well in North Wales. In Scandinavian countries, with their predominant Protestant tradition, there are just a few such places. One of them is St. Canute's or Odense Cathedral in Denmark, where the remains of King Canute, who was murdered in the church of St. Alban's Priory in 1086, and his brother Benedict are on display.

Northn European Orthodox and Old Believers often associate miracles with weeping, myrrh-streaming, and self-cleaning icons of Jesus, Mary, and the saints. For example, over several years ten icons were streaming myrrh in the branch of Riga St. Trinity-Sergiev Nunnery in Valgunde, Latvia. Additionally, in Latvia a myrrh-streaming icon of Saint Nicholas can be seen in the Orthodox Church of the Nativity of the Blessed Virgin in Ilukste. Myrrh-streaming figures are also found in paintings of the Resurrection, icons of the Theotokos, Saint Nicholas, Saint Seraphim of Sarov in the Orthodox Cathedral devoted to Saints Boris and Gleb in Daugavpils. Old believers of Daugavpils in their turn worship the myrrh-streaming cross. The self-cleaning icon of Saint Seraphim of Sarov is worshipped in the St. Trinity Cathedral, located in the territory of Riga St. Trinity-Sergiev Nunnery.

Further, across Northern Europe specific phenomena of belief in healing miracles are strengthened by a rapidly growing influence of different evangelical ministries. For example, healing ministries in Sweden, Denmark, and Norway where hundreds or even thousands of people were healed from all kind of diseases after spiritual prayers, and the baptism of the Holy Ghost have been widely described. When in 1374 the relics of Saint Birgitta of Sweden were translated to her homeland from Rome, the usual healings were recorded, but the Briggitines who carried her additionally received premonitions of war, which they were careful to avoid.

Belief in miracles also sometimes depends on returning to the pre-Christian religious traditions and some specific newly invented neo-pagan practices. Thus, all over Northern Europe, sacred stones, caves, trees, hills, and springs with miraculous healing power are being searched out and made sites for worship. For example, in Estonia there are around 2,000 sacrifice stones, and many of them are being honored at present. Some of them are so-called slide-down stones or fertility stones that, as evidenced by a number of reports, miraculously help women to conceive a child. Such stones are also used in Sweden. In northern Sweden, one of the best-known fertility stones is near the village of Jerstva, next to the Viking cemetery. In Latvia, thousands of people each year go to Pokaiņi, near the city of Dobele. Pokaiņi is considered a particularly sacred healing spot with stones, trees, hills, and springs, all endowed with curative power.

Solveiga Krumina-Konkova

Further Reading

Fröjmark, Anders. "*Ad portum non precogitatum:* The Homecoming of the Birgitta Relics to Sweden (1374)." *Analecta Bollandiana* 129(1) (2011): 81–104.

Shevzov, Vera. "The Struggle for the Sacred: Russian Orthodox Thinking about Miracles in a Modern Age." In *Thinking Orthodox in Modern Russia*, edited by Patrick Lally Michelson and Judith Deutsch Kornblatt, 131–150. Madison: University of Wisconsin Press, 2014.

Vail, Anne. *Shrines of Our Lady in England.* Herefordshire, UK: Gracewing Publishing, 2004.

Wigglesworth, Smith. *Ever Increasing Faith.* Radford, VA: Wilder Publications, 2007.

Novena

In Roman Catholic tradition, a novena is a prayer of petition typically repeated over nine days. The word "novena" is derived from the Latin *novem*, meaning "nine." The daily prayers can be offered in either private or public as an intercession for a blessing. These petitions may consist of the rosary or a devotional prayer dedicated to the Trinity, the Sacred Heart of Jesus, the Virgin Mary, or another saint and offered throughout the day. A celebration of the Eucharist may be held before or after a novena on the tenth day to complete the petition. A novena is a challenging form of prayer, requiring discipline and a mindful approach to the devotion.

A novena's nine consecutive days recall the amount of time Mary and the Apostles spent praying between Ascension Thursday and Pentecost Sunday. Considered the first novena, the future leaders of the new church were cloistered in continuous prayer in anticipation of the promised coming of the Holy Spirit. In Christian belief, the descent of the Holy Spirit on the tenth day led to the foundation of the Church.

Usually, novenas are prayers or devotions offered on nine consecutive days, but through the centuries the strict period of nine days has taken various forms. The series could take place over nine consecutive weeks or nine months, including devotions on nine First Fridays. Some local traditions include three-day or thirty-day novenas. Mother Teresa is credited with developing the emergency novena or express novena, consisting of nine consecutive *memorares*, a traditional prayer to the Virgin Mary.

Novena, as the feminine form of the medieval Latin word for "nine," probably dates back as a sacred number to at least the Roman Empire. The classical historian Livy described the Romans using nine days' solemnity of prayer and sacrifice to ward off supernatural portents, including a mysterious shower of stones, probably a meteor shower, that fell from the sky during the Punic Wars. The devotion was also informed by early Greek and Roman pagan customs memorializing the dead. Nine days of mourning followed by a feast celebrating a life on the tenth day helped shape the tradition that originated outside of Scripture. Nine may also represent the nine months of Mary's pregnancy with Jesus Christ in the womb.

A novena is a devotional practice that is separate from a liturgical action, external to the celebration of the Holy Eucharist and of the other sacraments, and therefore cannot be used during Mass. According to Catholic rule, novena prayers must first be approved for public use by a bishop or other ranking official. The Latin names for such approvals are *nihil obstat* ("nothing hinders" or "nothing stands in the way"), *imprimi potest* ("it can be printed"), and the imprimatur ("let it be printed"). The 1963 Constitution on the Sacred Liturgy issued by Pope Paul VI governs the rules of approval; these were updated in a more recent document, "Directory on Popular Piety and the Liturgy," published by the Congregation for Divine Worship in 2001.

There are four main kinds of novenas: of mourning, of preparation for feast, of prayers of petition both by individuals or groups, and of indulgence for the remission of sin. Novenas may be performed in church, at home, or anyplace where solemn prayers are appropriate, though some indulgenced novenas require church attendance and symbolic additions of incense or a perpetual candle. During the Middle Ages, novenas began to be used as preparation for a feast or for important liturgical events. The familiar Advent hymn "O Come, O Come Emmanuel" is part of the ceremony of Vespers, a nine-day preparation for the Christmas feast. The novena has grown in popularity and variety ever since the Middle Ages, with countless devotional novenas practiced today. The novena has always been more widespread in popular piety than as part of the Church's formal liturgical tradition. For two and a half millennia, novenas have been popularly believed to bring miraculous answers to prayers.

Nancy Lusignan-Schultz

Further Reading

Schultz, Nancy Lusignan. *Mrs. Mattingly's Miracle: The Prince, the Widow, and the Cure That Shocked Washington City*. New Haven, CT: Yale University Press, 2011.

Yuhaus, Cassian J., and Richard Frechette. *Speaking of Miracles: The Faith Experience at the Basilica of the National Shrine of Saint Ann in Scranton, Pennsylvania*. New York: Paulist Press, 2006.

O

Odor of Sanctity

Odor of sanctity refers to a scent that is said to emanate from bodies of saints recognized by the Catholic Church. In addition, in the Islamic tradition pleasant scents have been associated with both saints and martyrs. Although this scent is generally described as merely a fragrant aroma, it is more specifically associated with flowers and awakens the olfactory response in sometimes pronounced ways. For example, upon the death of Saint Teresa of Ávila (1515–1582), the water in which she bathed, the monastery where she lived, and the grave site in which she was buried were said to have smelled of roses. Incorruptibles—bodies of individuals, saints in particular—that seemingly do not undergo the natural process of decomposition are also said to exude the odor of sanctity.

Despite these more popular cases, this phenomenon is not exclusive to the circumstances of individuals' dying or even their postmortem states, as there are examples of individuals exuding such agreeable fragrances during their lives. Perhaps the most well-known example of this took place during the stigmata of Saint Pio of Pietrelcina, in which the blood that flowed from his wounds was said to have had a floral scent. The fragrance of flowers is an old trope. Saint Ambrose of Milan, writing in the fourth century, suggested that virgins "emit a fragrance through divine grace as gardens do through flowers, temples through religion and altars through the priest."

Some scholarship has suggested that olfactory systems played an important role in organizing the social order of religiosity from as early as Late Antiquity. Within this conceptual framework, individuals may have used scents associated with religious or nonreligious figures as at least one attribute in the informative process of designating such figures as sacred or secular. The scents also limned the boundaries between good and evil. Sweet spices were contrasted with more acrid or sulfuric ones. This is not a hard-and-fast rule, however. In the fifth century the Syrian stylite Symeon tended a malodorous and festering wound for years, yet his body is said to have emitted "sweet smells of asceticism."

Additionally, both the rituals that incorporate the stimulus of scent—thereby contributing to the establishment of a communal experience—and the participation in such rituals within which smells conjure up individual memories associated with a given event serve to enhance one's religious experience. In this way, the phenomenon of the odor of sanctity has the potential to lend itself to moments in which one may affirm or even reaffirm one's faith through the encounter of such fragrances. Further, the removal of foul scents and the perfuming of a cleansed body—as in the ritual ablutions for Muslims—is meant to make the believer a more acceptable oblation before God.

Salvador Murguia

Further Reading

Harvey, Susan Ashbrook. *Scenting Salvation: Ancient Christianity and the Olfactory Imagination.* Berkeley: University of California Press, 2006.

Rothkrug, Lionel. "The Odour of Sanctity and the Hebrew Origins of Christian Relic Veneration." *Historical Reflections* 8(2) (1981): 95–142.

Thurkill, Mary. "Odors of Sanctity: Distinctions of the Holy in Early Christianity and Islam." *Comparative Islamic Studies* 3(2) (2007): 133–144.

Oil

When an unctuous substance such as oil is tied to miraculous phenomena, it elicits a sensate reaction either through touch, taste, vision, or smell. Oil not only can be applied to objects such as bodies or statues but can be exuded from them as well. It is a means to the sacred and makes it tangible and immediate.

It had been the custom of the ancient Hebrew kings to be anointed with oil, a practice that stems from "Jacob's pillow," as explained in the book of Genesis. Jacob had a vision of a ladder leading to heaven, with God at the top. To mark the place, Jacob set up a "stone pillow" and, "pouring oil on it," consecrated it with the name "Beth-el" or "House of God" (Genesis 28:10–14, 28:18–22). In Genesis 31:13, God validates this name and the anointing such that by chapter 35 (9–15) Jacob's name is changed to Israel, and God's commitment to the covenant relation with Jacob and his descendants comes into closer view. So favorable is the practice of pouring out oil that the patriarch Moses is instructed to anoint the tabernacle and all the sacred vessels with it (Exodus 40:9). He later anointed the tabernacle again, together with its contents, as well as the altar of the Temple (Leviticus 8:10–11).

Links between leadership, power, and oil extend to others in the Hebrew scriptures. Aaron and his sons are made priests through the use of holy oil. Samuel anoints Saul as king, who in turn consecrates David to be ruler of Israel. They are anointed on the head.

When combined, the thickening agents for holy oil included myrrh, cinnamon or other perfumed spice, and a pure olive oil. They formed chrism, from the word *chrio* (to anoint). As a healing balm, it was frequently used medicinally so that by the time of the earliest Christians, the apostle James can be found instructing the other disciples to anoint the sick (James 5:14). Indeed, in the Christian gospels, the apostles are often found curing the sick with oil (Mark 6:13). The kingship theme is also found in Christian texts, though the accent is on humility. For instance, Jesus has his feet anointed by Mary of Bethany (the Magdalene) with a pure and expensive nard (John 12:3) and dries his feet with her own hair.

The liturgical use of oil is meant to convey the presence of God's Holy Spirit, marking the body and empowering it to do holy things. This is the nature of sacrament. Whether through priestly service, confirmation, or extreme unction, bodies are consecrated and glorified. It is easy to see why. Oil's natural properties suggest the ability to do the unexpected. Thus, oil can float on any liquid, soften things that are hard and chapped, sweeten the bitter, illumine the darkness, and supply nourishment to the body. Oil thus became sought after. Pilgrims around the Mediterranean would collect oil from the lamps of shrines in ampullae to bring home with them.

Perhaps most unusual of all, oil has been discovered emanating from three-dimensional objects such as statues, especially those composed to represent the Virgin Mary, bones, or tombs. In the eleventh and twelfth centuries the bones of Saint Nicholas of Bari were said to exude copious amounts of oil. Recent examples of this include a Marian statue in a Christian home in the town of Tarshiha, on Israel's northern border with Lebanon. It tends to "weep" oil, which continues even after being wiped from the statue.

Similarly, the case of the pictures and statues associated with the home and chapel of Audrey Santo (1983–2007) of Worcester, Massachusetts, has caused thousands of visitors to marvel. Santo had been bedridden for many years, and her sanctity has been promoted by family and friends since her death. The first reported manifestation of oil came in 1992 on a picture of Our Lady of Guadalupe in Audrey's room. The local bishop convened an investigation and, erring on the side of caution, released the following statement: "Is the presence of this 'mysterious' oil significant? The presence of oil is not proof, direct or indirect, of the miraculous. Paranormal activities in and of themselves, according to the perspective and practice of the Catholic Church, do not provide a basis for proving the miraculous. This has been the Church's confirmed directive for hundreds of years since Pope Benedict XIV (1740–1758). When one applies fundamental rules of logic to the situation, even if the presence of the oil cannot be explained, one cannot presume that the inability to explain something automatically makes it miraculous. It certainly calls for scientific research and we will continue to do so. We must be careful not to identify this oil as 'holy oil,' which could be used to anoint a person."

Patrick J. Hayes

Further Reading

"Diocese Issues Interim Findings on Miraculous Claims Statement by Most Rev. Daniel P. Reilly, Bishop of Worcester." The Diocese of Worcester, http://web.archive.org/web/20070928100126/http://www.worcesterdiocese.org/audrey.html.
Harvey, Susan Ashbrook. *Scenting Salvation: Ancient Christianity and the Olfactory Imagination.* Berkeley: University of California Press, 2006.
Mueller, Tom. *Extra Virginity: The Sublime and Scandalous World of Olive Oil.* New York: Norton, 2011.

Orthodoxy and Miracles

For Orthodox Christianity, the true miracle is the revelation and revolution inaugurated by Jesus Christ in the world: his birth, ministry, crucifixion, and, quintessentially, resurrection from the dead. The resurrection is the miracle par excellence, manifesting the good news of the Gospels. Jesus Christ empties himself into the fallen world of sin and death, the miracle of God's intervention through the birth of Jesus Christ. Moreover, Christ's crucifixion serves as testimony of his love for humankind whereby death is miraculously overridden through his resurrection. The power of the resurrection miracle is that humankind may share in the true miracle by participating in Christ's love and a life in Christ.

From this vantage point, while all miracles of Christ are recognized in Orthodoxy as extraordinary supernatural events, they remain secondary, as they are harbingers leading to the central resurrection miracle event. Instances of these events in which the lame and blind are healed are temporary or secondary, as those healed ultimately succumb to natural ends. However, the miracle of the resurrection of Jesus provides knowledge of the power and truth that prevail to the end of time, through eternity. Through the resurrection miracle Christ shows that he ruled over space and time but is not subject to either. Some Orthodox theologians have explored the significance of miracles for the faithful. Among the most notable is Sergei Bulgakov, who observes that the New Testament provides a series of texts that have one common theme: "The resurrection of Christ was accomplished in that 'God has raised up (in Greek, *anestesen*) Jesus of Nazareth.'"

Although Jesus performed miracles, he did not seek to attract those who sought out miracles as essential proof of his ministry and significance. The Gospels tell that the Pharisees remained unconvinced of Jesus's claims about himself after he cured a demon-possessed man who was both blind and mute. Following this event, the Pharisees accused Jesus of driving out demons by the power of Satan, and they asked him, "Teacher, we want to see a sign from you" (Matthew 12:38). When asked by the Pharisees for miraculous proof that he was indeed the Messiah, Jesus used a metaphor to reference his future crucifixion and resurrection: "A wicked and adulterous generation asks for a sign! But none will be given it except the sign of the prophet Jonah. For as Jonah was three days and three nights in the belly of a huge fish, so the Son of Man will be three days and three nights in the heart of the earth" (Matthew 12:39–40). In this way Jesus defines the true miracle, the resurrection.

Orthodox Christians affirm miracles of saints and miracle workers as occurrences that encourage and strengthen faith. Icons are venerated as holy objects believed to promote protection against evil and sickness, retaining miraculous energy, as icons are windows to the supernatural world. Orthodoxy is rich in its tradition of art through iconography, medallions, phylacteries, and artifacts utilizing such material objects as vehicles for divine healing. Sanctity of holy people and holy places is transferred through these art forms. For example, the sand of Jerusalem or soil around the grave of a saint may serve as a vehicle for miracles and healing.

Prayer and spiritual life of the early church evolved through liturgical services to healing services through prayers sanctified by anointment of pure olive oil in the sacrament of Holy Unction. In Orthodoxy, a healing tradition of holy men and women established a tradition of miracle workers. Within this miracle tradition, those maintaining contact with God, so-called saints, miracle workers, and holy men and women, tap into the healing power of the Holy Spirit with the capacity to initiate miracles on the spiritual, psychological, and physical plane. Volumes are written about hundreds of such saints who were empowered with divine gifts that mediated God's love and healing through their prayers, guidance, and blessings. The physical clothing or actual bones of such holy persons and merely visiting their homes or graves are reported to facilitate miraculous healing.

In line with a holistic understanding of healing over Cartesian divisions separating healing of body, mind, and soul, Orthodox faithful embrace the numerous miracles of fellow healers who seek to remedy illness and death through science and various healing acts. The Orthodox spiritual tradition affirms discovery of natural cures, whether through medicine or science, as proof of God's philanthropy and the goodness of creation. In Orthodoxy, miraculous, mystical, and supernatural experiences are not separate from theology but instead are the basis for theology. Healing as well as illness emerges out of the historical Judeo-Christian notion of wholeness between body, mind, and soul, reflecting on human nature as physical, psychological, and spiritual. Though the Orthodox tradition distinguishes between scientific and spiritual healing, it refrains from separating them. All of these efforts, both religious and scientific, are precursors to the world as it is suppose to be—healed and restored.

Throughout the history of the Orthodox church, from the fourth century the Eastern Roman Empire and the Byzantine Empire created settings where holistic healing, including miracles, occurred in *xenones* (places for strangers; hostels) and hospitals, drawing on both medical and spiritual resources for healing and collaborating with patients' initiatives with reference to their spiritual healing. Scholars detail a span of approximately 1,000 years during which Orthodox miraculous healings occurred in Byzantium, curing many of the same illnesses suffered by people today through miraculous healings at saints' shrines and sacred springs and contact with the coffins and relics of saints and through miraculous artifacts, such as icons, as well as miraculous healing events by living saints.

Miracles awaken people from their spiritual stupor, when faithful and unfaithful alike fail to recognize God in nature. For Orthodox Christians, miracles occur today similarly to affirm the Gospel. Orthodox Christians today participate in these same vital mediums for miracles in addition to resources of prayer, sacramental life, and modern secular healing methods.

John T. Chirban

See also: Byzantium, Miracles in; Resurrection/Resuscitation

Further Reading

Bulgakov, Sergei. *Relics and Miracles*. Grand Rapids, MI: William B. Eerdmans, 2011.

Chirban, John, ed. *Holistic Healing in Byzantium*. Brookline, MA: Holy Cross Press, 2010.

Efthymiadis, Stephanos, ed. *The Ashgate Research Companion to Byzantine Hagiography*, Vols. 1 and 2. Aldershot, UK, and Burlington, VT: Ashgate, 2011, 2014.

Fouka, Georgia, et al. "Health-Related Religious Rituals of the Greek Orthodox Church: Their Uptake and Meanings." *Journal of Nursing Management* 20 (2012): 1058–1068.

Meyendorff, John. "Miracles: Medical, Psychological, and Religious Reflections." In *Healing: Orthodox Christian Perspectives in Medicine, Psychology, and Religion*, edited by John T. Chirban, 51–55. Brookline, MA: Holy Cross Press, 1991.

Talbot, Alice-Mary, and Scott Fitzgerald Johnson, trans. *Miracle Tales from Byzantium*. Cambridge, MA: Harvard University Press, 2012.

Our Lady of Aglona

The veneration of Our Lady in Latvia has a long tradition, because historically this country has been known as Terra Mariana, so-named by Pope Innocent III in 1215. From the beginning, the first missionaries always emphasized devotion to the Virgin Mary. For example, when Bishop Albert built a cathedral in Riga in 1215, he dedicated it to the honor of the Assumption of Mary. Later the Dominicans also dedicated their churches in honor of Mary. One of the most well-known Dominican centers is Aglona in Latgale, in eastern Latvia.

Celebration of Our Lady of Aglona dates back to the end of the 1600s, when Countess Ewa Justyna Sielicka-Szostowicka invited Dominicans from Lithuania to establish the church and monastery and donated the land of Wyszkowo (today Aglona) to them. For the site of their church, Dominicans chose a spot in the pine forest between Lake Cīriss (Cīreits in Latgalian) and Lake Egle (Agles Azars in Latgalian), a nearby spring that had curative powers and was reputed also to protect against sorcery and the "evil eye." The monastery was built first, in 1699. The wooden church in honor of the day of the Most Holy Virgin Mary's Ascension was built in 1751. This church was destroyed during the fire of 1766, and in 1768 the Dominicans began to build the present stone church, which was finished in 1780. The church, in Italian Baroque style, is considered one of the most beautiful sacred buildings in Latvia.

The greatest treasure of the church is the historic icon of the Madonna and Child, popularly known as Our Lady of Aglona. The Aglona icon is thought to be a copy of the icon of the Virgin Mary at the Dominican church in Trakai, Lithuania. According to several sources, the Trakai icon is one of the so-called peripatetic or wandering Madonnas, painted by Saint Luke. A long-standing version says that this icon came from Constantinople to Lithuania in 1384 as a gift from Byzantine emperor Manuel II to Lithuanian grand duke Vytautas the Great in honor of the conversion of Lithuania. The icon was placed in his Trakai castle's Church of the Assumption of the Virgin Mary in 1409. At the end of the seventeenth century, a copy of the Trakai icon was made at the request of Aglona's Dominicans. The first historical reference to the Aglona icon is from 1718, when it was crowned—that is, a silver shroud with a crown above the head of both Mary and little Jesus was placed on the painting. The Trakai icon also was crowned in 1718.

There is a legend that the Aglona icon is the original painting, while the copy was mistakenly returned to Trakai between 1708 and 1710 during the Great

Northern War, when the Trakai icon had been brought to Aglona for safe keeping. This legend also tells that residents of Aglona village were saved from the plaque of 1708 thanks to the protection of Our Lady of Aglona.

There are hundreds of reports of miracles connected to the Aglona icon, and thousands of signs of gratitude for restored health or other favors, commonly called votas, are to be seen around the painting today. If in earlier times the Aglona icon was shown only during major religious celebrations, now it is displayed at each religious service. In the time between services, it is normally kept hidden by a painting of the Assumption of the Blessed Virgin that hangs in front of it.

According to tradition, on August 15, 1698, the Blessed Virgin Mary appeared to Latgalian orphan girl Anna from Wyszkowo estate when she was saying evening prayers. Therefore, the biggest religious feast with thousands of pilgrims has been the Assumption of the Blessed Virgin, on August 15.

In 1980 Pope John Paul II conferred the title of basilica (*basilicae minoris*) to Aglona's church, and now it is one of the eight international shrines recognized by the Holy See.

Solveiga Krumina-Konkova

Further Reading

Aglonas Bazilika—Basilica Aglonensis—Aglonos Bazilika. Sastādītājs Silvija Tulisa. Rēzekne: Katōļu Dzeive, 1993.

Latkovskis, Leonhards. *Aglona: A History of the Church and Monastery.* Rezekne: Publishing House of the Latgalian Culture Centre, 2009.

Our Lady of Akita

In 1973, Sister Agnes Katsuko Sasagawa (b. 1930)—a deaf nun residing in Akita, Japan—reported apparitions of the Virgin Mary, stigmatic occurrences, and the weeping of a Marian statue. Known as Our Lady of Akita, Sasagawa's account of these events has received a formal acknowledgment known as an "Approval of the Bishop" in the Catholic Church and is considered one of the more famous incidents of a Marian apparition in Asia.

In the summer of 1973, Sasagawa reported witnessing bright lights emanating from the altar's tabernacle, which she concluded were several spiritual beings engaged in worship of the Eucharist. Within days of these apparitions Sasagawa claimed to have had a stigmatic-like experience in which she began to bleed from a cross-shaped opening on her left hand.

On July 6, 1973, Sasagawa reportedly began receiving messages from a three-foot-tall Katsura-wood statue of the Virgin Mary. According to Sasagawa, the statue became illuminated and conveyed the first of three messages. In this message, the Virgin Mary acknowledged Sasagwa's stigmata and hearing impairment, then proceeded to instruct Sasagawa to pray the prayer of the "Handmaids of the Eucharist," an invocation of devotion that Sasagawa and the Virgin Mary prayed together. Recitation of this prayer, according to Sasagawa, would cure her deafness (which was reportedly temporarily cured one year later in 1974 and then permanently in 1982). Shortly after receiving this message, Sasagawa and at least two other nuns witnessed droplets of blood permeating from the statue's right hand. The statue was said to have bled on four occasions that year between July 6 and September 29, at which time the hole on the statue's right hand disappeared. In the moments that followed, Sasagawa and these nuns also reported witnessing sweating from the neck and forehead of the statue.

On August 3, 1973, Sasagawa received a second message from the statue in which the Virgin Mary encouraged the repentance of those who afflicted the will of God. This message also made references to how the Virgin Mary intervened to save humanity from the wrath of God and stressed the importance of prayer, penance, and sacrifice in assuaging his anger. Finally, this message concluded with guidance for Sasagawa to confirm her commitment to her faith through metaphor in which such commitment was likened to fastening oneself to the cross with three nails, as Christ was forced to endure. These three nails, according to the message, symbolized obedience, poverty, and chastity.

On October 13, 1973, Sasagawa received her third and final message, warning her of an impending cataclysmic disaster that could only be prevented if humans were to pray the rosary daily. The message also indicated that in the absence of prayer, the Catholic Church would be infiltrated by the devil, turning believers and nonbelievers alike against each other.

After the final message, the statue became animated for an extended period. On January 4, 1975, Sasagawa and a number of nuns witnessed the first instance in which the statue of the Virgin Mary reportedly wept tears. For nearly seven more years, Sasagawa and others claimed to have watched the statue weep on a total of 101 occasions.

Sasagawa's account was later reported in detail to Bishop John Shohiro Ito (1909–1993) of Nigata, who later consulted officials in Rome at the Sacred Congregation for the Doctrine of the Faith in 1975. This consultation led to the establishment of a church commission of inquiry, and after an eight-year investigation, Bishop Ito approved the incident in a pastoral letter recognizing its supernatural characteristics and authorizing the veneration of the "Holy Mother of Akita."

In 1988, Bishop Ito furthered his endeavors pertaining to the events by consulting Cardinal Joseph Ratzinger (later to become Pope Benedict XVI). Although Cardinal Ratzinger made no judgment about the credibility of the events, he issued no objections to the conclusions of Bishop Ito's pastoral letter.

Salvador Murguia

See also: Statues

Further Reading

Burke, Raymond L. *Mariology: A Guide for Priests, Deacons, Seminarians, and Consecrated Persons*. Goleta, CA: Queenship Publishing/Seat of Wisdom Books, 2008.
Yashuda, Teigi. *Akita: The Tears and Message of Mary*. Translated by John Haffert. Asbury, NJ: 101 Foundation, 1991.

Our Lady of Beauraing

In the context of the Great Depression of the 1930s and unemployment alongside the rise of Nazism in neighboring Germany, Belgium became the country that experienced an epidemic of apparitions of Mary in 1933 and 1934 (the greatest number in any one country in the twentieth century over a short period of time). Catholic culture in Belgium had come under pressure from growing support for socialism and falling church attendance, especially in French-speaking Wallonia. According to devotees and pilgrims, Mary came to provide reassurance to this country, which in 1940 would face the catastrophe of a second German invasion within 26 years.

The first apparition of the series occurred at Beauraing, a small town near Dinant and the Meuse River. On November 29, 1932, five children aged between nine and fifteen from the two families of Degeimbre and Voisin were gathered by a Lourdes grotto on the grounds of a convent where one of the girls went to school. The only boy in the group, Albert Voisin, shouted that he saw a beautiful, shining young woman above the railway bridge; golden rays of light surrounded her head like a crown, and her feet were hidden in a cloud. The others then saw her. Visions continued over the days ahead; the figure moved closer, alighting on the branches of a hawthorn bush. By the time of the last vision, somewhere in the region of 30,000 people were coming to Beauraing to witness the visions.

The messages were unremarkable but reassured many: Mary announced herself as "the Immaculate Virgin" (although in response to a question along those lines) and "the Mother of God and Queen of Heaven." She asked for a chapel to be built at the site and showed one girl her golden heart. Yet the event took a more dramatic turn with visions in the summer of 1933 to a 58-year-old, Tilman Côme, a pilgrim from a village 20 miles away who claimed to have been healed at Beauraing. Expectation of healings and miracles grew, and Côme mentioned an "invader" from whom Mary would protect Belgium: people interpreted this to mean Nazi Germany. He announced a day of great pilgrimage, August 5, 1933, when an estimated 150,000 attended. However, nothing sensational occurred, and interest in Côme began to wane.

Catholics in Belgium were divided on the apparitions. Many doctors attended, of whom a certain Dr. Maistriaux believed the children and wrote a supportive pamphlet; others, such as Dr. van Gehuchten and Dr. de Greeff, from Louvain University, regarded the visions as "unconscious simulation" and "auto suggestion," a view supported by the Belgian Carmelites and the English Jesuit Herbert Thurston. At the same time, the movement known as "Rex," which campaigned for a traditional and authoritative Catholicism, supported the visions. This increased publicity but added difficulties, as the Rexists became the Belgian fascists and were denounced by the church in 1937.

The Catholic diocesan bishops followed a time-honored strategy by choosing the least controversial of the visionaries and rejecting the rest. The visions of the children of Beauraing and of Mariette Beco—an eleven-year-old who had experienced visions of the "Virgin of the Poor" at Banneux between January 15 and March 2—were authenticated in 1949. The bishops of Namur (Beauraing) and Liège (Banneux) fought for the cause of the apparitions against considerable church opposition and were successful after the shrines proved durable during World War II. The shrines still draw considerable numbers today. Of the rest, Onkerzele in Dutch-speaking Flanders retains a following, and recent church relaxation of prohibitions has given its devotees hope that the cult will survive.

Chris Maunder

See also: Apparitions

Further Reading

Études Carmélitaines, Les Faits Mystérieux de Beauraing: Études, Documents, Réponses 1 (1933): 1–195.

Maunder, Chris. "The Footprints of Religious Enthusiasm: Great Memorials and Faint Vestiges of Belgium's Apparition Mania of the 1930s." *Journal of Religion & Society* 15 (2013): 1–17.

Thurston, Herbert. *Beauraing and Other Apparitions: An Account of Some Borderland Cases in the Psychology of Mysticism.* London: Burns, Oates and Washbourne, 1934.

Our Lady of Częstochowa

Częstochowa is a city located in the southern Silesian district or *voivodeship* of Poland. Clockwise, the city is circled by the major cities of Gdansk and Lodz to the north, Warsaw to the northeast, Kraków to the south, and Wroclaw and Poznan on Poland's western border. Częstochowa was founded as a Slavic community in the eleventh century and was granted a town charter in the mid-fourteenth century. With a population of 235,798 (2013 estimates), the city is regarded as the heart and soul of the Polish nation. Within the city is a Pauline monastery, Jasna Góra, founded in 1382 by Vladislaus II of Opole. Today it is one of the world's most sacred Marian pilgrimage sites, receiving upwards of 4 million tourists and pilgrims on an annual basis.

Enshrined within the sanctuary of the Jasna Góra complex is a chapel where the Icon of Our Lady of Częstochowa, also known as the Black Madonna of Częstochowa, beloved by Christians for centuries, is reverently displayed behind a silver screen. The diminutive image, a somber Hadigitria barely 32 inches by 40 inches, is painted on an old limewood panel. The original image is attributed to Saint Luke the Evangelist, reputed to have painted the image in Jesus's workshop while listening to Mary talk about the life of her son. Legend records that the image is one of the earliest in the Christian tradition, painted in the first century in Palestine. Saint Helen is said to have recovered the image in 326 CE in Constantinople, where she arranged to have the image enshrined. It is said that the image saved the city from destruction. During subsequent centuries the image was transferred until it came into the possession of Prince Vladislaus, who after surviving a Tartar attack on the Russian city of Belz immediately transferred the image to Bright Mountain and the Pauline monastery at Jasna Góra in 1384.

The monastery was prosperous and a target for thieves and looters. In 1430 during a Hussite attack, the painting was pierced twice on the cheek by a vagabond's sword. Today, the sword cuts and the Tartan arrow wound to the Madonna's throat are defining features that bring an unforgettable intensity to the efficacy of the image as a symbol of the Polish nation. The Madonna's miracles are legion, reflecting the power of symbols and created icons to perpetuate essential beliefs that define the multidimensional character of a culture and nation. Moreover, the image of the Black Madonna, the queen of Poland, serves as a powerful human archetype that unites the world of the sacred to its hierophanic manifestation in everyday life, creating a specific spatiotemporal plane of experience for self-reflection and the transformation of human values over time.

Contemporary scholars hotly debate the authenticity of the image as originating from the hand of Saint Luke. Countless studies of its multilayered matte of paint and fabric imply that the image may have been painted and repainted over time, leaving its original sources buried in ambiguity. That ambiguity presents an aesthetic continuum that intertwines Eastern and Western spiritual traditions in a timeless dimension that is at the same time active in the present moment. The icon's universal appeal is reinforced by the fact that it is often included within a particular genre of Marian icons known as Black Madonnas, numerous images that depict the Virgin and Child with physical features common to the multicultural Byzantine and early Christian communities.

Many stories of miracles are attributed to reverent devotion to the Madonna, the recitation of the rosary being considered a primary and most efficacious mode of recollection. The icon was considered miraculous at the time of its reception at Jasna Góra in 1384. The monastery houses a series of early miracle documents, including a listing found in the Jagiellonian Library at Kraków, dated to the 1470s; the Register of the Confraternity of the Order of St. Paul the First Hermit, dated 1517; the miracle book of the Pauline provincial Martin Lubnicensis, dated 1591; the *Historia Pulchra, et stupendis miraculis referta, imagines Maria quomodo et unde in Clarum montem Czastochovvie et Olsztyn advenerit*, published in Kraków in 1524; and a Polish translation of the *Historia Pulchra—Historya o obrazie w Czestochowie Panny Maryjej*, also published in Kraków in 1568. The fulfillment of the pilgrimage, the vows and votive offerings made to honor the request for particular aid, are essential components of many miracle narratives. Important miracle narratives include the defense and victory of the Jasna Gora monks over the marauding Swedes in 1655 (attributed to Abbot Augustine Kordeckiego), similar victories against the Austrians and Russians, and the defeat of the Bolsheviks on August 15, 1920.

Throughout the past millennium the church played an essential role in preserving Polish identity and culture. The walls of the chapel at Jasna Góra leading to the image of the Madonna are crowded with the votive offerings of countless pilgrims whose prayers were answered in miraculous ways during times of cultural and political malaise and disintegration. Of particular note are the rosaries of those survivors of the Polish *Ausschluss*. Alongside the elegant beads of royal patrons of the monastery hang those, made of black bread, fruit seeds, and string, fashioned by survivors of World War II extermination and labor camps. For countless Christians the prayerful meditation on the life and passion of Jesus helped them endure their own torture and suffering, and death. For those who survived, the rosary was an offering of thanksgiving for delivery and a token of memory for the millions of lives lost. It is estimated that from 1939 to 1945, 6 million Poles died, half of whom were Polish Jews. During the tumultuous years of the formation of Poland's Solidarity movement, the Black Madonna was the emblem of freedom for countless laborers. In 1983 the movement's founder, Lech Walesa, was awarded the Nobel Peace Prize, an honor he gave as an offering to the Madonna of Poland. In 2013 the image of the Black Madonna was carried across Europe and North America in a pilgrimage, "From Ocean to Ocean," coordinated by Human Life International, in defense of the miracle of life. The icon, a symbol of human life and family, is embraced by Catholic and Orthodox Christians alike.

Victoria M. Breting-Garcia

See also: Poland, Miracles in

Further Reading

Aradi, Zsolt. "The Black Madonna of Czestochowa." Catholic Culture, http://www .catholicculture.org/culture/library/view.cfm?recnum=2996.

Baeten, Elizabeth M. *The Magic Mirror: Myth's Abiding Power*. Albany: State University of New York, 1996.

Galland, China. *Longing for Darkness: Tara and the Black Madonna—A Ten-Year Journey*. New York: Penguin, 1990.

The Glories of Czestochowa: Miracles Attributed to Our Lady's Intercession. Stockbridge, MA: Marian Press, 2004.

Halecki, Oscar. "The Place of Czestochowa in Poland's Millennium." *Catholic Historical Review* 52(4) (January 1967): 494–508.

Maniura, Robert. *Pilgrimage to Images in the Fifteenth Century: The Origins of the Cult of Our Lady of Czestochowa*. Woodbridge, Suffolk, UK: Boydell, 2004.

Oleszkiewicz-Peralba, Malgorzata. *The Black Madonna in Latin America and Europe: Tradition and Transformation*. Albuquerque: University of New Mexico Press, 2007.

"Sanctuary of the Black Madonna of Czestochowa, Queen of Poland." Jasna Góra, http:// www.jasnagora.pl/en.

Scheer, Monique. "From Majesty to Mystery: Change in the Meanings of Black Madonnas from the Sixteenth to Nineteenth Centuries." *American Historical Review* 107(5) (December 2002): 1412–1440.

Swick, Thomas. *Unquiet Days: At Home in Poland*. New York: Ticknor and Fields, 1991.

Our Lady of Fatima

Fatima in Portugal is the most influential Marian apparition of the twentieth century. Like Lourdes, it created a template for apparitions of Mary for many that came afterward. The message of Fatima replays a centuries-old theme: future punishment for sin but the blessing of peace if Catholics turn to prayer and devotion.

In addition, Fatima's "miracle of the sun" has prompted many other reported sightings of sun phenomena: moving, spinning, and changing colors.

Fatima is a story of war and peace, as the apparitions took place during World War I. Portugal was in chaos in 1917: the republican government of 1910–1926 was highly unstable, probably the least secure in twentieth-century Europe. The country had entered the war on the side of Britain and its allies; the net result was turmoil, hunger, and casualties. Added to all these difficulties, the republic had enacted liberalizing laws that took moral authority and other powers away from the Catholic Church, threatening the Catholic way of life especially in rural areas. Portugal had followed France in disentangling the relationship between church and state.

Perhaps, then, it is no surprise that many thousands journeyed to the village of Fatima because of reports of apparitions of Mary. The visionaries were small children, Lucia Santos (age ten) and Francisco and Jacinta Marto (ages eight and seven, respectively). On May 13, 1917, they claimed to see a woman: young (apparently around midteens), bathed in light, and hovering above a small holm oak tree. She told them not to be frightened and that she had come from heaven, to where the visionaries themselves would go eventually. They asked about the war and how long it would last; this became a theme of the six apparitions. The vision—soon identified as Mary—urged them to say the rosary daily to bring about the end of the conflict.

Because of skepticism locally and in the Santos family (whereas the Martos's father was an early believer), the children asked the lady for a miracle so that everyone would believe them. This was promised for October 13, the date of the last apparition. A crowd of over 70,000 gathered, and many of them witnessed a descent of the sun. Although this could not have happened literally, the sun vision was seen by so many that it was pronounced a collective miracle, and many newspapers—even republican publications such as *O Seculo*—reported the event.

Jeffrey Bennett shows how pilgrimage to Fatima became a central feature in the reestablishment of a pro-Catholic state in the late 1920s and early 1930s. This regime lasted until 1974; although the relationship with the church was not always easy, the Catholic culture of Portugal was assured, and Fatima became its national shrine, with many millions visiting.

The apparitions were fully approved by the church on October 13, 1930, after an inquiry. However, the story of the apparitions was not yet complete. The children had indicated that secrets were given to them by the Virgin Mary. The principal seer, Lucia, the only survivor of the three visionaries after the postwar influenza epidemic, began to describe more details about the apparitions from the 1930s. She told of an earlier vision in 1916 of an angel who gave the children mystical communion and of the sacrifice and self-mortification undertaken by the three of them. The "secrets" were partly revealed in 1941. They included a vision of hell and a prophecy of the coming of World War II (however, the difficulty is that the war had already started, so the prophecy cannot be proven to be genuine). Lucia also wrote that Russia, the main source of communist ideology, would spread its "errors," but if that country were consecrated to the Immaculate Heart of Mary, it would be converted and there would be peace; devotion to the Immaculate Heart of Mary needed to be established on a worldwide scale if humanity wished to save itself from future wars. A third secret was written down in 1944 but sent to the Vatican, which declined to publish it.

The later developments of Fatima demonstrate why it has come to be seen as the most intriguing apparition miracle of the twentieth century. Pius XII carried out the consecration to the Immaculate Heart, but only John Paul II, in 1984, satisfied Lucia that he had followed her instructions in requiring that all the world's Catholic bishops should take part. Thus, many Catholics regard the coming of Mikhail Gorbachev to power in 1985 and the subsequent collapse of communism in Eastern Europe in 1989–1991 as the fulfilment of the prophecy.

In 2000, the Vatican finally published the third secret (with a commentary by Cardinal Ratzinger, the future Benedict XVI). It consisted of a vision of Catholic people, including a bishop in white, being shot and killed. Pope John Paul II interpreted the third secret of Fatima as a reference to the attempt on his life on the 64th anniversary of the first apparition (May 13, 1981) and thought that it described an atheistic assault on the church that would be repulsed by the Immaculate Heart of Mary.

There are still Catholics who hold a conspiracy theory that Lucia was forced to accede to these Vatican interpretations despite the fact that the prophecies were not truly fulfilled. Whatever the truth of the matter, Lucia, a lifelong nun who died in 2005 only weeks before John Paul II, had an enormous influence on the Catholic Church from 1917 onward. Her apparitions gave her the status of an unsurpassed mediator with Mary, and in all likelihood Lucia will follow other famous visionaries to eventual canonisation as a saint.

Chris Maunder

See also: Apparitions

Further Reading

Bennett, Jeffrey S. *When the Sun Danced: Myth, Miracles, and Modernity in Early Twentieth-Century Portugal.* Charlottesville: University of Virginia Press, 2012.

Bertone, Tarcisio, and Joseph Ratzinger. *The Message of Fatima*. Vatican City: Congregation for the Doctrine of the Faith, 2000.

Our Lady of Guadalupe

Though the miracle of the apparitions of Our Lady of Guadalupe (Nuestra Señora de Guadalupe) is said to have occurred in December 1531, most modern versions of the tale originate in two works from the seventeenth century. In 1648, Father Miguel Sánchez of Mexico City published *Imagen de la Virgen Maria, Madre de Dios de Guadalupe*. The following year, the tale was translated into the Nahuatl language by the vicar of Guadalupe, Father Luis Laso de la Vega. This version gave a slightly expanded narrative, incorporating fourteen miracle stories associated with the Virgin of Guadalupe.

The story is this, and it is rife with miracles. A man from Cuauhtitlan—a Nahua named Juan Diego—passed by the hill of Tepeyac and was entranced by some songbirds. The beauty of the place was a welcome distraction for this traveler, who was on his way to pay a visit to a sick uncle, Juan Bernardino. As Diego looked around, he discovered a maiden who instructed him to build a chapel on the site. She had the appearance of a native girl, the kind Diego would ordinarily see in any village—but she was different. She was Mary, the Mother of God, who was now occupying the site of a former mother goddess. Without any prompting, she also allayed his anxiety over the health of his uncle, who had been cured. As a way of convincing the local bishop, Juan de Zumárraga, to erect the chapel, she instructed Diego to pick Castilian roses and carry them to the episcopal palace in his *tilma*, or cloak. The roses were neither endemic to the region nor in season. He did as he was told, but as the roses spilled out before the bishop, an image of the Virgin of Guadalupe could be seen imprinting itself on the *tilma*. Today the image is enshrined at the Basilica of Our Lady of Guadalupe in Mexico City.

Some scholars have questioned the very existence of Diego, while others have sought to discredit the Marian image. It was decades after her apparition before the first mention of the picture is found in official records. Veneration at Tepeyac had been robust among the Nuatls, causing concern to many missionaries who feared that they might be backsliding into their pre-Christian superstitions. Diego himself is the object of intense scrutiny. His sainthood cause emerged in the mid-seventeenth century and was formally launched in 1723. It would take several hundred years to bring it to completion, largely owing to the fact that Bishop Zumárraga's own papers refer to neither Diego nor his miraculous cloak. Evidence in deer skin manuscripts and other texts led to broader acceptance. In 1987, Pope

John Paul II declared Deigo "venerable," and on May 6, 1990, he was beatified by the same pontiff in the Basilica of Our Lady of Guadalupe. In 2002, Diego was declared a saint.

The *tilma* has also undergone scientific scrutiny, though the last tests—photographic and biochemical—were completed in the early 1980s. Infrared photographs were taken and magnified. There is evidence that the image has brush strokes applied to it, which would negate the notion that the image is of a miraculous transfer of Mary's image to the cloth. However, the image itself had very little flaking or cracking except in those areas that had obviously been touched up. From the point of view of preservation, it has been able to remain in near-perfect condition for several hundred years, this despite a climate that is not always hospitable to such objects, an ammonia spill in 1791, and a bomb attack on the altar of the basilica in 1921.

Today the Virgin at Tepeyac and her mysterious image are both migratory and multiple. She crosses borders with ease, and her ubiquity makes her recognizable by believers and nonbelievers alike. As one explanation, some scholars suggest that the image goes back longer than when she first appeared in the Mexican hill country and instead may be found in medieval Iberia at Extramadura, Spain. There she was used to combat Muslim influence, and her Christian followers brought her to the Americas in the hope of converting the natives. She has been a symbol of indigenous Mexicans, and in the last two centuries when Mexico underwent widespread political and social turmoil, she has been a constant source of stability, perseverance, and hope. Today she is considered the patroness of the Americas.

Patrick J. Hayes

Further Reading

Brading, D. A. *Mexican Phoenix: Our Lady of Guadalupe; Image and Tradition across Five Centuries*. New York: Cambridge University Press, 2001.

Callahan, Philip. "The Tilma under Infra-Red Radiation." *CARA Studies in Popular Devotion* 2(3) (March 1981): 1–45.

Chávez, Eduardo. *Our Lady of Guadalupe and Saint Juan Diego: The Historical Evidence.* Lanham, MD: Rowman and Littlefield, 2006.

Harrington, Patricia. "Mother of Death, Mother of Rebirth: The Virgin of Guadalupe." *Journal of the American Academy of Religion* 56(1) (1988): 25–50.

Peterson, Jeannette Favro. *Visualizing Guadalupe: From Black Madonna to Queen of the Americas*. Austin: University of Texas Press, 2014.

Poole, Stafford. *The Guadalupan Controversies in Mexico*. Stanford, CA: Stanford University Press, 2006.

Poole, Stafford. "History vs. Juan Diego." *The Americas* 62 (July 2005): 1–16.

Poole, Stafford. *Our Lady of Guadalupe: The Origins and Sources of a Mexican National Symbol, 1531–1797*. Tempe: University of Arizona Press, 2001.

Our Lady of Knock

The Knock apparition in County Mayo, Ireland, on August 21, 1879, occurred in a time of intense economic and political pressure. The terrible national famine of 1847 still cast its shadow over rural Ireland, and in 1879 there was the threat of another (although this did not materialize). People farmed small plots of land and rented them from powerful landlords: the economic difficulties pushed rents up, and poverty caused widespread evictions. The Land League, a radical movement in opposition to landlords, was founded in County Mayo in that same year, 1879, yet it was criticized by Knock's diocesan bishop, Archbishop John MacHale of Tuam, previously regarded as a stalwart of the people and campaigner for justice. Father Cavanagh, parish priest of Knock, was likewise unpopular for his refusal to support the movement.

In the midst of this tense situation, an apparition was reported on the church wall in the village of Knock. Mary Beirne and Mary McLoughlin, two adult women, were the original visionaries, but they called others, and over a two-hour period fifteen people ages six to sixty-eight had witnessed the phenomenon. It consisted of a tableau on the wall that included figures: the central one was clearly the Virgin Mary. To her left was a man felt to be Saint Joseph; the man on her right wore a bishop's miter and was only identified later as Saint John the Evangelist. On the right of these three figures, a lamb stood on an altar underneath a cross with angels overhead. These figures and the ground beneath them remained dry, despite the heavy rain.

The news brought many pilgrims to Knock, some of whom recorded further apparitions. The pilgrims also removed cement from the church gable, regarding it as a miraculous substance, and healings were claimed. The church supported the apparition, and a commission of three priests interviewed the witnesses, coming to a positive conclusion although there was no official declaration of authentication in the manner of the French shrines. Irish pilgrims from overseas—especially America, Canada, and Australia—traveled to Knock in the 1880s including the archbishops of Hobart and Toronto, who gave thanks for cures that they attributed to the Knock apparition.

With the advent of a new archbishop in Tuam, McEvilly, Knock's cause was not pursued. Popular pilgrimage continued, but Knock did not become the national shrine that it is today until after the establishment of the Irish Republic in the 1920s. Then Judy and Liam Coyne campaigned for the revival of Knock, and this was achieved in the time of Archbishop Gilmartin, who was the first local archbishop to take part in pilgrimage in 1929. He opened a new commission that interviewed surviving witnesses in the 1930s and sent a positive report to Rome. Knock then took its place in Europe's national Marian shrines as the chief pilgrimage site of Ireland. Pope John Paul II visited in 1979, thanks to the organization of parish priest James Horan, who also campaigned for a local airport for pilgrims.

Two theories cast some doubt on the miraculous nature of Knock. The first was that the apparition—which, unlike other famous cases, did not move or speak—was cast onto the wall by a "magic lantern," an early type of film projector. The theory was refuted by an investigator's report in the *Daily Telegraph* in 1880, but it has proved persistent.

The second is the fruit of a scholarly analysis by Eugene Hynes, who argued that the tableau in the vision is actually a popular folk device created in order to criticize priestly behavior. The vision, with Mary at its center, reminds the priesthood of the need to support the people struggling against the burdens of tenant farming, high rents, and evictions. Whether Hynes's theory is correct or not, his work is a reminder that proper research into apparitions has to take into account their full historical, social, political, and cultural context.

Chris Maunder

See also: Apparitions

Further Reading

Hynes, Eugene. *Knock: the Virgin's Apparition in Nineteenth-Century Ireland*. Cork: Cork University Press, 2008.

Walsh, Michael. *The Apparition at Knock: A Survey of Facts and Evidence*. 2nd ed. Tuam: St. Jarlath's College, 1959.

Our Lady of LaSalette

On September 19, 1846, two young cattle herders were taking their cows for a stroll up Mont sous-les-Baisses near LaSalette, France. Melanie Calvat, age 15, and Maximin Giraud, age 11, were favored with an apparition of the Blessed Virgin Mary and heard her impart several warnings against those who had lost their faith, took up bad habits, and forsaken the Sabbath. Without obedience to God's laws, she said, "I will be forced to let go of My Son's Hand"—meaning that the end of the world was near. She worried that he could be no longer restrained: "I am growing tired" of preventing the destruction of the world.

The remedy for this crisis was a return to the rosary, prompt confession of sins, and amendment of the lives of Christians in France. Word of the apparition reached the ear of the local bishop on September 19, 1846. Bishop Philbert de Bruillard was skeptical and immediately sent a letter to all his priests "not to print or publish any new miracle, under any pretense of knowledge that it may be, if not from the authority of the Holy See or ours after an examination which cannot be but exact and severe." The bishop was then 82 years old, but he spent the next five years verifying the veracity of the children's claims.

The tearful Virgin had told each child a secret, though only Melanie's survives in published form. Finally Bishop de Bruillard gave his approbation, and Melanie Calvat turned over her secret to Pope Pius IX in 1851. The contents were dire: three-quarters of the French population would lose its faith, and peace would be frustrated by warring nations. Many have seen in these prophetic utterances a rise in secularization and the dawning of World War I.

The apocalyptic warnings of Our Lady of LaSalette were enough to prompt the establishment of a large shrine and the founding in 1852 of a missionary order dedicated to the promulgation of her messages. Charles Dickens wrote of the apparition in 1852 that the lady who appeared to these children could not be human. "Nobody except shepherds could climb such steep mountains," he said. While incorporating some elements of previous apparitions—a natural setting, an encounter with children, secret messages, and so on—LaSalette remains part of an ongoing dialogue between Mary and the world.

Patrick J. Hayes

See also: Bayside Apparitions; Lourdes; Our Lady of Lourdes

Further Reading

Dickens, Charles. "History of a Miracle." *Household Words: A Weekly Journal* 18 (June 1858): 37–42.

"La Salette: A Biblical Apparition Filled with Symbols." La Salette Missionaries, http://www.lasalette.org/about-la-salette/apparition/the-story.html.

Stern, Jean. *La Salette: Documents authentiques*. 3 vols. Paris: Desclée De Brouwer, 1980–1991.

Our Lady of La Vang

The image of Our Lady of La Vang (in Vietnamese, Duc Me La Vang) stems from an apparition of Mary, the mother of Jesus, to Catholics who sought refuge in the forest of the same name, in the Quang Tri province of Vietnam, about 37 miles from Huê. In the aftermath of pograms instigated by anti-Catholic sentiments arising from legislation of Emperor Canh Thinh in the late eighteenth century, Vietnamese Catholics sought to practice their faith, especially the recitation of the rosary, in the jungle. The Virgin, clad in a traditional Vietnamese garment and clutching the infant Jesus, appeared to such a gathering. She spoke to those assembled, telling them to boil leaves for medicinal purposes (the terms *la*, meaning "leaf," and *vang*, meaning "herb seeds"). The memory of this event—seen as a sign of God's favor for their faithfulness in trial—is retained to this day by Vietnamese Catholics around the world.

By 1820 a chapel was built on the site of the apparition, and for the next 50 years persecution remained the norm. During this period 117 martyrs were commemorated for their sacrifice, and in images of Our Lady of La Vang, they are often pictured crowded around her. A new chapel was built in 1886 and consecrated to Our Lady Help of Christians in 1901. Another was blessed by Bishop Eugene Maria Giuseppe Allys, the vicar apostolic of Huê in 1928 when the church finally became an independent parish large enough to accommodate pilgrims. Only in 1954, however, was the statue of Our Lady of La Vang ensconced in the church. In April 1961, the Vietnamese bishops made this church the national Marian shrine. Pope Saint John XXIII raised the church to a minor basilica a few months later, and this set in motion an extensive expansion of the parish boundaries. Unfortunately, the Vietnam War would bring the entire complex to ruin.

Without formal written testimony there is doubt over the actuality of the apparition, but the oral and pictorial tradition remains strong. Catholic Vietnamese exiles in the United States clung to their religious beliefs and established close-knit communities in places such as New Orleans and Houston. In the Catholic Diocese of Galveston-Houston alone, four parishes arose that were dedicated to the Vietnamese apostolate, including Giao Xu Duc Me La Vang (Our Lady of La Vang), a large building in the pagoda style. The church community serves as a touch point to the homeland insofar as catechesis is given and Mass is celebrated in Viet Ngu. But it is also a reminder of the sacral nature of maternal protection by Our Lady of La Vang under oppressive regimes and a sign of hope for future generations.

Patrick J. Hayes

Further Reading

Bangston, Carl L. "Vietnamese-American Catholicism: Transplanted and Flourishing." *U.S. Catholic Historian* 18(1) (Winter 2000): 36–53.
Our Lady of Lavang Parish, http://ololv.org.

Vu, Roy. "Natives of a Ghost Country: The Vietnamese in Houston and Their Construction of a Postwar Community." In *Asian Americans in Dixie: Race and Migration in the South*, edited by Khyati Y. Joshi and Jigna Desai, 165–189, Carbondale: University of Illinois Press, 2013.

Our Lady of Lourdes

The story of the apparition at Lourdes is remarkable because the location has become the most visited shrine in Europe, famous across the world for its healing waters. In Roman Catholic belief, Bernadette Soubirous experienced eighteen apparitions of the Virgin Mary between February 11 and July 16, 1858. Nevertheless, Bernadette did not identify her vision as the Virgin Mary; indeed, the fourteen-year-old visionary of below average height described her as a girl neither older nor taller than herself. Devotees created the maternal Mary of Lourdes according to their expectations.

A crucial moment occurred on March 25 when Bernadette, prompted by questions, asked the little lady who she was and received an answer in her native Bigourdan that was to shape Catholic visionary experiences for decades: "I am the Immaculate Conception." This was the doctrine that had been declared dogma by the Catholic Church just four years earlier, a cornerstone of Pope Pius IX's campaign to reestablish traditional Catholicism in a changing world. It convinced the parish priest and many others that Bernadette's companion, whom no one else could see, was indeed the Virgin Mary. The statement was unusual (Mary is not strictly the Immaculate Conception but the one who was immaculately conceived, as in the messages at the Rue du Bac in 1830). It may derive from paintings of Mary titled "the Immaculate Conception"—referring to the event rather than the person—that were common enough at the time. Yet it affirmed the simplicity and lack of theological sophistication of Bernadette, which were important characteristics of the nineteenth century Catholic visionary: for devotees, she had the quality of a pure vessel through which Mary could speak.

The rapidly expanding crowds played their part because they gave testimony to the charisma of Bernadette. Jean-Baptiste Estrade, a local tax collector who later wrote a book on the visions, referred to the transformation of Bernadette in trance. The serial nature of Bernadette's visions, which were expected during March 1858 at daily intervals, lent the phenomenon authenticity: people saw it happening, and so it could not easily have been fabricated by the visionary or other persons. Eventually the public excitement reached the empress of France herself, and she supported the shrine against local officials who wished to close it.

The messages of Mary at Lourdes are brief and therefore memorable. She wanted Bernadette to visit the grotto every day for a fortnight and then occasionally thereafter, wanted people to come on pilgrimage, wanted a chapel to be built, promised Bernadette happiness in the next world but not in this one, and asked for penance. Mary's actions were important. She prayed the rosary, and Bernadette did the same in reply; she told Bernadette to dig in the ground, from where water began to flow. This mountain spring became the source of holy water and healing baths for millions of pilgrims.

Mary was clothed in white with a blue sash, familiar colors for Mary after the Counter-Reformation and its artistic portrayals of her. This was the uniform of the Children of Mary, a society for devout Catholic women to which the sickly, poor, and uneducated Bernadette, daughter of an unemployed miller, could not have aspired. However, her visions not only gave her membership in the Children of Mary, but she became the society's inspiration.

The Cinderella story of Bernadette, later Sister Marie Bernarde of the Sisters of Charity at Nevers, is a story of transformation that is paralleled by the fortunes of the grotto itself. It had been a dirty and spooky site a little way out of town where one might have expected to meet spirits and fairies. It is now one of the holiest places in European Catholicism, visited regularly by popes and boasting two great basilicas: the older built in the years shortly after the apparitions were approved by the Church in 1862, and the more recent underground church accommodating the huge growth in the number of pilgrims. The third of Lourdes's transformations is in the pilgrims themselves: although miraculous healings authenticated by the medical bureau at the shrine are not numerous, many report spiritual healing and peace in the acceptance of incurable disease. There are also the helpers, whose journeys to Lourdes to aid the sick and disabled are also transformative, as they enjoy a community spirit that is rare and valuable.

Our Lady of Lourdes had many successors: in Lourdes itself, where Bernadette's visions inspired others that were not selected for authentication, and then in many other sites of apparitions, where visionaries referred to a Mary who was often known as "the Immaculate Conception." France was blessed with Lourdes, and other countries wanted their own version: hence in the 1870s, Marpingen was referred to as "the German Lourdes" and Knock "the Irish Lourdes." Yet none is quite like the original.

A common Catholic saying is that "Rome is the head of the Church, but Lourdes is its heart." This reflects how much of the experience of pilgrimage to Lourdes is intuitive and tactile, the rock of the grotto being touched by the pilgrims who also bathe in the water; the grotto shrine by the river is silent for prayer. Lourdes could be said to be maternal rather than paternal like Rome. This distinction draws on ancient stereotypes of gender: while Rome reflects the male priestly hierarchy of the church, led by the successors of Saint Peter, Lourdes's feminine qualities are due to the Virgin Mary and her visionary and chosen companion, Bernadette Soubirous. Numerous Lourdes grottos in many countries capture the intimacy of this relationship; despite the crowds that gathered from an early point in the series of apparitions, the representations include only these two figures. Lourdes is unusual in that Christ was not seen or mentioned in any of the eighteen apparitions.

As of 2015, there were 69 approved miracles that have taken place at Lourdes.

Chris Maunder

See also: Apparitions

Further Reading

Harris, Ruth. *Lourdes: Body and Spirit in the Secular Age*. London: Penguin, 1999.
Taylor, Thérèse. *Bernadette of Lourdes: Her Life, Death and Visions*. London: Burns and Oates, 2003.

Our Lady of Mount Carmel

A cultural fixture, most notably within Italian ethnic parishes and homes, Our Lady of Mount Carmel is a somewhat more nebulous patroness whose devotions stem from a unique association with the Brothers of Our Lady of Mount Carmel, a Roman Catholic religious order commonly called the Carmelites. The order began in the early 1200s as a collection of hermits gathered together in a semimonastic lifestyle on Mount Carmel in present-day Israel. They requested a rule of life from Saint Albert, the Latin-rite patriarch of Jerusalem, not long before his death in 1214. This original Carmelite foundation was under the patronage of Mary from the beginning. However, after the purported apparition of the Blessed Virgin Mary to Saint Simon Stock in the 1250s, in which she told him that those who died wearing the scapular of the Carmelite Order worthily would not suffer eternal fire, the Carmelites began to stress Marian devotion as a defining characteristic of their order and identity.

In particular, Carmelite spirituality emphasizes the imitation of the virtues of Mary as the best way to express devotion to her. The primary component of Carmelite spirituality is contemplative prayer, and Mary is venerated as the supreme example of one who "ponders in her heart" (Luke 2:19) the mysteries of God. The virginity of Mary mirrors the commitment to celibacy and purity of heart in Carmelite spirituality, as symbolized by the white mantle of the religious habit.

Mary's humility is seen in her acceptance of the words of the angel Gabriel in the Annunciation and in her silence, since she speaks on only four occasions throughout the Gospels. Her detachment from material goods is seen in her poverty and exile as expressed in the Gospel of Luke during the early years of Jesus's infancy and childhood. Her charity is seen in her visitation to her cousin Elizabeth and in her concern for the wedding couple who ran out of wine at Cana. Finally, her acceptance of God's will in all things, no matter how painful, is seen in her compassionate presence with Jesus at the foot of the cross.

All of these virtues of Mary are to be imitated by those following Carmelite spirituality. Humility, detachment, and charity were identified by Saint Teresa of Ávila (in her *Way of Perfection* 4:4) as the primary virtues that should be fostered by Carmelites, and contemplative prayer and silence are enjoined in the Rule of Saint Albert, mentioned above.

Carmelite spirituality also emphasizes relating to Mary in a familial manner. While Mary is certainly venerated as Queen and Splendor of Carmel, she is also seen as mother and even sister, as implied by the original name of the order. One of the most well-known Carmelite saints, Saint Therese of Lisieux (sometimes referred to as "Little Flower"), expressed this familial approach in the so-called Yellow Notebook entry of August 21, 1897, stating that for her, Mary was "more mother than queen."

The image of Mary as Our Lady of Mount Carmel is found in other miraculous events. Most famously, in the final apparition of Our Lady of Fatima on October 13, 1917, the Blessed Virgin Mary appeared to the children as Our Lady of Mount Carmel, clothed in the habit of the Carmelite order. This apparition is the only one in which the Blessed Virgin Mary is seen wearing the habit of a particular religious order.

Our Lady of Mount Carmel was proclaimed the patroness of Chile by the famed rebel Bernardo O'Higgins, who beseeched her aid against Spanish colonizers. When these were roundly defeated at Maipú in 1818, O'Higgins had a shrine erected there in her honor.

Because of the legend that the Blessed Virgin Mary miraculously appeared to Simon Stock in Aylesford, Kent, England, on July 16, 1251 (although modern historians may debate this date), the Roman Catholic Church continues to celebrate the feast of Our Lady of Mount Carmel as an optional memorial on July 16, and it is celebrated as a liturgical solemnity by all the branches of the Carmelite order today. The Carmelite monastery at Aylesford remains a site of pilgrimage to this day.

Jason Bourgeois

See also: Carmelites and Miracles

Further Reading

Clarke, John, trans. *St. Therese of Lisieux: Her Last Conversations*. Washington, DC: Institute of Carmelite Studies, 1977.

Miles, Margaret. *Maiden and Mother: Prayers, Hymns, Songs and Devotions to Honour the Blessed Virgin Mary*. London: A. and C. Black, 2001.

O'Donnell, Christopher. *A Loving Presence: Mary and Carmel; A Study of the Marian Heritage of the Order*. Melbourne, Australia: Carmelite Communications, 2000.

Rodriguez, Otilio, and Kieran Kavanaugh, trans. and eds. *The Collected Works of St. Teresa of Avila*, Vol. 2, *The Way of Perfection, Meditations on the Song of Songs, the Interior Castle*. Washington, DC: Institute of Carmelite Studies, 1980.

Smet, Joachim. *The Carmelites: A History of the Brothers of Our Lady of Mount Carmel*, Vol. 1, *ca. 1200 until the Council of Trent*. Revised ed. Darien, IL: Carmelite Spiritual Center, 1988.

Valabek, Redemptus Maria. *Mary Mother of Carmel: Our Lady and the Saint of Carmel*. 2 vols. Rome: Institutum Carmelitanum, 1988.

Our Lady of Perpetual Help

In this icon, the Blessed Virgin Mary, often depicted crowned, holds her child Jesus while the archangels Michael and Gabriel flutter on either side. The original painting—attributed by the devout to be the work of Saint Luke and attested by Theodore the Lector and John Damascene—has been lost, though the most authentic reproduction is ensconced above the main altar in the Redemptorist Church of Sant'Alfonso in Rome. It is in the Byzantine style and is the most replicated image of the Virgin in existence.

Among the icon's historians was Redemptorist Father Clemens Henze, C.Ss.R., whose studies between the 1920s and 1930s still stand the test of time. Henze claimed that it was painted by an unknown Greek artist in the thirteenth or fourteenth century, probably of a Cretan school, perhaps a Greek monk, done while contemplating the Hodegetria icon. It came to Rome through the stealthy influence of a merchant around 1490, who, before dying, confided it to a Roman. The legend has it that this man did little except to store the painting and for dishonoring the icon in this way died a horrible death. His six-year-old daughter had a vision in which Mary asked that her portrait be placed between the Basilica of Saint Mary Major and the Basilica of Saint John Lateran. It was moved to the Church of San Matteo sometime around March 1499, and the first miracle attributed to the portrait records that a paralytic was restored immediately thereafter. Scores of these cures followed.

After 1798 when the Augustinians ended their care for the Church of San Matteo, the icon was removed to another part of the city. San Matteo was a few blocks from the present Church of Sant'Alfonso, where the Redemptorist general house was located. On December 11, 1865, the Redemptorist superior-general, Father Nicholas Mauron, had an audience with Pope Pius IX, at which time he requested that the picture be brought to the Church of Sant'Alfonso, and the Augustinians were ordered to surrender it. As it was processed to the Redemptorist monastery and passed by the homes of two ailing children, the health of both was restored. It has been in the care of Redemptorists since, and its miracles and image are promoted by them worldwide.

The miraculous healings attributed to the icon were universally extended by touching copies to the original. The first copy came to America in February 1868 and was installed in the brothers' chapel at St. Mary's in Annapolis, Maryland. The first copy installed for public veneration was in the Church of St. James the Less in Baltimore in December 1868. Others were forwarded to Redemptorist parishes across the country. The most famous of these was installed in Boston's Church of Our Lady of Perpetual Help, also known as the Mission Church, on May 28, 1871. Between its installation and 1885, over 300 cures were documented by the Redemptorists. When the present Basilica of Our Lady of Perpetual Help was dedicated in 1878, the icon was removed to a side chapel, and a shrine was created in her honor. Today it is adorned with the crutches left by those who enjoyed cures wrought by the miraculous picture.

The Our Lady of Perpetual Help icon is today present in other cities with equally spectacular results. Weekly novenas to Our Lady of Perpetual Help, said before the image in churches around the world, have drawn millions. Beginning in July 1922 in St. Louis, Missouri, at the Redemptorist Church of St. Alphonsus (also known as the "Rock Church"), the city altered bus service to accommodate the throngs of worshippers—sometimes upwards of 10,000 people—who attended novenas each Tuesday afternoon. The weekly devotion was taken by priest missionaries of this province around the world. For instance, thousands attend the novena in places such as the National Shrine of Our Lady of Perpetual Help in Baclaran, the Philippines.

Patrick J. Hayes

See also: Mission Church; Redemptorists and Miracles

Further Reading

Buckley, Daniel J. *The Miraculous Picture of the Mother of Perpetual Help*. Cork: Mercier Press, 1948.

Eskildson, J. F. *Our Lady's Shrine: An Account of Some of the Miraculous Cures (with a History of the Miraculous Picture) Performed at the Mission Church, Boston Highlands, 1870–1883*. Boston: Cashman, Keating, 1883.

Ferrero, Fabriciano. "Nuestra Señora del Perpetuo Soccorro: Informacion Bibliografica y Cronologia General." *Spicilegium Historicum Congregationis SSmi Redemptoris* 38(2) (1990): 456–502.

Ferrero, Fabriciano. *The Story of an Icon*. Cambridge, UK: Redemptorist Publications, 2001.

Henze, Clement. *Mater de Perpetuo Succursu: Prodigiosae Iconis Marialis ita nuncupatae mongraphia*. Bonn: Collegium Josephinum, 1926.

Our Lady of Pontmain

The apparitions at Pontmain in Normandy, France, occurred during a time of national and regional crisis. The Franco-Prussian War was nearing its end; the Prussians had besieged Paris and were advancing on the town of Laval, not far from Pontmain. Four children, brothers Eugène and Joseph Barbadette (aged twelve and ten), and two girls, Françoise Richer and Jeanne-Marie Lebossé (aged eleven and nine), comprised the main group of visionaries. There were also three younger children who seemed to see something too. Adults—the parish priest, nuns, and lay people—gathered around the children and prayed but could not see the apparition. They later told authorities that they saw a cluster of stars in the vicinity of the apparition that were particularly bright. The children reported that up in the sky, there was a crowned Madonna with a gown of stars and a great message written: "But pray, my children, God will soon answer your prayer. My Son is willing to hear you." They saw her in an oval frame, surrounded by four candles that were successively lit; the Virgin held out a great red crucifix toward them. The apparition lasted three hours.

A Prussian army halted the very next day and did not take Laval. The outcome was uncertain for a few days. On January 20 Bishop Wicart of Laval organized a pilgrimage to the shrine church of Notre-Dame d'Avenières in the town and made a vow that he would restore the tower and steeple were the town to be saved by the "Immaculate Virgin." He was at that time unaware of the apparitions at Pontmain. This was one of several such initiatives in which the Virgin was petitioned for peace, both locally and in Paris.

The fact that the war ended on January 28 without the Prussians advancing into the devout northwest of France convinced Wicart and the parish priest, Richard Guérin, that the visions of Pontmain had constituted a miracle. The apparition was therefore authenticated more quickly than any other apparition in the modern era, the decision being declared on February 2, 1872. A basilica was built, and pilgrimage has continued through to the present day, being especially important during World War I and World War II in which France was in conflict once again with Germany.

Pontmain was in many ways the model apparition from the Catholic Church perspective. The message was simple and noncontroversial; children were the seers, but adults, including a priest and nuns, witnessed them; and the prophecy was apparently fulfilled within a very short time. The apparition occurred in a time of crisis, but there was a beneficial outcome locally (despite military defeat for France). It was not without its political implications. Cheryl Porte's work points out how the apparition supported a Catholic French identity at a time of ideological crisis during which the Third Republic was founded, with many detrimental consequences for the church.

Chris Maunder

See also: Apparitions; France, Miracles in

Further Reading

Laurentin, René. *Pontmain: The Apparition*. Pontmain: Sanctuaire de Pont-Main, 1987.
Porte, Cheryl A. *Pontmain, Prophecy, and Protest: A Cultural-Historical Study of a Nineteenth-Century Apparition*. New York: Peter Lang, 2005.

Our Lady of Subang Jaya

On November 9, 2012, an image of the Blessed Virgin Mary appeared on a glass window panel on the seventh floor of the outpatient center of Sime Darby Medical Centre, a private hospital in Subang Jaya, Selangor, Malaysia. The image was first seen by a window cleaner. Soon after, thousands of people gathered outside the hospital around the image to pray, offer flowers, light candles, and sing hymns. The image also drew the attention of people of other faiths. Visitors from East Malaysia and neighboring countries such as Brunei and Singapore came to view the image for themselves. Although the image could only be seen from the outside, as the access to the stairwell on the seventh floor was closed, those who managed to touch the panel claimed that it was not paint.

The image of Mary resembles popular Catholic art in which Mary is depicted as the Immaculate Conception. She stands upright, a halo around her head and dressed in a veil, a blue mantle, and a white tunic that is gathered at the waist. Her arms are outstretched in a gesture of embrace and welcome. Some onlookers also claimed that they could see an additional image of an adult Jesus Christ on a cross in a panel below that of Mary. They believed that the images of Mary and Christ were moving and gradually becoming clearer. Although some admitted that they saw an image, they were uncertain if it was of divine origin. The images were shared on various social media platforms.

Some believed that the appearance of Mary was a call for prayer and good deeds, particularly for world peace. They drew a parallel between this incident and the various apparitions of Mary around the world. Others understood the event as a test of faith. Many considered her appearance at a hospital to mean that infirmities could be healed through faith. Several people even claimed that they were physically cured and their prayers answered due to the miraculous appearance. Some regarded the appearance as a sign that God was reaching out to people and inviting them to follow the right path through Mary. Local clergy called for calm and prudence in relation to the incident.

Soon after the incident, St. Thomas More Parish in Subang Jaya sought permission from the hospital to have the old and delicate panels on which the images appeared removed and taken to the Church of Our Lady of Lourdes in Klang, approximately 21 kilometers (13 miles) away. The hospital agreed to this request, and the transfer was witnessed by the leaders and parishioners of St. Thomas More Parish. Since its transfer, the panels have attracted an average of 200 visitors on weekdays and between 800 and 1,000 on weekends. Local Roman Catholic authorities have since emphasized the need for an authentication of the images and the experiences of the witnesses.

Joseph N. Goh

See also: Apparitions

Further Reading

"Catholics Told to Remain Calm over 'Virgin Mary' Sighting." Malaysian Digest, November 12, 2012, http://goo.gl/vPJYfM.

Ng, Eileen. "'Virgin Mary' Glass Panes Moved to Klang." The Star, November 21, 2012, http://goo.gl/0dQxx2.

Prasena, Priscilla. "Apparition of Mary Continues to Draw Crowd." Free Malaysia Today, February 13, 2013, http://goo.gl/P1QNsM.

Tan, Thomas. "Image of Virgin Mary Appears at Subang Jaya Hospital." Citizen Journalists Malaysia, November 14, 2012, http://goo.gl/Kuy40R.

"Theologian: Virgin Mary's Apparition a Call to Return to God." Malaysian Digest, November 15, 2012, http://goo.gl/hJlKXn.

Toh, Terence. "Awestruck by Virgin Mary Image." The Star, November 11, 2013, http://goo.gl/mqPHuq.

Toh, Terence. "Image Becomes Clearer, Say Witnesses." The Star, November 12, 2012, http://goo.gl/XMnZoF.

Our Lady of Walsingham

Although the shrine or Our Lady of Walsingham is medieval in origin, 1997 marked the centenary of the restoration of devotional life at England's famed Marian shrine of Walsingham, Norfolk, England's Nazareth. The Walsingham Ballad, the name usually given to the earliest written (and subsequently printed) account of the miraculous events of 1061, was written in the mid-fifteenth century (ca. 1460) and printed by Richard Pynson in 1495. Though often referred to as "The Pynson Ballad," its author is unknown. The only extant copy was discovered in the Pepys Library at Magdalene College, Cambridge. According to this ballad, Our Lady appeared to a noble widow, Lady Richeldis de Faverches, in 1061, asking her to build a chapel. Mary led Lady Richeldis "in spirit" to Nazareth to show her the place where the Archangel Gabriel had greeted her and directed the widow to take measurements of the house so that she could build one like it at Walsingham. In this spot, the Virgin Mary explained, the people would celebrate the Annunciation, the "root of mankind's gracious redemption," and would find help in their needs. Three times Lady Richeldis experienced this vision and request. This confirmed her desire to have the chapel constructed, but the directions about the location were unclear to her and to the carpenters. When the carpenters could make no progress in building, Lady Richeldis spent the night in prayer. Her supplications were answered immediately, for the ballad recounts that Our Lady herself had angels complete the construction on the site she wanted, just 200 feet from where the workmen had labored.

As a site of pilgrimage, by 1500 Our Lady of Walsingham reputedly ranked second only to that of Thomas Becket in England and third in all of Europe behind Rome and Santiago de Compestella. Many miracles were attributed to her, but as a source of medieval miracles, the Pynson Ballad gives no specifics, merely vague references to the "Lame made hole and blynde restored to syghte / Maryners vexed with-tempest safe to porte brought / Defe, wounded and lunatyke that hyder haue sought / and also lepers." The anonymous author writes of people who suffered from "wicket spyrytes also moche vexacyon" and assures the reader "of thys is no dought" the "Dede agayne reuyued."

Of more certain documentation is a miracle that Edward I personally attributed to Our Lady of Walsingham. Having been saved from a piece of falling masonry, he is known to have made pilgrimages to the shrine in 1280 and 1296. Erasmus too made a pilgrimage to Walsingham and made light of a miraculous legend commonly held at that time. In 1314 a mounted knight, Sir Ralph Boutefort, was reputedly pursued by an enemy and, calling on Our Lady to rescue him, was given miraculous entry to the shrine via a low entrance that was far too small for him to pass through. The miracle is commemorated in the name of an adjoining street and in an entrance through the priory wall known as the Knight's Gate, which was reconstructed in the 1800s as a memorial to the original gateway.

In his *Life of Henry VIII*, Lord Bacon writes that Henry's father, Henry VII, "kept Easter, 1487 at Norwich, and from thence went in pilgrimage to Walsingham, where he visited Our Lady's church, famous for miracles, and made his prayers and vows for help and deliverance." When the king soon afterward gained a victory at Stoke, "he sent his banner to be offered to Our Lady at Walsingham, where before he made his vows." The same king, by his will, ordered an image of silver gilt to be set up in the shrine.

Henry's son, of course, was responsible for the downfall of the medieval shrine. The suppression of Walsingham priory came late in 1538, under the supervision of Sir Roger Townshend, a local landowner. John Hussey wrote to Lord Lisle in 1538: "July 18th: This day our late Lady of Walsingham was brought to Lambhithe (Lambeth) where was both my Lord Chancellor and my Lord Privy Seal, with many virtuous prelates, but there was offered neither oblation nor candle: what shall become of her is not determined." The shrine and priory buildings were looted and largely destroyed, but the memory of the shrine was less easy to eradicate. Sir Roger Townshend wrote to Cromwell in 1564 that a woman of nearby Wells (now called Wells-Next-the-Sea) had declared that a miracle had been done by the statue after it had been carried away to London. He had the woman put in the stocks on market day to be abused by the village folk but concluded that "I cannot perceyve but the seyd image is not yett out of the sum of ther heddes."

The revival of the shrine is itself seen as miraculous from an ecumenical perspective. It is perhaps the best example of Anglican–Roman Catholic rapprochement since before Vatican II and since then has only deepened, though this has been dampened somewhat of late by developments both on the Roman Catholic and Anglican sides, most notably the erection of the Ordinariate. However, as recently as 1982 when Pope John Paul II visited England, he celebrated Mass at Wembley with the image of Our Lady of Walsingham on the altar. The image was placed there by the director of the Catholic shrine and the administrator of the Anglican shrine. Thereafter Anglicans and Catholics have recognized each other in their publications and events.

Nathan J. A. Humphrey

Further Reading

"The Catholic National Shrine of Our Lady of Walsingham." Walsingham, England Nazareth, http://www.walsingham.org.uk.

Janes, Dominic, and Gary Waller, eds. *Walsingham in Literature and Culture from the Middle Ages to Modernity*. Aldershot, UK: Ashgate, 2010.

Rayne-Davis, John, and Peter Rollings. *Walsingham: England's National Shrine of Our Lady*. London: St. Paul's, 2010.

Waller, Gary. *Walsingham and the English Imagination*. Aldershot, UK: Ashgate, 2011.

P

Passionists and Miracles

Passionists proclaim that through participation in the sufferings of Jesus, humanity comes to understand God's love. Arriving in the United States in 1852, they were committed to adapting the vision of Italian founder Saint Paul of the Cross (Paolo Francesco Danei, 1694–1775) to preach Christ crucified. As a young man in Ovada, Italy, Paul grew to appreciate the sufferings of Christ as "the miracle of miracles of the love of God." Many of his biographers point to the saint's own propensity to perform miracles but in conformity with his message about the Passion of Jesus. A story is related that in 1738 when Paul was at Piagaro in the Diocese of Pieve, he closed a preaching tour stating that he would leave "one who will preach far better than myself." As he moved on from the church, a large crucifix was suddenly seen to sweat large quantities of a substance the color of blood. When parishioners caught up to him to relay this wonder, the saint simply replied that he already knew all about it. In another instance while hearing the confession of a soldier, the saint cradled a crucifix in his hands. Meditating on Jesus's wounds, Saint Paul enumerated all of the soldier's sins even before he spoke them. Astonished, the penitent acknowledged them all.

Passionist tradition understands miracles as rooted in sustained ministry emanating from diverse institutional apostolates such as pilgrimage devotions, conversions, preaching of retreats, and the cult of Passionist sanctity.

Pilgrimage devotions. The arrival of the bones of Saint Benedict at St. Michael's Monastery in West Hoboken (later Union City), New Jersey, in May 1877 marked this devotional site as a destination for pilgrims seeking healing. Prayers were answered in 1879 when Passionist Father Victor Carunchio blessed and healed Louise Lateau (1850–1883). The September 14, 1879, edition of the *New York Times* reported that the timely miracle would make the West Hoboken Passionist monastery as famous as Lourdes itself. Saint Michael's continued a weekly novena for decades thereafter, and though the monastery's novena had declined by the 1960s, Passionist devotional sites maintain historic and contemporary association to miracles.

Dedicated in 1898, visitors to Our Lady of Lourdes Grotto at Holy Cross Church, Mt. Adams, in Cincinnati, Ohio, experienced many healings. Crutches left behind serve as *ex votos* of thanksgiving. The weekly and annual week long St. Ann's Novena, held in Scranton, Pennsylvania, that began in 1924 continues to the present day. The faithful follow a prescribed ritual. Petitioners recite a common prayer, light a candle, and are blessed by holy oil and the relic of Saint Ann. By means of verbal witness or written letters, prayers answered are acknowledged to be everyday miracles or life-changing events.

Conversion miracles and sacraments. Beginning in the late nineteenth century and regardless of faith, the front door apostolate at Passionist monasteries attracted the spiritually downtrodden in need of solace or those searching for a renewed faith. Among the Passionists with a reputation for holiness in receiving new converts was Blessed Dominic Barberi (1792–1849), who had the distinction of establishing the order in Belgium and also received John Henry Newman into the Roman Catholic Church.

Counseling or confession provided spiritual reconciliation, and among its most dedicated ministers was Passionist Father Frederick Corcoran (1890–1957) at the Passionist monastery in West Springfield, Massachusetts. He was the porter at this monastery for three decades, faithfully responding to anyone who knocked, and earned a reputation as a converter of souls. His death in 1957 received front-page coverage in the *Springfield News*. Likewise, Passionist priests have often described the miracles of fallen-away Catholics who returned to the faith through confession.

Retreat preaching. During the 1920s, iconic Passionist preaching on the Passion and death of Jesus found a home in the Passionist worldwide retreat movement. After the 1960s, many retreatants continued to testify that personal time for prayer, reconciliation, solitude, and identification with the sufferings of Jesus allow for an oasis of healing.

Cult of sanctity. Miracles can sometimes be contentious. Because of the extraordinary cures of Passionist Saint Charles Houben (1821–1893) of Mount Argus, Ireland, his religious superiors subjected him to criticism and humiliation. In the end, devotional faith by the public praised his sanctity and kept his cult alive. In 1999, his assistance was implored by a Dutchman, Adolph Dormans, who hailed from the same birthplace in Munstergeleen. Complications from a ruptured appendix had done irreparable injury to his intestines, and his physicians instructed Dormans to prepare himself for death. But the Servant of God would not be denied; Dormans experienced a complete and inexplicable reversal, leading to his canonization as Saint Charles in 2007.

Robert Carbonneau

Further Reading

Carbonneau, Robert. "The Front Door and Parlor Apostolate of Passionist Fathers Frederick Corcoran, Michael Anthony Campbell, and Anthony Neary." *Passionist Heritage Newsletter* 9 (Winter 2002), http://www.cpprovince.org/archives/heritage/winter2002/winter02-1-2.php.

"Extraordinary Graces and Miracles of St Paul of the Cross." St Paul of the Cross, http://www.saintpaulofthecross.com/2009/09/miracles-of-st-paul-of-cross.html.

Gerald Laba, C. P., "The Passionists." In *The Encyclopedia of American Catholic History*, edited by Michael Glazier and Thomas J. Shelley, 1110–1116. Collegeville, MN: Liturgical Press, 1997.

Lachapelle, Sophie. "Louise Lateau and the Experience of Stigmata and Ecstasy." *Configurations* 12(1) (2004): 77–105.

Pius a Spiritu Santo (Devine). *The Life of St Paul of the Cross—Founder of the Congregation of Discalced Clerks of the Holy Cross and Passion of Our Lord, Usually Called Passionists*. New York and Montreal: D. and J. Sadlier, 1868.

Spencer, Paul Francis. *To Heal the Broken Hearted: The Life of Saint Charles of Mount Argus*. Glasgow, Scotland: Ovada Books, 2007.

Strambi, Vincent Mary. *The Life of the Blessed Paul of the Cross, Founder of the Congregation of the Barefooted Clerks of the Most Holy Cross and Passion of Jesus Christ*, Vol. 2. London: Thomas Richardson, 1853, http://www.passionists.com/Strambi%20-%20Volume%201.pdf.

Yuhaus, Cassian P., with Richard Frechette. *Speaking of Miracles*. New York: Paulist Press, 2006.

Physics

Physics is the science of understanding the natural laws of the universe, such as cause and effect, spatiality, gravity, fluidity, mass, temperature, or time. Underlying these laws is the epistemic possibility of actually explaining them in order to attain satisfactory and rational understanding of their principles. Miracles would flout this possibility and tend, at least in the popular mindset, to contradict or violate physical laws. Among many examples that could be offered, the miracle of levitation suspends the law of gravity, and the miracle of walking on water appears to transform an observably fluid surface into a firm mass.

If we grant that there are some universal laws by which we can make claims about reality that can be widely understood and accepted as true, a further theological postulate holds that there is a creative Being that has set these laws in place from eternity. Prescinding from the atheist's objection that there is no such being, an additional objection can be raised, as follows: if there is a God endowed with the most eminent reasoning capabilities and who set physical laws of the universe in place from eternity, why would there be a need to violate them with seeming impunity through the introduction of miraculous phenomena? While the objection has a certain logic to it, it nonetheless limits God's freedom or circumscribes divine activity to only those categories that mortal beings—none of whom have infinite insight—seem to have feebly grasped. The question of reversing the divine will is therefore made moot when considering that God's freedom is limitless and well beyond our knowledge.

In a similar way, the abilities of architects, for instance, to create sound buildings using methods standardized over time is challenged through feats of engineering marvels. Consider the Loretto Chapel staircase in Santa Fe, New Mexico. Built between 1877 and 1881 by an unknown craftsman, the spiral staircase has no center support and makes two 360-degree turns up a span of some 20 feet. It is constructed without glue or nails, and all of the risers are of uniform length. How does this staircase stand? Saint Augustine said, "Miracles are not contrary to nature, but only contrary to what we know about nature."

Quantum mechanics, however, hypothesizes that physical laws are not deterministic and are, in fact, much more elastic than normal sense experience suggests. Since the 1920s, quantum physics has all but put away the canard that the universe is uncompromising in its features or that all of its laws are determined from the ages. The logical extension of such a premise is that miracles are not only possible but are also undeniable. The challenges of both physics and quantum theory are perennial to religion, but their opposition is hardly locked down even by the most skeptical scientists and theologians. If one accepts that physics holds within it deep mathematical laws—ones that offer both precision and elegance in their explanation—it is not difficult to see in their creation and evolution the hand of the divine, even when they appear new or unexpected. The Hebrew scriptures note that "As far as the heavens are above the earth, are my ways above your ways and my thoughts above your thoughts" (Isaiah 55:9). God's ways may not be our own, but they show the same kind of surprising and beautiful aspects of world making that seems endemic to the human project.

Finally, physical laws do not countenance chaos theory, which would hold that there is nothing at all deterministic about the universe and that, in fact, its features are utterly random. Miraculous phenomena also confront chaos—not insofar as the miracle is unusual but because the requirement of normalcy is inherent in the identification of a miracle. That is, one cannot have a violation of the normal laws of the physical universe if everything is chaotic.

Patrick J. Hayes

See also: Hume, David

Further Reading

Barr, Stephen. *Modern Physics and Ancient Faith*. Notre Dame, IN: University of Notre Dame Press, 2003.

Berkovitz, Joseph. "On Supernatural Miracles and Laws of Nature." *Toronto Journal of Theology* 28(1) (2012): 145–174.

Carter, Tim. "The Loretto Chapel Staircase: A Lesson in Physics, Not Miracles." *Washington Post*, January 16, 2010, http://www.washingtonpost.com/wp-dyn/content/article/2010/01/15/AR2010011501810.html.

Jaki, Stanley. *Physics and Miracles*. West Chester, PA: Christendom Press, 2004.

Larmer, Robert. "Miracles, Divine Agency, and the Laws of Nature." *Toronto Journal of Theology* 27(2) (2011): 267–290.

Polkinghorne, John. *Quantum Physics and Theology: An Unexpected Kinship*. New Haven, CT: Yale University Press, 2008.

"Staircase." The Loretto Chapel, http://www.lorettochapel.com/staircase.html.

Pietism

The rise of Pietism in the late seventeenth century under the influence of Frankfurt pastor and theologian Philipp Jakob Spener (1635–1705) and lawyer Johann Jakob Schütz (1640–1690) brought with it a renewed emphasis in German Protestantism on the internalizing of the Christian experience. Church historian Johannes Wallmann has noted that Pietism was characterized by an emphasis on personal Bible reading, conventicles, and a delayed return of Christ. These particular characteristics grew out of an attention to individual conversion and a critique of the spiritual condition of the German Protestant Church. Spener and Schütz represent the two trajectories that Pietism took: churchly and radical. Churchly Pietists sought spiritual renewal within the boundaries of the Protestant Church's confessions, while radicals threw off such symbols for an imagined community of the reborn. Early Pietism nevertheless should be seen as a co-mixture of churchly and radical tendencies, which enabled a religious climate that encouraged what Ryoko Mori calls "supernatural signs of God."

In close connection to the Pietist controversy that occurred over the Leipzig ministry of August Hermann Francke (1663–1727), who was a follower and friend of Spener, groups of Pietists in the surrounding regions evidenced a period of heightened interest in the miraculous. During the first part of the 1690s there were several reports of visions, prophetic voices, and healings occurring among Pietists during worship services and conventicle meetings. Such ecstatic moments exemplify how the miraculous was encountered within a religious movement such as

Pietism, which emphasized the inner experience of God. Supernatural events served as both reminders of the "new life" that could be acquired through rebirth and testimonies to the intimate relationship individuals had with God. Furthermore, reports such as those that claimed miraculous levitation and the sweating and crying of blood substantiated a Pietist narrative that they were living in a special period of God's presence.

The so-called three ecstatic maids (*drei begeisterte Mägde*) provide a useful example of the presence of miracles in early Pietism. Catharina Reinecke, Magdalena Elrich, and Anna Maria Schuchart became known throughout much of the Pietist network for their trancelike states and visions. The testimonies given about these women's personal experiences included a healing from a near-death sickness, being fed with a heavenly food, and the sudden transformation of the level of language used during trances. Such reports even drew the attention and interest of Francke, who was working in Halle, on the Saale River, to implement his Pietist-oriented social reform plan.

Anti-Pietist advocates within Lutheranism, who are often given the label "Lutheran Orthodoxy," used such claims of miraculous events to construct polemics against the budding movement. As a result, those such as Spener, who had from the outset approached stories of the supernatural with suspicion, hardened their stance against such "wonders," which could threaten the influence of their ministries. From the standpoint of some radical Pietists, such occurrences remained badges of the true community of God. As testimonies to the inner, intimate work of God in individuals, miracles helped reify the boundaries set between the reborn and those deemed to be separated from the "true" church.

Peter James Yoder

Further Reading

Deppermann, Andreas. *Johann Jakob Schütz und die Anfänge des Pietismus*. Tübingen: Mohr Siebeck, 2002.

Mori, Ryoko. *Begeisterung und Ernüchterung in christlicher Vollkommenheit*. Tübingen: Max Niemeyer, 2004.

Wallmann, Johannes. *Der Pietismus*. Göttingen: Vandenhoeck and Ruprecht, 2005.

Pilgrimage

Pilgrimage, as a journey from the everyday world toward a sacred center, takes three different forms: existential, metaphorical, and physical. This entry focuses on the physical journey as well as what people do at these sacred places. Such "place pilgrimage" involves a complex and dynamic mixture of processes—ideological, political, economic, and psychological—and therefore extends beyond the sphere of institutional religion into secular activities. Although it is individually experienced, it is a process that can involve a specific group's understandings and behaviors and is developed iteratively over time; pilgrims walk in the footsteps of others.

Since the early 1990s, scholars have been examining secular forms of pilgrimage, which encompass any type of voyage considered hyper-meaningful by the travelers. It has traditionally been applied to journeys for spiritual or religious purposes, and it is particularly in this context that miracles are implicated. Mircea Eliade, the noted historian of religion, considered sites of pilgrimage as *axes mundi* (irruptions of the sacred) to which humans are drawn to recapture cosmological perfection amid the chaos of profane existence. They are often geographically removed from urban centers in which daily life takes its course. Victor Turner also sees pilgrimage sites as sacred centers "out there," peripheral to the institutional power structures in quotidian life. In this sense, pilgrimages are places par excellence for experiencing transcendence and divine intervention; they are often considered unique places to see and be seen by the divine, particularly in traditions such as Hinduism (*darshan*), Shinto (*kanko*), and the spiritual tradition of ancient Greece (*derkomai*). Indeed, the divine and its sacred mediators (such as saints or gurus) are often perceived as being present—often imbued in statues, graves, images, or relics, or in natural land forms such as mountains (i.e., Mt. Meru) or waterways (i.e., Ganges).

These elements of material culture are frequently considered to possess healing properties (i.e., Lourdes) or, in the case of the Ganges, a liberation from the suffering-filled cycle of reincarnation (*moksha; nirvana* in Buddhism). Indeed, there is considerable literature on the hermeneutics of suffering in pilgrimage, and a great many sites are explicitly associated with medico-miraculous narratives of healing, be they corporeal, spiritual, or psychological. The corporal miracle is particularly important, even for the object of pilgrimage: incorruptible bodies of saints as well as weeping, bleeding, or moving images are a particular draw. Narratives of suffering and healing and of suffering and redemption or revivification are so prominent that they help construct the significance of a site in sometimes contested ways. Pilgrimage therefore involves a dynamic relationship between persons, places, texts, and mobilities—both human and divine. Moreover, in Western societies, changing beliefs about the body are affecting how miracles are understood, with people looking beyond spectacular cures to more everyday "minimiracles."

While Islam obliges all those who are able to make a pilgrimage to Mecca (hajj), most other traditions see pilgrimage as a somewhat voluntary way to accumulate merit, which often translates into divine intervention in material affairs.

Pilgrimage itself is frequently seen or undertaken as a sacrifice: arduous, costly, time-consuming, and, in the past, quite dangerous. With the emergence of modern means of transportation and accommodation, which has lessened the innate difficulty associated with pilgrimage, many sites build in places where bodily toil or sacrificial rituals can be undertaken, such as walking a *via Crucis* (Stations of the Cross); fasting for days as in Croagh Patrick, Ireland; or climbing to the top of a mountain without the aid of a funicular. While once pilgrims walked from southern France to Spain's great sanctuary of Santiago de Compostela, for example, today the pilgrim office only grants the much sought-after *compostela* stamp to travelers who have walked or cycled 100 kilometers. Many Santiago pilgrims—whether they are undertaking the journey for religious or secular purposes—talk of their wounded feet and backs as evidence of their meritorious self-sacrifice.

Furthermore, to gain merit with a deity or saint, pilgrims are often compelled to make elaborate or costly donations and sacrifices or leave a votive offering to mark a vow made (*ex voto*) or, in the Catholic world, as thanks for a grace received. Pilgrims in Asia tie papers to sacred trees, affix gold leaf to an iconic statue, or publicly leave receipts attesting to the size of their monetary donation; in Catholicism, they leave plaques in thanksgiving, *ex votos* in the shape of a body part they hope will be healed, or even their crutches or bandages after experiencing a miraculous healing. While sometimes these donations are kept relatively private, in Southeast Asian forms of Buddhism, for example, they are very public, and devotees often compete with one another to secure the attention of the divine.

Hence, as some scholars have argued, the very significance of pilgrimage sites is constructed through these explicit and often public contestations and struggles among factions of devotees. This is not intended to be a unidirectional supplication, however; pilgrims strategically engage in a bargaining (or, as in the case of Saint Padre Pio's townsmen in Pietrelcina, a kinship) relationship with the divine whereby they seek to tie the saint or deity into a mutual obligation. The miracles that emerge are therefore considered not simply as the divine erupting uncontrollably into human society but are hopefully triggered by the devotee's vow, sacrifice, or gift.

Pilgrims will also frequently bring back souvenirs, relics, pieces of the land, or bottles of holy water to give to friends, families, and those in need of miraculous cures who could not make the pilgrimage. Even mundane souvenirs purchased at a pilgrimage site—plastic statuettes, rosaries, prayer cards, or images—may be turned into relics for this purpose; pilgrims will touch these objects to the sacred effigy in a transfer of so-called contagious magic, or an accompanying priest will engage in an informal rite of *inventio*, blessing bags of souvenirs at the end of a journey.

Pilgrimage is thus implicated in elaborate forms of reciprocity with the divine that largely circumvent the religious institutions and practitioners of the sacred who are otherwise mediators between devotees/congregations and the divinity. Victor and Edith Turner argued that pilgrimage can create a temporary sense of human commonality among pilgrims (*communitas*) that exists above and beyond the lived social structures of daily life—including the institutionalized religious organizations. For this reason, many orthodox religious hierarchies are ambivalent about such manifestations of popular piety and may either deter the faithful from engaging in pilgrimage or co-opt the charisma of the object of pilgrimage through ritualized authorization processes, such as canonization or verification of an apparition around which a pilgrimage site is created. At the least, they will maintain a watchful eye on the popular practices at pilgrimage sites, as the Israeli rabbinate does for pilgrimage to the tombs of holy people (*tsaddiquim*). Yet place pilgrimage is not so easily constrained, and the quest for miracles today takes diverse forms as spiritual pilgrims and religious tourists pursue their own agendas at officially religious shrines and develop alternative sites and cults in a religious free market.

Michael A. Di Giovine

See also: *Ex Voto;* Lourdes

Further Reading

Butler, E. *Ritual Magic*. Cambridge: Cambridge University Press, 1949.

Coleman, Simon, and John Eade. *Reframing Pilgrimage: Cultures in Motion*. London and New York: Routledge, 2004.

Coleman, Simon, and John Elsner. *Pilgrimage: Past and Present in the World Religions*. Cambridge, MA: Harvard University Press, 1997.

Di Giovine, Michael. "Padre Pio for Sale: Souvenirs, Relics, or Identity Markers?" *International Journal of Tourism Anthropology* 2(2) (2012): 108–127.

Eade, John, and Michael Sallnow, eds. *Contesting the Sacred: The Anthropology of Christian Pilgrimage*. New York: Routledge, 1991.

Eliade, Mircea. *The Sacred and the Profane: The Nature of Religion*. Translated by Willard R. Trask. New York: Harcourt, Brace, 1959.

Fedele, Anna. *Looking for Mary Magdalene: Alternative Pilgrimage and Ritual Creativity at Catholic Shrines in France*. Oxford: Oxford University Press, 2012.

Frey, Nancy. *Pilgrim Stories: On and Off the Road to Santiago*. Berkeley: University of California Press, 1998.

Harris, Alana. "Lourdes and Holistic Spirituality: Contemporary Catholicism, the Therapeutic, and Religious Thermalism." *Culture and Religion* 14(1) (2013): 23–43.

Harris, Ruth. *Lourdes: Body and Spirit in the Secular Age*. London: Penguin Books, 1999.

Morinis, Alan. *Sacred Journeys: The Anthropology of Pilgrimage*. Santa Barbara, CA: Praeger, 1992.

Nuttall, Deirdre. "Christian Pilgrimage: Miracles and Magic." *Sinsear* 8 (1995): 1–12.

Shoham-Steiner, Ephraim. "'For a Prayer in That Place Would Be Most Welcome': Jews, Holy Shrines, and Miracles—A New Approach." *Viator* 37 (2006): 369–395.

Turner, Victor. "The Center Out There: Pilgrim's Goal." *History of Religions* 12(3) (February 1973): 191–230.

Turner, Victor, and Edith Turner. *Image and Pilgrimage in Christian Culture.* New York: Columbia University Press, 1978.

Poland, Miracles in

With close to 90 percent of the population considering itself Catholic and with a historical affiliation to Christianity that goes back more than a millennium, the piety of the people of Poland is deep and wide. Included in that environment is the strong belief in miracles; up to 70 percent of students believe in supernatural phenomena created by God. As recently as 2008, Catholics in Sokolka in the Archdiocese of Bialystok were stunned one Sunday during Mass at the Church of St. Anthony. A communion wafer fell on the floor of the church and developed a bloody spot. This manifestation was later tested by two physicians, both of whom determined that the spot contained organic heart muscle tissue. Subsequently, believers insist that the host is a fragment of Jesus's own heart. It has been placed in a reliquary that is carried in procession each year through the little town, despite widespread skepticism.

Poland's saints and shrines are numerous. Like the Sokolka miracle, the miracles of saints and shrines are sources of national and local pride. Included in the catalog of saints are several bishops, including Saint Adalbert (d. 997) and Saint Stanislas (d. 1079), both of whom were martyred. Bishop Adalbert was martyred along the Baltic coast at the hands of the pagans he hoped to convert. When Christians were sent to retrieve his body for proper burial, the pagans demanded the bishop's weight in silver for its return. Scales were erected to exact the ransom, but by the time they tipped, only one silver coin remained. Bishop Stanislas's legend includes the tale of his resurrecting Peter, who goes on to serve as a witness on Stanislas's behalf in a legal skirmish with King Boleslaw. The bishop's row with the king ended when Boleslaw murdered him at Skalka outside Kraków. The bishop's body was then hacked to bits and strewn over a pond. According to one legend, the pieces then miraculously reassembled. Today the remains are interred in a silver sarcophagus in the Wawel Cathedral in Kraków, where they have become a point of national pilgrimage.

Two monarchs are on the list of Poland's royal saints. The first is Jadwiga (Hedwig) of Poland (1373–1399), whose "kingship" was marked by her extraordinary generosity, including refurbishment of an educational institution that grew into the Jagiellian University. While in a Corpus Christi day procession a young drowning victim was brought before her. She passed her cloak over the boy, who was instantly revived. Today her bones rest below a crucifix in the Wawel Cathedral before which she often prayed. According to legend, its corpus spoke to her. Saint Casimir of Poland (ca. 1458–1484), patron of the Polish and Lithuanian people, died in Grodno, and his remains are venerated in a reliquary ensconced in the cathedral at Vilna, Lithuania. The altar on which the reliquary rests became famous for miracles, including the revivification of a young boy. Casimir's first miracle was a postmortem appearance at the Battle of Polock (Polatsk) in 1518, where he was alleged to have led the Lithuanians to safe passage against Moscovite invaders. This prompted his elder brother to petition for his canonization cause to open, which was done immediately, so that by 1521 Pope Adrian VI beatified the young prince. Casimir was canonized in 1602. To these royals one could add two princesses: Saints Hedwig (1243) and Cunegund (1292).

Among other Polish saints, mention should be made of Saints Hyacinth (d. 1257), John Cantius (d. 1473), Stanislas Kostka (d. 1568), and Andrew Bobola (d. 1657). The twentieth century witnessed several saints, many of whom died for the faith in concentration camps. Two such martyrs include the Franciscan friar Maximilian Kolbe and Carmelite sister Teresa Benedicta of the Cross (Edith Stein). For Kolbe, his miracles included a July 1948 cure of intestinal tuberculosis in Angela Testoni and in August 1950 the cure of calcification of the arteries of Francis Ranier. For Teresa Benedicta, her final miracle before canonization came in 1987 when a young child named for her suffered from hepatic necrosis after ingesting lethal doses of Tylenol. Prayers for her intercession were launched by the child's family, and she recovered within days.

Finally, with respect to shrines, the most famous in the country is Our Lady of Częstochowa, housed in the Jasna Góra Monastery. The Black Madonna depicted in this icon has been widely replicated. Legends abound, including two prominent stories of the icon's ability to fend off a fire in the church where it was housed, though not before the Virgin and Child's complexions were darkened. Additionally, when the monastery was sacked and robbed of its icon by Hussites in 1430, their attempt to escape with it was foiled when the horses they rode refused to move. Perhaps the greatest miracle is the fidelity of the Polish people to their Madonna, where twentieth-century pilgrimage to Jasna Góra was meant to defy both Nazi occupation and communist tyranny.

Patrick J. Hayes

See also: Our Lady of Częstochowa

Further Reading

Plezia, Marian. "Męczeństwo św. Wojciecha" [The Martyrdom of St. Adalbert]. In *Średniowieczne żywoty i cuda patronow Polski* [The Medieval Lives and Miracles of the Holy Patrons of Poland], edited by Marian Plezia, 31–39. Warsaw: Instytut Wydawniczy Pax, 1987.

Pleziowa, Janina. "Cuda św. Wojciecha" [The Miracles of St. Adalbert]. In *Średniowieczne żywoty i cuda patronow Polski* [The Medieval Lives and Miracles of the Holy Patrons of Poland], edited by Marian Plezia, 81–95. Warsaw: Instytut Wydawniczy Pax, 1987.

Ketrzyński, Wydał Wojciech. *Vitae et miraculua sanctorum Poloniae patronorum Adalberti et Stanislai.* Lwów: Druk. Zakładu Narodowego im. Ossolińskich, 1883.

Klaniczay, Gabor. *Saints of the Christianization Age of Central Europe Tenth to Twelfth Centuries.* Budapest: Central European University Press, 2012.

Kuzmová, Stanislava. "Medieval Sermons on Saint Stanislas of Cracow and Their Role in the Construction of His Image and Cult." PhD dissertation, Central European University, 2010.

Pomponazzi, Pietro

Pomponazzi (1462–1525) was an Aristotelian philosopher who mainly taught at the universities of Padua and Bologna. He did not believe in the possibility of miraculous divine interventions into the ordinary course of nature and devoted a lengthy treatise, *De incantationibus*, to the subject. Pomponazzi approaches the topic in the context of peripatetic natural philosophy, contemporary medicine, and psychology. Even though he grudgingly bowed to ecclesiastical authority, admitting now and then the occasional miracle, Pomponazzi argues quite stringently that all miracles are merely caused by the influence of extraordinary heavenly constellations.

His novel suggestion that the miraculous abilities of certain human beings derive from the stars means that these bodies are capable of influencing the individual's physical and mental propensities. Such people may become prodigious healers as well as cause a lot of harm by redirecting powerful celestial forces onto other people's bodies and minds. To that aim they consciously or unconsciously use certain mental images, the phantasmata, which in the first place influence their own psychic conditions.

The medium of transmission to the outside world is an invisible subtle airy vapor produced by the most refined part of the human blood: the so-called *spiritus*. Originally a medical concept, the *spiritus* is the instrument by which individual souls are able to govern their own body as well as act upon the physical world.

Pomponazzi explains that this image-forming power of soul is attributed to the imagination and to the faculty of desire. Even though Pomponazzi admits that this idea is un-Aristotelian and perhaps fabulous, he subscribes to the theory that the soul may act externally through vaporous substances, because this explains all sorts of miracles or demonic events.

With that theoretical backdrop Pomponazzi also explains the natural causes of miracles that were experienced by more than one person. He discusses a case from Aquilea where a congregation of faithful was able to dispel a hailstorm and, by might of their prayers, cause an apparition in the sky of San Celestino, the town's patron saint. Pomponazzi says that such stunning visions are caused by a favorable astrological constellation (which stopped the hailstorm) and that the saint's apparition was caused by the collective emission of subtle material *spiritus* that had been fomented by local images of the patron saint. He thus argues that the people themselves caused the apparition by their collective and directed mental effort that materializes in subtle airy bodies. The prayers of the congregation were merely subsidiary because they have no power to influence God.

Such phenomena, Pomponazzi believed, was attributable to those particularly prone to falling totally under the influence of the stars. As a concept, the idea that the soul could act externally grew out of scholastic philosophy, especially Avicenna (*Liber sextus de naturalibus* 4, 5), who says that the human soul, through its imagination, is capable of affecting other bodies. Saint Thomas Aquinas objects to this opinion (*Summa Theologiae* I, q. 117, a. 3).

Sergius Kodera

Further Reading

Garin, Eugenio. "Fantasia e imaginatio fra Ficino e Pomponazzi." *Giornale critico di filosofia italiana* 64 (1985): 349–361.

Giglioni, Guido, 2010. "The Matter of the Imagination: The Renaissance Debate over Icastic and Fantastic Imitation." *Camenae* 8 (2010): 1–19.

"Pietro Pomponazzi." Stanford Encyclopedia of Philosophy, http://plato.stanford.edu /entries/pomponazzi/.

Pine, Martin L. *Pietro Pomponazzi: Radical Philosopher of the Renaissance*. Padua: Antenore, 1986.

Pomponazzi, Pietro. *De incantationibus*. Edited by Vittoria Perrone-Compagni. Florence: Olschki, 2011.

Pomponazzi, Pietro. *De naturalium efectuum admirandorum causis sive de incantationibus*. 1556; reprint, Hildesheim: Georg Olms, 1970.

Walker, Daniel P. *Spiritual and Demonic Magic from Ficino to Campanella*. London: Warburg Institute, 1958.

Postulator

A postulator is a duly authorized individual responsible for processing a sainthood cause. Postulators must be expert in canon law and theology and may be either clerics or lay people. Unlike an external assistant, who can be charged with developing a *positio* (biography) detailing a person's sanctity, the postulator has the power to direct all legal, procedural, and financial matters related to a cause, including the right to select a vice postulator. Postulators may also write the *positio* themselves.

Postulators are of two types: Roman and local. The Roman postulator is the principal advocate for a saint's cause before the Congregation for Saints' Causes in Rome. The local or vice postulator—sometimes called the diocesan postulator—is the individual who works with the Roman postulator at the locale where the Servant of God lived or was buried. Typically, the vice postulator assists the local bishop in the formation of a tribunal that investigates the cause for sainthood and does so through the instruction of the postulator. These tribunals can collect and examine documents by or about the candidate, make transcripts, present reports to the bishop, and call witnesses and depose them. Similarly, the postulator and vice postulator can direct inquiries into alleged miracles. They are responsible for advocating that the candidate's virtues are exemplary and that the miracles wrought by the candidate's intercession follow upon his or her purported sanctity.

Postulators need not confine themselves to one cause or set of causes for sainthood, and many Roman postulators have active practices that undertake the cases of numerous clients around the world. These petitioners or actors work in concert with the postulator, who is hired for a nominal fee. Postulators, in turn, take the information gathered about a case to relevant authorities, study the spirituality cultivated by the subject, and work with the people hoping to see their candidate advance as a Servant of God, a venerable, a blessed, and finally a saint.

Another specialized type of postulator is the postulator-general. This is a person selected by a religious order of women or men to seek canonization for one of the order's deceased members who had a particular reputation for holiness in life.

Some postulators have left detailed notes on their research and encounters with devotees of their saint. Redemptorist Father Francis Litz often marveled at the devotion to Saint John Neumann, the Catholic bishop of Philadelphia and first male saint of the United States. As vice postulator of the Neumann cause for canonization, Litz worked with a team of fellow Redemptorists in the United States and Rome to assemble all of the documentation necessary for advancing the cause. He was also present to oversee the exhumation of the saintly bishop when his remains were transferred to a glass-encased altar in the lower church of Saint Peter the Apostle in Philadelphia. The story is relayed that when Neumann was redressed in bishop's vestments, a miter was placed on his head. But it was so large that it could not fit comfortably inside the altar-reliquary. Litz managed to obtain a shorter miter from the local Episcopal bishop, proving that a postulator's ingenuity had to remain both constant and versatile.

Though it is not required of them, some postulators serve as unofficial historians of the causes of saints. The processes involved in assembling a cause can often take decades of work, and the transfer of responsibilities from one postulator to another is often caused by an abrupt death or advanced age. The enormity of the tasks involved in putting together a cause—from doing the necessary historical spade work on the *positio* to putting together the seating charts for a canonization Mass—are undertaken in humility.

Patrick J. Hayes

See also: Beatification; Canonization; Congregation for Saints' Causes; Marmion, Abbot Columba

Further Reading

Casieri, Antonio. *Postulatorum Vademecum*. 2nd ed. Rome: Congregation for Saints' Causes, 1985.

Hoegerl, Carl. "History of the Cause for Canonization of Blessed Francis Xavier Seelos, CSSR." *Spicilegium Historicum Congregationis SSmi Redemptoris* 49 (2001): 349–409, http://www.santalfonsoedintorni.it/Spicilegium/49/SH-49-2001%28II%29351-412.pdf.

Raquez, Olivier. "Memoirs of the Postulator for the Cause of Blessed Columba Marmion." *American Benedictine Review* 60(1) (2009) 27–43.

"Souvenirs of Father Olivier Raquez: Postulator for the Cause of Blessed Columba Marmion." Marmion Belgium, http://www.marmion.be/marm2214l.pdf.

Woestman, William B., ed. *Canonization: Theology, History, Process*. Ottawa: Faculty of Canon Law, St. Paul University, 2002.

Price, Richard

Richard Price (1723–1791) was an influential figure who counted among his friends persons such as Thomas Jefferson, David Hume, Adam Smith, and Mary Wollstonecraft. The literary executor of Thomas Bayes, the pioneer of Bayes's Theorem, Price edited Bayes's major work, *An Essay towards Solving a Problem in the Doctrine of Chances* (1763), and was elected a fellow of the Royal Society in recognition of his pioneering work in probability theory.

In his *Four Dissertions* (1772), Price criticizes Hume on the basis that Hume's grasp of probability theory was deficient and that Hume wrongly defines miracles as necessitating violation of the laws of nature. Regarding the first point, Price criticizes Hume's account of how testimonial evidence is to be evaluated. Regarding the latter point, Price draws an analogy between miracles and the acts of human agents, writing that "the supposition that a miracle . . . implies a *violation* or *suspension* of the laws of nature . . . is by no means necessarily included in the idea of a miracle. A sensible and *extraordinary effect* produced by *superior* power, no more implies that a law of nature is *violated* than any *common effect* produced by human power."

Robert Larmer

Further Reading

Price, Richard. *Four Dissertations: I. On providence; II. On Prayer; III. On the Reasons for Expecting That Virtuous Men Shall Meet after Death in a State of Happiness; IV. On the Importance of Christianity, the Nature of Historical Evidence, and Miracles.* 2nd ed. London: Printed for A. Millar and T. Cadell, opposite to Catherine-Street, in the Strand, 1768.

Prophecy

Prophecy is a communication either from God to human beings through an oracle or from human beings to one another. In a prophecy, some specific, unforeseen, future event or issue is identified and explained before its actual occurrence. The story of this prophetic moment is then disseminated to a wider public either by a prophet or a chronicler of the event. Prophecy is tied to miracles, because a prophet is typically conceived of as a person who is able to make complex predictions—without error—that then come true. Prophecy implies a miraculous knowledge of very specific material that could not have been contrived or so regularly predicted by human beings. A prophet, however, is also a person, and so having at one's disposal an otherwise supernatural power of prediction creates a sense of awe and wonder.

If faith comes through hearing (*fides ex auditu*), the prophet announces or articulates God's words in order to supply direction or make sense of faith's tenets. They are not mediums, which the Hebrew Bible forbid (cf. Deuteronomy 18:9–22); they seek no remuneration for their service. Real prophets are authenticated by their track record; they are always correct. Their words are linked to change (of the present to the future) and behaviors. Their focus is on that which will keep people holy and observant on questions of obligation or duty. Thus, for instance, the prophet Amos in the Old Testament turns the people by reminding them not to break mutual treaty obligations and to fulfill their duties toward the poor and needy. In Judaism, numerous prophecies were made by the patriarchs of the faith, Abraham and Moses, as well as prophets such as Isaiah, Ezekiel, and Joel, among others. Some of their prophecies were joyous. Elisha, for instance, predicted the birth of a son to a Shunammite woman, and despite her unbelief, it came to pass. Elisha was not a man to be trifled with. When he went up to the city of Bethel, some boys came out to jeer him: "Go up, baldhead! Go up, baldhead!" Their taunts were met with Elisha's curse. "Then two she-bears came out of the woods and tore forty-two of the children to pieces" (2 Kings 2:23–24).

An element of prophecy in first-century Palestine is the expectancy of the arrival of the Messiah. With its political overtones and tinged with Jewish apocalyptic, Yemot haMasheach, literally "blue sky," was to be a time of peace ushered in by the *Mashiach* ("anointed one"). There was a sense of something cataclysmic that would take place within a person's lifetime. Many writers supported the idea that the end of the world as they knew it was coming. When Jesus emerged in his public ministry, he noted ominously that "we do not know the hour" when "heaven and earth will pass away" (cf. Mark 13:21–37). His disciples could not be other than terrified by this, since Jesus reportedly knew the future like any of the prophets worthy of the title (cf. Mark 6:15; Luke 7:16; John 6:14, all of which describe Jesus as a prophet). Jesus had a way of predicting events that were often told cryptically, as with the predictions of his own passion and death (cf. Mark 8:31, 9:31, 10:33–34) and just as often without getting the message across to his immediate followers.

In Christianity, depending on how passages of the Bible are interpreted, prophecy makes up over 25 percent of the text. Many Jewish prophecies in the Old Testament are also prophecies in Christianity—the two religions follow many of the same prophets. In Islam, at least depending on tradition, there are eschatological prophecies such as the future coming of the Mahdi, the Twelfth Imam. Muhammad, the central figure in Islam, is also seen as a prophet—indeed, the last one—who is responsible for the culminating and unsurpassable holy Qur'an.

A prophet may be a divine agent but is also inescapably a human being. Abraham Heschel, one of the leading Jewish thinkers of the twentieth century, called attention to the role of prophets and their prophecies. In his book *The Prophets*, Heschel defines a prophet as "a person, not a microphone. He is endowed with a mission, with the power of a word not his own that accounts for this greatness—but also with temperament, concern, character, and individuality." There is a humanity to the prophet mixed with divine thought. The prophet has a "breathless impatience with injustice," which "may strike us as hysteria"; "often his words begin to burn where conscience ends." Prophets are extremely serious about issues of sin and expect society to change immediately.

The nature of the prophet is important in the context of miracles and to prophecy. Advocacy is often tinged with rhetorical skill, poetic words, patriotism, or statesmanlike bearing. Social criticism from the prophet is sharp and precise—beyond the normal range of predictive or caustic remarks. The prophet has a divine ability. He is able to speak into a society—and often a larger world—and talk about pertinent issues that can correct humanity in very specific ways. Heschel notes that "Prophecy is not simply the application of timeless standards to particular human situations, but rather an interpretation of a particular moment in history, a divine understanding of human history."

In the history of ideas, prophecy has been closely associated with miracles, as the twin pillars of revealed religion. Thus, for David Hume, "what we have said of miracles may be applied, without any variation, to prophecies; and indeed, all prophecies are real miracles, and as such only can be admitted as proofs of any revelation." When he sought to lay waste to the veracity of miracles, he was also calling into question the possibility of prophecies. Yet both miracles and prophecies are testimonies of a sort, ones that tend to confirm what we have come to know as true but that we would be circling around as if in a fog had there been no prophetic utterance, giving credence to the assertion that prophecies enjoy a "particular advantage above most other miracles, on the force of their duration."

Patrick J. Hayes

See also: Revelation

Further Reading

Amit, Yairah. "A Prophet Tested: Elisha, the Great Woman of Shunem, and the Story's Double Message." *Biblical Interpretation* 11:3–4 (2003): 279–294.

Harrison, Peter. "Prophecy, Early Modern Apologetics, and Hume's Argument against Miracles." *Journal of the History of Ideas* 60(2) (April 1999): 241–256.

Heschel, Abraham Joshua. *The Prophets.* New York: Jewish Publication Society of America, 1962.

Kaplan, Lawrence. "Maimonides on the Miraculous Element in Prophecy." *Harvard Theological Review* 70(3–4) (October 1977): 233–256.

Kselman, Thomas A. *Miracles and Prophecies in Nineteenth-Century France.* New Brunswick, NJ: Rutgers University Press, 1983.

Long, Burke O. "The Social Setting for Prophetic Miracle Stories." *Semeia* 3 (1975): 46–63.

Orton, David E., ed. *Prophecy in the Hebrew Bible: Selected Studies from Vetus Testamentum.* Leiden: Brill, 1999.

R

Redemptorists and Miracles

The Congregation of the Most Holy Redeemer (Redemptorists), founded in Italy in 1732 by Saint Alphonsus Liguori, counts among its members four saints, fourteen beati, and ten venerables. Two of these are Americans: Saint John Neumann (1811–1860) and Blessed Francis X. Seelos (1819–1867).

Neumann was the fourth bishop of Philadelphia, and almost immediately after his death miracles were reported. They continued over the next century, though faulty record keeping prevented Redemptorist postulators from submitting these cases for formal review. Favors were recorded both at the bishop's tomb and in Europe, especially cures of children and cancer victims. The two miracles used for his beatification included a cure in 1923 of an eleven-year-old girl, Eva Benassi, from the town of Sassuolo near Milan, Italy. She had contracted peritonitis, but recourse to Neumann made all her symptoms vanish. The second case occurred in 1946 to Villanova, Pennsylvania, native J. Kent Lenahan Jr. He was the victim of an automobile accident that crushed him between the car and a utility pole, resulting in a fractured skull and internal bleeding. A Neumann relic was applied to the injured man. Within hours his blood pressure and temperature were normalized, and a month later he walked out of the hospital. The miracle used in Neumann's canonization process centered on the case of Michael Flanagan. In 1962 at age five he developed bone cancer, which later spread to his lungs and jaws. He suffered over the course of the following year until he was blessed with a Neumann relic. Within six weeks, no trace of the cancer could be found. Neumann was canonized by Pope Paul VI on June 19, 1977.

Father Francis Seelos, a German missionary to America, died of yellow fever in New Orleans—a death he predicted (both in the manner and the time) a year prior. Unlike Neumann, miraculous phenomena were detectable during Seelos's life as well as after death. Two confrères approached him for cures (both for knee ailments), and their afflictions subsided. His cause for sainthood was promoted judiciously, with meticulous accounting of postmortem miracles. Among those used for his beatification was the case of Angela Maria Boudreaux (neé Governale) who was diagnosed with non-Hodgkin's lymphoma of the liver in 1967. She died in 2001 of an unrelated illness, though not before traveling to Rome in 2000 to witness the beatification of Blessed Seelos.

Saint Gerard Majella (or Maiella) was another Redemptorist saint for whom numerous miracles are attributed. Born on April 6, 1726, in Muro outside Naples, Italy, from an early age he was graced with visions of Mary and Jesus. Typically these occurred in a local chapel and were corroborated by Gerard's sister, who once witnessed a statue of the Virgin and Child come to life. His spiritual hunger was quenched in part by the Archangel Michael, who gave Gerard his first holy communion. As a teen he served the bishop of Lacedonia but one day accidentally dropped the key to the episcopal residence down a well. Gerard lowered a statue of the infant Jesus, and witnesses described the key's return in the figure's hand. As a Redemptorist brother, Gerard would periodically bilocate or read minds. His ecstasies while at prayer often were accompanied by levitations. He resuscitated a boy who had fallen from a cliff, multiplied bushels of wheat for a poor family, and guided a group of fishermen safely to shore after walking across stormy seas to meet them. A child named Amata Giuliani suffered burns from scalding water in April 1747, only to be healed by Gerard's touch. While visiting a local family, he gave over his handkerchief to one of the daughters. Many years later she was in the throes of child birth, the pangs of which were threatening her life. Calling out for Gerard's aid, she clutched the handkerchief, and almost immediately her labor was eased. Since his death from tuberculosis on October 16, 1755, he has continued to have the reputation of lessening the burdens of pregnancy and to this day remains the patron of those either seeking to become pregnant or of mothers confronted with difficult deliveries.

Finally, the life of Saint Alphonsus Liguori (1696–1787) was also fraught with miracles. Initially a lawyer and later a preacher and chaplain, the founder of the Redemptorists could often be found in the hill country around Naples. At several of his missions he appeared enthralled by a shaft of light emanating from an image of the Blessed Virgin Mary. His spirituality was so deep that he was often drawn bodily into the air. He appeared at the death bed of Pope Clement XIV in Rome on September 22, 1774, and simultaneously in another city. Today Saint Alphonsus is a doctor of the Church and patron of moral theologians and confessors.

Patrick J. Hayes

Further Reading

Brother Ernest. *The Miracle Man of Muro: A Story of St. Gerard Majella.* Notre Dame, IN: Dujarie Press, 1950.

Byerley, Timothy E. *Saint John Neumann: Wonder-Worker of Philadelphia, Recent Miracles, 1961–1991*. Philadelphia: National Shrine of St. John Neumann, 1992.

Ferrante, Constance Petrucelli. "A Walk through Time: A Symbolic Analysis of the Devotion to St. Gerard Maiella." PhD dissertation, Rutgers University, 1993.

Magnier, J. *Life, Virtues and Miracles of St. Gerard Majella, Redemptorist Lay Brother: The Wonder-Worker of Our Days*. St. Louis: Herder, 1902.

Nicastro, Thomas D. *The Feast of St. Gerard Majella, C.Ss.R.: A Century of Devotion at St. Lucy's, Newark, New Jersey*. Charleston, SC: History Press, 2012.

Rush, Alfred. *The Autobiography of St. John Neumann, C.Ss.R.* Boston: Pauline Books, 1977.

Saint-Omer, Edward. *St. Gerard Majella: The Wonder-Worker and Patron of Expectant Mothers*. Rockford, IL: TAN Books, 1999. Reprint of *The Wonder-Worker of Our Days: The Life, Virtues, and Miracles of Saint Gerard Majella*. Boston: Mission Church Press, 1907.

Savastano, Peter. "Changing St. Gerard's Clothes: An Exercise in Italian-American Catholic Devotion and Material Culture." In *Italian Folk: Vernacular Culture in Italian-American Lives*, edited by Joseph Sciorra, 171–188. New York: Fordham University Press, 2011.

Treece, Patricia. *Nothing Short of a Miracle: The Healing Power of Saints*. New York: Doubleday, 1988.

Reformation Europe, Miracles in

By 1500, Christian Europe was experiencing a surge of belief in the power of saints to heal and otherwise perform miraculous works. This trend was evident in the enduring popularity of saintly miracles in the *Legenda Aurea*, the multitudes of pilgrims who traveled each year to seek cures and redeeming grace at holy shrines, and the fascination with wonder books whose pages reported strange heavenly portents, hideous birth defects, and approaching natural calamities. Such obsessive belief in the cult of saints, pilgrimages, miracles, and other supernatural phenomena soon came under vigorous attack from the great religious reformers of the sixteenth century. Martin Luther, who initially authored the Protestant breach with Rome, seems in his early life to have shared these traditional beliefs in saints and miracles. In 1505, for example, he prayed to Saint Anne for safety during his famous thunderstorm experience, and in 1510–1511 he visited all the popular pilgrimage sites in Rome during his Augustinian mission to that city.

Luther's views on these holy wonders gradually began to shift, however, during the following decade. By the time he faced charges of heresy at the Diet of Worms in 1521, his revolutionary new doctrine of *sola fideism* (salvation by faith alone) had all but swept aside the need for saints and their confirming miracles. Luther argued that otherworldly occurrences were as likely to have demonic as sanctified origins, and he stressed faith and scripture as more legitimate verifications of religious truth than were miracles. He did acknowledge the miracles of the New Testament apostles but attributed such supernatural feats to the passionate faith that these "elect" men possessed as gifts from God, and he insisted that their miracles had simply been temporary tools of Christian recruitment in an earlier pagan age.

On the other hand, Martin Luther enthusiastically embraced natural abnormalities as likely revelations of divine will. In 1522 a deformed calf was born in Saxony that resembled a cowled monk, leading Luther to believe that the poor creature might be a sign of the coming Apocalypse. When his student Philip Melanchthon also claimed knowledge of a strange donkey-human-reptilian monster supposedly discovered near the pope's castle outside Rome, the two published *The Meaning of Two Horrific Figures: The Monk Calf and the Papal Ass* in 1523, accusing the papal Antichrist of bringing about the Last Days. Luther also referred at various times in his life to astrological marvels and bizarre human births so that even the great Reformer himself seems to have been, after all, a man of his own credulous age.

Other sixteenth-century evangelical reformers challenged Catholic belief in saints and miracles as well, even if their followers initially did not always support their views. John Calvin denounced miraculous works even more firmly than had Luther, condemned cures associated with the relics of saints as fraudulent and ungodly, and insisted that the age of miracles had long since ended. In his *Institutes of the Christian Religion*, Calvin agreed with Luther that the miracles of the biblical prophets and apostles had been gifts from God and that only Christ had possessed the divine power to perform his own true miracles. Another champion of Protestant reform, the Englishman John Foxe, compiled his *Acts and Monuments* in 1554–1558 to record the passions of thousands of martyrs from the apostolic age to the reign of Queen Mary. Like his mentor John Calvin, Foxe limited miraculous powers to the Christian victims of Roman persecution in the ancient world, allowing only supreme courage and steadfast faith to his more recent martyrs in Marian England.

Some reforming movements, however, appropriated the power of miracles to their own purposes. The radical Anabaptists who seized and created a "New Jerusalem" in Münster in 1534–1535 were one such group. In 1533 a future leader of the Münster occupation, Jan van der Leyden, was believed by his followers to have cured a sick girl in the town of Schöppingen simply by baptizing her. In 1534 an Anabaptist missionary named Henry Graes, who had been captured, tortured, and condemned to death in nearby Osnabrück, miraculously escaped his tormentors and returned to Münster with the reputed aid of a radiant angel. Thus, popular belief in the healing and saving power of miracles was slow to die even among some of the more radical sects of the Protestant Reformation. And, of course, the Roman Catholic Church itself underwent its own reformation in the midst of the sixteenth century. Its leaders chose at the Council of Trent to reaffirm the role of miracles in supporting the faith of European Catholics but ruled that such holy wonders could only be accepted as authentic if first investigated and confirmed by bishops or other ranking ecclesiastical officials.

Clayton J. Drees

See also: Calvin, John; Council of Trent

Further Reading

Harline, Craig. *Miracles at the Jesus Oak: Histories of the Supernatural in Reformation Europe*. New Haven, CT: Yale University Press, 2011.

Johnson, Trevor. *Magistrates, Madonnas and Miracles: The Counter Reformation in the Upper Palatinate*. Burlington, VT: Ashgate, 2009.

Parish, Helen L. *Monks, Miracles, and Magic: Reformation Representations of the Medieval Church*. New York: Routledge, 2005.

Soergel, Philip M. *Miracles and the Protestant Imagination: The Evangelical Wonder Book in Reformation Germany*. New York: Oxford University Press, 2012.

Relics

Within the shrine built by Charlemagne at Aix La Chapelle in Aachen, Germany, rests a golden reliquary housing the swaddling garment of the infant Jesus. Within the Basilica of St. Mary Major in Rome are the remnants of Jesus's crib. A short distance away are the bones of his disciples, the head of his cousin, Saint John the Baptist, and reliquaries containing some of the thorns that Jesus endured at his crucifixion. In Turin, Jesus's burial cloth, the Holy Shroud, takes pride of place.

The gathering and preservation of these and other relics go beyond the mere fascination with antiquity but lie at the heart of spiritual communion. The sacred thing becomes the locus for religion. The remains or objects associated with a saint or martyr were treated by the early Christians as having the power to connect people to God and to serve as weapons against harm, sources of strength, and standard-bearers of what counts as a virtuous life. The cult of the martyrs began almost immediately with the protomartyr Stephen and grew with every public execution experienced by the nascent Christian community throughout the Mediterranean world. Companions or followers gathered up the bodies for burial, which were frequently set aside until sufficient decomposition could allow for removal to an ossuary or specially designated tomb. What was left behind to be cherished helped to grow churches and encouraged a way of life marked by a communion with the saints. Relics act as the middle ground between heaven and Earth and demonstrate the power and importance of the cult of saints, which was echoed throughout the preaching of both the pre-Nicene and post-Nicene church.

It is impossible to overstate the importance of relics to medieval Christendom. If saints are ubiquitous, then so are the bodies, bones, and material remains associated with them. If we were to stumble into ninth-century Rome, as did the Carolingian courtier Einhard, we would encounter a thriving trade in bones and goods, available to the highest bidder. We would also see the rather shady characters sneaking into the Roman catacombs to liberate and free the bones of the saints from their tombs. Although Einhard wrote a rather stirring narrative depicting his theft as being at the behest of the saints themselves, it is nonetheless an excellent example of the sheer appetite of early medieval Christianity for relics. In the ninth century (801 and 813), Charlemagne decreed that all churches in his empire must have relics in their altars. It is possible, then, to speak of a real trade in relics existing across Europe. And it was one that interested the highest levels of political leadership, with important relics sought as plunder after wars and conflict or used in international diplomacy and gift exchange.

The relics can be broadly categorized into three types: primary, secondary, and tertiary. Primary relics are the corporal remains of a saint (or sections of those remains). These are perhaps the most powerful relics one can claim, and the miracles associated with them can be dramatic. Secondary relics are items that had direct contact with the saint (such as clothing or chains). Tertiary relics are those items that have had contact with primary or secondary relics. Some scholars note that while relics are essentially passive and neutral, it is the people who use them, discuss them, and emphasize their importance that give them meaning. It is they who create the cult of saints, who create the appetite for reliquaries and saintly remains. They belong to a wider religious and social theater. In the mind of the medieval monk, the saint and his power were enshrined within the relics associated with them. They were a real tangible presence.

Given their ubiquity and power, relics could fetch a considerable price or bring to the table a high value, depending upon the class of relic, its size, and its importance to the Christian story. The Veil of Veronica, for instance, could be considered more valuable—since it was mentioned in the Gospel—than a lesser saint's knee cap. The valuation of relics, however, invited mischief and abuse. Finally, Pope

Clement X in a brief of 1672 condemned the violation of cemeteries and burial sites for relic theft and sought to halt the incorporation of relics in private homes, ordering instead their rightful return to the church. Still, little has been done to comply with the papal edict. Even today, the relic trade has not diminished and is now an unseemly part of Internet trading, where in the absence of corporate policies, Ebay, for instance, maintains a healthy and lucrative bidding mechanism on relics.

Other religious traditions have a positive affinity for relic veneration, especially among the laity. Most noticeable are Buddhists, whose South Asian stupas—monuments that often contain the relics of deceased monks—are visible reminders of their importance. Worship of the relics of the Buddha likely predates the dawn of Christianity. In most Theravadan monasteries, the stupa is among the most precious objects and is routinely celebrated in prayer or other devotions. When Pope Francis paid a call at the Agrashravaka temple in Sri Lanka in January 2015, the monks favored the pontiff with the opening of a casket of relics of two disciples of the Buddha—an extraordinary privilege and break with monastic practice.

Anthony Smart

See also: Buddhism and Miracles; Maria Stein Shrine of the Holy Relics; Reliquary; Shroud of Turin; St. Anthony's Relic Chapel; Veil of Veronica

Further Reading

Bynum, Caroline Walker. "The Blood of Christ in the Middle Ages." *Church History* 71(4) (2002): 685–714.
Cruz, Joan Carroll. *Relics*. Indianapolis: Our Sunday Visitor Press, 1984.
Deuffic, Jean-Luc, ed. *Reliques et sainteté dan l'espace médiéval*. Saint-Denis: PECIA, 2006; vols. 8–11 of PECIA: Ressources en médiévistique, 2005.
Dutton, P. E. *Charlemagne's Courtier: The Complete Einhard*. Peterborough, Ontario: Broadview, 2003.
Geary, Patrick. *Furta Sacra: Thefts of Relics in the Central Middle Ages*. Princeton, NJ: Princeton University Press, 1990.
Nickell, Joe. *Relics of Christ*. Lexington: University Press of Kentucky, 2007.
Werner, Karel. "The Place of Relic Worship in Buddhism: An Unresolved Controversy?" *Buddhist Studies Review* 30(1) (2013): 71–87.

Reliquary

As containers for relics—bodies and body parts of sacred persons or objects associated with them—reliquaries have played a significant role in the veneration of holy figures. While they are largely associated with Christianity and the cult of saints, relics and reliquaries are also found in other religions, such as Buddhism.

Reliquaries have the dual purpose of protecting and displaying relics. They are housed in churches or chapels for regular veneration by the faithful but sometimes are carried in processions. They range widely in size. Given the importance of the objects they enclose, they are made of precious materials, such as gold, silver, or ivory, and often adorned with gems. In the early Christian period existing objects were sometimes reused for relics, but since the Middle Ages reliquaries have almost always been specially made. As a result, one may identify a number of types of reliquaries; often form relates explicitly to the sacred object.

Early Christian reliquaries were often made in the shape of a box or casket. As many relics were bodies or body parts, this form was a reminder of their funerary purpose. Simple forms were generally decorated with figures of saints or narrative imagery, painted, carved, or enameled on the sides. Over time these reliquaries became larger and more elaborate, such as the Shrine of the Three Kings at Cologne Cathedral (ca. 1170–1230).

Reliquaries could be made in the shape of a cross. These typically held relics of the True Cross (or other Passion relics). They were frequently decorated with Christological images, reinforcing their origin. Another form with a similar connection to Christ is derived from the monstrance. A monstrance displays the Eucharist, and its shape is subsequently adapted for the display of relics, including miraculous hosts (those that had bled or actively resisted desecration). Eucharistic miracles occurred frequently in the centuries following establishment of the doctrine of transubstantiation in 1215, but this type of reliquary was used for all sorts of relics, given that its form allowed for the relic to be visible.

Figural (full or partial body) or shaped reliquaries became popular in the Middle Ages. The bodies of saints were often fragmented and distributed; a reliquary shaped like the arm, foot, or head served to stand in for the whole. It should be noted that these figural reliquaries do not always contain the relics suggested by their form. The celebrated reliquary of Saint Foy at the abbey church in Conques depicts her full body but contains only her head.

Small relics could be encased in jewelry, such as rings or pendants. They were portable and also served a protective function. Charlemagne legendarily wore amulets containing fragments of the True Cross, drops of Holy Blood, or the hair of the Virgin Mary.

Finally, there are reliquaries closely associated with architecture. The reliquary of the Holy Corporal in Orvieto Cathedral is shaped to resemble the facade of the church housing it. Other reliquaries were constructed like small buildings, houses, or churches, often capped with domes or other architectural details suggesting the role of the relic or the specific audience who venerated it. Actual buildings could also be considered reliquaries if they enclosed very large relics or collections of multiple relics. Sainte-Chapelle in Paris, specially constructed to house the Crown of Thorns and other Passion relics acquired in the Holy Land by King Louis IX, is one good example of this type, as are the Sancta Sanctorum of the Lateran Palace in Rome and the Chapel of the Holy Shroud in Turin.

Alison C. Fleming

See also: Relics; Saint André Bessette's Heart and the Oratory of St. Joseph Shrine, Montreal; Thorns

Further Reading

Bagnoli, Martina, et al., eds. *Treasures of Heaven: Saints, Relics, and Devotion in Medieval Europe*. New Haven, CT: Yale University Press, 2010.

Deuffic, Jean-Luc. *Strange Beauty: Issues in the Making and Meaning of Reliquaries, 400–c. 1204*. University Park: Pennsylvania State University Press, 2013.

Deuffic, Jean-Luc, ed. *Reliques et sainteté dan l'espace médiéval*. Saint-Denis: PECIA, 2006; vols. 8–11 of PECIA: Ressources en médiévistique, 2005.

"Relics and Reliquaries in Medieval Christianity." Metropolitan Museum of Art, http://www.metmuseum.org/toah/hd/relc/hd_relc.htm.

Resurrection/Resuscitation

Resurrection is the postmortem rejuvenation of a life—body and soul. After ceasing all bodily functions and reaching the commonly held view of being clinically dead, that same body is said to rise again. All four gospels in the Christian canon of the scriptures mention the resurrection of Jesus Christ. It is the single most important aspect of Christ's life and ministry, the principal commemorative feast in the church calendar, and the miraculous sign of hope that death is not the final word on our individual and collective existence.

According to the Christian tradition, Jesus of Nazareth was crucified, died, and buried about the year 33 CE outside the city gates of Jerusalem. Many people witnessed his trial and subsequent condemnation. Many participated in his scourging, and his death was an event that drew perhaps scores of onlookers. After lying three days in the tomb, Jesus appeared as a living person, replete with wounds, to his followers and others for several weeks before his ascension to heaven.

Immortality was not an unknown teaching in first-century Palestine. Plato and Socrates both held that the reasoning intellect was immortal, so at least the mind of a human being was not subject to natural decay. But one of Jesus's contemporaries, Apollonius of Tyana, taught that there would be life after death in the physical sense as well. He would seem to be confirmed in this teaching by the Christian scriptures themselves, as when the Gospel of Mark tells the story of the raising of Jairus's daughter (Mark 5:21–24, 35–43) or when John's gospel relates the story of Lazarus (John 11:1–44). In both instances, Jesus confronts the problem of those who appear to be dead and restores them to life. The difference between them and Jesus's resurrection is that they were resuscitated through the power of another. Jesus's resurrection required no outside assistance because of his divinity.

The revivification of Jairus's daughter and Jesus's friend Lazarus are meant in a sense to prefigure the resurrection of Jesus. By alerting the reader about the possibility of this occurrence, believers identify with the resurrection as being applicable to ordinary mortals through the power of Christ. Jesus spells this out clearly in John's gospel: "I am the resurrection and the life. Those who believe in me, even though they die, will live, and everyone who lives and believes in me will never die" (John 11:25–26).

The triumphalism engendered by the resurrection texts has been enshrined in the Christian imagination through some of the great artists of Western civilization. One is immediately struck, for instance, by the glowering Christ of Pierro della Francesca emerging from the tomb and by Matthias Grunewald's resurrection scene, with a free-floating and happy Christ unbounded by his tomb. In the Eastern rites as well one notes the multiplication in the numerous Russian, Greek, and Coptic icons of the resurrection where the Christ is shown pulling the dead—now alive—from their tombs. The Easter experience is meant for all.

Patrick J. Hayes

Further Reading

Alkier, Stefan, Leroy A. Huizenga, and Richard B. Hays. *The Reality of the Resurrection: The New Testament Witness*. Waco, TX: Baylor University Press, 2013.

Brown, Raymond. *The Death of the Messiah: From Gethsemane to the Grave*. New York: Doubleday, 1999.

Bryan, Christopher. *The Resurrection of the Messiah*. New York: Oxford University Press, 2011.

MacGregor, Neil, and Erika Langmuir. *Seeing Salvation: Images of Christ in Art*. New Haven, CT: Yale University Press, 2000.

Moloney, Francis J. *The Resurrection of the Messiah: A Narrative Commentary on the Resurrection Accounts in the Four Gospels*. Mahwaw, NJ: Paulist Press, 2013.

Roch, Martin. "L'emergere del culto delle reliquie nei secoli IV–VI: Una manifestazione storica di una 'cultura della risurrezione.'" *Nuova Umanità* 32 (2010–2012): 279–297.

Retablo

The term *retablo* has different meanings based on its regional usage. Derived from a Latin term for "behind the board/table/altar," it is a Spanish designation for an altarpiece, featuring painted or sculpted religious figures built behind an altar or perhaps along the walls of a church. Such decorative iconographic ensembles developed in European sanctuaries by the late Middle Ages, and this architectural feature was transferred to church buildings established in the Spanish New World. In this ecclesiastical usage, a *retablo* exemplifies the church's art to be seen and enjoyed by the local community of the faithful. In the world of Latin American and especially Mexican folk/vernacular religious art, however, the words *retablo*, *lamina*, and *santos de hojalata* (saints on tinplate) also refer to more intimate personal art: small paintings of saints commissioned and created by untrained local artists for devotional usage by individual believers.

Retablos are paintings of Jesus, the Virgin Mary in her many forms, the pantheon of saints, the Trinity, the souls in Purgatory, etc., expressly meant to inhabit home or work spaces of believers and placed either on walls or within individual domestic altars. Such images were personally enshrined and lovingly maintained with candles, flowers, and perhaps some fabric as well as reminders of family members who needed protection. It has been estimated that their production in Mexico, where the tradition especially flourished between 1830 and 1910, created some one million such small devotional paintings.

Retablos do not usually carry dates or signatures by their artists, so art historians have often traced similarities in visual stylistic motifs from one *retablo* to the next to identify individual creators. Their subject matter was influenced by the statues and paintings of academically trained artists found in ecclesiastical settings as well as the variety of popular religious prints imported from Europe to the Americas. European imports also had a major influence on the actual substance on which the *retablo* images were painted. When Mexican independence (1821) stimulated new levels of goods and resources being brought across the Atlantic, thin sheets of tin plate became readily available. Ostensibly intended for use crafting such practical housing elements as water pipes and drain gutters, tin also began to be employed by local artisans for the development of two genres of religious art: *retablos* and *ex votos*. Such metal was inexpensive, making it affordable for both artists and the believers who commissioned or purchased creations from their makers. Tin also allowed for a smooth surface texture for the paintings, adding to their visual appeal and allure.

Ex voto paintings (also called *milagros*) were used as public expressions in churches of religious vow making and fulfillment of promises made and graces received by believers. Such humble paintings continued a European tradition in Mexico of the public visual expression in shrines of the results of intercessory prayer. The *retablo* in this devotional equation provided the prayerful and ocular focus from which the motivation to ask for an intercession and make a vow may have emerged. *Retablos* reminded the faithful of the cult of the saints and martyrs and helped drive devotions to the Virgin Mary (Guadalupe and other local Madonnas) or Jesus (the Sacred Heart, for example). The miraculous power of these heavenly friends, needed during accidents, crime, illness, etc., was called on frequently. The *ex voto* tradition spread to Mexico from Italy in the colonial period. It reached its height of production in the nineteenth century. *Ex votos* are still being made in the 21st century, but *retablo* production ceased by the first decades of the twentieth century. *Retablos* are now collected as valuable examples of religious folk art by collectors and sold by dealers and are readily available at such digital auction outlets as eBay.

Leonard Norman Primiano

See also: *Ex Voto*

Further Reading

Caswell, James, and Jenise Amanda Ramos, eds. *Saints and Sinners: Mexican Devotional Art*. Atglen, PA: Schiffer, 2006.

Egan, Martha. *Milagros: Votive Offerings from the Americas*. Santa Fe: Museum of New Mexico Press, 1991.

Giffords, Gloria Fraser. *Mexican Folk Retablos*. Albuquerque: University of New Mexico Press, 1992.

Zarur, Elizabeth, Netto Calil, and Charles Muir Lovell, eds. *Art and Faith in Mexico: The Nineteenth-Century Retablo Tradition*. Albuquerque: University of New Mexico Press, 2001.

Revelation

Three principle meanings of the word "revelation" may be related to miracles. First, a revelation is a heuristic device that points to something beyond itself. Thus, a cure, especially the elimination of an aggressive disease or other malady that has withstood conventional medical therapies, might suggest that the finger of God is here. Second, a revelation may be treated as a sign meant to convey a larger meaning. Thus, if there is no greater signification of the love of one person for another than the sacrifice made of one's own life, the martyr is the exemplar of such signs. Finally, a sign is a portent of things to come. What lies hidden just beyond the horizon of our knowing and is revealed through some sign or disclosed datum can give a foretaste of the future. Prophecy, a preternatural gift of foreknowledge, may be considered a miraculous example of such a sign.

In each meaning, there is a sense of "showing" or "making visible" something heretofore hidden or obscure. Etymologically the word "revelation" is drawn from the Latin word *revelatio*, meaning "to uncover" or "to remove the veil." If anything, miracles set our experiences of the world in greater relief. They show us that the natural world often defies our understanding, but they also clarify what counts as transcendent. In this respect they carry an intermediary function between that which is known and that of which we can take cognizance. As a sign, the object of our knowing becomes more greatly revealed, but this does not mean that the thing shown is anything more than the image of the object. Thus, to experience a miracle is to gain a glimpse of the transcendent being whom many people call God. It does not mean that the experience is a direct encounter with the divine. Miracles, then, assist in knowledge but confirm faith.

In Christianity many important theologians have discussed a theory of signs, though one, Saint Thomas Aquinas, was especially keen to link signs with miraculous wonders. In question 178 in the second part of his massive *Summa Theologica*, Saint Thomas expounds on the grace of miracles in two articles. In the first of these he wonders whether there is a gratuitous grace, and his affirmative reply rests in part on the test applied to wondrous events. "Just as the knowledge which a man receives from God needs to be brought to the knowledge of others through the gift of tongues and the grace of the word, so too the word uttered needs to be confirmed in order that it be rendered credible. This is done by the working of miracles, according to Mark 16:20: 'And confirming the word with signs that followed.'" In short, miracles confront our natural reason with glimmers of the supernatural objects of faith (God, heaven, salvation, perfection, etc.). For Aquinas, these signs do more than suggest themselves to our intellect. They move us to trust in the manifestations of the supernatural.

In some respects, Saint Thomas was speaking as a man of his time. In the Middle Ages, certain forms of miraculous phenomena were taken as signs of salvation. This included the stigmata that had already been prefigured, to an extent, in the New Testament's letter of Saint Paul to the Galatians: "I bear the marks of the Lord Jesus Christ in my body" (Galatians 6:17). Centuries of commentators on this passage made it somewhat easy for Saint Francis of Assisi, the first recorded instance of stigmatization, to go beyond the pious superlative and treat it as a sign of God's favor. Indeed, this form of miraculous suffering was a further sign that if Paul and Francis took on their suffering in imitation of Christ, neither should we be allergic to the pains of this world if we endure them for higher purposes.

The negative aspect of revelation comes through human psychosis, where so-called private revelations of individuals often have the character of a fantasy or are so incommunicable that the content begs description. Naturally, the subjective nature of private revelations also eliminates any possibility of verification. The case of the Bayside apparitions is illustrative. The so-called Seer of Bayside, Veronica Lueken, experienced numerous private revelations and ecstasies, but due to their peculiar nature and the decided lack of objective proof of their occurrence, Church officials have not only disavowed their authenticity but have warned Roman Catholics against participating in any of the Bayside movement's activities.

By contrast, some private revelations are acceptable to church authorities, though these are often accompanied by extensive examination of the subject. Saint Mary Margaret Alacoque, for instance, experienced revelations of the Sacred Heart of Jesus between 1673 and 1675. Her exceptional communications with the divine were not wholly integrated until many years later, but eventually they found their way into the devotional practices and liturgical rites of the church. Saint Catherine Labouré and her interactions with the Blessed Virgin Mary as well as Bernadette Soubirous and the Virgin at Lourdes are also examples that may be classed as private revelations, though they also exhibit a deep basis in faith.

Patrick J. Hayes

See also: Augustine, Saint; Bayside Apparitions; Lourdes; Miraculous Medal; Stigmata

Further Reading

Dulles, Avery. *The Assurance of Things Hoped For: A Theology of Christian Faith*. New York: Oxford University Press, 1994.

Dulles, Avery. "Faith and Revelation." In *Systematic Theology: Roman Catholic Perspectives*, Vol. 1, edited by Francis Schüssler Fiorenza and John Galvin, 89–128. Minneapolis: Fortress Press, 1991.

Dulles, Avery. *Models of Revelation*. Reprint ed. Maryknoll, NY: Orbis, 1992.

Jackson, B. Darrell. "The Theory of Signs in St. Augustine's *De Doctrina Christiana*." In *Augustine: A Collection of Critical Essays*, edited by R. A. Markus, 92–137. Garden City, NY: Doubleday, 1972.

Lawton, John S. *Miracles and Revelation*. New York: Association Press, 1960.

Laycock, Joseph. *The Seer of Bayside: Veronica Lueken and the Struggle to Define Catholicism*. New York: Oxford University Press, 2014.

Markus, R. A. "St. Augustine on Signs." In *Augustine: A Collection of Critical Essays*, edited by R. A. Markus, 61–91. Garden City, NY: Doubleday, 1972.

Muessig, Carolyn. "Signs of Salvation: The Evolution of Stigmatic Spirituality before Francis of Assisi." *Church History* 82(1) (2013): 40–68.

S

Saint André Bessette's Heart and the Oratory of St. Joseph Shrine, Montreal

The Oratory of St. Joseph is a Roman Catholic shrine, dedicated to Canada's patron saint, overlooking Montreal from the heights of Mount Royal. The oratory was the life's work of Saint André Bessette (1845–1937), who even during his lifetime was referred to as "The Miracle Man of Montreal."

Born in the village of Saint Gregoire in Quebec's Eastern Townships, Alfred Bessette was a poor and sickly child, largely uneducated, and orphaned at the age of twelve. He spent several years as an itinerant worker throughout Quebec and New England before entering the Congregation of Holy Cross in 1870 at the age of 25, ultimately taking André as his religious name.

Assigned as porter of the community's Notre Dame College in Côte-des-Neiges, Brother André maintained his lifelong devotion to Saint Joseph and soon developed a reputation as a healer. Several students of the college inexplicably recovered from illnesses after being visited by him, and even the college's skeptical physician came to believe in the holy man's healing power when his wife was inexplicably healed.

Brother André often instructed the sick and infirm to pray for healing through the intercession of Saint Joseph, to carry a medal of the saint, or to anoint themselves with oil from the lamps that burned in front of the saint's statue. As more and more of Brother André's petitioners experienced relief from their infirmities, the number of visitors to the college rose, sometimes numbering nearly 300 a day. Bothered by the disruption this caused, the college's administrators forced Brother André to receive his visitors at a nearby tram station rather than in the college parlor.

Despite the fact that even some members of his own religious community first thought him a charlatan, the visitors and reported cures continued, and Church officials inquiring into claims of healing repeatedly backed Brother

André's ministry. However, Brother André resolutely maintained that he was not responsible for any miracles, always deflecting credit to Saint Joseph and resolving to honor the saint by building a shrine in his name.

In 1904 a small wooden chapel was built on the mountainside facing the college with the assistance of Brother André's many friends and supporters. Not only did Brother André greet visitors there, but Mass was celebrated three times a day, and a fellow brother helped answer the 20,000 letters received each year. Over time, several slightly larger structures replaced the original chapel until work finally began in 1915 on the current oratory. The oratory was only completed in 1967 owing to financial struggles and work stoppages during the Great Depression. It boasts the third-largest dome of its kind and is the world's largest shrine to Saint Joseph. In 1954 the oratory was named a minor basilica by Pope Pius XII.

During Saint André's life, pilgrims who claimed to have been healed through his intercession placed thousands of canes and crutches on the walls of the oratory. These testimonies to their healing continue to adorn the oratory's crypt, where votive candles illuminate eight large sculptured plaques, each depicting Saint Joseph under his traditional titles. Some two million pilgrims continue to visit the oratory annually, many of whom ascend the shrine's 283 steps on their knees.

When Brother André died on January 6, 1937, nearly one million people braved a snowstorm to pay their respects as he lay in state. His tomb was placed in the crypt of the oratory, and at the request of Archbishop Georges Gauthier of Montreal, Brother André's heart was preserved in a reliquary as a sign of gratitude and devotion. The heart was stolen from the oratory in March 1973, and a ransom was demanded but never paid. The heart was only recovered in December 1974 when an anonymous source informed police that it was located in a locker in the basement of a Montreal apartment building.

The cause for Brother André's canonization was formally opened in 1940. The first miracle accepted for his cause was introduced in 1958. A New Yorker, Joseph Audiano, prayed to Brother André to reverse what doctors believed to be terminal cancer. The second accepted miracle delivered a boy from severe head trauma after being struck by an automobile. Pope Saint John Paul II beatified Brother André in 1982 and prayed before his tomb in the oratory while visiting Canada in 1984. Pope Benedict XVI canonized Saint André Bessette on October 17, 2010, making him Canada's first native male saint.

Stephen Koeth

See also: Canada, Miracles in; *Ex Voto;* Reliquary

Further Reading

Bergeron, Henri-Paul, and Rev. Real Boudreau. *Brother Andre: The Wonder Man of Mount Royal*. Montreal: Fides, 1958.

Dubuc, Jean-Guy. *Brother Andre: Friend of the Suffering, Apostle of Saint Joseph*. Notre Dame, IN: Ave Maria Press, 2010.

Hatch, Alden. *The Miracle of the Mountain: The Story of Brother André and the Shrine of Mount Royal*. New York: Hawthorne, 1962.

Ruffin, C. Bernard. *The Life of Brother Andre: The Miracle Worker of St. Joseph*. Huntington, IN: Our Sunday Visitor, 1988.

Scala Santa

After Roman emperor Constantine and his mother Helena converted to Christianity, she journeyed to the Holy Land, demonstrating her devotion. Contact with the sites and objects connected to Christ and the earliest Christians prompted her to recover relics and bring them back to Europe. Most celebrated is her recovery of the True Cross, a sliver of which was placed in her palace chapel (now the Church of Santa Croce in Gerusalemme) in Rome. However, Helena legendarily also returned with a staircase taken from the Praetorium, the palace of Pontius Pilate in Jerusalem. These steps, referred to in the Middle Ages as the *scali pilati* (steps of Pilate), are more commonly known today as the *scala santa* (holy staircase). They were placed in the Patriarchum, or Lateran palace, built on land ceded to the papacy by Constantine, in 314–315. They may constitute the largest Christological relic ever brought to Rome.

The staircase consists of 28 marble steps, revered as those walked upon by Christ, dripping blood, after the Flagellation. They were covered with wooden planks in the early eighteenth century, with openings that reveal the sacred bloodstains. Medieval guidebooks to Rome rarely mentioned the steps, but pilgrims must have visited, as the Church of San Giovanni in Laterano and the adjacent palace were important stops on their itinerary. They would have climbed the stairs on their knees—an act both protecting the sacred object and demonstrating their piety—to earn the plenary indulgence granted for this act.

The writer of the twelfth-century guidebook *Mirabilia Urbis Romae* refers somewhat obliquely to the staircase, stating that "In the Palace of the Lateran are things to be marveled at but not to be written." The precious relic of the stairs, and the other significant artifacts housed in the chapel above, may indeed be too extraordinary to be described in words. While the term *scala santa* may seem to reference only this particular object, it is one that generally refers to the entire building, which includes the Sancta Santorum (Holy of Holies). This private chapel of the pope was substantially renovated during the papacy of Nicholas III, with frescoes attributed to Pietro Cavallini. These paintings included narrative scenes (predominantly martyrdoms) and figures of saints that are connected to the relics housed in the chapel: Peter, Paul, Stephen, Lawrence, Agnes, and Nicholas of Bari. There are also fragments of the True Cross and other relics from the Holy Land—perhaps collected by Helena—and the icon known as the *Archeropita*, meaning "not made by human hands." This portrait of Christ was thought to have been painted by Saint Luke and an angel.

Pope Sixtus V substantially renovated the Lateran palace in 1585–1587, and the staircase was moved from the north side of the Patriarchum and enclosed. His architect Domenico Fontana, who was also responsible for moving obelisks in the city, described the move, which took place at night by torchlight. He also added flanking staircases to be used for visual effect and more efficient access for foot traffic, allowing the holy stairs to be reserved for pilgrims on their knees. When the devoted reached the top, they were afforded a view into the Sancta Sanctorum through a grated window. The shrine was entrusted to the Passionists in 1853 by Pope Pius IX; he was the last pope to ever climb the holy steps on his knees.

Alison C. Fleming

Further Reading

Cempanari, Mario. *Sancta Sanctorum Lateranense: Il Santuario della Scala santa delle origini ai nostril giorni*. Rome: Tipografia Città nuova, 2003.

Cempanari, Mario, and Tito Amodei. *Scala Santa e Sancta Sanctorum: Storia, arte, culto del santuario*. Vatican City: LEV, 2013.

Mirabilia Urbis Romae. New York: Italica Press, 1986.

Webb, Matilda. *The Churches and Catacombs of Early Christian Rome: A Comprehensive Guide*. Brighton, UK: Sussex Academic Press, 2001.

Scapular

A scapular is a sacramental garment of the Catholic Church, usually consisting of two pieces of sewn cloth attached by strings and worn over the shoulders, with one piece hanging over the chest and the other hanging over the back. The scapular was originally a component of some religious habits, the set of garments worn by members of a religious order, but later a smaller version (usually one inch by two inches) began to be worn under the clothes by laypersons who wished to associate with a particular religious order.

The most famous scapular is the Brown Scapular of Our Lady of Mount Carmel. The Brothers of Our Lady of Mount Carmel (commonly referred to as Carmelites) were originally founded as an order of hermits who lived together on Mount Carmel in Israel in the early 1200s.

According to legend, the Blessed Virgin Mary miraculously appeared to Saint Simon Stock, the prior-general of the Carmelite order on July 16, 1251, and promised that whoever died wearing the scapular of this order worthily would enter into heaven. Also according to legend, in 1322 the Blessed Virgin Mary miraculously appeared to Pope John XXII and extended the promise to include the so-called Sabbatine privilege, namely, that those who died wearing the scapular of the order and who fulfilled certain other conditions would be rescued by the Blessed Virgin Mary from the punishment of Purgatory on the first Saturday after their death. In the ensuing centuries, many laypersons were enrolled in the scapular by Carmelite priests or other designated priests as a result of these promises. Devotion to the scapular was an important component of the final apparition of Our Lady of Fatima in 1917 as well.

The Carmelite order has taken pains throughout the centuries to distance itself from a "magical" view of the scapular, as though simply wearing it was a "get out of Purgatory free" card. Rather, wearing the Brown Scapular is a visible expression of affinity with the spirituality of the Carmelite order, which emphasizes contemplative prayer, detachment from any created being that detracts from the primacy of God, and penance for the atonement of one's sins and for the sins of others. It is a sign of being clothed with the virtues of the Blessed Virgin Mary and under the mantle of her protection. A person who committed mortal sins without repentance would not be considered to be wearing the scapular worthily, and hence the promise of the scapular would not apply to that person.

Scapulars are often worn by members of a third order, consisting of laypersons who make a promise to live the spirituality of a religious order while living and carrying out their ordinary duties in the world. Members of a Carmelite third order (either the lay Carmelites or the Secular Order of Discalced Carmelites) wear a large brown scapular (approximately eight by six inches) outside of their clothes during their meetings or special religious ceremonies. Members of the Dominican third order (now called the Lay Dominicans) may wear a white scapular underneath their clothes as a sign of membership in the order.

Pope Gregory X (d. 1276) died in Arezzo, Italy, and was buried in the city's cathedral. Nearly six centuries later in 1830 his body was reinterred, but the scapular he had been wearing was still intact. It remains the oldest example of a scapular in existence. Other popes and saints have testified to its spiritual merits. Saint Alphonsus Liguori and Saint John Bosco both wore the scapular and were buried with it. Their tombs were opened for the process of canonization, and their scapulars showed no signs of decay even though their own bodies had deteriorated.

Scapulars are also sometimes worn to express a particular religious devotion. For example, the green scapular is worn to express devotion to the Immaculate Heart of Mary, with the intention of contributing to the conversion and salvation of the souls of nonbelievers.

Jason Bourgeois

See also: Carmelites and Miracles; Our Lady of Mount Carmel

Further Reading

Haffert, John M. *Sign of Her Heart*. Washington, NJ: Ave Maria Institute, 1971.
The Scapular of Our Lady of Mount Carmel: Catechesis and Ritual. Washington DC: Institute of Carmelite Sources, 2000.

Sherlock, Thomas

Thomas Sherlock (1678–1761) was a prominent figure in the extensive discussion of the rationality of belief in miracles that took place prior to the publication of Hume's *Of Miracles*. Sherlock is chiefly remembered for his *The Tryal of the Witnesses of the Resurrection of Jesus* (1729). Although writing in reply to Woolston's *Discourses on the Miracles* (1727–1728), Sherlock anticipates Hume's a priori epistemological argument of Part 1 of *Of Miracles*. One of Sherlock's points against this argument is that it does not take into consideration the theoretical possibility of oneself seeing a miracle. Once this possibility is granted, the claim that no quantity or quality of testimony could ever warrant belief in a miracle appears too strong, inasmuch as it does not allow the possibility of testimony correcting conclusions drawn on the basis of too narrow a personal experience. J. C. A. Gaskin takes *Of Miracles* to be, at least in part, a response to Sherlock's highly influential *Tryal of the Witnesses*, but R. M. Burns, while agreeing that Hume would have read the *Tryal*, suggests "that its contents must have become a hazy memory to him by the mid-1830s when 'the first hint' of the argument occurred to Hume at 'the place of its birth' (La Flèche)."

Robert Larmer

Further Reading

Burns, R. M. *The Great Debate on Miracles*. East Brunswick, NJ: Associated University Presses, 1981.

Gaskin, J. C. A. *Hume's Philosophy of Belief*. London: Macmillan, 1978.

Shipwrecks

When people live through an event such as a shipwreck, they may consider it a miracle and will use the term to label this unusual event in a positive way. It could be considered the result of divine, spiritual, supernatural, sacred, or numinous power represented in a personal or impersonal form.

One of the oldest and best-known accounts of a shipwreck involves miracles illustrated in the Bible. In the New Testament, Jesus calms the Sea of Galilee from a storm that would have ordinarily swamped his disciples' fishing boat (Mark 4:35–41). The scene was later immortalized by Rembrandt, whose depiction, *The Storm on the Sea of Galilee*, was stolen from the Isabella Stewart Gardiner Museum in Boston in 1990. Additionally, in the Acts of the Apostles, Saint Paul is arrested and, because he is a Roman citizen, is sent to Rome for trial (Acts 27). Paul is guided by God and foretells the danger of the voyage to a centurion, his jailer, but they continue on anyway. The ship is caught in a violent tempest that lasts for 14 days. During the storm, Paul would tell all the crew members of a miracle to come. They would survive if they would remain on the ship. Those who left the ship through lifeboat or attempted to swim to land would drown. The ship finally wrecked on the island of Malta, and all who rode out the storm, according to what Paul was told by God, survived.

A second account is that of the cargo ship *Lady Isabella*, which sank in 1902 a short distance from its destination. As it passed the island of Arran on its way through the Firth of Clyde, Scotland, it went into rough weather. It smashed onto a shoal some 200 meters from shore off Little Cumbrae Island, and its captain, while inspecting damage on deck, was washed overboard by a huge wave. Miraculously, he was tossed back on deck by another wave and managed to cling to the rigging of the ship's mizzen mast. The same wave that threw the captain into the sea took away the *Isabella*'s lifeboat. A decision to wait out the storm merely confirmed the inevitable: the ship had been ripped open by rocks, and water was in every hold. They had to get off somehow, and a valiant crew member swam the icy waters with a rope, which enabled the remaining crew members to disembark. As they reached safety, each noted "the glad, auspicious tidings of shore. The men clasped their hands, and looked toward Heaven with emotions of gratitude."

A third account of a shipwreck miracle comes from Gunner's Mate 2nd Class Hugh Wingo. Wingo recounts an attack by USS *Benham* some 600 miles off the coast of Japan. A Japanese torpedo hit the forward starboard side and blew off 40 feet of hull. It broke the keel about midship. According to Wingo, "By some miracle, they did not lose a single man, but one man was blown overboard. He was picked up the next day by Marines from Guadalcanal." The ship could not be saved; the crew was ordered to abandon ship and sink the vessel. Wingo attributes his survival and the lives of his fellow crew mates to a higher power. In similar battles, veterans often explain their survival as miraculous.

Literature is also full of shipwreck accounts and the miraculous tales of their survival. These stories can be found in numerous writings, some of which include classics such as Homer's *Odyssey*, plays such as Shakespeare's *Twelfth Night*, Edgar Allen Poe's short story "MS Found in a Bottle," poems such as Gerard Manley Hopkins's "The Wreck of the Deutschland," and novels such as *Robinson Crusoe, Gulliver's Travels*, and, most recently, *Life of Pi*.

Paula L. Webb

Further Reading

Bowery, John. "Hugo Wingo." Armed Forces Retirement Home, https://www.afrh.gov/afrh/hwingo.htm.

Defoe, Daniel, and N. C. Wyeth. *Robinson Crusoe*. New York: Scribner, 1983.

Homer, Robert Fagles, and Bernard Knox. *The Odyssey*. New York: Viking, 1996.

Hopkins, Gerard Manley. *The Poems of Gerard Manley Hopkins*. Edited by W. H. Gardner and N. H. MacKenzie. London: Oxford University Press, 1967.

Huntress, Keith G. *Narratives of Shipwrecks and Disasters, 1586–1860*. Ames: Iowa State University Press, 1974.

Martel, Yann. *Life of Pi: A Novel*. New York: Harcourt, 2001.

Poe, Edgar Allen. *Poetry and Tales*. Edited by Patrick F. Quinn and G. R. Thompson. New York: Library of America, 1996.

Praeder, Susan Marie. "Acts 27:1–28:16: Sea Voyages in Ancient Literature and the Theology of Luke-Acts." *Catholic Biblical Quarterly* 46(4) (October 1984): 683–706.

Shakespeare, William. *Twelfth Night: Or, What You Will*. New Haven, CT: Yale University Press, 1954.

Stevenson, Robert L., and Barry Menikoff. *Robert Louis Stevenson's Kidnapped: Or, the Lad with the Silver Button; The Original Text*. San Marino, CA: Huntington Library, 1999.

Swift, Jonathan. *Gulliver's Travels*. New York: Knopf, 1991.

Shrines

A shrine is a place of public worship where people, individually or collectively, perform religious rites outside their homes. Shrines are often marked by physical and evocative images that suggest the presence of a divine being. People, places, and things are enshrined because of what they represent in the religious or cultural life of a people. Shrines are usually associated with memorable persons or events and are regarded as the abode of God and marked as sacred. In predominantly Christian societies, for instance, most shrines are associated with the early Christian missionaries or leaders who made significant contributions in the propagation of the gospel. Such missionaries founded some of the early churches and sometimes paid with their lives, especially when the persecution of Christians was common. In some cases, the early church leaders were canonized by the church as saints before their remains were enshrined.

A shrine may be located in groves, in trees, on roadsides, at springs, on the banks of rivers, or in houses. Images or ephemeral decorations in shrines help in lifting believers into an exalted state of repentance and faith. Although images in shrines are human creations, devotees believe that they attract divine presence. Devotees attribute the artistic creation of shrine images by painters or sculptors to divine inspiration. The elevation of shrine images to divine inspiration explains why the images are considered sacred and capable of performing miracles.

The common understanding among different religious groups is that the objects of devotion or images in shrines are only media of divine presence, not the divine itself. Among Catholics, the images of Christ or Mary in shrines, for example, are revered in honor of the original person they represent. It is not about the images but the entity they represent. This has been a source of controversy between some Protestant churches and the Catholic Church. Some Protestant churches interpret reverence to holy images as idolatry. Such Protestant churches hinge their argument on the Ten Commandments in which God commanded the Israelites not to make for themselves any image in the form of anything in heaven, on Earth, or the earth beneath. Catholics, on the other hand, believe that they worship Christ and the saints through their images. Catholics share the same view with some religious groups, such as African Traditional Religion. Traditionalists in Africa use images to represent the divine. They see the images or sacred objects as a means to the divinity and not the divinity itself. Images in shrines are therefore perceived as the outward and visible symbol of the divine. Based on this conviction, believers approach the awe-inspiring images with the right spirit and in the right way, believing that they would receive divine intervention in their situations or needs.

Pilgrimage to shrines is one of the rituals that believers in some religions aspire to fulfill in their life time. People visit shrines for sanctity and spiritual reflection because of the sense of awe and wonder they evoke. Christians, for instance, visit shrines to renew and keep their spiritual light aglow. People also visit shrines for spiritual assistance. Beholding sacred images in shrines draws a believer closer to the divine, thereby making it possible for miracles to take place. There are abundant testimonies that sick and barren people who visited some shrines received miraculous healings and deliverance from spiritual problems. Some shrines are believed to be too holy and to attract more pilgrims because of testimonies of miracles. In such shrines, pilgrims take off their shoes as they enter. Water and objects from such shrines are believed to possess divine powers that can work miracles such as healing and protection from spiritual attacks.

However, people frequent popular shrines not just for their spiritual needs or the spiritual relevance of such sites but because of the atmosphere of sociability that such shrines provide. These social pilgrims see holy sites as avenues for mingling with people from different backgrounds. A visit to shrines provides an exciting and relaxing experience. While church leaders try to carry pilgrims along by creating some level of modernity around the shrines, they also struggle to maintain the spiritual relevance of the shrines. The tension between maintaining the purity of the shrines and adjusting to the pressures of modernity has been a source of concern to church leaders, especially in popular shrines where pilgrimage generates a lot of revenue through the sale of souvenirs.

The value of shrines differs in different religions. While some shrines are popular for the miracles and spiritual support they provide for their visitors, others are known for their cultural significance. In some African societies, for instance, people see shrines as cultural signposts that define village, community, or ethnic boundaries. Shrines in such societies are a symbol of identity and a group's claim to ownership of a piece of land or earlier settlement in a particular geographical area. The connection between shrine and land also reveals an aspect of African worldview: land is owned. Shrines that are associated with land in Africa are venerated with sacrifices of fowl or goat from the offspring of the animals of ancestors who founded the land. During occasional pilgrimage to shrines, people pray for miracles such as birth for the barren, protection from evil spirits, healing, and good harvest. They also make vows to the deities of such shrines, promising to come back to fulfill them if their requests are granted. Interestingly, many pilgrims come back to fulfill their vow after receiving their miracles. People who fail to come back to fulfill their vows at the shrines are sometimes afflicted with diseases by the deities until they fulfill their vows. While some Christian shrines attract pilgrims from different parts of the world, most of the shrines in African societies only attract people within the region where the shrines are located. The reason for the low patronage is not because of the absence of miracles but because Christians associate such holy sites with paganism. While Christian shrines are open to Christians and non-Christians, non-Christian shrines are mainly attended by non-Christians.

Arua Oko Omaka

See also: Pilgrimage

Further Reading

Blake, Liam. *Shrines*. Dublin: Real Ireland Design, 2001.

Dawson, Allan Charles. *Shrines in Africa*. Calgary: University of Calgary Press, 2009.

Pepin, David. *Discovering Shrines and Holy Places*. Oxford, UK: Shire Publications, 1980.

Ponsonby-Fane, R. A. B. *Studies in Shinto and Shrines*. London: Kegan Paul, 2004.

Taylor, William B. *Shrines and Miraculous Images: Religious Life in Mexico before the Reforma*. Albuquerque: University of New Mexico Press, 2010.

Shroud of Turin

This linen cloth, housed in Turin, Italy, is reputed to be the burial covering of Jesus of Nazareth. It measures 14 feet 3 inches by 3 feet 7 inches. A reddish-brown stain faintly portrays the front and back sides of a bearded man, flecked with bloodlike marks corresponding to the wounds of scourging and crucifixion described in biblical accounts of the Passion. It remains one of the most enigmatic objects in Christian history, subject to intense devotion and heated controversy.

The shroud has been contentious since its origins, which are most likely Western and medieval. It enters the historical record with a 1389 memorandum addressed to the antipope Clement VII and attributed to Bishop Pierre d'Arcis of Troyes, France, who denounced the shroud as fraudulent and sought to prohibit its exhibition. (In d'Arcis's account, the shroud first appeared in his diocese in 1355 or 1356, when the knight Geoffroi I de Charny displayed it in a church in the town of Lirey and invited pilgrims to venerate it as a relic.) Clement, however, ordered Arcis to continue to permit its display, with the caveat that pilgrims were to understand it as a picture to aid them in devotion, not a relic invoking the real presence of Christ. Yet the shroud's devotees rarely respected the papal distinction. Marguerite de Charny, a descendant of Geoffroi, continued to promote the shroud's authenticity throughout the early fifteenth century.

The shroud moved from place to place before settling in Turin. Marguerite ceded the shroud, probably in 1453, to the House of Savoy, which preserved it in 1502 in a chapel in Chambéry, France. A fire in 1532 nearly ruined the cloth, though Poor Clare nuns attempted to repair its damaged areas. In 1578 Emmanuel Philibert, the duke of Savoy, transferred the shroud to Turin, the new capital of his duchy. In 1694 it was installed in the royal chapel in the Cathedral of St. John the Baptist. Architect Guarino Guarani designed the chapel in an elaborate Baroque style to encourage its veneration.

A new era in the shroud's history began with the click of a camera in 1898. In this year amateur photographer Secondo Pia took the first photographs of the shroud, producing remarkable results. Pia noticed that the film's negative yielded a surprisingly lucid positive image, far stronger than the faint image visible to the naked eye. The face came into especially sharp focus. Pia's negative photograph of Jesus's face has since been widely replicated in diverse media such as prints, prayer cards, and medals. A sacred image in its own right, it plays a central role in the cult of the Holy Face, a popular Catholic devotional movement.

In the twentieth century the shroud became an object of extensive scientific investigations. The most well known of these attempts were conducted in 1978 by a group of mostly American scientists associated with the Shroud of Turin Research Project (STURP), which largely supported a hypothesis of biblical origins. STURP found itself subject to harsh scrutiny in the scientific community, as other scientists denounced its work as being driven by preestablished conclusions. Eventually, carbon dating performed in 1988 by another group confirmed its origins to range between the years 1260 and 1390, consistent with the historical record. Such evidence did little to quell debate, however. Other scientists have since raised concerns about improper procedures used in its carbon dating. Moreover, how the distinct image of a body and face came to be fixed on the cloth remains a scientifically unresolved problem, adding to its mystique. Some posit that the image was miraculously transferred in a burst of bright light at the moment of Jesus's resurrection.

Today, further speculations about the shroud continue to proliferate. Some Eastern Orthodox Christians, for example, support a theory that the shroud is the legendary Mandylion, or the Image of Edessa, stolen from Constantinople by crusaders in 1204. If the Shroud of Turin has at least one enduring power, it is the power to ignite religious imagination.

Sonia Hazard

Further Reading

Cormack, Robin. *Painting the Soul: Icons, Death Masks, and Shrouds.* London: Reaktion Books, 1997.

Kessler, Herbert L., and Gerhard Wolf, eds. *The Holy Face and the Paradox of Representation: Papers from a Colloquium Held at the Bibliotheca Hertziana, Rome, and the Villa Spelman, Florence, 1996.* Bologna, Italy: Nuova Alfa, 1998.

Mondzain, Marie-José. *Image, Icon, Economy: The Byzantine Origins of the Contemporary Imaginary.* Translated by Rico Franses. Stanford, CA: Stanford University Press, 2005.

Scott, John Beldon. *Architecture for the Shroud: Relic and Ritual in Turin.* Chicago: University of Chicago Press, 2003.

Zaccone, Gian Maria. "The Shroud from the Charnys to the Savoys." In *The Turin Shroud: Past, Present and Future: International Scientific Symposium, Torino 2–5 March 2000,* edited by Piero Savarino and Silvano Scannerini, 379–412. Turin, Italy: Centro Internazionale di Sindonologia and Effatà Editrice, 2000.

Sign

The word "sign" originates from the Latin word *signum* that in turn was adopted by Old French as *signe* and finally by Middle English as "sign," all of which refer to an image, a seal, or a token. In the Christian world the term has enormous importance and may be traced back to ecclesiastical thinkers who used biblical evidences for interpreting the miraculous "signs and wonders" performed by Christ and his disciples. Christian philosophers and theologians such as Origen Adamantius and Saint Augustine claim that the concept of signs alludes to miracles that in turn validate the presence of a creative power or an author who renders meaning to the world. It is believed that while a miracle is defined as a direct act of God that subverts natural law, signs become an important means of understanding a miracle, because the latter are most often hints through which God reveals himself to humankind.

Understandably, the belief in the essential invisibility of the divine compels God's followers to attach great significance to the interpretation of signs, since for them the divine manifests itself to human senses only through signs. Notably, among Christians the concept of signs has undergone many changes since its early stages. For instance, the earliest believers attached immense importance to signs and wonders, appropriating them as facts of sensible experience that validated the presence of God. However, over time scriptural passages have asserted that signs and wonders do not always prove the sanctity of a miracle worker, and hence they alert people against "false Christs, and false prophets, [who] shall show great signs and wonders: insomuch that, if it were possible, they shall deceive the very elect" (Matthew 24:24). Such discourses in skepticism were strengthened in the eighteenth century with the growing acceptance of scientific knowledge that in turn added to the ambiguity associated with signs and the fear of counterfeits and false prophets. Not surprisingly, these historical changes have gradually resulted in a reduction of the interpretative validity of all miraculous signs.

In contrast to its religious interpretations, the concept of signs in secular and intellectual practices has generated many complex and productive discourses. One of the most significant earliest examinations of signs inheres in Aristotle's *Rhetoric* (I, 1357 a32–b36), which states that "Anything which involves in its being, the being of something else, either at the same time or before or later, is a 'sign' of that thing or event." Aristotle's claim is bolstered by Cicero, who interprets the sign as phenomena that can serve as an evidence, a symptom, or a portent, all of which are open to inferences. Arguably, since the sign has been open to multiple inferences since Greco-Roman understanding up to the present times, it forms the basis of most contemporary structuralist and poststructuralist cultural theories with regard to language and signification. Theorists have employed the concept of signs, including Roland Barthes in his work *Mythologies* (1957), to examine how signs and signification determine sociocultural practices. Barthes interprets all value systems pertaining to modern civilizational practices and artifacts as signs functioning within linguistic structures that in turn generate cultural myths. According to Barthes, therefore, all popular and largely accepted meanings associated with everyday practices, such as wine drinking and wrestling, and with culturally celebrated personalities such as Charlie Chaplin function within the realm of signs and subsequently are open to multiple interpretations that may change over time and cultural contexts. Accordingly, it may be claimed that the one unifying characteristic defining signs across discourses is their ability to produce multiple interpretations and meanings.

V. Neethi Alexander

Further Reading

Barthes, Roland. *Mythologies*. London: Random House, 2009.

Daston, Lorraine. "Marvelous Facts and Miraculous Evidence in Early Modern Europe." *Critical Inquiry* 18(1) (1991): 93–124.

Harrison, Peter. "Miracles, Early Modern Science, and Rational Religion." *Church History* 75(3) (2006): 493–511.

Landrum, George. "What a Miracle Really Is." *Religious Studies* 12(1) (1976): 49–57.

Long, Cecil F. "Miracles." *Irish Church Quarterly* 9(33) (1916): 35–46.

Markus, R. A. *Signs and Meanings: World and Text in Ancient Christianity*. Liverpool: Liverpool University Press, 1996.

Markus, R. A. "St. Augustine on Signs." *Phronesis* 2(1) (1957): 60–83.

Oakes, Robert. "Life, Death and the Hiddenness of God." *International Journal for Philosophy of Religion* 64(3) (2008): 155–160.

Sikhism and Miracles

A comparatively young religion, Sikhism emerged in the last two decades of the fifteenth century with emphasis on one God, the Creator. Guru Nanak Dev (1469–1539), the founder of Sikhism, developed a religious philosophy, and followers were known as Sikhs (disciples). He was their first Guru. For Nanak, God was one, immortal, creator, timeless, and eternal. Monotheism became a cardinal principle of Sikhism. The three basic principles that Nanak formalized were *naam japna* (chanting the holy name of god), *kirat karo* (honest livelihood), and *wand chhako* (sharing with the needy). Whereas one finds a plethora of miracles and supernatural happenings in Hinduism, Buddhism, and Christianity, Sikhism abhors irrational phenomenon. Nanak commented that his greatest miracle was not to perform a miracle, even though he had the ability. But there are instances in Nanak's life story and the gurus who followed him that pertain to miraculous happenings. Some of the *kautak*, the Punjabi word for "miracles," have been interpolated. Even if the gurus performed miracles a few times, it was for a noble cause and never for personal glory.

The Janamsakhi (Life Story) literature recounted the birth and life of Guru Nanak and his successors. The beginning of the short narratives in the Punjabi language started around the end of the sixteenth century and passed on through successive years in diverse versions. This earliest work of Punjabi prose written in Gurumukhi script is full of mythical narratives about the founder's life. Nanak was interested in spiritualism from an early age. One story mentioned that once he neglected his duty as cattle watcher because he was deep in meditation. The cattle destroyed a nearby wheat field, and an inquiry team from the village came to inspect it. But to everybody's amazement, not a single crop was damaged. While working in a store in Sultanpur, Nanak was sometimes giving grain freely, and when the enraged boss came to see, he found heaps of grain intact. Other narratives have Nanak undergo a revelatory experience, with a vision of God commanding him that he was to be a guru or preceptor. Nanak realized that there was only one ultimate reality. The people were worried, as he had not returned home for three days after going to bathe in the Bein River. The interregnum was the time of Nanak's communion with this reality. The divinity offered him a cup of *amrit* (nectar) and asked to drink from the cup of "name adoration." Nanak began the mission of a new faith after being embellished with gift of "My Name" from the Supreme Being.

It was said that Nanak also received the gift of a robe from the heavenly court. He gave up all worldly possessions and began a long journey with the faithful Muslim attendant Mardana. Nanak toured extensively in the Indian subcontinent. While in Kashmir, he had a meeting with one Pundit Brahm Das, who had attained supernatural powers. Das had come in a flying carpet to meet Nanak to impress the guru but could not see Nanak, although the guru was sitting in front of Das along with other people. Das went away and came back the next day walking. Nanak replied that Das could not see him because of the arrogance of having a flying carpet. He advised the pundit to give up his ego and look for the inner truth.

While in Panja Sahib, Nanak's follower Mardana felt thirsty. The folkloric tradition mentions that water from a nearby spring trickled at the feet of the guru. When the owner of the spring Wali Shah made a boulder to rush down toward Nanak, the latter held it up with his palm. Sikh tradition claims that the guru had made *udasi* (trips) to Sri Lanka (formerly Ceylon), Mecca, Baghdad, and Turkey. He even undertook a journey to the moon and stars. The guru performed many miracles during his visits. While en route to Sri Lanka, he took rest in a *gurdwara* on the island of Rameshwaram. Water from the well inside the temple turned sweet by the mere presence of Nanak. Dressed as a holy man, Nanak entered in the precincts of the city of Mecca. While going to sleep, a fellow pilgrim asked Nanak not to turn his feet toward Kaaba. When the former in a fit of anger removed the guru's feet away from the direction of Kaaba, the latter also moved in that direction! Nanak was making the pilgrim to understand that God was everywhere. All the miracles of the guru mentioned in Sikh tradition and the Janamsakhi show Nanak to be not an ordinary person of this mundane world but rather a divinity himself.

Nanak passed away on September 22, 1539, and Angad (1504–1552) became the second guru. Amar Das (1479–1574), the third guru, began the *guru ka langar* (communal eating). The fourth guru, Ramdas (1534–1581), founded a colony called Ramdaspur, later christened as Amritsar. The fifth guru, Arjan Dev (1563–1606), compiled the *Guru Granth Sahib* and built Harmindar Sahib (the Golden Temple). He was executed by Jahangir (r. 1605–1627), and the martyrdom of the guru galvanized Sikhism. Har Govind (1595–1644), the sixth guru, constructed the Akal Takht in the Golden Temple and issued the *hukamnama* (edict) asking the Sikhs to put on arms for self-defense. The seventh and eighth gurus were Hari Rai (1630–1661) and Hari Krishan (1656–1664), respectively. Tegh Bahadur (1621–1675), the ninth guru, was executed by Aurnagzeb (1658–1707). The last human guru of the Sikhs was Govind Singh (1666–1708), who left behind a cohesive and militarized Khalsa. The lineage of the ten gurus came to an end, and the authority of the gurus was vested with the Adi Granth. Govind Singh had proclaimed that Scripture was the permanent guru and christened it as *Sri Guru Granth Sahib* on October 20, 1708. Apart from its ethical dimensions, it inculcated a spirit of unity among the Sikhs, who did not hesitate to fight against the forces of tyranny and oppression throughout the successive history of the Indian subcontinent. Thus, it was more than a miracle that a holy scripture could give an identity to the Sikh community.

As per tradition, some of the gurus were invested with supernatural powers. Mughal emperor Humayun (r. 1530–1540 and 1555–1556) wanted to strike the second guru, Angad, but Humayun's hand was stuck, and the sword did not come out of the sheath. The fourth guru, Ram Das, called "Lord of Miracles," was famous for mystical visions. One miracle of a big streak of lighting in the form of a ball occurring in April 1877 in the Golden Temple of Amritsar was attributed to the long-dead Ram Das. The British colonial government stopped the plan of taking over the temple after the incident.

Baba Atal Rai, a son of Guru Har Govind, raised the dead. Ram Rai, the son of Guru Hari Rai, performed 70 miracles. Among them is the story of a sheet of cloth that was spread over a well. Ram Rai was asked to sit on it. Nonetheless, he did not fall into the well. He once also showed two moons in the sky to the emperor.

Guru Hari Krishan, although a child of five years, possessed superhuman prowess. He cured leper patients and made illiterate persons recite the *Bhagavad Gita*. Govind Singh was able to take out water from the earth by his arrow. His companion Baba Deep Singh (1682–1757) defended the Golden Temple of Amritsar even after his head was cut off by an Afghan army.

According to Sikh belief, miracles are not confined to one place. In August 1976, another miracle happened in Great Britain. There was no rain for many days. Believers say that the continuous reading of the *Guru Granth Sahib* made it possible for the onset of rain. Whatever may be the cause of the rain, it is beyond doubt that miracles and supernatural elements have a role in Sikhism.

Patit Paban Mishra

See also: Asia, Miracles in

Further Reading

Agnihotri, H. L. *The Sikh Gurus*. Amritsar: Nanak Singh Pustak Mala, 2008.

All about Sikhs, http://www.allaboutsikhs.com.

Cole, W. Owen, and Piara Singh Sambhi. *The Sikhs: Their Religious Beliefs and Practices*. Brighton, UK: Sussex Academic Press, 2006.

Ghatage, Kusum. *Ten Gurus of the Sikhs: Their Life Story*. Mumbai: Bharatiya Vidya Bhavan, 2005.

Gill, Harjeet S. *Baba Nanak*. New Delhi: Harman Publishing House, 2003.

Goswami, Sandeep, and Malkiat Singh. *The Great Glory: Sikhism*. New Delhi: Rupa, 2006.

McLeod, W. H. *Essays in Sikh History, Tradition, and Society*. New Delhi: Oxford University Press, 2007.

Mishra, Patit Paban. "Dev, Nanak Guru." In *Encyclopedia of Modern Asia*, Vol. 2, edited by Karen Christensen and David Levinson, 270. New York: Scribner, 2002.

Mishra, Patit Paban. "Rites of Passage." In *Encyclopedia of American Folklore and Folklife*, Vol. 3, edited by Jonathan H. X. Lee and Kathleen M. Nadeau, 1030–1033. Santa Barbara, CA: ABC-CLIO, 2011.

Sikh Information, http://www.info-sikh.com/.

Singh, Darshan. *Martyrdom of Guru Tegh Bahadur*. New Delhi: Anamika Publishers, 2003.

Singh, Khushwant. *History of the Sikhs*. 2 vols. Princeton, NJ: Princeton University Press, 1963, 1966.

Singh, Nikky-Guninder Kaur. *Sikhism*. 3rd ed. New York: Chelsea House, 2009.

Singh, Pashaura, et al. *Sikhism and History*. New Delhi: Oxford University Press, 2004.

Singh, Prithi P. *The History of Sikh Gurus*. New Delhi: Lotus Press, 2006.

Solemnity of the Lord of Miracles (El Señor de los Milagros)

Originally this feast of the Catholic Church commemorated the Cristo de Pachacamilla, named after the neighborhood where a confraternity of pious men (*cofradias*) had their meeting house. The group could trace its roots to the Afro-Peruvian population in the city of Lima, Peru, and specifically to the site of the future Church of Las Nazarenas, which was erected in 1730. On two occasions the meeting house fell victim to earthquakes—first in 1655 and again in 1687. Each time the wall bearing an image of Christ painted by one of the members somehow stood firm. On account of this, some began to venerate the image. A small shrine was made around the site, but soon the confluence of Christian paraliturgy mixed with African cultural dance so that the archbishop sought to have the image painted over. Miraculously, the workman assigned this task either fell ill or fell victim to temporary paralysis in their limbs. With years of candle smoke rising up before the image, the picture of Christ began to take on a darker hue, and the cult of a "Black Jesus" took shape.

With the devastation caused by the earthquake of 1746, the cult took on greater significance. Subsequently, every October the devotees of the image, weighing nearly two tons, parade it through the streets of Lima from the Church of Las Nazarenas to the Church of La Merced. Everyone in the procession is clad in purple as a sign of penitence. To this day the streets of Lima are jammed for the procession of El Señor de los Milagros, and wherever Peruvians reside around the world, they gather in October to imitate their compatriots. To carry the enthroned image is considered a high honor, and the annual procession's organization is given episcopal approbation.

One legend of the Solemnity of the Lord of Miracles (El Señor de los Milagros) is that it cured a paralytic mulatto woman named Josefa (Pepa) Marmaguillo. In thanksgiving, she distributed a candy known as *turrón de doña Pepa*, and since her day this has been a traditional food associated with the feast. The Archdiocese of Lima is the official sponsor of the annual procession and has embraced social media around it—even creating an app for the event.

Patrick J. Hayes

Further Reading

Higgins, James. *Lima: A Cultural History*. New York: Oxford University Press, 2005.
"Inicio." Arzobispado de Lima, http://www.arzobispadodelima.org/index.php?option=com _content&view=article&id=293&Itemid=143.
Redding, Martha Manson. "In the Land of El Señor de Los Milagros: Peruvian Catholicism, 1919–1931; Religion in a Period of Societal Change." Senior thesis, Harvard University, 1990.

Spain, Miracles in

The Iberian Peninsula—comprising Spain and Portugal—is a diverse topographical land that has known drought and famine, invasion and reconquest, and violence and suffering. Its agonies have set the stage for numerous miracles. The implantation of Christianity—by tradition through the efforts of the Apostle James the Greater (or Elder)—was not an immediate success but rather a gradual evolution over centuries. The death of James, according to legend, came from his beheading by Herod Agrippa in Jerusalem. James's body was miraculously borne by an angel in a rudderless ship to the "ends of the earth" (Finesterra) in northern Galicia. Though there is considerable reason to doubt his missionary venture into Spain as well as the relics claimed by the Cathedral in Santiago de Compostela to be his, nevertheless it is here, at the end of the Camino de Santiago, that the focal point of the lengthy pilgrimage culminates. As it was said by Pope Calixtus II (d. 1124) on the occasion of the translation of his relics to the present church, "He was translated so that he may strengthen with his patronage, bestow with his benefits, look down with his miracles and prepare seats in the heavenly realm for those loving him with all their hearts, not only for the Galicians but also for those visiting his holy tomb." This homily forms part of the pope's *Codex Calixtinus*, a work that also documents 22 miracles of Saint James performed across the continent mostly for the benefit of pilgrims.

Pilgrimage became a central Christian and cultural practice by the fourth century. In later centuries Spain, like other European countries, witnessed its share of martyrs. In circa 303 Deacon Vincent of Saragossa was martyred in Valencia by order of Dacian, the local governor of Tarragona. Vincent's murderers tortured him with flesh-ripping hooks and seared him with hot metal plates. They then tied a millstone around his neck and threw him into the sea. His body, however, floated to the shore. Ravens are said to have protected the body of the deceased saint from wild beasts until his remains could be properly interred. His relics became important for veneration by the faithful who traveled on their way to Santiago de Compostela each year. The church that housed the relics later came under Muslim control, and by the twelfth century his body was in Lisbon—with a forearm given to the Cathedral at Braga and a femur to the treasury in Notre Dame in Paris.

Urged on by the monastics after the sixth century and later the mendicants after the twelfth century, pilgrimage to or from shrines became an ordinary part of Spanish national identity and made the trip to Compostela practically obligatory. In a way, it helped to keep Moorish advances on the peninsula in check. By 711 after the Berber invasion of Grenada, the Moors went north, building two major strongholds in Seville and Córdoba. By the end of the tenth century their forces had all but destroyed the Cathedral at Santiago de Compostela, and the stage was set for Christian reconquest. It was not until the twelfth-century Crusades that Islam's grip on the southern tier began to erode.

Mary's part in these Christian victories cannot be discounted, as one miraculous win after another was acknowledged to be from entreaties to her. Seville was finally taken back in 1248, and the king at the time, Fernando III, brought an image of the Virgen de los Reyes (Virgin of Kings) into the city, where he had it installed in the central mosque, a building soon converted to the Catholic cathedral. King Alfonso X of Castile, author of a book of praises to Mary, *Cantigas Santa Maria*, recounts some 356 Marian miracles, many of which are in relation to the reinvigoration of the Spanish Crown. The final blow came in 1492 with their expulsion of the Moors altogether. At the same time, Mary's usefulness crossed borders. With the new encounters between Europeans and the indigenous of the Americas, Mary was known variously as protectress and standard-bearer for the conquistadors.

Another main practice cultivated both locally and nationally are processions. Especially in the late Middle Ages, processions begot social cohesion, teamwork, and civic unity. Semana Sancta (Holy Week) processions are prodigious affairs in which thousands of onlookers can spill into the streets. Among the more grandiose is the parade in Seville, where hundreds of burly men carry two large thrones upon which sit the Virgin and Child and a crucified Christ. These bulky but ornately decorated seats are marched through the streets to a central meeting point in order that the Madonna can greet her son. They go well accompanied, typically by thousands of members of the local brotherhoods clad in festive hoods and gowns. For the faithful, this honors the principal miracle of Christianity—Christ's victory over death on the Cross.

Religious orders have added considerably to the stock of mystical writings and happenings throughout the Spanish countryside. A special word could be said about Franciscans, Dominicans, and Carmelites. Because of the close connection of their founder with the stigmata, the preaching of Franciscans often focused on wounds and blood, the resulting agony of Christ on the cross, and the need for penitence. Is it any wonder that so many miraculous crucifixes are so gruesomely bloodied? With Dominicans, the vitality of their preaching rested on the fine points of doctrinal accuracy, and their involvement in the Inquisition, the principal instrument for stamping out heresy, placed the role of authentication of visions or miraculous phenomena squarely within the jurisdiction of the Church hierarchy. Both of these mendicant orders have also made petitions for the souls in Purgatory and devotion to the rosary a lasting legacy.

With the Carmelites, the two reformer saints John of the Cross and Teresa of Ávila (1515–1582) have added immeasurably to the spiritual literature of the post-Reformation Church and continue to offer an important avenue toward deliverance from, as Saint John put it, the "dark night of the soul." The city of Ávila, situated between the university town of Salamanca and the capital of Madrid, was a barren place in the sixteenth century. It had numerous monastic foundations of women and men, but Saint Teresa's convent was not conducive to modernization after the Council of Trent. Sisters there were meant to pray and then not even for themselves but rather for the souls of the convent's benefactors. This Carmelite Monastery of the Incarnation was cloistered and highly ascetical. Teresa found her own spiritual longings to be routinely stifled.

In 1562 Teresa left to found another Carmelite monastery in Ávila in which she experienced mystical encounters with God, ecstasies she called the "transverberation of the heart" and made famous by Bernini's exquisite sculpture *St. Teresa in Ecstasy* in a side altar in Santa Maria della Victoria in Rome. Five years later Teresa began to found other Carmelite monasteries throughout Spain after the discalced or "shoeless" practice. Ultimately she would raise sixteen new foundations. Her chief collaborator among the males of her order, Saint John of the Cross, shared his own spiritual writings with her, and both learned from each another. Teresa died while traveling, and it is said that on the night she died her cell in her convent in Ávila was blessed with a pungent scent of flowers. When it was exhumed over three centuries later, Saint Teresa's tomb also carried a pleasant odor. She was canonized in 1622 along with two other Spanish saints: Ignatius of Loyola and his companion Francis Xavier. It belongs to Teresa, however, to carry the title "Doctor of the Church."

In Portugal, there was also a link between the Crown and sanctity. Saint Isabel (Elizabeth), wife of King Diniz and grandniece of Saint Elizabeth of Hungary, was a medieval philanthropist of extraordinary talent and virtue. She worked tirelessly on behalf of the poor and most vulnerable, eventually establishing a convent in Coimbra. Her husband, however, had restricted her charity. Once she had hidden in her apron some bread destined for her impoverished subjects but ran into the king, who inquired about what she was carrying. "Roses," she said, and miraculously displayed the contents of her bundle. The king was astonished that fresh roses should bloom in January when they were not in season, but he let her go on her way.

Like its Iberian neighbor, Portugal also sought the favor of the Madonna. Fatima is duly famous for its Marian apparition to three young children, its miracle of the dancing sun, and its pilgrimages but is a relative latecomer to the scene. When Portuguese explorers began their colonization efforts in Brazil, Marian images followed and became part of that cultural landscape as well. The statue of the Seven Dolorous Swords of the Holy Virgin—memorializing the seven pains Mary experienced as recorded in the gospels—is but one example of her ubiquitous image. Processions commemorating the Virgin of Nazareth, begun as early as 1616, will also often include a so-called miracle float where onlookers will toss *ex votos*—mainly plastic dolls' heads, arms, legs, or feet in thanksgiving for healing.

Images—especially Marian images—are thought to have power not only to control events but also to affect cultural behaviors. Thus, a mother leaving an abusive marriage will only gather her children and the image of the Madonna before departing. People cleave to the totem in which their faith is invested. Some preferred a more cerebral approach to Mary. Father Gonzalo de Berceo assembled his book *Milagros de Nuestra Señora* as an aid to sinners in need of repentance. Mary's miracles showed that true remorse could lead a penitent to redemption. On a collective level, vast processions of highly decorated images suggest that for many Spaniards, their faith is necessarily public and celebratory. It is one way that indigenous peoples in New Spain were brought into the Catholic Church. Spaniards have had cause for placing so much trust in Mary. In 1370, for instance, a group of Moors lay in wait at El Sotillo to ambush some passing Christians when Mary's presence illuminated the night sky. The exposure of the Moors took away their element of surprise, and they were summarily vanquished by some rather unforgiving Christians. Stories such as this helped to build Mary's cult but also fueled the impulses of conquest.

Scholars point to two particular Marian images in the late medieval period: Guadalupe and Montserrat. The confraternities that grew up around support for the churches dedicated to these Madonnas were extensive and loyal, routinely passing from generation to generation. Their devotion networked villages and produced much commerce, a system eventually transferred to New Spain. The little statue of the Black Virgin of Montserrat first came to prominence in the twelfth century, but it can be traced back to the eighth century. After a mysterious disappearance from the historical record, it reemerged in 880 when one night some sheepherders saw the night sky ablaze with light coming from the mountain of Montserrat. The local clergy investigated and found the statue hidden in a cave. A chapel was erected on the spot, and this later grew into an impressive Benedictine foundation. It was here that Saint Ignatius Loyola, the founder of the Jesuits, placed his sword before the Madonna before embarking on his spiritual quest. She is today the patroness of Catalonia and has lent her name and image to numerous churches in the former Spanish colonies of the Americas.

Of course, other shrines dedicated to Mary are strewn throughout the country, and those associated with miracles reach nearly 300. Among the more notable are Our Lady of Atocha near Madrid, Our Lady of Saragossa, and two in Cuenca: Our Lady of Socorro and La Concepción of Trascastillo. The verification processes of the miracles associated with these shrines involve a systematic and eventually formulaic notarization system so that anyone, for all time, can be assured of their stamp of approval. Some are more dubious than others, such as Our Lady of Pilar in Zaragosa. The first written version of this apparition site occurred some eight centuries after the event. Frequently, cures are effected at these shrines after a vigil in prayer. Typically, a petitioner will enter the shrine to pray and after a while will fall asleep. In the morning upon waking, the prayer is answered.

Apparitions in Spain are plentiful, too. Nuestra Señora del Pilar is the earliest. The Virgin of the Pillar appeared before Saint James the Greater, who had been preaching near Zaragoza. She instructed him to take heart that his preaching would win souls and to build a chapel on the site of the pillar on which she stood. For this wonder she became the patroness of Spain. In their day and age other apparitions were considered exceedingly important. These were the Crucifix of Christ in Limpias (Santander), whose eyes began to move in 1919; Our Lady of Ezquioga in the early 1930s; and Our Lady of Garabandal, where the Virgin appeared almost nightly to three girls between 1961 and 1965. Each is known for its longevity in the popular mindset of regional Catholics. Their stories can still be recounted precisely to this day.

Crucifixes that can move, sweat, bleed, or cry are also curiosities but are widely reported. During a parish mission preached by a Redemptorist priest in April 1903, the congregation saw a child with outstretched arms where the Eucharist should be in a monstrance. The parish church of San Sabastian in Madrid had a moving crucifix, and a crucifix sweated blood in a village in the province of Cadiz between 1907 and 1909. In Seville, a statue of the Virgin Mary was said to blink. By 1918 the Christ of Gandía began to move and work miracles, including the embrace of small children. A short time later the corpus of the crucifix at

Lampias did the same, though both of these moving Christs had the air of fraud about them.

Some objects of devotion are most unusual and continue to inspire, such as the famed Crystal Skull of Malaga, which is kept in the Santa Maria Cathedral. Supposedly the skull of a fourteenth-century monk, its fame is owed to its power to cure a wide variety of illnesses, including the more lethal such as leukemia and brain tumors. Additionally, Valencia claims a chalice that is reputed to be the one used by Jesus at the Last Supper, though this "Holy Grail" has proven notoriously difficult to verify.

Further, in Portugal, relics from distant lands have found homes. In a small village outside of Lisbon sits a relic chapel at Lumiar that has housed the head of Saint Brigid, patroness of Ireland, since the thirteenth century. In Lisbon's cathedral there are relics of Saint Vincent the Deacon as well as the right arm reliquary of Saint Gregory the Nazianzen. At Coimbra rest the relics of Saint Elizabeth of Portugal. At the Church of St. Anthony in Lisbon is the mummified sarcophagus of Saint Justina. Lisbon's Church of São Roque also contains a reliquary chapel filled with arm and bust reliquaries of various saints. At Fatima under the crown of the statue of the Virgin is the assassin's bullet removed from Pope Saint John Paul II in 1981, a gift of that pope in thanksgiving for his recovery.

Modern Spain of the twentieth century was deeply scarred by civil war. Tens of thousands of Catholic priests and nuns were tortured, starved, or shot in hatred of the faith. Many groups of these men and women are now being recognized officially by the church as martyrs, such as the 1987 beatification of 489 men and women, the largest collective beatification in history, and more recently the Redemptorists of Cuenca in 2014.

Patrick J. Hayes

See also: *Ex Voto;* Latin America, Miracles in

Further Reading

Christian, William A. *Apparitions in Late Medieval and Renaissance Spain*. Princeton, NJ: Princeton University Press, 1981.

Christian, William A. *A Divine Presence in Spain and Western Europe, 1500–1960*. Budapest: Central European University Press, 2012.

Christian, William A. *Local Religion in Sixteenth-Century Spain*. Princeton, NJ: Princeton University Press, 1989.

Christian, William A. *Moving Crucifixes in Modern Spain*. Princeton, NJ: Princeton University Press, 1992.

Christian, William A. *Person and God in a Spanish Valley*. Princeton, NJ: Princeton University Press, 1989.

Coffey, Thomas F., Linda Kay Davidson, and Maryjane Dunn. *The Miracles of Saint James: Translations from the Liber Sancti Jacobi*. New York: Italica Press, 1996.

Dunn, Maryjane, and Linda Kay Davidson, eds. *The Pilgrimage to Compostela in the Middle Ages*. New York: Routledge, 2000.

Echagüe, José Ortiz. *España Mística*. Madrid: Bolaños y Aguilar, 1943.

Fletcher, Richard A. *Saint James' Catapult: The Life and Times of Diego Gelmírez of Santiago de Compostela*. New York: Oxford University Press, 1984.

Flory, David A. *Marian Representations in the Miracle Tales of Thirteenth-Century Spain and France*. Washington, DC: Catholic University of America Press, 2000.

Fontaine, Jacques. "King Sisebut's *Vita Desiderii* and the Political Function of Visigothic Hagiography." In *Visigothic Spain: New Approaches*, edited by Edward James, 93–129. New York: Oxford University Press, 1980.

Hall, Linda B. *Mary, Mother and Warrior: The Virgin in Spain and the Americas*. Austin: University of Texas Press, 2014.

Hardy, Richard P. "Early Biographical Documentation on Juan de la Cruz." *Science et Esprit* 30(3) (1978): 313–323.

Lappin, Anthony. *The Medieval Cult of Saint Dominic of Silos*. MHRA Texts and Dissertations 56. Leeds: Modern Humanities Research Association, 2002.

Spells

A spell is a magic formula intended to produce a specified result. The elaboration of spells varies from simple rhymes to complex performances. A spell can involve the physical manipulation of objects, such as the so-called voodoo doll, or be expressed in material form, such as in amulets and talismans.

Stories of Egyptian magicians parting the waters, as Moses was later said to have done in the Tanakh book of Exodus, with a spell dating back to circa 3800 BCE. Most well known is the so-called ancient Egyptian *Book of the Dead*, a collection of funerary spells intended to guide and protect the soul after death. The oldest papyrus texts date to the fifteenth century BCE, but some point to older sources.

Early Greek references to the use of spells are found in Homer's *Odyssey* (eighth century BCE), notably the sorceress Circe's use of a charm to transform Odysseus's crew into swine. In addition to literary sources, surviving magical artifacts attest to the prevalence of spells well into the Roman period. Despite documented burnings of magical texts, many have survived, particularly from Greco-Roman Egypt of the second century BCE to the fifth century CE.

However, ecclesiastical zeal in destroying the magic of pre-Christian Northern Europe has left little in the way of evidence. What does remain points to a significant everyday use of spells to ensure the success of a range of ordinary activities. *Bald's Leechbook* of the ninth century CE contains the earliest of the Anglo-Saxon charms to have survived, and from the same period the so-called Merseburg Incantations are the only surviving charms in Old High German. The Middle Ages were dominated more by writings against spells than the writing of them, although some rare texts have been rescued and published. In the nineteenth century, Alexander Carmichael collected a Gaelic oral tradition of some antiquity from among the people of the Scottish Highlands and Islands, including many spells, such as the poetic *Invocation of the Graces*, a blessing recited over young people that had a dual function: protection and the installation of virtue.

The Reformation saw a significant emphasis being placed on the role of the Devil pact. While there are few examples of such pacts or spells to that effect, the turn toward demonic invocation is especially marked. Looking at the New World, spell use has been documented at one time or another among most of its inhabitants (e.g., Native Americans and German settlers).

Leo Ruickbie

Further Reading

Betz, Hans Dieter. *The Greek Magical Papyri in Translation*. Chicago: University of Chicago Press, 1992.

Budge, E. A. Wallis. *Egyptian Magic*. London: Kegan Paul, Trench, Trübner, 1901.

Carmichael, Alexander. *Carmina Gadelica: Hymns and Incantations*. 2 vols. Edinburgh, UK: Constable, 1900.

Fanger, Claire, ed. *Conjuring Spirits: Texts and Traditions of Medieval Ritual Magic*. Stroud, UK: Sutton, 1998.

Faulkner, R. O. *The Ancient Egyptian Book of the Dead*. London: British Museum Publications, 1990.

Graf, Fritz. *Magic in the Ancient World*. Cambridge, MA: Harvard University Press, 2000.

Grimm, Jacob. "Über zwei entdeckte Gedichte aus der Zeit des deutschen Heidenthums." *Abhandlungen der Königlichen Akademie der Wissenschaften zu Berlin* (1844): 21–22.

Kieckhefer, Richard. *Forbidden Rites: A Necromancer's Manual of the Fifteenth Century*. Stroud, UK: Sutton, 1997.

Kilpatrick, Alan. *The Night Has a Naked Soul*. Syracuse, NY: Syracuse University Press, 1997.

Milnes, Gerald C. *Signs, Cures, and Witchery*. Knoxville: University of Tennessee Press, 2011.

Paine, Sheila. *Amulets*. London: Thames and Hudson, 2004.

Ruickbie, Leo. *Faustus: The Life and Times of a Renaissance Magician*. Stroud, UK: History Press, 2009.
Wright, C. E., ed. *Bald's Leechbook: British Museum Royal Manuscript 12 D.XVII*. Copenhagen: Rosenkilde and Bagger, 1955.

Spinoza, Baruch

Baruch Spinoza (1632–1677) was born into the Portuguese Jewish community of Amsterdam. His father was a leader in the synagogue and the yeshiva that Baruch attended. Baruch was gifted, and it was expected that he would become a rabbi. However, he did not engage in advanced Talmudic study. He began working at his father's business at the age of 17 after the death of his older brother. At 20, he began to study Latin with Frances van Enden, who was a Jesuit before becoming a physician and Latin tutor. Van Enden likely taught him classics, physics, anatomy, and modern philosophy, especially Descartes.

After their father died in 1653, Baruch's younger sister disputed the inheritance. After defeating her in court, he renounced his claim. He then moved in with van Enden and changed his first name to its Latin form, Benedict. He began to teach for van Enden and to associate with a number of dissident Christian groups. Van Enden eventually would be hung in Paris in 1674 for his political activity.

Spinoza's theology was problematic for a religious minority group existing on the good graces of its host city. That theology was also problematic within the Jewish community. When two synagogue members questioned him about some of his specific theological stances, his fate with the community was sealed. At the age of 23, he was banned from the community and declared to be damned. Not long before this, he was attacked as a heretic on the synagogue steps by a knife-wielding man. Spinoza would leave the family business in the wake of his ban.

The break was inevitable, as Spinoza held a number of other positions that would have caused separation. Chief among those was his rejection of the claim that Moses wrote every word of the Pentateuch (the first five books of the Hebrew Bible). Spinoza's efforts were the foundation of what became known as higher criticism of the Hebrew Bible.

Spinoza left Amsterdam. He returned for a time, teaching philosophy and lens grinding, but left for good in 1661, spending the rest of his life in Rijnsburg and Voorburg.

Spinoza wrote four works that were published during his life, only one of which his name appeared on, *The Priniciples of Cartesian Philosophy*. The others were too religiously charged to claim authorship, though it was an open secret as to who their author was. After his death, two completed and one unfinished work were published.

The ingesting of the ground matter from his vocation of lens grinding no doubt contributed to his death at the age of 44 of some lung ailment. He never married but was enamored of van Enden's daughter, Clara Maria. She married Dirck Kerckring in 1671.

Much of what Spinoza is remembered for concerns his position on miracles. Paradoxically, his denial of miracles is based upon his affirmation that there is indeed a God who is in control of the universe.

For Spinoza, all that appears miraculous is an aberration. There is some underlying, undiscovered explanation. The problem with miracles is that they ultimately are a denial of the laws of nature. For Spinoza, God is nature. In a famous passage, he states that the "eternal and infinite being we call God, or Nature, acts from the same necessity from which he exists." The Latin phrase *Deus, sive Natura*, declares that the two are interchangeable. It is the regularity and infinity of nature that points to God. To lessen the absolute power of nature (through miracles) is to deny the omnipotence of God.

God is the source of the laws of nature. It is the regularity of nature in accordance to its laws that is the true demonstration of divine power. God's understanding is identical to his will. His infinite knowledge and power are on display in a universe that functions flawlessly, according to its laws. Nature, ultimately, "pursues a fixed and immutable course" that makes the presence of miracles a "patent absurdity."

For Spinoza, God is necessary, infinite, and uncaused, the mirror image of Aristotelian proofs. Spinoza wants to avoid anthropomorphisms, which give God a body and emotions, subject to change. God is ultimately the only substance of the universe. It is our finiteness that produces the illusion of separate substances and entities. The universe came into being not by divine whimsy and fiat, by a willful act that could have just as easily not been chosen; rather, the universe is a necessary and infinite product of God's nature. That God exists means that the universe must necessarily exist; the universe cannot exist apart from God but only as a product of his nature. For God to exist, miracles cannot happen.

Spinoza was labeled an atheist during his life. He has been called "God intoxicated" for his expansive view of God. Spinoza denied being a pantheist. He is best understood as a panentheist, one who believes that God penetrates and exceeds all of nature. However one wishes to understand *Deus, sive Natura*, what is clear from his thought is that miracles count against the existence of God. Albert Einstein once stated that he did believe in the God of Spinoza.

Mark Anthony Phelps

Further Reading

Garrett, Don, ed. *The Cambridge Companion to Spinoza*. New York: Cambridge University Press, 1995.

Goldstein, Rebecca. *Betraying Spinoza: The Renegade Jew Who Gave Us Modernity*. New York: Schocken, 2006.

Nadler, Steven. *Spinoza: A Life*. New York: Cambridge University Press, 1999.

St. Anthony's Relic Chapel

The largest collection of relics outside the Vatican can be found in St. Anthony's Chapel in Pittsburgh, Pennsylvania. The chapel is home to the skeletal remains of Saint Demetrius, the skulls of the martyred companions of Saint Ursula, a piece of the table from the Last Supper, and a tooth that once belonged to Saint Anthony. The collection totals approximately 5,000 pieces.

Contemporary pilgrims' guides and newspaper articles from the 1880s provide two important clues as to how the relics came to rest in Pittsburgh: a dynamic priest and the political upheavals of European nation-state making.

St. Anthony's Chapel is the handiwork of Father Suitbert Mollinger. Born in 1800 to aristocratic parents and trained as a physician, Mollinger heard the call to be a priest and took on his ministry—an effort that blended medicine and relics—with gusto.

Mollinger arrived in Pittsburgh in 1868 with a few relics already in hand. In the years leading up to the completion of the chapel (it would be completed in 1892), he traveled to Europe to acquire more relics. The market opened up when the Kulturkampf and the Risorgimento jeopardized the ability of monasteries to house relics—and Mollinger got them on the cheap. He procured some from pawn shops.

Mollinger gained a region-wide reputation as a pharmacist and a divine intermediary in the 1880s. Sought out by the region's sick, he prescribed medications, prayers to the saints, and rounds of the sacraments. Between 1888 and 1892, thousands of cure seekers consulted Mollinger and prayed in the presence of the relics. Many walked away cured.

When St. Anthony's Chapel was completed in 1892 (at Mollinger's expense), the relics had a permanent home. Pilgrims made the journey to St. Anthony's in search of cures, relics, and a special space. Such journeys continue today.

Peter Cajka

Further Reading

Saint Anthony Chapel, http://saintanthonyschapel.org/.

Schorr, W. David, and Louis Baysek. *St. Anthony's Chapel in Most Holy Name of Jesus Parish*. Pittsburgh: J. Pohl, 1997.

Statues

Statues are not inanimate objects. In the eyes of believers, they are dynamic and powerful. They can bleed, cry, and move, or they can intervene in human affairs. They are also stone screens onto which any number of social, political, or religious concerns can be projected. This is a phenomenon of especial importance within Catholicism. In Spain, when the public reporting of visions went into decline after the Inquisition, reports of miraculous statues and images rose reciprocally. Sightings of moving, bleeding, or weeping statues, which did not challenge Church authority, thrived in Catholic lands in the seventeenth century. Unlike personal visions, miraculous statues did not challenge the priest's role as intermediary with the divine. The miraculous statues were usually already in churches. In cases where they were in private homes, they were soon moved to churches. Such statues remain sites for pilgrimage today.

A large proportion of the early modern Spanish cases occurred during epidemics or the fervor of Holy Week celebrations. The Christ of Burgos is said to have sweated blood during a drought in 1698. Later incidents often had a more political context. In the Papal States, there occurred a wave of weeping and eye movements of statues in 1795–1796 in advance of the Napoleonic invasion. In contrast, miraculous statues were exceedingly rare in Protestant Europe. Crying statues are sometimes connected to other important religious sites, such as the chapel of the Daughters of Charity in Paris. It was there in 1830 that Catherine Labouré received successive visions of the Immaculate Conception. It was in that same year and location that a twelfth-century statue of Mary was said to have wept profusely, such that the superior had to sop up the tears with a cloth. This was largely an internal and localized occurrence, free from the public's eyes.

In Catholic parts of Germany, though, the Marpingen visions of 1878 became a mass phenomenon during the rapid industrialization of the nineteenth century. Many copy cat visionaries in the wake of Marpingen were convicted of fraud, mostly on account of trying to peddle healing water or tonics. Likewise, miraculous statues were again a mass phenomenon in Spain in the twentieth century, in the context of the upheaval of the civil war and Franco's rule. Such events tend to cluster in time, and modern media has often been a factor in their dissemination.

Though later discredited, visions associated with a bleeding image in Templemore in Ireland in 1921 were directly influenced by contemporaneous events in Spain. The Irish case was also partly a reaction to the violence of the war of independence, while contemporary Spanish cases were linked to anxieties about secular socialist rule.

Ireland was also the site for miraculous statues phenomena starting in 1985 and continuing sporadically after that. Again, this was in response to serious social upheaval in a rapidly secularizing society. Indeed, the speedy collapse of Catholic authority goes some way toward explaining the popularity of the phenomenon. It was also a phenomenon aided by the modern media and thus one of the best-documented cases.

The 1985 Irish moving statues began in Ballinspittle in County Cork before spreading island wide. As in many other instances, the original seers were children, while the later pilgrims tended to be adults. Those interviewed at the scene by journalists often expressed the view that these visions were warnings to a secularizing Ireland increasingly seen as wayward and immoral. The sightings also tended to take place in grottos or shrines, reflecting greater suspicion of a clerical leadership that was seen as weak and ineffectual in the face of secularization.

The Irish case is a rarity, though. Scholars have suggested that many and perhaps most encounters with supernatural phenomena go unreported and remain personal, or family or community bound. Moreover, the suspicion within Protestantism, Islam, and Judaism of graven images explains their absence within these religious cultures. Miraculous statues, however, are not unheard of in Hinduism and Orthodox denominations of Christianity, both of which share Catholicism's affinity for icons and powerful religious imagery.

Aidan Joseph Beatty

See also: Carmelites and Miracles

Further Reading

Beatty, Aidan. "Irish Respectability and the Politics of Contraception, 1979–1993." *New Hibernia Review* 17(3) (2013): 110–118.

Blackbourn, David. *The Marpingen Visions: Rationalism, Religion and the Rise of Modern Germany.* London: Fontana, 1995.

Christian, William A., Jr. *Divine Presence in Spain and Western Europe, 1500–1960.* Budapest: Central European University Press, 2012.

Christian, William A., Jr. *Moving Crucifixes in Modern Spain.* Princeton, NJ: Princeton University Press, 1992.

Jung, Jacqueline. "The Tactile and the Visionary: Notes on the Place of Sculpture in the Medieval Religious Imagination." In *Looking Beyond: Visions, Dreams, and Insights in*

Medieval Art and History, edited by Colum Hourihane, 203–240. Princeton, NJ: Index of Christian Art, 2010.

Nickell, Joe. *Looking for a Miracle: Weeping Icons, Relics, Stigmata, Visions and Healing Cures*. Amherst, NY: Prometheus, 1998.

Peabody, Norbert. "In Whose Turban Does the Lord Reside? The Objectification of Charisma and the Fetishism of Objects in the Hindu Kingdom of Kota." *Comparative Studies in Society and History* 33(4) (1991): 726–754.

Stigmata

Stigmata are marks on a body that replicate the wounds of Christ during the Passion that have not been induced through ascertainable natural intervention. Most often these occur on the hands, feet, and side—corresponding to the wounds Jesus received during crucifixion—but sometimes stigmatics manifest wounds on the head representing Christ's crown of thorns or whip marks on the back from Jesus's scourging, both of which occurred at the beginning of his Passion; one case of oral lesions was interpreted as representing the piercing of Jesus's mouth by the hyssop branch that carried the vinegar-soaked sponge, his last drink before he died (John 19:29). The term has also referred to the imprint of a crucifix on one's forehead or chest or unexplained bleeding from other orifices, such as the ear canals or eyes; the German stigmatic Therese Neumann (1898–1962) famously bled tears as well as carried crucifixion marks, perhaps in an *imitatio* of the miraculous bleeding or crying Madonnas common in popular Catholicism.

While some definitions include invisible stigmata (sharp pains in the hands, feet, and side, sometimes accompanied by red marks and nonbleeding lesions), most use the term to describe physical marks from which blood or other liquid flows forth; they are often characterized medically as psychogenic purpura (spontaneous hemorrhaging with no natural cause) and may also include forms of cutaneous lesions (skin lesions) or psychogenic ecchymosis (bruising, or bleeding under the skin, through no known natural cause). However, as studies of Saint Francis of Assisi (ca. 1181–1226)—the first recognized stigmatic in the Catholic Church—in the earliest hagiographical account of Saint Francis's life, written by Tommaso di Celano, suggest, Francis's wounds on his hands and feet did not bleed but were raised, black bumps resembling the actual nails that affixed Jesus to the cross.

While most stigmatics experience recurrent bleeding, the actual time that blood would come forth from the wounds is often specific intervals, such as every Friday (the day of the week Jesus died), during particular activities (such as receiving Holy Communion), or during liturgical feasts or seasons associated with Jesus's

Passion (such as during Good Friday or during all of Lent). Somewhat uniquely, the wounds of Saint Padre Pio of Pietrelcina (1887–1968) bled continuously for 50 years, leading some to argue that he fraudulently kept the wounds open with carbolic acid. Furthermore, the exact manifestation of the stigmata on an individual's body strongly depends on the types of imaginaries of Jesus and/or Saint Francis to which the victim was privy; this is particularly the case with the side of the abdomen on which Jesus's spear wound would appear on the stigmatic, which the Jesuit doctor and theologian Herbert Thurston found to correspond to the position of the wound on a crucifixion image with which the stigmatic was familiar.

Categorized as a mystical experience, the stigmata is frequently accompanied by visions of seraphim or the Passion. Prior to receiving the stigmata, many stigmatics had already expressed a desire to suffer—and in some cases, such as that of Margaret Maria Alacoque (1647–1690), were wont to engage in extreme physical mortifications—and these wounds were often accompanied by extreme pain, which the sufferer supposedly accepted with obedience. There is also a high correlation between a manifestation of the stigmata and the mystical experience of *inedia*, subsistence on only the Eucharist for spiritual nourishment with no noticeable physical change.

From an anthropological perspective, the stigmata can be considered a culture-bound syndrome (sometimes called a folk illness) that only manifests itself within the bounds of a particular society—in this case, the Judeo-Christian worldview. Indeed, the majority of cases have occurred in Italy, though high-profile cases have been reported in the United States, Ireland, the United Kingdom, the Netherlands, Belgium, and Germany. Indeed, the stigmata experience is clearly an *imitatio Cristi,* or imitation of Christ, though the message of how the stigmatic imitates God and the behaviors it shapes vary throughout time. For Saint Francis, it was a personal gift from God (via a seraph) that marked the monk's personal assumption of Christ's behaviors and teachings; it was manifested in private (perhaps with one witness, but the hagiographies dispute this) and was only revealed to the public upon his death. For Padre Pio, however, it marked the beginning of a very public ministry that centered on Pio's suffering as a proxy for his followers' sins and is in line with victim soul mysticism of the nineteenth and twentieth centuries.

Although Saint Francis and Saint Padre Pio—the two most popular stigmatics in history—are male, 87–91 percent of the victims were women, and often these cases would be psychologically diagnosed as hysteria, a particularly gender-specific female affliction. Furthermore, until the twentieth-century case of Padre Pio, a Capuchin friar, no priest has been recognized as a stigmatic. This can also be interpreted as symptomatic of the need of the stigmatic to transcend typical gender and vocational roles in Catholic culture; a priest is already theologically considered an *alter Cristus*, with Christ present during the Eucharistic rite (transubstantiation), and therefore has little need to manifest physical signs of his Christological affinity.

Beginning with a sweeping 1894 study by French Catholic physician Antoine Imbert-Gourbeyre, research into stigmata increased in the twentieth century, likely because of advances made in psychotherapy and epidemiology as well as in the global reach of sensationalist media that circulated images and writings of stigmatics such as Gemma Galgani (1878–1903), Neumann, and Pio. Indeed, while Pio, the first stigmatic priest in history, kept his stigmata covered by fingerless gloves except when celebrating the Eucharist—thereby increasing the stigmatic's mystique and inducing curiosity seekers to attend Mass—Neumann, a laywoman not bound by affiliation to a particular religious order, allowed herself to be photographed by news media, doctors, and theologians.

Although most stigmatics tend to be Catholic, contemporary medical researchers looking for a universal scientific basis for the stigmata have emphasized the limited cases among atheists, Protestants, Muslims, and Jews. An interesting case study of a young Jewish man who bled from his hands and had apparently never heard of the religious stigmata was published in a psychology journal in 1943; the therapist determined that it was a psychosomatic response to guilt over masturbating and tensions in his sexual orientation. Indeed, there is actually little scriptural basis for the stigmata, and the term only occurs in the Bible once, in which Saint Paul states that "I bear on my body the marks [stigmata] of Jesus" (Galatians 6:17). However, it is generally agreed that Paul was speaking figuratively; stigmata were proprietary marks branded on Roman slaves. Indeed, prior to Saint Francis of Assisi, the Church persecuted male and female stigmatics as heretics. As the Church modernized in the contemporary era, it also took a skeptical view; Thurston largely dismissed the high-profile cases of Neumann and Pio as a psychological "crucifixion complex." The stigmata furthermore has never been the sole basis for canonization—if anything, it draws more attention to the canonical need to assess that the would-be saint was of a sound psychological state and exercised obedience to the Church hierarchy and teachings despite the charisma that the marks often produce.

Michael Di Giovine

Further Reading

Carroll, Michael P. "Heaven-Sent Wounds: A Kleinian View of the Stigmata in the Catholic Mystical Tradition." *Journal of Psychoanalytic Anthropology* 10(1) (1987): 17–38.

Davidson, Arnold. "Miracles of Bodily Transformation, or How St. Francis Received the Stigmata." In *Saints: Faith without Borders*, edited by Françoise Meltzer and Jaś Elsner, 451–480. Chicago: University of Chicago Press, 2011.

Di Giovine, Michael. "Making Saints, (Re-)Making Lives: Pilgrimage and Revitalization in the Cult of St. Padre Pio of Pietrelcina." PhD dissertation, University of Chicago, 2012.

Imbert-Gourbeyre, Antoine. *La Stigmatisation*. 2 vols. Translated by Joachim Bouflet. Paris: J. Millon, [1894] 1996.

Margnelli, Marco. "An Unusual Case of Stigmatization." *Journal of Scientific Exploration* 13(3) (1999): 461–482, http://www.scientificexploration.org/journal/jse_13_3_margnelli.pdf.

Ratnoff, Oscar D. "Stigmata: Where Mind and Body Meet." *Medical Times* 97(6) (1969): 150–163.

Thurston, Herbert. *The Physical Phenomena of Mysticism*. Edited by J. H. Crehan. London: Burns Oates and Washbourne, 1952.

Sufism and Miracles

For Sufis, the prospect of a saint's miracles is possible as long as the acknowledged source is God. In this respect Sufis do not differ from Christians. The Sufi has firm evidence that this is permitted within the pages of the Qur'an and the Sunna, or commentary, of the Prophet Muhammad. The prospect of sharing *barakah*—a grace or blessing—comes through the imparting of wisdom from a sheikh, or master. The master leads one to God, and it is God alone who sources the goodness behind the blessing. The possibility of attaining the miraculous blessing comes about for the sheikh only by passing through stages on the path (*tariqa*), and even then the miraculous can impede the ultimate pursuit of self-realization.

Miracles can become distractions along the way. In contrast to the sheikh, the imam or religious teacher is thought to have the ability to perform miracles from birth. While imams also have the ability to share blessings with the devoted, they are endowed with an intrinsic ability. Though these men may be able to perform miracles, for the Sufi the miracle itself is by God's gracious favor (*karamat*). They may be performed by two types of individuals: saints and prophets. *Karamat* (*charismata*) applies to the saints who, by their very actions, amaze. They do so because of their closeness and friendship with God. Examples include the attempted murder of Bastami, a mystic, who remained unscathed even while wounds were transferred to his assailants. *Mujizat* applies to prophetic persons whose powers are extraordinary (*khariq*) and unrepeatable for the vast majority of creatures. Fertility miracles occur under this heading whereby prediction is but child's play, though such prognostications hardly defy the natural order.

Sufi mystics, however, are often thought to be able to perform miracles practically at will. Their visions hold out an admixture of fantasy and pious hope. With the mystic Bistami we find him ascending to heaven, and he described his passage to the Footstool of God as fraught with tests but also home to angels who flew to Earth 100,000 times a day. The purity of his quest did not escape God, who turned Bistami into a bird who flew closer and closer to the Divine Footstool. At its threshold he met an angel who handed over to him a pillar of light that guided him to the Throne of the Almighty, whereupon God called to him and drew him close, for the purity of Bistami's desire to see the Holy One could not be doubted. And there in God's presence Bistami dissolved "as lead melts" when heated in fire, becoming like the souls of those who were not yet created, before there was existence of any kind, when only God "abode in solitude."

This intimacy with the transcendent is a particular kind of friendship reserved for the most devout. Often when encountering the writings of these "friends of God" they are drawn up with miracle stories as well as a teaching about the meaning of the miracle. Rumi is notable in this regard. In addition to an explication of a miracle, Rumi's narratives explore the dual effects of the relationship between the friends and God, namely, prophethood and law. In the divine communication there is the special grace whereby the mortal creature is made both aware and responsive. Prophecies are received from God and then communicated publicly. They are never stored up. True prophets were nearly always discouraged from learning this craft or technique through books. Abdul-Qadir Gilani is said to have bleached out by a miracle a philosophy text that he found objectionable. Other Sufis were instructed in dreams to throw their books into a river. *Firasa* (discernment) was also a common miracle worked by Sufi masters so that the uninitiated were cautioned to beware him who could read thoughts and hearts, for they see "by God's light."

Sharia also figures in the mystical union with the divine. Behavior is regulated accordingly; that is, with the advent of miraculous performances, the law becomes practically immaterial. If one is captivated toward positive ends, he or she can be capable of anything. The moral tenet does not hold when a person's mind, for all intents and purposes, is entranced by someone or something. Thus, the story of al-Haddad the blacksmith is told. He was a leading Sufi of the ninth century: "One day he was sitting in his shop listening to a blind man who was reciting the Koran in the bazaar. He became so absorbed in listening that he put his hand in the fire, and without using pincers, drew out a piece of molten iron from the furnace."

The mystic literature is supplemented by those who practice. Among the most visible practitioners are the dervishes. Within the Sufi moral tradition, the dervish is known not only for dancing in a whirling motion but also for supplying a short vignette that carries a life lesson. Thus, a story relates how a dervish was approached by a tax collector in his village. The dervish had earned his living by cultivating the land around his home, but the tax collector demanded a portion: "Look how many years you have cultivated land without paying any share of your produce, despite the abundance of your grain. Either pay your overdue taxes or perform a miracle." The dervish wondered what sort of miracle the tax collector expected of him, and so, refusing to pay up, the dervish was ordered to "Walk on the river, if indeed you can perform a miracle!" So the dervish set foot on the river and walked across to the other side as if walking on land. When he reached the far shore, he called back to the tax collector to send a boat to bring him back. "Why don't you just walk back?" he replied. The dervish answered, "One should not pander the lower self, otherwise it might think, 'At last I've become something!'"

The famed whirling dervish, a technique for meditation marked by spinning with outstretched hands, is mesmerizing. For the dervish, however, the mind is said to be transported to the realm of the divine. This takes work, and so the miraculous element in breaking free of this world to meet God is looked upon as both ridiculous and lazy by some Sufi writers. They see miracles as a short cut. Such subordination of rigorous training can draw out epithets. As one writer put it, "Miracles are the menstruation of men." Performing miracles, which demands a public audience for the wonder to take place, may be viewed as a form of narcissism.

That Sufis experience miracles of numerous varieties, however, is something the naysayers must confront. 'Abd ar-Rahman Jami, the celebrated poet and Sufi author from the second half of the fifteenth century, wrote that "There are very many types of events that disrupt conventions [*khavaraq-i 'adat*], such as making present something nonexistent and eliminating something existent; manifesting something hidden and obscuring something apparent; positive acceptance of invocatory prayer; covering the distance to a far-off place in a short period," and so on. Levitation is not unknown. Multiplication of foodstuffs is also common in Sufi literature. In any case, the mystical elements are of a piece with the moral components of such examples whereby the Sufi's ascetical life is made deeper.

Patrick J. Hayes

Further Reading

Aigle, Denise, ed. *Miracle et Karama: Hagiographies médiévales compares*. Turnhout: Brepols, 2000.

Bashir, Shahzad. *Sufi Bodies: Religion and Society in Medieval Islam*. New York: Columbia University Press, 2013.

Cornell, Vincent. *Realm of the Saint: Power and Authority in Moroccan Sufism*. Austin: University of Texas Press, 1998.

Dihlavī, Hassan, ed. *Nizam Ad-din Awliya: Morals for the Heart: Conversations of Shaykh Nizam Ad-din Awliya Recorded by Amir Hasan Sijzi*. Mahwah, NJ: Paulist Press, 1992.

Mojaddedi, Jawid. *Beyond Dogma: Rumi's Teachings on Friendship with God and Early Sufi Theories*. Oxford: Oxford University Press, 2012.

Renard, John, ed. *Tales of God's Friends: Islamic Hagiography in Translation*. Berkeley: University of California Press, 2009.

Schimmel, Annemarie. *Mystical Dimensions of Islam*. Durham: University of North Carolina Press, 2013.

Takim, Liyakat N. *The Heirs of the Prophet: Charisma and Religious Authority in Shi'ite Islam*. Albany: SUNY Press, 2012.

T

Televangelists

Television evangelists, or televangelists, are a new breed of preachers using television for religious discourse. These electronic broadcasts are also referred to as "electronic church." Television burst into the mass media scene around the 1950s, and gradually religious preachers made use of this powerful electronic medium to disseminate the teachings of Jesus Christ. By the 1970s and 1980s, the televangelist gurus made their presence in American homes. People preferred to listen to the gospel inside their home without going to churches. There were about 220 Christian networks and 1,370 religious radio stations by the 1980s. Religious broadcasting in the golden age of televangelism—from approximately 1980 to 1987—witnessed evangelical preachers telecasting sermons as well as asking for donations from the audience.

After the traditional missionaries, radio broadcast in the 1920s was the medium to preach the gospel. Radio evangelists soon gave way to televangelists. Catholic bishop Fulton J. Sheen was the the first televangelist in the early 1950s. Billy Graham took center stage afterward and became a world pastor with his nobility and integrity of character. The televangelists focusing on saving souls and reinforcing Christian life as per the teachings of Jesus garnered the audience support of viewers and gradually developed financial support. Some notable television preachers are Pat Robertson, Jim Bakker, Jimmy Swaggart, Joel Osteen, Jerry Falwell, Robert Schuller, Rod Parsley, Mark I. Pinsky, and Oral Roberts. Television evangelism has become a multimillion-dollar industry with an audience of over 20 million viewers globally. Televangelists endeavor to draw audiences to their ministries, as competition is stiff among them.

Televangelists are adept in telling about their ability to heal by extraordinary miraculous powers. Pat Robertson claimed to have direct communion with God. As a storm chaser, he could change the direction of hurricanes! Robertson's prediction of a global economic collapse in 1985 proved to be false. The televangelist

Peter Popoff talked of "miracle water" that would free a person from debt, and he marketed it through a website. In their broadcasts, some televangelists boasted of making people in wheelchairs walk and persons with back problems dance. Televangelists also claim to possess the power to heal by prayer. The claims are unverified, but the preachers harp on their miracles. Sexual misconduct and financial improprieties have sullied the reputation of televangelists. The Maryland pastor Robert J. Freeman ended up behind bars in a bankruptcy case. Televangelists had lavish lifestyles, with private jets, fleets of expensive cars, and millions of dollars stashed in banks. Broadcasters such as Kenneth and Gloria Copeland, Creflo and Taffi Dollar, Joyce and David Meyer, Benny Hinn, Eddie L. Long, and others have come under congressional investigation.

The majority of televangelists capitalize on Christianity and have proved to be false prophets. To their good fortune, they have gullible people in audiences believing in their so-called supernatural powers. As long as these gurus confined themselves with sermons and salvations, they were truly religious persons. But once they cross the boundary and begin soliciting money and hoodwinking desperate persons, their true nature is revealed.

Patit Paban Mishra

Further Reading

Hadden, J. K., and A. D. Shupe. *Televangelism*. New York: Holt, 1988.

Martz, Larry, and Ginny Carroll. *Ministry of Greed: The Inside Story of the Televangelists and Their Holy Wars*. New York: Weidenfeld and Nicolson, 1988.

McElvaine, Robert S. *Grand Theft Jesus: The Hijacking of Religion in America*. New York: Crown, 2008.

Schultze, Quentin J. *Televangelism and American Culture: The Business of Popular Religion*. Grand Rapids, MI: Baker, 1991.

Walton, Jonathan L. *Watch This! The Ethics and Aesthetics of Black Televangelism*. New York: New York University Press, 2009.

Thaumaturgy

The word "thaumaturge" comes from the Greek *thaumaturgos* and designates a person who works (*ergon*) wondrous things (*thaumathos*). Christianity took the word from Greek and transformed the wonder-worker into a miracle maker, one who could defy the laws of nature in the name of God. Such miracles can only operate in a differentiated world, one that offers a clear view of what belongs to the natural course of things and what constitutes a supernatural event. In such societies, certain individuals can be considered sacred, meaning that their closeness to the invisible provides them with the power and the ability to manifest divine will (hierophany). These people are not sacred by themselves; it is the social function they embody that allows them to act and to be recognized as such. In some cases, physical differences separate them from the normal world and qualify them as holy; such may be the case of albinos, dwarves, or twins. Holiness grants access to the divine without being the divine.

Thaumaturgy, as it is performed by individuals filling sacred social functions, is a miracle of healing. Through a divinity's will, the sick can be cured if deemed worthy of such grace. Accounts of thaumaturgy miracles performed by priests, saints, kings, prophets (such as Jesus Christ), the Virgin Mary, "monsters," sacred places, or objects show an impressive range of illnesses or weaknesses. Some of these, such as paralysis (total or partial), blindness, cough, rheumatism, hernia, or leprosy, constitute a fairly simple range of problems. Other cured afflictions prove to be more complex and must be apprehended in a particular social context. Christianity, for example, considered throughout Late Antiquity and the Middle Ages that illnesses were the work of the Devil. Thaumaturgy, in that case, is as much the action of healing the body as it is the purification of the soul. In some cases, the miracle can be directed at a situation such as imprisonment, a fighting wound, or the resurrection of a stillborn baby.

Individuals practicing thaumaturgy are said to be invested by holiness. In order to be recognized by their peers, they have to participate in an established institution. More precisely, the signs that are manifested through the miracle of healing or solving a disorderly situation have to be understood by everyone in order to be effective. The role of thaumaturgists as keepers of social order provides them with the power to restore that order when it is disrupted, elevating their miracles to more than simple generous gestures.

Thaumaturgy is usually achieved through direct ritual contact with the sacred through *virtus*, or holy power. However, while the touch of a holy person has been known to be effective, it is not absolutely necessary, as some objects and places are contaminated with the holiness of the original bearer. These objects, known as relics, become the host of divine power in what can be considered a substitution process. Relics vary in shape and form and can be classified in three main categories:

1. Bodily relics: hair, teeth, maternal milk, bones, skin, foreskin, etc.
2. Contact relics: clothes, thorn from a crown of thorns, cramp-rings used by the king of England, wax from a candle used in a sanctuary, water fountains, lakes, caves, etc.

3. Picture relics: the picture of a holy person can be used to perform a miracle by applying the picture on the part of the body that needs to be cured. The holy individual may also appear in dreams and vision and be as effective as the "real" person.

The ability to perform miracles, known as thaumaturgy, always depends on a divine will. Kings of France, Italy, Germany, and England have been known to cure various disease conditions, but it is important to remember that this power (the royal touch) was given to them by contact with the holy anointing oil. It is their function, not their personal charisma, that gives them *virtus*.

Geneviève Pigeon

Further Reading

Bloch, Marc. *The Royal Touch: Monarchy and Miracles in France and England*. New York: Dorset, 1990.

Eliade, Mircea. *The Sacred and the Profane: The Nature of Religion*. San Diego: Harcourt Brace Jovanovich, 1987.

Weber, Max. *The Sociology of Religion*. Boston: Beacon, 1993.

Thomas of Cantilupe

Saint Thomas Cantilupe (ca. 1218–August 25, 1282) is also known as Saint Thomas of Hereford for the cathedral in England where he was bishop from 1275 until his death. Thomas was descended from Norman barons on both sides. His father William of Cantilupe was seneschal during King John's reign, and his uncle Walter became bishop of Worcester in 1236 and was a close friend of Simon de Montfort during the Baron's Rebellion. Thomas studied at Oxford and Paris, attended the first Council of Lyons in 1245, and became a papal chaplain under Pope Innocent IV. After more studies in civil and canon law in Orleans and Paris, Thomas joined the faculty at Oxford in 1255 and was elected chancellor of the university in 1261.

In the fourteen years before he became bishop of Hereford Cathedral, Thomas supported Simon de Montfort in his cause against King Henry III, and after Simon's victory at the Battle of Lewes in May 1264, Thomas was elected chancellor of England until Henry's victory over Simon at the Battle of Evesham in August of that year. A stint as a teacher in Paris, a second term as chancellor at Oxford, and the gradual addition of ecclesiastical prebends eventually led to the bishopric at Hereford. As a councilor to King Edward I, Thomas held high standing until an argument with the archbishop of Canterbury in 1282 led to his excommunication. Thomas was appealing this sentence directly to the pope when he died in Italy that same year. Thomas's bones were laid to rest at Hereford Cathedral.

Miracles associated with Thomas were first recorded in 1287, the same year when his bones were moved to a new tomb in the north transept of the cathedral. An aggressive campaign for Thomas's canonization was undertaken by his successor at Hereford, Bishop Richard Swinfield, who spent the next 15 years compiling the necessary documentation and letters of support, including many from King Edward I and King Edward II. A number of inquiries, commissions, and hearings were held in England and Avignon between 1307 and 1320 until Pope John XXII finally canonized Saint Thomas in 1320 and set his feast day on October 2. King Edward II immediately started collecting donations for a new shrine for the saint, which wasn't completed until 1349. It is recorded that King Edward III, who had fallen ill on his way to the translation ceremony, was miraculously cured.

Saint Thomas's popular cult and the details of his many miracles are well documented. Recent scholars have pointed to the shockwave effect fanning out from the saint's tomb from 1287 through 1307 as well as the marked change in registered pilgrims from female to male as the saint's prestige and healing power became known. One of the interesting effects of Saint Thomas's sainthood was the establishment of a unique liturgical use at Hereford with its own set of rites and procedures. Although not as famous as the Sarum Use at Salisbury Cathedral, which actively competed in prestige and practice with the Roman rite during the late medieval period, the Hereford Use was one of only a few medieval English rites, with Sarum, York, and Lincoln perhaps the best known.

Among the more spectacular tales of miraculous intervention attributed to Saint Thomas was the release of a condemned Welsh man, William Cragh, who was dropped from the gallows in 1289 and, before nine witnesses, hung until dead. Cragh was removed from the place of his demise and, while presumed to be deceased, had entreated the saintly bishop to save him. Indeed, Cragh was resuscitated and became a witness in the canonization proceedings.

Bradford Lee Eden

Further Reading

Alington, Gabriel. *St. Thomas of Hereford*. Leominster, MA: Gracewing, 2001.

Bartlett, Robert. *The Hanged Man: A Story of Miracle, Memory, and Colonialism in the Middle Ages*. Princeton, NJ: Princeton University Press, 2004.

Finucane, Ronald C. *Miracles and Pilgrims: Popular Beliefs in Medieval England*. Totowa, NJ: Rowman and Littlefield, 1977.

Jancey, E. M. *St. Thomas of Hereford.* Isle of Wight: J. Arthur Dixon, 1978.
Jancey, E. M., ed. *St. Thomas Cantilupe, Bishop of Hereford: Essays in His Honour.* Hereford, UK: Friends of Hereford Cathedral, 1982.

Thorns

Pain is evocative of so much emotion, and the shock of a weapon such as a thorn piercing the flesh of another human being would make most cringe or recoil in disgust. That the human mind could fashion a vine of thorn branches into an instrument to encircle the cranium, thrusting it into the scalp and drawing out blood, is among the most barbarous acts ever devised. What is the value of such torture? For Christians, and especially those who accept a penal-substitution theory of Jesus Christ's crucifixion, his pain has redemptive purchase. The tangible relics of this event have been treasured as markers of the salvation of the world. Among these are the individual thorns that pierced his head.

According to three of the canonical Gospels, a woven crown of thorns was an instrument of Jesus's suffering and death on Golgotha. It is mentioned in the gospels of Matthew (27:29), Mark (15:17), and John (19:2, 5). After the death of Jesus, however, the gospels remain silent on what happened to the instruments of the Passion, though many believe that these were collected by his disciples and preserved near the sacred sites important for his life. They begin to appear with greater regularity, both for devotional purposes and thanks to the lifting of legal restrictions on Christian practice, only in the late fourth century.

Mention is made by those traveling through Jerusalem on pilgrimage of the great relics from biblical times. Egeria, a fourth-century Spanish pilgrim, notes how important it was for her to be in physical proximity to the things that she read about in the scriptures. It was her good fortune to be in Jerusalem during Holy Week—the seven days preceding Easter—when on Good Friday the cross of Christ was shown to the people. It had to be kept under heavy guard, she said, because once a pilgrim drew close to it and bit off a portion (*Itinerarium Egeriae*, 81:16–18). The preservation of passion relics were thus of paramount concern. They were coveted by the devout. Makrina (d. 379), the sister of the Church Father Gregory of Nyssa, carried a splinter of the cross in a ring around her neck.

Among contemporary writers of this period was Bishop Paulinus of Nola, who spoke about "the thorns with which Our Saviour was crowned" in addition to the cross and pillar upon which Jesus experienced the scourging (now in the Church of St. Prasseda in Rome). Saint Paulinus had owned a splinter of the cross, a portion of which he gave to a fellow bishop, Sulpicius Severus, and lodged the remainder in the altar in his cathedral at Nola. Saint Paulinus entrusted this gift to Severus with the admonition not to focus on the paucity of the relic but rather on the magnitude of what it represents. Big things come in little packages, he seemed to say.

For centuries the crown of thorns remained intact, at least up to the point when Gregory of Tours wrote his book *Glory of the Martyrs* (ca. 583–594). He records that the crown had miraculously maintained its youth, appearing still green hundreds of years later. Antoninus of Piacenza stated that the crown was on display in the Church on Mount Zion, and later reports suggest its presence there up to at least the year 870. At some point—again, not known precisely—Jesus's crown of thorns was entirely dismantled, and the thorns were parsed out to various sovereigns and bishops. Their multiplication seemed endless, and some scholars now put the number of extant thorns near 700. Emperor Justinian had already had a thorn removed and sent to Saint Germain, the bishop of Paris, sometime before the former died in 565. Around the turn of the century (ca. 800) Empress Irene sent a large cache of relics, including several thorns, to her son Charlemagne that now reside at the cathedral in Aachen, Germany. Many of these were later farmed out to important abbeys or families of Europe.

Thorn reliquaries were crafted to house the sacred relics in specially built chapels. The French were masters at this and often knit together both ecclesial and political power with the patronage of artisans who assembled these repositories. Between 1239 and 1241, Emperor Baldwin II of Constantinople supplied the crown of thorns reliquary to his cousin King Louis IX of France, partly as an attempt to cement better relations between East and West and to generate needed income in his battle with Bulgars and Greeks. The crown accompanied a string of other Passion relics, including remnants of the True Cross. Louis's piety found him humbly stripping off his royal robes and walking bare foot through Paris carrying the crown. It was ensconced in Sainte-Chapelle—a special reliquary chapel built for the reception of the crown—but now rests in the Cathedral of Notre Dame in Paris.

The large number of thorns that believers have suggested are relics of Christ's Passion invariably fail to mention that the thorns themselves may count as relics of greater or lesser importance, having merely been touched to original thorns over the years. Some indeed have been considered originals that pierced the flesh of Christ and drew some of the divine blood. Other thorns on the crown likely did not touch the sacred head but came into contact with other thorns nearby. Still others were later touched to the originals. Thorn reliquaries containing the spiny needles may be subject to disclaimers. Aside from the provenance of the thorns, however, is the prestige factor: who gives the thorn and to whom is it given? Many of

Europe's monarchs were honored to present the supposed relic, and the recipients took great pleasure in the ceremony and privilege of accepting. The Holy Thorn Reliquary in the British Museum, a gift of Ferdinand de Rothschild containing one thorn, was made for the French royal Jean, duc de Berry (1340–1416), in the 1390s, who was the recipient of many thorns from his brother, Charles V, as well as members of his family who were aware of Jean's devotions to Christ's Passion. The thorn is profusely ornamented with pearls, gold, and white enamels. The fact that this reliquary survived the British invasion of France—where after their victory at Agincourt Jean's possessions were destroyed—is testament to its miraculous power.

A catalog and gazetteer of thorns has been developed that attempts to account for the whereabouts of each thorn relic. For instance, two thorns given by Mary, Queen of Scots, to Thomas Percy, the earl of Northumberland, can be found in St. Michael's in Ghent and at Stonyhurst College in Lancashire, England. In Prague's St. Vitus Cathedral there is a thorn in the cross at the top of the crown of Saint Wenceslas, part of the Czech crown jewels. In Germany in the Trier Cathedral there is another thorn. Among the stational churches of Rome is the Basilica of Santa Croce in Gerusalemme, where a side chapel holds a reliquary with two thorns from the crown of thorns. In Spain in the Cathedral of San Salvador in Oviedo, there are five thorns. These are in the company of another famous relic, the ark containing the Sudarium, a blood-stained cloth alleged to have been wrapped around the head of Jesus Christ after he died (cf. John 20:6–7). Even in the United States, at St. Anthony's Chapel in Pittsburgh there is a single thorn from the crown.

Today the crown of thorns is somewhat indecorously made a part of lifelike reenactments in Passion plays around the globe. In the Philippines, Mexico, and even San Antonio, Texas, actors are made to suffer the torments inflicted on Christ, part of which includes a crowning with thorn branches.

Patrick J. Hayes

See also: Relics; Reliquary; St. Anthony's Relic Chapel

Further Reading

Bagnoli, Martina, et al. *Treasures of Heaven: Saints, Relics, and Devotion in Medieval Europe*. London: British Museum Press, 2011.

Cherry, John. *The Holy Thorn Reliquary*. London: British Museum Press, 2010.

Dillenberger, John. *Images and Relics: Theological Perceptions and Visual Images in Sixteenth-Century Europe*. New York: Oxford University Press, 1999.

Evans, Joan. "The Duke of Orléans' Reliquary of the Holy Thorn." *Burlington Magazine for Connoisseurs* 78:459 (1941): 196, 200–201.

Robinson, James. *Finer Than Gold: Saints and Their Relics in the Middle Ages*. London: British Museum Press, 2011.

Smith, Bennet. "The Holy Thorn Reliquary Reconsidered." PhD dissertation, Courtauld Institute of Art, 2006.

"Treasures of Heaven: Saints, Relics, and Devotion in Medieval Europe." Columbia University, http://www.columbia.edu/cu/arthistory/faculty/Klein/Sacred-Things-and -Holy-Bodies.pdf.

Van Dam, Raymond, trans. *Gregory of Tours: Glory of the Martyrs*. Liverpool: Liverpool University Press, 1988.

Tomb

Burial chambers of the deceased have been the site of innumerable miracles over the centuries. For Christians, the early martyrs were interred in catacombs, the niches of which served as a temporary resting place until such time as only the bones remained and could be placed in a charnel house or ossuary. The bone fragments of martyrs were treated with special reverence and were either marked as the location of a holy person's final place of rest or placed in a reliquary for preservation and display, often on the occasion of the anniversary of the person's death. Gradually these locations became sites of pilgrimage, particularly if the martyr's tomb had gained a reputation for miraculous cures.

Among the earliest narratives on the importance of a tomb as the locus for miraculous phenomena is the *De miraculis sancti Stephani*. This fifth-century text emerged from Uzalis, the site of the protomartyr Stephen's relics, and had been translated from Jerusalem. It describes a number of unusual occurrences around the tomb, from the reception of dreams and dialogues with Saint Stephen to the healing of a Carthaginian's jaw bone and the conversion of a pagan. In one of his sermons (323) Saint Augustine relays a separate story of a young catechumen who perished before baptism. His mother took him to the shrine of Saint Stephen, and the lad was revived long enough to be baptized and thus earn his heavenly reward.

Tombs as pilgrimage sites are legion in the Christian world. Among the more famous is the crypt at the Cathedral of Santiago de Compostela, Spain, where relics of Saint James the Apostle repose. It is the culmination of the Camino pilgrimage from the French Pyrenees to Galicia in northwestern Spain. In the Middle Ages, thieves often sought to rob tombs of the remains of holy people in order to sell them or enhance collections. The market for these relics among pious Christians was no doubt fueled by Rome itself. The city built a large economy on the strength of those buried there and the wonders that emerge around tombs.

Less well-known sites include the tomb of François of Paris, a Jansenist deacon whose tomb became renowned for miracles and was the controversial source of the movement that came to be known as the Convulsionnaires of St. Médard. Very quickly, the deacon's tomb was visited by pilgrims, who sought a bit of earth from the grave site as a relic of the holy man. Miracles were reported not only by those touching the gravestone but also by those who ingested a portion of the soil collected at the tomb. In 1728 about a year after François's death, the local bishop inaugurated a tribunal to investigate the alleged miracles. No one disputed his holiness in life, and his extreme asceticism and work on behalf of poor people were widely admired. Five miracles were brought forward for inspection, and in the end Cardinal Louis Antoine de Noailles pronounced François a blessed, though not in a canonical sense. At the urging of some Jansenists in Paris, the cardinal opened beatification proceedings for the deacon. In a few years some 800 cures were cataloged in a sensational three-volume study and ultimately proved to be the downfall of the movement. Many highly placed prelates and philosophers cast doubt on the cases so that within a decade, the tomb and the convulsionnaires became subject to ridicule and disdain.

In the last century in the United States, Father Patrick Power's tomb in Malden, Massachusetts, was also a temporary but highly sensational site for alleged miracles. The young priest had died of tuberculosis in 1869. Sixty years later during the very week of the stock market crash of 1929, Power's grave was making headlines for purported cures. Soon a steady stream of pilgrims were coming to Holy Cross Cemetery, and the Catholic cardinal of Boston, William O'Connell, was forced to close the cemetery for fear of the enormous crowds who jostled for a small sample of earth from around Power's grave. Many were there to collect "holy water" that had collected in an imprinted chalice carved into the grave's marble slab. Today the tomb is often visited by local devotees who leave *ex votos* or small slips of paper attached to the fence surrounding the tomb. For the untold favors granted, the notes typically read "Thank you, Father Power."

Patrick J. Hayes

See also: Martyrs

Further Reading

Collins, Joseph. *The Miracles at the Tomb of B. François de Paris*. New York: William Wood, 1908.

"De miraculis sancti Stephani libri duo, II.2." In *Les miracles de saint Étienne: Recherches sur le recueil pseudo-augustinien (BHL 7860–7861) avec édition critique, traduction et commentaire*, edited by Jean Meyers, Hagiologia 5. Turnhout: Brepols, 2006.

Geary, Patrick. *Furta Sacra: Thefts of Relics in the Central Middle Ages*. Princeton, NJ: Princeton University Press, 1991.

Hayes, Patrick J. "Massachusetts Miracles: Controlling Cures in Catholic Boston, c. 1929." In *Saints and Their Cults in the Atlantic World*, edited by Margaret Cormack, 111–127. Columbia: University of South Carolina Press, 2007.

Strayer, Brian E. *Suffering Saints: Jansenists and Convulsionnaires in France, 1640–1799*. Brighton, UK: Sussex Academic Press, 2008.

Toothache Cures

Toothache was a major problem in medieval Europe. The pattern of dental disease was different from that found today, and chronic gum disease was particularly common because of poor oral hygiene. Unlike modern times, there was little in the way of dental treatment and certainly no anaesthetics. One could try one of the herbal remedies recommended for toothache, possibly have recourse to an itinerant tooth drawer, or visit the local blacksmith to have an aching tooth extracted, but if that was not possible, what else was available? Fortunately, there was a patron saint for sufferers of toothache: Saint Apollonia, an aged virgin, martyred in 249 CE, having first had all her teeth knocked out before being burned to death. Many people would have sought the prayers of Saint Apollonia to help cure their toothache. Her popularity can be seen from the fact that there are over 60 representations of her (shown holding a pair of pincers containing an enormous molar) in medieval churches in England, mainly in the eastern and southwestern counties. Other people would have prayed to their own favorite saint, perhaps the saint whose name they bore. Besides Saint Apollonia, there were other saints who seem to have had a specialty for curing toothache. A review of the literature, both in printed form and online, will reveal quite a long list of saints said to have provided miracle cures for toothache. However, there is little good evidence to support such claims. The saints for whom there are primary sources (contemporary documents) or reliable secondary sources to support these miracle claims include Saint Thomas of Canterbury, Saint William of Norwich, and Saint Osmund (bishop of Salisbury), the latter for whom one witness is quoted in the petition for canonization as stating that he knows of more than 100 miracles of curing toothache brought about by the bishop. Sometimes a specific relic had to be visited in order to receive the miracle, such as going on pilgrimage to Thetford in Norfolk to where the smock of Saint Etheldreda of Ely was kept.

John F. Beal

Further Reading

Blanton-Whetsell, Virginia. "Tota integra, tota incorrupta: The Shrine of St. Ethelthryth as Symbol of Monastic Autonomy." *Journal of Medieval and Early Modern Studies* 32(2) (Spring 2002): 227–267.
Phillips, David. *Exhibiting Authenticity*. Manchester, UK: Manchester University Press, 1996.

Transcendentalism and Miracles

A debate over biblical miracles contributed to the formation of the loose coalition of American Transcendentalists. The New England polemic erupted in 1836, when Unitarians Andrews Norton and George Ripley squared off in a pamphlet war over Christ's miracles. When Ripley championed an intuition-based religious experience and critiqued the evidentialist tie between Jesus's miracles and his Gospel message, Norton damned his reasoning as heretical and forcefully reasserted the link between Christian faith and the historicity of the New Testament accounts of Christ's miracles. This first foray in the miracles controversy helped establish boundary markers between Unitarians, who grounded their faith in historical evidences, and Transcendentalists, who posited that religious truth emanated from outside and above temporality.

In his infamous Harvard Divinity School Address (1838), Ralph Waldo Emerson delivered a powerful blow against the Unitarian position. He agreed that Christ "spoke of miracles" but in the sense that "man's life was a miracle." The Galilean's salvific message rested not in atonement but rather in the fact that he was "the only soul in history who has appreciated the worth of man." Drawing attention to the assumed dichotomy between nature and miracle, the Sage of Concord lamented that the word "is not one with the blowing clover and the falling rain." He proposed that verbal misuse had turned "Miracle" into an epistemological "Monster." Belief in Christianity had mistakenly come to rest on whether or not the Gospels' miracles reflected ancient realities. In stressing the indwelling presence of the divine in nature and, above all else, in the soul, Emerson struck at Unitarianism's foundation of belief.

Fellow Transcendentalist Theodore Parker, who uniquely wrestled with German biblical scholarship, acutely understood the potential danger involved in constructing Christian faith on history's shifting grounds. He most fully entered the debate through a pseudonymous 1839 publication, written in response to Norton's latest attack. Parker traced the universal presence of an innate religious sense. He found in Christianity "the highest form of religion" and believed that "Jesus . . . wrought miracles" but saw "not how a miracle proves a doctrine," which allowed him to sidestep "some historical difficulties in the way of establishing *all* the miracles which [Jesus] wrought."

Attending to context, Parker pointed out the "tendency to the marvelous in all ancient nations, especially among the Jews," and of the evangelists he argued that "their inspiration did not free them from the notions of the age and nation." He still believed in "the *general* accuracy of their history of Christ." The issue was not whether Christ had existed or performed miracles but whether the truth of Christianity rested on the miracles he had presumably performed.

When figures such as Norton argued that historical circumstances shaped biblical content but resisted viewing descriptions of Christ's miracles as historically conditioned productions, Parker highlighted the shakiness of their chosen foundation. "You make our religion depend entirely on something outside, on strange events which happened, it is said, 2,000 years ago, of which we can never be certain." Historical distance fostered historical skepticism, and Parker preferred a foundation less susceptible to deterioration.

The miracles controversy followed from a number of developments, including the growing emphasis on a historical explication of the Bible, and had a number of implications, including the establishment of religious identities on historical and nonhistorical foundations. Thus, the sustained focus on Christ's miracles gave impetus and shape to the formation of Transcendentalism in response to Unitarianism.

Jordan Tuttle Watkins

Further Reading

Blodgett, Levi [Theodore Parker]. "The Previous Question between Mr. Andrews Norton and His Alumni Moved and Handled, in a Letter to All Those Gentlemen (1840)." In *Transcendentalism: A Reader*, edited by Joel Myerson, 260–280. New York: Oxford University Press, 2000.

Emerson, Ralph Waldo. "An Address Delivered before the Senior Class in Divinity College." In *The Collected Works of Ralph Waldo Emerson*, Vol. 1, edited by Robert E. Spiller and Alfred R. Ferguson, 76–93. Cambridge, MA: Belknap Press of Harvard University Press, 1971.

Grodzins, Dean. *American Heretic: Theodore Parker and Transcendentalism.* Chapel Hill: University of North Carolina Press, 2002.

Hurth, Elizabeth. *Between Faith and Unbelief: American Transcendentalists and the Challenge of Atheism.* Leiden: Brill, 2007.

Trees

Cross-culturally and certainly in many religious traditions, trees are not just natural resources or aesthetically pleasing but are significant phenomena imbued with power capable of miracles. Trees have been part of human spirituality and belief since time immemorial. Sacred trees relate to the idea of creation, fecundity, initiation, reality, immortality, and the supernatural. Whether individually or collectively, standing or carved, trees have symbolic meanings that transcend the social, economic, political, and religious spectra of human life. The miraculous nature of trees among the world's belief systems is often linked to the veneration of saints, and trees are made the objects of prayer, healing, and ritual pilgrimage.

In the New Testament, trees are often employed as teaching devices by Jesus. In the miracle of the fig tree, for instance, we find that once cursed by Jesus it withers (Mark 11:12–14, 20–24). The parable is not lost on listeners, who take it that the same fate could befall Israel.

Sacred trees in Irish history span from pre-Christianity through the Christian eras. The Abbey of Fore in County Westmeath in Ireland boasts a nearby tree that could not burn. One legend attaching to it is its association with the abbey's founder, Saint Feichin, in the seventh century. The water collected by this tree is also believed to miraculously heal sick children. Another ancient Irish saint was Saint Brigid (sometimes Brigit or Bridget), who established her famed monastic community at Cill-Dara—the "Church of the Oak"—now known as Kildare, which once possessed an oak tree important to druids. Among Brigid's miracles is the curse she placed upon fruit trees belonging to a greedy person. They were immediately made barren. Conversely, a generous person was granted the favor of a large tree whose produce was twofold. Another famous Irish saint, Columba, is said to have raised his hand against an apple grove that produced bitter fruit, turning the apples to a most favorable sweetness.

Other Christian contexts involved the veneration of trees. Apart from trees serving as sites of worship and fellowship, some early Christian legends describe how saints could move trees by supernatural utterances through prayer and faith. Martin of Tours, for instance, was in the process of cutting down a sacred pine tree of the pagans. Just as it began to tip in his direction, he stretched out his hand and made it sway toward the unbelievers. In the seventeenth-century Low Countries, fascination with miracle trees continued unabated. Just outside of Brussels sat a large oak containing a carving of the Virgin Mary with her child Jesus in her arms, placed there by survivors of the plague in 1637. Many miracles were attributed to the so-called Jesus Oak—including over 400 between 1920 and 1940.

Trees have been employed in reckoning with natural disorders of various kinds. Among the Mapuche people of South America, shamans of the *foye* tree are consulted for provision of water in times of drought. They are also believed to have divine healing power over any kind of sickness. In some African religions it is believed that the nuts of palm trees could miraculously make a barren woman mother of many offspring. Often trees have been used to miraculously cure a victim or the land. The *obo* tree (*Erythrophleum surveolens*) is sacred in the Yoruba religion, mostly practiced in southwestern Nigeria. Its importance is vested in Yoruba cosmology. Among other uses, the *obo* is known for its power to repel evil spirits or witches. In traditional Yoruba beliefs, the *obo* tree or any of its elements, such as bark or leaves, provides a recipe for miraculously walling off evil spirits or witches, effectively extinguishing their power. The tree is also used to prepare concoctions or sacrifices to heal a victim of the attack of the evil spirits or witches.

Trees may also be agents of miracles because of their economic and ritual values. The palm tree (*Elaesis guineisis*) is a good example. Among the Yorubas all parts of a palm tree, from the fruit to the root, are useful for livelihood. Palm oil is extracted from the fruit, and palm kernel oil is used in soap making or as oil lotion. The nutshell is used as fuel in industrial or domestic firing, and brooms are made from the leaf veins. Palm wine is tapped from the tree, the trunk is used in construction, and the roots are used as herbs, mostly for medicinal purposes. In addition, the leaf is considered sacred to ward off intruders and evils. Palm leaf is regarded as the cloth of the deities.

Abidemi Babatunde Babalola

See also: Ireland, Miracles in; Jesus, Miracles of

Further Reading

Awolalu, Omosade. *Yoruba Beliefs and Sacrificial Rites*. London: Longmans, 1979.

Bagigalupo, Ana Mariella. *Shamans of the Foye Tree: Gender, Power, and Healing among Chilean Mapuche*. Austin: University of Texas Press, 2007.

Cusack, Carole. *The Sacred Tree: Ancient and Medieval Manifestations*. Newcastle, UK: Cambridge Scholars Publishing, 2011.

Harline, Craig. *Miracles at the Jesus Oak: Histories of the Supernatural in Reformation Europe*. New York: Doubleday, 2003.

Zucchelli, Christine. *Trees of Inspiration: Sacred Trees and Bushes of Ireland*. Wilton, CT: Collins, 2009.

U

Understanding, Miracles of

The ability to understand, interpret, or cognitively absorb complex data, especially in spectacular fashion or despite intellectual deficits, is sometimes called miraculous. Ordinary predictability of some turn of events could also be confounded by the gift of understanding, which is somehow able to factor all variables and lay the odds correctly every time. From prognostication to mind reading, the ability to overcome barriers that are generally normal aspects of uncertainty or misunderstanding places the actions of agents in a different light.

The world's religions have named this power variously. For Buddhists, for instance, the power of extraordinary knowledge is called *abhijñā*. Those savants who are able to remember past lives or comprehend reality with absolute purity and truth are said to have become awakened. In the process, successful attainment of this state, *rddhi*, means that they can perform additional feats that defy the natural order: flying through the air, passing through solid objects, bilocation, and so forth. In some traditions, especially in South Asia, Buddhists see certain yogic practices as paving the way toward *rddhi*, and the texts of the Pali canon are instructive. The practice of mindfulness (*sati* in Pali) can be seen as a kind of exercise for memory and learning that allows people to cut through the extraneous or obfuscating elements of daily life. Such an unclouded vision of reality enables the practitioner to achieve understanding, which ultimately eschews attachments to the natural world in order to yield complete freedom.

In Christianity the sense of clarity of comprehension is sometimes described as xenoglossa—a kind of gift of tongues. The prospect of absorbing information and interpreting or translating it despite one's particular intellectual or social deficits has been considered of supernatural origin. No human power could arrive at such wisdom. This was especially true for the medieval beguine communities, where devout lay women would often parse biblical narratives well beyond their knowledge. Thus, the Spiritual Franciscan Angelo Clareno (d. 1337) is said to have mastered the whole Greek language in the space of one evening in order to translate difficult theological texts into Latin. Saint Catherine of Siena reported to her spiritual director Raymond of Capua that she had the good fortune of being taught to read and write by none other than Saints John the Baptist and Thomas Aquinas. They came to her in her dreams, she said, and empowered her—an otherwise illiterate woman—to read the Psalms and other prayers of the Divine Office.

Whether schooled by grace or some other means, Christian saints have also had remarkable abilities to read minds or know the thoughts of others. Saint Pio of Pietrelcina is one such case. Not only could this friar read thoughts, especially in the confessional, but he was often apparently precognizant of future events. One might call this a kind of Rain Man syndrome in which, though rare, certain individuals on one end of an autism spectrum are equipped with problem-solving abilities beyond those of ordinary human beings.

Patrick J. Hayes

Further Reading

Clough, Bradley S. "The Higher Knowledges in the Pāli *Nikāyas* and *Vinaya*." *Journal of the International Association of Buddhist Studies* 33(1–2) (2010): 409–433.

Cooper-Rompato, Christine F. *The Gift of Tongues: Women's Xenoglossia in the Later Middle Ages*. University Park: Pennsylvania State University Press, 2010.

Fiordalis, David. "Abhijñā/Rddhi (Extraordinary Knowledge and Powers)." Oxford Bibliographies, http://www.oxfordbibliographies.com/view/document/obo-9780195393521/obo-9780195393521-0112.xml.

Fiordalis, David V., ed. "Miracles and Superhuman Powers in South and Southeast Asian Buddhist Traditions." *Journal of the International Association of Buddhist Studies* 33(1–2) (2010): 381–554.

Jacobsen, Knut A., ed. *Yoga Powers: Extraordinary Capacities Attained through Meditation and Concentration*. Leiden: Brill, 2012.

United States, Miracles in

The peculiar puzzle of the United States, from its pre- to postcolonial past, is an amalgam of Spanish and French interests that eventually brush up against an English presence that controls up until the turn of the nineteenth century. The religious history of the places where these nations held sway is particularly fraught. But whereas Spanish and French missions into the northern and southern tiers of what eventually became America helped to give a particular religious language and set of traditions to the people there, the English uncorked a largely experimental form of Christianity that set itself apart from the Catholics (and Protestants) of Europe. Only in the last two centuries has Catholic Christianity been assimilated and then only gradually.

The concept of miracles arising in the English colonies was polemically charged. Some of this was carried over from popular diatribes published in England. The sixteenth-century English controversialist John Foxe wrote a lengthy and polemical treatise, which has come to be known as Foxe's Book of Martyrs, about the indignities visited upon Anglicans by Catholics under the reign of Catholic monarchs. "Papists," as he referred to Catholics, were evil. Persecution, according to Foxe, was inherent in their nature, and so they were worthy of being loathed. For Foxe, "it is only when the heart has been renewed and sanctified by divine grace that men have rightly understood and practiced the true principles of toleration." The book was published well into the nineteenth century in the United States, helping to fuel concern over the immigration of Catholics into the new republic.

The Puritans saw miracles as being confined to the biblical narratives and looked askance at the suggestion that they continued to occur to ordinary mortals. Jonathan Edwards, writing in 1723, noted that papist Catholics wished to pervert the term by calling their Eucharistic theology a parody of the truth. "Another miracle that they make men believe they work, is the changing of bread and wine into the body and blood of Christ, making ten thousand bodies of Christ, that shall yet be the same body, and the same with that in heaven. This is a miracle indeed! None of the prophets, nor apostles, nor Jesus Christ himself, ever did the like of this. This is a miracle that God himself cannot do!" Nevertheless, by the time of Edwards's own great awakening, people routinely reported "angel sightings" that helped to give them a sense of comfort over against a determinative worldview. Such visions, however, probably had more to do with the anxieties of early American settlers than the intrusion of God into human affairs.

Subsequent generations of American clergymen were no less sanguine about the power of miracles, at least as they were expressed by Catholics. Alexander Campbell (1788–1866), a Scotch-Irish immigrant and ordained minister in the United States, was a reformer in the Restoration Movement, also known as the Stone-Campbell Movement, whereby followers of Barton Stone merged with those of Campbell. Their congregations self-identified as Disciples of Christ, among other appellations. Campbell was greatly influenced by Scottish Enlightenment philosophy and called miracles, in the Jewish and Christian sense, displays of supernatural power in attestation of the truth of a message from God. In brief, the biblical prophecies of yore, some of which were playing out before contemporary American eyes, had to be shored up with evidence. Miracles had a utilitarian function, "for with us miracles or supernatural facts are alike necessary to true morals as to true religion. Evidence and authority are demanded alike by conscience as by reason, before we make a perfect surrender of ourselves to the dictates of piety and humanity." In other words, the claims of religion upon any thinking being demand a proof. For Campbell, "miracles are a seal of a [biblical] message."

The linking of miracles to the wider problem of the supernatural was forcefully argued by Horace Bushnell in his book *Nature and the Supernatural*. Against a more Transcendentalist view that the realm of nature was wholly distinct from what lay above it in the celestial realm, Bushnell sought to make it abundantly clear that the bonds between the natural and supernatural worlds were tighter than one might imagine. Later, theologians at Princeton, including James McCosh, the university's president (1868–1888), debated the necessity of miracles in coming to faith. These preachers and academics were supplemented in their studies by lesser lights such as Emma Hardinge Britten, who sought to collect numerous accounts of "spiritualist" happenings from around the globe but particularly in the United States. Her book *Nineteenth Century Miracles* took up a broad subject matter: drawings by spirit power, the passage of matter through matter, and hauntings and obsessions, or speaking in foreign tongues. For the general population, the prospects of confusing miracles and magic were as likely as investing faith in advertised potions or elixirs to cure various ailments.

Catholics, however, made their mark in America through the lives of their seventeenth-, eighteenth-, and nineteenth-century saints. Many of these were martyrs. In 1930, Pope Pius XI canonized six French Jesuit missionaries and their two lay companions. Three of these men, the famous Isaac Jogues (1607–1646) and his two donnés, or lay assistants, René Goupil (1608–1642) and Jean de la Lande (d. 1646), endured violent deaths near Albany, New York, between 1642 and 1646. The other five Jesuits included Jean de Brébeuf (1593–1649) and his confrères Gabriel Lalemant (1610–1649), Antoine Daniel (1610–1648), Charles Garnier (1605–1649), and Noël Chabanel (1613–1649). These priests died at the hands of the Iroquois in present-day Ontario between 1648 and early 1649. These men, America's first saints, are better known collectively as the North American Martyrs. More than one commentator, however, dismissed their miracles—as well as their sainthood—as mere Catholic superstition.

It therefore became important for Catholics in America to give their Protestant neighbors some signs that miracles could occur in the United States, that it was not merely a European phenomenon, and that they could attach to American citizens, both the foreign-born transplants and natives. Beginning in the 1820s, Ann Mattingly—a devout Catholic and sister of a Washington, D.C., mayor—developed breast cancer that put her through terrible agonies. From her home in Georgetown, however, she and her associates joined the prayer novena of Father Alexander Leopold Franz Emmerich, prince of Hohenlohe-Waldenburg-Schillingsfürst (d. 1849) and miracle-working priest in Germany. Her cure was not immediately accepted by Washington society, in part due to antiforeign sentiment then circulating in Washington, the culmination of which came from President James Monroe's famous doctrine of European nonintervention.

Similarly, miracles for the cause of Saint Peter Claver also had a tepid reception. Though all of the miracles used in his canonization cause originated in the United States, he was a saint from another continent in the era of Spanish colonization. But for ethnic German Catholics in mid-nineteenth-century America, his story was readily adopted because all of the cures favored this group. One of Claver's miracles included the healing of Ignatius Strecker, a German immigrant and father of nine living in St. Louis. He had worked in a soap-making factory when in 1861 his breastbone was struck by a piece of heavy machinery. An infection set in, and he developed symptoms of tuberculosis coupled by intense pain. As the malady progressed, he prepared himself for death but not before acquiescing to his wife, who hoped that a final visit to his local church of St. Joseph would bring some relief. That came on March 16, 1864. At the time, a Jesuit missionary named Francis Xavier Weninger was passing through with a relic of the Jesuit Peter Claver, the so-called Apostle to the Negroes. Weninger preached on Claver's curative powers and after services applied the relic to whomever wished. Mrs. Strecker believed that Claver was the only one who could help her husband. According to the contemporary description of the event, "The next day, with the last ounce of his strength, he literally dragged himself to St. Joseph's Church and came in just as Father Weninger was blessing the sick with the relic. With sincere faith and strong confidence he placed himself in the line of the sick. Father Weninger blessed him and allowed him to kiss the relic." By the time Strecker returned home his wounds were already healing, and within 10 days all signs of his tuberculosis had vanished. There was no relapse. Strecker died in 1880 of typhoid. The miracle was authenticated in 1887, and Claver was canonized the following year.

The first American citizen to be canonized as a saint was Mother Francesca Cabrini (1850–1917), who was raised to the altars in 1946. The saintly convert Elizabeth Ann Seton (1774–1821) was the first native-born American canonized in 1975. Most recently, the so-called Lily of the Mohawks, Kateri Tekakwitha (1656–1680), was canonized by Pope Benedict XVI in 2012—a significant moment for the Americas in that her canonization made her the first female from an indigenous population to be recognized, and her cause was active the longest.

Most miracles attached to members of the clergy or to nuns. Of the scores of miracles attributed to America's first male saint, Saint John Neumann, three were used for his canonization cause. The first is that of an eleven-year-old Italian girl, Eva Benassi, who in 1923 was healed from an acute case of peritonitis. She had received the last rites of the Church when her teacher, Sister Elizabeth Romoli, began to pray to Bishop Neumann for a miracle. The nun applied a picture of the bishop to Eva's abdomen. Both the family and her convent joined in prayer for the little girl, and the next morning the life-threatening illness had vanished. By December 1960 in the last examination before Neumann's beatification, Eva, then 48 and a mother of two, was in perfect health.

Neumann's other two miracles both occurred in the United States. On July 8, 1949, nineteenth-year-old Kent Lenahan of Villanova, Pennsylvania, was standing on the running board of a moving car. Suddenly the car swerved out of control, crushing Lenahan against a utility pole. When he arrived at Bryn Mawr Hospital his skull was crushed, his collarbone was broken, and one of his lungs was punctured by a rib. He was bleeding from ears, nose and mouth and was comatose. His temperature and pulse were elevated. Doctors thought that there was no hope of recovery. Lenahan's parents prayed while in front of Bishop Neumann's tomb and later applied a first-class relic to their son. Shortly afterward a marked response was seen in Kent's vital signs. Five weeks after the accident, Lenahan walked unaided from the hospital.

Finally, a West Philadelphia six-year-old, Michael Flanigan, was suffering from Ewing's Sarcoma, a form of bone cancer. The cancer had spread, and as with the others, no hope of recovery was offered. The Flanigan family took Michael to the Bishop Neumann Shrine at St. Peter the Apostle Church, and after several visits to the bishop's tomb, he began to exhibit signs of renewed health. By Christmas of 1963, though he was near death, all signs of Ewing's Sarcoma had vanished. In December 1975 after a final examination of Michael's medical records, the Medical Board of the Vatican's Congregation for Saints' Causes declared that his cure was "scientifically and medically unexplainable."

Among women religious, aid was given to a Colorado Springs boy in 1999 when two Sisters of St. Francis of Perpetual Adoration prayed to their foundress, Mother Theresia Bonzel (d. 1905). The nuns hoped their prayers would be answered, curing then four-year-old Luke Burgie from a severe gastro-intestinal condition that his doctors couldn't relieve. He suffered for six months with episodes of diarrhea eight to ten times a day. He was deprived of schooling, stopped growing, and was slowly wasting away. The illness vanished suddenly on February 22, 1999, just as two members of Bonzel's order finished praying a novena.

In July 2013, the cure of eight-year-old Michael Mencer's irreversible juvenile macular degeneration in the 1960s was accepted as medically inexplicable by panels of ophthalmologists in Rome and in the United States. The Congregation for Saints' Causes determined that the miraculous restoration of sight to Michael

Mencer occurred by prayer through the intercession of Venerable Sister Miriam Teresa Demjanovich (1901–1927). Her beatification—the first to take place on American soil—occurred on October 4, 2014, at the Cathedral Basilica of the Sacred Heart in Newark, New Jersey.

Other causes for sainthood involve clerics. In June 2014, a miracle attributed to the erstwhile televangelist Catholic archbishop Fulton Sheen (d. 1979) was confirmed by the Congregation for Saints' Causes. It involved a baby born in September 2010. He showed no signs of life for an hour after birth, despite the best efforts of medical professionals to revive him. The boy's family prayed to Sheen for help, and the child's health was inexplicably restored.

Another is that of Father Michael McGivney, a nineteenth-century priest of the Archdiocese of Hartford and founder of the Knights of Columbus. His cause for sainthood began in 1997. Born in Waterbury, Connecticut, he was ordained in Baltimore in 1877. He began his ministry in New Haven, where he founded the Knights of Columbus, but was transferred to Thomaston in 1884 to take up a pastorate there. In 1890 he contracted pneumonia and died at age 38. Many favors have been credited to him: from relieving a toothache to surviving cancer to a deathbed recovery.

Among other priests awaiting recognition of miracles are Monsignor Nelson Baker, a priest who served the Diocese of Buffalo and has been declared venerable. Priests whose causes are in the preliminary stages include the Reverend Vincent Robert Capodanno, a military chaplain killed in Vietnam, and the Reverend Augustus Tolton of Chicago, who was the son of slaves and is said to have been the first American diocesan priest of African descent. There is also the cause of the Servant of God Joseph Parater, a seminarian who died in 1920 of rheumatic fever while in studies in Rome. He is buried in the North American College Mausoleum in the Campo Verano cemetery in Rome.

Unusual phenomena have occurred in every state in America and in a variety of ways. Some are tied to a particular place, such as a church, shrine, or tomb. Apparitions of the Blessed Virgin Mary began in the mid-nineteenth century. Among the earliest and best documented is the one occurring on October 9, 1859, to a Belgian farmer named Adele Brise (1831–1896). The first appearance near Robinsonville, Wisconsin, took place in a wooded area, where Mary dazzled in a long white gown with a yellow sash. A crown of stars illumined her head—not unlike the Virgin who appeared to Saint Catherine Labouré (d. 1876). The Madonna instructed Adele to evangelize and spread the catechism. When she told her parents what happened, they thought she was out of her mind, but while Adele was on her way to Mass on October 15, the Virgin appeared again, announcing herself as the "Queen of Heaven who prays for the conversion of sinners." Mary departed with a warning that if people did not convert, her son would be obliged to punish them. For the next two years, Adele was busied building a chapel and St. Mary's Academy on the site.

In October 1871 the largest fire ever recorded in American history—approximately 1.2 million acres—swept through northern Wisconsin, encircling Adele's chapel and school. She invited many local residents to take shelter from this fire, and the property was the only patch of earth for miles that was not reduced to ash. By then Adele's cult was growing, and the local bishop, Joseph Melchior, sought to reign her in. As a modern-day Joan of Arc, Adele's voice would not be quieted. In 1880 a third chapel of brick was built, and for the next sixteen years Adele taught catechism classes and conducted paraliturgies until she died in 1896. For two generations, the memory of Adele Brise was kept alive. In 1941, Bishop Paul Rhode of Green Bay laid the cornerstone for the present church—Our Lady of Good Help. In 2009 an investigation was opened on Adele's visions, and the following year Bishop David Ricken of Green Bay declared them authentic, making them the first approved apparitions in the United States. Today the shrine is dressed with crutches from miracle cures and other *ex votos*.

Miracles are not bound geographically, but place seems to matter. In Canton, Ohio, for instance, a home once owned by Rhoda Wise (1888–1948) became a local legend. Ill or near death for much of her later years, Wise recited prayers to Jesus for consolation and healing. She also turned to Saint Thérèse of Lisieux, whose cult was wildly popular during the Great Depression. One night Jesus appeared while Wise was having difficulty recuperating after surgery to remove a large tumor. Wondering whether Jesus was there to collect her, he replied that her time had not yet come. Apparitions of Saint Thérèse followed after attempts to repair a malformed foot. The saint told her to get up and walk after her cast was split open from top to bottom. The sight caused Wise's husband to give up drinking and reform as a father to their adopted daughter. Eventually Wise was gifted with the stigmata, wounds that afflicted her for two years. Statues that surrounded her at the end of her life wept, and visitors to her makeshift shrine were cured. Some of Wise's friends who learned of these happenings had brought rose petals for Jesus and Saint Thérèse to bless. Many left seeing that the petals had an image of the saint emblazoned on them.

Finally, in an age when newspapers could rally the attention of thousands virtually overnight, two miracle narratives inflamed the devotions of Catholics in Boston and New York as well as other parts of the world. The first involved the grave site of a Boston priest, Patrick Power. Buried since 1869 in the priests' plot of Holy Cross Cemetery in Malden, Massachusetts, his tomb had dozens of purported miracles associated with it beginning in 1929. Pilgrims came from all over the United States to collect a bit of earth near the grave or to scoop out rainwater that had collected in the chalice of his tombstone. Crowds grew so unwieldy and unrelenting that the cardinal of Boston closed the cemetery to all but family. A clamor was raised to nominate Power for sainthood, but no action was ever taken. Generations later, people still leave *ex votos* around the site.

In the Bronx, young Joseph Vitola Jr., age nine, became a minor celebrity when the Virgin Mary appeared to him on the Grand Concourse in 1945. In the days that followed, and after much ink was spilled in the local press, Vitola joined about 25,000 others in a prayer vigil on the spot where Mary initially greeted him. The press continued to hang on his every word, and a grotto resembling the apparition at Lourdes was built nearby, lending credence to the observation that Vitola, like Bernadette Soubirous, was a poor child and visionary who fell into a classic pattern for visits by the Blessed Virgin.

Patrick J. Hayes

See also: Georgetown Miracles; Hohenlohe-Waldenburg-Schillingsfürst, Prince Alexander Leopold Franz; Latin America, Miracles in; Redemptorists and Miracles; Stigmata

Further Reading

Anderson, Emma. *The Death and Afterlife of the North American Martyrs*. Cambridge, MA: Harvard University Press, 2014.

Britten, Emma Hardinge. *Nineteenth Century Miracles: Or, Spirits and Their Work in Every Country of the Earth; A Complete Historical Compendium*. New York: William Britten, 1883.

Bushnell, Horace. *Nature and the Supernatural as Together Constituting the One System of God*. 4th ed. New York: Scribner, 1859.

Campbell, Alexander. *The Writings of Alexander Campbell: Selections Chiefly from The Millennial Harbinger*. Edited by W. A. Morris. Austin, TX: Eugene Von Boeckmann, 1896.

Curran, R. Emmett. "The Finger of God Is Here: The Advent of the Miraculous in the Nineteenth-Century American Catholic Community." *Catholic Historical Review* 73(1) (1987): 41–61.

Hall, David D. *Worlds of Wonder, Days of Judgment: Popular Religious Belief in Early New England*. Cambridge, MA: Harvard University Press, 1990.

Hall, Linda B. *Mary, Mother and Warrior: The Virgin in Spain and the Americas*. Austin: University of Texas Press, 2004.

Hayes, Patrick J. "Jesuit Saint Making: The Case of St. Peter Claver's Cause in Nineteenth-Century America." *American Catholic Studies* 117(4) (Winter 2006–2007): 1–32.

Hayes, Patrick J. "Massachusetts Miracles: Controlling Cures in Catholic Boston, 1929–1930." In *Saints and Their Cults in the Atlantic World*, edited by Margaret Cormack, 111–127. Charleston: University of South Carolina Press, 2007.

McGreevy, John T. "Bronx Miracle." *American Quarterly* 52(3) (2000): 405–443.

Mullin, Robert Bruce. *Miracles and the Modern Religious Imagination*. New Haven, CT: Yale University Press, 1996.

Munson, Paul. "Sacred Seeds: The French Jesuit Martyrs in American Catholic Historiography." *Logos: A Journal of Catholic Thought and Culture* 17(4) (2014): 87–107.

Park, Karen E. "The Negotiation of Authority at a Frontier Marian Apparition Site: Adele Brise and Our Lady of Good Help." *American Catholic Studies* 123(3) (2012): 1–26.

"A Place for Saints." Diocese of Saint Cloud, http://visitor.stcdio.org/place-saints/.

Rhoda Wise House & Grotto, http://rhodawise.com/.

Schultz, Nancy Lusignan. *Mrs. Mattingly's Miracle: The Prince, the Widow, and the Cure That Shocked Washington City*. New Haven, CT: Yale University Press, 2011.

Shrine of Our Lady of Good Help, www.shrineofourladyofgoodhelp.com.

Shrine of St. Joseph, www.shrineofstjoseph.org.

"Testimonials." The Catholic Diocese of Richmon, http://www2.richmonddiocese.org/parater/testimonial.htm.

"Venerable Michael McGivney," http://www.fathermcgivney.org/en/index.html.

V

Veil of Veronica

The Veil of Veronica is a Roman Catholic relic. It consists of a piece of fabric bearing a miraculous imprint of the face of Christ. Also called a *sudarium* (sweat cloth), legend identifies it as the cloth that Saint Veronica presented to Christ on the Via Dolorosa. During the late Middle Ages (ca. 1300–1500), the Veil of Veronica was one of the most widely reproduced images in Europe. It has been associated with many miraculous events, including causing blindness, reproducing itself, and rotating spontaneously. Several extant and lost relics have claimed to be the original Veil of Veronica, but their historicity remains in question.

Tradition considers the Veil of Veronica an *archeiropoieton*. This term describes an image of miraculous origin, one made "without human hands." Very few Roman Catholic images of Jesus belong to this category, with the Shroud of Turin being another famous example. According to the most authoritative legend, Saint Veronica presented Christ with a piece of her veil to wipe the sweat and blood from his face on his way to the crucifixion. After he returned the cloth, Veronica realized that it contained a perfect imprint of the Holy Face. The image's miraculous creation confirmed that the relic presented the "True Image," a rare, genuine likeness of Christ.

While the veil itself did not enjoy widespread fame in Europe until the mid-thirteenth century, its claims to the status of "True Image" tied the relic to a much older visual tradition. In the Eastern Orthodox Church, the Mandylion of Edessa held the title of "True Image" since before the sixth century. Similar in style and subject, some historians consider the Veil of Veronica to have been the Mandylion's primary competitor in the Western Church. Possession of these miraculous likenesses confirmed divine approbation for emperors and church patriarchs. The True Image could legitimize a civil ruler's authority or authorize new religious practices a bishop instituted. During their sack of Rome in 1527, Lutheran soldiers tried to destroy the symbolic power of the True Image by removing the Veil of Veronica from St. Peter's and auctioning it at a local tavern. As a relic with claims to be the True Image, the Veil of Veronica served as a flashpoint in power struggles between East and West, civil and religious authorities, and interpretations of Christianity.

West European veneration of the Veil of Veronica increased dramatically after a miraculous event in 1216. As Pope Innocent III carried it in a procession from St. Peter's Basilica to the hospital of San Spirito, the face on the cloth turned itself upside down. In response, Innocent granted an indulgence of ten days for those who said a prayer before an image of the veil. While most indulgences applied to pilgrims who visited a particular relic, Innocent's indulgence extended to those who said the prayer before *any* image of the Veil of Veronica. Consequently, images of Saint Veronica and her veil began appearing in countless artworks. From Rome to Scotland, pictures of the Veil of Veronica helped fuel the growing popularity of image veneration in medieval Catholicism.

Andrew Coates

Further Reading

Clark, Anne I. "Venerating the Veronica: Varieties of Passion Piety in the Later Middle Ages." *Material Religion* 3(2) (July 2007): 164–189.

Kuryluk, Ewa. *Veronica and Her Cloth: History, Symbolism, and Structure of a True Image.* New York: Blackwell, 1991.

Morgan, David. *The Embodied Eye: Religious Visual Culture and the Social Life of Feeling.* Berkeley: University of California Press, 2012.

Wolf, Gerhard. "From Mandylion to Veronica: Picturing the 'Disembodied' Face and Disseminating the True Image of Christ in the Latin West." In *The Holy Face and the Paradox of Representation*, edited by Herbert L. Kessler and Gerhard Wolf, 153–179. Bologna: Nuova Alfa, 1998.

Victim Soul

Though for Christians the extent of the merits of Jesus Christ for the salvation of the world are without limit, in a mystical way from time to time in order to appease God on account of human ingratitude, certain persons are chosen to endure extreme forms of suffering for the sake of others. That they have different trials visited especially on their bodies is observable, but for many there is also a terrific battle against psychotic breaks and the less visible elements of mental illness. This is often spiritualized, and thus their souls undergo intense assault and wounding.

By willing acceptance of their torment and transforming that pain into something positive, their action redounds to God's glory. While self-sacrifice lies at the heart of this acceptance and helps to model the virtue to others, in some cases the relief of those who transfer their suffering to the recipient is considered miraculous. The one on whom pain is deposited is called a victim soul.

It is generally accepted today that this category of mystic is one whose holiness is manifest through unconventional methods. It can be of two types: active and passive. Examples of the former include Saint Catherine of Siena and Saint Faustina Kowalska, whose "spiritual stigmata" were born from desire or even a hunger to unite to the divine. By contrast, Audrey Santo, a young paraplegic from Worcester, Massachusetts, who lay in a persistently vegetative state from early childhood, was considered a passive sufferer of physical ailments par excellence. Those who visited with her at her bedside felt the weight of their problems or the corporeal healing of their bodies occur through her intercession. In each instance, the broken body grows closer to Christ precisely through suffering. Thus, it is not a bar to the divine but a means or vehicle toward it.

The language of the victim soul is almost always the same. Words such as "pain," "piercing," "wounding," "immolation," and "blood" as well as other terms associated with victimhood are commonplace. Yet the words are rendered powerless by the victim soul's ability to transform something universally understood as negative into a more positive creation. The sinfulness of another, which rots the soul, can be undercut by the atoning sacrifice of a victim soul. Additionally, victim souls will usually try to cover up their victimhood or otherwise submit to the whims of their supporters or devotees. Victim souls rely on the recognition of the devout; they do not remain anonymous.

Victim souls differ from stigmatics insofar as their bodies do not typically or spontaneously reproduce the wounds of Christ on their person. However, some stigmatics may take on aspects of victim souls. Saint Pio of Pietrelcina is an example of someone who was favored with the characteristics of the stigmata but also was known for combating the devils that tormented those he encountered who were spiritually troubled. It is the combination of the physical and spiritual wounds incurred that suggests that the person is a victim soul.

The concept of a victim soul seemed to gain traction with the release in 1984 of Saint Pope John Paul II's encyclical *Salvifici Doloris* (On Human Suffering). In that text, redemptive suffering is viewed as both edifying and instructive, though the text stops short of suggesting that the more excruciating the pain, the greater the salvific force. Further, the pope never indicated approval of the concept of a victim soul, and to this day it remains a matter of theological speculation.

Patrick J. Hayes

Further Reading

Kane, Paula M. "'She Offered Herself Up': The Victim Soul and Victim Spirituality in Catholicism." *Church History* 71(1) (March 2002): 80–119.

Korson, Gerald. "What Is a Victim Soul." Our Sunday Visitor, https://www.osv.com /TodaysIssues/Article/TabId/599/ArtMID/13753/ArticleID/10338/What-is-a-Victim -Soul.aspx.

Vincentians and Miracles

Among the leading charitable organizations in the world is the St. Vincent de Paul Society, with a membership of nearly one million, begun in 1835 by the French layman Blessed Frederic Ozanam. As of 2014 he still had but one miracle to his credit: the case of a Brazilian infant, Fernando Luis Benedito Ottoni, whose incurable diphtheria subsided after his grandfather sought Ozanam's spiritual aid. Ozanam's sainthood cause was introduced only a year earlier, in 1925. He was proclaimed a venerable on July 6, 1993, by Pope John Paul II, and this same pontiff signed the decree recognizing the Ottoni miracle as valid in 1996. Consequently, Pope John Paul beatified Ozanam on August 22, 1997, in the Cathedral of Notre Dame in Paris during one of the gatherings of World Youth Day.

The society's namesake, Saint Vincent de Paul (1581–1660), the spiritual father to the Congregation of the Mission (Vincentians) and the Sisters of Charity, is today thought by some to have no miracles to his credit, believing instead that Roman authorities granted the favor of the canonization principally due to Vincent's widespread charitable works through France and eventually into mission territories around the globe. Modern-day authors look back to the biography of Bishop Louis Abelly of Rodez, a contemporary of Vincent's, whose factual data is often in doubt. Abelly maintained that no miracles were manifest through Vincent but that this was inconsequential. However, the beatification record attests to eight cases of miraculous healings, four of which were authenticated and two of which were accepted for the cause: the cure of a nun from ulcers and another woman from paralysis.

Vincent's sainthood cause began in 1709 and was approved by the Holy See in 1713. Pope Clement XII declared him a saint on June 16, 1837. When Vincent's body was exhumed 50 years after his death, it was found to be incorrupt, though today the bones and fragments are encased in a wax figurine in the Chapel of St. Vincent on the Rue de Sèvres in Paris. His heart was encased in a glass reliquary and is now displayed in Paris in the Chapelle Notre-Dame de la Medaille Miraculeuse, a short distance from St. Louise de Maurillac, Vincent's companion in charity.

Among the notable Vincentian sisters whose miracles have touched supplicants is the first American-born saint, Mother Elizabeth Ann Bayley Seton (1774–1821), foundress of the Sisters of Charity. In 1880, James Cardinal Gibbons of Baltimore launched the preliminary investigations into her life and reputation for holiness. These culminated in the brief submitted to the Roman postulator in June 1911. Three principal miracles were used in her canonization cause, all of which took place in the United States. The first miracle was for Sister Gertrude Korzendorfer (1872–1942), a Daughter of Charity from St. Louis who was relieved of pancreatic cancer in 1935 after her sisters commenced a novena to Seton. An autopsy showed no sign of any previous damage to the pancreas, and further tests indicated that she died of a heart ailment unrelated to her previous illness. Ann Teresa O'Neill (Hooe) at age 4 was cured of acute lymphatic leukemia after a second-class relic of Mother Seton was pinned to her hospital gown and a novena was said. The miracle was accepted when O'Neill was fifteen years old and had remained cancer free. In 1963 Carl Kalin, a Lutheran from New York, was cured after a novena was commenced and a bone fragment of Mother Seton's was brought to his bedside. He had suffered from complications of red measles, resulting in primary fulminating reubeola meningo-encephalitis (prior to Seton's canonization, Kalin converted to Catholicism). Seton was declared venerable in 1959 by Pope John XXIII and was beatified in 1963 and canonized on September 14, 1975, by Pope Paul VI.

Additionally, a Sister of Charity of St. Elizabeth, Miriam Teresa Demjanovich (1901–1927)—a daughter of Slovak immigrants who settled in Bayonne, New Jersey—was beatified by Pope Francis on December 18, 2013. Sister Miriam made her religious profession while on her deathbed on April 2, 1927, and died the following month. Her only authorized miracle to date was the healing in 1964 of a boy blind from a rare form of macular degeneration.

Elsewhere in the world, notoriety has been given to the Vincentian Father Gui Tianjue, the first martyr of the Diocese of Yujiang in China. After being tortured, he died in prison at the hands of communists in 1953. The herbs growing at his grave site are purported to hold healing power. Gong De was cured of a protracted stomach ailment after ingesting an herbal brew, and a certain Father Zeng, a curate in the diocese, was cured of cancer after drinking a similar herbal concoction.

Finally, the canonization record of a French martyr hung for the faith, Saint John Gabriel Perboyre, CM (1802–1840), shows a striking coincidence, namely that on the very morning of his beatification, November 10, 1889, a Daughter of Charity of Héverlé, Sister Gabrielle Isoré (1851–1906), was healed of a type of paralysis through a novena to Perboyre arranged by her fellow sisters. At first diagnosed as myelitis, Sister Gabrielle's actual malady turned out to be acute ascending spinal lepto-meningitis when she was 38 years old. With her health restored, she continued in ministry until her death at age 55.

Patrick J. Hayes

Further Reading

D'Amico, Robert. "The Causes for Canonization in the Vincentian Family." *Vincentiana* 40(4–5) (July–October 1996): 387–404.

Davitt, Thomas. "The Cause for the Canonization of John Gabriel Perboyre." *Vincentian Heritage Journal* 16(2) (1995): 209–213.

Davitt, Thomas, trans. "Fr. Gui Tianjue, C.M.: Confessor of the Faith in China." *Vincentiana* 39(1) (January–February 1995): 60–61.

"Elizabeth Ann Seton." Famvin, http://famvin.org/wiki/Elizabeth_Ann_Seton.

"Miriam Teresa Demjanovich." Famvin, http://famvin.org/wiki/Miriam_Teresa_Demjanovich.

Ristretto Cronologico della Vita, Virtù, e Miracoli del B. Vincenzo de Paoli, Fondatore della Congregazione della Missione e della Serve de'Poveri, Dette le Figlie della Carità. Ferrara: Giuseppe Barbieri, 1732, http://catalog.hathitrust.org/Record/009314993.

Sheldon, William W. "Canonization of Frederick Ozanam: History of the Cause." *Vincentian Heritage Journal* 17(1) (1996): 51–62.

Voice

In most contexts in life, those who hear voices are often assumed to be under the sway of some form of psychosis, delusion, or mental impairment. In religion, however, those who hear voices are assumed to be under the sway of prophecy, divine inspiration, or spiritual grace. Stories of miraculous voices in the Bible are well known, but less familiar and more surprising are the abundant stories of miraculous voices in the Talmud.

The belief that human beings on Earth can hear voices from heaven was implanted in Jews by biblical stories such as 1 Samuel 3, where God's voice can be heard by human beings, even if this voice can easily by confused with normal human voices. In fact, 2 Kings 19:11–13 indicates that God is more likely to appear to human beings through a "still small voice" (v. 13) than through more overt means. These and other biblical examples became the basis for subsequent folkloric tales of miraculous voices. Such biblical stories served as precedents for the principle that human beings can receive forms of heavenly communication and that while the voice of God cannot always be heard, voices that represent God may still be heard. Such voices teach religionists that even though God's presence may no longer be as keenly felt as it was in the days of yore, God's law is still binding because God is still present in the world, albeit in a less manifest manner. Indeed, the *bat kol* (heavenly voice, lit. "daughter of voice") persisted as a significant miracle trope in Jewish legal literature, particularly in the Talmud. Examples of Talmudic accounts of miraculous voices can be found in the Babylonian Talmud (*Eruvin* 13b, 54b) as well as the Jerusalem Talmud (*Berakhot* 1:6, 3b), wherein a celestial voice (*bat kol*) is heard rendering a legal judgment.

The notion that heavenly voices and other miracles can render legal judgments is not sui generis to Talmudic law (see Babylonian Talmud, *Eruvin* 64b), for according to traditional Judaism, the entire basis of Mosaic law is miraculous: it was communicated by God to men (Mishnah, *Avot* 1:1). Moses received the 613 commandments of the Torah (the written law) and their accompanying legal interpretations (the oral law) via direct divine communication. The Prophet Isaiah was believed to have received certain laws regarding the Sabbath from the heavenly voice of God as well (the laws in the books of Ruth and Esther, notwithstanding their context in the biblical canon, do not appear to have been communicated to men via heavenly voices). When contrasted with the heavenly voice believed to have dictated the law to men at Sinai, the *Bava Metzia* (59a–b), in which a heavenly voice heard rendering a legal judgment is ignored, thus represents a novel position that such voices are no longer heeded in Jewish law.

According to traditional Judaism, prophecy—a phenomenon in which the miraculous perception of heavenly voices was constitutive of the prophetic experience—persisted through biblical times and ceased in the beginning of the Second Temple era (the date usually attributed to the cessation of prophecy is 450 BCE). By the advent of the era of the Men of the Great Assembly, the hearing of heavenly voices was no longer a regular occurrence, and isolated incidents of such miracles were assessed on an individual basis. If heavenly voices were to have binding importance in Jewish law, compelling reasons would have to be adduced to override the baseline presumption that "heavenly voices [*bat-kol*] are not considered" in adjudicating *halakhah*, because the law is no longer in heaven (Deuteronomy 30:12). However, according to the sage R. Avdimi, after the destruction of the Second Temple, sages were allowed to receive a form of heavenly communication that was once only in the preserve of the prophets (Babylonian Talmud, *Bava Batra* 12a–b).

In the Christian New Testament, the public aspect of the divine voice is exemplified in each of the synoptic gospels at the baptism of Jesus by John (Matthew 3:13–17; Mark 1:9–11; Luke 3:21–23), where onlookers or the gospel writers hear a voice from heaven proclaim that Jesus is the beloved Son of God and on him favor rests.

Daniel Goodman

See also: Revelation

Further Reading

Batluck, Mark Daniel. "Revelatory Acts of God in the Gospels: How Divine Visions and Voices Promote Reverence for Jesus within the Canonical Narratives." PhD dissertation, University of Edinburgh, 2013.

Goodich, Michael. *Miracles and Wonders: The Development of the Concept of Miracle, 1150–1350.* Burlington, VT: Ashgate, 2007.

Freze, Michael. *Voices, Visions, and Apparitions.* Huntington, IN: Our Sunday Visitor, 1993.

Scholem, Gershom. *The Messianic Idea in Judaism: And Other Essays on Jewish Spirituality.* New York: Schocken, 1971.

Voodoo

Voodoo is a genuine African religion that was mainly transformed in Haiti due to the influence of a petit bourgeois milieu of former slaves who were allowed to farm their own estates as a consequence of the end of the sugar boom and an increasing need for coffee planters. Voodoo also had an integrative function that helped to overcome the destroyed family bonds of the former slaves by creating a new and more religiously motivated family. As a practice, Voodoo cleaves to mystical symbols and ritualized performance that engage both nature and magic.

When the sugar boom ended in the second half of the eighteenth century, St. Domingue, the most important French colony, which would become Haiti in 1804, transformed into a coffee-planting colony where former slaves from Africa were allowed to cultivate their own land. This special status with regard to colonial surroundings allowed them to develop their own religious beliefs as well. As a consequence of the French Revolution, a rebellion broke out in St. Domingue too. Voodoo played a unifying role for the rebels, and we can trace an interrelationship of religion and revolution in the Latin American country, which declared independence in the aftermath.

Voodoo communities understand themselves as spiritual extended families where the cult leaders—*oungan* (male) and *mambo* (female)—lead the members (*ounsi*) in a spiritual way. They are called mother or father by the members and are responsible for the organization of the Voodoo temple, which is the center of spiritual life and—in contrast to Western images—not just a single building.

Due to the fact that Haiti was separated from the Catholic Church between 1804 and the 1860s, Christian symbols were also adapted into Voodoo rituals. One example is the statue of Legba, a Voodoo god, depicted as Saint Lazarus that protects the entrance of Voodoo temples, which are complexes of different houses for the *ounsi* as well as the Voodoo gods.

The highest of these is Bondye, who is deistic, meaning that he does not interfere in human affairs. In contrast to him, there are two groups of gods (*lwa*) who do interfere. The *rada* are gentle and reliable, while the *petwo* are aggressive and moody. They construct a natural hierarchy, led by the highest one, Danbala. Each goddess has her own favorite food, color, and even a favorite day of the week and is said to have other special characteristics. The *lwa* have houses that are part of the Voodoo temple and are summoned to take part in the ceremonies during celebrations. The reason for such a celebration could be the birthday of one of the several gods or the wedding of a special *lwa* with a community member.

By using ceremonial dance, the gods are summoned by the community, and when the members fall into trance, a god will take possession of a human, who will lose his identity and imitate one of the several different *lwa* who may be in possession. Due to a Voodoo wedding, such a bond is knit forever, and the human must remain sexually abstinent on the special day of the married *lwa*. As a consequence of the fact that there exists white and black magic in the Voodoo religion, people fear that if such a bond is not dissolved after their death, they will become a zombie, who could be controlled by a bad magician. The spirit will not be released from Earth and will become the zombie slave of someone else. It was this imagination that made Voodoo well known outside Haiti, as did the popular image of the Voodoo puppet.

In actuality, these puppets are used during Voodoo ceremonies but not to control a person or to hurt them; rather, they are used merely to knit or solve love bonds between two persons. In general, Voodoo is more of a self-help religion, and the cultural leaders are trying to help their community members with the problems that arise in daily life by acting as healer or mediator who can ask the gods for their impression of a single problem. This ability to provide practical help made Voodoo successful, even outside Haiti.

Frank Jacob

See also: Caribbean, Miracles in the

Further Reading

Brown, Karen McCarthy. *Mama Lola: A Vodou Priestess in Brooklyn*. Berkeley: University of California Press, 1991.

Davis, Wade. *Passage of Darkness: The Ethnobiology of the Haitian Zombie*. Chapel Hill: University of North Carolina Press, 1988.

McAlister, Elizabeth. *Rara! Vodou, Power, and Performance in Haiti and Its Diaspora*. Berkeley: University of California Press, 2002.

W

Warfield, Benjamin

As a professor of didactic and polemic theology at Princeton Seminary, Benjamin Warfield (1851–1921) was a distinguished and prolific author generating both academic tomes and popular articles. A staunch defender of Calvinistic orthodoxy and confessions, especially the Westminster Confession of Faith, he is perhaps best known for *The Inspiration and Authority of the Bible* in which he sets out to defend the Bible from both its religiously liberal and secular critics. His views on the inerrancy of scripture shaped the early fundamentalist movement in the United States and continue to wield great influence among many evangelicals to this day. While he staunchly believed the religion of the Bible to be a supernatural religion with a God who intervenes in human history in extraordinary ways, he also believed and taught that miraculous gifts within the church ceased after their God-ordained role in authenticating the apostolic witnesses and the final formation of the New Testament canon was complete.

Warfield's influential book *Counterfeit Miracles*, based on a series of lectures, set out to thread the needle between the rising antisupernaturalist modernism of his day, the post–New Testament miracles of Roman Catholicism, and the emerging Protestant Higher Life, Keswisk, and Pentecostal movements. He endorsed the controversial Anglican cleric Conyers Middleton's *A Free Inquiry into the Miraculous Powers*, which limited miracles to the immediate apostolic activity of Jesus's chosen twelve disciples and to those on whom they confer such gifts. Upon the death of the last of the twelve apostles, such gifts can no longer be conferred and therefore cease with the death of those on whom these miraculous gifts were given. There is no apostolic succession in this regard. Besides, argued Warfield, the internal witness of the New Testament is that such extraordinary gifts are no longer needed. The Spirit-led and Spirit-breathed formation and completion of the New Testament canon makes such gifts obsolete. Warfield therefore considered all other extraordinary manifestations as counterfeit and fodder for polemic argument against later Roman Catholic miracles, heretical movements, and what he considered Protestant deviants.

In this way, Warfield wrote in *The Inspiration and Authority of the Bible*, believers had to defend against "two movements of thought, tending to a lower conception of the inspiration and authority of Scripture": (1) The "Rationalistic view," which sought to "distinguish between inspired and uninspired elements within the Scriptures," and (2) the "Mystical view," which enables something residing within the Christian to discern what portions of the Bible or aspects of spiritual experience are to be trusted and valued. Here he identifies the subjective apologetic of Friedrich Schleiermacher as a great threat that has "broken in upon the church like a flood, and washed into every corner of the Protestant world."

Warfield's view on the cessation of the miraculous gifts was widely influential not only among like-minded Calvinists but also among Dispensationalists, who used its arguments in their polemical arguments with Pentecostal and Charismatic Christians. The belief in the cessation of miraculous gifts that became enshrined in interpretive Dispensational notes of the Scofield reference bible ensured that this view was not some theological nicety but rather a popular belief that is contested to this day.

Douglas Milford

Further Reading

Brown, Colin. *Miracles and the Modern Mind*. Grand Rapids, MI: William B. Eerdmans, 1984.

Marsden, George M. *Fundamentalism and American Culture: The Shaping of Twentieth Century Evangelicalism, 1870–1925*. New York: Oxford University Press, 1980.

Ruthven, Jon Mark. *On the Cessation of the Charismata: The Protestant Polemic on Post-Biblical Miracles*. Tulsa, OK: Word and Spirit, 2011.

Warfield, Benjamin B. *Counterfeit Miracles*. New York: Scribner, 1918.

Warfield, Benjamin B. *The Inspiration and Authority of the Bible*, 2nd printing. Philadelphia: Presbyterian and Reformed Publishing Company, 1948.

Zaspel, Fred G. *The Theology of B. B. Warfield: A Systematic Summary*. Wheaton, IL: Crossway, 2010.

Water

Water is a key symbol and often a principal vehicle for miraculous phenomena. As an elixir for all life, water is one of the four elements that lay the foundations of natural philosophy. With its counterparts—earth, wind, and fire—water is the substance of life's primordial origins and animates all human creation mythologies. It remains archetypal as a symbol of death and rebirth. Water is sacred in its transparency, fluidity, and capacity to restore purity. Its cleansing properties in the natural world translate easily in spiritual contexts, where its power to loosen and dissolve obstruction is symbolized in the forgiveness of sin or the miraculous restoration to life. Immersion in water lies at the heart of ritual baptism. Similarly, water is used in the ritual bathing of the dead in preparation for the soul's journey across the waters of death to the otherworld of eternity.

Waters that spring from the earth are universal sources of miraculous healing, as they are living waters that nourish and restore life. The story in the New Testament of the man born blind is a classic example of water's restorative power. In the ninth chapter of John's gospel, Jesus encounters a blind man and, after making a mud paste with his own spittle, smears the man's eyes. Jesus then tells him to wash in the pool of Siloam, whereupon the blind man was given the power to see.

All over the world, wellsprings, rivers, rain rocks, stone circles, and cupolas retain their deep cultural significance as sacred places where all living creatures find rest and healing. Water can also set the stage for the spectacular, as when Jesus turns water into choice wine at the wedding at Cana (John 2:1–11) or walks out on the waters of the Sea of Galilee to meet his disciples in their boat (Matthew 14:29). These narratives have touched the lives of millions of people, in faith and in the miraculous experience of God's love and healing.

Victoria M. Breting-Garcia

See also: Lourdes Water

Further Reading

Alter, Stephen. *Sacred Waters: A Pilgrimage up the Ganges River to the Source of Hindu Culture*. New York: Harcourt, 2001.

Emoto, Masaru. *The Miracle of Water*. New York: Atria Books. 2007.

Fagan, Brian. *Elixir: A History of Water and Humankind*. New York: Bloomsbury, 2011.

Grigsby, Bruce H. "Washing in the Pool of Siloam: A Thematic Anticipation of the Johannine Cross." *Novum Testamentum* 27(3) (1985): 227–335.

Macaulay, David. *Elemental Philosophy: Earth, Air, Fire, and Water as Environmental Ideas*. Albany: State University of New York Press, 2010.

Ortlund, Dane. "The Old Testament Background and Eschatological Significance of Jesus Walking on the Sea." *Neotestamentica* 46(2) (2012): 319–337.

Toussaint, Stanley D. "Significance of the First Sign in John's Gospel." *Bibliotheca Sacra* 134(533) (January–March 1977): 45–51.

Varner, Gary R. *Sacred Wells: A Study in the History, Meaning, and Mythology of Holy Wells & Waters.* 2nd ed. New York: Algora Publishing, 2009.

Varner, Gary R. *Water from the Sacred Well: Further Explorations in the Folklore and Mythology of Sacred Waters* (originally published as *Water of Life Water of Death: The Folklore & Mythology of Sacred Water*). Raleigh, NC: Lulu, 2010.

Weeping

Weeping refers to instances in which inanimate objects—mostly statues and pictures—secrete tears. Popularly believed to be outright miracles or signs of impending disasters, the true meaning of these instances is largely unknown and often undergoes extensive scrutiny.

The vast majority of such phenomena have been associated with the Roman Catholic and Eastern Orthodox traditions, wherein adoration of physical statues and icons is incorporated among religious belief and practice. Yet virtually every reported case of weeping has been determined to be a hoax. In Brooklyn, New York, a priest in 1985 was ordered to stop selling statues of the Blessed Virgin Mary because customers were reporting that they wept. The Diocese of Brooklyn later found the stories (and the priest) to lack credibility. Perhaps one of the most well-known hoaxes took place in 2002 when a passerby in Messina, Sicily, reported seeing a red substance, believed to be blood, secreting from a statue of Saint Padre Pio of Pietrelcina (1887–1968). Catholic officials ordered an investigation, and although the substance was indeed confirmed to be blood, it was later revealed that it was placed on the statue by an individual from the local community. The problem with these instances is that they take an enormous amount of time and energy to investigate and often distract the faithful from more worthy objects of devotion.

Building upon the extensive incidents of fraud, skeptics have gone to great lengths to debunk new and emerging cases of weeping objects. For example, physicist Shawn Carlson of the Lawrence Berkeley National Laboratory introduced the notion that it was possible to engineer a weeping object. Although he never actually revealed his method, in 1987 he did demonstrate how such weeping could materialize, using an image of the *Mona Lisa*.

Despite the bulk of fraudulent instances and the efforts of skeptics to expose them, there is at least one popular case in which the Catholic Church has conferred some form of approval. In this case, known as Our Lady of Akita, the events received a form of acknowledgment known as an Approval of the Bishop. In this instance, a three-foot-tall wooden statue of the Virgin Mary in Akita, Japan, was said to have shed tears on at least 101 occasions between 1975 and 1981. After Sister Agnes Sasagawa (b. 1930), a nun who witnessed each of these occasions, reported the details of the weeping to Bishop John Shohiro Ito (1909–1993), Ito later approved the incident in a pastoral letter recognizing its supernatural characteristics and authorizing the veneration of the Holy Mother of Akita. In 1988 Bishop Ito furthered his endeavors pertaining to the events by consulting Cardinal Joseph Ratzinger. Although Cardinal Ratzinger made no judgment about the credibility of the events, he issued no objections to the conclusions of Bishop Ito's pastoral letter.

Salvador Murguia

See also: Compunction (Tears); Our Lady of Akita; Statues

Further Reading

Lutz, Tom. *Crying: The Natural and Cultural History of Tears*. New York: Norton, 2001.

Nicholl, Joe. *Looking for a Miracle: Weeping Icons, Relics, Stigmata, Visions, and Healing Cures*. Amherst, NY: Prometheus Books, 1993.

Patton, Kimberley Christine, and John S. Hawley. *Holy Tears: Weeping in the Religious Imagination*. Princeton, NJ: Princeton University Press, 2005.

Yashuda, Teigi. *Akita: The Tears and Message of Mary*. Translated by John Haffert. Asbury, NJ: 101 Foundation, 1991.

Wells

A well is a site where local geology causes subterranean water to rise to the surface. Because of the spontaneous way that water appears from deep within the earth, wells are associated with purity and portals to the spirit realm in many world traditions. There is archaeological evidence of votive offerings and animal sacrifices at well sites worldwide dating at least as far back as the Neolithic Age. Wells are also associated with purification rituals such as the *mikvah* in Judaism and the *chōzuya* at Shinto shrines. In Christian tradition there are numerous examples of wells that were created through miracles or that possess miraculous healing properties. Beliefs in holy wells are highly diverse—ranging from world-famous Lourdes to thousands of lesser-known well sites that are part of local folklore.

While there are a few biblical accounts of miraculous wells, such as Moses drawing water from a rock (Exodus 17:2) or the healing well of Bethesda in Jerusalem (John 5:2–4), their appearance in Christian culture likely owes more to religious syncretism with Celtic and Greco-Roman traditions. The pre-Christian landscape of Europe was dotted with shrines at sacred wells in locations ranging from remote forest groves to highly developed complexes, such as the Castalian Spring at Delphi. Some of these places were converted into Christian sites such as Bath Abbey in Somerset or incorporated into Christian folklore such as the Fontaine-de-Vaucluse in southern France.

Because of the association of wells with pagan traditions, some early Christian writers regarded them with suspicion. Martin of Braga (ca. 520–580) claimed that many of the demons that had been cast out of heaven inhabited bodies of water on Earth and were worshipped by pagans. Despite such condemnations, miraculous wells were adopted into official practices. The well of Saint Mary of the Healing Spring in Istanbul dates at least as far back as the fifth century CE. There are also examples of miraculous wells appearing at the tombs of saints, such as Nicholas in Myra and Peter of Luxembourg in Avignon.

More common, although less documented, are wells connected with popular culture, where heterodox practices and possibly pagan survivals are most evident. A dramatic example of this is the well of Saint Guinefort near Lyon in France. There, a thirteenth-century Dominican monk investigated a shrine to a martyred greyhound where local women practiced a curative ritual for sick children. Many of these medieval well sites were suppressed by the Church or fell into disuse with the establishment of Protestantism.

Modern interest in holy wells dates back to the seventeenth and eighteenth centuries, when early antiquarians and folklorists first began to record them. More recently, there has been a revival of interest in wells among the neo-pagan and New Age communities. Many of these sites are still visited today by pilgrims who leave votive offerings. Thousands of holy wells in Europe have been cataloged, particularly in parts with Celtic roots such as Brittany, Wales, Cornwall, and Ireland, which are typically affiliated with obscure local saints. This has led to the theory that these sites were originally pagan shrines that were rebranded with the advent of Christianity. However, because there is so little historical documentation of holy wells and pre-Christian religious practices, it is impossible to draw any certain conclusions about their antiquity or past significance.

There are examples of holy wells appearing in the modern era. The most famous of these is Lourdes in southwestern France, but there are lesser-known examples such as the fountain of Szentkút in Doroslovo, Serbia. These modern wells are typically affiliated with the Virgin Mary, suggesting a rupture with the past tradition of wells being associated with local saints in post-Tridentine Catholicism.

Eric F. Johnson

See also: Ireland, Miracles in

Further Reading

Carroll, Michael P. *Irish Pilgrimage: Holy Wells and Popular Catholic Devotion.* Baltimore: Johns Hopkins University Press, 1999.

Harris, Ruth. *Lourdes: Body and Spirit in the Secular Age.* New York: Viking, 1999.

Holy Wells Research and Preservation Group. *Source: Journal of the Holy Wells Group.* Northampton, UK: Northampton Press, 1985–.

Martin of Braga. *De Correctione Rusticorum.* Translated by Claude W. Barlow. Washington, DC: Catholic University of America Press, 1969.

Schmidtt, Jean-Claude. *The Holy Greyhound: Guinefort, Healer of Children since the Thirteenth Century.* Cambridge: Cambridge University Press, 1983.

Varner, Gary R. *Sacred Wells: A Study in the History, Meaning, and Mythology of Holy Wells & Waters.* New York: Algora Publications, 2009.

Whately, Richard

Richard Whately (1787–1863) is chiefly remembered for his first published work, *Historical Doubts Relative to Napoleon Buonaparte* (1819). Rather than directly attack the argument in Part 1 of Hume's "Of Miracles," Whately employed what logicians term an indirect proof, the method of *reductio ad absurdum* whereby one conditionally accepts the premises of an argument and then shows that they lead to a contradiction—that is, absurdity. Specifically, Whately argued that if one accepts Hume's argument, the same principles of reasoning undermine accepting the existence and exploits of Napoleon. Given that Napoleon was still alive and had posed such a threat to Britain, the absurdity of such a conclusion would not have been lost on Whately's audience.

The crux of Whately's criticism is that miracles are only one type of unusual event believed on the basis of testimonial evidence. Inasmuch as Hume's argument counts not only against miracles but also other unusual events reliably believed on the basis of testimony, the argument proves too much and must be rejected. Whately was writing for a popular audience, but C. D. Broad later made the same criticism in a more academic context. Whately's positive views on Christian apologetics, as opposed to his destructive critique of Hume's argument, are found in his *Introductory Lessons on Christian Evidences* (1856) and in his comments to the 1859 edition of William Paley's *View of the Evidences of Christianity.*

Robert Larmer

Further Reading

Broad, C. D. "Hume's Theory of the Credibility of Miracles." *Proceedings of the Aristotelian Society* 17 (1916–17): 77–94.

White, Ellen G.

Ellen Gould (née) Harmon was born in 1827 in New England at the height of the Second Great Awakening. White converted to the Methodist Church in 1842, after feeling drawn to the faith following attendance at a camp meeting. Her views at that time were especially influenced by the work of William Miller, who preached an imminent second coming, or advent of Christ, thus founding the Adventist movement. When this event did not occur within Miller's specified time frame, resulting in what was known as the Great Disappointment, many Millerites left the tradition. White, however, was not among them. After professedly having a vision that the Adventists would one day participate in Christ's return and enter the kingdom of God, she gained recognition as a religious visionary.

Debates continue among Adventists and non-Adventists to the present day as to whether or not White's visions were triggered or predisposed by a serious childhood head injury in which she was struck by a rock thrown by another child, leaving her unconscious for weeks and with permanent facial disfigurement. White deflected attention away from her role as prophetess, on one occasion writing that "I have had a great light from the Lord upon the subject of health reform. I did not seek this light; I did not study to obtain it; it was given to me by the Lord to give to others" (E. G. White, "Sunnyside," Manuscript 29, 1897).

With her husband James and fellow Adventist Joseph Bates, Ellen White took a marginalized Protestant sect and turned it into a successful and lasting American faith tradition, largely through the influence of her incredible visions. Most prominent among these revelations, believed by Adventists to have been received by White directly from God, were the many health and dietary reforms adopted by the tradition in the latter half of the nineteenth century. Subsequent to a 45-minute vision of comprehensive health reforms at a tent meeting in Michigan in 1863, Adventist followers were called to strict adherence to a vegetarian diet—free from meat, tobacco, alcohol, and spicy and rich foods. Regular exercise and curative water treatments were also to be undertaken in order to help prepare Adventist bodies for what they believed would be a corporeal reunion with the divine.

In this worldview, the body became a vessel for the sacred rather than being viewed as something corrupt and disposable after life and was thus meant to be kept pure and in good condition. Adventist motives to perfect the body as well as the spirit continued to be thought of as direct revelations from God and were taken seriously by practitioners of the faith. With the help of Dr. John Harvey Kellogg, White's religious health reform movement gained scientific support, as many of her visions and teachings were in line with heightened understandings of scientific approaches to medicine in her day. These reforms were carried out with no greater care than in the sanitariums formed by White and Kellogg. These were havens where Adventists, and later many non-Adventists, would seek healing and respite.

In a time in American history in which some of the population was already skeptical about the effects of prepackaged nutrient-depleted foods on health and well-being, White's divinely mandated regimen of a meatless diet filled with whole grains and a lifestyle in which exercise, sunlight, clean air, and proper hydration were key became increasingly popular. Her visions would have a lasting effect on practitioners of the Adventist faith as well as American health reform as the twentieth century commenced.

Emily Bailey

Further Reading

Bull, Malcolm, and Keith Lockhart. *Seeking a Sanctuary: Seventh-Day Adventism and the American Dream*. 2nd ed. Bloomington: Indiana University Press, 2007.

Numbers, Ronald L. *Prophetess of Health: A Study of Ellen G. White*. 3rd ed. Grand Rapids, MI: William B. Eerdmans, 2008.

White, Ellen G. *The Ministry of Healing*. Washington, DC: Review and Herald Publishing Association, 1905.

Woolston, Thomas

Thomas Woolston (1670–1733) was notorious for his attack on belief in the literal occurrence of miracles, advocating that Christian Scripture must be interpreted allegorically. In *The Moderator between an Infidel and an Apostate* (1725) and *Six Discourses on the Miracles of Our Saviour* (1727–1728), he denied existing grounds for believing in the miracles of the New Testament. One of his central themes was that the miracles attributed to Jesus are inconsistent with God's moral perfection and thus inherently unbelievable. Woolston writes, in typically polemical fashion, that Jesus's miracles "if literally true . . . are enough to turn our Stomachs . . . [and] enough to make us take him for a *Conjuror*, a *Sorcerer*, and a *Wizard* rather than the *Messiah*." Although Woolston's views led to him being charged and convicted of blasphemy—he died in prison, being unable to pay the fine—he influenced the debate over the rationality of belief in miracles not only in Great Britain but also on the European continent. Voltaire appears to have admired Woolston's extreme polemical style and views, writing that "no one before him [Woolston] had taken boldness and offensiveness this far, [treating] the miracles and the Resurrection of our Saviour as puerile and extravagant stories."

Robert Larmer

Further Reading

"Thomas Woolston Bibliography." 18th Century Bibliography, http://www.c18th.com /author-works.aspx?id=74.

Woolston, Thomas. *A Discourse on the Miracles of Our Saviour*. 4th ed. London, 1728.

Bibliography

Abou-El-Haj, B. *The Medieval Cult of Saints: Formations and Transformations.* New York: Cambridge University Press, 1994.

Acta Sanctorum, http://acta.chadwyck.co.uk/.

Adams, William. *An Essay in Answer to Mr. Hume's Essay on Miracles.* 3rd ed. London: B. White, 1767.

Ahern, Dennis M. "Hume on the Evidential Impossibility of Miracles." *American Philosophical Quarterly* (1975): 1–31.

Anderson, Emma. *The Death and Afterlife of the North American Martyrs.* Cambridge, MA: Harvard University Press, 2013.

Antonelli, Francesco. *De inquisitione medico-legali super miraculis in causis beatificationis et canonizationis.* Studia Antoniana 18. Rome: Antonianum, 1962.

Arlandson, James. "Bibliography on Miracles." Biblical Studies, http://www.biblicalstudies .org.uk/pdf/jma/miracles_7_arlandson.pdf.

Ashley, Kathleen, and Pamela Sheingorn. *Writing Faith: Text, Sign, and History in the Miracles of Sainte Foy.* Chicago: University of Chicago Press, 1999.

Babbage, Charles. *The Ninth Bridgewater Treatise.* London: John Murray, 1837.

Baldwin, Lou. *Saint Katharine Drexel: Apostle to the Oppressed.* Philadelphia: Catholic Standard and Times, 2000.

Bartlett, Robert. *The Hanged Man: A Story of Miracle, Memory, and Colonialism in the Middle Ages.* Princeton, NJ: Princeton University Press, 2004.

Bartlett, Robert. *Why Can the Dead Do Such Great Things? Saints and Worshippers from the Martyrs to the Reformation.* Princeton, NJ: Princeton University Press, 2013.

Basinger, David, and Randall Basinger. *Philosophy and Miracle: The Contemporary Debate.* Lewiston, ID: Edwin Mellen, 1986.

Baumgarten, A. I. "Miracles and Halakah in Rabbinic Judaism." *Jewish Quarterly Review* 75(3) (January 1983): 238–253.

Bayne, Stephen M. "Hume on Miracles: Would It Take a Miracle to Believe in a Miracle?" *Southern Journal of Philosophy* 45(1) (2007): 1–29.

Beard, John Relly. *Voices of the Church.* London: Simpkin, Marshall, 1845.

Beckett, Edmund. *A Review of Hume and Huxley on Miracles.* New York: E. and J. B. Young, 1883.

Beckett, Thomas, and Shelley Mydans, eds. *The Life, Passion, and Miracles of Thomas Beckett*. New York: Doubleday, 1965.

Bell, Rudolph M., and Cristina Mazzoni. *The Voices of Gemma Galgani: The Life and Afterlife of a Modern Saint*. Chicago: University of Chicago Press, 2003.

Bennett, Jeffrey S. *When the Sun Danced: Myth, Miracles, and Modernity in Early Twentieth-Century Portugal*. Charlottesville: University of Virginia Press, 2012.

Benvenuti, Anna, et al. *Storia della santità nel cristianesimo occidentale*. Rome: Viella, 2005.

Benvenuti, Anna, and Marcello Garzaniti, eds. *Il tempo dei santi tra Oriente e Occidente: Liturgia e agiografia dal tardo antico al concilio di Trento; Atti del IV Convegno di studio dell'Associazione italiana per lo studio della santità, dei culti e dell'agiografia, Firenze, 26–28 ottobre 2000*. Rome: Viella, 2005.

Best, John H. *The Miracles of Christ in Light of Our Present-Day Knowledge*. London: SPCK, 1967.

Bigger, Matthew C. "Hume and Miracles." *Journal of the History of Philosophy* 35(2) (1997): 237–251.

Birnbaum, Ruth. "The Polemic on Miracles." *Judaism* 33(4) (Fall 1984): 439–447.

Blackbourne, David. *Marpingen: Apparitions of the Virgin Mary in Nineteenth-Century Germany*. New York: Knopf, 1994.

Blackman, Larry Lee. "The Logical Impossibility of Miracles in Hume." *International Journal for Philosophy of Religion* 9(3) (1978): 179–187.

Blaher, Damian Joseph. *The Ordinary Processes in Causes of Beatification and Canonization: A Historical Synopsis and a Commentary*. Washington, DC: Catholic University of America Press, 1949.

Blumenfeld-Kosinski, Renate, and Timea Szell, eds. *Images of Sainthood in Medieval Europe*. Ithaca, NY: Cornell University Press, 1991.

Boesch-Gajano, Sofia, and Marilena Modica, eds. *Miracoli: Dai segni alla storia*. Rome: Laterza and Figli, 2000.

Bowie, Fiona. "Miracle in Traditional Religions." In *The Cambridge Companion to Miracles*, edited by Graham Twelftree, 122–137. New York: Cambridge University Press, 2011.

Boyarin, Adrienne Williams. *Miracles of the Virgin in Medieval England: Law and Jewishness in Marian Legends*. Woodbridge, Suffolk, UK: D. S. Brewer, 2010.

Boyer, O. A. *She Wears a Crown of Thorns: Marie Rose Ferron (1902–1936) Known as "Little Rose"; The Stigmatized Ecstatic of Woonsocket, R.I.* 2nd ed. Ellenberg, NY: Self-published, 1940.

Brading, D. A. *Mexican Phoenix: Our Lady of Guadalupe; Image and Tradition across Five Centuries*. New York: Cambridge University Press, 2003.

Brown, Candy Gunther, ed. *Global Pentecostal and Charismatic Healing*. New York: Oxford University Press, 2011.

Brown, Colin. *Miracles and the Critical Mind*. Grand Rapids, MI: Eerdmans, 1984.

Brown, Peter. *The Cult of the Saints: Its Rise and Function in Latin Christianity*. Chicago: University of Chicago Press, 1982.

Brownson, Orestes A. *Saint Worship/The Worship of Mary*. Edited by Thomas R. Ryan. Paterson, NJ: St. Anthony Guild Press, 1963.

Buckle, S. "Marvels, Miracles, and Mundane Order." *Australasian Journal of Philosophy* 79(1) (2001): 1–31.

Burns, Robert M. *The Great Debate on Miracles from Joseph Glanvill to David Hume*. London and Toronto: Associated University Presses, 1981.

Burton, Richard E. *Holy Tears, Holy Blood: Women, Catholicism, and the Culture of Suffering in France, 1840–1970*. Ithaca, NY: Cornell University Press, 2004.

Byerley, Timothy E. *Saint John Neumann: Wonder-Worker of Philadelphia*. Philadelphia: National Shrine of St. John Neumann, 1992.

Bynam, Caroline Walker. *Holy Feast, Holy Fast: The Religious Significance of Food to Medieval Women*. Berkeley: University of California Press, 1987.

Bynam, Caroline Walker. "Wonder." *American Historical Review* 102 (1997): 1–26.

Bynam, Caroline Walker. *Wonderful Blood: Theology and Practice in Late Medieval Northern Germany and Beyond*. Philadelphia: University of Pennsylvania Press, 2007.

Campbell, George. *A Dissertation on Miracles*. 1762; reprint, London: Thomas Tegg, 1839.

Canetti, L. *Santità e agiografia nell'Ordo praedicatorum: Il culto e l'immagine di san Domenico nella formazione dell'identità domenicana (1221–1260)*. Milan: Università cattolica del Sacro Cuore, 1994.

Carroll, Michael P. *Catholic Cults and Devotions: A Psychological Inquiry*. Kingston, ON: McGill-Queen's University Press, 1989.

Carroll, Michael P. *The Cult of the Virgin Mary: Psychological Origins*. Princeton, NJ: Princeton University Press, 1992.

Carroll, Michael P. *Veiled Threats: The Logic of Popular Catholicism in Italy*. Baltimore: Johns Hopkins University Press, 1996.

Casieri, Antonio. *Postulatorum Vademecum*. 2nd ed. Rome: Congregation for Saints' Causes, 1985.

Casieri, Antonio, et al., eds. *Bibliotheca Sanctorum: Appendice*. 2 vols. Rome: Città Nuova, 1987–2000.

Cavadini, John C., ed. *Miracles in Jewish and Christian Antiquity: Imagining Truth*. Notre Dame, IN: University of Notre Dame Press, 1999.

Channing, William Ellery. *A Discourse on the Evidences of Revealed Religion Delivered before the University in Cambridge at the Dudleian Lecture, March 14, 1821*. Boston: Cummings and Hilliard, 1821.

Christian, William A. *Moving Crucifixes in Modern Spain*. Princeton, NJ: Princeton University Press, 1992.

Christian, William A. *Person and God in a Spanish Valley*. Revised ed. Princeton, NJ: Princeton University Press, 1989.

Chryssides, George. "Miracles and Agents." *Religious Studies* 13 (1977): 319–327.

Cicognani, Amleto. *Sanctity in America*. Paterson, NJ: St. Anthony Guild Press, 1945.

Clarke, Steve. "Hume's Definition of Miracles Revised." *American Philosophical Quarterly* 36(1) (1999): 49–57.

Coleman, Dorothy P. "Hume, Miracles and Lotteries." *Hume Studies* 14(2) (1988): 328–346.

Composta, Dario. *Il miracolo: Realtà o suggestione? Rassegna documentata di fatti straordinari cinquantennio 1920–1970.* Rome: Città Nuova 1981.

Congregation for Saints' Causes. *Miscellanea in occasione del IV centenario della Congregazione per le Cause dei Santi (1588–1988).* Vatican City: Congregation for Saints' Causes, 1988.

Connell, Janice T. *The Visions of the Children: The Apparitions of the Blessed Mother at Medjugorje.* New York: St. Martin's, 1992.

Cooper, Kate, and Jeremy Gregory, eds. *Signs, Wonders, Miracles: Representations of Divine Power in the Life of the Church,* Studies in Church History 41. Suffolk, UK: Boydell and Brewer, 2005.

Cooper, Thomas. *The Verity and Value of the Miracles of Christ.* London: Hodder and Stoughton, 1876.

Cotter, Wendy. *The Christ of the Miracle Stories: Portrait through Encounter.* Grand Rapids, MI: Baker Academic, 2010.

Cotter, Wendy. *Miracles in Greco-Roman Antiquity: A Sourcebook for the Study of New Testament Miracle Stories.* New York: Routledge, 1999.

Craig, William Lane. "The Problem of Miracles: A Historical and Philosophical Perspective." In *Gospel Perspectives VI: Miracles of Jesus,* edited by David Wenham and Craig Blomberg, 9–40. Sheffield, UK: JSOT Press, 1987.

Cranston, Ruth. *The Miracle of Lourdes.* New York: McGraw-Hill, 1955.

Crislip, Andrew. *Thorns in the Flesh: Illness and Sanctity in Late Ancient Christianity.* Philadelphia: University of Pennsylvania Press, 2012.

Craughwell, Thomas J. *Saints Preserved: An Encyclopedia of Relics.* New York: Image, 2011.

Crook, John. *The Architectural Setting of the Cult of Saints in the Early Christian West, c. 300–c. 1220.* New York: Oxford University Press, 2000.

Cruz, Joan Carroll. *Eucharistic Miracles and Eucharistic Phenomena in the Lives of the Saints.* Rockford, IL: TAN, 1987.

Cruz, Joan Carroll. *Relics.* Huntington, IN: Our Sunday Visitor, 1984.

Cunningham, Lawrence. *The Meaning of Saints.* New York: Harper and Row, 1980.

Dalarun, Jacques. *The Misadventures of Francis of Assisi: Toward a Historical Use of the Franciscan Legends.* Translated by Edward Hagman. St. Bonaventure, NY: Franciscan Institute, 2002.

Dal Santo, Matthew. *Debating the Saints' Cults in the Age of Gregory the Great.* New York: Oxford University Press, 2012.

Danaher, James P. "David Hume and Jonathan Edwards on Miracles and Religious Faith." *Southwest Philosophy Review* 17(2) (2001): 13–24.

Daston, Lorraine, and Katharine Park. *Wonders and the Order of Nature, 1150–1750.* New York: Zone Books, 1998.

Davies, Edward O. *The Miracles of Jesus: A Study of the Evidence.* London: Hodder and Stoughton, 1913.

DeCerteau, Michel. *The Possession at Loudun*. Translated by Michael B. Smith. Chicago: University of Chicago Press, 2000.

Delehaye, Hippolyte. *The Legends of the Saints*. Translated by Donald Attwater. New York: Fordham University Press, 1962.

Deuffic, Jean-Luc, ed. *Reliques et sainteté dan l'espace médiéval*. Saint-Denis: PECIA, 2006; vols. 8–11 of PECIA: Ressources en médiévistique, 2005.

DiOrio, Ralph. *A Miracle to Proclaim: Firsthand Experience of Healing*. New York: Image Book, 1984.

Douglas, John. *The Criterion or, Rules by Which the True Miracles Recorded in the New Testament Are Distinguished from the Spurious Miracles of Pagans and Papists*. 4th ed. Oxford: Oxford University Press, 1832.

Duffin, Jacalyn. *Medical Miracles: Doctors, Saints, and Healing in the Modern World*. New York: Oxford University Press, 2009.

Earman, John. *Hume's Abject Failure: The Argument against Miracles*. New York: Oxford University Press, 2000.

Efthymiadis, Stephanos, ed. *The Ashgate Research Companion to Byzantine Hagiography*, Vols. 1 and 2. Aldershot, UK, and Burlington, VT: Ashgate, 2011, 2014.

Eszer, Ambrose. "Il concetto eroica nella storia della virtu." In *Sacramenti, Liturgy, Cause dei Santi: Studi in onore del Cardinale Giuseppe Casoria*, 605–636. Naples: Campania Notizie, 1992.

Eszer, Ambrose. "Miracoli ed altri segni divini: Considerazioni dommatico-storiche con special riferimento alle cause dei santi." In *Studi in onore del Card: Pietro Palazzini*, 129–158. Pisa: Giardini Editori e Stampoatori, 1987.

Evans, George P. *101 Questions and Answers on Saints*. New York: Paulist Press, 2007.

Farmer, Hugh. *A Dissertation on Miracles*. London: T. Cadell, 1771.

Faupel, J. F. *African Holocaust: The Story of the Ugandan Martyrs*. Kampala: St. Paul Publications, 1984.

Finucane, R. C. *Contested Canonizations: The Last Medieval Saints, 1482–1523*. Washington, DC: Catholic University of America Press, 2011.

Finucane, R. C. "The Use and Abuse of Medieval Miracles." *History* 60 (1975): 1–10.

Flew, Antony. "Miracles." In *Encyclopedia of Philosophy*, V:346–353. New York: Macmillan and Free Press, 1967.

Fogelin, Robert J. *A Defense of Hume on Miracles*. Princeton, NJ: Princeton University Press, 2003.

Force, James E. "Hume and Johnson on Prophecy and Miracles: Historical Context." *Journal of the History of Ideas* 43 (1982): 463–476.

Freeman, Charles. *Holy Bones, Holy Dust: How Relics Shaped the History of Medieval Europe*. New Haven, CT: Yale University Press, 2012.

Frey, E. F. "Saints in Medical History." *Clio Medica* 14(1) (1979): 35–70.

Gannon, John Mark. *The Martyrs of the United States of America*. Easton, PA: Mack, 1957.

Garnet, Jane, and Gervase Rosser. *Spectacular Miracles: Transforming Images in Italy from the Renaissance to the Present*. New York: Reaktion Books, 2013.

Garrett, Don. "Hume on Testimony Concerning Miracles." In *Reading Hume on Human Understanding: Essays on the First Enquiry*, edited by Peter Millican, 301–334. New York: Oxford University Press, 2002.

Gaskin, J. C. A. "David Hume and the Eighteenth-Century Interest in Miracles." *Hermathena* 99 (1964): 80–91.

Geivett, R. Douglas, and Gary R. Habermas, eds. *In Defense of Miracles: A Comprehensive Case for God's Action in History*. Downer's Grove, IL: IVP Academic, 1997.

Gibbons, John. "Some Sicknesses and Their Saints." *New Blackfriars* 10(115) (October 1929): 1392–1395.

Goldish, Matt. *Spirit Possession in Judaism: Cases and Contexts from the Middle Ages to the Present*. Raphael Patai Series in Jewish Folklore and Anthropology. Detroit: Wayne State University Press, 2003.

Goodich, Michael. *Lives and Miracles of the Saints: Studies in Medieval Latin Hagiography*. Aldershot, UK: Ashgate, 2004.

Goodich, Michael. *Miracles and Wonders: The Development of the Concept of Miracle, 1150–1350*. Aldershot, UK: Ashgate, 2007.

Goodich, Michael. "The Politics of Canonization in the Thirteenth Century: Lay and Mendicant Saints." *Church History* 44 (1975): 294–307.

Goodich, Michael. *Vita Perfecta: The Ideal of Sainthood in the Thirteenth Century*. Monographien zur Geschichte des Mittelalters 25. Stuttgart: Anton Hiersmann, 1982.

Goodich, Michael. *Violence and Miracle In the Fourteenth Century: Private Grief and Public Salvation*. Chicago: University of Chicago Press, 1995.

Gordon, David M. *Invisible Agents: Spirits in a Central African History*. Columbus: Ohio University Press, 2012.

Gordon, George Angier. *Religion and Miracle*. London: Clarke, 1910.

Gower, Barry. "David Hume and the Probability of Miracles." *Hume Studies* 16(3) (1990): 17–31.

Graef, Hilda C. *The Case of Therese Neumann*. Westminster, MD: Newman, 1961.

Graves, Wilfred. "Popular and Elite Understandings of Miracles in Enlightened England." PhD dissertation, Fuller Theological Seminary, 2007.

Graziano, Frank. *Cultures of Devotion: Folk Saints of Spanish America*. New York: Oxford University Press, 2007.

Graziano, Frank. *Wounds of Love: The Mystical Marriage of Saint Rose of Lima*. New York: Oxford University Press, 2004.

Greer, Allan. *Mohawk Saint: Catherine Tekakwitha and the Jesuits*. New York: Oxford University Press, 2005.

Greer, Rowan A. *The Fear of Freedom: A Study of Miracles in the Roman Imperial Church*. University Park: Pennsylvania State University Press, 1989.

Gregory, Lady. *Visions and Beliefs in the West of Ireland Collected and Arranged by Lady Gregory: With Two Essays and Notes by W. B. Yeats*. New York and London: Putnam, 1912.

Grey, William. "Hume, Miracles, and the Paranormal." *Cogito* 7(2) (1993): 100–105.

Haar, Gerrie ter. "A Wondrous God: Miracles in Contemporary Africa." *African Affairs* 102 (2003): 409–428.

Hagiography Circle, http://hagiographycircle.com/index.htm.

Hagiography Society, http://www.hagiographysociety.org/.

Hahn, Cynthia. *Portrayed on the Heart: Narrative Effect in Pictorial Lives of Saints from the Tenth through the Thirteenth Century.* Berkeley: University of California Press, 2001.

Hahn, Cynthia. *Strange Beauty: Issues in the Making and Meaning of Reliquaries, 400–c. 1204.* University Park: Pennsylvania State University Press, 2013.

Hájek, Alan. "Are Miracles Chimerical?" In *Oxford Studies in Philosophy of Religion*, Vol. 1, edited by Jonathan Kvanvig, 82–104. New York: Oxford University Press, 2008.

Hájek, Alan. "In Defense of Hume's Balancing of Probabilities in the Miracles Argument." *Southwest Philosophy Review* 11(1) (1995): 111–118.

Hamburger, Robert. "Belief in Miracles and Hume's Essay." *Noûs* 14(4) (1980): 587–604.

Harline, Craig. *Miracles at the Jesus Oak: Histories of the Supernatural in Reformation Europe.* New York: Doubleday, 2003.

Harris, Ruth. *Lourdes: Body and Spirit in the Secular Age.* New York: Penguin Compass, 2000.

Harrison, Peter. "Miracles, Early Modern Science, and Rational Religion." *Church History* 75 (2006): 493–510.

Harrison, Peter. "Prophecy, Early Modern Apologetics, and Hume's Argument against Miracles." *Journal of the History of Ideas* 60(2) (1999): 241–256.

Harvey, Warren Zev. "Spinoza on Biblical Miracles." *Journal of the History of Ideas* 74(4) (2013): 659–675.

Hayes, Patrick J. "Jesuit Saint Making: The Case of St. Peter Claver's Cause in Nineteenth-Century America." *American Catholic Studies* 117(4) (Winter 2006–2007): 1–32.

Hayes, Patrick J. "Massachusetts Miracles: Controlling Cures in Catholic Boston, 1929–1930." In *Saints and Their Cults in the Atlantic World*, edited by Margaret Cormack, 111–127. Charleston: University of South Carolina Press, 2007.

Head, Thomas, ed. *Medieval Hagiography: An Anthology.* New York and London: Routledge, 2001.

Heffernan, Thomas J. *Sacred Biography: Saints and Their Biographers in the Middle Ages.* New York: Oxford University Press, 1987.

Heike, Behrend, and Armin Linke. *Resurrecting Cannibals: The Catholic Church, Witch-Hunts, and the Production of Pagans in Western Uganda.* Woodbridge, Suffolk, UK: Boydell and Brewer, 2011.

Hellé, Jean. *Miracles: A Discussion of the Authenticity of Modern Miracles.* Translated by Lancelot C. Sheppard. New York: David McKay, 1952.

Hesse, Mary. "Miracles and the Laws of Nature." In *Miracles: Cambridge Studies in Their Philosophy and History*, edited by C. F. D. Moule, 33–42. London: A. R. Mowbray, 1965.

"Historical Summary of Our Lady of the Cape Shrine." Our Lady of the Cape Shrine, http://www.sanctuaire-ndc.ca/en/historical.html.

Holder, Rodney D. "Hume on Miracles: Bayesian Interpretation, Multiple Testimony, and the Existence of God." *British Journal for the Philosophy of Science* 49(1) (1998): 49–65.

Holmes, Megan. *The Miraculous Image in Renaissance Florence*. New Haven, CT: Yale University Press, 2013.

Houdini, Harry. *Miracle Mongers and Their Methods: A Complete Expose of the Modus Operandi of Fire Eaters, Heat Resisters, Poison Eaters, Venomous Reptile Defiers, Sword Swallowers, Human Ostriches, Strong Men, Etc.* New York: E. P. Dutton, 1920.

Houston, J. *Reported Miracles: A Critique of Hume*. New York: Cambridge University Press, 1994.

Howard-Johnston, James, and Paul Antony Hayward, eds. *The Cult of Saints in Late Antiquity and the Middle Ages: Essays on the Contribution of Peter Brown*. New York: Oxford University Press, 2002.

Hume, David. "Of Miracles." In *An Enquiry Concerning Human Understanding*, 79–95. New York: Oxford University Press, 2008.

Hynes, Eugene. *Knock: The Virgin's Apparition in Nineteenth-Century Ireland*. Cork, Ireland: Cork University Press, 2008.

Jackson, Deirdre E. *Marvelous to Behold: Miracles in Illuminated Manuscripts*. London: British Library, 2007.

Jacobus de Voragine. *The Golden Legend: Readings on the Saints*. 2 vols. Princeton, NJ: Princeton University Press, 1993.

Jefferson, Lee M. *Christ the Miracle Worker in Early Christian Art*. Minneapolis: Augsburg Fortress Press, 2014.

Joassart, Bernard. *Hippolyte Delehaye: Hagiographie critique et modernisme*. Subsidia Hagiographica 81. Brussels: Société des Bollandistes, 2000.

Johnson, David. *Hume, Holism and Miracles*. Ithaca, NY: Cornell University Press, 1999.

Joly, Henri. *The Psychology of the Saints*. London: Duckworth, 1898.

Joskowicz, Ari. "Selma the Jewish Seer: Female Prophecy and Bourgeois Religion in Nineteenth Century Germany." *Journal of Modern Jewish Studies* 13 (2014): 1–19.

Joyce, George Hayward. *The Question of Miracles*. St. Louis: B. Herder, 1914.

Justice, Steven. "Did the Middle Ages Believe in Their Miracles?" *Representations* 103(1) (2008): 1–29.

Katajala-Pelomaa, S. *Gender, Miracles, and Daily Life: The Evidence of Fourteenth-Century Canonization Processes*. Turnhout: Brepols, 2009.

Kaufman, Suzanne K. *Consuming Visions: Mass Culture and the Lourdes Shrine*. Ithaca, NY: Cornell University Press, 2005.

Kee, Howard Clark. *Medicine, Miracle, and Magic in New Testament Times*. New York: Cambridge University Press, 1986.

Kee, Howard Clark. *Miracle in the Early Christian World: A Study in Sociohistorical Method*. New Haven, CT: Yale University Press, 1983.

Kelhoffer, James A. *Miracle and Mission: The Authentication of Missionaries and Their Message in the Longer Ending of Mark*. Tuebingen: Mohr Siebeck, 2000.

Kemp, E. W. "Pope Alexander III and the Canonization of Saints." *Transactions of the Royal Historical Society*, 4th series, 27 (1945): 13–28.

Kempf, Constantine. *The Holiness of the Church in the Nineteenth-Century*. Translated by Francis Breymann. New York: Benzinger Brothers, 1916.

Keneer, Craig S. *Miracles: The Credibility of the New Testament Accounts*. 2 vols. Grand Rapids, MI: Baker Academic, 2011.

Kieckhefer, Richard. *Unquiet Souls: Fourteenth-Century Saints in Their Religious Milieu*. Chicago: University of Chicago Press, 1987.

King-Farlow, John. "Historical Insights on Miracles: Babbage, Hume, Aquinas." *International Journal for Philosophy of Religion* 13(4) (1982): 209–218.

Klaniczay, Gábor, ed. *Medieval Canonization Processes: Legal and Religious Aspects*. Collection de l'École Française de Rome, Vol. 340. Rome: École Française de Rome, 2004.

Kleinberg, Aviad. *Flesh Made Word: Saints' Stories and the Western Imagination*. Translated by Jane Marie Todd. Cambridge, MA: Harvard University Press, 2008.

Kleinberg, Aviad. *Prophets in Their Own Country: Living Saints and the Making of Sainthood in the Later Middle Ages*. Chicago: University of Chicago Press, 1992.

Kleinberg, Aviad. "Proving Sanctity: Selection and Authentication of Saints in the Later Middle Ages." *Viator* 20 (1989): 191–197.

Knowles, David. "Great Historical Enterprises: Problems." In *Monastic History*, 3–32. London, Thomas Nelson and Sons, 1963.

Koopmans, Rachael. *Wonderful to Relate: Miracle Stories and Miracle Collecting in High Medieval England*. Philadelphia: University of Pennsylvania Press, 2011.

Koskenniemi, Erkki. *The Old Testament Miracle-Workers in Early Judaism*. Tübingen: Möhr Siebeck, 2005.

Koudounaris, Paul. *Heavenly Bodies: Cult Treasures and Spectacular Saints from the Catacombs*. London: Thames and Hudson, 2013.

Kreiser, B. Robert. *Miracles, Convulsions, and Ecclesiastical Politics in Early Eighteenth-Century Paris*. Princeton, NJ: Princeton University Press, 1978.

Kuefler, Mathew. *The Making and Unmaking of a Saint: Hagiography and Memory in the Cult of Gerald of Aurillac*. Philadelphia: University of Pennsylvania Press, 2013.

Lacey, Thomas Alexander. *Nature, Miracle, and Sin: A Study of St. Augustine's Conception of the Natural Order; The Pringle Stuart Lecture for 1914*. London: Longmans, Green, 1916.

Lachapelle, Sofie. *Investigating the Supernatural: From Spiritism and Occultism to Psychical Research and Metapsychics in France, 1853–1931*. Baltimore: Johns Hopkins University Press, 2011.

Langtry, Bruce. "Hume, Probability, Lotteries and Miracles." *Hume Studies* 16(1) (1990): 67–74.

Langtry, Bruce. "Miracles and Rival Systems of Religion." *Sophia* 24 (1985): 21–31.

Larmer, Robert. "Against 'Against Miracles.'" *Sophia* 27 (1988): 20–25.

Larmer, Robert. "C. S. Lewis' Critique of Hume's 'On Miracles.'" *Faith and Philosophy* 25(2) (2008): 154–171.

Larmer, Robert. "Interpreting Hume on Miracles." *Religious Studies* 45(3) (2009): 325–338.

Larmer, Robert. "Miracles and Overall: An Apology for Atheism?" *Dialogue* 43 (2004): 555–568.

Larmer, Robert. *Water into Wine? An Investigation of the Concept of a Miracle.* Toronto: McGill-Queen's University Press, 1988.

Latourelle, René. "Miracle et Révélation." *Gregorianum* 43 (1962): 492–509.

Latourelle, René. *The Miracles of Jesus and the Theology of Miracles.* New York: Paulist, 1988.

LeBec, E. *Medical Proof of the Miraculous.* Translated by H. E. Izard. London: Harding and More, Ambrosden Press, 1922.

Legg, Catherine. "Naturalism and Wonder: Peirce on the Logic of Hume's Argument against Miracles." *Philosophia* 28(1–4) (2001): 297–318.

Leuret, François, and Henri Bon. *Modern Miraculous Cures: A Documented Account of the Miracles of the Twentieth Century.* Translated by John Barry and A. T. Macqueen. London: Peter Davies, 1957.

Levack, Brian P. *The Devil Within: Possession and Exorcism in the Christian West.* New Haven, CT: Yale University Press, 2013.

Levine, Michael. *Hume and the Problem of Miracles: A Solution.* Dordrecht: Kluwer Publishers, 1989.

Lewis, C. S. *Miracles: A Preliminary Study.* New York: Macmillan, 1947.

Lias, John James. *Are Miracles Credible?* London: Hodder and Stoughton, 1883.

Locke, John. *A Discourse of Miracles.* London, 1706.

Lockyer, Herbert. *All the Miracles of the Bible: The Supernatural in Scripture—Its Scope and Significance.* Grand Rapids, MI: Zondervan, 1961.

Love, Velma. *Divining the Self: A Study in Yoruba Myth and Human Consciousness.* University Park: Penn State University Press, 2012.

Lukwago, Juliet. "The Journey of the Uganda Martyrs." *New Vision*, October 22, 2010, http://www.newvision.co.ug/D/9/183/735826.

Mackie, J. L. *The Miracle of Theism.* Oxford: Oxford University Press, 1982.

Mackler, Aaron L. "Eye on Religion: A Jewish View on Miracles of Healing." University of Chicago, https://pmr.uchicago.edu/sites/pmr.uchicago.edu/files/uploads/Mackler,%20Eye%20on%20Religion-%20a%20Jewish%20View%20on%20Miracles%20of%20Healing.pdf.

Manchingura, Francis. "The Significance of Glossolalia in the Apostolic Faith Mission, Zimbabwe." *Studies in World Christianity* 17(1) (April 2011): 12–29.

Marx, Jacques, ed. *Sainteté et martyre dans les religions du livre.* Brussels: Éditions de l'Université de Bruxelles, 1989.

"The Mary Page: About Mary." University of Dayton, http://campus.udayton.edu/mary/aboutmary2.html.

Mavrodes, George I. "David Hume and the Probability of Miracles." *International Journal for Philosophy of Religion* 43(3) (1998): 167–182.

McCready, William David. *Miracles and the Venerable Bede.* Toronto: PIMS, 1994.

McCready, William David. *Signs of Sanctity: Miracles in the Thought of Gregory the Great*. Toronto: PIMS, 1989.

McGreevy, John T. "Bronx Miracle." *American Quarterly* 52(3) (2000): 405–443.

McGrew, Timothy, and Lydia McGrew. "The Argument from Miracles." In *The Blackwell Companion to Natural Theology*, edited by William Lane Craig and J. P. Morel, 593–662. New York: Blackwell, 2008.

Mejia, A. Royo. "Notes on the Historical Evolution of the Concept of the Heroic Virtues Applied to the Causes of Saints." *Spanish Journal of Canon Law* 52 (1995): 519–561.

Meltzer, Françoise, and Jaś Elsner, eds. *Saints: Faith without Borders*. Chicago: University of Chicago Press, 2011.

Merbeck, Mitchell B. *Pilgrimage and Pogrom: Violence, Memory, and Visual Culture at the Host-Miracle Shrines of German and Austria*. Chicago: University of Chicago Press, 2012.

Mercati, Angelo. *"Bollandiana" dall'Archivio Segreto Vaticano*. Miscellenaea Historiae Pontificiae III:4–5. Rome: Casa Editrice SALER, 1940.

Mesley, Matthew M., and Louise E. Wilson, eds. *Medium Aevum*, Vol. 32, *Contextualizing Miracles in the Christian West, 1100–1500*. Oxford, UK: Society for the Study of Medieval Languages and Literature, 2014.

Metzer, Françoise, and Jaś Elsner, eds. *Saints: Faith without Borders*. Chicago: University of Chicago Press, 2011.

"Miracle." Jewish Encyclopedia, http://www.jewishencyclopedia.com/articles/10869 -miracle.

The Miracle Hunter, http://www.miraclehunter.com/.

"Miracles." Stanford Encyclopedia of Philosophy, 2005, http://plato.stanford.edu/archives /fall2010/entries/miracles/.

"Miracles." Stanford Encyclopedia of Philosophy, 2014, http://plato.stanford.edu/entries /miracles/.

Miracles of the Church, http://www.miraclesofthechurch.com.

"Miracle Stories." Facebook, https://www.facebook.com/miraclenewsservice.

Molinari, Paolo. "Saints and Miracles." *The Way* 17 (1978): 287–299.

Molinari, Paolo, and Peter Gumpel. "L'istituto della beatificazione: A proposito d'uno studio recente." *Gregorianum* 69(1) (1988): 133–138.

Monden, Louis. *Signs and Wonders: A Study of the Miraculous Element in Religion*. New York and Paris: Desclée, 1966.

Montgomery, John Warwick. "Science, Theology, and the Miraculous." *Journal of the American Scientific Association* 30 (1978): 145–153.

Moore, R. I. "Between Sanctity and Superstition: Saints and Their Miracles in the Age of Revolution." In *The Work of Jacques Le Goff and the Challenges of Medieval History*, edited by Miri Rubin, 55–67. Woodbridge, UK: Boydell and Brewer, 1997.

Mozely, James Bowling. *Eight Lectures on Miracles*. London: Rivingtons, 1865.

Mullin, Robert Bruce. *Miracles and the Modern Religious Imagination*. New Haven, CT: Yale University Press, 1996.

Mullin, Robert Bruce. "Science, Miracles, and the Prayer-Guage Debate." In *When Science and Christianity Meet*, edited by David C. Lindberg and Ronald L. Numbers, 203–224. Chicago: University of Chicago Press, 2003.

Nambowa, Carol. "Finding Answers at the Uganda Martyrs' Shrine." *Daily Monitor*, June 2, 2013, http://www.monitor.co.ug/Magazines/Life/-/689856/1868284/-/f0i989/-/index .html.

Nelson, John O. "The Burial and Resurrection of Hume's Essay 'Of Miracles.'" *Hume Studies* 12(1) (1986): 57–76.

Newman, John Henry. *Two Essays on Biblical and Ecclesiastical Miracles*. London: Longmans, Green, 1918.

Oleszkiewicz-Peralba, Malgorzata. *The Black Madonna in Latin America and Europe: Tradition and Transformation*. Albuquerque: University of New Mexico Press, 2009.

Olsen, Karin E., Antonia Harbus, and Tette Hofstra, eds. *Miracles and the Miraculous in Medieval Germanic and Latin Literature*. Leuven: Peeters, 2004.

O'Malley, Vincent J. *Saints of North America*. Huntington, IN: Our Sunday Visitor, 2004.

Overall, Christine. "Miracles and God: A Reply to Robert H. Larmer." *Dialogue* 36 (1997): 741–752.

Overall, Christine. "Miracles and Larmer." *Dialogue* 42 (2003): 123–135.

Parigi, Paolo. *The Rationalization of Miracles*. New York: Cambridge University Press, 2012.

Parish, Helen L. *Monks, Miracles and Magic: Reformation Representations of the Medieval Church*. New York: Routledge, 2005.

Park, Karen E. "The Negotiation of Authority at a Frontier Marian Apparition Site: Adele Brise and Our Lady of Good Help." *American Catholic Studies* 123(3) (2012): 1–26.

Peterson, Janine Larmon. "Contested Sanctity: Disputed Saints, Inquisitors, and Communal Identity in Northern Italy, 1250–1400." PhD dissertation, Indiana University, 2006.

Peterson, Janine Larmon. "Episcopal Authority and Disputed Sanctity in Late Medieval Italy." In *Saintly Bishops and Bishops' Saints*, edited by John S. Ott and Trpimir Vedris, 201–216. Bibliotheca Hagiotheca Series Colloquia II. Zagreb: Hagiotheca/Humaniora, 2012.

Peterson, Jeannette Favrot. *Visualizing Guadalupe: From Black Madonna to Queen of the Americas*. Austin: University of Texas Press, 2014.

Petroff, Elizabeth. *Consolation of the Blessed*. Millerton, NY: Alta Gaia, 1979.

Phillippart, Guy. *Hagiographies: Histoire internationale de la littérature hagiographique latine et vernaculaire en Occident des origines à 1550*, Vols. 1–6. Turnhout: Brepols, 1994–2014.

Phillippart, Guy. "Hagiographies et hagiographie, hagiologies et hagiologie: Des mots et des concepts." *Agiografia* 1 (1994): 1–16.

Pilgrimage & England's Cathedrals, Past and Present, http://www.pilgrimageandcathedrals .ac.uk.

Porterfield, Amanda. *Healing in the History of Christianity*. New York: Oxford University Press, 2005.

Pyysiäinen, Ilkka. *Magic, Miracles, and Religion: A Scientist's Perspective*. Walnut Creek, CA: Alta Mira, 2004.

Radner, Ephraim. *Spirit and Nature: The Saint-Médard Miracles in 18th-Century Jansenism*. New York: Crossroad, 2002.

"Relics and Reliquaries in Medieval Christianity." The Metropolitan Museum of Art, Heilbrunn Timeline of Art History, http://www.metmuseum.org/toah/hd/relc/hd_relc.htm.

Rennard, Étienne, Michel Trigalet, Xavier Hermand, and Paul Bertrand, eds. *Scribere sanctorum gesta: Recueil d'études d'hagiographie médiévale offert à Guy Philippart*, Hagiologia: Études sur la Sainteté en Occident—Studies on Western Sainthood 3. Turnhout, 2005.

Reynolds, Joseph William. *The Mystery of Miracles*. London: C. Kegan Paul, 1879.

Rüth, Axel. "Representing Wonder in Medieval Miracle Narratives." *MLN*, supplement, 126(4) (2011): 89–114.

Sanchez, Roberto. "The Black Virgin: Santa Efigenia, Popular Religion, and the African Diaspora in Peru." *Church History* 81(3) (September 2012): 631–655.

Schlesinger, George. "Miracles and Probabilities." *Nous* 21 (1987): 219–232.

Schoen, Edward L. "David Hume and the Mysterious Shroud of Turin." *Religious Studies* 27(2) (1991): 209–222.

Scholz, Bernhard W. "The Canonization of Edward the Confessor." *Speculum* 36(1) (January 1961): 38–60.

Schulenburg, Jane Tibbetts. *Forgetful of Their Sex: Female Sanctity and Society, ca. 500–1100*. Chicago: University of Chicago Press, 1998.

Schutte, Anne Jacobson. *Aspiring Saints: Pretense of Holiness, Inquisition and Gender in the Republic of Venice, 1618–1750*. Baltimore: Johns Hopkins University Press, 2001.

Schutte, Anne Jacobson, trans. and ed. *Cecilia Ferrazzi: Autobiography of an Aspiring Saint*. Chicago: University of Chicago Press, 1996.

Scott, Robert A. *Miracle Cures*. Princeton, NJ: Princeton University Press, 2010.

Sharpe, Richard. *Medieval Irish Saints' Lives: An Introduction to Vita Sanctorum Hiberniae*. New York: Oxford University Press, 1991.

Shaw, Jane. *Miracles in Enlightenment England*. New Haven, CT: Yale University Press, 2006.

Sheingorn, Pamela, trans. *The Book of Sainte Foy*. Philadelphia: University of Pennsylvania Press, 1995.

Sigal, P.-A. "Les voyages de reliques aux onzième et douzième siècles." In *Voyage, quête pèlerinage dans la littérature et la civilisation médiévales*, edited by H. Taviani, 73–103. Paris: C.U.E.R.M.A., 1976.

Sigal, P.-A. *L'homme et le miracle dans la France médiévale (XIe–XIIe siècle)*. Paris: Les Éditions du CERF, 1985.

Slater, Candice. *Trail of Miracles: Stories from a Pilgrimage in Northeast Brazil*. Berkeley: University of California Press, 1984.

Smoller, Laura Ackerman. *The Saint and the Chopped-Up Baby: The Cult of Vincent Ferrer in Medieval and Early Modern Europe*. Ithaca, NY: Cornell University Press, 2014.

Sobel, John H. "Hume's Theorem on Testimony Sufficient to Establish a Miracle." *Philosophical Quarterly* 41 (1991): 229–237.

Sobel, John H. "On the Evidence of Testimony for Miracles: A Bayesian Interpretation of David Hume's Analysis." *Philosophical Quarterly* 37(147) (1987): 166–186.

Société des Bollandistes, http://bhlms.fltr.ucl.ac.be/.

Société des Bollandistes, http://www.bollandistes.org/.

Soergel, Philip M. *Miracles and the Protestant Imagination: The Evangelical Wonder Book in Reformation Germany*. New York: Oxford University Press, 2012.

Steinmeyer, Franz Ludwig. *The Miracles of Our Lord in Relation to Modern Criticism*. Edinburgh, UK: T. and T. Clark, 1875.

Stempsey, William E. "Miracles and the Limits of Medical Knowledge." *Medicine, Health Care and Philosophy* 5(1) (2002): 1–9.

Swinburne, Richard. *The Concept of a Miracle*. London: Macmillan, 1971.

Swinburne, Richard, ed. *Miracles*. New York: Macmillan, 1989.

Szynkowski, Eugene N. *Virtues and Glories of Mary Rose Ferron: Little Rose*. Detroit: Eugene Szynkowski, n.d.

Talbot, Alice-Mary. "Pilgrimage to Healing Shrines: The Evidence of Miracle Accounts." *Dumbarton Oaks Papers* 56 (2002): 153–173.

Taylor, James E. "Hume on Miracles: Interpretation and Criticism." *Philosophy Compass* 2(4) (2007): 611–624.

Taylor, Thérèse. *Bernadette of Lourdes: Her Life, Death, and Visions*. London and New York: Burns and Oates, 2003.

Taylor, William B. *Marvels and Miracles in Late Colonial Mexico: Three Texts in Context*. Albuquerque: University of New Mexico Press, 2011.

Taylor, William B. *Shrines and Miraculous Images: Religious Life in Mexico before the Reforma*. Albuquerque: University of New Mexico Press, 2011.

Theissen, Gerd. *The Miracle Stories of the Early Christian Tradition*. Philadelphia: Fortress Press, 1983.

Théodoridès, J. "Saints in Medical History (A Complement)." *Clio Medica* 14(3–4) (1980): 269–270.

Treece, Patricia. *Nothing Short of a Miracle: The Healing Power of the Saints*. New York: Doubleday, 1988.

Trench, Richard Chenevix. *Notes on the Miracles of Our Lord*. 2nd ed. London: John W. Parker, 1847.

Tucker, Aviezer. "Miracles, Historical Testimonies, and Probabilities." *History and Theory* 44 (2005): 373–390.

Turner, Edith. *Experiencing Ritual: A New Interpretation of African Healing*. Philadelphia: University of Pennsylvania Press, 1992.

Twelftree, Graham H. *Jesus the Miracle Worker: A Historical and Theological Study*. Downer's Grove, IL: IVP Academic, 1999.

Twelftree, Graham H. *Paul and the Miraculous: A Historical Reconstruction*. Grand Rapids, MI: Baker Academic, 2013.

Twelftree, Graham H., ed. *The Cambridge Companion to Miracles*. Cambridge: Cambridge University Press, 2009.

Tweyman, Stanley, ed. *Hume on Miracles*. Bristol, UK: Thoemmes Press, 1996.

Tylenda, Joseph M., ed. *Portraits in American Sanctity*. Chicago: Franciscan Herald Press, 1982.

Van Dam, Raymond. *Saints and Their Miracles in Late Antique Gaul*. Princeton, NJ: Princeton University Press, 1993.

Vanderburgh, William L. "Of Miracles and Evidential Probability." *Hume Studies* 31(1) (2005): 37–61.

Van Hove, Alois. *La Doctrine du miracle chez Saint Thomas et son accord avec les principes de la recherche scientifique*. Wetteren: J. De Meester et Fils, 1927.

Vauchez, Andre. "La religion populaire dans la France meridionale au XIVe siecle d'apres les proces de canonisation." *Cahiers de Fanjeaux* 11 (1976): 91–107.

Vauchez, Andre. *La sainteté en Occident aux derniers siècles du Moyen Age d'après les procès de canonization et les documents hagiographiques*. Rome: École Français de Rome, 1988. English translation, *Sainthood in the Later Middle Ages*, translated by Jean Birrell. New York: Cambridge University Press, 1997.

Veraja, Fabijan. *La beatificazione: Storia, problem, prospettive; Sussidi per lo studio della cause dei santi 2*. Rome: Sacra Congregazione per la Cause dei Santi, 1983.

Veraja, Fabijan. *Le Cause di Canonizazione dei Santi: Commento alla Legislatione e Guida Pratica*. Rome: Congregation for Saints' Causes, 1992.

Walker, D. P. "The Cessation of Miracles." In *Hermeticism and the Renaissance: Intellectual History and the Occult in Early Modern Europe*, edited by Ingrid Merkel and Allen G. Debus, 111–124. Washington, DC: Catholic University of America Press, 1988.

Ward, Benedicta. *Miracles in the Medieval Mind*. Philadelphia: University of Pennsylvania Press, 1987.

Ward, Keith. "Believing in Miracles." *Zygon* 37(3) (2002): 741–750.

Wardlaw, Ralph. *On Miracles*. Edinburgh, UK: A. Fullarton, 1852.

Warfield, Benjamin. *Counterfeit Miracles*. New York: Scribner, 1915.

Weddle, David. *Miracles: Wonder and Meaning in World Religions*. New York: New York University Press, 2010.

Weinstein, Donald, and Rudolph M. Bell. *Saints and Society: The Two Worlds of Western Christendom, 1000–1700*. Chicago: University of Chicago Press, 1982.

Whatley, E. Gordon, trans. and ed. *The Saint of London: The Life and Miracles of St. Erkenwald*. Binghampton, NY: Center for Medieval and Renaissance Studies, 1989.

Whitney, Loren Harper. *A Question of Miracles: Parallels in the Lives of Buddha and Jesus*. 2nd ed. Chicago: Library Shelf, 1910.

Wilkinson, James C., trans. and ed. *Exemplary Lives: Selected Sermons on the Saints from Rheinau*. Milwaukee: Marquette University Press, 2006.

Williams, Joseph W. *Spirit Cure: A History of Pentecostal Healing*. New York: Oxford University Press, 2013.

Williams, T. C. *The Idea of the Miraculous: The Challenge to Science and Religion.* Houndmills, Basingstoke, Hampshire, and London: Macmillan, 1990.

Wilson, Stephen, ed. *Saints and Their Cults: Studies in Religious Sociology, Folklore, and History.* New York: Cambridge University Press, 1986.

Winstead, Karen A. *Virgin Martyrs: Legends of Sainthood in Late Medieval England.* Ithaca, NY: Cornell University Press, 1997.

Woestman, William H., ed. *Canonization: Theology, History, Process.* 2nd ed. Ottawa: Faculty of Canon Law, Saint Paul University, 2014.

Wolf, Kenneth Baxter. *The Life and Afterlife of St. Elizabeth of Hungary: Testimony from her Canonization Hearings.* New York: Oxford University Press, 2010.

Woodward, Kenneth L. *The Book of Miracles: The Meaning of the Miracle Stories in Christianity, Judaism, Buddhism, Hinduism, and Islam.* New York: Simon and Schuster, 2000.

Woodward, Kenneth L. *Making Saints: How the Catholic Church Determines Who Becomes a Saint, Who Doesn't, and Why.* New York: Simon and Schuster, 1996.

Yarrow, Simon. *Saints and Their Communities: Miracle Stories in Twelfth-Century England.* New York: Oxford University Press, 2006.

Yazicioglu, Isra. *Understanding Qur'anic Miracle Stories in the Modern Age.* University Park: Penn State University Press, 2013.

Ziegler, Joseph. "Practitioners and Saints: Medical Men in Canonization Processes in the Thirteenth to Fifteenth Centuries." *Social History of Medicine* 12 (1999): 191–225.

Zimdars-Swartz, Sandra L. *Encountering Mary: From LaSallette to Medjugorje.* Princeton, NJ: Princeton University Press, 1991.

About the Editor and Contributors

PATRICK J. HAYES, PhD, is the archivist for the Redemptorists of the Baltimore Province, based in Philadelphia, Pennsylvania. In addition to archival conservation of Redemptorist heritage materials, he edits and contributes to the *Redemptorist North American Historical Bulletin*, an online publication. Hayes's doctorate is in ecclesiology from the Catholic University of America (2003). He has taught at various colleges and universities in the United States and in West Africa. Hayes is the author of *A Catholic Brain Trust: The Catholic Commission on Intellectual and Cultural Affairs, 1945–1965* (University of Notre Dame Press, 2011), editor and contributor to the two-volume *The Making of Modern Immigration: An Encyclopedia of People and Ideas* (Greenwood/ABC-CLIO, 2012), coeditor of *A Realist's Church: Essays in Honor of Joseph Komonchak* (Orbis Books, 2015), and author of numerous articles and essays in the field of church history.

Guy Aiken
Department of Religious Studies,
University of Virginia

V. Neethi Alexander
Department of English, Indian Institute
of Technology Hyderabad, India

Abidemi Babatunde Babalola
Department of Anthropology, Rice
University

Emily Bailey
Department of Religious Studies,
University of Pittsburgh

Vincent Bataille
Abbot emeritus, Marmion Abbey,
Aurora, Illinois

John F. Beal
Independent scholar

Aidan Joseph Beatty
Department of History, University of
Chicago

Stefan Bosman
Tyndale House, Cambridge
University

Jason Bourgeois
*Librarian, The Marian Library,
    University of Dayton*

Victoria M. Breting-Garcia
Independent scholar

Jamie L. Brummitt
*Department of Religion, Duke
    University*

William E. Burns
*Department of History, George
    Washington University*

Peter Cajka
Department of History, Boston College

John Cappucci
*Faculty of Arts and Sciences,
    University of Windsor*

Robert Carbonneau
*Ricci Institute, University of San
    Francisco*

Raeleen Chai-Elsholz
Independent scholar

John T. Chirban
Harvard Medical School

Randy Clark
*Department of Theater, Clayton
    University*

Andrew Coates
*Department of Religion, Duke
    University*

Stavroula Constantinou
*Department of Byzantine and
    Modern Greek Studies, University
    of Cyprus*

Wendy Cotter
*Department of Theology, Loyola
    University of Chicago*

Geoffrey Dennis
*Department of Jewish Studies,
    University of North Texas*

Philip Deslippe
*Department of Religious Studies,
    University of California at Santa
    Barbara*

Michael A. Di Giovine
*Department of Anthropology and
    Sociology, West Chester University
    of Pennsylvania*

Clayton J. Drees
*Department of History, Virginia
    Wesleyan University*

Glen Duerr
*Department of History and
    Government, Cedarville University*

Bradford Lee Eden
*Dean of Library Services, Valparaiso
    University*

David J. Endres
*Department of Church History,
    Mount St. Mary's Seminary of
    the West*

Richard Kent Evans
*Department of History, Temple
University*

Patrick Flanagan
*Department of Theology and Religious
Studies, St. John's University*

Alison C. Fleming
*Department of Art and Visual Studies,
Winston-Salem State University*

Elizabeth Georgian
*Department of History, University of
South Carolina–Aiken*

Joseph N. Goh
*School of Arts and Social Sciences,
Monash University of Malaysia*

Daniel Goodman
*Yehsivat Chovevei Torah Rabbinical
School, Israel*

Robert Hauck
*Department of Religious Studies,
Gonzaga University*

Patrick J. Hayes
*Archivist, Redemptorist Archives of the
Baltimore Province, Philadelphia,
Pennsylvania*

Sonia Hazard
Department of Religion, Duke University

Brett Hendrickson
*Department of Religion, Lafayette
College*

John C. Hirsh
*Department of English, Georgetown
University*

Nathan J. A. Humphrey
*vicar, St. John's Church, Newport,
Rhode Island*

Frank Jacob
*Department of History, Heinrich Heine
University of Düsseldorf*

Eric F. Johnson
*Department of History, Kutztown
University*

Margaret John Kelly
*Vincentian Center for Church and
Society, St. John's University*

Sergius Kodera
*dean of the Faculty of Design, New
Design University, St. Pölten,
Austria*

Stephen Koeth
*Department of History, Columbia
University*

Anton Karl Kozlovic
*School of Humanities, Flinders
University, Australia*

Solveiga Krumina-Konkova
*Institute of Philosophy and Sociology,
University of Latvia*

Robert Larmer
*Department of Philosophy, University
of New Brunswick*

Elizabeth Lev
Independent scholar

Nancy Lusignan-Schultz
Department of English, Salem State University

Chris Maunder
Department of Religious Studies, York St. John's University

Alison McLetchie
Department of Sociology, Clafin University

Douglas Milford
Corporate MBA Programs, University of Illinois at Chicago

Patit Paban Mishra
College of Law, Government and International Studies (COLGIS), Universiti Utara Malaysia

Paul G. Monson
Department of Theology, Marquette University

Salvador Murguia
Department of Sociology, Miyazaki International College, Japan

Judith S. Neulander
Department of Religious Studies, Case Western Reserve University

Arua Oko Omaka
Department of History, McMaster University, Canada

Mark Anthony Phelps
Department of History, Ozarks Technical Community College

Geneviève Pigeon
Département des sciences des religions, Université du Québec à Montréal

Leonard Norman Primiano
Department of Religious Studies, Cabrini College

Leo Ruickbie
Independent scholar and associate, Kings College of the University of London

Francesco G. Sacco
Postdoctorate research fellow, University of Calabria, Italy

Andrew Salzmann
Department of Theology, Benedictine College

Fortune Sibanda
Department of Philosophy and Religious Studies, Great Zimbabwe University, Zimbabwe

Anthony Smart
Department of History, York St. John University

Swathi Krishna S.
Department of English, Indian Institute of Technology Hyderabad, India

Molly Pulver Ungar
Department of History, University of the Fraser Valley

Hana Videen
Department of English, Kings College of the University of London

Jordan Tuttle Watkins
Department of History, University of Nevada–Las Vegas

Paula L. Webb
Librarian, Government Documents Library, University of South Alabama

Nicholas R. Werse
Department of Religion, Baylor University

David White
Department of Philosophy, St. John Fisher College

Sophia Wilson
Department of English, Kings College of the University of London

Peter James Yoder
Fellow in residence, Leibniz-Institut für Europäische Geschichte (IEG) BMBF-Nachwuchsgruppe "Europabilder ev. Missionare" and Department of Religion, Berry College

Index

Entries in **bold** indicate a main entry.